Health Psychology

Biopsychosocial Factors in Health and Illness

Health Psychology
Biopsychosocial Factors in Health and Illness

Larry C. Bernard
Loyola Marymount University

Edward Krupat
Massachusetts College of Pharmacy and
Allied Health Sciences

Harcourt Brace College Publishers

Fort Worth Philadelphia San Diego New York Orlando Austin San Antonio
Toronto Montreal London Sydney Tokyo

Publisher	Ted Buchholz
Acquisitions Editor	Eve Howard
Developmental Editor	John Haley
Senior Project Editor	Kay Kaylor
Production Manager	J. Montgomery Shaw
Art Directors	Priscilla Mingus, Melinda Huff

Cover Illustration © 1993 Fred Otnes

Address for Editorial Correspondence: Harcourt Brace College Publishers, 301 Commerce Street, Suite 3700, Forth Worth, TX 76102

Address for Orders: Harcourt Brace & Company, 6277 Sea Harbor Drive, Orlando, FL 32887; 1-800-782-4479 or 1-800-433-0001 (in Florida)

ISBN: 0-03-074417-2

Library of Congress Catalog Card Number: 93-78967

Printed in the United States of America
3 4 5 6 7 8 9 0 1 2   039   9 8 7 6 5 4 3 2 1

PREFACE

■ BACKGROUND

When we began our studies as graduate students in psychology in the late 1960s and 1970s, health psychology did not exist. One of us (L.B.) was intent on becoming a clinical psychologist, the other on becoming a social psychologist. A book like this one—on the topic of health for psychology classes—was inconceivable.

What has changed in psychology since we began our graduate studies to bring us to writing this book? First, the strict separation between psychology and medicine has relaxed. Psychologists now work alongside colleagues in many health care disciplines, providing direct care to patients who are physically ill. Second, psychologists have participated in the creation of a substantial amount of new knowledge concerning illness prevention and health promotion.

We are excited by these changes, which have resulted in a rare occurrence—the birth of a new content area within an established academic field: the emergence of health psychology. This has happened over the last decade with the introduction of health psychology to the curriculum at many colleges and universities. Being relatively new to the curriculum, health psychology draws from many areas of the field, including, but not limited to, clinical, physiological, and social psychology. Health psychology will, in all likelihood, continue to expand in the foreseeable future, so we have avoided writing a "closed book" on the subject. Instead, we present health psychology as an open and emerging area where models and knowledge are not fixed.

■ ORIENTATION

Because knowledge in health psychology is not fixed, it is necessary to provide students who are introduced to the field for the first time with a solid reference point, a firm foundation from which to explore it. For us, this foundation is the *special perspective* that psychologists bring to questions of health and illness, regardless of their area of focus. This special perspective is grounded in the history, tradition, and science of psychology, and it involves an experimental analysis of behavior and the mental processes that underlie it.

ORGANIZATION

This book is divided into three parts that reflect the special perspective of health psychologists and equally emphasize topics in behavioral health and behavioral medicine.

PART I: FOUNDATIONS OF HEALTH PSYCHOLOGY

Part I introduces the psychological perspective on health. *Chapter 1* begins with a conceptual history of health psychology, its current scope, and its relationship to other health care disciplines. It emphasizes what is unique about health psychology and identifies it both within psychology and in relation to other disciplines. Health psychology's philosophical framework is discussed with respect to the classic debate between dualism and holism. The biomedical and biopsychosocial models are described, and health is defined. *Chapter 2* continues by explaining how health psychologists acquire and apply knowledge to promote well-being. Major research methods are described, and the experimental method in health psychology is illustrated with an example of an experiment to lower cholesterol that takes both biological and psychosocial factors into account. The various roles that health psychologists have as researchers, clinicians, and consultants are described, and the general approaches to intervention that health psychologists use are reviewed.

The remainder of the book builds on the introductory foundation of Part 1. We believe that students deserve a comprehensive and balanced introduction to health psychology. The collaboration in the writing of this book between a clinical psychologist with a background in behavioral medicine and a social psychologist with a background in behavioral health combines different areas of expertise. We strive for a balance that equally emphasizes health promotion and illness intervention, behavior and cognition, and research and applications.

PART II: BIOPSYCHOSOCIAL FACTORS IN HEALTH

Part II provides the theoretical groundwork for psychologists' understanding of how people behave when they are ill and how the health care system responds to them. *Chapter 3* presents several of the current models that help us conceptualize the experience of health and illness. It also describes health promotion and education and explores how people deal with the symptoms of illness. *Chapter 4* focuses on the practitioner–patient relationship, issues of adherence, medical education and practice, and alternative methods of health care delivery. Finally, *Chapter 5* deals with two important influences on individual health: the developmental challenges that occur across the life span and the effects of the environment. Chapter 5 also introduces three health-related variables, the effects of which we follow throughout the book: stress, personal control, and social support.

PART III: BIOPSYCHOSOCIAL FACTORS IN ILLNESS

Part III is more clinically oriented, drawing heavily from medical psychology and behavioral medicine and integrating the psychosocial with the biological and medical aspects of illness. In order to accomplish this, Part III is organized by physiological systems of the body within which traditional psychosocial topics are discussed. This serves two purposes: First, it provides students of psychology a bridge to biology and medicine. Second, it helps students who are more biologically oriented integrate psychosocial topics within a familiar framework. The result is that the book makes health psychology accessible to students in psychology and the social sciences as well as to those in medicine, dentistry, nursing, pharmacy, and other health professions.

Part III is divided into two sections. *Section 1* involves the function and organization of the nervous and endocrine systems, and related psychosocial health issues take up its four chapters. The first two chapters cover two of the most important topics in health psychology—"Stress" (*Chapter 6*) and "Pain" (*Chapter 7*). The next two explore "Addiction" (*Chapter 8*) and "Disability" (*Chapter 9*). Each of the remaining four chapters in Part III, in *Section 2*, deals with the function and organization of a specific physiological system and its related psychosocial health issues: *Chapter 10*, "The Immune System"; *Chapter 11*, "Cardiovascular and Respiratory Systems"; *Chapter 12*, "Digestive System"; and *Chapter 13*, "Reproductive System."

The chapters in Part III can stand alone and may be assigned in any order. Case examples are used to enliven and illustrate the concepts in Part III. They are based on actual patients whose identity is concealed. The examples are woven into the text and follow a typical clinical course in that they begin with a presentation of symptoms, continue through the discussion of related research, lead to an assessment and differential diagnosis, and end in a description of the treatment. These case examples illustrate how treatment follows from theory and research.

We conclude with *Chapter 14*, "Improving Health and Well-Being," which provides an integrative summary of current knowledge in health psychology. It is a practical, research-based guide to optimizing wellness that summarizes four variables affecting individual health: lifestyle, personality, social support, and personal control. Each one is discussed in a way that maximizes students' utilization of this knowledge in their own lives.

■

PEDAGOGY

Throughout the book, we consider illness and health from a biopsychosocial perspective—one that takes into account the biological, psychological, and social factors in health and illness. We believe that this perspective is closest to mind/body holism, which is the philosophy that seems to be driving much of the interest in health psychology. However, much of what is purveyed in the public arena as mind/body holism today is unfounded, if not potentially harmful. So, we strove to provide an up-to-date research-based introduction to health psychology.

This proved to be a challenge for two reasons. First, as the more than 2,000 references cited in this book exemplify, there is a vast literature to be surveyed. Second, health psychology research and applications are developing so rapidly that in some areas they evolved quite literally while we were in the process of writing this book. Keeping up with that has made writing this book exasperating at times but always exciting and worthwhile.

Acknowledging this vast literature and also recognizing that this book is an introduction to the field, we have chosen to discuss in detail only those studies that we consider seminal. We believe that this will maintain students' interest and preserve for them some of the excitement of research in health psychology. We have also incorporated several learning aids to help students master the material.

MODULAR ORGANIZATION

In each chapter (except Chapters 1 and 14), related material is treated in smaller units called *modules*. This allows students to concentrate on a single topic at a time, and it also provides instructors with more flexibility in making assignments. Instructors may assign only certain modules within a chapter, or they may assign modules in an order that better fits their own sequence of topics for the class. Those who prefer frequent examinations may test by module, whereas those who prefer comprehensive examinations may test by chapter or by each of the book's three parts.

MODULE SUMMARIES

Each module ends with a point-by-point summary of the major concepts covered. In our experience, it sometimes helps students who are having trouble mastering an unfamiliar area to read the module summaries first before learning the details in order to find out what the authors believe are the important concepts.

USE OF FIGURES

The biopsychosocial perspective increases the number of factors students must consider. Therefore, we have made liberal use of figures and diagrams to help students picture how biopsychosocial factors are related to the phenomenon at hand. Many of these were developed especially for this book (for example, stress, immune system, addiction).

BOLDFACE TERMS

Every important term and concept is highlighted in boldface, described when first introduced, and included in the Glossary. This alerts students to significant new terms and concepts and helps them find and review them when studying.

GLOSSARY

A comprehensive glossary at the back of the book helps students find a term even if the module it was first used in cannot be recalled.

■

ACKNOWLEDGEMENTS

First and foremost, I (Larry) would like to thank Douglas "Wordsmith" Hutchinson, who read and re-read every version of the manuscript from its inception, making important suggestions on grammar, style, and form. I am also grateful to my many students who contributed to this endeavor, especially Christine-Sartiaguda, Myra Alves, and Pamela Pennington, all of whom helped acquire material and whose energy and good cheer never wavered. I would also like to thank all of my faculty colleagues at LMU for their understanding, encouragement, and helpful comments during this project.

I (Ed) would like to thank my wife Barbara and my sons Jason and Michael. They have provided sustenance of every kind throughout and provided encouragement and support in just the right doses when I needed it most. At MCP/AHS, I want to acknowledge my colleagues, especially Mark Mesler and the members of the Liberal Arts Department, for providing useful feedback and an atmosphere that helped sustain my efforts. Special thanks go to librarians Julie Whelan, Peg Hewitt, and Nancy Occhialini for their expert assistance and to Janet Post, who helped type, manage, and coordinate work on the project with immense skill, patience, and good humor.

Any text owes a great deal to the efforts and insights of those individuals who lend their expertise to the reviewing process. This text is no exception. Many thanks to our reviewers, whose comments and suggestions proved invaluable:

Karen Anderson	Santa Clara University
Andrew Baum	Uniformed Services University of the Health Sciences
Ann Bristow	Frostburg State University
John Cavenaugh	Bowling Green State University
Bob Croyle	University of Utah
Robert Emmons	University of California at Davis
Lou Fusilli	Monroe Community College
Eugene Gilden	Linfield College
Bonnie Gray	Mesa Community College
William Heater	Lansing Community College
Francis Keefe	Duke University Medical Center
Kristi Lane	Winona State University
Edward Lichtenstein	Oregon Research Institute
Leon Rappaport	Kansas State University
Karen Rook	University of California at Irvine

Ilene Siegler	Duke University Medical Center
Rebecca Warner	University of New Hampshire
Josephine Wilson	Wittenburg University
Brian Yates	The American University

Finally, we would both like to thank our editors: Eve Howard for bringing the project to Holt, Rinehart and Winston/Harcourt Brace and providing crucial feedback early in the book's development, and to John Haley for his dedication and skill in developing the project and his help in improving its organization and style. Their efforts are sincerely appreciated.

Larry C. Bernard
Edward Krupat

Contents in Brief

CONTENTS

II BIOPSYCHOSOCIAL FACTORS IN HEALTH

3
UNDERSTANDING HEALTH-RELATED BEHAVIOR 63

INFLUENCES ON HEALTH 163

III BIOPSYCHOSOCIAL FACTORS IN ILLNESS

6
STRESS 233

7

PAIN 279

8

ADDICTION 323

11

CARDIOVASCULAR AND RESPIRATORY SYSTEMS: FUNCTION AND ORGANIZATION 467

12

DIGESTIVE SYSTEM: FUNCTION AND ORGANIZATION 517

13

REPRODUCTIVE SYSTEM: FUNCTION AND ORGANIZATION 565

14

IMPROVING HEALTH AND WELL-BEING 611

FOUNDATIONS OF HEALTH PSYCHOLOGY

How does your health relate to your state of mind? Does the mind influence your state of physical health and illness? Does your physical state influence your mental health? Or, do your mental and physical states exist symbiotically—each influencing the other?

These questions lie at the root 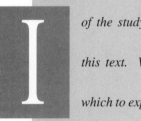 *of the study of health psychology and will be explored throughout this text. We begin in Part 1 by presenting a firm foundation from which to explore the relatively new field of health psychology.*

Chapter 1 places health psychology in context, defining how it has historically evolved as a discipline and how it relates to other health care fields. This chapter also presents some important concepts and introduces the biopsychosocial model.

Chapter 2 discusses research and intervention—two crucial areas to health psychology. It is through research and intervention that new understandings of the relationships between physical and mental health are discovered and then applied in the clinical setting.

1

THE EMERGENCE OF HEALTH PSYCHOLOGY

What do these people have in common: a 19-year-old male, premed student with several recent colds and injuries; a 47-year-old male salesperson with heart disease; a 27-year-old female real estate agent with chronic low back pain; a 23-year-old male police officer with paraplegia from a spinal cord injury; a 35-year-old female with bulimia; and a 29-year-old female with sexual arousal disorder that has affected her ability to conceive? Each has benefitted from knowledge acquired by health psychologists. Their illnesses were also treated by health psychologists who, in conjunction with physicians and other health care workers, helped them cope with their illnesses and improve their health. You will become more familiar with these people and their stories—all true—later on.

MODELS OF HEALTH AND ILLNESS

Health psychologists study how the mind and behavior influence *physical* health and illness, and vice versa. They are interested in preventing illness, in treating those who are ill, and in improving people's general physical and mental well-being. The existence of health psychology is itself an acknowledgment of the relationship between the mind and the body. However, the precise nature of this relationship is one of the most long-standing debates in philosophy. On one side of this debate are the **dualists,** who believe that the mind and body are separate, and on the other side are the **holists,** who believe that the mind and body are one. The two models of health and illness that we describe in this section reflect this debate. The traditional biomedical model of illness is dualistic, while the newer biopsychosocial model is holistic.

THE RISE OF THE BIOMEDICAL MODEL

DUALISM   Ancient Greek dualists took the position that the mind and the body are separate entities, while holists (from the Greek word "holos," which means whole) took the position that they are one. René Descartes (1596–1650), a Renaissance dualist who is often called the father of modern philosophy, believed that the mind and the body are fundamentally different substances. He believed that the body is "extended substance," part of the physical world, obeying physical laws and operating mechanistically, while the mind is "unextended substance," nonmaterial, much like the soul. Descartes was familiar with Harvey's discovery of the circulation of the blood in 1628, one of the first scientific discoveries to influence modern medicine, and it fit well with his concept of the body as a *machine* (Boring, 1950).

Dualistic philosophy has dominated Western thought for hundreds of years. Yet it has always posed a problem for philosophers: How can the material body be affected by the nonmaterial mind? How are two fundamentally different substances connected? Descartes proposed that the mind and the body were somehow connected in the pineal gland. This appealed to his sense of logic because the pineal gland is located in the center of the brain and it is the only part of the brain that is not duplicated in two halves. Since no one knew what the pineal gland did anyway, it was as good a choice as any. (We now know that the pineal gland is part of the endocrine system. Although it is still only partly understood, one of its functions seems to be maintaining circadian rhythms such as the sleep/wake cycle.) Descartes' solution to the mind–body problem is known as **interactionism**, which means that the mind and body interact while preserving their separateness.

Figure 1.1 is a representation of this interaction. Visual images are transmitted by the eye to the brain which, through a type of "hydraulic" system, causes the arm to move and the finger to point to the image. Notice that the pineal gland is located between the incoming visual image and the movement of the arm and hand, because that is the point at which the mind presumably interacts with and influences behavior.

THE BIOMEDICAL MODEL   Descartes's dualistic interactionism has dominated medicine and psychology for 300 years. It is responsible for the belief held by many physicians *and* psychologists that the physical and mental aspects of our health are separate and subject to only limited interaction. It also provides an important foundation for the **biomedical model** of illness that dominates medicine today (Engel, 1977; Schwartz, 1982). This model has four characteristics:

1. *Dualistic* Physical and psychosocial processes are separate, and disease is not influenced by the latter.
2. *Mechanistic* The body is like a machine and disease occurs when the normal operation of the body machine is disrupted by a foreign agent.

3. *Reductionistic* Ignores the complexity of factors—some psychosocial, some physical—that are involved in the health of the whole person by focusing solely on one disease or physical system.
4. *Disease oriented* "Health" is defined as the absence of disease, and efforts rarely go beyond the elimination of disease.

THE GERM THEORY OF DISEASE   The biomedical model's influence in medicine has come largely through the **germ theory** of disease. During the second century A.D., Galen (*ca.* 129–199 A.D.), a Greek physician living in Rome, proposed that disease is caused by a **pathogen**, a foreign agent that disrupts the normal operation of the body (Stone, 1979a). Although Galen was correct about the cause of many diseases, it would take well over a dozen centuries, the invention of the microscope, and the maturing of the experimental method before his theory could be validated.

Figure 1.1   RENÉ DESCARTES'S MIND/BODY INTERACTIONISM

Woodcut demonstrating René Descartes's version of mind/body interactionism. In it, the mind and body are separate but linked at the pineal gland at the center of the brain, where the mind asserts its influence over the visual image transmitted from the eyes and the pointing response of the arm and finger.

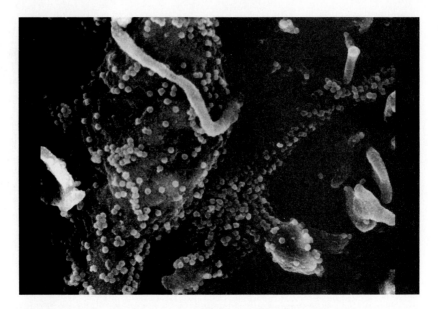

Many small, round herpes-type viruses cover the surfaces of these dead cells.

Galen's theory was validated at the end of the 19th century when the German pathologist, Rudolf Virchow (1821–1902), found microscopic organisms that disrupt the normal operation of the body and cause disease (Kaplan, 1985). Eventually, medical researchers found hundreds of bacteria, viruses, and other pathogens that cause disease. Thus was born the **germ theory** of disease in which each pathogen causes a specific **disease**, a characteristic grouping of physical signs and symptoms. Standard medical references like *Harrison's Principles of Internal Medicine* (Isselbacher, Adams, Braunwald, Petersdorf, & Wilson, 1980) describe most recognized diseases, their symptoms, and causes.

ADVANTAGES OF THE BIOMEDICAL MODEL   The germ theory and the biomedical model encouraged enormous research efforts to find specific pathogens that cause disease and treat them without concern for the psychological effects caused by the disease or by the treatment. Physicians did not have to consider that the mind might be involved in the development of diseases that affect the body. This led to the development of specific aggressive physical treatments for disease: (a) medications that destroy pathogens or ease pain and suffering were discovered in nature or created synthetically; (b) vaccines to protect against viral diseases (for example, polio); (c) medical technology to diagnose disease (for example, x-rays and new imaging devices); and (d) new surgical procedures (antiseptics and anesthetics) to reduce complications and save lives.

These developments have been responsible for some of the greatest health advances in human history. Many diseases that caused untold suffering and loss of life from the beginning of history were understood for the first time, not as plagues from unhappy gods or as demonic possession, but as the result of identifiable pathogens. Hundreds of diseases caused by a variety of pathogens can now be prevented or treated: athlete's foot, hepatitis B, influenza, malaria, mumps, measles, pneumonia, rabies, tetanus, tuberculosis.

In fact one disease, smallpox, was the first to be entirely eliminated from the human and animal population. Smallpox was known as early as the second century B.C., and its symptoms included fever and scarring pustules on the skin, particularly the face, where they resulted in grotesque disfigurement and blindness. Two smallpox epidemics in seventeenth century Europe left more than half the population facially scarred. The introduction of smallpox to the new world, where it became a scourge of the Native Americans who had no resistance, is one of the reasons that the Europeans were able to conquer them.

In 1796, Edward Jenner, an English country doctor influenced by the germ theory, developed the first vaccine for smallpox. It took many years for people to become convinced of its safety and effectiveness, but eventually, with improved vaccines, the disease was eliminated. The last case occurred in the United States in 1949. In 1977, the world was declared free of the smallpox virus. Today, it exists only as a frozen sample in vaults in Moscow and in the Centers for Disease Control in Atlanta.

THE RISE OF THE BIOPSYCHOSOCIAL MODEL

Despite the advantages of the biomedical model, it has been challenged by two recent trends (Engel, 1977; Knowles, 1977). One is the changing pattern of illness, the other is the escalating cost of health care.

THE CHANGING PATTERN OF ILLNESS
The pattern of illness has changed dramatically during the twentieth century (see Figure 1.2). In 1900, many of the leading causes of death were contagious diseases—influenza, pneumonia, tuberculosis, measles, and typhoid fever. However, by 1950, the incidence of these diseases had declined dramatically, while, in contrast, the incidence of noncontagious diseases linked to behavior or lifestyle—heart disease and cancer—was rising (U.S. Department of Health and Human Services [USDHHS], 1992). Today, 50% of mortality from the 10 leading causes of death may be attributed to lifestyle (Hamburg, Elliot, & Parron, 1982; U.S. Department of Health, Education, and Welfare [USDHEW], 1979a).

This changing pattern is the result of several factors (USDHHS, 1992). First is the decline in contagious diseases, due partly to the success of the biomedical approach, which has led to the development of vaccines, better medical treatment, improved public hygiene, and better sanitation (Grob, 1983).

Second is the decline in the rate of infant mortality (see Figure 1.3). Finally, total mortality also fell from 1,720 to 870 per 100,000 in the population in the last 90 years (U.S. Bureau of the Census, 1975, 1990).

In contrast, the increase in noncontagious diseases is largely the result of people living longer and engaging in health-compromising behaviors. A lack of physical activity, poor nutrition, cigarette smoking, and alcohol and drug abuse all contribute to the development of noncontagious diseases such as heart disease, cancer, and stroke. Also, because of medical advances in the prevention and treatment of infectious disease, more people live into their 60s, 70s, and 80s, so there is more time for them to develop diseases that arise as a result of behavior and lifestyle. The result is that well over half of all deaths in the United States in 1988 were linked to lifestyle or behavior (see Figure 1.4).

Figure 1.2   DISEASE MORTALITY TRENDS

The changing pattern of disease is indicated in mortality trends of contagious diseases—such as influenza and pneumonia—which have decreased, and noncontagious diseases—such as heart disease and cancer—which have increased during the twentieth century.

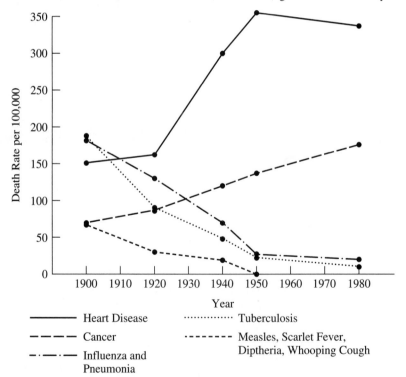

Source: U.S. Bureau of the Census, 1990, Statistical abstracts of the United States: 1990, 110th ed. (Washington, D.C.: U.S. Government Printing Office); U.S. Bureau of the Census, 1975, Historical statistics of the United States: Colonial times to 1970, Part 1 (Washington, D.C.: U.S. Government Printing Office).

Figure 1.3   INFANT MORTALITY TRENDS

Infant mortality has declined dramatically from 1900 to 1987. Total mortality has also declined during this period.

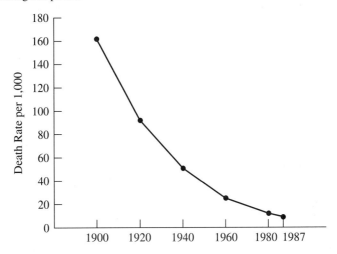

Source: U.S. Bureau of the Census, 1990, Statistical abstracts of the United States: 1990, *110th ed. (Washington, D.C.: U.S. Government Printing Office); U.S. Bureau of the Census, 1975,* Historical statistics of the United States: Colonial times to 1970, Part 1 *(Washington, D.C.: U.S. Government Printing Office).*

Figure 1.4   LEADING CAUSES OF DEATH IN THE U.S. IN 1988

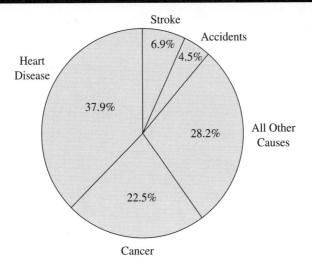

Source: U.S. Bureau of the Census, 1990, Statistical abstracts of the United States: 1990, *110th ed. (Washington, D.C.: U.S. Government Printing Office).*

ESCALATING HEALTH CARE COSTS   The other challenge to the biomedical model has been the dramatically escalating costs of health care. The
Department of Health and Human Services reported that, in 1989, more than
$600 billion was spent for health care in the United States. (Rosenblatt, 1990).
In 1960, medical services accounted for just 5% of the Gross National Product
(GNP) of the United States, but by 1990 they were estimated to have risen to
12% (USDHHS, 1992). When this figure is added to the lost economic productivity caused by illness, which is another 18% of the GNP, total costs to the
country are 30% of the annual GNP.

Yearly per capita health care expenditures have risen faster than inflation
and total nearly $2000 for each man, woman, and child in the United States
(see Figure 1.5). The biggest categories of health care spending in 1989 were
hospitals, at $232.8 billion; doctors' services, at $117.6 billion; nursing home
care, at $47.9 billion; medications, at $44.6 billion; and dentists' services, at
$31.4 billion (Rosenblatt, 1990).

While the costs of treating contagious diseases are relatively low, the cost
of the advanced medical technology necessary to treat lifestyle or behavioral

**Figure 1.5   YEARLY PER CAPITA HEALTH CARE
EXPENDITURES, 1960–1987**

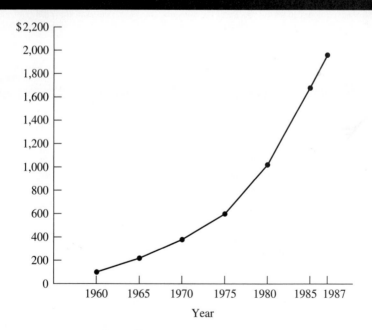

*Source: U.S. Bureau of the Census, 1990, Statistical abstracts of the United States: 1990, 110th ed.
(Washington, D.C.: U.S. Government Printing Office).*

diseases is quite high. Patients may require open heart surgery or heart transplants, and radiation or chemotherapy, all of which are expensive. In this case, it would be much more cost efficient to *prevent* the development of these diseases—that is, to employ behavioral and lifestyle changes before disease develops—than to treat them later.

LIMITATIONS OF THE BIOMEDICAL MODEL   The changing pattern of illness and the escalating cost of health care revealed weaknesses in the biomedical model (Ahmed, Kolker, & Coehlo, 1979). Put simply, it is incomplete. While it works well when applied to contagious diseases with specific pathogens, it is too limited to take into account the "interactions among social and psychological as well as biological factors in the etiology, course, and treatment of [lifestyle or behavioral] disease" (Jemmott & Locke, 1984, p. 78).

The fact that a comprehensive model of illness would have to take psychosocial factors into account received support when researchers discovered that psychotherapy, even in a brief form and even when there was no mental disorder diagnosed, resulted in an unintended but significant decrease in the utilization of medical services (for example, Follette & Cummings, 1967; Schlesinger, Mumford, & Glass, 1980). Consistent with this discovery is other evidence that people in poor mental health make frequent use of medical care, while people in poor physical health make frequent use of mental health services (for example, Aronowitz & Bromberg, 1984; Kessler et al., 1987; Vaillant, 1979; Ware et al., 1984). At the same time that the limitations of the biomedical model were being realized, researchers were finding a link between poor mental health and poor physical health.

THE BIOPSYCHOSOCIAL MODEL   Psychiatrist George Engel (1977) was the first to propose a **biopsychosocial model** of illness. He stated that a "medical model must take into account the patient, the social context in which he lives and the complementary system devised by society to deal with the disruptive effects of illness" (p.132). By stating that a model of disease must take the patient into account, Engel repudiated the biomedical model and dualism. Rather, he recognized that illness and health must involve a whole person. He was not alone in this position, because others also recognize that people are "individual mind–body complexes ceaselessly interacting with the social and physical environment in which they are embodied" (Lipowski, 1977, p. 234). Physician John Knowles (1977), stated it this way:

Over 99 percent of us are born healthy and made sick as a result of personal misbehavior and environmental conditions. The solution to the problem of ill health in modern American society involves individual responsibility, in the first instance, and social responsibility through public legislative and private voluntary efforts, in the second instance (p. 58).

However, rather than a new approach, the biopsychosocial model is actually a return to *holism,* which existed at the time of Hippocrates (*ca.* 460–370 B.C.), the "father of medicine" (Boring, 1950; Gentry & Matarazzo, 1981). In it, health and illness are states of being that result from multiple factors and have multiple effects. These multiple factors include biological and physiological processes, pathogens, and chemical imbalances, as well as psychosocial processes, personality, and behavior (see Figure 1.6). The mind and body are not separate, independent entities; rather, they are two aspects of a whole person. Health and illness are not physical *or* mental; rather, they are physical *and* mental. Health care that accommodates the physical and mental aspects of illness is sometimes referred to as holistic because it encompasses the whole person, but unfortunately "holism" and "holistic" have been used too loosely and unscientifically in fringe medicine and "pop" psychology.

Because it is holistic, the biopsychosocial model is more complex than the biomedical model. Researchers and health care workers must take many more factors into account in order to define health and to treat illness, but this model probably represents reality better than the biomedical model's forced separation of mind and body, mental and physical health (Schwartz, 1984). A new model of health necessitates a new definition as well.

A NEW DEFINITION OF HEALTH

What is health? How do you know when you are healthy? To answer these questions, let's first consider what illness is. We have previously defined a *disease* as a characteristic grouping of physical signs and symptoms; it is given a specific name and can often be traced to a specific causal agent. **Illness,** however, is a broader term that involves people's *beliefs* about the state of their physical well-being and the resulting *behaviors* they engage in (see Module 3.3). Illness beliefs may be the result of a specific disease or just the way we feel when we *say* we are ill (even when there is no evidence of a disease). Illness is important because it is what motivates people to seek out a physician. A disease is what the physician recognizes as a specific disorder based on known signs and symptoms (Kleinman, 1988). Therefore, a physician is likely to define health as the absence of disease, while the average person might define health more broadly, as the absence of *any* ill feelings (the sick role and illness behavior are discussed in more detail in Module 3.3).

In both of these definitions, however, health is described in terms of what it is *not*—as the *absence* of disease or illness. A better definition conceives of illness and wellness as opposite ends of a single continuum (Antonovsky, 1979). Although this concept still lends itself to a view of health as the absence of illness, it is reciprocal, because it also views illness as an absence of health.

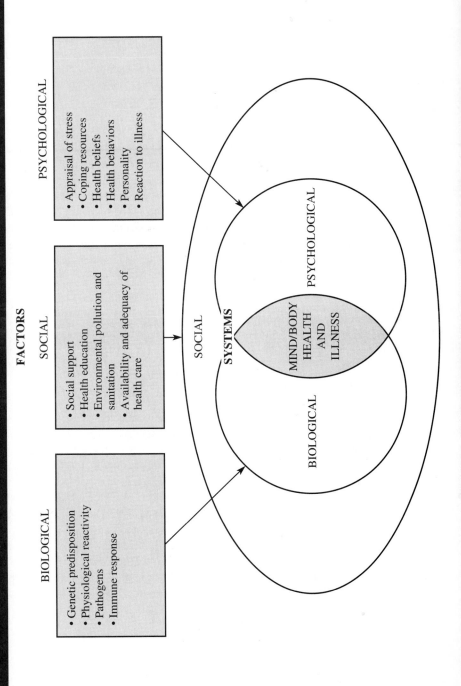

Figure 1.6 **THE BIOPSYCHOSOCIAL MODEL FROM TWO PERSPECTIVES: FACTORS AND SYSTEMS**

FACTORS

BIOLOGICAL
- Genetic predisposition
- Physiological reactivity
- Pathogens
- Immune response

SOCIAL
- Social support
- Health education
- Environmental pollution and sanitation
- Availability and adequacy of health care

PSYCHOLOGICAL
- Appraisal of stress
- Coping resources
- Health beliefs
- Health behaviors
- Personality
- Reaction to illness

SYSTEMS

SOCIAL

PSYCHOLOGICAL

BIOLOGICAL

MIND/BODY HEALTH AND ILLNESS

More importantly, it permits attention to be focused on what factors help people stay well, rather than solely on what makes them ill. Figure 1.7 shows how the biomedical and biopsychosocial models might be combined. The biomedical "ladder" addresses the "climb" from illness to the health midpoint, which represents the absence of disease, whereas the biopsychosocial model addresses the continued climb to wellness, or optimum health.

SYSTEMS THEORY

Many of the factors that help people stay well are systemic. A system is any regularly interacting or interdependent group of elements that form a unified whole. **Systems theory** attempts to understand the behavior of these dynamic, interrelated elements, and has had an important impact on family and community psychology. In health psychology, an individual may be thought of as a system, with the various organs being its elements. There are, however, many overlapping systems that exist on different levels of complexity. For example, on the micro level, each organ is itself a separate system and its elements are

Figure 1.7　ILLNESS–WELLNESS LADDER

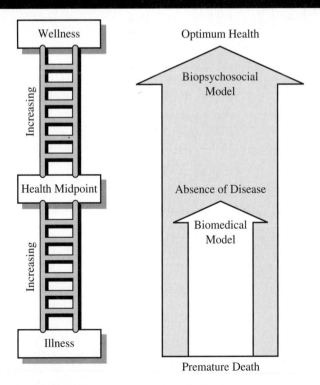

individual cells, while on the macro level, people are the elements in family or community systems.

How does systems theory relate to health? It is not an integral part of the biopsychosocial model, nor is it necessary for a definition of health, but it is quite compatible with both (Engel, 1980; Schwartz, 1983). First, it recognizes that an individual's health is partly dependent on internal systems—each must be operating well in order for an individual to achieve optimum health. Second, system theory recognizes that individual health is also affected by external systems in the larger community. The relationship between systems theory and health will become clearer when the concept of homeostasis or balance is taken into account.

HEALTH AND BALANCE

Homeostasis, which refers to equilibrium or balance among the various elements of a system, is an important concept in systems theory and health psychology. Health is characterized as a smoothly functioning and regulated system in a state of homeostasis. Homeostasis is maintained by the feedback of information. There are two kinds of feedback: (a) *negative feedback,* which causes the system or one of its elements to *decrease* activity in order to achieve homeostasis; and (b) *positive feedback,* which causes the system to *increase* activity in order to achieve homeostasis. Positive feedback can be detrimental to a system if it leads to overactivation; likewise, negative feedback can be detrimental if it leads to underactivation.

A simple thermostat on a heating system provides a good example of homeostasis and feedback. Homeostasis would be defined as a comfortable, preset temperature, perhaps 70°. When the temperature drops below 70°, the thermostat sends a message to activate the furnace (positive feedback). When the temperature returns to 70°, the thermostat sends a message to deactivate the furnace (negative feedback) and homeostasis is reestablished. In order to understand the implications of homeostasis and feedback for health, imagine what would happen if something went wrong, if the thermostat failed to send negative feedback or if it did, but the furnace did not respond. The temperature would rise unchecked and disaster could result.

Homeostasis and feedback are important principles that underlie many of the body's basic regulatory mechanisms and feature prominently in processes to maintain health and to sustain life. For example, body temperature, blood sugar, respiration, and immune system functioning are all regulated by homeostatic processes. Consider the regulation of blood sugar. It rises after a meal, but too high a level of sugar in the blood produces discomforting symptoms: flushing, vomiting, thirst, damage to internal organs, and even coma. To prevent this, when blood sugar rises, the pancreas reacts like a thermostat and releases the hormone insulin into the bloodstream. Insulin reduces blood sugar by allowing it to pass from the blood into cells where it can be metabolized, and blood sugar falls toward a homeostatic or nonharmful level. If blood sugar

Regular physical activity helps maintain health when it is balanced by periods of relaxation and more sedentary activity.

falls too low, the pancreas again reacts like a thermostat and releases another hormone, glucagon, which causes the level of blood sugar to rise. Thus, the pancreas maintains homeostasis in the level of blood sugar. Dysfunction of this mechanism results in diabetes (discussed more fully in Part III, in the introduction to the nervous and endocrine systems).

Systems theory provides a framework for classifying and understanding the many factors involved in the biopsychosocial model, while homeostasis and feedback describe the dynamic flow of information and its effects within a system. Gary Schwartz (1984), former president of the Health Psychology Division of the American Psychological Association (APA), has suggested that the brain might be the body's executive homeostatic coordinator. Provided that the individual pays attention and does not distort the feedback received by the brain, it can lead to improved self-care and health, according to Schwartz.

In order to summarize the new definition of health, the following concepts must be integrated: the biopsychosocial factors depicted in Figure 1.6, systems theory, and homeostasis. A helpful way to accomplish this integration is to imagine that each person contains a number of internal elements and that each element has its own thermostat, which controls various homeostatic processes necessary for health. These thermostats are all interrelated (one possibility is through the brain), such that changes in one thermostat affect the others. Systems theory also implies that individuals are loosely involved in larger systems with other people. Some people may be interrelated to many others, while others may be related to only a few. This suggests that people in a family or neighborhood system can affect the health of one another. Therefore, in addition to the absence of illness, a definition of health should incorporate the notion of homeostasis, of both internal and external systemic balance.

OPTIMUM HEALTH

Julius Seeman (1989) argued in the *American Psychologist* for a definition of *positive* health that would be completely independent of any notion of illness. Seeman based his concept of health on the definition adopted by the World Health Organization of the United Nations at its founding in 1946: "Health is a state of complete physical, mental and social well-being, and not merely the absence of disease and illness" (cited in Sullivan, 1974, p. 2). This definition goes beyond even the illness–wellness continuum, because health requires not just optimal physical functioning, but optimal *mental* and *social* functioning as well.

This definition is also compatible with the biopsychosocial model, because it recognizes the three broad categories (physical, psychological, and social) of factors involved in illness and health. Also, it defines health as an *optimum* state (a state of well-being), rather than as just a neutral state. Therefore, health should be defined as freedom from illness, as homeostatic balance, and as optimal physical, mental, and social functioning. This expanded definition has important ramifications, for it implies that health is broadly related to the overall quality of life—that is not just an internal state, but involves the external community in which one lives as well.

PSYCHOLOGY AND HEALTH

This definition of optimum health clearly implies a role for psychologists in health. In fact, psychologists have been interested in physical health for a long time, but health psychology has taken a while to develop to its current state.

SOMATOFORM DISORDERS

Sigmund Freud actually provided one of the first modern links between medicine and psychology, although, in true dualistic fashion, Freud gave up medicine to study the mind. Freud was a physician trained in neurology, but he observed that some patients had physical symptoms (like numbness, blindness, or paralysis) in the absence of any known organic pathology. He attributed these symptoms to unconscious mental conflicts and called the disorder **"conversion hysteria,"** because he believed that the mental conflicts were being *converted* into physical symptoms (Alexander, 1950; Davison & Neale, 1990). Because medical techniques were ineffective in treating conversion hysteria, Freud abandoned them to develop his own purely psychological "talking cure," which he named "psychoanalysis."

Today, conversion hysteria is among a category of psychological disorders called **"somatoform"** ("soma" is Greek for body), which are characterized by physical symptoms generated by psychological processes. Table 1.1 contains descriptions of the somatoform disorders. You might think of these disorders as "psychosomatic," but health psychologists use the term "psychosomatic" differently (see the next discussion).

Table 1.1   SOMATOFORM DISORDERS

Body Dysmorphic Disorder
   Preoccupation with an imagined defect in the body in a normally appearing person

Conversion Disorder
   Loss or alteration in physical functioning typically mimicking neurologic disease (for example, paralysis, blindness), but it also may mimic disease of the autonomic or endocrine systems; the person is *not* aware of intentionally producing the symptoms.

Hypochondriasis
   Preoccupation with the fear of having a disease or the belief that one has a serious disease in the absence of any physical evidence

Somatization Disorder
   Recurrent *multiple* physical symptoms and complaints (for example, vomiting, pain, shortness of breath, amnesia, difficulty swallowing, burning sensations, painful menstruation)

Somatoform Pain Disorder
   Experiencing pain in the absence of physical evidence that can account for it

---

Source: American Psychiatric Association, 1987, Diagnostic and Statistical Manual of Mental Disorders, *3rd. ed., rev. (Washington, D.C.: Author.).*

Under the dualistic tradition, physicians have been involved only when there is verifiable *organic* pathology, and somatoform disorders have been regarded as the domain of psychiatrists and psychologists. Within psychology, somatoform disorders are studied by clinical psychologists and considered in courses like abnormal psychology or psychopathology. Consistent with the dualistic tradition, somatoform disorders are not considered part of health psychology, although, ironically, the very existence of somatoform disorders can be interpreted as support for mind–body holism, because it demonstrates that physical symptoms can be mentally controlled.

PSYCHOSOMATIC MEDICINE

The ancient Greek holists, Hippocrates among them, would not have appreciated our modern separation of mind and body into psychology and medicine. Neither did all of Freud's psychiatric contemporaries, for several remained interested in research on physical as well as mental problems throughout the 1930s. Their field became known as **psychosomatic medicine**, combining the Greek word "psyche" for mind and the word "soma." They believed that the mind and the body should not be separated and studied independently. They began to publish the journal *Psychosomatic Medicine* in 1939 and formed the American Psychosomatic Society several years later. Until the 1960s, their work remained heavily influenced by psychoanalytic theories. However, as biopsychosocial advances began to challenge the biomedical model, the field of psychosomatic medicine broadened (Totman, 1982; Lipowski, 1986). Today, health psychologists are regular contributors to *Psychosomatic Medicine.*

BEHAVIORAL MEDICINE

Psychology developed over the same time period as psychoanalysis, beginning in the late 1800s. However, the two fields developed independently. While Freud was primarily a clinician, interested in treating patients, psychologists in Freud's time were primarily researchers, interested in understanding psychological processes and behavior through laboratory and field research. One of the early trends in psychological research was **behaviorism**, the study of how behavior is *learned* through conditioning.

American psychology was dominated by behaviorism throughout the first half of the twentieth century. John Watson, its first proponent, maintained that psychologists should only study observable behavior. Later, B. F. Skinner's research led to a more "radical behaviorism" in which all behavior was believed to be under the control of external reinforcement. By the 1970s, researchers had demonstrated impressive results in modifying behavioral and emotional problems (Rimm & Masters, 1979), and the behavioral perspective is one of the most important contributions psychology has made to the study of health and illness, particularly in the realm of intervention.

Another traditional area of psychological research is known as physiological or **biopsychology**. Biopsychologists study brain function and the relationship between physiology and mental states. Again, by the 1970s, psychologists like Neal Miller had applied the principles of behaviorism to basic physiological processes and shown that they could be affected by conditioning (Dienstfrey, 1991). One important discovery was that people could learn to control physiological processes if they were provided with feedback on their operation (Miller, 1969). Eventually this came to be called **biofeedback** (Rimm & Masters, 1979; described in more detail in Module 2.2). Both behavioral and biopsychology contributed to the development of the new field of **behavioral medicine**.

A conference of psychologists and physicians was held at Yale University in 1977 with the goal of formally defining this new field (Pomerleau, 1982). Shortly after the conference, the Society of Behavioral Medicine and the Academy of Behavioral Medicine Research (of the National Academy of Sciences) were formed and the *Journal of Behavioral Medicine* began publication. Behavioral medicine was defined as an

> *interdisciplinary field concerned with the development and integration of behavioral and biomedical science knowledge and techniques relevant to health and illness and the application of this knowledge and these techniques to prevention, diagnosis, treatment and rehabilitation.* (Schwartz & Weiss, 1978, p. 250)

One of the most important aspects of behavioral medicine is that it seeks to combine the biomedical and behavioral sciences, with the goal of *treating* people who are ill (see Dreher, 1992, for a report on current approaches to treatment). To this end, it remains an interdisciplinary field, involving biologists and physicians, among others, as well as psychologists (Gentry, 1984).

Notice that the definition of behavioral medicine mentions health and prevention along with illness. Those concerned primarily with the enhancement of health in healthy individuals eventually formed a subfield within behavioral medicine called **behavioral health** (Matarazzo, 1980). Behavioral health is more concerned with reaching optimum health (Matarazzo, 1984), while behavioral medicine is more concerned with achieving an absence of illness (refer to Figure 1.7). Like behavioral medicine, behavioral health is also interdisciplinary, including dieticians, epidemiologists, and health educators, in addition to psychologists.

Health Psychology

Although psychologists were involved in the developing fields of behavioral medicine and behavioral health, interest in health was also growing within the APA. At first, very few psychologists were directly involved with health research and only about 50 health psychologists were identified in 1974

(APA Task Force, 1976; Stone, 1982). By 1978, however, the Division of Health Psychology was formed within the APA. In 1982, it began publishing a journal, *Health Psychology,* and by 1987, the division had 3,000 members (Houston, 1988).

Joseph Matarazzo, the first president of the Division of Health Psychology provided this definition of health psychology:

> **Health psychology** *is the aggregate of the specific educational, scientific, and professional contributions of the discipline of psychology to the promotion and maintenance of health; the prevention and treatment of illness; the identification of etiologic and diagnostic correlates of health, illness, and related dysfunction; and to the analysis and improvement of the health care system and health policy formation (1982, p. 4).*

This definition includes an important aspect of health that had not yet been considered: the improvement of the health care system itself. Other than that, health psychology is concerned with the same aspects of wellness and illness that behavioral medicine and behavioral health are concerned about.

Today, all of these fields accept the biopsychosocial model of health and illness, and psychologists may be involved with any or all of these organizations. Then why the need for health psychology if it overlaps so much with behavioral medicine and health? The reasons are partly historical and organizational.

The most important reason for maintaining a distinction is that behavioral medicine and behavioral health are interdisciplinary, encompassing a variety of health-related fields, whereas health psychology is a subfield strictly *within* psychology. As such, it maintains connections to the many other diverse and productive subfields of psychology (for example, biopsychology, clinical psychology, social psychology). Therefore, it profits from advances in these subfields and it maintains a broad perspective in keeping with the biopsychosocial model. Table 1.2 lists some contributions to health psychology made by some of the subfields in psychology.

In summary, we have answered the question, "What is health psychology?" Health psychology is the application of psychological research and practice to the improvement of efforts to prevent and treat illness and to optimize health. Health psychologists often work jointly with other disciplines to obtain these goals. Health psychologists have backgrounds in a variety of subfields within psychology that they bring to these joint ventures. Yet, what sets health psychologists apart from other psychologists is their focus on physical illness and health.

HEALTH PSYCHOLOGY AS A CAREER

By now it is probably evident that health psychologists work as either researchers or practitioners, although some are both. Because of this dichotomy, which runs throughout psychology, we will discuss a career in health psychology in terms of research and practice.

RESEARCH Medical schools employ a variety of scientists as teachers. These academics typically hold Ph.D. degrees and come from many fields. Among them are substantial numbers of psychologists, and virtually every medical school in the U.S. employs psychologists as faculty (Lubin, Nathan, & Matarazzo, 1978). Their colleagues on medical school faculties come from the major life science fields such as anatomy, biology, and pathology. Psychologists who work in behavioral medicine may conduct research jointly with those in the basic life sciences. Other fields with whom health psychologists may conduct joint research include medical sociology, medical anthropology, and epidemiology.

PRACTICE In psychology, practice means the application of psychological knowledge to enhance people's well-being. Most people are probably familiar with the traditional role of the clinical (or counseling) psychologist. **Clinical psychologists** utilize psychological knowledge in a therapeutic way with individuals or small groups. Their goal is usually to reduce psychological distress and change maladaptive behavior. The difference between clinical psychologists and clinical health psychologists is that the former work with people who have psychological problems, while the latter work with people who have physical problems.

Table 1.2 CONTRIBUTIONS OF PSYCHOLOGY'S SUBFIELDS TO HEALTH PSYCHOLOGY

PSYCHOLOGY SUBFIELD	CONTRIBUTION
Physiological/Biological	Interrelationship of the brain and the immune system (for example, see "Psychoneuroimmunology" in the Introduction to Chapter 10)
Clinical	Psychological and behavioral approaches to treatment (for example, see Changing Behavior in Module 2.2)
Cognitive	Models of health-related behavior (for example, see the Health Belief Model in Module 3.1)
Developmental	The effects of growth and aging on health and illness (see Module 5.1)
Social	Health promotion and education (see Module 3.2)

Health psychologists who work clinically with ill people are usually referred to as **medical psychologists**. Medical psychologists often interface with physicians, who usually specialize in one of the many medical specialty areas, including cardiology, immunology, and neurology, or today's equivalent of the "general practitioner" (specialists in family practice, internal medicine, or pediatrics). Health psychologists also work alongside other health care workers who are not physicians, such as nurses, pharmacists, and physical therapists. Medical psychologists utilize treatments and techniques currently derived from the mainstream of clinical psychology. These treatments and techniques are described in Module 2.2.

In a newer role, **applied psychologists** utilize psychological knowledge in consultation, usually with large groups such as businesses, institutions, or government (Gregory & Burroughs, 1989). Their goal is to *prevent* the development of psychological distress and maladaptive behavior. They must have effective communication skills to be able to get along in the milieu in which they work, and they must be able to translate and apply psychological knowledge in order to achieve practical results. Applied health psychologists might work as consultants within businesses, communities, and government to develop programs that prevent illness and optimize health.

EDUCATION AND TRAINING   The APA maintains the doctorate in psychology as the minimum achievement for identification as a psychologist in any subfield. Doctoral programs in departments of psychology offer similar core courses, such as clinical, developmental, or social psychology, which graduate students in health psychology also take. In this way, health psychologists learn to apply the "accumulated knowledge from the science and profession of generic psychology to the area of health" (Matarazzo, 1987, p. 55). In addition, they often take such elective courses as epidemiology, biostatistics, public health, or physiology.

Beyond the core courses, psychology graduate students typically receive training in research, teaching, and/or the application of psychology through consulting or clinical practice. All students in doctoral programs complete a dissertation, which must be an original contribution to the field in which the student is training (for example, health). Those who obtain the Ph.D. receive additional training in research and teaching, and their dissertation is research based. Those who obtain the Psy.D. receive additional training in clinical practice, and their dissertation may not be research based. The typical doctoral program requires five to six years, although it is not uncommon for students to take longer. Students whose emphasis is in clinical or counseling psychology must also complete a year of supervised internship training before obtaining their degree (this would include health psychologists who intend to provide services to patients).

At the present time, very few departments offer a formal program in health psychology, and today most health psychologists have backgrounds in another subfield of psychology. Some departments have incorporated a health emphasis within an existing program (for example, social or clinical; Belar, Wilson, & Hughes, 1982; Sheridan et al., 1988). Graduate students interested in becoming health psychologists often study in an existing program in a department that offers outside opportunities to take elective courses related to medicine and health.

Whereas graduation from a Ph.D. program is usually considered sufficient training for a career in research and teaching in any area of psychology, further training and experience is the norm for those planning to do applied or clinical work. The National Working Conference on Education and Training in Health Psychology has recommended two years of additional training in a formal residency program *after* receipt of the Ph.D. or Psy.D. *and* completion of at least one year of formal internship experience (Stone, 1983). During this program, specific skills and techniques should be learned (see Table 1.3). At present, these recommendations have not been implemented. Students who are interested in becoming a health psychologist should contact the APA's Division of Health Psychology for the latest developments.

Table 1.3 **REQUIREMENTS FOR CLINICAL POSTDOCTORAL RESIDENCY***

Relaxation Therapies
Short-term individual psychotherapy
Group therapy
Family therapy
Consultation skills
Liaison skills
Assessment of specific patient populations (for example, pain patients, spinal cord injury patients)
Neuropsychological assessment
Behavior modification techniques
Biofeedback
Hypnosis
Health promotion and public education skills
Major treatment programs (for example, chemical dependence, eating disorders)
Compliance motivation

---

*At least six of these techniques and skills should be acquired in a two-year clinical postdoctoral residency in health psychology.

Source: Sheridan, E. P., Matarazzo, J. D., Boll, T. J., Perry, N. W., Jr., Weiss, S. M., & Belar, C. D., 1988, Postdoctoral education and training for clinical service providers in health psychology, Health Psychology, 7, 1–17.

CHAPTER SUMMARY

You should now have a better understanding of the history of health psychology and the biomedical and biopsychosocial models of illness. You should have a good definition of health psychology, know a little bit about what health psychologists do and what is required to become one, and realize how health psychology relates to subfields of psychology and other health-related fields.

Health psychology is a vibrant and growing field in which psychology may potentially make its greatest contributions in the coming decades. Virtually unknown a few years ago, today health psychology is the most popular area of clinical research in doctoral programs (Sayette & Mayne, 1990). In addition, with the World Health Organization's emphasis on psychosocial and behavioral factors in health, international interest in health psychology is beginning to develop (Diekstra, 1990a; Jansen, Methorst, & Kerkhof, 1990), although currently the U.S. and Canada are the only countries with formal training programs (Methorst, Jansen, & Kerkhof, 1990).

Chapter 2 will introduce the methods health psychologists use to conduct research, treat illness, and enhance well-being. However, before continuing, review the following points made in this chapter:

1. One of the most long-standing debates in philosophy is over the relationship between the mind and body. Dualism, which is associated with the biomedical model of illness, maintains that the mind and body are separate entities, while holism, which is associated with the biopsychosocial model of illness, maintains that they are one.
2. In addition to being dualistic, the biomedical model is mechanistic, reductionistic, and disease oriented. However, these features have resulted in advantages that gave rise to the germ theory of disease and effective prevention and treatment for many diseases.
3. Since the beginning of the twentieth century, illness patterns have changed. Deaths caused by contagious diseases have decreased, while deaths caused by noncontagious lifestyle diseases such as cancer and heart disease have increased. In addition, people are living longer due to vaccines, better medical treatment, improved public hygiene, and better sanitation.
4. More recently, health care costs have escalated dramatically. This partly reflects the more expensive medical technology involved in treating the lifestyle diseases.
5. Because of the changing patterns of illness and escalating health care costs, the limitations of the biomedical model have become more apparent. The biomedical model is incomplete, and because it does

not take psychosocial factors into account, its effectiveness in dealing with lifestyle diseases is limited.

6. The biopsychosocial model represents a better alternative for dealing with lifestyle diseases because it takes biological as well as psychosocial factors into account. It also fits well with systems theory and the concept of homeostasis.

7. Systems theory can be applied to internal bodily subsystems as well as external systems, such as the family or community within which a person lives. Homeostasis recognizes that optimum functioning depends on balance among the elements of a system. Many of the body's systems are homeostatic and illness can result from disequilibrium in them.

8. Health is defined as freedom from illness, as homeostatic balance, and as optimal physical, mental, and social functioning.

9. When physical symptoms are generated by psychological processes, they are termed "somatoform," not "psychosomatic." Traditionally, these somatoform disorders are treated by psychiatrists and clinical psychologists. The term "psychosomatic" is used to describe a holistic mind–body approach to illness.

10. Behavioral medicine is an interdisciplinary field that integrates behavioral psychology and biomedical science to treat illness, whereas behavioral health, also an interdisciplinary field, is more concerned with wellness and optimizing health in healthy individuals.

11. Health psychology is a subfield of psychology. It combines an orientation toward illness and wellness, treatment and prevention. The APA maintains the doctoral degree as the minimum achievement for identification as a psychologist.

12. Health psychologists are trained in doctoral programs that encompass the same core psychology courses that all psychologists study. They also take additional courses related to medicine and health. Health psychologists may work in research, teaching, or practice. They often work alongside colleagues from a variety of medical and health disciplines.

2

ACQUIRING AND APPLYING
KNOWLEDGE IN HEALTH PSYCHOLOGY

2.1 Research
2.2 Intervention

A solid foundation in health psychology requires an appreciation of how health psychologists acquire and apply knowledge. Module 2.1 explores the research enterprise in health psychology and illustrates the process with an example of an experiment to test two behavioral methods of lowering blood cholesterol, a major risk factor in heart disease. Module 2.2 describes the ways in which health psychologists apply the knowledge acquired through research to help people.

RESEARCH

ACQUIRING KNOWLEDGE

Can stress cause heart attacks? Can exercise prevent them? Why is it so hard for some people to maintain their weight? Are depression and cancer related? How effective are stop-smoking treatments? You've probably thought about one or more of these questions yourself, and maybe that is why you are taking this class. Perhaps you already have opinions about them, but where did those opinions come from? If you are like most people, they probably came from reports in the media and anecdotes that you have heard over the years.

ANECDOTES

An **anecdote** is a report of an experience that someone else has had or a brief narrative of an interesting or biographical event. People often tell health-related anecdotes. Take this one for example, which was overheard in a doctor's office:

> First it was exercise, now they tell us fiber prevents heart attacks. I don't think doctors know what they're talking about. They still say that cigarettes cause cancer, but I don't believe it. My husband smoked a pack-and-a-half every day of his life from the time he was 13—37 years—and he never had cancer. He was strong as a bull until the day he was hit by a truck.

Anecdotes such as this do not help us acquire knowledge in health psychology. First, details may be left out of the story or this woman may not realize that the detrimental effects of smoking are cumulative and that it may be many years before health problems arise. When her husband met his untimely demise at 50 years of age, he would just have been entering the period when cancer and heart disease begin to occur with some frequency in smokers. An autopsy would probably have revealed considerable tissue damage from smoking. Second, even if an autopsy revealed no damage, her husband may just have been a rare exception. It is also important to know what happens to other people who smoke cigarettes. The unsystematic and personally biased nature of anecdotes serves as a contrast to the systematic way in which psychologists usually acquire knowledge.

However, do not get the idea that health psychologists are not interested in people's stories, because they certainly are. Anecdotes reveal how people think about illness and health. On a clinical level, they help us understand the individual and the meaning of health in his or her life. On a societal level, they can provide direction for the planning and promotion of health and education programs.

Researchers often gather useful information by listening to people's anecdotes. Early in an epidemic, public health researchers interview and carefully record people's reports regarding their symptoms. Using such interviews, they can sometimes find a convergence of information that leads to a hypothesis about what is happening. In fact, anecdotal reports were used early in the epidemic of Acquired Immune Deficiency Syndrome (AIDS) to help generate hypotheses about what causes the disease. One research technique, called the case study, specifically focuses on individuals.

CASE STUDIES

There are two types of **case studies**, each of which involves a single subject. A *clinical case study* is an in-depth report of an illness and its treatment. It is often used for rare diseases where groups of subjects cannot be studied or for studying the effects of an experimental treatment. The background and characteristics of the subject are described in great detail, as are the symptoms, treatment, and outcome.

The *research case study* is used frequently by behavioral psychologists (Christensen, 1991). An individual's behavior is studied while a variable is manipulated. In this way, the effect of the manipulated variable on the behavior can be determined. If the behavior changes after the variable is manipulated, it is assumed that they are causally related.

For example, if a parent wanted to increase the activity level of a child who watched too much television, the child could be relieved of doing one chore (for example, taking out the trash or mowing the lawn) for each hour spent engaged in a physical activity during the week instead of watching television. If physical activity level went up over the next few weeks, we could conclude that relief from chores increases this child's activity level. We could be even more confident in our conclusion if the parent stopped relieving the child of chores and the child's physical activity level dropped.

Research case studies are helpful in determining potential cause-and-effect relationships between variables. However, there is little basis to apply the results of one person to anyone else, so it is said that they do not *generalize* well. In order to generalize the results, experiments with more subjects must be conducted. The case study is an economical first step, because if a relationship cannot be demonstrated with one person, it may not be worth conducting a larger experiment.

SYSTEMATIC RESEARCH

Illness is a universal experience. All people face it and are naturally interested in it. People want to know about illness because such knowledge can help them live better, healthier lives. For example, when researchers found a link between diets high in cholesterol and heart disease, new low cholesterol labels quickly appeared on food packages. In this way, manufacturers took advantage of people's awareness of the link between dietary cholesterol and disease. Meanwhile, other researchers found that blood cholesterol could be reduced through behavioral changes—by increasing dietary fiber and exercise.

How did these researchers come by this knowledge in the first place? Knowledge can be acquired in a variety of ways. Some knowledge is just plain *superstition;* some is based on *logical reasoning;* and some is based on *empiricism,* which is experience gained through observation (Helmstadter, 1970). Science, the method used by researchers in health psychology, is a systematic way of obtaining data in an unbiased manner. The **scientific method** does not accept superstition; instead, scientists make use of logical reasoning and empiricism. Logical reasoning is used to develop theories and hypotheses, and empiricism is the process of collecting and observing objective data instead of relying on anecdotes. The scientific process usually begins with a theory.

THEORY   A **theory** is a set of organized and related ideas about natural phenomena (Christensen, 1991). Theories serve several useful purposes. First, they seek to explain by organizing and making sense out of individual facts. Second, they help us to make predictions about variables and their relationships. Third, they stimulate research by generating hypotheses. Although, ideally, scientists would like to believe that the process proceeds in an orderly fashion from theory to hypothesis to research, this is often not the case. Sometimes individual hypotheses are formulated and researched and the theory develops after the fact as a means of explaining the results.

HYPOTHESIS   A scientific study is almost always conducted to test a specific **hypothesis,** which is the best prediction or tentative answer to a research problem or question. It is important to note that, as useful as theories and hypotheses may be, scientists learn not to view them as absolute, for they are always subject to change as more is learned through scientific study.

Once a hypothesis has been formulated, the next step is to determine what research design to use.

Research Designs

There are three basic types of research designs—descriptive, correlational, and experimental—and one that is a combined correlational-experimental design called quasi-experimental.

Descriptive Research

This may, in fact, be the most widely used method of research (Helmstadter, 1970). If you have ever seen a poll by Gallup, you have seen the results of descriptive research. Descriptive research attempts to obtain accurate data that describe a situation or phenomenon. The data may come from existing records such as the U.S. Census (for example, the proportion of the population with a disability), or researchers may conduct a survey to answer a specific question (for example, asking all mothers of premature infants in a particular state if they drank alcohol while pregnant). Descriptive data are only as good as the sample from which they come.

Descriptive research is used by **epidemiology,** a branch of medicine that studies how a disease occurs or spreads in a population (epidemiology also uses the other types of research designs described here, particularly correlation). Epidemiologists make frequent use of descriptive research to determine the *incidence* and *prevalence* of disease in a population. **Incidence,** which refers to the *frequency* of new cases of a disease during a specific period of time, and **prevalence,** which is the *proportion* of a population that has a disease at a specific point in time, are important terms in epidemiology and health psychology.

Epidemiological studies that examine how a disease spreads through a population can actually help determine its cause. For example, early epidemiological evidence suggested that AIDS appeared to be caused by an infectious agent. It also suggested that this infectious agent was a virus because it appeared to spread through sexual contact, just like the spread of the virus responsible for hepatitis B.

Descriptive research helps identify important factors in illness and health, especially in large populations. It is also useful to determine the status of a situation, such as how much is being spent on health care or what the infection rate is for a disease. However, it is the most limited type of research because it cannot establish associations among variables or cause-and-effect relationships.

Years of descriptive research preceded the generation of the example hypothesis used in this module. Researchers noticed that in certain countries with high fiber diets people also had low levels of blood cholesterol. They also noticed that people in jobs requiring more physical activity had lower blood cholesterol. This led researchers to suspect that there would be a *correlation* between dietary fiber, physical activity, and blood cholesterol.

CORRELATIONAL RESEARCH

Correlational studies attempt to establish the degree of association that exists between two or more variables. When there is an association, changes in one variable correspond to (but do not necessarily cause!) changes in the other variable. The degree of association is expressed as a number called the **correlation coefficient,** which ranges from −1.00 through 0.00 to +1.00. The minus and plus signs indicate the *direction* of the association. A *positive* correlation means that both variables rise together. For example, a *positive* correlation would indicate that, as weight increases, so does the rate of diabetes. A *negative* correlation does *not* mean "no correlation"; it means that as the value of the first variable rises, the value of the second variable falls (that is how they *are* associated). For example, there is a negative correlation between dietary fiber and cholesterol and between activity level and cholesterol. This indicates that as dietary fiber and activity level increase, the level of cholesterol in the blood decreases.

The *strength* of the association is given by the size of the correlation coefficient, either from 0.00 to −1.00 or from 0.00 to +1.00. Correlations of −1.00 and +1.00 are *perfect* correlations, that is the two variables are highly related (these rarely occur in nature). Correlations of −0.50 and +0.50 indicate the same *strength* of association, and both would be considered *moderate*. When a correlation coefficient is near zero, whether positive or negative, it indicates no association between the variables.

Correlational studies allow us to *predict.* For example, a person with a low level of physical activity is more likely to have a high blood cholesterol level. Variables (for example, lack of physical exercise) related to certain diseases (such as heart disease) are called **risk factors** and are associated with development of the disease. Risk factors represent, to greater or lesser degrees, the probability that a person with a certain condition will develop a specific disease. They are based on the finding that the conditions occur with greater frequency in people with the disease than in those without it. However, because risk factors are determined by correlational studies, we cannot say that they *cause* the disease. A low activity level is a risk factor for high cholesterol, but high cholesterol (and heart disease) is caused by a combination of factors, and activity level may not even be the most important one. Risk factor determination is an important part of epidemiology and health psychology.

Correlational studies can never establish cause-and-effect relationships. One important reason for this is that another (third) variable that was not included in the study may be responsible for the observed correlation. This is known as the "third variable problem." For example, we know that the weight of parents and children is correlated; overweight parents tend to have overweight children. It would be tempting to conclude from this correlation that being overweight is caused by the environment—that the parents eat a lot of food and that they feed their children a lot too. However, it is possible that a third variable—their similar genetic inheritance—may actually be responsible for the fact that both parents and children are overweight. One way of evaluating this would be to include environmental and genetic variables in the same study. However, this still could not establish cause and effect because there are literally hundreds of potential third variables and we cannot be certain that all possible ones have been included.

Researchers did find that the intake of dietary fiber and the level of physical activity were low to moderately negatively correlated with cholesterol. Therefore, experiments that could potentially establish a cause-and-effect relationship would be the next logical step. If a significant correlation between the variables had not been found, there would be no basis for conducting an experiment because it would be highly unlikely to support the hypothesis.

EXPERIMENTAL RESEARCH

Only experimental studies can establish cause-and-effect relationships among variables. A psychological **experiment** is "an objective observation of phenomena which are made to occur in a strictly controlled situation in which one or more factors are varied and the others are kept constant" (Zimney, 1961, p. 18). Christensen (1991) has provided an analysis of the various components of this definition:

1. *"Objective observation"* refers to the potential for the researcher to bias the results. Knowing of this potential, researchers attempt to construct the conditions of the experimental procedure so as to minimize any personal effect they may have on it.
2. *"Phenomena which are made to occur"* refers to some measurable outcome. This measurable outcome is also called the **dependent variable**. In the present example, the dependent variable is each subject's blood cholesterol level.
3. *"A strictly controlled situation"* is one in which we have eliminated any effects on the dependent variable from other sources beside the one we are interested in (in other words, all "third" variables).
4. *"One or more factors (that) are varied"* refers to the manipulation of one or more **independent variables** that are expected to cause a change in the dependent variable. The independent variables are manipulated individually and sometimes in combinations to see how they effect the dependent variable. Activity level and fiber intake are independent variables in our example. They will be manipulated separately and then together.

Before proceeding, the hypothesis for our example experiment must be stated so it conforms exactly to what will actually happen in the experiment:

Increasing subjects' level of aerobic exercise and the amount of fiber in their diets will each cause a lower blood cholesterol level and increasing both exercise and fiber will cause an even lower blood cholesterol level.

Once the hypothesis is stated, an experiment is likely to follow a standard procedure, which is illustrated for our example in Figure 2.1-1.

First, subjects must be selected with some rationale. This type of study requires subjects with a relatively high level of cholesterol at the beginning. You might obtain such subjects through physicians. In order to isolate the cause of any changes in the subjects' cholesterol levels, they would not be permitted to take cholesterol-lowering medication during the study. Ethical standards require that the researchers discuss the possible health consequences of this with each subject, who would then have to give informed consent in order to participate. Although it is unlikely that this experiment would endanger subjects' health, some risk is involved in many experimental studies.

Next, subjects are **randomly assigned** to the independent variables—this is done to make sure they would be exposed to them by chance alone (one simple way of doing this would be to pull their names out of a hat). Random assignment distributes the effects of third variables (for example, height, weight, medical history) randomly across the various groups in the experiment. This experiment would require four groups, one for each of the independent variables (exercise and diet), one for their combination, and one that receives no treatment (against which the comparison of effectiveness will be measured). Cholesterol levels would be taken before the experiment begins. Then the subjects would begin their treatment and continue for six months (except for the nontreatment group, which would continue in their normal routine).

After the treatment, cholesterol levels would again be taken and compared with the pre-experimental level. If the cholesterol levels of the exercise and diet groups were lower than the nontreatment group's, the first part of the hypothesis is supported; if the combined treatment group's cholesterol level is lower than both the exercise and diet groups', then the second part of the hypothesis is supported. Statistics provide a method of determining that these lower levels did not just happen by chance. By convention, psychologists call a result "significant" if the probability that it happened by chance is less than 20 to 1. This is what is meant by the term "significant" in this book.

The most important advantage of experimental studies is that they can establish causal relationships. This advantage occurs because of the strict control used, which eliminates influence from other sources, and also because of the manipulation of the independent variable, which occurs when we compare the different treatments with a nontreatment group. In the preceding example, we could conclude that aerobic exercise and a high fiber diet each reduce cholesterol and that together they reduce it more.

Before this discussion of experimental studies is complete, it is necessary to introduce two topics that are very important in experimental research: placebos and blind research.

Figure 2.1-1 DESIGN OF AN EXPERIMENT

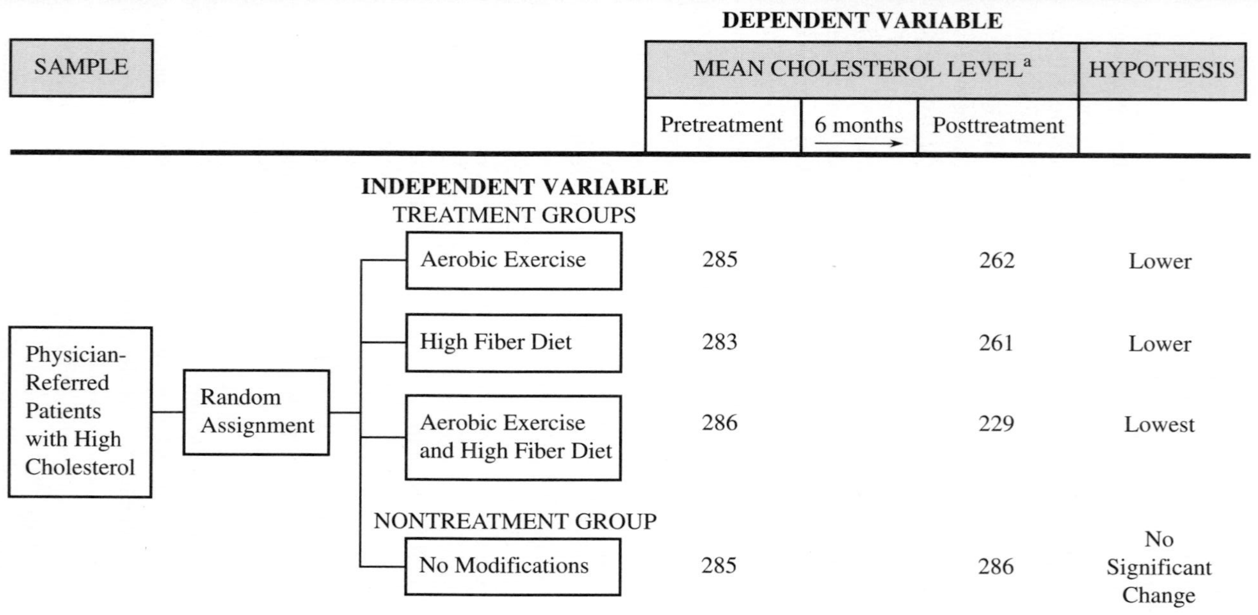

DEPENDENT VARIABLE

SAMPLE		MEAN CHOLESTEROL LEVEL[a]		HYPOTHESIS
		Pretreatment	6 months → Posttreatment	

INDEPENDENT VARIABLE
TREATMENT GROUPS

	Pretreatment	Posttreatment	Hypothesis
Aerobic Exercise	285	262	Lower
High Fiber Diet	283	261	Lower
Aerobic Exercise and High Fiber Diet	286	229	Lowest

NONTREATMENT GROUP

	Pretreatment	Posttreatment	Hypothesis
No Modifications	285	286	No Significant Change

Random Assignment

Physician-Referred Patients with High Cholesterol

*Cholesterol levels are hypothetical but based on typical results from similar experiments.

Regular aerobic exercise, whether done in a formal class or solitarily, may have a healthy effect on cholesterol.

PLACEBO   **Placebo** is Latin for "I shall please," but it has a special meaning in research. Long ago, researchers discovered that people do not always "act normally" when they are subjects. They try to figure out what the experiment is about and then act the way they *think* they should be acting. They may try to please the experimenter by producing what they believe should be the effects of the independent variable.

You have probably heard that people are sometimes given sugar pills as placebos, and the term "placebo" has even come to mean "pill" in some cases. That is because the ability of inert and innocuous substances in pill form to "cure" a variety of disorders is well known (Wolf, 1950). It should come as no surprise after what you have already learned about the mind–body relationship that placebos can produce physiologically *real* results. That is, they can sometimes produce the same results as biologically active substances (Levine, Gordon, & Fields, 1978; Sobel, 1990). This makes the placebo effect a problem for medical and psychological research alike (for example, Schachter & Singer, 1962).

How can we tell whether the results of an experiment are due to an independent variable or just a placebo? To determine this, researchers use a placebo group to which subjects are also randomly assigned. The placebo group is *not* a nontreatment group, for its subjects do receive a placebo that takes the same form as, and substitutes for, the treatment the other groups receive, but it does not contain the active ingredient under study.

When evaluating the effects of a new medication, the placebo may be a sugar pill, but one that looks and tastes exactly like the medication. The effect of the medication is then compared to the effect of the placebo. The medication's effect must be significantly greater; otherwise, we would have to conclude that it is just the act of taking the pill and believing that it will work that produces the effect, not what is in the pill.

A placebo group would also strengthen the design of our experiment to lower cholesterol, but psychological and behavioral placebos are more tricky than the typical medical placebo. There would have to be an additional group that received some form of physical exercise that was *not* aerobic and still another group that received a dietary change that did *not* affect their natural intake of fiber. Some of you skeptical mind–body dualists out there are probably thinking, "Okay, I understand how a placebo might work on someone who had conversion hysteria, it's all in their mind anyway. But could a subject's *belief* in the effects of exercise or diet change their cholesterol level?" The answer is yes, at least for a certain percentage of subjects. As a matter of fact, both medical and psychological placebos are effective (Blanchard & Andrasik, 1982), and they both produce an improvement rate of about 35% across all kinds of studies (Evans, 1985).

BLIND EXPERIMENTS   The other subject that is related to placebo and is also very important in health-related research is "blind" experiments. In a **single-blind** experiment, subjects are kept unaware of to which group they belong. In a **double-blind** experiment, neither the subjects nor the experimenters know to which group the subjects belong (the treatment or the placebo). In that way, the researchers cannot inadvertently communicate to the subjects what changes are expected of them.

Again, it is relatively simple to conduct double-blind studies in medical research, because biologically active and inactive placebo pills can be made to look identical and then coded by someone not connected with the research. The code is broken only after the study is completed. However, although it is possible to conduct single-blind studies of psychological or behavioral treatments, it is more difficult to conduct double-blind studies. That is because psychological and behavioral treatments rely on people to conduct them, and people can usually tell when they are conducting the placebo treatment.

SUMMARY AND CRITIQUE   The experimental method has been criticized for the artificiality of its conditions, the very conditions (control and manipulation) that allow it to establish cause and effect. Critics have claimed that this artificiality produces results that cannot be applied in the "real" world.

However, such criticism can be refuted because experiments do not take place in a vacuum (Christensen, 1991). First, there are field experiments that use the same experimental conditions but in real-life settings, and field and laboratory experiments can be used to complement one another. An experiment done first in the laboratory may be repeated in the field. Second, the different types of research designs are often used in conjunction, in a logical, step-by-step progression, like the one illustrated by the example of cholesterol research.

Descriptive studies provide evidence that the phenomenon exists in the real world, that low blood cholesterol levels are found where people had relatively high fiber diets and higher levels of physical activity in their jobs. Then correlational studies demonstrate a naturally occurring association among the variables. Finally, an experiment is conducted to establish the causal relationship. In this way, each type of research design is important and all contribute to the final picture. This is, of course, an ideal—research is not always conducted in so logical a sequence.

The last topic in this module concerns a special type of research design—quasi-experimental. It is emphasized because it is a very important and frequently used design in health psychology.

QUASI-EXPERIMENTAL RESEARCH

Quasi-experimental studies are a special category of correlational research. They resemble an experiment because they have separate groups of subjects. However, they are *not* true experiments because subjects are not randomly assigned to groups representing the independent variables. Instead, the groups are based on some predetermined characteristic such as race, gender, weight, or whether or not the subjects have a particular disease. Although researchers call the characteristics "independent variables," they are not manipulated like the independent variables in experimental studies. (Quasi-experimental studies are sometimes called "ex post facto" because the independent variables are selected "after the fact," that is, after the characteristic [for example, having a certain disease or gender] has been determined, rather than manipulated.)

Quasi-experimental studies are used frequently in health psychology research, but because quasi-experiments do not involve manipulation, they cannot establish cause-and-effect relationships between independent and dependent variables. ("Mixed studies" employ both ex post facto and manipulated independent variables, so it is sometimes possible to make limited inferences about causal relationships, but only for the manipulated variable.)

Why use quasi-experiments when they cannot establish causality? There are two reasons. First, some independent variables cannot be manipulated for ethical reasons. For example, it would be unethical to deliberately *raise* someone's cholesterol level to see if they developed heart disease. Second, some variables cannot be manipulated at all, yet we may still want to include them to find out if they are related to health or illness. For example, we may want to find out if men and women receive the same cholesterol-lowering benefits from aerobic exercise and diet. This would necessitate a mixed study, with gender as an additional independent variable. Obviously, subjects cannot be randomly assigned to be males or females, so relatively equal numbers of male and female subjects would need to be randomly assigned to each of the four groups, which would then be analyzed by gender.

It would also be necessary to ensure that the male and female subjects are equivalent on other factors, such as age, that could influence the dependent variable. To do that a technique called **matching** would be employed. In order to match the males and females on age, individuals would be added or subtracted from each group to reduce any significant difference in their mean ages.

There are several variations of quasi-experimental designs. Two major variations developed by epidemiologists and often used in health psychology research are called "retrospective" and "prospective."

RETROSPECTIVE RESEARCH   A **retrospective study** looks *backward* from a specific point in time. Typically, we are interested in subjects who already have a particular condition or disease—for example, high cholesterol. We match them with a group of subjects who do not have the condition or disease and then look backward through the histories of both groups for factors on which they differ significantly. This is a quasi-experiment because cholesterol level is not manipulated.

PROSPECTIVE RESEARCH   In contrast, a **prospective study** begins with subjects who do *not* have the condition or disease of interest and looks *forward* in time. In our example, we would begin by measuring factors, such as exercise level and diet, that are hypothesized to be related to the condition or disease of interest—cholesterol level. We would then follow the subjects over a period of time to see who develops a high cholesterol level. At the end, we would compare those whose cholesterol level became high with those whose level did not to see if there were significant differences in exercise and diet *before* the development of disease.

Prospective studies provide stronger evidence of a relationship because factors of interest are measured before the development of disease. Also, retrospective studies are dependent on the accuracy of historical records and sometimes rely on subjects' own recall, which may be distorted by the fact they already have the disease. However, prospective studies are much more expensive to conduct because they must follow subjects over time.

Two special types of retrospective and prospective designs—called "cross-sectional" and "longitudinal"—have long been used by developmental psychologists to study the effects of age.

CROSS-SECTIONAL RESEARCH   **Cross-sectional studies** are *retrospective* designs that use groups made up of subjects of different ages (for example, one group 20–30 years of age may be compared with another group 40–50 years of age) on a dependent variable.

LONGITUDINAL RESEARCH **Longitudinal studies** are *prospective* designs that follow a single group of subjects over time *as they age* (for example, at the start all subjects would be the same age, perhaps 20, and then they might be followed until they were 50 years of age). Longitudinal, like prospective studies, are more expensive but provide stronger evidence of associations among variables.

THE REPETITIVE PROCESS OF SCIENCE   The repetitive process of science refers to the fact that scientific studies are usually repeated. They are repeated not because the scientist made a mistake (although that could happen), but because sometimes the results of a study support the hypothesis, and sometimes they do not. When results support the hypothesis, it is taken as *evidence* that the hypothesis may be correct, but never as proof. When results do not support the hypothesis, it is evidence that the hypothesis may be incorrect and it might be modified or discarded.

Scientists are extremely cautious about making claims from the results of a single study. They are used to waiting for many studies to be conducted before taking the accumulated weight of the evidence in support of a hypothesis. Studies must be **replicated**, that is repeated, usually by other researchers in other circumstances, before the results are accepted by the scientific community at large.

The repetitive process of science is depicted in Figure 2.1-2. Notice that there are two loops. The larger one represents the general flow of the scientific process from theory; to hypothesis; and to research, which either does or does not support it. The smaller loop represents the necessity to replicate results from any study several times before proceeding back to accept, modify, or reject the hypothesis.

Figure 2.1-2   **THE REPETITIVE PROCESS OF SCIENCE**

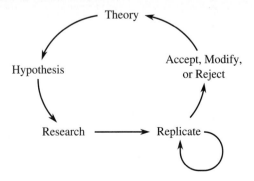

MODULE SUMMARY

Scientists seek to acquire knowledge using an objective method that minimizes bias. The objectives of science are to describe, explain, predict, and ultimately influence (Christensen, 1991). This section has described the various types of studies that relate to each of these objectives: Case studies and descriptive research provide a description of naturally occurring phenomena; correlational and quasi-experimental studies allow scientists to describe, explain, and predict these phenomena; and experimental studies help us to understand the cause-and-effect relationships among them.

Figure 2.1-3 depicts a hierarchy that orders the types of research design according to the four objectives of science. It moves from left to right in terms of increasing influence. All four scientific objectives are important, but health psychologists, in particular, are interested in how to influence people in order to help them produce and maintain healthy behavior.

Module 2.2 describes how health psychologists try to influence people to decrease unhealthy and increase healthy behaviors, but first review this point-by-point summary of how psychologists acquire knowledge:

1. Anecdotes are personal reports or narrative stories that may provide an understanding of the meaning of illness to an individual or provide helpful information in public health research, but are too unsystematic and biased to substitute for the scientific method.

2. Case studies are a systematic approach to acquiring knowledge that use only one subject. Clinical case studies are in-depth reports of an illness and its treatment that are used for rare diseases. Research case studies involve manipulated variables and can establish cause-and-effect relationships, although caution must be used in generalizing their results.

3. The scientific method is systematic and strives toward observing data in an unbiased manner. It relies on logical reasoning and empiricism, but not superstition.

4. Ideally, the scientific method begins with a theory, which is a set of organized and related ideas about natural phenomena that allows predictions to be made about variables and their relationships.

5. Hypotheses are predictions or guesses about natural phenomena that drive research. Ideally, hypotheses are derived from a theory. Along with theory, they represent the use of logical reasoning in science.

6. Scientists are very cautious about accepting the result of a single experiment and usually require that it be replicated several times. Scientists rely on this repetitive process and the accumulation of evidence in support of hypotheses and theories.

Figure 2.1-3 RESEARCH DESIGN HIERARCHY

Type of Study	ANECDOTAL	DESCRIPTIVE	CORRELATIONAL	QUASI-EXPERIMENTAL	EXPERIMENTAL
Research Purpose	Information	Description	Relationship		Cause and Effect
Moves toward Increasing Influence →					
Scientific Goal	None	Description	Explanation and Prediction		Influence
Independent Variable	None	None	No Manipulation	Limited Manipulation	Manipulation
Sampling and Assignment	None	Representative Sample	Representative Sample	Equivalent (Matched) Groups	Randomly Assigned Groups
Placebo and Blind Research				Placebo/ Single or Double-Blind	

7. Descriptive research is very widely used and provides data that describe a situation or phenomenon. Two forms of descriptive data used by epidemiologists and health psychologists are incidence, or the frequency of new cases of a disease during a specific time, and prevalence, or the proportion of a population that have a disease at a given time. Descriptive research helps identify factors that may be important in health.

8. Correlational research establishes the degree of association between two or more variables. Health predictions are based on correlations, but they cannot establish cause-and-effect relationships. Risk factors are variables that are related probabilistically to the development of diseases.

9. Experimental research relies on the manipulation of one or more independent variables while measuring their effects on a dependent variable. It also relies on random assignment of subjects to treatment and nontreatment groups. Experiments can establish cause-and-effect relationships. Placebos control for the effects of subjects' expectancies or beliefs on the dependent variable. In a single-blind study, subjects do not know if they are receiving the placebo and in a double-blind study, both the experimenters and the subjects do not know. This maintains the integrity of the placebo effect.

10. Quasi-experimental research is a special category of correlational research in which subjects are not assigned randomly to groups because it is either unethical or impossible to do so. Some mixed quasi-experimental studies do have random assignment within them.

11. In retrospective studies, groups of subjects with and without a condition are constituted and their histories are examined for factors that differ between them. In prospective studies, subjects who do not have a condition are assessed on certain factors and then followed over time to see who develops the condition and what factors are related to its development. Prospective designs provide stronger evidence of relationships.

INTERVENTION

███

APPLYING KNOWLEDGE

Some health psychologists produce and disseminate knowledge. An example of their work is the experiment in Module 2.1 on the effects that increased dietary fiber and exercise have on lowering cholesterol. Researchers naturally hope that results like these will influence people to change their behavior, and conducting an experiment such as that can be rewarding because the results may help save people's lives.

However, *do* people change just because they know what is good for them? Unfortunately, they often do not, and as many health psychologists can attest, good intentions and motivation are sometimes not enough. So, the work of health psychologists does not stop with knowledge acquisition. Some health psychologists are interested in **intervention**—in directly applying knowledge about health and illness to help people change their lives.

LEVELS OF INTERVENTION

Intervention can occur on three levels: primary, secondary, and tertiary (Caplan, 1964). *Primary intervention* is concerned with the *prevention* of illness but it can also refer to the *promotion* of optimum physical, mental, and social well-being. Primary intervention is both cost effective for society and advantageous for the people who remain healthy longer. Unfortunately, motivating people who are not ill to change their lifestyle or behavior can be very difficult because it usually does not result in immediate benefits (Miller, 1983).

In contrast to primary intervention, secondary and tertiary intervention both involve people who are already ill. *Secondary intervention* is concerned with determining whether or not certain symptoms mean that a disease process is present. Secondary intervention efforts are directed at detecting disease early and reversing its progress. *Tertiary intervention* is concerned with treating people whose disease is already fully established. Intervention efforts are directed at arresting the disease process and reestablishing the person's health.

A survey of the content of journal articles in health psychology published during 1988 and 1989 revealed that health psychologists in clinical settings focused most of their efforts on secondary intervention (Duncan, 1990). It also found that their primary prevention efforts were concentrated in school and work environments. Traditionally, psychologists intervene in one of two roles: as clinicians, at the secondary or tertiary levels directly with patients, or as consultants, at the primary level through other professionals and institutions.

CONSULTING HEALTH PSYCHOLOGY

Consultation is an indirect method of service. Some health psychologists consult with health care workers to improve their effectiveness when working with patients. For example, physicians may be taught how to communicate better with their patients so as to maximize adherence to a healthy lifestyle (Ray & Donohew, 1990). Other health psychologists may consult with institutions such as community organizations, employers, or government. For example, they may consult with a congressional committee on national health care promotion objectives (for example, Harris, 1980).

Because consulting health psychologists are concerned with primary intervention efforts, they are in a seeking mode—they seek to bring services to people and to the community at large (Rappaport & Chinsky, 1974). In health psychology, primary prevention is also known as health promotion. **Health promotion** attempts to improve people's health by helping them gain control over it. Module 3.2 discusses health promotion in greater detail.

Given the changing pattern of disease and the escalation of health care costs, consulting health psychologists may be able to make very important contributions to the future of health in our society. However, as successful as health promotion may eventually become, some people will develop illness and need secondary and tertiary care, which are provided by clinical health psychologists.

CLINICAL HEALTH PSYCHOLOGY

Imagine that your doctor has just told you that you have high blood cholesterol and that it puts you at risk for premature death from heart disease. Your doctor, who is up on the latest research, then prescribes a cholesterol-lowering program that begins with reducing the intake of fat and cholesterol, increasing the fiber in your diet, and starting an aerobic exercise program. You are given an informational pamphlet on how to do this and told to return in six months to retest your cholesterol level. What is the probability that you would increase the fiber in your diet? What is the probability that you would begin to exercise regularly? If you are like most people, it is much less than 50-50.

You may *intend* to do these things, but somehow your follow through is lacking. When you return to the doctor, your blood cholesterol level is unchanged. You did reduce your cholesterol and fat intake somewhat and you added a little oat bran to your cereal in the mornings, but you just could not start exercising. So, your doctor gives you two options: (a) referral to a health psychologist, who might be able to help you put your intentions into action; or (b) begin anticholesterol medication, which you would have to take indefinitely and which is costly and has several unwanted side effects (for example, constipation, stomach upset, liver damage).

What would happen if you chose to see a health psychologist? While many health psychologists work in professional offices, others provide inpatient and outpatient treatment in hospitals (Enright, Resnick, DeLeon, Sciara, & Ranney, 1990). They may work through hospital departments of behavioral medicine, or they may be members of interdisciplinary healthcare teams. They may work with general medical patients, or they may specialize in certain types of problems, such as pain or addiction or specific populations of patients such as those with a spinal cord injury or those undergoing cardiac rehabilitation.

Although it is controversial, psychologists recently have had the opportunity to join hospital medical staffs alongside physicians in the new role of "attending clinician" (Enright, Welch, Newman, & Perry, 1990). As attending clinicians they admit, diagnose, formulate a treatment plan, and discharge patients, much as physicians or surgeons do. That is how your doctor found the psychologist to whom you have been referred. The psychologist works in the behavioral medicine department of a nearby university hospital.

A psychologist's work usually consists of two tasks: *assessment* and *treatment*. Assessment involves gaining an understanding of the person and the problem. You would be interviewed and probably given some questionnaires and forms to complete. You also might be asked to keep track of some of your behaviors between sessions, perhaps recording what you eat and your activity level. One to three sessions would probably be devoted to assessment. After a complete understanding of you and your situation has been gained, the psychologist would discuss it with you and make recommendations for intervention.

METHODS OF CLINICAL INTERVENTION

Health psychologists have several treatment approaches at their disposal, depending on the goal of treatment: to gain insight, to change behavior, or to change cognitions. They also may combine approaches.

GAINING INSIGHT

Psychosomatic medicine developed as a result of Freud's psychoanalytic and psychiatric contemporaries who remained interested in physical as well as mental problems (see Chapter 1). They were strongly influenced by psychoanalytic concepts and believed that some forms of physical illness originated in unresolved unconscious conflicts (for example, Alexander, 1950). They attempted to treat physical conditions with insight therapy in order to uncover these unconscious conflicts. **Insight therapy** includes forms of psychological treatment that assume that disordered behaviors, emotions, and thoughts are due to conflicting needs and drives of which the person is *unaware* (London, 1986).

Insight therapies share a common technique: the reliance on some form of verbal interchange between client and therapist aimed at making the client more fully aware of these conflicts (hence Freud's "talking cure"). Included among the insight therapies are Freud's *psychoanalysis;* its modified form, *psychodynamic* or *ego therapy* (see Hartmann, 1958); *humanistic therapy* (see Rogers, 1961); and *existential therapy* (see Ford & Urban, 1963; Frankl, 1963).

Let us assume that there is no deep conflict of which you are unaware that is preventing you from following your doctor's advice. Like many people, you find it hard to change long-standing lifestyle habits; therefore, the therapeutic goal the health psychologist recommends is to change your behavior.

Changing Behavior

When the goal of treatment is to change behavior, psychologists have three approaches that can be used: classical conditioning, behavior modification, and modeling. We introduce these approaches here, but we will evaluate their effectiveness in relation to specific conditions in subsequent chapters.

CLASSICAL CONDITIONING   One method of changing behavior is **classical conditioning**, which had its origins in Pavlov's (1927) experiments that conditioned dogs to salivate to a bell. It is used to condition *involuntary* behaviors, such as basic physiological responses.

In classical conditioning, two stimuli that occur together become associated with the *same* response. One of these stimuli—the *unconditioned stimulus*—is the one that is naturally associated with the response. The other stimulus—the *conditioned stimulus*—is not naturally associated with the response but eventually, by repeated association with the unconditioned stimulus, elicits the response by itself. The response is initially called the *unconditioned response* when it is associated only with the unconditioned stimulus. The response is called the *conditioned response* after it becomes associated with the conditioned stimulus. If this sounds confusing, perhaps the following examples will help.

There are two types of therapeutic techniques based on classical conditioning: Aversion therapy and relaxation training. In **aversion therapy** an aversive stimulus, that is something disliked or repugnant, is paired with a stimulus that elicits an unwanted response. Although controversial, aversion therapy has been widely used to change unhealthy behaviors, but usually only after other methods have been tried and failed (Rimm & Cunningham, 1985).

Consider this example of a treatment used for alcohol abuse. Alcohol is an unconditioned stimulus that naturally produces pleasurable effects such as relaxation, which would be the *unconditioned response*. In aversion therapy, the patient takes a medication that causes extreme nausea and vomiting whenever alcohol is ingested. When even a sip of alcohol reaches the stomach, it causes violent illness and retching. Eventually, the alcohol becomes the *conditioned stimulus* that leads to the nausea and vomiting which is the new *conditioned response*. Then when the alcoholic even thinks about drinking, he or she feels nauseous; alcohol is no longer appealing and the link is broken.

You may wonder, "Can't alcoholics just stop taking the drug when they want a drink?" It turns out that it is not that simple. Remember that classical conditioning works at a physiological level on involuntary responses. Therefore, alcoholics will continue to experience the conditioned response of nausea to the smell or taste of alcohol even in the absence of the medication (at least for awhile).

However, there are problems using this technique. Eventually, in the absence of the medication, over time the association weakens and the conditioned response is extinguished. Nevertheless, aversion conditioning is a potent technique for changing unhealthy behaviors (for example, Lazarus & Wilson, 1976; Sandler, 1975).

Relaxation training, is one of the oldest and most widely used treatments in health psychology, probably because it requires little expertise and no equipment (Blanchard & Andrasik, 1985). It consists of learning two behaviors that result in the reduction of tension in the body: deep breathing and muscle relaxation. Edmund Jacobson's (1938) early work in the 1920s at the University of Chicago led to the development of progressive muscle relaxation training. Jacobson, who was studying the knee jerk reflex, discovered that the degree of tension a patient was under influenced the extent of the knee jerk response. As tension was reduced, so, too, was the extent of the response.

Jacobson's *progressive muscle relaxation* consists of having patients learn the difference between a state of tension and a state of relaxation in muscles by alternately and deliberately tensing and relaxing them. This is done with each of the major muscle groups progressively working from head to toe or vice versa, inducing a state of muscle relaxation throughout the body. No more than about 10 sessions are sufficient to teach the technique, after which it can be practiced independently.

An alternative is Benson's (1975) *progressive muscle relaxation with controlled breathing*. This method incorporates features from yoga, such as its focus on breathing and use of a repeated, mantra-like sound. Controlled breathing is taking deep, measured breaths at the rate of about six to eight a minute (the normal rate is 17 per minute, and when people are anxious the rate goes much higher). Controlled breathing reduces blood pressure and heart rate and increases the concentration of oxygen in the blood.

Joseph Wolpe (1958, 1987) is credited with applying these relaxation techniques in a classical conditioning therapy called **systematic desensitization**, developed to treat anxiety disorders. First, anxious people describe their fears (specific anxiety arousing stimuli) and rank them in a hierarchy from lowest to highest. Then they are taught relaxation. Next, while in a state of relaxation, they are exposed through mental images to the anxiety arousing stimuli, beginning with the lowest and moving up the hierarchy in systematic steps.

To illustrate this process, imagine a person who has a fear of syringes and needles and so avoids necessary injections. At the low end of the hierarchy, he or she might picture a syringe; in the middle, he or she might imagine watching a nurse prepare an injection; and at the top, he or she might imagine the nurse wiping his or her arm with an alcohol swab and then inserting the needle. The patient must remain in a state of relaxation throughout each step in the hierarchy, otherwise the therapist backs up and reinduces relaxation. Systematic desensitization works through ***counter*conditioning**, which occurs when an incompatible *response* (relaxation) is associated with a stimulus (syringe and needle) that once produced anxiety. Relaxation and anxiety are antagonistic responses, and the goal of systematic desensitization is to countercondition the stimulus to elicit relaxation.

You may have noticed that the syringe example took place entirely in the patient's imagination. While this is sometimes sufficient to produce the desired result, most of the time it is followed by moving up the hierarchy into reality. This is done via exposure to real-life situations while in a state of relaxation (Lazarus & Wilson, 1976). Usually, the anxiety response is reduced enough by the imagined hierarchy to make real-life desensitization possible.

You have probably already realized that the problem for which you are seeing the health psychologist is not how to rid yourself of a health-inhibiting behavior like substance abuse or anxiety. Your problem is how to *add* two new health enhancing behaviors. For that, the health psychologist would probably use behavior modification.

BEHAVIOR MODIFICATION   **Behavior modification** is the term generally applied to techniques intended to change behavior through the principles of operant conditioning. **Operant conditioning** is based on principles of learning first described by E. L. Thorndike (1898) and later developed by B. F. Skinner (1953). It is used to condition *voluntary* behaviors that may be quite complex (like changing your diet). It rests on the proposition that behaviors can be increased or decreased depending on the consequences that follow them. **Reinforcement** is the general term for the consequences: *Reward* will increase the likelihood of a behavior occurring again, while *punishment* will decrease the likelihood. Two types of consequences can follow behavior and reward it and two types of consequences can follow behavior and punish it (see Figure 2.2-1).

Generally, reward works better than punishment. In other words, operant conditioning is more effective at increasing behaviors than at decreasing them.

That is because punishment can have unintended side effects. Even when it effectively reduces a response, it can result in the general suppression of behavioral activity (Van Houten, 1983). In particular, physical punishment can result in strong emotional responses and can increase aggressive behavior. Therefore, instead of using punishment to decrease a behavior, often reward is used to increase an alternative behavior.

Since your doctor has referred you to the health psychologist with a prescription to increase two discrete behaviors—eating more fiber and getting more exercise—reinforcement would be used. The first step in behavior modification is to break a complex behavior down into small units of behavior. Using walking or jogging as an example, this might involve increasing periods of time spent at the activity or increasing the distance covered. The next step is to come up with ways that you can be rewarded for the increases. What is reward or punishment to one person may not be to another. Each behavior modification program must, therefore, be customized to the individual. Some people find money rewarding, some find certain activities rewarding (for example, going out to dinner), some find praise rewarding, and some find the achievement of a goal rewarding. It is the role of the psychologist to help you discover your rewards and to arrange them so they support your exercising. For example, if you enjoyed going to the movies, you would only do so after a successful week of exercising.

MODELING **Modeling** is behavior change that results from watching another person perform a behavior. There is no reinforcement of the observer. Instead, observing the reinforcement of the model is the mechanism of learning (Bandura, 1977, 1986). It might be said that, "We learn by others' suc-

---

Figure 2.2-1 TYPES OF REINFORCEMENT AND THEIR CONSEQUENCES AND EFFECTS ON THE TARGET BEHAVIOR IN OPERANT CONDITIONING

REINFORCEMENT	CONSEQUENCES		TARGET BEHAVIOR
	Add (+)	Take Away (−)	
Reward	Pleasant	Unpleasant	Increases
Punishment	Unpleasant	Pleasant	Decreases

cesses (rewards) and failures (punishments)." Sometimes modeling is called observational or vicarious learning. It is quite a successful method of behavior change. Modeling is also responsible for a substantial amount of original learning of both healthy and unhealthy behaviors, a process that takes place in large part during childhood.

In a variation of counterconditioning, people who observe a model engaging in an anxiety-provoking activity (for example, receiving an injection), have their own anxiety reduced when they see that the activity does not lead to negative consequences (Bandura, 1969). However, it is necessary for the observer to be able to identify with the model. Models and situations cannot be idealized. Models should be similar to observers. They must be seen to be undergoing at least a moderate amount of anxiety. The results of one experiment on relieving children's fear of injections demonstrated this (Vernon, 1974). Children were randomly assigned to one of three groups: (a) those viewing an idealized, unrealistic film of children receiving injections without pain or emotion, (b) those viewing a realistic film of children receiving injections with moderate pain and emotion but handling it well, and (c) a nontreatment group that saw no film.

Afterwards, the children in all three groups received an injection. Those who saw the realistic film experienced less pain than the nontreatment group, while those who saw the idealized film experienced *more* pain than the nontreatment group.

The psychologist might also use modeling by having you join an exercise group. Ideally, it would be comprised of people like you who have a good medical reason to exercise but have avoided it in the past. The example of those who have been with the group for a while could serve as vicarious reinforcement to you. Of course, modeling would work best if you were a socially oriented person.

CHANGING COGNITIONS

It is just a small step from understanding how modeling works to recognizing the important role that cognitive processes play in behavior. Bandura (1986) made a distinction between *learning,* which is a cognitive process, and *behavior,* which is only a visible indication of learning. Behavior-change therapies tend to ignore cognitive processes altogether, focusing only on the target behavior. With cognitive processes, however, we have another method of influencing health.

Cognitive processes may affect health in one of two ways. First, they can *mediate behavior* (Thoresen & Mahoney, 1974). In classical conditioning terms, they can intervene between a stimulus and a response, affecting the association between them. In operant conditioning terms, cognitions can affect the very manner in which reward and punishment are perceived, even defining which consequences are rewarding and which ones are punishing to the individual. There may also be specific cognitions in the chain of mental events that precede a behavior and increase its likelihood of occurring (for example, a bulimic's purging behavior may be preceded by feelings of guilt for overeating). Finally, personal goals, which are also cognitions, influence behavior. People determine their own goals, make plans for the future, and behave in ways that move them toward their goals (Leventhal, Zimmerman, & Gutmann, 1984).

The second way cognitive processes may affect health is *directly,* by triggering neuroendocrine responses that can affect homeostasis, enhancing or impairing physiological functioning throughout the body (this is described in more detail in Part 3). Cognitions are both a product of brain activity and they influence it. The brain monitors and can affect many physiological processes in the body (for example, immune system functioning). Therefore, one's perceptions, beliefs, attitudes, feelings, thoughts, and goals have the potential to affect physiological processes within the body. That is another reason why health psychologists are interested in changing cognitions.

Cognitive therapy refers to a variety of approaches that have as their goal changing maladaptive thought patterns and beliefs that affect people behaviorally and emotionally (for example, Beck, 1987; Ellis, 1987). In recent years, these techniques have been put to increasing use by health psychologists, some of them are described in Box 2.2-1.

The approaches used to change behavior and those used to change cognitions have a great deal in common. In fact, there are very few "pure" behavior or cognitive therapists, and the similarity of these two approaches is acknowledged by a term that joins them—**cognitive-behavioral**. Cognitive techniques are considered to be at least as effective as behavioral techniques for treating specific health problems, especially those involving anxiety, stress, and pain.

One therapeutic approach, called "multimodal," uses a wide range of cognitive-behavioral techniques (Lazarus, 1971). In multimodal therapy, attention is paid to many aspects of the person: biology, affect, sensory, intellect, cognition, interpersonal relationships, and drugs or medication. Any or all of these aspects may be identified as contributing to a person's problem and he or she may be treated by a variety of primarily cognitive-behavioral techniques.

However, this is not a "shotgun" treatment approach, in which many techniques are used in the belief that at least one will be effective and more might be more effective. A careful and comprehensive assessment procedure should tailor the therapy to the client, but some programs uniformly treat clients with as many treatment components as possible. Two principles guide the selection of treatments in medicine and psychology: (a) they must be safe *and* (b) they must be effective. Therefore, psychologists must be careful when combining techniques, because it is possible that individually effective techniques, when combined, may hinder improvement (Brownell, Marlatt, Lichtenstein, & Wilson, 1986).

Box 2.2-1 COGNITIVE THERAPY TECHNIQUES

Homework assignments are devised by the therapist as a follow-up and review of therapy sessions and sometimes to provide additional practice as in relaxation training (Shelton & Levy, 1981). They typically reflect what is happening in therapy. For example, in your exercise program, you might be asked to keep track of the time spent exercising during the week. This produces a useful record to monitor therapeutic progress, and it involves clients in the therapy, allows them to take responsibility, and increases their self-control. When clients keep track of problem behaviors such as smoking, it makes them more aware of the behavior and what circumstances are involved in its occurrence. Homework assignments are used frequently in treating health problems. One survey found that they were used in 75% of weight loss programs, in 71% of rehabilitation programs and programs treating physical illnesses, and in 54% of smoking cessation programs (Shelton & Levy, 1981).

Contracting between therapist and client involves making each of their roles in the therapy process explicit. This lets clients know what to expect of the therapist and what the therapist expects of them, again allowing clients to feel more responsible and in control. A special form called "contingency contracting" is often used in behavior modification (Thoresen & Mahoney, 1974). Rewards and punishments are listed in the contract and made contingent on clients' behavior. For example, in your exercise program, a contract might call on you to deposit a sum of money with the psychologist (perhaps $500) out of which you would receive rewards for staying with the program (perhaps $25 for each week as your weekly goals were reached).

Self-conditioning (also called "self-reinforcement") is a method of behavior self-control in which clients reward and punish themselves following certain behaviors. Self-reinforcement and self-punishment consist of the same potential consequences as they do in operant conditioning. Generally, the results of self-reinforcement parallel those of external reinforcement procedures (Thoresen & Mahoney, 1974). Self-reward is at least as effective as external reward, and, as we would expect, self-reward works better than self-punishment.

Cognitive restructuring is one of the most comprehensive and widely used approaches to self-control cognitions, which involves modifying cognitive processes, sometimes referred to as the "internal monologue" (Hollon & Beck, 1986; Thoresen & Mahoney, 1974), often through the use of operant conditioning principles (Kanfer, 1971; Mahoney, Thoresen, & Danaher, 1972). Health-supporting cognitions are developed to replace maladaptive ones and clients are taught to self-administer them. Cognitive restructuring uses education, modeling, self-reinforcement, rehearsal, and finally practice in real situations (an example is given in Module 5.3).

Skills Training Often, maladaptive behavior is perpetuated because people lack certain social skills. Being unable to perform skillfully in social situations can cause anxiety and distress, which can lead to other problems such as smoking cigarettes, drinking alcohol, or overeating to gain some temporary comfort (Chaney, O'Leary, & Marlatt, 1978). Also, without social skills, people may be unable to overcome their anxiety and distress, because they rarely receive the natural reinforcements that occur in many social situations (Putallaz & Gottman, 1981). Social skills training is often undertaken in conjunction with treatments for other health-related problems.

OTHER CLINICAL INTERVENTIONS

Health psychologists have used several other therapeutic approaches: family intervention, group intervention, meditation, biofeedback, and hypnosis.

FAMILY INTERVENTION   Recall from systems theory how the social systems in which a person participates can influence health beliefs and behavior (Sallis & Nader, 1988). One of the most important social systems is the family. Family based interventions use education and group forms of behavioral and cognitive change therapies to modify health habits of the entire family system, thereby improving the health of its members. Family therapy is considered a particularly promising means of preventing lifestyle health problems that develop over long periods of time, such as cardiovascular disease and obesity (Sallis & Nader, 1988).

Physical illness in a family member also affects the family system and hence other family members. In that case, family counseling is usually supportive rather than directed toward change. Supportive counseling resembles insight therapy in that it is a verbal interchange, except that the goal is not to uncover conflicts of which the person is unaware. Instead, supportive therapy is educational, providing information to family members about a patient's condition and its ramifications, and allowing the family a chance to talk through and organize coping strategies to help the patient and other family members. Family based therapy is becoming an important part of treatment for many serious or chronic health problems.

GROUP INTERVENTION   Group intervention is another format for the delivery of therapeutic services. Almost every type of individual therapy has been used in group form (Davison & Neale, 1990). Health psychologists have adapted several of the approaches described in this section (particularly cognitive and behavioral techniques) to group intervention, and groups are used extensively in the treatment of smoking and obesity. Many self-help organizations such as Alcoholics Anonymous have also made extensive use of groups.

Groups have two general advantages. First, they are economical, allowing a number of people to be treated simultaneously. Second, they provide a social environment that is particularly well suited for employing modeling and social skills training.

MEDITATION   Sometimes used in place of or as an adjunct to relaxation training, meditation has been practiced in Asia where it has had religious associations for thousands of years. One form that has achieved popularity is transcendental meditation (Orme-Johnson & Farrow, 1977). Although transcendental meditation (TM), too, has religious associations, meditation used as a relaxation technique does not (Shapiro, 1985).

Two versions of meditation are thought to have potential in health psychology to promote relaxation. In *non-structured meditation* (Carrington, 1978), the subject sits in a comfortable position in quiet surroundings and repeats a sound called a "mantra" *mentally* without its being linked to breathing. In *structured meditation* (Benson, 1975), which closely resembles TM, the subject sits as before, but the sound (often simply the word "one") is linked to breathing and repeated each time the subject exhales. Meditation sessions for relaxation last approximately 20 minutes.

BIOFEEDBACK   Biofeedback brings modern technology to therapeutic interventions. It consists of electronically sensing and amplifying physiological responses, and then providing immediate information (feedback) about them to the patient. The typical responses that have been monitored consist of changes related to sympathetic arousal of the autonomic nervous system (described in the Introduction to the Nervous and Endocrine Systems). These forms of biofeedback are described in Box 2.2-2.

Box 2.2-2   **FORMS OF BIOFEEDBACK**

The clinical importance of biofeedback derives from the fact that both animals (for example, Miller, 1969) and humans (for example, Brown, 1970) can learn to control and alter these biological responses through reinforcement.

Electromyograph (EMG) biofeedback is measured through electrodes placed on the surface of the skin that reflect the electrical discharge of the muscles as they contract. EMG is used for clinical symptoms of stress that involve muscle tension such as low back pain and headaches.

Temperature biofeedback is measured by a temperature-sensitive resistor also placed on the skin surface that senses changes in skin temperature reflecting constriction or dilation of blood vessels. Temperature biofeedback is used for specific disorders such as migraine headache and Raynaud's disease (where vasoconstriction produces restriction of blood flow and pain).

Electrodermal (EDR) biofeedback is a measure of electrical conductance on the surface of the skin, which increases with perspiration. (A related measure of perspiration is also given by galvanic skin response biofeedback or GSR.) EDR is considered one of the best research measures of stress and anxiety, although it is not widely used in clinical practice because perspiration levels vary, making it difficult to get a reliable reading (Schuman, 1982).

Electroencephalograph (EEG) biofeedback is measured by placing electrodes on the scalp that monitor the electrical activity of the brain. EEG is used because the production of alpha brain waves does appear to be related to a state of relaxed wakefulness (Olton & Noonberg, 1980). Because EEG training is quite lengthy and costly, it is not as popular as other methods.

Therapeutic biofeedback involves the monitoring of physiological functions such as muscle tension (EMG) or skin conductance (EDR). Here a patient is undergoing electroencephalographic (EEG) monitoring of brain-wave activity with the objective of learning how to produce increased "alpha" waves, which are associated with a relaxed state of mind.

H Y P N O S I S Hypnosis is the oldest of all of the intervention techniques reviewed here. It was certainly around before psychology began, having been used by physicians for at least 200 years (Hilgard & Hilgard, 1983). It probably existed long before modern medicine. Yet, even with its lengthy history, and recent intense scientific study, we still do not know exactly what hypnosis is. There are two theories, each with relatively good support. One theory proposed by Ernest Hilgard (1979; Hilgard & Hilgard, 1983) views hypnosis as an altered state of consciousness. In this theory, a person must undergo an **induction**, during which he or she is placed in a hypnotic state ("trance") by concentrating and focusing attention. The other view, proposed by Theodore X. Barber (1980, 1982), is that hypnosis is based on a trait called "suggestibility." In other words, some people are either more or less suggestible when others tell them to do something. No special induction is necessary.

Both Hilgard and Barber agree that hypnotizability seems to be normally distributed in the population. Approximately 20% of all people can achieve a deep state of hypnosis—that is, they are able to hallucinate or to withstand what would be extreme pain and discomfort under normal conditions—and it appears that about 20% of people cannot be hypnotized at all. The balance of the population falls somewhere in between, being able to be hypnotized to some extent.

Although this normal distribution tends to support Barber's trait theory, most of the research supports Hilgard's theory of altered consciousness (for example, Orne, 1977, 1980). However, these theories are not mutually exclusive, and perhaps both are correct. Hypnosis might be based on a trait of suggestibility and it may be an altered state of focused attention. Despite this disagreement over what exactly hypnosis is, it is a definite phenomenon. Hilgard (1979) has described four features related to the phenomenon of hypnosis (see Box 2.2-3).

■■■

MODULE SUMMARY

Health psychologists have a variety of techniques available to influence people to change. This has been just a brief survey and introduction to some of the most widely used ones. The use and effectiveness of these techniques will be discussed in Part III in relation to specific health problems. For now, review the following information about how health psychologists apply knowledge:

1. Intervention can take place on three levels: primary, which is involved with illness prevention and health promotion; secondary, which is concerned with early detection and reversal of the disease process; and tertiary, which is concerned with treating people with a fully established disease.

Box 2.2-3   HILGARD'S FOUR FEATURES OF HYPNOSIS

Increased Suggestibility
When people are hypnotized they are more susceptible to the suggestions of the hypnotist than when they are not.

Enhanced Imagery and Imagination
Hypnotism seems to allow for more vivid mental images and sensory experiences; people appear to recall remote past events with more ease and greater detail.

Disinclination to Plan
During hypnosis people prefer to be directed by the hypnotist, and they get annoyed if they are asked to plan to do something on their own.

Reduction in Reality Testing
Under hypnosis there is an apparent suspension of normal logic that allows perceptual distortions and apparent hallucinations to occur.

2. Consulting health psychologists, who work with other professionals and institutions, intervene at the primary level. Cinical health psychologists or medical psychologists, who work directly with patients, intervene at the secondary or tertiary level.

3. The tasks of a clinical health psychologist include assessment and treatment. There are several major treatment approaches available, depending on the goal: gaining insight, changing behavior, or changing cognitions.

4. Gaining insight refers to making people aware of unconscious conflicts that may contribute to ill health. There are many forms of insight therapy: psychoanalysis, psychodynamic or ego therapy, humanistic therapy, or existential therapy. They all share the common technique of reliance on verbal interchange between client and therapist to make the client fully aware.

5. Changing behavior depends on one of three approaches: classical conditioning, behavior modification, or modeling.

6. Classical conditioning is effective for reducing unwanted, involuntary behaviors. Two primary forms are aversion therapy, which pairs an aversive stimulus with a stimulus that elicits an unwanted response, and relaxation training, which pairs the response of relaxation with a stimulus that formerly elicited anxiety or tension.

7. Behavior modification uses the principles of operant conditioning to change, usually add and shape, new voluntary behaviors. This is done by arranging the reinforcement (the reward and punishment) that follow behavior. Generally, reward is preferred to punishment.

8. Modeling is behavior change that occurs from watching another person receive reinforcement when performing a behavior.

9. Changing cognitions typically involves restructuring one's maladaptive thoughts, emotions, beliefs, and attitudes in order to bring about behavioral change. A variety of techniques include homework, contracting, self-conditioning, and skills training.

10. Cognitive and behavioral techniques are often combined in treatment. Multimodal therapy is a cognitive-behavioral approach that might even be considered holistic because it takes many aspects of the person into account.

11. Family based intervention may help people avoid lifestyle problems that develop over long periods of time. Supportive family counseling may also help families deal with the physical illness of a member.

12. Group therapy is a form of treatment, not a type. Groups provide economic advantages because many people can be treated at one time and they provide a social environment that works well for modeling and social skills training.

13. Meditation is sometimes used as an adjunct to relaxation training. Biofeedback uses electronic amplification to provide information (or

feedback) about internal physiological states to help people gain control over them.

14. Hypnosis is not well understood, but it is widely used. It may be an altered state of consciousness (trance) or it may simply be a trait representing suggestibility.

BIOPSYCHOSOCIAL FACTORS IN HEALTH

Part II is concerned with the ways that biological, psychological, and social factors come together to affect our health. For instance, why do some people run to the doctor at the first sign of a cold, whereas others never seem to notice those little aches and pains that we all experience? What do people like **II** *most and least about their doctors, and how can the doctor-patient relationship affect your health? Why do people so often fail to take their medicine, and what consequences can that bring? And how do environmental factors combine with developmental changes to affect our health and well-being? These issues, and more, are addressed in this part.*

Chapter 3 deals with the role of health-related behavior. Module 3.1 begins with an exploration of the various models that have been developed to understand when and why we act on behalf of our health. Health education and promotion programs and their effectiveness are evaluated in Module 3.2. Module 3.3 explores how people cope with the symptoms of illness.

Chapter 4 looks more specifically at the health care system. Module 4.1 analyzes the patient–practitioner relationship and its effect on health. The factors that affect adherence with medical advice are explored in Module 4.2. Module 4.3 evaluates the delivery of health care and its effect on health.

Chapter 5 is concerned with two important influences on health: human development and aging (Module 5.1) and the environment (Module 5.2).

3

Understanding Health-Related Behavior

3.1 Models of Health-Related Behavior
3.2 Health Promotion and Health Education
3.3 Dealing with the Symptoms of Illness

Among humans, disease and illness are not interchangeable concepts (Kleinman, 1988; Mostofsky, 1981). "Disease" is something that can be detected and defined objectively as the result of physical examination and tests. It is diagnosed as part of a process in which a physician looks for and discovers a set of physical indicators, referred to as *signs*, which demonstrate that the body is not functioning as it should.

"Illness," however, is something that is far more subjective and much harder to define. It is a state that is mediated not only by physical signs, but by **symptoms**, which are personally experienced feelings and sensations. Therefore, feeling ill is determined greatly by the cognitions and motivations that people bring to a situation. As Barnlund (1993) has stated, "Human illness is not only a physical condition but a symbolic one as well. No animal talks itself into becoming sick, suppresses its symptoms because it fears diagnosis, prolongs recovery because of the symbolic payoff it receives, or spontaneously recovers because it has redefined its situation" (p. 32). Yet, of course, the human animal is capable of all these things. Some people seek out the advice of a health professional at the first sign of a cold, while others delay seeking help in the face of the most severe symptoms. Some people tolerate tremendous pain and go on with their everyday endeavors, while others become obsessed with the slightest discomfort.

Throughout this chapter we will consider the ways people think and act in relationship to their health. We will introduce theories, models, and research that help clarify how people relate to everyday issues of health and illness, and we will review the manner in which health promotion and lifestyle modification have become an integral part of our public consciousness. We will consider the ways people evaluate the sensations and symptoms their bodies present, and how commonsense models of illness guide behavior. In addition, we will review factors that help determine why and when people act—or fail to act—when faced with a threat to their health.

MODELS OF HEALTH-RELATED BEHAVIOR

When it comes to health, people are constantly acting and reacting. They engage in a wide variety of behaviors to maintain and improve their health when they feel well. They seek out advice, information, and clarification when they are troubled or concerned about their state of health. And, they submit to the recommendations and treatments prescribed for them when they have a recognized health problem.

HEALTH-RELATED BEHAVIORS

Kasl and Cobb (1966) have classified health-related behaviors according to three categories: (a) **health behavior**, which involves actions aimed at promoting good health and preventing illness; (b) **illness behavior**, which is aimed at clarifying one's health status and seeking help if necessary; and (c) **sick role behavior**, in which people who have been diagnosed as ill take action to restore their health.

HEALTH BEHAVIOR

Health behavior has also been referred to as health promotion or disease prevention behavior. It involves actions taken by people in the absence of signs and symptoms aimed at remaining well or improving their state of well-being. Specific behaviors that fall under this category range from wearing seat belts to getting immunized before the flu season, from jogging to getting a regular medical checkup. And people vary quite a bit in the degree to which they engage in these kinds of activities.

Health habits involve the most basic of health behaviors. They are learned at an early age as a result of observation and reinforcement from the child's role models, and they come to be performed almost without awareness. In their classic Alameda County study, Belloc and Breslow (1972) identified a set of specific health habits that might be associated with good or poor health, and then followed the mortality rate of more than 2,000 Californians who either did or did not practice these habits. They found that five health habits were significantly related to lower mortality rates: sufficient sleep, moderate drinking, not smoking, regular exercise, and weight control. For instance, Berkman and Breslow (1983) found that among men between the ages of 30 and 49, those who reported regularly practicing fewer than three of these habits had a rate of mortality that was almost 8 1/2 times higher than those who practiced four or five of these habits. Surprisingly, however, in this and other studies of health behaviors, specific forms of preventive health behavior are relatively uncorrelated (Rosenstock & Kirscht, 1979). The person who brushes three times a day may or may not wear a helmet when biking, and there is no guarantee that those who take vitamins regularly install smoke alarms in their homes.

ILLNESS BEHAVIOR

Illness behavior consists of all those actions that people engage in when faced with uncertainty in order to clarify and understand their status. These actions represent a response to signals from the body that something may be wrong. This category refers to behaviors such as seeking advice from friends and family as well as from people who have knowledge and training in health care. Illness behavior is, therefore, a form of help seeking as well as information seeking, although doing nothing—just waiting to see if the problem will go away on its own—is also one of the most prominent forms of illness behavior. In contrast to health behavior, where preventive actions are relatively independent of one another, people appear to be far more consistent in their willingness or unwillingness to seek out help for different problems and symptoms (Tracey, Sherry, & Keitel, 1986).

SICK ROLE BEHAVIOR

Consistent with traditional medicine's focus on illness and disease rather than on prevention, a great deal of attention has been devoted to the third category—*sick role behavior.* This category deals with all those actions to restore or rehabilitate health taken by people who have been labeled as ill. Talcott Parsons, the noted sociologist, has described the sick role in great detail (Parsons, 1951; 1975). Parsons believes that people who occupy the sick role have certain rights and privileges, and in return they must fulfill certain duties or obligations.

PRIVILEGES   Two privileges are particularly important in the Parsonian description of the sick role. First, when people are ill, they are not seen as being at fault for their condition. Rather than blame sick people for their condition, others feel sympathy for them and maintain a desire to help them.

Second, people who are sick are exempted from their normal duties and responsibilities. Known as the "secondary gain of illness," this allows sick people to be excused from having to go to work, to take exams, or to do the dishes, for example.

Parsons assumed that freedom from blame existed for all conditions and problems. However, in several important exceptions we unfairly question victims and sufferers. For instance, when a woman is raped or when a person contracts AIDS, many people will improperly question that person's behavior, asking whether the victim could have avoided the predicament had he or she acted differently. More generally, while the growing emphasis in our society on personal responsibility for maintaining health has many positive aspects, sometimes we are guilty of "blaming the victim" (Ryan, 1971). On hearing that a person has lung cancer, one person will offer sympathy and assistance, but another may state, "What do you expect? The fool smoked a pack a day." As we will discuss in Module 3.2, this is one potentially negative aspect of the growing health promotion movement (Becker, 1986, 1991).

The privilege of being exempted from normal responsibilities is quite widespread, yet even here important exceptions exist. Some people, such as those who are new to a job or feel insecure about their position, may be reluctant to be released from their obligations. Others, such as single mothers, must continue to fulfill their duties unless they are truly incapacitated because nobody else is available. Still others may feel that accepting the sick role is a threat to their self-image and reject a reduction in their load (Rosengren, 1980). Half seriously, Parsons (1978) has referred to people who shun the sick role as "*hyper*chondriacs." Although some people avoid the sick role, it is more common for people to overuse it to avoid responsibility or to gain sympathy. For instance, workers may use the sick role to gain lighter assignments (Shuval, Antonovsky, & Davies, 1973), or the elderly may use it to gain support for dependent behavior (Nuttbrock, 1986).

OBLIGATIONS   In return for their privileges, people who are not feeling well are faced with certain duties or responsibilities. They are obligated to recognize their current state as undesirable, and must take steps to get well. Therefore, they must seek out competent treatment and comply with a program designed to restore them to health. In stating these obligations, Parsons describes the person as dependent upon the medical establishment, a point for which he has been both applauded and criticized. It is important that patients be motivated to return to a healthy, productive state, and seeking a physician's care is the standard route by which to carry this out. However, some have suggested that Parsons has overemphasized the doctor's role, thereby overlooking the role of friends, family, and other health practitioners, as well as the role that patients themselves may play. They believe that Parsons has characterized the patient's role as passive and dependent, and that this is both an inappropriate and inaccurate description (Haug & Lavin, 1983; McCormack, 1981).

CRITIQUES OF PARSONS   The Parsonian view of the sick role is one of the most influential descriptions of patient behavior and has generated a great deal of discussion, both positive and negative (Freidson, 1970; Wolinsky, 1988a). The Parsonian model has been criticized because it presents itself as a universal model; yet, research has shown that it does not apply equally well to all illnesses and all people. The sick role is best applied to individuals with acute medical problems who may return to their regular roles once a specific episode has been treated and cured. Those who have chronic conditions, are terminally ill, or have a permanent disability do not fit the model very well. Chronic patients can never quite return to "normal," and therefore, it is unclear how or whether they can be excused from their regular duties. Also, chronically ill patients are likely to want to play a larger role in treatment decisions since these affect them over the long term. As a result, the relationship between doctor and patient may be marked by conflict and a struggle for power rather than with compliance and agreement.

A second important criticism of the Parsonian model is that it applies only to American sick role patterns, more specifically to those of middle-class America (Pill & Stott, 1982). Working-class people may be blamed more often for acting sick, and their right to be exempt from their duties for reasons of poor health may not be respected. Also, in many non-Western cultures, conceptions of the causes and cures of illness are very different from ours, and the concept of nonresponsibility for illness does not exist. Arctic Indians who are sick may perceive the experience as losing a part of their soul, and the treatment can involve confession or even sacrifice (Witte, 1991). Sickness in one Japanese sect is often attributed to neglect of religious duties, and recovery is accomplished through prayer (Lebra, 1972).

In summary, the actions that people take play a large part in determining how they feel. Health behaviors have the goal of maintaining or improving a person's positive state of health, illness behaviors represent attempts at coping with potential problems, and sick role behaviors involve actions that people take to restore themselves to a healthy state. An important question that must be asked is, What factors determine the extent and kind of actions that people take to maintain and restore their health?

■

THE HEALTH BELIEF MODEL

Psychologists have long been interested in generating theories and models to explain and predict why and when people act—or fail to act—to maintain or restore their health. Probably the most influential and studied of these is the **Health Belief Model** (Becker, 1974; Rosenstock, 1966). The Health Belief Model grew out of the efforts of psychologists in the Public Health Service in the 1950s to understand why people often failed to take advantage of available programs and services (Rosenstock, 1990).

In an early attempt to explain why so few people participated in neighborhood tuberculosis screenings provided in mobile x-ray units, Hochbaum (1958) asked people in these neighborhoods two types of questions. First, to what extent did they believe that they were susceptible to tuberculosis? Second, did people feel they could derive real benefits from participation in the program; did they believe that x-rays could detect tuberculosis in the absence of symptoms and that early detection was important? Of those people who held both beliefs, who not only felt susceptible but also accepted the benefits of early detection, 82% went for at least one chest x-ray. In contrast, only 21% of those people who held neither belief bothered to participate. The Health Belief Model grew out of early work such as this, and has been utilized to explain the full range of health, illness, and sick role behaviors.

ELEMENTS OF THE MODEL

The Health Belief Model is based on what is known as *value-expectancy* formulation. Its authors believed that people will take action when behavior leads to an outcome that is valued and when they have an expectancy that the outcome can be achieved. Having been revised and expanded several times, the key variables in the current version of the model are illustrated in Figure 3.1–1. They involve (a) beliefs about the nature of the threat, (b) beliefs about the nature of the action, and (c) beliefs about one's abilities to accomplish relevant actions. Specifically, these include perceived threat, efficacy of the behavior, and self-efficacy.

PERCEIVED THREAT   This variable is composed of two elements: *perceived susceptibility* and *perceived severity*. Perceived susceptibility refers to the degree to which people feel vulnerable to a given health problem. Could it happen to *me,* could *I* actually come down with this disease? The importance of this factor can be seen in the reaction of young people to basketball star Earvin Magic Johnson's announcement in November of 1991 that he had tested positive for the AIDS virus. Instead of feeling that AIDS was a health threat only to gay people or intravenous drug users, many people realized that if a young, strong, heterosexual athlete could contract the virus, it could happen to them as well.

Perceived severity deals with the seriousness of contracting an illness. It poses the question, What are the medical and clinical consequences (for example, discomfort, pain, or even death) as well as the social consequences (for example, loss of ability to work or to function as part of a group) that the condition brings? Put simply, we ask ourselves, "How bad is this condition? Is it

life threatening? Will it keep me from doing the things I like?" When seriousness and susceptibility are both high, the Health Belief Model predicts that
people will be motivated to take action to deal with the threat to their health.

EFFICACY OF THE BEHAVIOR   Feeling threatened, people must decide
what to do. Should I get that flu shot? Should I have my cholesterol tested?
Should I wait and see if my symptoms go away, go get some medication on
my own, or should I go see a doctor right away? To choose among alternative
courses of action, the Health Belief Model suggests that people go through a
form of mental cost-benefit analysis. This consideration involves two elements, *perceived benefits* and *perceived barriers.*

Perceived benefits involves the questions, "What's in it for me? If I take
my pills will the pain go away? If I practice safer sex, will that prevent me
from getting AIDS?" People take action when they feel it is likely to work.
When multiple possibilities are available, they select the one they believe will
work best.

Figure 3.1-1   THE HEALTH BELIEF MODEL

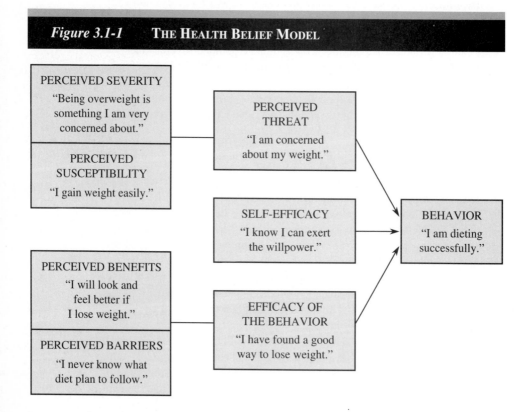

Perceived barriers refer to the drawbacks of a given course of action. Before choosing one path or another, people want to know its costs, risks, and dangers. We ask ourselves, "What will happen if the operation is not a success? Does this medication have side effects that are unpleasant, and how much will it cost?" In choosing among several options, people weigh the perceived benefits of the action against its perceived costs, choosing the path that maximizes the net result of gains minus costs.

SELF-EFFICACY   This last factor, which is a recent addition to the Health Belief Model (Rosenstock, Strecher, & Becker, 1988), focuses on Bandura's concept of *self-efficacy* (Bandura, 1977, 1982). Self-efficacy refers to a person's belief that he or she can successfully accomplish the action required to achieve a goal. People who are high on self-efficacy, not surprisingly, are more likely to initiate and maintain a program of behavior change (Bandura, 1986; Marlatt & Gordon, 1980). Self-efficacy takes on its greatest significance in relation to long-term actions, especially those that involve changing one's lifestyle.

Maddux and Rogers (1983), working in the tradition of a related model—Protection Motivation Theory—found an even more powerful effect of self-efficacy in relation to smoking. They reported that people who did not even feel particularly vulnerable to the negative effects of smoking indicated that they intended to quit as long as they felt that they could do so effectively. In effect, these people were taking a precautionary strategy, saying, "Even though smoking doesn't concern me too much, why continue as long as I feel capable of quitting?" In this way, a sense of self-efficacy seems to be the minimal condition for translating a health concern, whether it be strong or mild, into a pattern of action.

In addition to these variables, the Health Belief Model has incorporated others throughout its history. Most important among these are demographic variables (such as age or sex), personality characteristics, knowledge about and interest in health, and past experience, each of which may serve as modifiers of perceived threat. In addition, cues to action are considered necessary to trigger a given response. These cues may be internal, such as the recognition of a symptom, or external, such as a media campaign or a reminder from a friend or relative.

APPLICATIONS OF THE MODEL

Since its development, numerous research and intervention programs have been based on the Health Belief Model. These range from breast self-examination (Champion, 1990; Wyper, 1990) to compliance with a diabetic regimen

(Heiby, Gafarian, & Mcann, 1989), and from AIDS prevention (Brown, DiClemente, & Reynolds, 1991; Montgomery et al., 1989) to safety belt promotion (Nelson & Moffit, 1988). In a recent study, for instance, Oldridge and Streiner (1990) surveyed 120 males with coronary artery disease who were part of a cardiac rehabilitation program. Combining items based on the Health Belief Model, they were able to predict which individuals dropped out and which remained in the six-month program in 65% of the cases.

Testing the effectiveness of this model in a very different way, Larson et al. (1979) sent 3 types of postcards to 283 elderly people urging them to get flu shots. The first type, a "neutral" card simply announced the availability of the vaccine. The second, a "personal" card, was signed by a physician and referred to the person by name. A third "Health Belief Model" card, which was not personalized, reminded people of the risk and seriousness of the flu, as well as the effectiveness of the vaccine and the very low risk of negative side effects. The neutral postcard generated a participation rate of 25%, only slightly above the 20% rate of those in a control group who received no card. The personal card raised participation to 41%. However, the highest level, 51%, was found among those who got the nonpersonalized Health Belief Model card.

CRITIQUES OF THE MODEL

The Health Belief Model remains one of the most respected and widely used models in health psychology. However, the role of each of the specific elements of the model, as well as the power of the combined factors to predict health, illness, and sick role behavior, has been the subject of debate. In a thorough review of 46 Health Belief Model studies that were conducted prior to the incorporation of self-efficacy, Janz and Becker (1984) found that the single most powerful predictor of behavior across all studies was perceived barriers. Perceived susceptibility was best able to predict preventive health behaviors, while perceived benefits was stronger for sick role behaviors. Perceived severity was the weakest of the factors overall, although its effect was most noticeable among sick role behaviors.

Critics of the Health Belief Model have also pointed out that it is not well organized. They state that it is a catalog of interesting and relevant variables, but that its formulators have never proposed just how these should be measured, quantified, and combined. Another problem with the Health Belief Model is that it attempts to account for behavior strictly in terms of attitudes and beliefs. It therefore leaves out important environmental and social factors that influence people's actions. Another approach, the Theory of Reasoned Action, combines cognitive (belief) factors with social factors, and it is to this approach that we turn.

THE THEORY OF REASONED ACTION

The **Theory of Reasoned Action** (Ajzen & Fishbein, 1977; 1980) and its extension, the Theory of Planned Behavior (Ajzen, 1985), represent another much researched and utilized approach for understanding and predicting when and why people take health-related actions. This theory did not develop from a specific interest in health; instead, it grew out of a general desire to understand the role that cognitive factors, especially attitudes, played in deciding to take action.

ELEMENTS OF THE MODEL

As outlined in Figure 3.1-2, Ajzen and Fishbein believe that the best way to predict behavior is to know a person's *behavioral intentions.* A behavioral intention represents a person's commitment to act and is strongly predictive of actual behavior (Fishbein, Ajzen, & McArdle, 1980). In order to assess intentions, Ajzen and Fishbein suggest that the question be as specific as possible to the behavior. Rather than ask, "How do you feel about seat belts?", the question, "How likely is it that you will wear your seat belt when you go out today?" is a more direct and powerful predictor. The more a person intends to perform a given act, the greater the person will try, and the greater the probability that the behavior will actually be performed.

Rather than propose that attitudes alone predict intentions and behavior, Fishbein and Ajzen suggest that intentions are a product of three factors. The first factor is represented by a person's *attitude toward the behavior.* That is, to know if a person intends to wear a seat belt, we should know how this person feels about wearing them. This attitude is the result of (a) the belief that this behavior will lead to certain outcomes, combined with (b) an evaluation of that outcome as a positive one.

The second factor that influences intentions and behavior, however, is not a personal or internal factor such as attitude, but rather a social factor, a response to external pressures. People respond to *subjective norms,* their perception of how others expect them to behave combined with their motivation to comply with these expectations. In this case, we would want to know the answers to two questions: "How much pressure do you feel from your family (or friends or experts) to wear your seat belt?" in addition to "How important do you consider it to act as these others expect you to?"

The third factor, recently added, is the matter of control, or more accurately, *perceived control.* This parallels quite closely the concept of self-efficacy that was added to the Health Belief Model and deals with the question

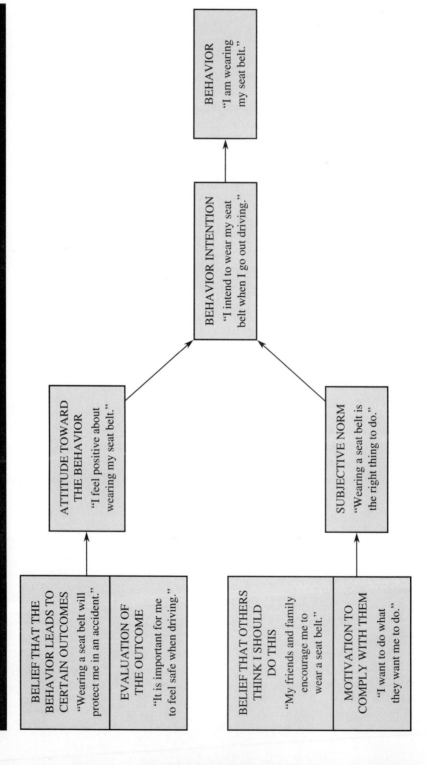

Figure 3.1-2 THE THEORY OF REASONED ACTION

BELIEF THAT THE BEHAVIOR LEADS TO CERTAIN OUTCOMES
"Wearing a seat belt will protect me in an accident."

EVALUATION OF THE OUTCOME
"It is important for me to feel safe when driving."

ATTITUDE TOWARD THE BEHAVIOR
"I feel positive about wearing my seat belt."

BEHAVIOR INTENTION
"I intend to wear my seat belt when I go out driving."

BEHAVIOR
"I am wearing my seat belt."

BELIEF THAT OTHERS THINK I SHOULD DO THIS
"My friends and family encourage me to wear a seat belt."

MOTIVATION TO COMPLY WITH THEM
"I want to do what they want me to do."

SUBJECTIVE NORM
"Wearing a seat belt is the right thing to do."

We engage in behaviors such as seat-belt wearing because we recognize that important others want us to.

of resources and opportunities. People who feel that they lack the resources or opportunities to engage in a given behavior are unlikely to generate a strong intention to engage in it even when they hold a favorable attitude and recognize that others would have them do so. In essence, it is a necessary condition for action. For example, no matter how strongly you might want to start an exercise program, you will not begin if you perceive that there is no time, no nearby health club, or nobody with whom to exercise.

APPLICATIONS OF THE MODEL

The Theory of Reasoned Action has also been applied to a range of health-related behaviors from high blood pressure (Norman et al., 1985) and family planning (Fishbein et al., 1980) to substance abuse (Beck, 1981) and medication adherence (Ried & Christensen, 1988). Attitudes and subjective norms have been shown to be highly related to intentions, as in a study by Jaccard and Davidson (1972) where these two factors accounted for almost 80% of the variance in the intention of female college students to use birth control pills. Olson and Zanna (1987) have offered a set of recommendations for promoting physical exercise based on this model, as shown in Table 3.1-1. They propose that specific forms of exercise (swimming or jogging rather than exercise in general) ought to be encouraged, emphasizing how each one can make you feel good or look better. Social pressures need to be exerted so people will feel that significant others want them to exercise. Finally, it is important that each person be made to feel that exercise is easy, and that he or she can really carry it out.

The Theory of Reasoned Action, like the Health Belief Model, grows out of a value-expectancy orientation and relates action to the health-oriented cognitions that people hold. This theory, however, allows for more careful measurement of its concepts and specifies in far more detail the interrelationship and paths of causation by which the variables influence each other. A particular contribution is its focus on the *intention* to act as a key mediator between attitudes and behavior, although intention does not always predict actual behavior, especially when the time frame between intention and action is long (Mullen, Hersey, & Iverson, 1987). Another important difference between the two theories is that this one focuses on the ways people react to the influence of others rather than those factors that arouse fear such as perceived susceptibility and seriousness. In this way, it provides a joint focus on external factors as well as internal ones, offering a broader view on the determinants of health-related behavior.

Table 3.1-1 **RECOMMENDATIONS FOR ENCOURAGING EXERCISE BASED ON THE THEORY OF REASONED ACTION**

RECOMMENDATIONS FOR PROMOTING PHYSICAL ACTIVITY

1. Promote specific exercises (jogging, swimming, walking, etc.):
    a. Emphasize the positive personal consequences that will result from performing the exercise.
    b. Explain how negative personal consequences that can result from the exercise are avoidable.
2. Communicate the negative personal consequences of not exercising ("fear appeals"), but also include information about how to avoid those consequences (i.e., how to begin exercising).
3. Create perceived social pressure for exercising:
    a. Communicate that "important others" want the target person to perform specific exercises.
    b. Involve "opinion leaders" from the community in the campaign.
4. Increase perceived control over exercising:
    a. Explain that exercising regularly is compatible with any lifestyle.
    b. Explain that everyone can engage in some form of activity.
5. Provide basic, detailed information about how to perform the exercise (or specify where such information can be obtained).

Source: Olson, J.M., & Zanna, M.P., 1987, Understanding and promoting exercise: A social psychological perspective, Canadian Journal of Public Health, 78, *S1–7.*

PUTTING IT ALL TOGETHER

The Health Belief Model and the Theory of Reasoned Action are two of the most influential models of health-related behavior that we have. They can be used to account for health behavior, illness behavior, and sick role behavior as well. As cognitive models, they emphasize that our actions are guided not simply by the events around us, but by these events and circumstances *as they are interpreted* by the individual. Two individuals may be in the same objective circumstances; yet, one may feel vulnerable while the other may not. Both people may be equally capable, but one may feel a greater sense of self-efficacy than the other. The Theory of Reasoned Action, in addition, points to the role of social pressures, as they are perceived, and how these also affect behavior. In recent years, several attempts to compare the predictive strength of these models with one another (Hennig & Knowles, 1990; Ross & Rosser, 1989; Ronis & Kaiser, 1989) have met with varying results. More important, however, would be an integration of these into a single all-encompassing and integrated approach. Although this has not yet been accomplished, the existing models and theories do offer us a meaningful view of the many factors that enter into the mental equation that determines when and why people take action on behalf of their health.

MODULE SUMMARY

1. Health behavior involves all those actions that people engage in when they feel well to promote good health and prevent illness. These actions range from regular exercise to getting immunizations, from regular checkups to wearing seat belts.
2. Illness behavior refers to the things people do when they suspect something may be wrong with their health in order to understand their status better. It includes both help seeking and information seeking, although one popular strategy is the wait and see, maybe-it-will-go-away approach.
3. Sick role behavior refers to those actions people take when they are labeled ill in order to restore and rehabilitate their health. The sociologist, Talcott Parsons, has developed the most widely regarded model of this behavior.
4. According to Parsons, people in the sick role are not blamed for their condition and are exempted from their normal obligations. In return, they are expected to seek competent medical help and to cooperate fully in getting well.

5. The Health Belief Model is one of the most widely used models in health psychology. It was developed to explain why and when people fail to take preventive measures, but it has been applied to the full range of health-related behaviors.

6. According to the Health Belief Model, people's actions are determined by three key variables: (a) the degree to which the problem is perceived as a threat; (b) the extent to which the available action is perceived as effective; and (c) the person's belief in his or her ability to carry out the action, known as self-efficacy.

7. The Theory of Reasoned Action is another well-respected approach to understanding health-related behaviors. It developed out of a desire to understand the manner in which attitudes affect behavior in general, and it has been applied to a wide range of topics from exercise to birth control.

8. The Theory of Reasoned Action contains two unique aspects. First, it suggests that the best way to predict action is to measure a person's behavioral intentions. Second, it notes that the expectations of others serve as an important factor determining intention. It therefore incorporates both internal and external pressures on behavior.

9. Both of these models share one common focus. They suggest that our actions are not determined by circumstances and events as they exist but as they are perceived or interpreted by the individual. In spite of recent attempts to compare the predictive power of these two models, further efforts need to be directed at developing a more integrated, all-encompassing approach.

HEALTH PROMOTION
AND HEALTH EDUCATION

A commercial for an automobile oil filter appeared on television a few years back that captured, by analogy, the essence of the health promotion concept. In it, a mechanic is seen working on an expensive and difficult transmission job. The mechanic speaks to the audience, suggesting that the whole operation could have been avoided by simple, inexpensive preventive maintenance. Pointing first to the $2 oil filter, hesitating, and then turning to the expensive work being performed on the disabled car, he says, "It's your choice. You can pay me now—or you can pay me later." The message is clear and fits neatly with one of our oldest homespun sayings: An ounce of prevention is worth a pound of cure.

THE RISE OF HEALTH PROMOTION

This point seems evident to everyone, and few people would disagree with it. Yet if this is so, how does it fit with the following facts? In 1982, the cost of all goods and services provided by the American medical care system was 287 billion dollars. Of that money 96% was spent on the treatment of illness; 4% was spent on prevention and health promotion.

Ainsworth (1984) has provided an answer to this paradox in a brief history of the American medical system and the public's response to it. Over much of the twentieth century the medical community focused its attention on controlling and curing disease. As medical discoveries multiplied, faith in the medical system grew, and people began to feel less and less responsible for their own health. Health was only a matter to think about if something went wrong, and even then, people believed that modern medical technology could provide the solution to their problems. Surely, when a new health threat reared its head, another vaccine would be found, or medical science would at least develop a new drug to treat or cure it.

Compared to 1900, when infectious diseases such as influenza, pneumonia, and tuberculosis were the leading causes of death in the United States, by 1990 hardly any of the top 10 killers were infectious. Chronic diseases such as cancer, stroke, and heart disease replaced them at the top of the list. But these were more problematic than everyone had assumed. No miracle cures existed for them because no single virus or germ could be identified and conquered by laboratory scientists or clinical practitioners. Instead, these were diseases of **lifestyle**, where risk was not determined primarily by any doctor's actions. Risk was determined instead by behavior, by diet and stress, and by the use of alcohol, tobacco, and drugs.

Currently, one in every six deaths in the United States can be attributed to smoking (U.S. Dept of Health and Human Services, 1989), and dietary practices and alcohol consumption contribute to 8 of the top 10 leading causes of death (Surgeon General's Report on Nutrition and Health, 1988). In fact, the Centers for Disease Control estimated in 1980 that 48% of the mortality in the United States was due to unhealthy behavior or lifestyle compared to 26% due to biological factors.

Little by little, disease *prevention* rather than disease *treatment* became a major focus of attention as people began to recognize the critical role they could play in staying healthy. Oat bran products sold like wildfire and whole grain breads were consumed as people attempted to lower their risk of heart disease and colon cancer through their diet. Yet the change was still not as fundamental as might first appear because the focus remained on illness, even if people were talking about its prevention rather than its treatment.

In recent years, however, the change has come full circle as people have come to think in more positive terms, to consider the effects of their behavior on *health* as well as on disease. As a result, concepts such as *wellness* that focus on the positive side of health have entered into our collective consciousness as people go about seeking health, an optimal state of mind and body, rather than simply avoiding illness. This emphasis has even been officially recognized by governments, as reflected in the report *Healthy People 2000: National Health Promotion and Disease Prevention Objectives* published by the U.S. Department of Health and Human Services. Acknowledging that illness is rooted in human behavior, it goes one step further by focusing positively on quality of life, not just on length of life.

HEALTH PROMOTION AND HEALTH EDUCATION

With this growing emphasis, the fields of *health promotion* and *health education* have also grown. Health promotion and health education are two closely related terms, each referring to a process by which people make informed and responsible choices that lead to improved health. **Health promotion** is the science and art of assisting people to change and reorient their lifestyle toward a state of optimal health. Health promotion efforts begin by changing individual behavior, but they do not stop there (Epp, 1986). Health promotion also encompasses changes in health policy, the creation of supportive environments, and the reorientation of health services beyond treatment and cure. It therefore includes not only health education, but also health advocacy (Minkler, 1989).

Although we sometimes use the two terms interchangeably, the concept of **health education** is usually thought of in a somewhat more specific manner as "any combination of learning experiences designed to facilitate voluntary adaptations of behavior conducive to health" (Green et al., 1980, p. 7). Health education is an instrument of social change by which individuals, groups, and whole populations are offered skills, knowledge, opportunities, and resources to improve their present and future health. The ultimate goal is to help people to change old behaviors and adopt new ones in order to pursue the positive goal of good health as defined in emotional, social, intellectual, and spiritual as well as physical terms (Green et al., 1980).

THE SCOPE OF HEALTH EDUCATION AND PROMOTION

The range of health education and health promotion issues and activities is almost limitless. Some programs focus on increasing positive behaviors such as exercise, proper diet, and stress management. Others are aimed at the elimination of health compromising behaviors such as smoking and drug and alcohol dependence. More traditional efforts aimed at disease prevention and control continue as well. Vaccination and immunization programs attempt to eliminate diseases such as measles and polio, while screening programs for problems such as cancer, hypertension, and tuberculosis focus on early detection. Interventions in each of these areas can involve a broad spectrum of settings, groups, and types.

SETTINGS

Health education programs can be found in any number of different sites. The school setting, from nursery school through college, has been a particularly prominent site for health education programs that address such issues as smoking prevention and alcohol and drug abuse. Teacher training and the creation of changes in the school environment complement traditional classroom efforts to educate young people.

In recent years, worksite health promotion programs have also grown in number and variety. Programs involving stress management and time management are

Health promotion programs often target special populations, such as programs that encourage women to engage in breast self-examination.

extremely popular, as are efforts directed at exercise, smoking, and nutrition (Weiss, Fielding, & Baum, 1991). Health care settings have become extremely active in providing education and training for employees and their families in addition to continuing education and inservice training for health care providers. In addition to traditional settings such as hospitals and doctors' offices, health maintenance organizations (HMOs), with their emphasis on prevention, have become prominent in sponsoring programs. Figure 3.2-1 presents an example of the programs offered by one particular HMO.

Although it is often not formally recognized as a setting for health education, the consumer marketplace now represents one of the largest and most pervasive settings for health education. People have been encouraged to read labels to find out the percentage of fat from calories in a given product, check whether the ingredients are "all natural," and investigate each product's nutritional value. We should be aware, however, that commercial claims have the primary purpose of promoting products rather than health, and they may be misleading or only partially accurate.

POPULATIONS

In order to be most effective, health promotion programs should be targeted at specific audiences and tailored to their problems, concerns, and needs, as well as their learning styles and requirements. At-risk groups, such as those with a family history of an inheritable disease or those who engage in high risk

Figure 3.2-1   A MENU OF COURSES OFFERED BY A LARGE HMO

Harvard Community
Health Plan

Health Center Division
Program Descriptions

A selection of our most popular courses are described below. Members of any HCHP health center or medical group are welcome to attend any program – at any location – for the reduced member fee; most courses are also open to the public. For more information or to register, please call: 731-7311.

HEALTH HABITS AND LIFESTYLE

Alcohol and Drug Education Group
A four-part program designed to answer basic questions about drug and alcohol use: "How can I tell if I have a problem?" What is a healthy use of these substances?" How can I help someone with a problem?"

Back School
A program that helps acute and chronic back-pain sufferers understand the cause of their back pain and teaches proper body mechanics and exercises for pain relief.

Basic Cardiac Life Support (BCLS)
An eight-hour certification program designed to teach cardio-pulmonary resuscitation (CPR) – the emergency plan of action to use after an adult's breathing has stopped. (All participants must be at least 13 years old).

Couples Communication Workshop
A four-session workshop that focuses on common communication patterns and blocks. The couple learns new skills to promote effective dialogue. Lecture, discussion, classroom, and home exercises included. (Advanced Couples Communication Workshops are also offered.)

First Visit to the Dentist
Preschoolers acquire good habits to prevent tooth decay, explore what happens at the dentist, and reduce dental anxiety by such activities as "riding" in the dental chair.

Freedom From Smoking™
A seven-session educational and support group (developed by the American Lung Association) for smokers who want to kick the habit.

Stress Management
Provides information and techniques helpful in understanding and managing stress.

Tension Relaxation Workshop
A one-session program designed to teach an effective method of relaxation.

NUTRITION

Cholesterol Education Class
Learn about healthy low-fat cholesterol-lowering meals and snacks, as well as the latest research, label-reading, new product guidelines, shopping, and hints for dining out.

Feeding Ourselves™
A ten-week comprehensive program for people with compulsive eating, weight, and body-image problems. The approach combines psychological awareness with behavioral techniques to achieve weight loss and a positive relationship to food.

Infant Nutrition
A program for parents of babies (one to ten months old), covering the introduction of solid food, the transition from baby food to table food and the components of a balanced diet.

Light Chinese Cooking
A hands-on workshop that teaches preparation of low-salt, low-fat and low-cholesterol Chinese food.

The N.E.W. HCHP Weight Loss Program
Nutrition, Exercise Guidelines, and Weight Management: A long-term program teaching you methods to alter the way you eat and exercise to achieve weight loss.

Sports Nutrition Workshop
Learn about good nutritional habits for your exercise program; topics include carbohydrate-loading, vitamins, fluids and caffeine.

Toddler Nutrition
A 90-minute program for parents of toddlers (12–24 months), covering the components of a nutritious diet, media influence on children's eating behavior, and imaginative ways to help children eat healthy foods.

Weight Loss – Getting Started
Learn the basic techniques to achieve and maintain weight loss, as well as options for follow-up.

PARENTING

Infant Care Series
A series of three child-care classes for parents. "Caring for Your Newborn", for expectant parents, including bathing the infant and selecting equipment. "When Your Baby is Ill" covers common illnesses and treatments for newborns to six months. "Keeping Your Baby Safe" covers common safety hazards for six-month to two-year-olds.

Parent Effectiveness Training™
A research-tested program that teaches communication techniques for building more effective relationships between adults and children (of any age). Listening, confrontation and problem-solving skills are emphasized.

SEXUALITY & REPRODUCTION

Pregnancy Past 30
Probes the medical concerns of prospective parents over 30.

Prepared Childbirth Program
Labor, the delivery process, breathing exercises and postpartum concerns are discussed, plus a tour of the hospital labor and delivery area.

Preparing for Pregnancy
Explores physical preparation for pregnancy (e.g., prenatal screening, medications, nutrition) and HCHP's labor and delivery policies.

Source: Harvard Community Health Plan, Health Center Division, flyer.

behaviors, have been identified and encouraged to modify specific practices. Programs are also aimed at people at various stages of their life cycle such as infants, teenagers, and the elderly. Others are designed for people who differ in their place of residence, for instance inner city versus rural dwellers, or who differ in their lifestyle, for instance heterosexual versus homosexual people. And still others have been designed for the health problems of women, for those with chronic diseases, and for specific cultural or racial groups.

MODALITIES OF INTERVENTION

If you wanted to have a great impact on the health of the public, how would you go about gaining the largest effect? Would you work with people one-on-one or in small groups? Would you place advertisements in the local newspaper and national television, or would you lobby to have laws changed? These are some of the options and dilemmas that constantly face people engaged in health promotion.

ONE-ON-ONE   At one end of the spectrum, we have the individual approach. Here professional and client interact one-on-one. This approach typifies the traditional model of medical and psychological therapy, but it can apply to a wide range of situations. The practitioner might be a nurse or pharmacist as well as a doctor, or a physical therapist as well as a psychotherapist. At this modality, education and therapy are individualized and can be tailored to meet the specific needs of the client.

THE SMALL GROUP   If you wanted to have a broader impact, you would work at the small group level. At this level, small numbers of people interact, discuss, role play, and support one another in a joint effort to deal with a problem. They may be a natural unit such as a family, club, or workplace team, or they may be groups of strangers who come together to deal with a common health concern. Groups typically share information, provide mutual support, and act as models for one another's actions.

The work of Evans (1984) on the prevention of smoking among teenagers is a good example of the group level approach. It rests on the assumption that peer group members are greatly responsible for inducing teenagers to begin smoking. In small groups, students learn how to resist peer pressure, practicing and discussing resistance among themselves. Worksite smoking cessation programs with adults also utilize small-group instruction and discussion (Fielding, 1991a, 1991b).

COMMUNITY WIDE   If you wanted to have an impact broader than that of the small group, you could initiate community wide programs. Community programs involve whole geographical or political units and usually utilize several different components. Early efforts of this type were often in the form of screening programs; however, more recent efforts have featured the use of mass media to educate and change behavior. Campaigns utilizing radio, newspapers, and especially television have grown in sophistication over the past years. They have been utilized widely, most notably in substance abuse campaigns (DeJong & Winsten, 1990) and major heart disease prevention programs (Flora, Maibach, & Maccoby, 1989).

Social marketing is another broad-based approach to health promotion. It involves the adaptation of the methods and approaches of commercial marketing to the arena of ideas and social causes (Bloom, 1980; Kotler, 1982). Using this approach, the population is considered in terms of relevant subgroups or segments. Then products and programs are tailored so that they will fit best into the beliefs, values, and lifestyles—and budgets—of these specific segments of the population. DeJong (1989) points out that social marketing programs to promote condoms for contraceptive purposes have been successful in developing countries and recommends that similar programs be adopted in the United States to limit the spread of AIDS.

P U B L I C   P O L I C Y   If you wanted to have the broadest impact, it would be best to affect institutional or public policies. Health promotion at the policy level affects whole populations of individuals by creating rules and regulations that require certain health-promoting behaviors, such as the wearing of seatbelts, or restrict other forms of health-compromising behaviors, such as smoking on air flights. Although attempts to make smoking illegal have not gotten very far, local, state, and federal governments have imposed considerable restrictions on the advertising and use of tobacco ever since the first Surgeon General's report on the dangers of smoking were issued (U.S. Dept. of Health, Education and Welfare, 1964). A few companies have even adopted the highly controversial policy of restricting the hiring of new employees to nonsmokers (Winett, King, & Altman, 1989).

W H I C H   I S   B E S T ?   Approaches to health promotion using each of these modalities have both advantages and disadvantages. At the individual modality, the impact of any given intervention is most intensive in that each person involved receives individual time and attention from a health educator. On the other hand, interventions at this level have been criticized in several ways. Some believe they are noncost-effective and inefficient because the one-to-one ratio of health educator to client limits their scope. Others are concerned about its potential social class bias, suggesting that the people who receive this sort of assistance are those who can most afford to pay rather than those who need it most.

Broad-based community interventions have reverse problems. While the impact may be quite wide as defined by the number and kind of people affected, the true effect of this sort of approach has been questioned. If the result of an intervention is superficial or only short lived for the majority of those targeted, we may ask what has truly been accomplished. Finally, approaches that affect policy, while sometimes successful, have been criticized for running counter to the very philosophy of health promotion, which is to assist people in making healthy *choices* rather than to require them to act in specific ways. In response to the question of which is best, Winett, King, and Altman (1989) have argued strongly that we must take a *multimodality approach,* analyzing a problem from diverse perspectives and dealing with it at a number of different levels in a number of different ways.

TECHNIQUES AND APPROACHES

A great many techniques exist that can encourage people to change their health-related behaviors. Should we teach people specific individual skills based on cognitive and behavioral principles? Should we try to frighten them into changing their behavior by saying, "You had better change or else face the consequences?" Or should we take a more positive approach and offer them incentives to engage in new and different behaviors? It is to these questions that we now turn.

COGNITIVE-BEHAVIORAL TECHNIQUES   As discussed in Module 2.2, a wide variety of one-on-one techniques have been applied to the modification of health-related behaviors. Behavior therapy, utilizing the principles of learning theory, focuses on the circumstances and conditions that elicit and maintain behavior. It helps people change their behavior by recognizing the ways environmental factors affect them. In contrast, cognitive therapy focuses on internal representations, the ways people see events and themselves. Once thought of as mutually exclusive, cognitive-behavioral approaches have recently been applied to a great many health-related behaviors. Under this combined approach, behavior is modified by changing the external conditions that give rise to it in combination with the thoughts, beliefs, and images that people hold.

FEAR APPEALS   In any large-scale effort directed at getting people to adopt positive health behaviors, four factors determine its success (Hovland, Janis, & Kelley, 1953). These include: (a) the characteristics of the communicator, (b) the characteristics of the message, (c) the channel to be used, and (d) the characteristics of the audience. In short, the question is, Who communicates what, by what means, to whom? Although each of these factors can

Campaigns that attempt to inspire fear have met with mixed results at best.

make a substantial difference in the effectiveness of a campaign, a key issue involves the content of the message itself. In particular, is it necessary or desirable to scare people in order to get them to change their behavior? When people are frightened, are they more or less likely to quit smoking, see their doctor, or change their diets?

Yul Brynner, an actor well known for his role as the king in the play *The King and I,* appeared on television several years ago to announce that he was dying of lung cancer. He noted that he was suffering from this fatal disease because he had smoked for most of his adult life and pointed out that it was too late for him to do anything about it. He told viewers that smoking was likely to kill them if they continued, and he implored them to quit before it was too late for them as well. He died shortly after those announcements came on the air. Is this sort of hard-hitting, emotional campaign likely to be effective?

The first part of the answer is that people in general *believe* that fear is effective. In research by Janis and Feshbach (1953) and Evans et al. (1970), those exposed to a high fear communication reported that they had been most influenced by this type of message. Yet in both cases the fear message actually created less attitude and behavior change than more positive approaches. The second half of the answer is that the majority of the evidence suggests that most fear-based campaigns do not work (Job, 1988). This is not necessarily due to problems inherent in the use of fear as a motivator, but to the misapplication of the findings concerning fear in the design of many health promotion campaigns.

Fear campaigns that merely threaten people do not work very well. In fact, sometimes they even boomerang and have an opposite effect to what was intended. People who are made to feel especially vulnerable are often left with no means to deal with their anxiety. As a result they may choose to ignore or deny a health threat instead of acting on it. In a study by Jepson and Chaiken (1986), subjects read an article urging regular checkups to avoid cancer. The more anxious that the subjects became about the topic, the less they recalled the content of the article and the less they were persuaded by its argument. In another study performed in the United Kingdom, posters and television advertisements graphically emphasized the dangers of AIDS. These high fear messages significantly increased anxiety among students who were at low risk, but they had no effects on the drug users who were the target of the campaign (Sherr, 1990).

In order for a fear arousing message to be successful, the threat must seem both immediate and likely. Most important, people must also be given information and alternative responses that will allow them to cope with the threat. When useful advice is given—if along with the fear comes one or more effective responses—then fear-arousing messages can be effective in inducing change. When no alternatives are provided, the shock value of fear may quickly disappear or even work in the opposite direction.

In a report of an early failure to reduce AIDS risk among heroin users in 1985, health care workers at San Francisco General Hospital put up a large poster on a wall with an eight-foot-long syringe. It read, "DON'T SHARE." Although the reported rate of needle sharing had been steadily dropping previously, sharing went up 8% a month after the poster's appearance (Sorenson & Guydish, 1991). In a similar vein, Evans (1988) has been critical of the antidrug "Just Say No" campaign because it arouses fear without giving alternative responses. To be successful, Evans believes that people must know *how* to say no. They must learn what to say to resist peer pressure so they do not lose face when standing up for themselves.

In comparison to these attempts, a successful road safety intervention project in Australia played on people's fear of arrest for drunk driving, going beyond the simple warning "Don't drink and drive." The message reminded people about a range of available alternatives such as taking a taxi, staying at a friend's house, or getting a lift with a friend (Job, 1985). Recently, the idea of having a "designated driver" has been proposed and popularized for groups of drinkers as another alternative to drinking and driving.

THE USE OF INCENTIVES   Although you may know that exercise would be good for you and that you should cut down on fatty foods, you may have found that you could never quite get yourself to do it. However, if someone offered you $10 for every hour you spent exercising, or a gift certificate to your favorite store for every 5 pounds you lost, would that make the behavior more attractive or more likely? The evidence suggests that people can and do change their behavior when offered concrete incentives.

Programs based on the use of incentives and competitions, often organized around the workplace, have generated high levels of short-term and long-term success (Fielding, 1991a; Jason et al., 1990). These have been applied most widely in smoking cessation programs (Klesges & Cigrang, 1989), but also in interventions involving blood pressure control (Shephard et al., 1979), weight loss (Stunkard, Cohen, & Felix, 1989), and the wearing of seat belts (Simons-Morton, Brink, & Bates, 1987). Although these programs can sometimes be expensive, their cost seems reasonable compared to the $29 to $61 billion dollars a year that smoking-related problems cost American industry (Office of Technology Assessment, 1990).

Incentive programs can work in a number of ways. In the Live for Life program of the Johnson & Johnson Company, employees who participated in a smoking control program earned play money that could be redeemed for athletic clothing and health-oriented products (Breslow et al., 1990). At the Bonne Belle Company, employees could earn a significant amount of money, $250, for quitting smoking. However, they also had to pledge to pay twice that amount if they resumed, a factor that discouraged the participation of some, but enlisted the long-term commitment of those who did sign up for the program (Jeffrey et al., 1988). Shepard et al. (1979) offered people at a hypertension clinic the opportunity to earn up to $16 per visit if they maintained their blood pressure at an agreed-on goal. They found that 81% of those in the incentive group (as opposed to 66% who received "standard care") met the goals set.

The use of competition in addition to incentives increases the rate of participation in smoking programs, and increases both initial and one-year cessation rates compared to behavioral approaches alone (Fielding, 1991b). In one program, workers earned $10 for attending each of six group counseling sessions, and $1 a day for the next 180 days that they kept from smoking. After 60 days all participants who had refrained from smoking had their names entered in a lottery for a large prize. Workers in the program also formed three-person teams competing for an additional prize of $300 for the team with the greatest number of nonsmoking days (Jason et al., 1990).

Providing joint rewards for people working together in teams allows people to provide social support for one another, and it leads them to exert social pressure within the group to maintain the behavior change. In the smoking competition just described, many workers said that they avoided smoking when tempted only because they did not want to ruin the chances of others who were counting on them.

THE PROCESS OF HEALTH EDUCATION

Health educators, being action oriented, often spot a problem and devise a solution without careful consideration of its design and evaluation. Lawrence Green, a highly respected health educator, has proposed the **PRECEDE model** for health education to encourage more careful planning and evaluation

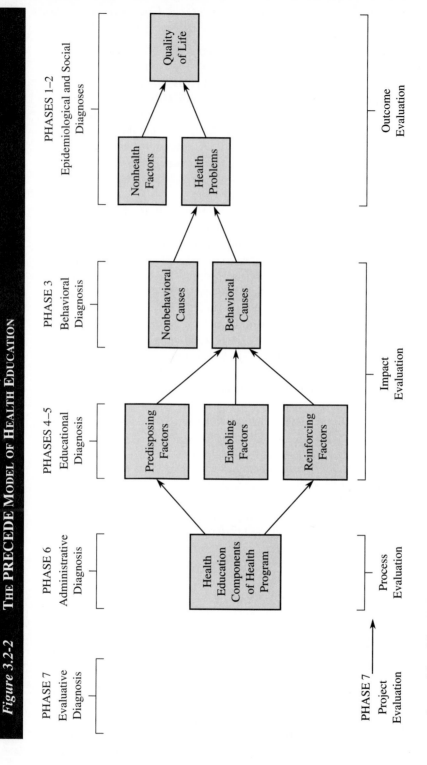

Figure 3.2-2 **The PRECEDE Model of Health Education**

Source: Adapted from L.W. Green, M.W. Kreuter, S.G. Deeds, and K.B. Partridge, eds., 1980, Health Education and Planning: A Diagnostic Approach (Palo Alto, CA: Mayfield Publishing).

(Green et al., 1980). The PRECEDE model, which stands for Predisposing, Reinforcing, and Enabling Causes in Educational Diagnosis and Evaluation, proposes a seven-step process (see Figure 3.2-2).

Phases 1 and 2 of PRECEDE are critical because they carefully define the problem. The process begins by considering the quality of life in a given population (such as students, workers, or patients), and then identifying specific health problems that seem to contribute to it. Knowledge of epidemiology, the study of the distribution and determinants of disease, is particularly useful at this point.

Phase 3 involves behavioral diagnosis linking specific modifiable actions to the health problems that have been identified. For instance, to what extent do exercise, diet, and smoking contribute to the problem? Nonbehavioral factors such as economic forces, family history, and the environment, which may place limitations on the interventions, are also considered here.

Phases 4 and 5 involve a diagnosis of the most important classes of factors affecting the behavior, as well as the decision about which factors to target for change. *Predisposing factors* involve the beliefs, attitudes, and perceptions of the target population that provide motivation or a lack of motivation for change. *Enabling factors* refer to the availability of skills, facilities, and personal and community resources that might facilitate or hinder the change. *Reinforcing factors* involve the kinds of consequences and degree of encouragement received from others that provide personal or social rewards for behavioral changes. Many of these elements bear a close resemblance to those of the Health Belief Model and the Theory of Reasoned Action discussed in Module 3.1.

Phase 6 involves the actual development of a program and its implementation. Choices of approaches and levels must be made, and practical and administrative problems must be overcome. Phase 7 involves the evaluation and assessment of impact. This stage of program assessment, which is crucial, is often done unsystematically or not at all. However, when it is performed carefully, it offers a clear picture of the success of the intervention and provides direction for the development of future programs.

HEALTH PROMOTION IN ACTION

Having outlined the how and the why of health promotion in general, we will now consider prevention and health promotion efforts related to two of our most pressing health problems, heart disease and AIDS. In doing so, we can get a sense of the variety of activities and approaches that have been tried, and can also come to appreciate the obstacles each has faced.

PROTECTING THE HEART

As we will discuss in greater detail in Module 11.1, many of the risk factors for coronary artery disease are associated with behaviors that can be modified. A person under age 45 who smokes more than 20 cigarettes a day has four times the risk of a nonsmoker of having a heart attack. And a person under age 55 with a high cholesterol level runs seven times the risk of someone whose cholesterol is not elevated.

Risk reduction programs for heart disease have been directed at a wide variety of groups. These range from young children who are taught good heart habits at an early age (Berenson et al., 1991; Luepker & Perry, 1991) to adult managers working under job-imposed and self-imposed stress (Roskies et al., 1986). Several major programs have focused on the community as a whole.

The Stanford Heart Disease Prevention Program under the direction of social psychologist Nathan Maccoby and physician John Farquhar (Farquhar et al., 1977; Meyer et al., 1980) was one of the first community-wide programs attempted, and has served as a model for many that have followed. The goal of the project was to modify knowledge, attitudes, and behavior of the residents of three semirural California communities in reference to smoking, diet, and exercise. Prior to the beginning of the program, the researchers contacted a large random sample of residents between the ages of 35–59 concerning their knowledge and behaviors related to these three factors, and they also assessed residents' weight, blood pressure, and cholesterol levels.

Over the next three years, one community was the object of an intensive media campaign. Television and radio announcements designed to inform and motivate people to change were heard often both in English and in Spanish (since 20% of the population was of Hispanic origin). Local newspapers carried columns about health; billboards contained messages; and booklets, cookbooks, and calendars were designed to reinforce the message. In a second community, those at highest risk received special intensive instruction in addition to the media campaign. The instruction was conducted in small groups, or if not possible, was carried out individually in the participants' homes. In this community, people also learned behavior change techniques and methods of self-control with the goal of reducing risky behaviors. A third community served as a control, and although measures of attitudes and behaviors were taken, no intervention program was offered to the residents.

Within a year of the program's beginning, people in the media-plus-counseling community showed significantly greater changes in smoking, blood pressure, consumption of saturated fats, and cholesterol compared to the control community. These changes also occurred in the media-only community, but not until two years into the program. Using a risk factor index, the researchers found that the media-plus-counseling community reduced its risk by 28% in the first year alone, and maintained that level during the next two years. The media-only community had a 25% reduction by the second year, but that fell slightly during the third year. In the control community, the risk reduction index never varied by more than 6%.

Encouraging results were also found in a large-scale community project in North Karelia, Finland (Salonen et al., 1981), that entailed not only mass media and health education efforts, but also changes in local health services, in the training of health providers, and in the environment. In this project, actual drops in the incidence of disease were found in addition to risk factor reductions. After 5 years, men had a 17% reduction in heart attacks and a 13% reduction in strokes. For women, heart attacks were reduced 10%, and strokes decreased 35%.

Another large-scale risk reduction program that focused specifically on small group intervention is the multiple risk factor intervention trial (Shekelle et al., 1985; Caggiula et al., 1981) known by its acronym MRFIT (pronounced "Mr. Fit"). Begun in 1973, the study followed 13,000 men between the ages of 35 and 57. These men had no prior symptoms of heart disease but were at high risk because of smoking, high cholesterol, and high blood pressure. In contrast to a control group that received "standard care," the intervention group began with 10 small group counseling sessions. At these sessions, the men and their wives received information and engaged in behavior modification procedures to control their smoking and blood pressure, and they learned how to change their cooking and eating patterns in order to reduce cholesterol. Additional counseling took place over the course of the seven-year study.

At the beginning of the study, both the control and intervention groups had an average daily intake of 450 milligrams of cholesterol. However, by its end the average daily intake of the intervention group dropped to 267 mg, whereas the control group had dropped to only 425. In addition, the results were apparently greatest among those with the highest risk levels. For instance, men in the intervention group with an initial high cholesterol level of 300 mg reduced their level an average of 15%, as compared to those in the more moderate range of 220–239 whose levels dropped by only 4%.

Building on these pioneering studies, other programs have used an even greater variety of change strategies. The Family Heart Study (Carmody et al., 1986) also began with the standard educational program about cholesterol and diet but involved the entire family. In group sessions, all the adults and children got together on a monthly basis to share their efforts, exchange recipes, and provide group support and reinforcement for one another.

In the Minnesota Heart Health Program (Jeffery, Hellerstedt, & Schmid, 1990), incentives were tried as part of a larger program. People were encouraged to enlist in a correspondence program involving monthly newsletters containing quizzes, recipes, tips, and information about weight control. Half the people recruited were offered the possibility of enrolling for a $5 fee. The other half was told that the fee was $60 but that the cost was totally refundable if they met a weight loss goal they set for themselves. Although the $5 program enrolled significantly more people than the incentive program, those who did join the incentive program lost twice as much weight.

Preventing the Spread of AIDS

Programs to educate and change behaviors to reduce the spread of AIDS are still in their infancy compared to those aimed at heart disease. Moreover, they face practical, political, and moral roadblocks similar to no other health threat that we face today (Fineberg, 1988). First, several distinct and different targets exist, ranging from heterosexual teenagers to intravenous drug users to gay men. These last two groups are considered by some to be deviant subcultures, and efforts to direct resources toward them have met with considerable resistance. In addition, intravenous drug users are often difficult to reach, with the result that many channels traditionally used in other programs have not been effective.

Second, moral and political conflicts have surrounded efforts to reduce high risk behaviors since these deal with sexual behaviors and illegal drug use. Many health officials and health educators have advocated the distribution of condoms in schools and communities as a means of preventing the spread of AIDS; others find this morally objectionable and instead have advocated the preaching of abstinence, a strategy that has met with little success. The use of bleach to clean the needles of intravenous drug users is a highly effective means of controlling the rate of AIDS in that population; however, in 1989 the United States Congress nearly banned the use of federal resources to distribute this product (Des Jarlais & Bailey, 1990).

Finally, the sexual and drug-related behaviors that AIDS educators are trying to affect are not only spontaneous and unplanned much of the time, but they are clouded in misconceptions and ignorance. The use of condoms has been resisted because they are unfamiliar and embarrassing to some people, and they are seen as compromising of sexual pleasure. A survey of the American public in 1987 showed that 92% of the people are aware that you can get AIDS by having sex with an infected person, and 80% believed that condoms are effective in preventing the disease. Still, 47% thought that AIDS can be transmitted by sharing eating utensils with an infected person, 38% believed that it can be transmitted by mosquito bites, and 31% felt that the use of public toilets presents a likely route of transmission (Dawson, Cynamon, & Fitti, 1987).

Given the lack of knowledge about the nature of AIDS and the means by which it can and cannot be spread, it is not surprising that many of the early AIDS prevention campaigns were primarily informational (Becker & Joseph, 1988). Results from a community-wide media campaign in London (Sherr et al., 1986) and small group education in Pittsburgh (Valdiserri et al., 1987) show that education has been effective in producing a more informed public. However, in these and other studies, changes in knowledge have not been predictive of long-term changes in behavior.

Knowledge may be a necessary prerequisite to change, but once we reach a certain threshold, increases in information are ineffective (Becker & Joseph, 1988). At that point, information needs to be supplemented by techniques that increase motivation, provide skills and resources, and change the social environment (Fineberg, 1988; Wermuth, Sorenson, & Franks, 1991). Consistent

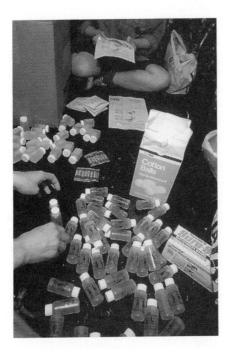

Attempts to teach drug users to use clean needles have run into moral, political, and practical roadblocks.

with this position, a variety of programs have been introduced, often with considerable success. Programs for needle exchanges have been developed (Marks & Parry, 1987), gay men have received training in self-management and sexual assertiveness skills (Kelly et al., 1990), and opinion leaders in the gay community have been enlisted to change perceptions as well as provide information (Kelly et al., 1991). Addressing a different population, workers in inner city prenatal clinics have been trained to provide women with the necessary medical and social services they need to deal with the threat of AIDS (Mason et al., 1991). While few large-scale, coordinated, national campaigns have been devised or reported, we can expect that these will be developed soon as all the theories, techniques, and approaches of health education and health promotion are applied to this most frightening disease.

HEALTH PROMOTION: A CRITICAL ANALYSIS

The health promotion movement has become a part of our lives. Self-help, fitness, and diet books fill the shelves of every bookstore, memberships in health clubs are at an all-time high, and it would be hard to spend a day without getting some form of reminder about eating well, exercising, or watching one's weight. Yet it was not always that way. One critical factor is the shifting pattern of morbidity and mortality in modern society toward diseases that are chronic rather than acute, and toward health problems that we have the potential to affect through our behavior patterns, the so-called lifestyle diseases.

A second factor involves the disenchantment many people have come to feel with the traditional medical model, and with it, an increased skepticism toward its practitioners (Haug & Lavin, 1983). In the last decade, power has shifted away from the traditional establishment, and people have placed an increased emphasis on self-help, self-care, and self-control. Finally, as the cost of medical care in the United States has gone sky high, the focus has shifted from cure to prevention, and from illness to health in an attempt to contain costs.

Most health psychologists as well as health care practitioners in general would agree that the health promotion movement has been a positive one. People have come to take an active rather than passive role in their everyday lives in order to create a state of wellness, to act, feel, and *be* healthy. Rates of smoking are down and so are rates of lung cancer. The consumption of fats in our diet has decreased and so have cholesterol levels and heart disease. While it is difficult to demonstrate a cause-and-effect relationship in each of these and other instances, few people believe that these are coincidences.

In spite of the great strides made by the health promotion movement, several prominent health psychologists have warned about promising more than we can possibly deliver (Evans, 1988; Brownell, 1991). Questions have arisen such as, Will all behavior change interventions have a strong and positive impact? Are all behavior changes reflected in changes in morbidity and mortality? And will behavior-focused interventions prove to be cost-effective or better than other types of medical or social interventions?

In his 1991 presidential address to Division 38, the Health Psychology Division of the American Psychological Association, Kelly Brownell warned not against health promotion itself but in taking it too far. He notes that a concern with health is a positive sign, but an obsession with it may be "unhealthy." Referring to Barsky's (1988) book, *Worried Sick: Our Troubled Quest for Wellness,* he says that we should avoid becoming "healthy hypochondriacs" full of "dis-ease" who end up "worrying ourselves to death."

He argues, first, that each individual should exert personal control but also recognize its limits. Health and illness are a product of many factors, and people should exercise reasonable but not excessive concern with their own personal responsibility for well-being. Second, people should avoid "blaming the victim," attributing blame to others who are unhappy or suffering. As the concept of the sick role implies, people should not be held responsible for becoming ill. They deserve to receive care and sympathy, not to have guilt and blame placed on them.

Third, he argues that we should not overemphasize individual control and responsibility while neglecting other factors. When workers experience stress on the job, the recommendation is often that they take a time management or stress management course, that the environment is reasonable but the individual is somehow deficient. Health promotion should not keep us from looking

Self-help books of every kind line the shelves of bookstores, reflecting our near obsession with health.

at environmental and organizational factors as key determinants. We may find that when you change the job or the structure of the organization, you do not have to worry nearly as much about changing the person.

Finally, as Evans (1988) has emphasized, we must remember that health promotion is not an ideological position that must be publicized, advanced, and defended at all costs. The media often prefer to portray the impact of health promotion efforts in a dramatic manner and to encourage great claims for new approaches to self-control activities. But that is not an accurate portrayal of the way science and health care advance. Science is a "business of probabilities," not absolutes, and progress in reducing risks is made in small increments (Becker, 1986; 1991). When we understand these things, we understand the important role that health promotion can play in creating a healthy population, but we avoid unreasonable concerns and excessive claims for the role of behavior in determining each individual's state of health or illness.

MODULE SUMMARY

1. Health promotion is the science and art of assisting people to change and reorient their lifestyles toward a state of optimal health. It encompasses changes in individual behavior, public policy, and the physical environment.

2. The health promotion movement has grown in response to a changing pattern of illness and causes of death. As infectious diseases have been conquered, the greatest threats to life are now diseases of "lifestyle" wherein people's behavior can place them at greater or lesser risk.

3. Health promotion and health education take place in many settings. Schools and the workplace have been primary sites, but health education takes place as well in hospitals, health maintenance organizations, and the consumer marketplace.

4. Health promotion efforts are most effective when targeted at specific audiences. Populations that have been addressed include children, the elderly, women, minority groups, and various at-risk populations.

5. Intervention can take place at many levels, depending on the goals of the program. Successful efforts have been reported at the one-on-one level, the small group level, the community level, and the public policy level.

6. Individual level programs are most intensive, but their scope is extremely limited. Community wide programs reach a far wider audience, but have been questioned as to their long-term impact.

7. Cognitive and behavioral techniques have proven successful in changing specific health-related behaviors. These techniques help people recognize the way their behavior is affected by external events as well as their representations of the environment and themselves.

8. Fear messages have generally been ineffective in changing behavior. If fear campaigns are to work at all, they must be accompanied by effective responses for overcoming the threat presented.

9. Incentives such as money and prizes have been used with considerable success to promote healthy behaviors. When people work in groups to compete for these incentives, they can support and encourage one another's positive actions.

10. The PRECEDE model of health education emphasizes the role of systematic analysis and design of programs. It also underlines the role of careful evaluation of program effectiveness.

11. Risk reduction programs for heart disease have been initiated at many levels and designed for many groups. The Stanford Heart Disease Prevention Program, one of the classics in the field, demonstrated that media programs could be successful, especially when combined with small group counseling.

12. Programs to prevent the spread of AIDS are still relatively new, and they face particularly difficult practical, moral, and political roadblocks. Information campaigns have had only limited success. In addition to knowledge, target populations must also receive motivation, skills training, and resources.

13. The health promotion movement has been a positive influence in modern society. However, we must be careful not to become obsessed with the health implications of every behavior, and we must avoid blaming those who become ill.

DEALING WITH THE SYMPTOMS OF ILLNESS

No matter how careful you are, and in spite of all of the efforts you make at maintaining and protecting your health, you will nonetheless experience episodes of illness. The odds of facing a major problem such as cancer are about one in three, and minor problems such as colds, sore throats, fatigue, and stomach aches are, as Mark Twain has said, as inevitable as death and taxes.

THE PREVALENCE OF SYMPTOMS AND PROBLEMS

Take a look at the checklist in Table 3.3-1, and think of how many of these physical symptoms you have experienced over the past month. When a group of college students responded to this list, they reported that they had experienced approximately 17 of these per month on the average (Skelton, 1980; Skelton & Pennebaker, 1978). In another study, 70% of the college students surveyed reported that they had experienced headaches, colds, or sore throats at least once during the previous year (Comstock & Slome, 1973); and 78% of the general public report that they have personally encountered at least 1 of 12 selected symptoms such as headache, dizziness, or heart palpitations (National Center for Health Statistics, 1970). At any given moment somewhere between 75% to 90% of the public has a condition that could be diagnosed and treated by a health professional (Kellner, 1986). Yet, it will come as no surprise that the majority of these conditions will go away without medical care, and the majority of people will not seek medical attention for them (Kosa & Robertson, 1975).

WHEN SHOULD HELP BE SOUGHT?

But what of those people who decide that a symptom is not important when it is? And conversely, what about those instances when a person seeks medical

Table 3.3-1   SYMPTOM LIST

On this page several common symptoms or bodily sensations are listed. Most people have experienced most of them at one time or another.

On the answer sheet, next to the number corresponding to the symptoms shown below, blacken the circle that indicates how frequently you experience that symptom. For all items, use the following scale:

A	B	C	D	E
Have never or almost never experienced the symptom	Less than 3 or 4 times per year	Every month or so	Every week or so	More than once every week

For example, if your eyes tend to water once every week or two, you would blacken the circle marked *D* next to item #1 on your answer sheet.

1. Eyes water	28. Swollen joints
2. Itching or painful eyes	29. Stiff muscles
3. Ringing in ears	30. Back pains
4. Temporary deafness or hard of hearing	31. Sensitive or tender skin
5. Lump in throat	32. Face flushes
6. Choking sensations	33. Severe itching
7. Sneezing spells	34. Skin breaks out in rash
8. Running nose	35. Acne or pimples on face
9. Congested nose	36. Acne or pimples other than face
10. Bleeding nose	37. Boils
11. Asthma or wheezing	38. Sweat even in cold weather
12. Coughing	39. Strong reactions to insect bites
13. Out of breath	40. Headaches
14. Swollen ankles	41. Sensation of pressure in head
15. Chest pains	42. Hot flashes
16. Racing heart	43. Chills
17. Cold hands or feet even in hot weather	44. Dizziness
18. Leg cramps	45. Feel faint
19. Insomnia	46. Numbness or tingling in any part of body
20. Toothaches	47. Twitching of eyelid
21. Upset stomach	48. Twitching other than eyelid
22. Indigestion	49. Hands tremble or shake
23. Heartburn	50. Stiff joints
24. Severe pains or cramps in stomach	51. Sore muscles
25. Diarrhea	52. Sore throat
26. Constipation	53. Sunburn
27. Hemorrhoids	54. Nausea

Source: Pennebaker, J. W., 1982, The psychology of physical symptoms *(New York: Springer-Verlag).*

treatment for a condition that is self-limiting, that would take care of itself without any medical intervention? In each case, an error has been made, and that error has important consequences. When patients enter the medical system for a problem that does not require professional care, medical and personal resources have been misused. The physician has spent time that could have been better directed to a more needy case, and the patient has lost time, been inconvenienced, and wasted money. Seeing patients who have no serious medical problem is a source of dissatisfaction in the everyday work of physicians, and patients who repeatedly return in the face of self-limiting conditions come to be known as hypochondriacs or "crocks" (Freidson, 1961; Haug & Lavin, 1983).

When patients misjudge a potentially dangerous condition to be nonthreatening, or when they delay in seeking medical care, however, the consequences can be disastrous. In a study of women with breast cancer, Neale, Tilley, and Vernon (1986) report that those who had delayed in seeking treatment less than 3 months had an 8-year survival rate of 50% as compared to 31% for those who had delayed 6 months or more. Women who had been diagnosed before the cancerous cells had metastasized (spread to other parts of the body) had a 68% survival rate compared to only 6% for those women whose cancer had not been diagnosed until it had spread to multiple sites throughout the body.

But chest pains can be caused by indigestion—or by a heart attack. That small mole on a person's skin can be absolutely insignificant—or an early sign of cancer. In this module, we consider how people come to notice physical symptoms and how they interpret and act on these symptoms. Decisions and actions relating to symptoms and disease can be thought of as part of a three-stage process: (a) becoming aware of sensations, (b) interpreting symptoms, and (c) planning and taking action. It is to these stages that we now turn.

■

THE RECOGNITION OF SENSATIONS

Many different stimuli compete for our attention at any given moment. Some are noticed, while others are not. Why do certain sensations become salient, or highly noticeable, while others never capture our attention? The answer to this question begins with several basic principles of attention and perception (Berlyne, 1960). Sensations that are recognized have several properties. They are likely to be strong, novel, and persistent (Pennebaker, 1982; Pennebaker & Brittingham, 1982), as well as painful and disruptive (Jones et al., 1981). The throbbing pain, the clogged sinuses, and the itchy rash all call themselves to your attention.

FOCUS OF ATTENTION

Even when sensations have properties that call attention to themselves, a second factor that determines whether we notice them or not is the person's focus of attention. The more our attention is drawn toward the outside, the more we are busily engaged in various pursuits or thoughts, the less we notice bodily sensations. It is amazing how people can become aware of every little ache and pain when they are lying in bed at night in a dark, quiet room not able to fall asleep. And have you ever wondered why dentists play music or jiggle a person's lip when they are injecting novacaine. The more attention you pay to those external stimuli, the less you attend to the pain or discomfort of the procedure.

In an interesting empirical demonstration of this competition-for-attention hypotheses, James Pennebaker (1980) took the response of coughing as an example. Coughing is a reaction to the perception of an itching or tickling throat, even though most people are not consciously aware of their perception or reaction. Pennebaker reasoned that people should cough less when they are interested in or distracted by an activity but more when they are bored and therefore internally focused. To test this, he had students watch a short movie, and he monitored the number of coughs in the room every 30 seconds. Since each consecutive 30-second segment had been previously rated for its degree of interest, he was able to measure the relationship between interest level and coughing. The correlation was $-.57$, which is quite high. The less people were distracted the more they coughed. Likewise, it has been found that people who live alone and those who are unemployed or have boring jobs report more symptoms than their counterparts whose attention is more often directed outward (Skelton & Pennebaker, 1982).

INDIVIDUAL DIFFERENCES

Differences in the dispositions and moods of individuals can also determine the noticing of sensations. Individual differences in self-monitoring and coping style have been related to awareness and accuracy of symptom reporting using measures such as the Miller Behavioral Style Scale (Miller, Brody, & Summerton, 1988), the Repression-Sensitization Scale (Byrne, Steinberg, & Schwartz, 1968), and the Private Body Consciousness Scale (Miller, Murphy, & Buss, 1981). Mechanic (1979) asserts that searching for symptoms is something that children learn from their parents at an early age. And Leventhal, Nerenz, and Steele (1984) suggest that medical complaint making represents a stable personality characteristic over the life cycle. In addition to relatively permanent dispositions, a person's temporary mood state can affect awareness. Salovey and Birnbaum (1989) induced negative or positive moods in people who were acutely ill. They found that those who felt momentarily sad reported more aches and pains and greater discomfort than people who felt happy.

The Interpretation of Sensations

Once a bodily sensation has been noticed, a person must determine what it means. When does a "sensation" come to be seen as a "symptom"? People interpret sensations and make attributions about them according to their context. They look to external events or circumstances, seeing whether or not they can explain their sensations as normal (Cioffi, 1991; Cacioppo et al., 1986). A sensation such as shortness of breath will be thought of as a symptom of an underlying health problem if you experience it as you get out of bed, but as a "normal" sensation, that is nonsymptomatic, when experienced at the end of a two-mile run.

Common Sense Epidemiology

Even when we define something as a symptom, it is still difficult to determine its true meaning because most symptoms are vague, ill-defined, and ambiguous. A headache could be an indicator of a wide variety of health problems, from the most insignificant to the most life threatening. Maybe you need a new pair of glasses, maybe you are tense, or perhaps this is the first sign of a brain tumor. To understand the meaning of their symptoms, people engage in a form of **common sense epidemiology** in which they generate hypotheses about the nature of their problem and engage in a search for additional information to confirm these. This closely parallels the actual process that trained health professionals carry out, although it is not as systematic or as well informed when conducted by the layperson.

Research has shown that while sensations and symptoms are the starting point for speculation about people's state of health, we generate common sense representations of illnesses in order to integrate and organize our information (Leventhal, Meyer, & Nerenz, 1980; Bauman et al., 1989; Lau & Hartman, 1983; Lau, Bernard, & Hartman, 1989). These cognitive representations have five elements. They are as follows.

1. *Identity*—the abstract label or verbal tag placed on a set of symptoms.
2. *Time line*—beliefs about the course of the illness, such as how long it will last and whether it is chronic or acute.
3. *Consequences*—the effects of the illness, both short and long term.
4. *Cause*—the beliefs people hold about the factors that brought about the problem.
5. *Cure*—what the person must do in order to recover from the illness.

Using these dimensions, it has been found that the way people represent their illness affects a range of behaviors. Cancer patients who thought of their illness as potentially curable and acute rather than chronic were more likely to supplement their chemotherapy with various forms of self-treatment (Leventhal et al., 1986). And patients recently diagnosed with hypertension (a chronic disease) were more likely to drop out of treatment if they thought of their condition as acute (Meyer, Leventhal, & Gutmann, 1985). Across a range of health problems, people are more likely to visit a physician if they had strong identity (What is my illness?) and cure (How do I get better?) components in their illness cognitions (Lau, Bernard, & Hartman, 1989).

Prototypes and Expectancies

The identification and labeling of a person's physical state is of great importance because it serves to direct future action. In formulating a diagnosis, we use **disease prototypes**, which are idealized conceptions of what symptoms go together for any given health problem (Bishop, 1990; Bishop & Converse, 1986). Based on experience, we know that nasal congestion accompanied by an itchy nose and teary eyes means one thing (hay fever, most likely), but it means quite another when it is accompanied by headache and a temperature (a cold or the flu). Based on these prototypical conceptions, we formulate hypotheses about the identity of the problem and engage in a directed search for confirming information.

The nature of this search has been demonstrated in several ways. Ruble (1972) told one group of women that she had determined by sophisticated instrumentation that they were 10 days away from their period and told a second group that they were only a day or two away. Actually, the women in both groups were approximately one week away. She then had all the women fill out a questionnaire asking them about possible premenstrual symptoms such as cramping, irritability, and swollen breasts. Even though both groups were at identical stages in their menstrual cycles, those women who carried the expectancy that their period was due any day reported more of these symptoms, both psychological and physiological, than those who believed that they were between periods.

In other research, people who were told that they had elevated blood pressure reported more symptoms they believed to be associated with that condition than those with equivalent blood pressure who were not told (Baumann et al., 1989). Also, subjects who were told that their skin temperature might increase or decrease as a result of ultrasonic noise (actually they heard nothing but a low-volume tone) reported that their temperatures had risen or fallen in accord with their expectations (Pennebaker & Skelton, 1981).

Although the expectancies in these experimental studies were induced by the researchers, many studies have demonstrated the important role that self-induced expectancies can play in the search for and interpretation of meaning in symptoms (Jones, 1990; Ditto & Hamilton, 1990). Perhaps the most fascinating example of symptom interpretation at work is **medical students' disease**. This is not a real disease, but rather a phenomenon that many fatigued and anxious medical students experience. As a new disease is introduced, some proportion of the class typically interprets their own stress-induced symptoms as consistent with the condition being studied. Usually, once a new topic is introduced, the affected students "recover" fully, although sometimes only to fall prey to the next condition being studied (Hunter, Lohrenz, & Schwartzman, 1964; Mechanic, 1972; Woods, Natterson, & Silverman, 1966).

THE CIOFFI MODEL   Noting that the same sensation can lead to multiple interpretations, Cioffi (1991) has developed a model that incorporates all of the factors we have discussed. As outlined in Figure 3.3-1, a physical change, let us say a drop in hand temperature, may be noticed or not. If it is not noticed, then no further action is possible or necessary. Once noticed, however, the person places a label on it, saying something like, "I have cold hands." At that point, an attributional search is set in motion in which the person looks for possible causes of this sensation. The search is guided by the person's expectancies and prior experiences, and hypotheses are formulated about what might be happening. This process is mediated by a range of factors such as the person's dispositional characteristics, mood, goals, coping style, and motivation. If interpreted as a normal reaction to external circumstances, no health-related action is necessary (although the person might put on a pair of gloves). But if the person determines that he or she is experiencing a specific symptom, then a decision must be made about symptom monitoring and/or help seeking.

THE ROLE OF CULTURE   The work discussed up to now deals with the way symptoms are interpreted *in general.* However, cultural differences may greatly affect the ways different groups of people interpret symptoms and experience illness. In Latin American folk culture, the commonsense conceptions that people hold of *cause* and *cure* differ significantly from that of Western medicine. In Puerto Rico, diseases can be thought of as hot or cold, and medications to cure are conceived of as hot, cool, or cold, even though these designations may have nothing to do with temperature (Harwood, 1971). Arthritis, colds, and upset stomachs are cold diseases, and these must be cured by "hot" foods and medicines such as vitamins or garlic. "Hot" diseases such as rashes and ulcers require "cool" foods such as bananas and coconut.

In a classic study, Zola (1966) found that the way people present and react to the same physical complaints may also vary according to culture. Zola studied 144 patients of Italian and Irish descent who came to an outpatient clinic for eye and ear problems. He found that the Irish patients tended to limit and understate their symptoms, often denying pain and referring to very specific symptoms and dysfunctions. In contrast, Italian patients were more likely to dramatize their problems, and to describe a variety of problems linked to several body parts.

Figure 3.3-1   INTERPRETATION OF BODILY SENSATIONS
(BASED ON CIOFFI, 1991)

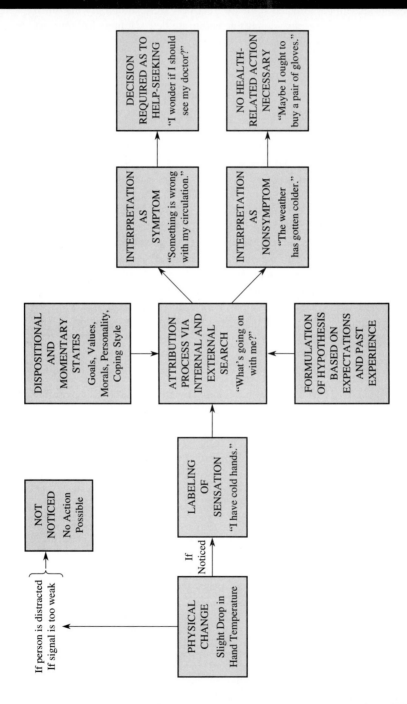

106

Thinking of culture in a very different vein, we find that differences exist in the very ways that the "medical culture" and the "lay culture" think about symptoms. In a study by Jones and Wiese (1982), medical students and rural adults were asked to sort a set of physical symptoms according to how much each possible pair was likely to occur together. For the medical students, the perceived relationships among symptoms was influenced almost exclusively by how life threatening they were. Among the lay group, however, this dimension was hardly used at all. Instead, the symptoms were sorted according to how painful and embarrassing they were.

DELAYING VERSUS TAKING ACTION

Once people recognize a set of symptoms and realize that these *could* indicate a medical problem, they have several options. They may choose to ignore the symptoms, denying their significance or hoping that the symptoms will go away on their own. They may monitor them carefully, deciding that if the symptoms worsen or do not disappear in a specified time period, they will take action. They may seek advice from the **lay referral network**, family and friends who supply information and suggestions about what to do (Freidson, 1970). They may seek help from alternative healers such as herbalists or spiritual advisors. Or finally, they may seek medical help, entering the traditional health care system for assistance. In Module 3.1, we reviewed several broadly defined approaches to questions of health-related behavior such as the Health Belief Model and the Theory of Reasoned Action. Here, we will consider several specific factors that influence illness behavior in the face of physical symptoms, noting how these are similar to some of the factors discussed previously.

THE DELAY BEHAVIOR MODEL

Most people who have no medical training find it difficult to know how long to wait before seeking help for a possible problem. Martin Safer and his colleagues (Safer et al., 1979) have developed a model of **delay behavior**, the time between recognizing a symptom and actually seeking help for it, that describes the delay process in terms of three decision making stages. As presented in Figure 3.3-2, the first decision involves the most basic of questions, "Am I ill?" As Cioffi (1991) has described, this is the first step in which the person asks whether the symptom is unimportant and nonthreatening or something to be concerned about. The time it takes to determine the severity and threat of the symptom is referred to as *appraisal delay*. Once the person has decided that the symptom is worthy of concern, a second decision must be made. It involves the question, "Do I need professional care?" Known as *illness delay*, this is the time between the recognition of a symptom as a threat and the decision to seek care. At the third stage, *utilization delay* refers to the time between decision and action in response to the question, "Is the care worth the costs?" Some people may implement their decision immediately, while others may keep putting off going for help. This would be, in terms of the Theory of Reasoned Action, a discrepancy between intention and action. Safer et al. (1979) point out that a person will actually enter treatment only after all three questions have been answered positively.

In trying to account for the factors that discriminate between those instances in which people do or do not take action, many variables have been investigated. Demographic factors such as social class, education, and age have been studied, with the finding that the lower one's level of education and income, and the older one is, the greater the delay (Safer et al., 1979; Berkanovic, Telesky & Reeder, 1981; Gortmaker, Eckenrode, & Gore, 1982). Two major factors that discourage low-income people from taking action are the cost of services and limited accessibility, referred to as "barriers" in the Health Belief Model.

For the elderly, an important and overlooked cause of delay behavior involves the relationship between senior citizens' commonsense models of illness and their commonsense models of aging. In this population, Prohaska et al. (1987) found that many symptoms, even severe ones such as walking pneumonia, were attributed to aging rather than disease. When symptoms were perceived to be caused by or associated with the aging process rather than disease, the response was more passive and the tendency toward delay was greater.

UNREALISTIC OPTIMISM

At the other end of the age spectrum, it has been suggested that young people, adolescents in particular, delay because of a sense of invulnerability and a

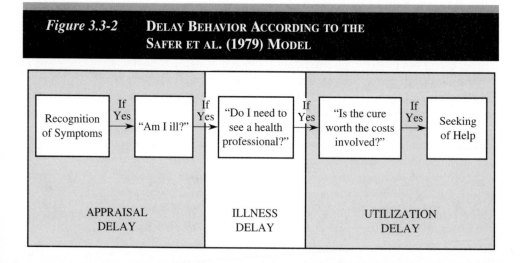

Figure 3.3-2   DELAY BEHAVIOR ACCORDING TO THE SAFER ET AL. (1979) MODEL

resulting unrealistic optimism about susceptibility to health problems (Weinstein, 1984; Weinstein & Lechandro, 1982). In a survey of people between the ages of 18–65, Weinstein (1987) has found, however, that people of all ages are quite optimistic, rating themselves as less likely to encounter health problems *compared to others their own age*. Although this has not been tested directly, it is reasonable to suggest, however, that the older people get, the more they feel vulnerable in an absolute sense.

TRIGGERS TO ACTION

Instead of focusing on factors that contribute to delay, many researchers have turned the question around to consider those factors that set people in motion. Zola (1973) has described five triggers to action. Combining his work with others who have studied this matter (Jones et al., 1981; Mechanic, 1968; Turk, Rudy, & Salovey, 1986), these cues can be conceptualized in terms of two broadly defined sources: (a) the person's symptoms and (b) the person's circumstances.

Symptoms trigger behavior in several different ways. First, various physical and perceptual characteristics of symptoms call attention to themselves. Symptoms that are visible, painful, intense, frequent, and persistent lead to action. Second, the *appraisal* of symptoms can set off behavior. When people believe that their symptoms are serious and unusual and that they can be controlled or affected through medical intervention, they take action (Ditto, Jemmott, & Darley, 1988). In particular, people often reason from past experience with a symptom or disease label and act when symptoms are perceived as new and different or as old and serious (Mechanic, 1968; Turk et al., 1985). One exception to this rule may occur when people fear that they may be very ill. In this case, they may delay rather than seek out help, especially if they are fearful of the treatment (Safer et al., 1979).

A third way action is related to symptoms has to do with their effects or consequences. When symptoms threaten normal relations with friends and family, or when they disrupt regular patterns of interaction, people seek help. An excellent example is the man who finally decided to go for treatment for his ulcer. Citing a personal disruption that touched him deeply, he stated, "If you can't drink beer with friends, what the hell" (Zola, 1973, p. 684).

A person's circumstances determine action in several ways as well. Zola (1973) suggests that an interpersonal crisis can trigger medical treatment. After experiencing marital or work-related difficulties, or when problems are mounting up, some people may seek refuge in the sick role. To the extent that the physician is seen as warm, the person may seek help in the form of emotional support as much as for the symptom itself. The person's financial circumstances affect action as well. People delay when money serves as a barrier, and they seek help when they can afford it. Finally, consistent with the Theory of Reasoned Action, people take action when they are encouraged by others to do so and when they realize that others with the same problem are also seeking help.

In sum, although we all respond to sensations and symptoms in unique ways, our actions are dependent on our commonsense representations of illness. Just as epidemiologists try to understand the nature of disease and consider its causes and distribution in the population as a whole, each of us as a commonsense epidemiologist tries to reduce uncertainty and minimize anxiety by understanding the consequences, causes, cures, duration, and identity of the health problems that we face. This information seeking and processing helps guide our decisions about whether to wait or whether to act. It is hard to know just when to go for medical attention, but people generally do seek out help when appropriate (Turk et al., 1985). Still, although people sometimes hesitate to act until they are certain of sufficient justification, they must be careful to avoid undue delay when action might alleviate suffering and even save their lives.

■

MODULE SUMMARY

1. At any given moment, 75% to 90% of the population has a condition that could be diagnosed or treated by a health professional. The majority of people will not seek out care, and the majority of problems will go away by themselves.

2. People must determine when they should seek professional health care. If they go too soon, they are wasting time, money, and the resources of the system. If they wait too long, they may be risking their own health.

3. Bodily sensations become noticeable when they are strong, novel, persistent, painful, or disruptive. When attention is drawn outward, people are less likely to be aware of sensations of all sorts.

4. Personality differences such as self-monitoring and coping style can affect the recognition of sensations and symptoms. Negative mood states can also increase the reporting of bodily discomfort.

5. When a sensation is noticed, people make attributions about it by looking at their circumstances. For instance, shortness of breath will be considered normal at the end of a run, but not on getting out of bed.

6. People hold commonsense representations of illness to integrate and organize information about health threats. The elements of these representations are identity, time line, consequences, cause, and cure.

7. Disease prototypes are idealized conceptions of how symptoms fit together for specific problems. We use prototypes and expectancies to better understand what health problems we may be experiencing.

8. Medical students' disease refers to a phenomenon whereby some medical students come to believe that their own stress-induced symptoms are consistent with the condition being studied at the moment.

9. Cultural differences affect the ways in which people experience symptoms and disease. In many cultures, commonsense conceptions of cause and cure differ greatly from those of Western medicine.

10. Delay behavior refers to the time between recognizing a symptom and actually seeking help for it. It consists of three stages: appraisal delay ("Is it important?"), illness delay ("Should I seek help?"), and utilization delay ("Is it worth the cost and effort?").

11. People may fail to seek help because of unrealistic optimism about susceptibility to health problems. People of all ages are quite optimistic, although adolescents feel particularly invulnerable.

12. Symptoms trigger action in several ways. They are most likely to lead to help-seeking when they disrupt normal patterns, occur in the midst of a personal crisis, or are recognized as new and different or familiar and serious.

4

ENCOUNTERING THE HEALTH CARE SYSTEM

When people decide that they have a medical problem, they come into contact with the health care system. This chapter is about that system and these encounters. Instead of focusing on the strictly medical aspects of treatment, which would be consistent with the biomedical model, we are going to take a broader approach. Consistent with a biopsychosocial perspective, we will investigate health care as an interpersonal process and consider what determines the quality and success of that process.

Module 4.1 begins by considering the doctor–patient relationship, asking how we can best characterize this tenuous, but important set of interactions. We then consider the extent to which people are satisfied with their physicians in general and ask what specific aspects of physician behavior they are most and least pleased with. Having done this, we will review research aimed at strengthening the relationship and generating more satisfied patients.

In Module 4.2, we review one major consequence of this relationship, the degree to which patients adhere to or comply with the recommendations and medication regimens that they are given. We will review the factors associated with good and poor adherence and review the particular problems faced by the elderly and people with hypertension. At that point, we shall consider ways in which this behavior can be increased.

The health care system and its centerpiece, the hospital, will be the topic of Module 4.3. We will note how the delivery of health care has evolved from a simple one-on-one arrangement into a complex bureaucratic process, and we will consider how social and economic forces have changed the very nature of health care. We will review some of the reasons that health care costs have skyrocketed and describe various attempts to control these. Finally, we will look inside the modern hospital, tracing its roots back in time and contemplating its present and future. Just as we began the chapter by looking at sources of satisfaction and dissatisfaction in the doctor–patient relationship, we will close it with a consideration of hospitalization from the patient's point of view, asking what patients like most and least about their hospital care.

THE PATIENT-PRACTITIONER RELATIONSHIP

Modern medicine has progressed to a point beyond the imagination of early health practitioners. Technological advances and medical breakthroughs have given the physician the ability to diagnose and treat that would have been considered science fiction only years ago. Yet, in spite of these great discoveries—or in part because of them—all is not well with modern medicine. For all the growth we have witnessed on the technical side of medicine, the interpersonal side, involving the human element of care, has not kept pace. In fact, several observers, including doctors, have asked whether this aspect of medical care has suffered with the advent of modern technological and bureaucratic medicine.

THE ART AND SCIENCE OF MEDICINE

The idea of treating the body by attending to the spirit has always caused tension in medicine. Although the philosopher Descartes expounded on the duality of body and mind, early physicians relied heavily on their interpersonal skills. In fact, sometimes they could offer little more than compassion, hope, and an effective bedside manner. The early Greek Hippocrates, known as the father of medicine, once wrote that it is possible that a patient "may recover his health through his contentment with the goodness of his physician."

In modern health care, the general practitioner and the small town doctor who ministered to all of a family's problems, physical as well as personal, are quickly disappearing. Increasingly, patients are being seen in large medical complexes by teams of highly specialized practitioners who diagnose via computer and treat using the latest technology. As a result, the technical quality of care has improved, but patients often report that "something is missing" in their relationship with their physician. As stated by one concerned physician, "Increasingly, people feel that their doctors do not or cannot listen, and are too caught up in struggles for money, status, knowledge, and power. . . . The

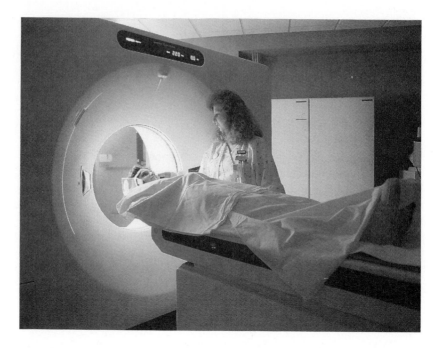

High-tech medicine, for all its advances, may be contributing to a trend toward impersonal health care.

patient and doctor no longer know and appreciate each other as people, working toward a common goal." (Roter & Hall, 1992)

This discussion underlines the distinction between the *art* and the *science* of medicine (Bloom, 1963; DiMatteo, 1979), between the tasks of *caring* versus *curing*. Yet, health psychologists feel strongly that the interpersonal and technical sides of medicine cannot be separated, that a health professional must combine both in order to provide effective treatment. In referring to the perspective of health psychologists, Friedman and DiMatteo (1979) have stated:

> *They are not merely saying that the physician should smile, as did the old family physician, while prescribing a particular treatment regimen. Nor are they saying that modern physicians should remember that the patient is a person with feelings, and should be treated as such as a matter of civility. Rather they are proposing that interpersonal relations are a part of the basic process of healing. . . . Ignoring these factors is not an error of ethics or courtesy; it is a scientific error (p. 4).*

The Nature of the Patient–Practitioner Relationship

It is curious that the term "relationship" has been used to describe what goes on between a physician and a patient. Some people have preferred to use the more neutral term "encounter" (Anderson & Helm, 1979) or the term "health transaction" (Stone, 1979) to capture its more business-oriented or problem-centered side. The concept of relationship does fit, however, because it captures the essential elements of what goes on in all relationships: Two people come together and enter into an agreement to engage in some form of exchange with the purpose of accomplishing one or more goals. When a patient and practitioner enter into a relationship, their goals may be well defined or vague; mutually agreed upon or not; and the interaction may differ in terms of its length, commitment, or intensity. Still, a bond is formed between the two participants about a key issue for them both, the patient's health (Krupat, 1983).

The Szasz-Hollender Models

In a classic paper, Szasz and Hollender (1956) have described three different types or models of patient–practitioner relationship. In the first, the model of activity-passivity, a great asymmetry of power exists, almost like the relationship between a parent and a very young child. The doctor is in complete control, and the patient is passive, little more than a work object to whom things are done. The treatment of the patient is almost totally determined by the physician and takes place independent of any preferences or contributions of the patient. Clinically, this might be appropriate in cases of acute trauma where the patient is bleeding, or when the patient is anesthetized or in a coma.

The second model, guidance-cooperation, underlies much of modern medical practice, especially in the treatment of acute illness. In this model, the patient's thoughts, feelings, and desires are made known, yet they still only serve as background for the choice of the physician. The patient has a problem and seeks answers from a knowledgeable health professional, readily willing to cooperate with the solution generated. An asymmetry of power still exists, but in contrast to the activity-passivity model, it is closer to that between a parent and adolescent.

The third model is mutual participation. This relationship is characterized by mutual respect, information sharing, and a decision-making process in which both participants have equal input. This is the sort of adult-to-adult partnership more likely found in the treatment of chronic disease, and it is often advocated by those who have taken a more activist stance.

In the model of guidance-cooperation, the doctor advises, and the patient listens with interest.

THE CONSUMER MODEL

Although it is difficult to estimate how common each of these models has become, there has been a clear trend away from patient passivity. The old authority relationship in which absolute trust was placed in the physician is slowly but surely eroding, and in its place we see one in which the physician's automatic right to govern is being challenged, and the patient's rights to participate and decide are being demanded (Haug & Lavin, 1983). Conceptualizing these models somewhat differently, Roter and Hall (1992), have included a consumerist model, which was not even considered by Szasz and Hollender when they were writing in the 1950s (see Table 4.1-1).

The consumerist model goes one step beyond the mutual participation model in reversing the balance of power between patient and practitioner. It envisions a health care relationship in which the practitioner is more of a skilled consultant who responds to the directives and needs of an informed and increasingly skeptical health care consumer. The consumerist model has been embraced by many but criticized by others for going too far. Its critics argue that those who take this orientation may underutilize the health professional's skills and expertise, placing themselves in a position of conflict and lack of trust (Stewart & Roter, 1989).

Patient versus Disease Centeredness

Parallel to the Szasz-Hollender models, which focus on the issues of power and control, other researchers have looked at this relationship from a different angle, contrasting a patient-centered style with a disease-centered orientation (Henbest & Stewart, 1990; Byrne & Long, 1976; Mishler, 1984). The *disease-centered* perspective is dominated by "the voice of medicine" (Mishler, 1984). It reflects a scientific and detached attitude, in which the physician's main goals are to understand the patient's problem in relation to organic pathology and to make an accurate diagnosis. The focus is on *the body* rather than *the person,* wherein the physician determines what information is relevant and what is not. If the patient is to gain an understanding of the problem, it is by entering into and accepting the practitioner's perspective on the problem.

A patient-centered orientation implies a more participatory or partnership-oriented relationship (Balint et al., 1970; Levenstein et al., 1989). In adopting this style, "the physician tries to enter the patient's world, to see the illness through the patient's eyes by behavior that invites and facilitates openness." (Levenstein et al., 1989, p. 111) Four key elements in this approach are: (a) understanding patients' ideas about what is wrong with them; (b) eliciting their feelings about their illness, especially their fears; (c) determining the impact of their problems on their everyday functioning; and (d) exploring their expectations about what should be done (Weston, Brown, & Stewart, 1989).

In Box 4.1-1 we have two versions of a medical interview between a physician and a retired Catholic priest who has recently had colon surgery. Taking a disease-centered approach, the physician's highest priority is to determine whether postoperative problems exist. Other issues are either irrelevant or of secondary importance. He uses *close-ended questions,* those that require brief, often one-word answers, which give the patient little opening to express his feelings, and he consistently misses cues that would lead toward an exploration of the patient's emotional concerns.

Table 4.1-1 **Types of Doctor–Patient Relationships**

	PHYSICIAN CONTROL	
PATIENT CONTROL	**Low**	**High**
Low	Default	Paternalism
High	Consumerist	Mutuality

Source: Roter, D. L., & Hall, J. A., 1992, Doctors talking with patients—Patients talking with doctors *(Westport, CN: Auburn House).*

Box 4.1-1   CONTRASTING STYLES OF PATIENT INTERVIEWING

The Disease-Centered Interview

Doctor: Hello, Father Smith, how are you today?

Patient: Fine—except for my headaches. . .

Doctor: . . . and your operation, how's that going?

Patient: Fine.

Doctor: Bowels working?

Patient: Yes.

Doctor: Appetite?

Patient: A bit poorly.

Doctor: Have you lost any weight?

Patient: No.

Doctor: Well, obviously your loss of appetite hasn't affected anything, so it can't be too bad. . . . Any nausea or vomiting?

Patient: None.

Doctor: Any pain at the operation site?

Patient: Not really.

Doctor: Are you eating the bran we recommended?

Patient: No.

Doctor: You must please stick to our recommendations. We don't want any recurrences.

Patient: (Sighing) Yes.

Doctor: Good, well the operation seems to have been a success and there don't seem to be any complications. Have you any other complaints?

Patient: I have this headache.

Doctor: Is your vision affected?

Patient: No.

Doctor: Any weakness or paralysis of your limbs?

Patient: No.

Doctor: Where are your headaches?

Patient: At the back of my head.

Doctor: How long do they last?

Patient: About four hours.

Doctor: What takes them away?

Patient: I just lie down.

Doctor: How often do they come?

Patient: About twice a week.

Doctor: How long have you been having them?

Patient: Ever since I've been at the home.

Doctor: Good, well you needn't worry—it can't have anything to do with your operation. They are tension headaches. Perhaps we can give you some paracetamol for them. The home you have just moved into seems to have beautiful gardens.

Patient: Yes.

Doctor: It really is good of the church to care for its elderly and it must be comforting to have company.

Box 4.1-1   CONTRASTING STYLES OF PATIENT INTERVIEWING (*CONTINUED*)

Patient: Yes.
Doctor: Well, good. Come and see me in a month's time and we'll see how things are going. Take care.

The Patient-Centered Interview

Doctor   Hello, Father Smith, how are you today?
Patient: Fine, except for my headaches.
Doctor: What about your headaches?
Patient: Well, I've been getting them about twice a week at the back of my head and they bother me so I can't do anything, and I have to lie down.
Doctor: You can't do anything . . . what's that like for you?
Patient: It's frustrating, they're interfering with the writing I want to get done and nobody seems to understand . . .
Doctor: Understand?
Patient: All the other priests are so old and decrepit in that place. All they can talk about is their aches and pains. I'm ashamed to say they make me sick.
Doctor: Why are you ashamed?
Patient: Well, I shouldn't really talk that way about them, they mean no harm . . . I feel so guilty about it.
Doctor: What do you mean guilty?
Patient: I feel that my anger is unjustified, I'm so frustrated that no one understands that I wish to write.
Doctor: It must be frustrating . . .
Patient: Yes, it is and my headaches—my headaches make it worse.
Doctor: When did they first start?
Patient: Ever since I've been at the home.
Doctor: Why do you think that is?
Patient: I . . . don't know. I haven't really thought about it . . . do you think it's tension? . . . . I mean, the people at the home . . . is it possible?
Doctor: What do you think?
Patient: Well, the whole situation at the home does trouble me.
Doctor: Would you like to talk about it more?
Patient: No, not now, perhaps later.
Doctor: Well, feel free to discuss it anytime you like.
Patient: Mmm, mmm, I will.
Doctor: Well, how are things going after your operation?
Patient: It seems okay.
Doctor: What do you mean, it seems okay?
Patient: Well, I don't seem to be eating well and I can't stand that bran. In fact, I have no appetite for food.
Doctor: What do you think that could be due to?
Patient: I wonder if it's due to the tension I'm feeling?
Doctor: Mmm, mmm.
Patient: I will really think about what we've said and come back to see you again.
Doctor: Fine, anything else today?

Box 4.1-1   CONTRASTING STYLES OF PATIENT INTERVIEWING (CONTINUED)

Patient: Fine, everything is fine, except I get a funny feeling on my scar.
Doctor: A funny feeling?
Patient: Yes, it seems a bit numb . . . I am afraid it may be serious.
Doctor: It's probably a little nerve that supplies the skin that was cut during the operation. Nothing to be concerned about.
Patient: I'm glad it's only that. I was quite worried.
Doctor: Anything else you'd like to discuss?
Patient: No, everything else is fine.
Doctor: Good. Would you like something for your headaches?
Patient: Thank you, but I don't think it's necessary.
Doctor: I'd like to see your wound in a month's time, but we can get together earlier if you'd like to.
Patient: Fine. I'll be in touch, Doctor.
Doctor: Anything else you'd like to discuss?
Patient: No, everything else is fine.

Source: Levenstein, J. H., Brown, J. B., Weston, W. W., Stewart, M., McCracken, E. C., & McWhinney, I., *1989, Patient-centered clinical interviewing. In M. Stewart & D. Roter (Eds.),* Communicating with medical patients *(Newbury Park, CA: Sage).*

The patient-centered doctor's interview has a broader agenda that can be addressed, even though the patient is allowed to guide the course of the interview. The physician uses *open-ended questions* that facilitate the patient's expression of feelings and concerns and encourages the patient to elaborate by picking up on subtle cues. In both interviews, the physician follows up on the patient's lack of appetite, but by taking a patient-centered perspective he gets a different and more accurate understanding of it.

PATIENT SATISFACTION

At the heart of the discussion of patient–practitioner relations are two basic questions: To what extent are people satisfied with the medical care that they receive? And what aspects or elements are they most satisfied and dissatisfied with? These questions have been difficult to answer for several reasons. First, different studies of satisfaction have defined and measured satisfaction in unique ways, making cross-study comparisons difficult. Second, the degree of satisfaction found differs somewhat depending on how specifically the question is asked. The more specific the question ("How satisfied are you with your last visit with your doctor?" versus "Are you satisfied with the health care system?"), the more satisfied people report that they are (Hall & Dornan, 1988a). Third, the level of satisfaction reported depends on whom is asked, and when (Ross, Wheaton, & Duff, 1981).

Recently, Judith Hall, Debra Roter, and their colleagues (Hall & Dornan, 1990; 1988a; 1988b; Hall, Roter & Katz, 1988) have applied the method of meta-analysis, a statistical technique that allows the results of many different studies to be combined and compared, to summarize the results of more than 200 satisfaction studies. Overall, they found very high levels of satisfaction, averaging 81% and ranging from a high of 99% to a low of 43% (Hall & Dornan, 1988a).

Satisfaction has been divided into many different categories (Ware & Hays, 1988; Ware, Davies-Avery, & Stewart, 1978; Pascoe, 1983). In Table 4.1-2, we present the 10 specific aspects of care evaluated by Hall and Dornan ranked according to patient satisfaction. In spite of concerns about the interpersonal skills of physicians, humaneness is the factor with which patients are most satisfied, followed closely by the competence of physicians and the outcomes of care. In the bottom half, we find two types of issues. The first involves the patient's relationship to the system, as represented by concerns over cost, access to care, and bureaucracy. The second deals with the amount of information patients receive, and whether they are treated by their doctors as something more than a narrowly defined medical problem.

Table 4.1-2   **OVERALL RANKING OF SATISFACTION WITH 10 SPECIFIC ASPECTS OF MEDICAL CARE BASED ON 107 STUDIES**

ASPECTS	RANK
Humaneness	1
Competence	2
Outcome	3
Facilities	4
Continuity of care	5
Access	6
Informativeness	7
Cost	8
Bureaucracy	9
Attention to psychosocial problems	10

Source: Hall, J. A., & Dornan, M. C., 1988a, What patients like about their medical care & how often they are asked: A meta-analysis of the satisfaction literature, Social Science and Medicine, 27, 935–939.

DOCTOR-PATIENT COMMUNICATION

Patients seem to be least satisfied with the degree to which doctors address their psychosocial concerns, treating them as whole people within the broader context of their lives. For instance, a study of 75 women who were receiving radiotherapy following a mastectomy showed that one third developed sexual problems and one quarter showed signs of clinical depression within a year of their operations. However, none of the sexual problems were identified by their physicians, and only half of the depressed women were identified and treated for this problem (McGuire et al., 1978). It is easy to see how these psychological and sexual problems might be missed if we assume that the physicians were taking a disease-centered approach. When physicians define the problem narrowly according to the biomedical model, they may look no further than the malignancy and miss other important aspects or consequences of the illness experience that are not technically a part of the physical ailment.

INFORMATION SHARING

Information giving, which is the single variable that best predicts satisfaction, ranked 8 out of the 10 dimensions measured (Hall, Roter, & Katz, 1988). During a typical visit, doctors and patients do not spend a great deal of time together, an average of 16.5 minutes according to research by Howard Waitzkin (1984). Of that time, 1 minute and 18 seconds, less than 10%, involves information giving by doctor to patient. Still, when asked how much time they had spent giving information, on the average the doctors responded almost 9 minutes, overestimating by a factor of almost 7. And when asked how much information their patients wanted, the physicians underestimated the amount desired in 65% of the cases.

Although it might be easy to blame doctors for this lack of information giving, patients typically ask no more than 3 or 4 questions per visit (Roter, 1984), and question-asking time ranges from 0 to 97 seconds, averaging an unbelievably low 8 seconds (Waitzkin, 1984). Still, patients report that they would like more information about their diagnosis, the prognosis for recovery, and the origins of their condition (Kindelan & Kent, 1987), as well as more complete disclosure about the risks of procedures and medications (Faden et al., 1981; Keown, Slovic, & Lichtenstein, 1984).

INFORMATION AND POWER To explain the lack of time allotted to information giving and question asking, a broad range of possibilities exists. Several noted researchers (Waitzkin, 1985; Waitzkin & Stoeckle, 1976; Freidson, 1970) believe that doctors avoid giving information and leave patients in a state of uncertainty to preserve power, that the doctor–patient relationship is a "micropolitical situation" in which the doctor withholds information to maintain dominance and patients seek it to challenge that dominance. Yet, to the extent that the doctor and patient are in a "struggle" over information, much of the evidence suggests that patients do not put up much of a fight. Many patients hesitate to ask for information, clarification, or additional information for fear of appearing ignorant, while others fear that they are taking time from more pressing requirements of the doctor or other more needy patients (Tuckett et al., 1985).

Although some doctors may withhold information to maintain power, the patient's desire for information is not necessarily accompanied by a desire to challenge the physician's right to make decisions (Beisecker & Beisecker, 1990). When technical knowledge is needed for decision making, people are generally willing to let the person with more expertise do so. However, when a choice must be made between equally effective treatments, in this case patients want some control over the decision (Kaplan, 1991; Pitts et al. 1991).

PATIENT CHARACTERISTICS   Another explanation for the lack of information exchange between patient and provider focuses on the characteristics of the patient (Clark, Potter, & McKinlay, 1991). In general, patients who are white, older, or female, as well as those with greater education and from the middle and upper classes, are given more time, ask more questions, and get more explanations. The more serious the diagnosis and the longer the doctor and patient have known each other, the greater the exchange of information as well (Hall, Roter, & Katz, 1988; Waitzkin, 1985). These findings suggest that physicians probably spend more time with people with whom they are most comfortable, and they dispense more or less information according to how much they believe patients want or can benefit from it. However, these assessments may often be inaccurate when they are based on stereotypes about race, sex, and class.

QUALITY OF DOCTOR-PATIENT COMMUNICATION

More than the mere *quantity* of information conveyed, what can we say about the *quality* of doctor–patient communication? In a classic study, Barbara Korsch and her colleagues (Korsch, Gozzi, & Francis, 1968) tape recorded 800 pediatric visits in a hospital outpatient clinic and then conducted follow-up interviews with the mothers. The communication tone of the visits was generally very technical and narrowly focused—that is to say, disease centered. The mothers reported that their emotional concerns were rarely addressed, and approximately one quarter did not have the opportunity to express the single most important problem on their minds. Twenty percent felt they were not given a clear explanation of what was wrong with their child, and almost half were unsure of what had caused their child's illness. Although these interactions involved white American, middle-class physicians with patients who were predominantly poor and black, similar findings have been reported in a wide variety of settings and with different patient populations in different countries (Ben-Sira, 1985; Clark, Potter, & McKinlay, 1991; Pendleton & Bochner, 1980).

Even when information is conveyed from doctor to patient, it is not always understood. In another classic study, Bonnie Svarstad (1976) observed patients at a neighborhood health center reputed to be one of the best of its kind. She found that more than three out of four times the physicians failed to give explicit instructions about how prescribed drugs should be taken, and when they did, the instructions were often ambiguous. In fact, more than half of the patients interviewed misunderstood the very purpose for which they were taking their medications. Some of the patients who had received prescriptions to control their blood pressure reported that the drug was meant to treat symptoms as diverse as asthma, palpitations, and lower back pain. Even more notably, Svarstad reported that many times she herself could not understand the directions offered to the patients. Even for something as basic as naming a condition, Hadlow and Pitts (1991) report that patients often misunderstand a range of terms such as "eating disorder," "migraine," and "stroke."

MEDICAL JARGON   Some of the failure of communication between patient and practitioner can be traced to the use of medical **jargon**. Defined as the specialized or technical language of a trade, jargon allows doctors to speak to one another in a strange dialect that is all their own. Pediatrician Perri Klass (1987), telling of her experience in learning this new language, offers one such example:

> *"Mrs. Tolstoy is your basic L.O.L. in N.A.D. admitted for a soft rule-out M.I.," the intern announces. I scribble that on my patient list. In other words Mrs. Tolstoy is a Little Old Lady in No Apparent Distress who is in the hospital to make sure she hasn't had a heart attack (rule out myocardial infarction). And we think it's unlikely that she has had a heart attack (a soft rule-out). (p. 73)*

Physicians even use terms that laypeople cannot understand even when there are simpler ways of saying things. They might say, "He had a pneumonectomy" instead of, "He had a lung removed." At other times they may communicate almost completely in numbers, noting that "his PO_2 is 45; pCO_2, 40; and pH 7.4" (Johnson, 1980). After a while, "doctor talk" becomes so natural that physicians forget when they are speaking it.

Jargon serves several purposes for health professionals. It allows them to communicate with one another in a fast, efficient manner and creates a sense of professional spirit and identification among people who are working under daily stress. Jargon helps to distance health professionals from the strong emotions that come with their work, yet it can distance them from their patients as well. When patients hear their doctors talking to one another about them in

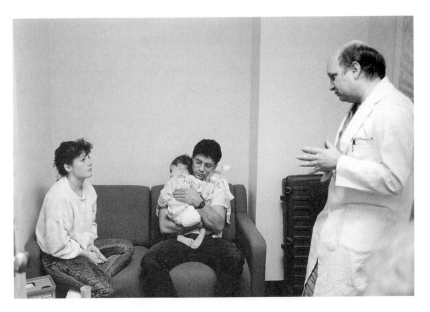

Words are not necessary to recognize the concern of both the parents and the doctor.

technical language, or when they are offered explanations in terms that they cannot understand, it makes them feel left out and leaves them frustrated.

Waitzkin (1984) has recommended that the communication ability of physicians be assessed according to how often physicians use *multilevel explanations* and *nondiscrepant responses*. Multilevel explanations offer a technical explanation accompanied by an explanation in everyday terms. In this way the physician educates the patient in the jargon, while at the same time offering understandable information. Nondiscrepant responses are answers given by physicians at the same level of technicality as the question asked by the patient. By giving complex answers to complex questions (and vice versa), physicians indicate that they have listened carefully, and they offer useful information by speaking in a language that matches the patient's level of sophistication.

NONVERBAL COMMUNICATION   In addition to the content of verbal communication, we have become increasingly aware of the importance of nonverbal communication. The messages that gestures, tone of voice, posture, and facial expressions convey can be every bit as important as those communicated by words. Physician behaviors that express a warm social climate such as sitting close, maintaining eye contact, leaning forward, and nodding in response to patient comments are associated with patient satisfaction (Hall, Roter, & Katz, 1988). In addition, physicians who have greater nonverbal sensitivity both in their ability to decode patients' emotions and to express their own feelings have more satisfied patients (DiMatteo, Hays, & Prince, 1986; DiMatteo et al., 1980; Friedman, 1982).

In sum, what do patients want from their doctors? A simple answer is difficult because patients differ according to their orientations, values, and needs. Some desire an active, involved relationship while others are satisfied to remain passive (Haug & Lavin, 1983; Krantz, Baum, & Weideman, 1980; Woodward & Wallston, 1987). However, we can make some generalizations that hold for a large part of the populace. People want to be treated with warmth and respect, to be given good technical care but related to as "whole people," not just as medical conditions. When they begin to interact with a physician in what is known as the history section of a medical encounter, they want the opportunity to express their concerns in their own words. And at the end, in the conclusion section, they want to be provided with information and have the chance to engage in feedback exchanges that build a partnership between doctor and patient (Stiles et al., 1979a, 1979b).

IMPROVING DOCTOR–PATIENT RELATIONS

Doctor–patient communication and patient satisfaction are not just topics of academic interest. Dissatisfied patients are more likely to shop around for doctors, to change health plans, to fail to follow medical advice, and even to sue (Kaplan & Ware, 1989). Conversely, greater patient involvement and satisfaction have been directly associated with better patient health outcomes (Greenfield, Kaplan, & Ware, 1985; Greenfield et al., 1988).

Several programs to improve satisfaction and communication have been initiated. One focus has been on the training of physicians. Medical schools such as those at Harvard, the University of New Mexico, and McMaster in Canada have been leaders in integrating the behavioral sciences into medical study and in highlighting the teaching of communication skills (Nooman, Schmidt, & Ezzat, 1990; Tosteson, 1990). At Long Beach Memorial Medical Center in California, residents are actually required to spend time as hospital patients to truly appreciate the patient's perspective.

Programs working with practicing physicians have also been effective. At the Johns Hopkins Hospital, a series of tutorial sessions were set up for physicians using the Health Belief Model as a guide for interviewing. The doctors were asked to inquire about patients' attitudes, beliefs and perceptions concerning their condition rather than focusing on physical signs and complications. After a single session, the physicians in this program were found to spend more time on patient teaching and to generate greater patient knowledge than physicians who did not receive this training (Inui, Yourtee, & Williamson, 1976). Bertakis (1977) encouraged physicians to end their medical sessions by having patients repeat information in their own words, clarifying anything that was confusing or adding relevant information that was omitted. When questioned later on, patients were not only more satisfied, but recalled 20% more information than a control group.

Other programs have focused on the patient rather than on the physician. Roter (1984) encouraged patients to identify questions they would like answered during their visit. She reported that this intervention increased question asking compared to a control group, although on the average patients did not end up asking as many questions as they initially intended. More recently, Thompson, Nanni, & Schwankovsky (1990) had one group of women write down questions to ask their doctor before a visit. A second group received a brief note from their doctor encouraging question asking, and a third (control) received no special treatment. The researchers found that both intervention groups were more likely to ask what was on their minds, felt more in control, and were also more satisfied with their visits.

Using a more comprehensive approach, Greenfield, Kaplan, & Ware (1985) reviewed patients' medical records with them, went over methods of treatment, and coached them in how to discuss and negotiate with their doctors. Patients who received this 20-minute coaching session were significantly more active and assertive with their doctors, received more information, and indicated that they liked taking a more active role. Most important, they reported fewer physical limitations during the 8 weeks following the study.

Programs such as these, which involve only small investments of time on the part of patients and doctors, have been quite successful and are likely to grow in the future. They acknowledge that every encounter between a doctor and patient represents a therapeutic opportunity, and that technical skill and knowledge must be accompanied by equal amounts of caring and communication. As we incorporate this into everyday practice, the doctor–patient relationship will improve, and so will medical care.

MODULE SUMMARY

1. Modern medicine has made great technological strides. However, many people believe that the interpersonal element of modern health care has suffered rather than improved. This underlines the importance of the *art* as well as the *science* of medicine, of caring as much as curing.

2. Szasz and Hollender have proposed three models of doctor–patient relationships. In the active-passive model, the doctor alone dictates treatment, and in the guidance-cooperation model, the doctor determines treatment based on patient input. In the mutual participation model, doctor and patient form an equal partnership.

3. Another model of doctor–patient relationships, the consumer model, describes a situation in which the doctor serves as more of a skilled consultant under the direction of an informed and skeptical patient.

4. Doctors who take a disease-centered orientation seek to understand the patient in terms of organic pathology, focusing on *the body* rather than on *the person*. In contrast, those taking a patient-centered orientation focus more on the patient's perceptions, fears, and expectations.

5. On the average, patients are quite pleased with their doctors. They rate them highest on humaneness and technical competence. They are least satisfied with cost and access to care as well as the amount of information they receive.

6. Studies indicate that doctors spend less than 10% of a visit giving information to patients. Some have explained this by suggesting that physicians withhold information as a means of control, while others believe that information is dispensed according to doctors' perceptions of how much patients want or can benefit from it.

7. The quality of communication between doctor and patient is often poor. Doctors often fail to address patients' emotional concerns and offer diagnoses and instructions that patients cannot understand properly.

8. The use of jargon is a major factor contributing to poor communication. Jargon serves several functions when health professionals need to communicate among themselves, but its use with patients most often confuses and alienates them.

9. Nonverbal communication between doctor and patient can also play an important role. When physicians sit close, lean forward, and maintain eye contact, they convey a warm and caring attitude.

10. Many recent programs have been initiated to improve the doctor–patient relationship. Several medical schools have expanded their course requirements and clinical experiences to emphasize the role of health psychology and communications.

11. Other programs to improve this relationship have focused on the patient. When patients are encouraged to ask questions and become involved, and are taught how to do this, the evidence suggests that outcomes improve for both doctor and patient.

Adherence

When a patient leaves the doctor's office, the health care process has not ended. In fact, it has only begun. As a result of the consultation, the patient has probably been given a plan of treatment, a recommendation for a follow up, or most likely, a prescription. Doctors scribble prescriptions in some unintelligible shorthand, pharmacists somehow decipher them, and patients take their medications. Or do they?

This question presents us with the issue of **adherence,** or as it has been called more traditionally, **compliance**. Adherence refers to the extent to which a person's behavior is consistent with or follows from expert advice, most typically that of a health care practitioner (Haynes, 1979). Prior to the 1940s physicians tended to see the following of advice as a moral matter. When patients failed to act as directed, it was taken as an act of bad faith, a failure on their part. Thus, the term compliance was used, which implied personal inadequacy and patient blame. We can see this in the words of the ancient Greek physician Hippocrates who advised, "Keep watch also on the faults of patients, which makes them lie about the taking of things prescribed" (Jones, 1923).

The matter of nonadherence has been with us since its first instance in the Garden of Eden (Haynes, 1979), although the first published research did not appear until 1943 (Koltun & Stone, 1986). In contrast to earlier approaches, the modern view avoids patient blaming. Instead, it considers nonadherence a matter on which both patient and physician must collaborate and for which each must take responsibility.

The Extent and Consequences of Nonadherence

Adherence can take on many forms. Although the emphasis has most often been on the extent to which people take their medications, there are several other realms in which patients may or may not act in accord with professional advice. These include the keeping of appointments, adherence to doctor's advice to change behavior or lifestyle, and entry into treatment or prevention programs.

How Common Is Nonadherence?

The figures on the extent of nonadherence are troubling to health profession-als. About half of all patients do not adhere to their medication regimens (Sackett & Snow, 1979), with even a higher rate for long-term conditions. In a survey of 33 studies, the rate of adherence ranged from a high of 92% to a low of 4%. Table 4.2-1 presents figures for specific types of actions. It docu-ments the wide variety of rates as well as some astoundingly low adherence rates for important behaviors such as insulin injections for diabetes (48%) and appointment-keeping for hypertension checkups (30%). Between 3% to 6% of the prescriptions filled each year are never even picked up (Boyd et al., 1974; Taubman, 1975).

Nonadherence for medications can take on several different forms. Patients often take their medications at the wrong time, in the wrong sequence,

Table 4.2-1 RATES OF PATIENT ADHERENCE

TREATMENTS	% COMPLIANCE RATE
Treatment for hypertension	53
Tuberculosis drugs	55
Antiasthmatic drugs	46
Antibiotic treatment	33
Insulin injection for diabetes	48
PHYSICIANS' ADVICE	
Quitting smoking	29
Weight-reducing diet	20
Kidney disease diet	28
Hemodialysis diet	70
APPOINTMENT KEEPING	
Dental checkup	72
Psychiatrist visit	60
Pap test	52
Hearing and eyesight, follow-up with doctor	35
Hypertension, follow-up after diagnosis	58
Hypertension treatment, annual check	30

Source: Burrell, C. D., and Levy, R. A. (1985). Therapeutic consequences of noncompliance. In Improving Medication Compliance: Proceedings of a Symposium *(Reston, VA: National Pharmaceutical Council).*

In institutional settings, adherence is not a major problem. However, most of the time patients must remember to take medications on their own.

and for the wrong reasons (Burrell & Levy, 1985). They may double up on doses when they have missed a pill, sometimes creating a toxic level of medication in their bloodstream, or take expired medication that is no longer therapeutically effective. Patients borrow medication from friends or discontinue their medications when their symptoms go away, even though they have been instructed not to. They combine medications prescribed by different physicians so the drugs counteract each other's effects or combine to cause harm rather than good.

THE CONSEQUENCES OF NONADHERENCE

No drug, no matter how powerful, works in the medicine cabinet. When a medication is underutilized, the patient is deprived of its benefits, and the disease process as well as its outward symptoms go untreated. In the reverse case, overutilization can also be a problem. For instance, a physician may prescribe a drug and then, presuming proper adherence, increase the dosage to improve its effect. If the formerly nonadherent patient then takes this new prescription, he or she may experience greater side effects or other negative consequences. Of course, some instances of overutilization are less complicated. Some patients reason that if one tablet is doing a good job, two tablets will be twice as effective (Hussar, 1985). About 35% of all patients misuse their medications in one way or another to such an extent that their actions pose a threat to their own health (Latiolais & Berry, 1969).

The costs of nonadherence can be measured in several ways (Smith, M.C., 1985). McKenney and Harrison (1976) found that slightly over 10% of the admissions to a hospital could be traced back to adherence problems. This occurred because patients were not taking (or not taking properly) their medications to prevent seizures, hypertension, or diabetic complications. Overall, Levine (1984) has estimated that 125,000 deaths and several hundred thousand hospitalizations each year result from the failure to use medications properly. This translates to $1½ billion of lost earnings, and 20 million lost workdays, as well as discomfort and suffering that cannot be calculated in dollars and cents.

MEASURING ADHERENCE AND NONADHERENCE

The ideal way to assess patient adherence would be to follow each person around and determine whether he or she took the medication as directed. Since this is hardly practical, researchers have had to develop alternative methods. No single technique, however, has met with universal approval. In an attempt to identify adherence levels accurately and objectively, one method used widely is the pill count. This technique has the potential to be simple and straightforward, yet it has many problems (Moriskey, 1986). Patients often do not bring their pill containers with them to medical visits, and if home visits are made to monitor adherence, patients may discard their pills to appear more adherent than they are. Since medications are not always begun on time, and people sometimes place more than one type of medication in a given container or share them with friends and family, estimates based on this method usually tend to overestimate levels of adherence when compared to other measures (Inui et al., 1980).

A potentially more accurate measure involves the use of biochemical analysis and chemical markers. By doing chemical analyses of blood or urine, or by placing a harmless marker substance in the medication, it is possible to determine the level of medication in the person's system. However, this method has severe limitations because it is inconvenient and invasive and therefore not practical in most settings. Moreover, blood levels of a drug are less than reliable indicators because they can be affected by a host of factors, such as metabolism rate, diet, and weight (Gordis, 1984).

Researchers originally believed that physicians would be best able to judge their patients' levels of adherence. To determine the accuracy of their judgments, medical residents and senior physicians were asked to estimate the amount of antacid their patients had taken and to rank order them from the most to the least compliant (Roth & Caron, 1978; Caron & Roth, 1971). The researchers found absolutely no relationship between the doctors' rankings of the most and least adherent patients and the actual rankings based on direct observation of the patients' behavior made by the nurses and the researchers. In this as well as other research (Norell, 1981), physicians generally overestimated the degree of their patients' adherence and proved to be unreliable judges of adherence.

Although it has not been useful to ask physicians about adherence, patients can be surprisingly good sources of adherence information. When patients are asked directly and noncritically by their physicians whether they are taking the drugs prescribed for them, the information obtained tends to be quite accurate (Moriskey, Green, & Levine, 1986; Klein et al., 1984). In one study, Sackett (1976) inquired about adherence by prefacing the question with a statement that allowed patients to answer more honestly. The researcher said, "Most people have trouble remembering to take their medication. Do you have trouble remembering to take yours?" Using this strategy, Sackett found that people were willing to admit they had problems. In addition, those who were willing to admit that they were less than compliant were also among the patients who benefitted most from the adherence-enhancing strategies offered by the researchers.

In comparing the different ways of assessing adherence, several studies have indicated that the patient interview is as good or better than any of the other methods studied (Gerbert et al., 1988; Haynes et al., 1980). Therefore, while none of the available methods are perfect, complicated methods such as pill counts and chemical analyses do not improve on the simple self-report of patient to physician when this is done carefully.

ACCOUNTING FOR ADHERENCE AND NONADHERENCE

Having recognized the magnitude of patient nonadherence and its importance in health care, the next question is, What causes it? By knowing what factors are associated with nonadherence, it may then be possible to address these and improve adherence.

CHARACTERISTICS OF THE PATIENT

Early practitioners who studied adherence reasoned that it makes no sense for a patient to take the time, money, and trouble to consult a health professional and then not to follow up on the advice given or not to take the medication prescribed. It must be that such a person was "deficient" in some way. Perhaps these people were lacking in the ability to understand, or they were poorly educated, or they had certain negative personality characteristics. As noted earlier, the very term "noncompliant" took on a negative connotation, associating a problematic *behavior* with problematic *people*.

When this view was tested, however, it fell apart. Numerous studies associating adherence rates with demographic and personality factors have generated findings that are weak, inconsistent, or nonexistent. Variables such as education, social class, age, race, gender, intelligence, occupation, marital status, and religion show no clearcut relationship to patient adherence (Diehl, Bauer, & Sugarek, 1987; Masur, 1981; Stone, 1979). In the self-management of diabetes, for instance, age is associated with adherence to certain aspects of a complex regimen but not with others (Goodall & Halford, 1991). In fact, studies that have investigated the adherence behavior of physicians themselves find that their rates of adherence are no better than the public at large (Blackwell et al., 1978; Shangold, 1979). In short, the matter of adherence is far more complicated than blaming those who do not follow advice.

CHARACTERISTICS OF THE ILLNESS

Depending on the health problem, the taking of medication and the following of physician advice vary a great deal. In general, rates of adherence are higher for acute rather than chronic illnesses, for highly threatening ones more than mild ones, and for problems that involve pain more than those that do not (Buckalew, 1991; Stone, 1979). When we think of these findings, they make perfect sense. Chronic illnesses often involve long-term, complex lifestyle changes, and these are difficult to fully adhere to (Glasgow, McCaul, & Schafer, 1987). Consistent with the Health Belief Model, people are less likely to take action when they perceive their diseases to be mild rather than serious (Becker, 1985). Last, why would people *not* take their pain medications? There is an automatic reminder ("When I forget, the pain comes back") and an automatic reinforcement for adherence ("I feel much better after I take it.") This line of thinking leads us toward a different analysis of adherence, one that looks more closely into the patient's understanding, relationships, and circumstances.

INFORMATION AND ADHERENCE Good communication and high adherence go hand in hand. As discussed in Module 4.1, patients often leave their physicians without a complete understanding of their problem or its solution. Physicians often fail to give enough information to their patients or they offer it in jargon that cannot be understood. Patient passivity, often due to fear of looking stupid, also contributes to a lack of understanding. Take the following example, as offered by DiMatteo and DiNicola (1982):

"You have essential hypertension," said the physician to his patient. "I'd like you to take hydrochlorothiazide b.i.d. to eliminate fluid retention. You should also reduce your sodium intake." "Thank you," said the patient (p. 42).

Although no results of this interaction are reported, it would not be very difficult to guess how adherent this patient is likely to be. The patient has (a) little information about the nature and risks of the disease, (b) little understanding of the treatment and its benefits, and (c) little understanding of the details of the regimen. These pieces of information are essential for adherence with short-term medication regimens.

In general, physicians ought to provide more information for their patients. Yet when physicians provide *too much* information, patients may become overwhelmed, and they may also fail to comprehend or remember what they have been told. In a series of studies, Ley (1982a; 1982b) has concluded that even when information is communicated clearly, patients often forget half of what they were told within a very short time. This is not that surprising when taken in perspective. Imagine the following: You are feeling quite anxious and are listening to a brief lecture on a technical topic with which you have little familiarity. You are trying to take all this in and understand it, but you are not taking any written notes. Even if you felt that you basically understood the material at the time, would it shock you to find that the next day you could not reconstruct very clearly what had been said? These are exactly the circumstances under which patients receive information from their physicians. As a result, physicians have to decide what information is most essential, explain this as clearly as possible, check for understanding, and supply written information as a backup to what was said.

CHARACTERISTICS OF THE REGIMEN   The more complex the procedures required to manage or cure a health problem, the less likely the person will be fully adherent. People who have been diagnosed with diabetes must engage in several different activities that may include several insulin injections daily, medication to control blood sugar levels, regular exercise, a strict diet, and constant self-monitoring. Because of its complexity, relatively few people are perfectly adherent with all these elements. In fact, there is little relationship between adhering to one aspect of the regimen versus another (Glasgow, McCaul, & Schafer, 1987; Goodall & Halford, 1991).

Complexity is related to adherence even for medication taking. The more often a drug must be taken daily, the greater the opportunities for errors and forgetting. In addition, patients who are taking multiple drugs make more errors and forget more doses. This is especially a problem for the elderly, who often take several drugs a day for different health problems.

Proper adherence is complicated by even the simplest of problems, even for those who are fully motivated and knowledgeable. In one study of pedi-

The more pills the patient takes, the greater the chances of errors and nonadherence.

atric patients, the researchers measured the actual volume held by the tea-spoons the parents were using to measure their children's dosage. They found that the teaspoons varied anywhere from two to nine milliliters in volume, so some children were receiving too much medicine while others were receiving too little (Mattar, Markello, & Yaffee, 1975).

SPECIAL CHALLENGES FOR MEDICATION ADHERENCE

Although adherence problems exist for many different populations, these can be critical for some. We have chosen two such groups, people with hyperten-sion and the elderly, whose problems are particularly important and challeng-ing. While the sources of their difficulties may be different, we will note in the final section of this module that good communication can help overcome the barriers for both groups.

ADHERENCE AND HYPERTENSION

As we will note in greater detail in Module 11.1, hypertension is a major health threat. Still, health experts believe that this problem would virtually disappear if every person with high blood pressure would be identified and then adhere to the therapy prescribed for them. Instead, between 50% to 70% of all hypertensives do not have their problem under effective control even though effective methods are readily available. Why is this so?

Hypertension, otherwise known as high blood pressure, is a disease with unique characteristics. Unlike almost all other conditions that have some form of outward manifestation, hypertension is *a*symptomatic. A person can have high blood pressure without being aware of any symptoms at all. In addition, hypertension cannot be *cured,* but it can be *controlled.* Therefore, when drug therapy is prescribed, it is for life. People cannot take the medication "until it goes away" because they cannot tell when their blood pressure is up or down, and when they stop, the medication's positive effects quickly disappear.

Consider the following scenario: A thirty-year-old man feeling perfectly healthy goes to his doctor for a checkup. After placing the blood pressure cuff on his arm, the doctor announces that it looks like he has hypertension. "But I feel perfectly fine," complains the patient. "You may feel fine, but you have a serious health problem that could cause a stroke or heart disease if not treated." The doctor then prescribes a medication, most often a diuretic, which is likely to have side effects such as frequent urination, muscle weakness, cramps, and possibly diarrhea, dizziness, or nausea. To treat his condition, the patient will have to take expensive medication for the rest of his life that will probably make him feel worse rather than better. All of this is in return for the probability that he may avoid serious health problems many years in the future. Is it any wonder that compliance may be a problem for this individual?

Looking at patients' commonsense representations of hypertension, Howard Leventhal and his colleagues report that cognitive representations of hypertension closely resemble representations of other diseases (Meyer, Leventhal, & Gutmann, 1985; Baumann & Leventhal, 1985). In general, people believe that hypertension is of limited duration, and that it is caused by factors such as stress at work or home. They feel strongly that they can recognize when their blood pressure is up by monitoring symptoms such as headaches or a flushed face, and they resist changing their beliefs even in the face of contrary evidence. Although it would seem appropriate to correct these inaccurate beliefs, a paradox exists. In one study, the researchers found that those who were most adherent and had their blood pressure under control were those who believed that their treatment was having a beneficial effect on their "symptoms" (Meyer, Leventhal, & Gutman, 1985).

These "commonsense" beliefs make hypertension adherence a particularly difficult problem. However, Orth et al. (1987) found that good communication between doctor and patient could help overcome these problems.

Based on the tape recordings of more than 200 hypertensive patients, the researchers concluded that adherence rates were highest when people had the chance to explain their concerns in their own words at the beginning of the medical interview, and when providers gave a good deal of information and explanation at the end.

COMPLIANCE AND THE ELDERLY

People over age 65 comprise somewhat more than 11% of the U.S. population, yet they account for about 25% of the 11.2 billion dollars spent annually for prescription and nonprescription drugs. By the year 2030, it is estimated that 17% of the population will be over age 65, and they will be purchasing 40% of all the drugs in America (Green, Mullen, & Stainbrook, 1985; Richardson, 1986). In addition to the nonprescription drugs they may be taking, older people average anywhere from 2 to 3.4 prescriptions, and many are on 4–6 different drugs a day (Ascione et al., 1980; Lundin, 1978).

Other issues further complicate the problem of the elderly and drugs. The cognitive deficits that some older people experience give them particular difficulty understanding and remembering the complex information they receive, and physical problems of strength, vision, and coordination make self-care problematic. Side effects from medications, adverse reactions from multiple medications, and increased sensitivity are also more likely among older people (German & Burton, 1989).

For the elderly, it seems particularly important that one individual, most likely a pharmacist who sees the person for all of his or her prescriptions, should keep track of the various medications used in order to check for potentially dangerous interactions. In addition, instructions should be paced to the ability of the person, and individualized question-asking should be encouraged (Kim & Grier, 1981; Lipton, 1982). Color coding of tablets and the use of memory aids and inventive packaging strategies have also proven to be effective in reducing medication errors among the elderly (Crome et al., 1982; Hurd & Blevin, 1984).

IMPROVING ADHERENCE

Every patient has the potential to be nonadherent, regardless of age, education, race, gender, condition, or medication. The challenge for health professionals is to increase adherence so people may benefit most from the expert advice that they receive. To begin, the regimen must be made as simple and uncomplicated as possible. The way to minimize errors, omissions, and confusion is to modify the program so unnecessary drugs are eliminated and those that must be used do not tax the person's ability to administer and coordinate them. Beyond this, however, several issues stand out.

PATIENT-PRACTITIONER INTERACTION

As implied in Module 4.1, two dimensions of the patient–practitioner relationship are relevant to outcomes such as adherence. These are (a) the emotional atmosphere and level of comfort and attachment created between patient and practitioner; and (b) the task-related functions involved with providing complete, accurate, and useful information.

SATISFACTION, INVOLVEMENT, AND ADHERENCE   Several studies have demonstrated that positive feelings and a perception that one's physician is warm and caring have been associated with medication adherence as well as appointment keeping (Hulka, 1979; DiMatteo, Prince, and Taranta, 1979). Conversely, actions that anger patients and lead to dissatisfaction, such as requiring people to wait a long time, are associated with lower levels of adherence (Linn, Linn, & Stein, 1982). Of particular importance for people with chronic conditions is that physicians who involve their patients as active participants in the treatment process generate a significantly higher rate of adherence than those who do not. A first guideline, therefore, is that health professionals should show care and respect and involve their patients in planning therapeutic and lifestyle changes.

INFORMATION AND ADVICE   The evidence is more complex concerning the effect of communication and patient education on adherence. Bartlett and his colleagues (Bartlett et al., 1990) noted that when patients inform their physicians of problems with adherence, many doctors assume that their patients simply lack knowledge or motivation. They launch into lengthy technical explanations, explaining the pathophysiology of hypertension or motivate their patients through the use of scare tactics, although neither of these techniques have been proven effective. Since this does not work, what should a provider do?

While offering some degree of information about the nature of the illness and the treatment is an absolute prerequisite, abstract information does not significantly improve compliance. Instead, health professionals should provide specific information, especially about how and when to take the medication as well as its likely benefits (Becker, 1985; Haynes, Wang, & Gomes, 1987). They must also check for understanding, invite question asking, and supplement verbal instructions with written information. Patients should be encouraged to self-monitor their progress, and providers should also continue to monitor their patients' behavior after they have begun treatment (Tindall, Beardsley, & Kimberlin, 1989). Pharmacists, located in the community and in contact with patients for their different medications, are in an ideal position to enhance compliance and are an underutilized resource.

Former Surgeon General C. Everett Koop (1985) has pointed out that health professionals should not make the mistake of assuming that medication taking is the person's most significant activity each day. The taking of drugs must revolve around the person's normal routine, not vice versa, and medication taking should be tailored to the individual's lifestyle and tied to everyday activities. These points as well as others offered in this section are summarized in Table 4.2-2.

THE USE OF AIDS TO ADHERENCE

Beyond attentive care, good information, and follow-up, compliance aids such as medication calendars, drug reminder charts, and special pill dispensers are very useful. Even the packaging of medication, such as that used for oral contraceptives, can help people understand how and when to take prescribed medicines. Labels on the medication container itself, which are required in some states, can also serve as useful reminders.

A technique that has seen limited use, but great success, is the patient contract (Janz, Becker, & Hartman, 1984; Swain & Steckel, 1981). Patient contracts usually contain an outline of expected behavior and specific goals that the patient and practitioner have agreed on, as well as rewards (such as free lottery tickets) for meeting the goal. The contract not only provides incentives for action, but its development increases adherence by engaging the patient in the decision making process and in making goals clear and specific.

Table 4.2-2   **A DOZEN SUGGESTIONS FOR INCREASING MEDICATION ADHERENCE**

- Explain the importance of adherence
- Explain how the medication is to be taken
- Emphasize key points (prioritize)
- Simplify complex or multiple regimens
- Make written supplements available
- Tailor the regimen to existing habits
- Anticipate problems and ask for feedback
- Encourage questions and patient involvement
- Encourage self-monitoring and engage in follow-up contacts
- Be warm and accepting
- Make available compliance aids such as calendars and special packaging
- Enter into a contract with patient and use incentives

GENERATING SOCIAL SUPPORT

Patients do not live in a vacuum, yet many health professionals treat them as if they did. There is a story about the physician who told a 55-year-old factory worker that he should cut out salt in his diet to lower his blood pressure, only to find out two months later that the patient's blood pressure level had not improved. The patient said he had changed his *eating* habits, having completely stopped putting salt on his food. Further probing, however, revealed that no one had ever consulted with his wife about her *cooking* habits, which resulted in the patient's continuation on a high salt diet.

Family members should be involved in treatment planning and enlisted as a source of encouragement and support. Their beliefs and actions can cue appropriate behaviors and discourage inappropriate ones. For instance, when friends or family volunteer to exercise with the patient or remind the patient to take his or her pills, the evidence consistently shows that adherence rates increase (Becker, 1985; Haynes, 1976).

In summary, no single easy path to patient compliance exists, yet several different routes hold great promise. At the least, people must receive clear information and solid support to have the motivation and means to be adherent. In addition, health professionals must monitor and assist their patients over time, making adherence a matter of mutual responsibility. If this occurred more consistently, the "problem" of adherence would begin to disappear. In fact, it might become one more "condition" that modern medicine has brought under control, in this case with information and care rather than with drugs and vaccines.

■■■

MODULE SUMMARY

1. Adherence refers to the extent to which a person's behavior is consistent with or follows from expert advice, most typically that of a health professional.
2. The term *adherence* is generally preferred over the more traditional term *compliance*. Compliance has taken on negative connotations, implying that it is the patient's fault for not following advice. Adherence is more neutral and implies a mutual responsibility between doctor and patient.
3. About half of all patients do not adhere to their medication regimens. In addition to simply not taking their medications, patients may take them for the wrong purposes, in incorrect dosages, or at the wrong times.

4. Nonadherence can lead to several negative consequences. It has been estimated that each year 125,000 deaths and several hundred thousand hospitalizations can be traced back to the improper use of drugs.

5. Levels of adherence are difficult to assess. Methods used include pill counts, biochemical analyses, physician estimation, and patient self-reports. When questioned carefully and sensitively, patients' reports can be as accurate as any method available.

6. It had been believed that patients who were nonadherent were different than those who took their medications properly. However, associations between adherence and variables such as social class, race, sex, education, and intelligence have been inconsistent or nonexistent.

7. Several factors relate closely to adherence. These include good rather than poor communication, and simple rather than complex regimens. When proper treatment of a disease has multiple requirements (as in diabetes), or when drugs must be taken many times a day, greater opportunities for forgetting and errors exist.

8. Hypertension, because it is chronic and has no outward symptoms, represents a particular adherence problem. It has been suggested, however, that if all hypertensives were adherent, this condition could be virtually eliminated.

9. Adherence is a particular problem for the elderly, who take a great many prescription and nonprescription drugs. Health professionals must take into account the physical and cognitive deficits that many older people have when prescribing and instructing.

10. Many efforts have been made to improve patient adherence. In general, programs that lead to greater patient satisfaction and involvement have shown improvements. Information about the likely benefits of the medication and how and when to take it are more effective than abstract information about the disease state.

11. Aids to compliance such as medication calendars and special pill dispensers have proven useful complements to education and communication. Patient contracts can also succeed by involving the patient in setting reachable goals.

12. Social support ought to be enlisted to help patients be more adherent. Family members and friends can remind, encourage, and assist people to follow recommendations and take medications.

HEALTH CARE DELIVERY

Health care in the United States has evolved tremendously. No longer considered a privilege for the few but a human right, it has grown in cost and complexity. In 1929, the United States spent 3.5% of its Gross National Product (GNP) on goods and services associated with health care. By 1986 this cost had skyrocketed to 11% of the GNP, a figure of 468 billion dollars (McCarthy & Thorpe, 1986). Unless the Clinton administration succeeds in curtailing costs, by the year 2000 this will seem like a trifle because the United States will likely spend 15% of its GNP, an annual figure of $1.5 trillion, to care for its populace (Health Care Financing Administration, 1987). The organization of health care and its financing is a matter of public policy and public debate, and although we sometimes take it for granted, it is an issue that affects everyone, young and old.

THE TRADITIONAL MODEL OF HEALTH CARE

In the beginning of this century, health care delivery could be easily explained. When people felt sick, they went to see their family physician, or if they were too ill the doctor made a house call. The doctor would render the necessary services and send the patient a bill. Although the system was not always quite this simple, this description captures four key elements of the system.

1. Health care consisted of a series of encounters between patients and personally chosen, independently practicing providers.
2. Those providers had a great deal of autonomy over the nature of practice. They set their own schedule of fees and exercised almost complete control over the amount and kind of treatment they provided.
3. Physicians' incomes depended on maintaining a large group of satisfied, returning patients and varied according to the number and kind of services provided.
4. The method of payment was "out of pocket" on a "fee-for-service basis." That is, doctor bills were paid directly by each patient or family in the same manner they took care of any other product or service.

The house call, once a common practice of physicians, is almost nonexistent now.

Although this model of practice and payment still exists, it is no longer the dominant one. In this modern age of bureaucratic medicine, specialists, government regulation, and third-party payments play an increasingly large role, and the nature of medical practice, payment, and delivery have changed drastically. Let us take a brief historical look at this evolution and then consider some of the major issues involved.

THE EVOLUTION OF HEALTH CARE FINANCING IN THE UNITED STATES

Before Blue Cross, which first offered prepaid insurance for hospital bills in 1929, the concept of health insurance did not exist (Eng, 1991). And until 10 years later, when Blue Shield first began offering coverage for doctors' bills, all health care was paid for like any other commodity, out of pocket (Larson, 1991). By World War II less than 1/3 of the population had any form of health or hospital insurance, and even then the extent of coverage was small. In 1950, for instance, only 12% of doctor bills and 37% of hospital bills were covered by any form of private insurance (Roemer, 1980).

Although health insurance was available individually, most people who had coverage received it as part of a group policy through their place of work. Yet, what coverage was available for those who were disabled or retired, unemployed or poor? In 1965, the federal government first attempted to address the social inequities and economic barriers that existed for these and other underserved groups by enacting Medicare and Medicaid as a form of public health insurance. Medicare, which is a federal program, deals with hospital care for those over 65. Medicaid, which is a joint federal–state program, deals with (nonhospital) health care costs for the poor, regardless of age. Both programs have had their share of successes and failures in providing adequate coverage of costs for patients, and each is the subject of constant debate. But together they have had a major, although unintended, effect on health care costs, causing them to spiral upward.

Government intervention pumped billions of new dollars into the system by providing payment for those previously without coverage. With a huge influx of capital and with payment assured, providers were quick to take advantage of this golden opportunity by increasing the number and price of their services. With much new money available, health care institutions built new facilities, modernized older ones, and acquired the latest in technological advances without great regard to cost. By the late 1960s, it was clear that the initial estimates for the cost of these programs were far too low.

With medical expenses rising out of hand, the focus of the federal government since the 1970s has been on cost control. A basic problem existed: Since fees could be virtually assured by some form of private or public financing, and since physicians' salaries increased according to the volume and expense of their services, few incentives existed for physicians to cut costs. In fact, they had just the opposite incentive. It would take a completely different type of financial reimbursement setup to encourage providers to streamline services and to offer only what was needed. Yet, how would this affect the very nature of health care delivery, and would the change be for the better? As we will see, the answer is still very much up in the air.

MANAGED CARE AND THE HEALTH MAINTENANCE ORGANIZATION

The term **managed care** refers to efforts by the health care system to control the cost of, access to, and quality of health care services. The many different forms of managed care have a basic set of characteristics in common. All of them group or "bundle" related services in reference to cost and attempt to control or channel utilization. In addition, attempts are made to maintain and monitor quality control in the provision of services, and all provide some mechanism for controlling or regulating the price of services (Curtiss, 1991).

Forms of managed care, such as the health maintenance organization (HMO) and the preferred provider organization (PPO), have grown tremendously. In 1984, 89% of those who paid for health care services did so through traditional fee for service arrangements as compared to 11% in some form of managed care. By the year 1997, it is predicted that this arrangement will be completely reversed such that 90% of health care costs will be covered through a form of managed care as opposed to 10% by fee for service arrangements (Kenkel, 1988).

HMOs are one of the most common forms of managed care in this country. They have existed here since the early twentieth century, but did not prosper until the early 1970s. Although many different types of HMO currently exist, the initial model could be distinguished from other forms of health care delivery by five specific features. HMOs have (a) an enrolled population of members who (b) prepay their premiums for health care services; (c) the coverage is comprehensive in nature, and (d) the services are provided in centralized health care or hospital facilities by (e) salaried practitioners who are on staff (Curtiss, 1991).

The key characteristic common to all HMOs that is critical to the projected cost savings is the concept of *prepayment*. Each member of an HMO is entitled to a full range of physician and hospital services, but with the exception of a small copayment fee (of approximately $2 to $5), cost is not dependent on usage. No matter how many or how few visits the patient makes to the doctor, or whether the patient is sick or well, the single prepaid premium covers all medical services. Another cost saving feature of many HMOs is that the physicians are paid employees, not independent practitioners. Their salaries are set regardless of the number of procedures performed, and therefore the incentive to "overserve" is eliminated. In fact, the more streamlined the operation is and the more that unneeded services are reduced, the greater the savings to the HMO. Another factor meant to contribute to cost savings is the idea that the HMO would truly live up to its name. That is, it would focus on health maintenance and emphasize preventive services, which would prove cost-effective in the long run.

HMOs AND COST REDUCTION

Has the HMO lived up to its promise? Does it offer quality care at a reduced cost? The answer varies, depending on the yardstick one uses, and even then the results are mixed (Curtiss, 1991). The HMO industry has been successful, for instance, in reducing hospital costs and services. For HMO patients under age 65, the hospital utilization rate is 351 inpatient days per 1,000 people compared to a national average 606 per 1,000, a reduction of 58% (Group Health Association of America, 1988). In 1987, the expense of a day's care in the hospital cost HMOs 17% less than those paying on a fee-for-service basis (Kenkel, 1988). On the other hand, this does not mean that HMOs in general were doing well financially. Approximately 3/4 of the HMOs in this country lost money in 1987, with the total loss estimated at a figure of 700 million dollars (Curtiss, 1991).

HMOs and Quality of Care

Whereas fee-for-service physicians have a financial incentive to offer unnecessary services, HMO physicians have the reverse incentive. Because their patients pay no more for their care no matter how extensive it is, people have asked whether HMO physicians will cut corners and limit their services to reduce costs, thereby providing less than optimal care.

In a landmark study, more than 1,500 people in Seattle, Washington, were randomly assigned to either an HMO or a fee-for-service plan, and were then followed over time (Ware et al., 1986). Healthy people in the two systems showed no differences in medical outcomes, but for those with health problems when the study began, differences did exist. High income HMO members who were initially ill became significantly healthier over time compared to fee-for-service patients. On the other hand, low-income HMO patients who began with health problems reported more serious symptoms and spent more time bedridden over the period of the study than fee-for-service patients.

Another recent study assessed comparative quality of care in a different manner (Udvarhelyi et al., 1991). Although patients were not randomly assigned, fee-for-service versus prepaid patients were seen by the same physicians. This was possible because the physicians were part of a network model HMO in which they saw some patients on a fee-for-service basis while other patients came to see them as part of a prepaid plan.

This study showed that prepaid patients visited their doctors for care more often. The likely reason for this is that the fee, which serves as a barrier or "disincentive" to a doctor visit, is not a factor in a prepaid system. In this study, prepaid patients were under better control for high blood pressure and received better care for preventive services, such as breast examinations, mammograms, and cervical cancer screenings. In sum, the results of these and other studies comparing fee-for-service versus HMO care show no consistent differences in patient care that clearly favor one system over the other (Hornbrook & Berki, 1985; Wolinsky, 1980).

Physician and Patient Satisfaction

When physicians join an HMO they become employees of a large organization, subject to policies that regulate the pace and routines of work and to formal bureaucratic review by the organization and its clients. This is a fundamental change in the nature of standard medical practice. Physicians join HMOs for reasons such as the desire to have a more predictable lifestyle with

Long waits and a clinic atmosphere are problems that HMOs have worked hard to overcome.

regular hours and a guaranteed salary (Smith, C.T., 1985). Yet, when they become employees, they give up a portion of their autonomy, rated by some as the most cherished aspect of their profession (Ku & Fisher, 1990; Starr, 1982). A study of physicians who switched from traditional forms of practice to an HMO in Madison, Wisconsin, found that HMO physicians recognized and accepted these tradeoffs. Although they had concerns about a potential loss of income and the quality of care they would be able to offer their patients, these physicians were generally satisfied and reported that neither income nor quality of care declined (Schulz et al., 1990).

Patients' reports on their satisfaction with HMOs are also mixed, although the reasons for dissatisfaction vary considerably. Mechanic (1976) has made an analogy between the use of an HMO versus a private physician and the experience of shopping at a large chain store versus a small boutique. At the chain store, you know that the prices are competitive, many services can be found at the same location, and you will not be misled or shortchanged by a disreputable dealer. Much the same can be said for an HMO. On the other hand, some of the personal amenities that one gets by shopping at the "finer establishments" may be missing. People have to learn how to navigate their way through the system, they may run into bureaucratic problems, and personal attention may be at a premium.

The early research evidence on patient satisfaction with HMOs found members upset about "continuity of care." This occurred because many

HMOs were originally set up as clinics where a patient might see a different provider each time rather than have a regular personal physician (Pope, 1978; Scitovsky, Benham, & McCall, 1979). Once this problem was identified, however, most HMOs were quick to arrange for each patient to choose a personal physician, and this source of concern was eliminated.

Some evidence has suggested that HMO patients are less satisfied with their doctor's warmth and personal interest in them (Luft, 1981); however, other studies have found no differences on the willingness of the physician to provide personalized care (Holloway, Matson, & Zismer, 1989; Rossiter et al., 1989). Weiss and Senf (1990) studied satisfaction by asking why people left one health plan for another during an open enrollment period at work. Dissatisfaction with the quality of care accounted for 17% of the reasons mentioned, while a lack of concern for patients was a reason cited for changing plans by only 8%. The reason mentioned most often was a desire to see another physician who was not available at their plan.

COMPARATIVE SYSTEMS: CANADIAN AND U.S. HEALTH CARE

The American health care system, which offers an ever-changing mix of public and private funding and a combination of state, federal, and free market regulation, has been the subject of widespread criticism. In spite of the many new programs and policies that have been initiated, it has not been able to control costs nor provide quality coverage to all of the population.

According to Rodwin (1990), health care systems can be categorized as fitting into one of five types (see Table 4.3-1). The private system, as existed in the United States and Western Europe in the nineteenth century, has already been described. In such a system, powerful, solo entrepreneurs serve people according to their ability to pay. A second type, pluralistic systems, are those in which public and private financing and ownership are combined, and health care is seen as a widely available consumer good or service. The current U.S. system is a good example of this. A national health insurance system, such as that seen in Canada, France, and Japan, differs on one critical dimension: Health care is *guaranteed* to *all* people in the system, although private ownership and support still complement the public sector. In a national health insurance system, as currently practiced in Great Britain, health care is not only guaranteed, but it is a state-supported activity in which the government owns most facilities and plays a major role in the formation of policy. Finally, in a socialized health care system, as practiced in the Soviet Union until its breakup, all health care workers are employees of the state, and the state has almost total influence over all financing and allocation decisions.

Table 4.3-1   **Types of Health Systems**

Health System	Type 1 Private	Type 2 Pluralistic	Type 3 National Health Insurance	Type 4 National Health Service	Type 5 Socialized Health Service
General definition	Health care as an item of personal consumption	Health care as predominantly a consumer good or service	Health care as an insured, guaranteed consumer good or service	Health care as a state-supported consumer good or service	Health care as a state-provided public service
Position of physician	Solo entrepreneur	Solo entrepreneur and member of variety of groups, organizations	Solo entrepreneur and member of medical organizations	Solo entrepreneur and member of medical organizations	State employee and member of medical organizations
Ownership of facilities	Private	Private and public	Private and public	Mostly public	Entirely public
Prototypes	U.S., Western Europe, Russia in 19th century	U.S. in 20th century	Sweden, France, Canada, Japan in 20th century	Great Britain in 20th century	Soviet Union in 20th century

Source: From Rodwin, V. G., 1990, Comparative health systems. In A. R. Kavner, ed., Health care delivery in the United States (New York: Springer).

Social experiments in health care delivery and funding have been tried in states such as Hawaii and Oregon, and their success and generalizability have been debated. In the search for a better way to handle health care, a great deal of interest has focused on the Canadian system as a possible model for the United States. Canada's system of National Health Insurance (NHI) is a public, nonprofit system in which federal funds pay about 40% of the total health care costs and the provincial governments furnish the rest. In the United States, approximately 37 million people have no health insurance, but in Canada coverage is universal. All citizens, regardless of their age, health, or employment status, are insured. Yet Canada still spends less of its gross national product, approximately 9%, on health care. In the Canadian system, benefits are comprehensive, meaning that, with only few exceptions, Canadians pay no doctor or hospital bills. In addition, the benefits are "portable," meaning that citizens are covered even when they are temporarily out of the country.

Physicians in Canada are paid on a fee-for-service basis, but the fees are carefully negotiated, and hospital budgets and expenses are tightly controlled by the federal government. The average cost per person for physicians' services in Canada is $202 as compared to $347 in the United States, and fees charged by American doctors for specific procedures average more than three times those charged in the Canadian system (Fuchs & Hahn, 1990). Although there is significant disagreement about this (see Sheils, Young, & Rubin, 1992), a recent report suggests that the "Canadianization" of our health care system would have reduced U.S. health care spending by more than $100 billion in 1991 (Woolhandler & Himmelstein, 1990).

The Canadian system is hardly perfect. Because of strict cost controls, high-technology medical equipment is relatively scarce in Canada compared to the United States, and waiting times for some services, especially those involving high-tech equipment, are generally much longer. Also, because physicians are still reimbursed on a fee-for-service basis, the incentive to eliminate unnecessary tests and procedures is not as strong as it might be. Still, surveys of Canadian citizens indicate that they are highly satisfied with their system of care (Starfield, 1991). Likewise, physicians in Canada are generally satisfied with their system and feel that the quality of care given to patients remains high.

■

THE HOSPITAL

The hospital is the centerpiece of the American medical system. It houses the best and brightest of practitioners and the most advanced technological equipment. In it new knowledge is developed, and lifesaving interventions take place on a daily basis. Yet it was not always that way. The modern hospital bears little resemblance to its early predecessors.

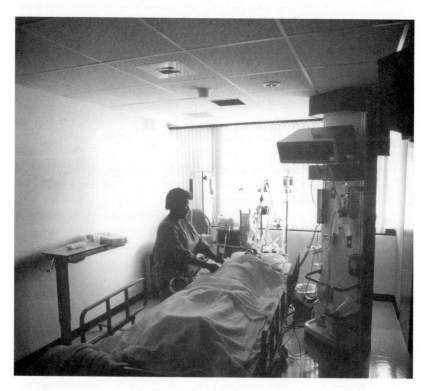

Modern hospitals bear little resemblance to their early predecessors. However, in spite of their ability to cure, hospitals can be particularly cold and unwelcoming.

The ancient Romans first established medical facilities that came to be known as hospitals, although the roots of the modern hospital are usually traced back to the rise of Christianity. Medieval hospitals were run by the church to assist the sick and needy, but they were really little more than shelters where the poor received prayer and nourishment. Hospitals became more secular by the end of the sixteenth century, but mostly they housed orphaned children or adults who were homeless, mentally or physically disabled, or unable to care for themselves due to age.

By the eighteenth century, medical treatment had become the primary function of the hospital. Still, the physical condition of these hospitals was outrageous by modern standards. Sanitation and ventilation were extremely poor, and the spread of infection was high. Antiseptic measures were unknown, and surgery was limited to amputation and childbirth (Coe, 1978). The first hospitals in the United States appeared in the 1700s. In 1751, Benjamin Franklin and his colleagues founded the Pennsylvania Hospital, the first in this country exclusively for the purpose of treating the sick (Cockerham, 1989).

From these humble beginnings, the standards of hospital practice have risen and great technological advances have been introduced. This growth has not been without its downside, however. The most commonly cited negatives of the modern hospital in many ways parallel those of the health care system in general. These negatives include cost and interpersonal relations.

THE COST OF HOSPITAL CARE

Hospitals have led the way in increasing medical costs. In 1970, the average cost per day of being hospitalized in the U.S. was $74. Ten years later, the cost had more than tripled to $245, and in 1990 that figure had almost tripled again to $687 (American Hospital Association, 1992). Today, approximately 60% of all health insurance claims are for expenses related to hospitalization.

Various attempts have been made to control hospital costs. The *prospective payment system* (PPS), which regulates the way hospitals are reimbursed by the government, is a hotly debated cost control policy. The PPS system classifies patients and procedures into *diagnosis related groups* (DRGs) based on a statistical evaluation of the average length of hospitalization and the cost for patients in a given grouping. The government then designates a fixed amount that it will reimburse a hospital for all patients in a given DRG. If the hospital can treat its patients less expensively or discharge them in a shorter period, it still receives the full fee. However, if the patient requires a longer or more costly hospitalization, then the hospital must cover the additional cost itself. Clearly, this system provides strong incentives for efficient treatment and quick discharge that may save the hospital and the system money and allow the patient to go home sooner.

Critics of DRGs have asserted that this program compromises the quality of care in the name of economic responsibility. They believe that it encourages premature discharge for patients who are not fully recovered or who suffer from complications. These issues were addressed in a major national survey of 297 hospitals in five states (Kahn et al., 1990; Rogers et al., 1990). The researchers compared the medical records of elderly Medicare patients in these hospitals for equivalent periods before and after the PPS system was put in place. They found that the length of hospitalization was significantly reduced, decreasing 24% after the DRG system was adopted. As for quality of care, overall outcomes and mortality rates did not appear to be negatively affected, although some patients were discharged home in an unstable condition. The debate over DRGs remains a lively one, and we can expect that this system will be monitored and will continue to evolve over the next decade.

THE EXPERIENCE OF HOSPITALIZATION

The modern hospital exists to help people. Its practitioners seek to diagnose, treat, and cure, yet the hospital is still dominated by the mindset of the bio-medical model. As a result, it is a place where the *body* gets first rate care, but the *mind* and the *spirit* are often neglected. All too often the medical staff think of their patients in terms of their condition and nothing more. Patients become "the rash in Room 408" or "the broken leg in 502," not whole people whose needs and fears must also be attended to.

THE PATIENT'S PERSPECTIVE   Those who run hospitals often forget to see the experience of hospitalization from the patient's perspective. Let us take a look. Patients typically arrive for a hospital stay with a great deal of anxiety (Newman, 1984). They are concerned about their diagnosis and their prognosis for recovery, about costs and time away from work and family, and whether and when they will be able to resume a normal life on discharge. They first encounter a clerk who probably has not had any special training designed to ease the patient into the hospital and who may be insensitive to these concerns.

Once inside, patients find that their control is extremely limited. Their clothes, their valuables, and to some extent their identity, are all stripped away. They are placed in a bare white room and given a "johnny," a hospital gown that is open in the back. Their mobility is limited by hospital rules, and their access to visitors is subject to restrictions. Routines are determined for all patients regardless of their individual needs or preferences, and it is not unusual for a patient who is resting peacefully to be awakened by the staff for breakfast, even though that person would have much preferred to remain asleep.

Most important, patients are often given limited information about their condition and what they should expect. The medical chart, full of facts and findings, is typically not shared with patients, with the result that they wonder and worry why information is being withheld from them. Sometimes whole medical teams come into a patient's room, aligning themselves on opposite sides of the bed discussing "the case" as if the patient did not exist.

DEPERSONALIZATION   The term **depersonalization** has been used to describe the manner in which hospitals remove the individuality of patients, treating them all alike in terms of hospital requirements and routine (Goffman, 1961). Referring to his own hospitalization and the depersonalizing treatment he received at an otherwise first-rate hospital, author Norman Cousins (1979) has noted, "I had a fast-growing conviction that a hospital was no place for a person who was seriously ill."

How do patients actually understand the hospital patient role, and how do they respond to the treatment they receive? In a classic study by Tagliocozzo and Mauksch (1979), a variety of hospitalized patients were asked what they believed was expected of them. Typically they felt they were supposed to be cooperative, not too demanding, and respectful and trusting in regard to their doctors. When asked what their rights were, one quarter of the patients said that they had no idea, while many others stated that they did not think they had any.

GOOD PATIENTS AND BAD PATIENTS   In another classic study, Judith Lorber (1975) focused on the reactions of the hospital staff to those patients who were passive versus those who were more demanding. About one quarter of those being treated came to be labeled "good patients" by the staff, while another quarter were labeled "problem patients." The "good" patients were obedient, undemanding, and cheerfully stoic regardless of the seriousness of their condition or the discomfort they were in. Very simply, they required the least time and attention of the staff.

"Bad" patients were much the opposite. They were judged to be uncooperative, complaining, and overly emotional. They were suspicious that they were not receiving the truth and sometimes reacted with anger to those treating them. These demanding patients, who tended to be younger and better educated, took up more time than the staff felt was warranted and might be sedated or even referred to the psychiatry department.

In commenting on the good patient-bad patient distinction, Shelley Taylor (1979) has added an important conceptual element. Taylor argues that the key issue that the hospital patient must deal with is the *loss of control*. The response of problem patients is one of **reactance** (Brehm, 1966; Brehm & Brehm, 1981). They feel that their freedom is being threatened, and they respond by actively taking steps to restore and assert personal control. They challenge, complain, and demand attention, all to demonstrate that *they* are the ones in charge.

The good patient is coping with the same loss of control but in the opposite way, by acceptance and passivity. While at first it might seem more adaptive to become a good patient, Taylor points out that it is not always "good" to be a good patient. When patients become withdrawn or depressed, when they deny fear or discomfort, they are working against their own recovery in at least two ways. Informationally, passive patients may fail to report problems or symptoms, and their needs may be neglected by a busy, overworked staff.

Biologically, depression is often accompanied by depletion of norepinephrine. As a result, the patient's physiological reserves, which normally help the body in its efforts against disease, may not be mobilized effectively. In this way, good patients may actually be lessening their chances of a speedy recovery.

RESTORING CONTROL   Having recognized the negative consequences of a loss of control, health psychologists and hospital staff have made significant attempts to counteract this. Several programs have been designed to provide patients facing surgery and other anxiety-producing procedures with a greater sense of control by providing information of two kinds (Egbert et al., 1964; Mathews & Ridgeway, 1984; Thompson, 1981). *Sensory information* tells patients what sensations they will experience as a result of the procedure. Is some pain normal? Will I feel tired or uncomfortable, and how long will that last? *Procedural information* offers patients knowledge of the sequence of procedures they will be exposed to so they will be able to anticipate just what will happen to them, as well as when and why.

Anderson (1987) has looked at the effects of information on patients about to have coronary bypass surgery. A control group received "standard preparation," which consisted of a discussion between the nurse and the patient about two pamphlets the patient had been given. The experimental group watched a videotape that followed previous bypass patients through all stages of their stay from hospital admission through discharge (procedural information), as well as an audiotape detailing how they might feel at each of the various stages of their stay (sensory information). Although both groups were equally anxious on admission, those in the experimental group were far less anxious before and after their surgery. No differences were found between the groups on the use of pain medication or the length of stay, but fewer of the experimental patients required medication for acute hypertension during recovery.

In reviewing more than 20 studies on this issue, Suls and Wan (1989) concluded that a combination of procedural and sensory information offers consistent positive benefits, that sensory information alone provides inconsistent results, and that procedural information alone generates only small effects. Researchers have also noted, however, that offering people more information than they can handle or information that is confusing can have negative effects (Miller & Mangan, 1983; Wallace, 1986). Therefore, just as biologically oriented researchers must test drugs to determine their best dosage levels and methods of administration, health psychologists must continue to investigate the kinds of information and control that are most useful, as well as the best ways of administering these to hospital patients.

SATISFACTION WITH HOSPITAL CARE   Spurred by growing concerns about the interpersonal element in health care and increasing competition among hospitals, research on hospital patient satisfaction has grown recently. One major study surveyed more than 2,000 patients from 10 hospitals across the United States, finding that patients evaluated hospital care along 6 dimensions (Ware & Berwick, 1990). These were nursing and daily care, hospital environment and ancillary care, medical care, information, admissions, and discharge and billing. The researchers reported that the first factor, nursing and daily care, was the best predictor of patient satisfaction as well as their intention to return to the same hospital if they were ill again.

Boston's Beth Israel Hospital conducted an even larger study of well over 6,000 patients from 62 hospitals all over the country, focusing on patients' beliefs about how they were treated as people (Cleary et al., 1991; Delbanco, 1992). Overall, patients' ratings of their hospital care were extremely high; 49% rated their care excellent, and only 6% rated it as fair or poor. Ninety-four percent said they would recommend their hospital to family or friends. Yet, some of the nation's "best hospitals," as judged by their reputation and prestige, were in fact some of the worst as judged by patient satisfaction.

In spite of the high overall ratings, patients did report many problems with specific aspects of their care. For instance, lack of emotional support and poor communication was mentioned by more than 20% of all patients; almost 1/2 complained that they had never been told what to expect of the hospital's daily routine; more than 10% felt that they had significant pain that could have been relieved by prompt attention, but was not; and more than 30% said that they were not informed about important side effects of their medications (Cleary et al., 1991; Knox, 1991).

Surprisingly, patient satisfaction with the hospital was not strongly related to their health status nor to personal characteristics such as age or income. Consistent with other research, the single variable that predicted satisfaction best was the degree to which patients felt cared for by those in the hospital (Cleary et al., 1991). In summarizing what patients want from their hospital care, Delbanco (1992) also tells us what patients want from the medical care system in general:

> *They want to be able to trust the competence and efficiency of their caregivers. They want to be able to negotiate the health care system effectively and be treated with dignity and respect. Patients want to understand how their sickness or treatment will affect their lives, and they often fear that their doctors are not telling them everything they know. Patients worry about and want to learn to care for themselves away from the clinical setting. They want us to focus on their pain, physical discomfort, and functional disabilities. They want to discuss the effect their illness will have on their family, friends, and finances. And they worry about the future (p. 414).*

It is highly encouraging that the findings of the Beth Israel study are not simply collecting dust on shelves. The results of this program are being fed back to each of the cooperating hospitals, and numerous projects have been initiated to improve quality of care in response to these surveys (Fullam, 1991;

Simon, 1991). Efforts such as these result in an ever-evolving health care system, one that is responsive to patient needs and works toward the generation of more positive health outcomes.

MODULE SUMMARY

1. In the traditional model of health care, patients choose independently practicing physicians who provide services and set prices as they please. People pay their doctors "out of pocket" on a fee-for-service basis.
2. Insurance to cover health care costs began in 1929 and has expanded in scope over time. In 1965, the federal government set up Medicare and Medicaid to help cover costs for the elderly and poor.
3. Medical costs skyrocketed as a result of federal health care spending. Because payment could be assured, physicians increased the number, kind, and expense of their services, and institutions invested in new equipment and facilities.
4. The Health Maintenance Organization (HMO) represents a new form of health care delivery that attempts to offer low cost, high quality services. HMO members prepay premiums rather than paying for care on a fee-for-service basis.
5. HMOs have received mixed grades on cost reduction and quality of care. In general, patients report high levels of overall satisfaction, and physicians seem pleased even though they are now employees rather than independent practitioners.
6. The Canadian health care system differs from the American in that almost all medical costs for all Canadian citizens are covered by the government through a system of National Health Insurance. Overall, health costs in that system are less and quality remains high.
7. Hospitals originated as little more than shelters for those who were homeless, elderly, or physically or mentally ill. In the United States, the first hospitals devoted solely to the treatment of physical illness began in the mid-1700s.
8. The average cost of a day's hospitalization went up over 900% between 1970 and 1990. A significant cost-cutting measure has been the Diagnosis Related Group (DRG) system, in which the government reimburses hospitals a fixed amount for patients in each DRG. This allows the hospitals to profit from early discharge as the result of efficient treatment.
9. While technical care in hospitals has improved, interpersonal care has not kept pace. Hospitals often fail to attend to patients' anxieties and concerns.

10. Hospitals depersonalize patients by removing their individuality and treating them alike in terms of hospital requirements and routine. People often do not know what their rights are as patients.
11. "Good" and "bad" patients are both responding to a loss of control. "Bad" patients fight to reassert control by being challenging and demanding, whereas "good" patients are more accepting and passive.
12. Patients feel a greater sense of control when they receive information about what will happen to them (procedural information) and how they are likely to feel (sensory information). Several informational programs have proven effective in treating patients.
13. Satisfaction with hospital care is generally quite high, although people still report problems concerning information and prompt attention to pain. Patients are most satisfied when they feel cared for by the hospital staff.

5

INFLUENCES ON HEALTH

5.1 Life Span Development
5.2 The Environment

Throughout their life span, all people change and develop, and all people exist in some degree of relationship to the sociophysical environment. Therefore, people's experiences of health and illness take place in a context that includes their own development and aging and their relationship to the environment. Developmental and environmental psychology study two of the most important contextual influences on health.

Module 5.1 traces the influence of human development on health across the life span, from gestation to old age. It also considers such topics as the major causes of death and illness, health challenges at various stages of development, suicide, and death. Module 5.2 explores an environmental model of stress and health, as well as various environmental factors that affect health and well-being such as crowding, noise, occupational stress, urban living, and commuting.

LIFE SPAN DEVELOPMENT

OVERVIEW

Danelle is a 67-year-old retired elementary school teacher who has had back pain for several years. She had looked forward to retirement as a time to travel with her husband, but now she finds her activities restricted by constant pain. Danelle has **osteoporosis**, *a reduction in bone tissue mass that leaves older people more vulnerable to fractures from even slight pressure (Berkow & Fletcher, 1987).*

Osteoporosis results from several factors: (a) an inadequate diet during childhood and adolescence that hinders the development of sufficient bone mass, (b) the additional loss of bone following menopause, and (c) a gradually less physically active lifestyle. Danelle's situation demonstrates the importance of a developmental perspective on health. Well-being in later life is affected by lifelong habits that take a cumulative toll on health status.

Developmental health psychology studies the interrelationship of health and aging. Developmental psychologists usually divide the life span into a succession of stages: infancy (birth to 2 years of age), early childhood (2 to 6 years of age), middle childhood (6 to 12 years of age), adolescence (13 to 20 years of age), young adulthood (20 to 40 years of age), middle adulthood (40 to 65 years of age), and later adulthood (above 65 years of age).

HEALTH STATUS

Of course, illness or death can occur at any age, but the factors that determine general health status are different at the various stages of development. The challenges to health, the types of illnesses encountered, and the causes of death vary according to age. In this section, we investigate how these factors change across the life span.

PREGNANCY

There are many risk factors related to birth defects, called **teratogens**. Generally, what is healthy for the mother is healthy for her fetus. Using both animal and human subjects, researchers have been able to determine a number of teratogens. From the list in Table 5.1-1 (pp. 168–69), it is apparent that the health behavior of the mother is of overriding importance for the healthy development of her fetus.

INFANCY

Teratogens also affect health and development after birth, because they are related to low birth weight, one of the greatest health challenges to newborns. Delivery *before* the 37th week is considered **preterm birth** (Duffy, Als, & McAnulty, 1990). Preterm babies usually weigh less than 2.5 kg (5.5 lbs), and they account for about 60% of low birth weight babies. For the remaining 40% of low birth weight babies, growth was slowed due to other factors. Although delivery may have been after the 37th week, the baby weighs less than 90% of babies of the same age. This baby is called **small for date**.

LOW BIRTH WEIGHT

About 7% of all newborns in the United States are low-birth-weight babies and they are 40 times more likely to die during the neonatal period than normal weight babies (Behrman, 1985; Brown, 1985). About 60% of all babies who die within the first year of life—25,000 per year in the United States—are low birth weight (USDHHS, 1992). Socioeconomic status is related to lower birth weights in general, and African American newborns are twice as likely as European American to be low-birth-weight babies (Morbidity and Mortality Weekly Report, 1987).

In spite of its imminent risk to life, low-birth-weight is only inconsistently associated with long-term physical and psychological problems. Although 80% of babies weighing less than two pounds at birth die, 80% of the survivors may have no major handicaps 6 months to 3 years later (Bennett, Robinson, & Sells, 1983; Greenberg & Crnic, 1988). Even newborns who weighed less than three pounds may have normal IQ scores and may be doing well at 5 years of age (Klein, Hack, Gallagher, & Fanaroff, 1985).

However, there is evidence of mild cognitive impairment in children who had a low birth weight (for example, Barrera, Rosenbaum, & Cunningham, 1986). At the age of 5 years, children who weighed less than 1500 gms (3.25 lbs) at birth scored significantly below well-matched normal weight children on an index of general cognitive ability (Smith, Knight, & Eveline, 1990). Therefore,

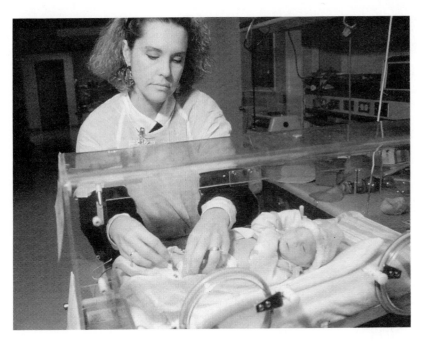

Preterm infants require the protective environment of an isolette.

even though not all studies show it, there is a strong suspicion that low birth weight is related to poorer cognitive development.

A number of risk factors for low birth weight have been reviewed (Brown, 1985). These are primarily maternal risk factors (see Table 5.1-2). A recent study of 771 African American and 1,223 European American first-time pregnant women found that lower birth weight babies were born to mothers who were younger, less educated, gained less weight during the pregnancy, and were African American (Ketterlinus, Henderson, & Lamb, 1990). Some of the risk factors for low birth weight—particularly those linked to socioeconomic status—are not easily remedied, but others can be altered (for example, the adequacy of medical care and the mother's behavior).

PREVENTING LOW BIRTH WEIGHT　Prenatal health care reduces the incidence of low birth weight, so government programs have focused on encouraging and providing access to it (USDHHS, 1992). However, whether or not women avail themselves of good prenatal care even when it is available is dependent on many factors. A study that compared African American, European American, and Native American women found that three types of

Table 5.1-1	TERATOGENS

TERATOGENIC AGENT	PROBABLE AFFECTS
Substances	
Alcohol	Anatomic dysmorphology (first trimester); low birth weight (third trimester); behavior disorders; **fetal alcohol syndrome (FAS)**—characterized by slow prenatal and postnatal development, body malformations, brain dysfunctions, hyperactivity, attention deficits, learning disabilities, and motor impairments in childhood.
Tobacco	*Fetal tobacco syndrome*—effects similar to FAS (Naeye & Peters, 1984; Nieburg, Marks, McLaren, & Remington, 1985).
Marijuana	Effects similar to FAS (Hingson et al., 1982); premature and low birth weight (Fried, Watkinson, & Willan, 1984).
Opiates	Sudden infant death (Cobrinck, Hood, & Chused, 1959; Ostrea & Chavez, 1979); retarded growth and behavior and learning problems (Householder, Hatcher, Burns, & Chasnoff, 1982; Wilson, McCreary, Kean, & Baxter, 1979).
Anticonvulsants	Anatomic dysmorphology.
Illnesses and Infections	
HIV	Physical abnormalities and failure to grow normally (Iosub, Bamji, Stone, Gromisch, & Waserman, 1987; Marion, Wiznia, Hutcheon, & Rubinstein, 1986); HIV is transmitted from infected mothers to their infants in 20%–30% of cases (Levine & Dubler, 1990).
Syphilis	Anatomic dysmorphology.
Gonorrhea	Infects the newborn, causing conjunctivitis and corneal ulcerations
Genital herpes	Infects the newborn, causing brain damage and death.
Diabetes	A threat to the pregnant mother as well as the fetus if not managed properly.
Rubella	Serious birth defects including deafness and heart abnormalities if contracted before the sixteenth week (Miller, Cradock-Watson, & Pollock, 1982).

barriers were related to inadequate care: (a) psychosocial (personal and emotional problems), (b) structural (for example, availability of child care and transportation), and (c) sociodemographic (poverty) (Lia-Hoagberg et al., 1990). Of these, poverty impacts all three barriers. For example, poor mothers often cannot afford to eat nutritious meals, even if they are aware of the importance of good nutrition through prenatal care.

In addition to poverty, the mothers' *perceptions* of the barriers and of how they are treated by health care providers are also significant predictors of the adequacy of the care they receive. In other words, the mothers' *beliefs* were more important than the actual barriers. Also, their health beliefs and social support can be important *motivators* to overcoming perceived barriers. Those who believe they can overcome the barriers are more likely to do so.

Environmental Hazards	
X-radiation	Retarded growth (third trimester).
Nuclear radiation	Prenatal chromosomal abnormalities and Down syndrome (West Berlin Human Genetic Institute, 1987).
Lead	Delayed behavior development and disordered learning.
Solvents	Disordered learning and memory.
Malnutrition	Low birth weight and delayed neurological development.
Heat	Low birth weight (third trimester).
Crowding	Behavior disorders.
Psychosocial Hazards	
General stress	Premature birth and disturbed temperament—slow adaptability, negative mood, and distractibility (Rutter & Quine, 1990).
Job stress	Preterm delivery and low birth weight (Homer, James, & Siegal, 1990).
Lack of social support	Preterm birth (Pagel, Smilkstein, Regen, & Montano, 1990)
Father's Role	
Alcohol, nuclear radiation, marijuana, lead, x-radiation, and pesticides	Abnormal sperm (Lester & Van Theil, 1977; Marieb, 1989).
Tobacco	Abnormal sperm; father's second-hand smoke also affects the fetus adversely through the mother (Rubin, Krasilnikoff, Leventhal, Weile, & Berget, 1986).

General Sources: Berkow, R., and Fletcher, A. J., 1987, The Merck manual of diagnosis and therapy *(Rahway, NJ: Merck Sharp & Dohme); Huffman, L. C., and del Carmen, R., 1990, Prenatal stress, in L. E. Arnold, ed.,* Childhood stress, *141–171. (New York: John Wiley & Sons).*

CHILDHOOD

As children mature, they are largely at the mercy of the environment and their caregivers. Because the major contagious illnesses that used to cause many children's deaths—measles, mumps, influenza, polio, diphtheria, and whooping cough—are controlled in the U.S. through vaccinations, today the leading cause of death and disability in childhood is accidents. Accidents annually kill about 16,000 and permanently injure between 40,000 and 50,000 children (Cataldo et al., 1986; USDHHS, 1982; Waller, 1987). Nearly half of all of children's deaths are due to accidents—half of these deaths involve motor vehicles (USDHHS, 1992). That is why all 50 states require that young children be physically restrained in cars.

Table 5.1-2   RISK FACTORS FOR LOW-BIRTH-WEIGHT BABIES

Mother's Background

Age <17 or >34
Low socioeconomic status
Race (African American; but this may be confounded with socioeconomic status)
Unmarried
Low educational level
No children or >4
Low weight for height
History of genital or urinary abnormalities or surgery
Chronic disease (specifically diabetes and hypertension)
Lack of immunity to infections such as Rubella
Previous low birth weight baby
Previous multiple spontaneous abortions
Genetic factors (for example, mother was a low birth weight baby)

Mother's Behavior

Smoking
Poor nutrition
Abuse of alcohol and other drugs
Exposure to environmental toxins
Residing in high altitudes

Mother's Medical Status During Pregnancy

Multiple pregnancy
Poor weight gain (<14 pounds)
Prior pregnancy within 6 months
Low blood pressure
Hypertension or toxemia
Infections such as Rubella or urinary infections
Anemia or abnormal hemoglobin
Fetal abnormalities
Incompetent cervix
Spontaneous premature rupture of membranes
Bleeding in the first or second trimester
Placental problems

Health Care

Premature delivery by induced labor or cesarean section
Inadequate health care

Source: Adapted from Brown, S. S., 1985, Can low birth weight be prevented?, Family Planning Perspectives, 17, *112–118.*

Several psychosocial factors contribute to the occurrence of childhood accidents (Mofenson & Greensher, 1978; Wright, Schaefer, & Solomons, 1979). Stress increases their likelihood. Accidents are more likely to happen when children are hungry or tired (before meals or naps), in a new surrounding (after moving to a new home or on a vacation), when there is a new caretaker, or when there is an illness or death in the family.

The second and third leading causes of death in children are the same as in adults: cancer and heart disease. Heart disease affects about 1 in 120 newborns and is more likely caused by birth defects rather than lifestyle factors, such as poor diet or exercise (Berkow & Fletcher, 1987). Children and young adults tend to have certain cancers—lymphoma, leukemia, and Hodgkin's disease—much more often than adults. Fortunately, advances in the treatment of these cancers are responsible for nearly a 50% reduction in the death rate from childhood cancer since 1950 (USDHHS, 1982).

In early childhood, children average between seven and eight colds a year, twice as many as adults, largely due to the immaturity of their immune systems (Denny & Clyde, 1983). Exposure is also a major risk factor in illness. The close physical contact among children, the sharing of food, and children's propensity to put objects into their mouths can all spread disease. That is why children who spend more time around other children are sick more often (Loda, 1980; Wald, Dashevsky, Byers, Guerra, & Taylor, 1988).

The spread of infection can be minimized by teaching children healthy behaviors such as not to put anything in their mouths beside food and to wash their hands after using the toilet and before meals. Caregivers should also wash their hands frequently, and they should see that high standards of cleanliness are used in food preparation and serving areas. In spite of the increased exposure, children are actually healthier overall when they attend day care centers if the centers follow high standards of nutrition, cleanliness, and preventive health care (AAP, 1986).

As the immune system matures, the frequency of colds decreases slightly in middle childhood to about six per year (Behrman & Vaughn, 1983; Denny & Clyde, 1983). Meanwhile, the widespread use of vaccines has made middle childhood one of the most disease-free periods of life. Because accidents also decrease from their peak in young childhood, this is one of the healthiest periods of life. One longitudinal study followed the health of mostly European American, middle-class children over a six-year period (Starfield et al., 1984). Although 90% had minor illnesses (mostly colds) and 80% had minor injuries, only slightly more than 10% developed serious chronic problems.

According to one theory, children's frequent illnesses may actually have beneficial effects on cognitive and emotional development (Parmelee, 1986). When children recover from illness, they experience the return of good health and physical strength. Theoretically, this provides children opportunities to develop a sense of confidence and teaches them how to cope with illness. Empathy may also develop when children see their classmates, siblings, and parents undergo the symptoms of illness.

ADOLESCENCE

Adolescence is characterized by rapidly increasing physical maturity, a high degree of experimentation, and ever widening exposure to the culture at large and its potentially health-threatening aspects—for example, cigarette smoking, alcohol and drugs, and sexual activity. Therefore, adolescence entails changing health hazards and it is a critical transitional period for the development of health habits (Cohen, Brownell, & Felix, 1990).

Accidents remain the leading cause of death in adolescence. About one-half of all deaths among people 15 to 24 years of age are due to accidents and three-fourths of these involve motor vehicles (USDHHS, 1992). Between 15 and 19 years of age, males are more than twice as likely to die in a traffic accident than females (Matarazzo, 1984). Intoxication is directly related to motor vehicle accidents and a reduction in the incidence of drinking and driving could result in fewer deaths among teenagers.

The fact that accidents are the leading cause of teenage deaths indicates that adolescence is a period of relatively little disease. Adolescents have survived the diseases of childhood and are not yet facing the lifestyle diseases of adulthood. There are, however, two other major causes of teenage deaths—suicide and homicide.

Healthy coping requires a repertoire of behavioral skills, which are also developing at the same time (Rice, 1990). Therefore, adolescents may not yet have the skills to cope with their growing challenges. Teenagers may feel overwhelmed and stressed. Stress is related to depression in adolescence (Daniels & Moos, 1990) and depression is a serious health risk for teenagers, particularly for those who lack social support. Adolescents unable to cope with the challenges may look for a way out through suicide.

Although identity seeking and maturation can be turbulent for many teenagers, these changes do not result in hopelessness and psychological pain for the majority of adolescents. In fact, less than 1% of teenagers attempt suicide (Petersen, 1987). Nevertheless, from 1950–1987, the rate of adolescent suicide more than tripled, making it the third leading cause of death—only accidents and murder are higher—and many of those accidents *may* be suicide (USDHHS, 1992).

Between the ages of 15 and 24, approximately 23 of every 100,000 people take their own lives each year, while 100 times as many may attempt it. More girls than boys attempt suicide but more boys are successful because they use more violent methods such as guns instead of drugs (Petzel & Cline, 1978). Seventy-five percent of adolescents who commit suicide are white, middle-class boys. The rate of suicide among African American adolescents is only one-half that of European Americans.

Surprisingly, factors such as poverty and deprivation, pregnancy, drug use, and sexually transmitted diseases are usually *not* related to suicide (Wynne, 1978; Yankelovich, 1981). Adolescent suicide is associated primar-

Table 5.1-3   Suicide Warning Signs

- Preoccupation with thoughts of death or suicide
- Previous suicide attempts
- Depression
- Giving away cherished possessions, making a will or other final arrangements
- Sudden dramatic changes in behavior patterns (for example, eating, weight, school)
- Social withdrawal or isolation
- Sudden personality changes (for example, moodiness, nervousness, hostility, lack of concern about health or appearance, or dramatic uplift in mood)
- Recent loss (break up of relationship, death of friend or parent)
- Suicide of friend or family member
- Drug or alcohol abuse (because they affect cognition)

ily with relationship and family conflicts, followed by career or job problems (Rich, Warstradt, Nemiroff, Fowler, & Young, 1991). Among 50 adolescents who poisoned themselves, 80% were having problems with their parents, nearly 60% were having school problems, and more than 50% were having relationship problems (Hawton et al., 1982). Therefore, most suicide attempts seem to be desperate cries for attention and help when adolescents feel unable to cope (Curran, 1987).

Up to three-fourths of people who attempt suicide have given one or more warning signs (Pokorny, 1968). Because of the ambivalence of those who attempt suicide, these warning signs (see Table 5.1-3) should be taken as help-seeking behavior requiring treatment (Shneidman, 1987).

In contrast to their relatively low suicide rate, African American adolescents are far more likely to be the victims of murder (USDHHS, 1992). The homicide rate for young black men is nearly 86 per 100,000, 7 times that of young white men. Low socioeconomic status is a major risk factor for homicide, while it is *not* for suicide. This suggests that poverty rather than race is involved in the high murder rate.

YOUNG ADULTHOOD

Most people coast into adulthood very healthy. They know it too: 90% of people 17 to 44 years of age believe that their health is good to excellent (USD-HHS, 1986e). The decade of the 20s begins at the peak of well-being with maximum stature and physical ability, strength, and endurance. Also, people rarely notice the slow decline in physical functioning that begins in the 30s.

Automobile accidents remain an important cause of death in young adulthood. After age 35, however, the lifestyle diseases—coronary artery disease, cerebral vascular disease, and cancer—surpass them (USDHHS, 1985, 1986e). This is the first time since infancy that illness asserts itself so strongly.

Overall, men are twice as likely as women to die in young adulthood (USDHHS, 1986e). In fact, women have lower death rates throughout adulthood. Why? Men may be more vulnerable to genetically linked diseases. In addition, hormones such as estrogen, which women have in higher concentration than men, may provide a protective edge in some illnesses such as heart disease. Behaviors also play a role: Women outlive men because they are more aware of health issues, know more about them, and do more to prevent them (Nathanson & Lorenz, 1982). However, even though women have a lower death rate than men, they do not have fewer health *problems*. In fact, they have higher rates of many nonfatal illnesses (Verbrugge, 1985).

African Americans are also twice as likely as European Americans to die during this period (USDHHS, 1986e). Socioeconomic factors may account for this because more African Americans are poor and poverty hinders access to medical care and education. There is a strong relationship between social class, education, and preventive health practices (Calnan & Rutter, 1986). Socioeconomic factors are also related to knowledge about disease. The less education people have, the more likely they are to contract a disease, be seriously affected by it, or die from it (Pincus, Callahan, & Burkhauser, 1987).

One healthful aspect of young adulthood is that usually people's habits have begun to stabilize, and they are less likely to *begin* to smoke, drink, or use drugs than they were in adolescence. The 1980s witnessed the lowest percentage of young adults smoking than at any time since 1955 when figures were first collected (USDHHS, 1987). Intoxication may be less of a problem too, for although 28% of adult drivers report that they sometimes drive after drinking, 70% never do (Prevention Research Center, 1986).

Middle Adulthood

The overwhelming majority of adults in middle age, 82%, report that their health is good to excellent (USDHHS, 1986e), only a slight decrease from young adulthood. In our affluent society, this is a time of relatively good physical health and well-being. People are usually at the peak of their earning potential and feel financially secure.

However, middle adulthood does not remain the healthy coasting period that young adulthood is. By middle adulthood, the lifestyle diseases are firmly entrenched as the top 3 causes of death (USDHHS, 1982, 1986e). The death rate doubles from 35 to 45 years of age, and it doubles again from 45 to 55 years of age. Even so, over the last 4 decades, the death rate during middle adulthood has *declined* 27%. During this period, the chance of dying from heart attacks and strokes has decreased, but even though the death rate from many cancers has also gone down, overall deaths from cancer have increased because lung cancer deaths have gone up so dramatically (USDHHS, 1992).

PHYSICAL CHANGES   In middle age, physical declines become more obvious, and there are some changes that do affect well-being. The reduction of **reserve capacity**—the ability of the body's organ systems to put forth several times more effort than usual under demand (Fries & Crapo, 1981)—is one of the most important health changes. Reserve capacity represents an extra margin of safety to resist disease, withstand stress, or endure physical hardship. By middle adulthood, maximum heart rate and cardiac output, glucose tolerance, vital lung capacity, cellular immunity, and kidney function have declined, leaving less resistance to physical challenges (Berkow & Fletcher, 1987).

Another change, referred to as **climacteric**, involves the reproductive system. The climacteric female has undergone **menopause**, the cessation of ovulation and menstruation. Menopause typically begins at 49 or 50 years of age and takes about 2 to 5 years (Berkow & Fletcher, 1987). Experience varies, but the climacteric female can experience "hot flashes," urinary problems, fatigue, insomnia, irritability, and thinning of the vaginal lining resulting in more painful intercourse (Ballinger, 1981; Neugarten, Wood, Kraines, & Loomis, 1963). One long-term health risk, however, is the development of osteoporosis, which was a factor in Danelle's back pain.

Much less is known about the climacteric male. Men usually maintain their reproductive capability until 60 years of age, but some reduction in fertility and frequency of orgasm does occur in middle adulthood (Beard, 1975). As men move towards later adulthood, there are hormonal fluctuations, and there is more variation in the male climacteric pattern (Kimmel, 1980; Weg, 1987).

LATER ADULTHOOD

Because people are living longer, the percentage of Americans over 65 has increased steadily from 4% in 1900 to 12% in 1988. This growth in the oldest segment of the population is expected to continue, reaching 22% by 2030 (USDHHS, 1992). Overall, for Americans born in 1987, average life expectancy was 81.4 years, compared to only 47 years in 1900. This increase is the result of decreases in infant mortality; the development of medical treatments, medications, and vaccines for many previously fatal illnesses; and dietary and other behavioral changes.

Life expectancy, however, is not the same for all Americans. African Americans born in 1987 have a shorter life expectancy than European Americans—only 69.4 years overall. Also, the vulnerability of males reduces their numbers throughout the life span, resulting in a life expectancy of only 79.8 years for those born in 1987 compared to females' life expectancy of 83.7 years.

While, generally, people who are 65 years of age can expect to live an additional 16.4 years, only about 12 of those years can be considered "healthy" (USDHHS, 1992). The implications for social and economic policy of the 4.4 unhealthy years that will be experienced by a projected 12% to 22% of the population are tremendous and that is why **gerontology**—the study of the aging process—has become important today.

Forty-five percent of deaths among those over age 65 are from heart disease, making it the leading cause of death in late adulthood (U.S. Bureau of the Census, 1983). Cancer accounts for an additional 20% of deaths in late adulthood and stroke for 11%. But is ill health inevitable in old age? Some gerontologists believe that it is not. They conceptualize *primary aging* as the physical and largely *genetic* process of gradual deterioration and *secondary aging* as the result of *nongenetic* factors like disease, abuse, and disuse that occur throughout the life span (Busse, 1987; Horn & Meer, 1987). People have control over secondary aging; eating well and keeping active and fit may help delay it. Danelle, by age 67, had been experiencing the chronic pain of osteoporosis for several years. In her case, bone loss resulting from menopause is an example of primary aging, and her less physically active lifestyle is an example of secondary aging.

The percentage of older adults who describe their health as good to excellent is 68%, with about 30% describing it as poor (USDHHS, 1986e). So, although the vast majority of older adults consider themselves to be in good health, it is clear that a large number report problems.

The majority of people over age 65 do have at least one chronic condition (for example, arthritis, hypertension, or heart disease) but they report fewer colds or influenza (AARP, 1986). Some of the chronic conditions result from the physical changes of aging. Older adults can do many of the same activities that younger adults do, but they are slower and have less endurance and strength (Birren, Woods, & Williams, 1980). In addition, both hearing and visual loss progress. These chronic conditions contribute to an increase in accidents of all kinds, including automobile accidents, and exacerbate chronic conditions such as asthma and arthritis (Birren, 1974; Sterns, Barrett, & Alexander, 1985).

The reduction of reserve capacity begun in middle adulthood continues in later adulthood. Older adults have less capacity to deal with stressful situations and chronic health conditions. Even a minor illness can be serious and involve a longer course of treatment because it occurs in the context of reduced reserve capacity. Older adults require more medical care, are hospitalized more frequently, and remain in the hospital longer (Binstock, 1987).

THREE VARIABLES RELATED TO HEALTH ACROSS THE LIFE SPAN

Even though general health status changes at different developmental stages, three variables seem to influence health to a greater or lesser degree across the life span. These variables—stress, personal control, and social support—are among the most extensively researched in health psychology, and they will be encountered throughout Part III. This section provides an introduction to them and explores how they affect health at each stage of development.

STRESS

Stress is a complex phenomenon involving three components: external (environmental) circumstances, a cognitive appraisal of these circumstances, and internal physiological responses. All of these components are considered in Chapter 6, while this section deals primarily with the relationship between developmental stressors and health. Stress is generally believed to affect health adversely, but the experience of being born reminds us that is not always the case.

THE STRESS OF BIRTH Birth is a challenge for both the mother and baby. Imagine yourself spending several hours crammed in the narrow birth canal gradually being squeezed out headfirst. With each contraction, your placenta, umbilical cord, and head are compressed. This results in oxygen deprivation—you literally suffocate temporarily—and, if this is prolonged, you could suffer brain damage or death. If all goes well, you emerge from the warm, dark, secure womb into the cold, bright, bustling, and alien environment of the delivery room.

By physiological measures, birth may be one of the most stressful experiences of life. As depicted in Figure 5.1-1, the newborn's adrenal glands release up to 10 times more catecholamines (epinephrine and norepinephrine) at birth than do men who are exercising. These hormones—involved in the adult "fight or flight" response to threat (see Module 6.1)—are believed to prepare the newborn for adaptation to the first challenges of life outside the womb (Lagercrantz & Slotkin, 1986). They arouse the sympathetic nervous system, helping to clear the lungs of fluid, and they increase metabolism, heart rate, and blood flow to the brain. These biological responses make the newborn more alert, which may facilitate its bonding with the mother. Therefore, the stress of birth appears to be adaptive because it promotes bonding and physical survival.

EARLY AND MIDDLE CHILDHOOD Many common stressors in childhood involve school: bullies, parental pressure to achieve or parental lack of interest in achievements, failing an exam, or conflicts with teachers (Sears & Milburn, 1990). However, young children are also affected by family stress.

Children from families that experience 12 or more stressful life events have more minor illnesses and accidents, are twice as likely to see a doctor for a medical problem, and are 6 times more likely to be admitted to the hospital than children in families that experience 4 or less stressful life events (Beautrais, Fergusson, & Shannon, 1982). Research indicates that children's physiological responses to stress may be related to susceptibility to illness (Jemerin & Boyce, 1990; Lewis, Thomas, & Worobey, 1990).

Stressful events might not be directly related to illness in children. It may be that stressful events reduce *parents'* coping abilities so that children are put more at risk. For example, marital discord and the physical health of four- and five-year-old children are related (Gottman & Katz, 1989). Perhaps marital strife makes parents less effective in teaching cleanliness or safety health behaviors.

Divorce is a major stressor, affecting approximately 1 million children under the age of 18 each year (Wegman, 1986). It also seems to be related to children's health. In comparing the health of 341 first, third, and fifth graders from divorced families to that of 358 similar children from intact families, it was found that children *and* parents in intact families had better health than those from divorced families (Guidubaldi & Cleminshaw, 1985). Of course, there may be other explanations beside divorce. It is even possible that illness contributes to family strain and divorce, rather than the other way around.

Divorce often results in children living in single-parent families. About 20% of European American children and almost 50% of African American children are being raised by single parents (U.S. Bureau of the Census, 1985). Although research has indicated that children are better off in a single-parent home than in a home where two parents are in conflict (Rutter, 1983), there are potential stressors inherent in single-parent homes. First, these homes do not

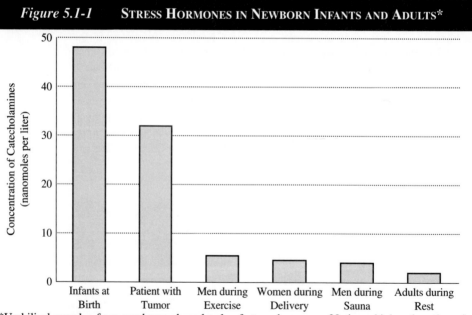

Figure 5.1-1   Stress Hormones in Newborn Infants and Adults*

*Umbilical samples from newborns show levels of stress hormones 20 times higher than those in resting adults. The surge of hormones during birth is also greater than is found in adults who are exercising or under great physical stress.

Source: Lagercrantz, H., & Slotkin, T. A., 1986, The "stress" of being born, Scientific American, 254, 100–107.

have two adults to share the strain and responsibilities of child rearing. Second, single-parent homes tend to have lower incomes, raising the specter of poverty.

ADOLESCENCE Stress is related to depression and the high suicide rate among adolescents as well as to substance abuse and eating disorders (Hendren, 1990). Typical adolescent stressors include physical and sexual maturation, changing relationships to parents, cultural and societal expectations, and peer pressure. These stressors are all initiated by the hormone-mediated processes of puberty. It was once thought that hormones directly influenced adolescent behavior and stress, but there is little research to support this belief (Hendren, 1990). Instead, it appears that adolescent behavior and stress are a *reaction* to the physical changes brought about by the hormones.

Teenage mothers are also more likely to suffer stress (Blinn, 1990; Dillard & Pol, 1982). The younger a woman is when she has her first child, the more tension and sadness she will experience later in life (Brown, Adams, & Kellam, 1981). The incidence of these feelings is 4 times higher in mothers who had their first child when the were less than 18 years of age, compared to those who first gave birth between 25 and 29 years of age.

YOUNG ADULTHOOD Young adults are typically involved in many life transitions: developing relationships, embarking on a career, getting married, and having children. These transitions make young and middle adulthood one of the most stressful periods of life (Moos & Schaefer, 1986). Sixty percent of young and middle adults report that they feel great stress at least weekly, and 27% report that they feel it at least 3 times a week (Prevention Research Center, 1986).

Many young adults become parents, which can entail an even more dramatic increase in stress than does getting married. The birth or adoption of a first child may initiate a crisis for each parent as well as for the marriage (Dyer, 1963; LeMasters, 1957). Even if it is a good experience, parenting still presents new stresses that must be coped with (Hobbs & Cole, 1976; Hobbs & Wimbish, 1977). These new stresses can include changes in the dynamics of family relationships; additional income, housing, and child-care needs; and renewed conflicts with one's own parents. Depending on the person, some will have difficulty coping with these, while others may gain a better sense of self-esteem through competent mastery of them (Valentine, 1982).

MIDDLE ADULTHOOD Stress continues at its highest level early in this period. When children are in their school years, marital satisfaction declines. Yet, marital satisfaction increases and stress decreases when children are grown and beginning independent lives (Schumm & Bugaighis, 1986). Then, middle adults have the time and money to enjoy the fruits of their labors, and advances in medicine and changes in lifestyle and behavior have contributed to people being more fit and healthy well into middle age. They also have years of accumulated life experience, and they may have gained in self-esteem from successful mastery of prior developmental transitions.

LATER ADULTHOOD   Men between the ages of 65 and 74 have the highest rate of attempted suicide of any group (U.S. Bureau of the Census, 1989), and the stress of poor planning for retirement and poor adjustment to it seem to be important factors in suicide attempts among the elderly (Marshall, 1978; Miller, 1978). However, at this age, *completed* suicides are relatively rare. Instead, older men seem to be oriented toward self-destruction—suicidal thoughts and self-neglect—rather than actively pursuing it (Kastenbaum, 1990).

Older adults experience many losses. Stress from grief can affect immune system functioning and increase illness (see Chapter 10), but such changes may only be temporary. In some cases, the health of the survivor actually improves after death, which may bring some relief to the prolonged stress of caring for an ill person (George & Gwyther, 1984).

PERSONAL CONTROL

Personal control is the ability to exert an influence on events in one's life, although, from a strictly cognitive perspective, the *belief* in one's ability to control events may be sufficient when it comes to promoting health and well-being. Control is related to the health behavior model (described in Module 3.2), and predicts whether a person will engage in health enhancing behaviors. Control also mediates the experience of stress.

INFANCY   Infants have not developed the cognitive capacity to exercise conscious control over events, but their reflexes (for example, crying) can elicit responses from caregivers. Nevertheless, the lowest level of personal control in life is during infancy.

EARLY AND MIDDLE CHILDHOOD   Between 6 and 12 years of age, children become more independent, and they begin to develop the cognitive capacity to understand their own behavior and its consequences. This can lead to the potential for more personal control, but it still remains relatively low. Middle childhood is a transition period for cognitive development that ultimately allows most children to assume control over their own health (Burbach & Peterson, 1986; Maddux et al., 1986). Roger Bibace and Mary Walsh (1979) have proposed a six-stage theory of development of children's conceptions of illness (see Box 5.1-1, pp. 182–83) that parallels Swiss psychologist Jean Piaget's (1983) description of general cognitive development.

ADOLESCENCE   As cognitive abilities and independence grow during adolescence, the potential for personal control increases. However, adolescents may not have had enough experience yet to develop a flexible repertoire of coping behaviors. Adolescence is a transition period to maximum personal control.

ADULTHOOD   More than any other age group, adults have the opportunity to assume personal control of their health (USDHHS, 1992). Young adults have the cognitive abilities, independence, and coping experiences to exercise personal control. As an example, the productivity of industrial workers actually *improves* during middle age, because they have more experience and better judgment so there are fewer injuries on the job (Belbin, 1967; Hunt & Hunt, 1974). Experience and wisdom seem to make up for the decline in physical abilities during middle adulthood.

LATER ADULTHOOD   Personal control begins to decline during older adulthood and one of the most dramatic examples is institutionalization of the elderly. Yet, even in institutions, personal control is strongly related to well-being. In a classic study, Langer and Rodin (1976, 1978) conducted an experiment in which some nursing home residents were accorded more personal control and responsibility. Forty-seven residents on one floor of a nursing home were told that they had control over their health care, daily routine, visitors, and leisure time. They were also offered a plant to take care of as they wished (all accepted it). Meanwhile, 44 residents on a different floor of the nursing home, who were similar in sex, age, health, and socioeconomic status, were used as a nontreatment group. They were not accorded personal control and, although also given a plant (they had no choice), were told that the nurse would take care of it. Otherwise, both groups received the same attention from the staff.

At the end of 3 weeks, 93% of those given personal control gained in mental *and* physical well-being and were more alert and active, while 71% of those not given control remained the same or became worse. On follow-up 18 months later, the personal control subjects continued to do better, even though most of the them were now living on different floors. This experiment suggests that institutions should not be warehouses where people are kept dependent until they expire. Instead, older adults can be more active and have a better quality of life even within a nursing home, if they are allowed to control their lives.

In contrast, older adults report *less* of a desire for control, particularly with regard to health matters (for example, Smith et al., 1988; Woodward & Wallston, 1987). They prefer that health professionals make decisions for them. Some health care workers worry that older adults may be less likely to take an active role in their health care when they are most at risk, but perhaps control is less important to people at this stage than the comfort of depending on others.

DEATH AND DYING   Ironically, control remains an issue even at death. Unless death comes suddenly or accidentally, a person usually has some awareness of it and some time to prepare. In all age groups, people strongly prefer to know the truth about their health care and to participate in decision making, even when dying (Justin, 1988). This may seem at odds with the finding that older adults prefer to yield control and to let health care professionals make decisions for them, but the giving up of control may pertain only to routine medical care and not to *decisions* about dying.

Generally, older adults are less anxious about death than others (Bengtson, Cuellar, & Ragan, 1975). A survey of people between 61 and 97 years of age, 40 of whom were voluntarily institutionalized and 40 of whom were not, found that only 1% had a strong fear of death (Myska & Pasewark, 1978). Fifty-one percent were "absolutely unafraid" and 40% were "indifferent."

Box 5.1-1   DEVELOPMENT OF HEALTH COGNITIONS IN CHILDREN

Before age 5, children tend to be egocentric and do not have much flexibility in their thinking. This period is represented by Bibace and Walsh's *phenomenism* and *contagion* stages.

Phenomenism

Illness is defined by single symptoms and the sensation they cause. Children may resort to far-fetched or magical explanations for the symptoms, such as "a demon is in my belly" (Perrin & Gerrity, 1981).

Contagion

Illness is still defined by a single symptom, but children are beginning to understand physical cause. They may realize that some diseases are contagious, but not fully understand the mechanism. They may also think that they are somehow responsible for causing the illness (Brewster, 1982).

Between 5 and 11 years of age, children can use mental symbols (representations of objects and events that are not immediately present) in their thinking, but their learning is still closely tied to physical experience. This period corresponds to Bibace and Walsh's *contamination, internalization,* and *physiological* stages.

Contamination

Children now begin to define illness by multiple symptoms. Their understanding about cause develops further, and they may have a concept that germs or dirt are related to illness. Their understanding of how to prevent contamination is still primitive and they may resort to magical behaviors like sleeping with a protective stuffed animal.

Internalization

Children's internal health locus of control develops during this stage (Perrin & Shapiro, 1985), and they begin to see themselves as capable of preventing illness. They realize that some illness results from contaminants getting inside the body, and they may even understand that lifestyle is related to heart attacks.

Physiological

Children have a more sophisticated understanding of the organs in the body and how their functioning can be disrupted by illness.

Perhaps older adults have had more time to adjust to death with the passing of friends and relatives so they become desensitized. Or, perhaps as their health fails, they experience less pleasure in living. Recently, public attention has focused on new approaches to death and dying—each of which gives people more control (see Box 5.1-2).

SOCIAL SUPPORT

Social support involves both the quantity and quality of one's acquaintances and relationships. How does social support affect health? The social support research is, of necessity, largely correlational and subject to interpretation problems. Although social isolation is related to mortality, the mechanism has still

By age 12, children may be able to apply their mental processes to abstract concepts, and this relates to Bibace and Walsh's *psychophysiological* stage, during which children can appreciate the relationship between illness and abstract psychological phenomena like stress.

Psychophysiological
   Children appreciate that illness is a complex process and that contact with germs does not always lead to disease, nor does avoiding germs always prevent it. They understand that illness may be due to both physiological and psychological causes. This stage lays the foundation for preventive health behavior in children as they enter adolescence.

Research suggests that Bibace and Walsh's stages may not fit all children (Siegal, 1988), but they do provide a framework for understanding cognitive development and the beginning of health beliefs. This theory suggests that efforts to develop positive health behaviors should be directed to children aged 11 or 12—when abstract thinking has developed.

Reaching the psychophysiological stage of understanding illness would seem necessary for preventive health behavior, but not sufficient. Children also need to develop **self-regulation**—the ability to effectively control one's behavior—in order to benefit from their more mature understanding of illness. Self-esteem relates to how well children are able to self-regulate behavior. In a nationally representative sample of children 6 to 12 years old, self-esteem was the most prominent factor relating to children's illness orientations (Lau & Klepper, 1988).

Source: Bibace, R., and Walsh, M. E., 1979. Developmental stages in children's conceptions of illness, in G. C. Stone, F. Cohen, and N. E. Adler, eds., Health psychology—A handbook *(San Francisco: Jossey-Bass).*

not been identified (Coyne & Delongis, 1986; Wallston, Alagna, DeVellis, & DeVellis, 1983). Perhaps socially involved people have more access to information and advice, or perhaps others encourage them to practice better health care or to seek help. Also, people who are more actively involved may feel that they have more control over events in their lives.

Social support is related to the perception of health and to health behavior (Connell & D'Augelli, 1990), and adults with more social ties engage in more health-promoting and fewer risk-taking behaviors (Hibbard, 1988). Intriguingly, there is some evidence that social support may influence the immune system (Cohen, 1988), although the precise mechanisms are not well established (Geiser, 1989).

INFANCY   Infants are entirely dependent on social support and it has major consequences for future development and health. For example, the amount and quality of stimulation in the early environment influences the development of the brain (Boll & Barth, 1981). Brain development, as well as development of an infant's height, weight, and emotional well-being, are dependent on caregivers providing good nutrition through regular and adequate feedings

Box 5.1-2   NEW APPROACHES TO DEATH AND DYING

One new approach to death and dying is an institutional alternative to hospitals called a hospice. A **hospice** provides an alternative to hospital care for people who are terminally ill. The goal of the hospice is to ease the patient's passing in a warm and supportive environment with a minimum of pain. Families are often a central part of the care. Medical care (for example, pain medication) is provided, but aggressive, life-prolonging treatment is not. When compared to hospitals, hospice care may not be any less expensive nor effective in reducing pain or suffering, yet it can result in more peace of mind for both patients and their families (Kane et al., 1984).

Another approach to death that society is grappling with is **euthanasia**—which literally means "mercy killing," usually of terminally ill patients, often in pain, who feel there is little quality left in their lives. Some believe that it represents the ultimate form of personal control over death, but physicians generally believe that their duty is to prolong life, not to shorten it. Many physicians are reluctant to consider euthanasia and actively use medical technology to prolong life. However, a poll taken in 1984 revealed that, while not directly condoning euthanasia, 77% of people (and a majority of both genders, all ages, incomes, and education levels of African and European Americans) agreed that doctors should stop using medical technology to prolong life if a terminally ill person requests it (*New York Times*/CBS, 1984).

The end of life can be difficult for some people to face, but apparently three-quarters of Americans are willing to endorse the individual's right to refuse life-prolonging medical procedures. We ultimately will have to give up life, but perhaps control and a sense of well-being may be preserved to the very end, making the passing a bit easier for all involved.

One of the first sources of social support is the infant's mother.

(Valenzuela, 1990) and supportive parenting (for example, cuddling and physical contact; Ainsfield, Casper, Nozyce, & Cunningham, 1990).

Supportive parenting is also called attachment. **Attachment** is an active, affectionate two-way relationship between parent and child (Bowlby, 1982; Kochanska, 1991). The critical period for attachment is between 1 and 4 years of age and any stressors that interfere during that time are particularly harmful to the child (Barton & Zeanah, 1990).

In forming an attachment, the quality of the mother–infant relationship, her affection, attention, and consistency of responsiveness, are more important than her caretaking skills or the amount of time she spends with the infant (Clarke-Stewart, 1977). Attachment provides the security on which later independence is based. *Nonattached* infants become insecure, anxious, and dependent children.

Infants can influence the development of attachment because almost any behavior they generate—smiling, crying, sneezing, burping—can elicit a response from adults. Unfortunately, babies that are hard to care for, developmentally delayed (showing fewer active behaviors), or seem to react negatively to physical contact are more difficult to form an attachment with (Egeland & Farber, 1984). The term "supportive parenting," however, stresses the need for the *parent* to be understanding and encouraging, since the infant is incapable of it.

What are the health effects for infants who lack supportive parenting? They are twofold, affecting both psychosocial and physical development. Babies that lack a secure attachment are less enthusiastic, persistent, and cooperative at the age of two (Matas, Arend, & Stroufe, 1978); less socially involved, curious, and actively engaged at the age of three (Stroufe, 1979); and less competent and independent at the age of five (Stroufe, Fox, & Pancake, 1983). Some of these characteristics are related to later health, stress, vulnerability, and addiction. However, infants that lack supportive parenting face an even more immediate threat to their survival—failure to thrive.

Failure to thrive is a delay in achieving expected height, weight, or motor development caused by emotional neglect and inattention and not by any known organic factor. It is an excellent example of a biopsychosocial interaction in which stress interferes with biological development (Lobo, 1990). Failure to thrive is likely to occur in a home environment that is disorganized and with a caregiver who is unresponsive or ignores or restricts an infant's activities (Bradley & Casey, 1984). One longitudinal study found that infants from emotionally nonsupportive environments have physical, intellectual, and emotional problems even into their teens (Oates, Peacock, & Forrest, 1985). However, when infants who fail to thrive are raised in a supportive environment, the effects can be reversed (see Box 5.1-3).

CHILDHOOD   Children's major source of social support is the family and their primary caregivers. Poverty greatly influences whether or not caregivers

Box 5.1-3   A CASE OF FAILURE TO THRIVE

Consider the case of a little girl who was admitted to the hospital at eight months of age because she was emaciated (Newberger, Newberger, & Harper, 1976). Unlike other eight month olds, she could not sit up alone and was unresponsive when people talked to her. While hospitalized, she began to gain weight, smile, and play. Eventually she was well enough to return home. However, she was readmitted two months later, again gaunt, feeble, dirty, and apathetic. This time the impoverished mother, who had four children, no husband, and little social support, was treated, too. She received dental care for bad teeth and medicine for a urinary infection. A homemaker, a public health nurse, and a social worker provided psychosocial support. The mother was visited at home daily and received counseling. She had been depressed but gradually recovered and began to find the energy to nurture her baby. The girl, back at home, gained weight, grew taller, and developed normally. By five years of age, she was reported to be doing well.

This case demonstrates the effectiveness of early, comprehensive intervention with failure-to-thrive infants. The treatment was complex, intensive, and expensive, requiring several professionals, but it could probably be streamlined. Fewer professionals could be used, but frequent home visits would probably still be required.

In adulthood, social support is derived from enduring relationships.

are able to provide social support during childhood. Nearly a quarter of all children in the United States live in a family with an income below the federal poverty level (USDHHS, 1992). Poverty has an important relationship to general health. In fact, it may be the most important risk factor for ill health in children (Brown, 1987). Poverty is a barrier to adequate prenatal maternal nutrition and health care, and it is a risk factor for low birth weight. Poor children often start life with a disadvantage, and the effects of poverty can continue after birth as well. Poor children have more illness, psychological disorders, learning disabilities, and behavior problems (Brown, 1987; USDHHS, 1992).

In addition, poor parents are more likely to be hungry, weak, and vulnerable to disease, so they may be unable to provide supportive parenting to their infant (Rosetti-Ferreira, 1978). This problem is further compounded because infants that lack adequate nutrition do not have the energy to engage their mother's or others' attention to get what they need (Lester, 1979).

ADOLESCENCE During the teenage years, new sources of social support develop outside the family. Wider friendship networks increase the potential for social support, but not all social support is beneficial. The values and behaviors of one's peer group may or may not enhance health and well-being.

ADULTHOOD Social isolation is related to higher death rates in middle and later adulthood (Berkman & Syme, 1979), but patterns of social support and isolation begin earlier. One of the most important social relationships is marriage. Married people are generally healthier than those who are separated, divorced, or widowed, with never married people in-between (Doherty & Jacobson, 1982; Verbrugge, 1979). When hospitalized, married people are discharged sooner, and married people have fewer limitations on their activities due to chronic health problems or disabilities. These data are correlational, however, so marriage may contribute to health, or healthy people just may be more likely to get married. Nevertheless, spouses probably do look out for each other, offer mutual support, and encourage each other to lead healthier lives.

Social relationships and activities are related to health even after we account for prior health status, weight, habits (cigarette and alcohol consumption), education, occupation, and age (House, Robbins, & Metzner, 1982). However, the particular social factors differ for men and women. Men have a better survival rate if they are married, have more relationships, are involved in voluntary organizations, and are engaged in active leisure social activities. Women have a better survival rate if they frequently attend religious activities, infrequently watch television, and do *not* enjoy voluntary organizations (a surprising finding). Overall, it seems to be the frequency more than the quality of social contacts that is related to health, but some researchers maintain that the *quality* of social support is also important (Reis et al., 1985).

LATER ADULTHOOD   Just 5% of older people have never married (AARP, 1986). Those who remain married into later adulthood report as much satisfaction with their marriages as younger adults and more than middle aged adults, perhaps due to a reduction of stress from middle adulthood (Gilford, 1986).

Divorce is extremely rare in later adulthood. Only about 4% are divorced (AARP, 1986). However, people who divorce in later adulthood have more difficulty adjusting and feel more hopeless (Chiriboga, 1982), and this probably affects their psychological and physical well-being. Divorced older adults

Box 5.1-4   PETS FOR THE ELDERLY

Can pets replace a dwindling social network? Although they cannot provide the same active help a human can in times of need, pets have been suggested as companions for the elderly (Schmall & Pratt, 1986). Pets offer affection and make older people feel needed (Beck & Katcher, 1983), both of which are important in maintaining psychological well-being. One study suggested that pets have an indirect effect on health, which is achieved by improving morale (Lago, Delaney, Miller, & Grill, 1989). Therefore, pets may be a reasonable substitute for those elderly who are lonely and in need of stimulation.

have higher death rates and are more likely to experience mental illness than married older adults (Uhlenberg & Myers, 1981).

Being married is the most important factor associated with *not* being institutionalized (AARP, 1986). As people age, the likelihood of living in an institution increases (Health Care Financing Administration, 1981). When a spouse dies, it may be more difficult for the older adult survivor to continue living independently. Also, some older adults who have chronic conditions or impairments may require more assistance than a spouse or family can provide. So, a nursing home is the final living situation for many elderly people.

Older adults are the most likely to need and to receive social support, but they also seem to have smaller social networks (Arling, 1987). One problem of aging is that social support networks may suffer attrition so fewer people are available when help is needed. One suggestion is for elderly adults to adopt a pet (see Box 5.1-4).

The ratio of widows to widowers is about five to one across middle and later adulthood (U.S. Bureau of Census, 1990). Survivors of widowhood often face emotional, economic, and health problems (Bound, Duncan, Laren, & Oleinick, 1991). Because women live longer than men, the health problems of late adulthood tend to be women's health problems. The vast majority of morbidity and disability among older Americans is concentrated in the lower socioeconomic level of society (House et al., 1990), and it primarily involves women. Many women end their lives ill, lonely, dependent, and poor (Katz et al., 1983).

Early research suggested that widowhood and bereavement take a toll on health, because shortly after the death of a spouse women have an increase in disabling chronic conditions (Verbrugge, 1979); men are more likely to die (Parkes, Benjamin, & Fitzgerald, 1969); and men and women are more likely to suffer depression and other mental problems (Balkwell, 1985). However, later research revealed that most of the variance in health and depression of women survivors appears to be accounted for by their lower economic status and prior illnesses (Lowenstein & Rosen, 1989; Murrell, Himmelfarb, & Phifer, 1988).

CONCLUSION

Although disease is more common in the elderly, normal aging is not the same thing as disease (Siegler, 1989). Also, most diseases common in later life do not start there, but are influenced by a lifetime of health habits. As noted by Siegler and Costa, "Behaviors at all stages of the life cycle, including health-related behaviors in later life, may well produce changes in life expectancy in the coming decades" (1985, p. 147). Future health may be influenced by the manner in which stress, personal control, and social support change across the life span.

MODULE SUMMARY

1. During pregnancy a variety of teratogens can cause birth defects and affect health across the life span. Low-birth-weight babies have significant health risks and have a high probability of dying during the first year of life, and those who survive may develop poorly. Low birth weight can be prevented in many cases by good prenatal care, but there are many barriers to obtaining it—poverty and the mother's perceptions being among the main ones.

2. During early childhood, accidents are the leading health risk with cancer and heart disease second and third. Although this is a period of many illnesses, they are minor because vaccinations control many of those that were once life threatening. Successfully negotiating frequent illnesses may have beneficial effects on cognitive and emotional development, helping children develop a sense of self-confidence.

3. In middle childhood, the frequency of illness goes down and some children begin to develop a psychophysiological conception of illness and self-regulation.

4. Accidents are the leading cause of deaths among adolescents, and adolescents have a high rate of suicide and homicide.

5. Young adulthood is the most disease-free period of life, with accidents remaining the leading cause of death. At 35, however, disease reasserts itself as cancer and heart disease overtake accidents. People's habits stabilize and they generally do not start smoking or begin other health-compromising habits during this period.

6. During middle adulthood, physical deterioration becomes more obvious and reserve capacity is reduced. The lifestyle diseases are the leading causes of death—heart disease, cancer, and cerebral vascular disease.

7. In later adulthood, the fewest people report that they are in good or excellent health and the majority of people have one or more chronic conditions. Women outlive men, but they often end up in poverty and ill health.

8. Each period of life poses a different set of health challenges, yet three health-related factors—stress, personal control, and social support—can be evaluated across the life span.

9. Physiologically, stress is highest at birth. Stress involves the basic survival needs—adequate nutrition and supportive parenting—in infancy. It is generally low during childhood, but can occur in the form of family problems. Stress is more prevalent in adolescence because of dramatic physical and physiological changes as well as the struggle for independence. It reaches a peak again in early and middle adulthood because of the transitions that take place; and varies in later

adulthood, depending on the circumstances of one's life—widowhood, chronic ailments, retirement, and so on.

10. The *potential* for personal control at birth is zero. It rises very little throughout infancy, and it begins to increase during childhood as cognitive abilities develop. Personal control increases when adolescents gain more independence, and it rises to its highest level in young and middle adulthood. It recedes in older adulthood as older adults relinquish some control, at least over medical matters.

11. The importance of social support is probably no more strongly related to physical health than during infancy and childhood, when the family provides it almost exclusively. In adolescence, social support includes networks of people and activities outside the family. In young and middle adulthood, social support appears to help people to better withstand the stressors of life. And in later adulthood, although social support is still important for well-being, it may become more difficult for some people to obtain due to the shrinking of social networks.

ENVIRONMENT

Is crowding associated with higher blood pressure readings? Can chronic stress caused by the fear of toxic exposure impair immune functioning? Can buildings make people sick? Is job strain related to heart attacks? Is commuting bad for your health? These questions are considered in the study of environmental psychology. *Environmental psychology* "is the study of the interrelationship between behavior and experience and the built and natural environment" (Bell et al., 1990). This definition recognizes the *interrelationship* between people and their environment—that people affect the environment and are affected by it. This definition also acknowledges that the environment includes nature as well as that which people have built.

Environmental psychology is a rich and diverse field (Bell et al., 1990; Heimstra & McFarling, 1978; Holahan, 1986). Many of the efforts of environmental psychologists have been directed at "basic research," studying the mechanisms of environmental perception and cognition and how environmental factors influence mood, behavior, and cognition, although some efforts have been directed at studying health.

ENVIRONMENTAL HEALTH MODEL

Environmental psychologists have proposed several theoretical models to account for interrelationships between the environment and behavior. However, one widely used model—the *environmental stress/adaptational model* (Baum, Singer, & Baum, 1971; Evans & Cohen, 1987; Saegert & Winkel, 1990)—is regarded as particularly comprehensive and mature (Saegert & Winkel, 1990). This model integrates several of the dominant theoretical perspectives in environmental psychology (see Figure 5.2-1).

The model begins with the *environment*—the objective physical conditions that exist independent of the individual. Next comes *perception* of the environment, which is influenced by individual psychological differences. From this point, two cognitive paths diverge. One path represents environments perceived as optimally stimulating and leads to *homeostasis*, or a state of well-being. The other path represents environments perceived as outside the range of optimal stimulation. It leads to *arousal and/or stress* and attempts

Figure 5.2-1 BELL ET AL.'S MODEL OF ENVIRONMENT BEHAVIOR RELATIONSHIPS

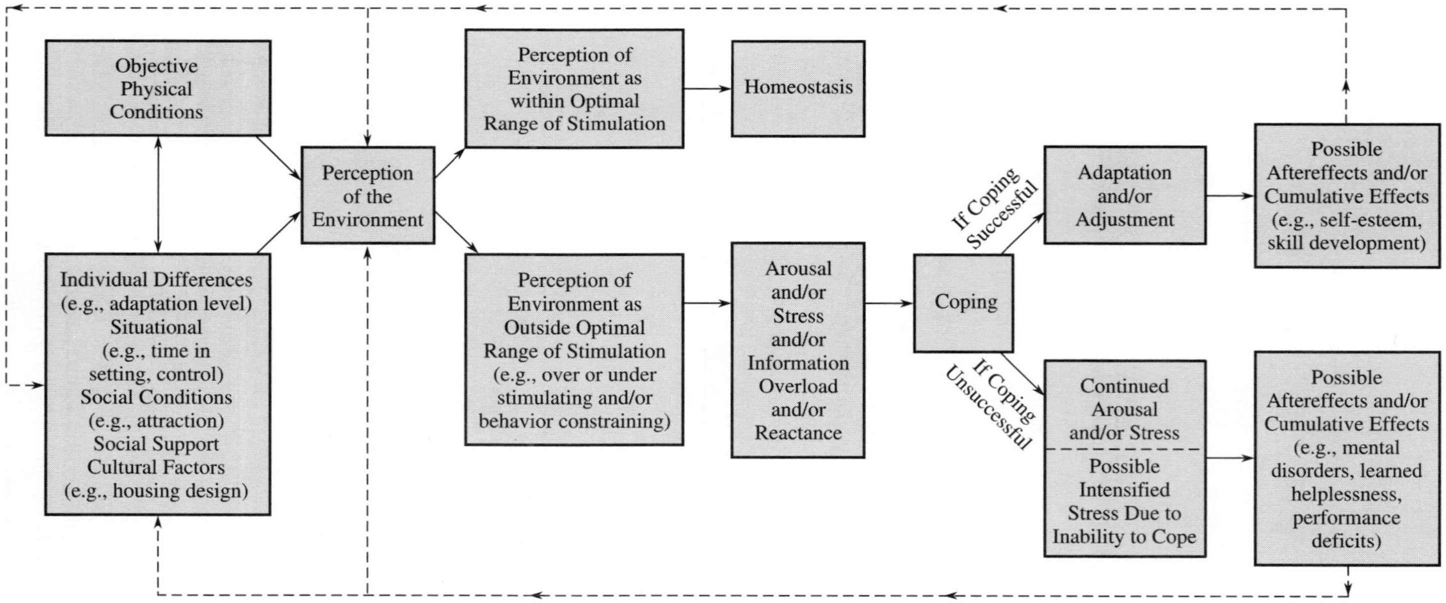

Source: Bell et al., 1990.

the range of optimal stimulation. It leads to *arousal and/or stress* and attempts at *coping*.

Coping also diverges into two paths. One leads to *adaptation or adjustment* and positive after effects. The other pathway leads to *continued arousal or stress* and negative after effects, and it is potentially linked to illness. The stress/adaptational model is helpful from a theoretical viewpoint, although it may not be entirely supported by data (Bell et al., 1990). Although this model has acknowledged limitations, one advantage is that it deals with outcomes that are important to people, particularly health and well-being. It also helps link environmental psychology and health psychology and is similar to the biopsychosocial model of stress used in Chapter 6.

■■■

ENVIRONMENTAL FACTORS RELATED TO HEALTH

Environmental psychologists have researched many physical factors related to psychological and physical well-being. Among them are the topics of this module: density and crowding, disasters and technological catastrophes, and environmental sensitivity. Each of these is viewed as a potential stressor in the environmental stress/adaptational model, but whether well-being is disrupted depends on an individual's perceptual processes and coping abilities.

DENSITY AND CROWDING

Environmental psychologists distinguish between density and crowding (Bell et al., 1990). **Density** is an objective *physical situation* having to do with the number of people in a certain space. High density involves a large population in a limited space and entails *potential* inconvenience. Whether or not an individual is inconvenienced depends on factors such as personality, social relationships, and what is being done in the situation. **Crowding** is a *psychological* state resulting from an individual's perception of high density and his or her subjective experience of confinement. It entails stress and can motivate people to take action to reduce discomfort.

EFFECTS OF CROWDING John Calhoun (1962) conducted early research to study the effects of high density on rats. He started with a small population of rats in pens that were designed to accommodate 40 to 50 comfortably. The rat population multiplied rapidly. As it increased, the normal behavior patterns of the rats changed in ways that affected their health and the survivability of the colony. Some rats became withdrawn and passive, while others became highly aggressive. Reproductive patterns of courting, nest

The density of city streets often leads to feelings of crowdedness.

building, and nursing were disrupted; some males mounted males and females indiscriminately; few females became pregnant; and there were higher rates of miscarriage and infant mortality.

In one very dramatic version of the experiment, an initial colony of 8 mice grew to 2,200 in 6 months, then the population began a steady decline (Marston, 1975). Even when the density fell, normal behavior patterns were never reestablished, and the last mouse in the colony died a little over 4 years after the experiment began.

High density and crowding also affect human behavior. Just as with rats and mice, density and crowding are associated with aggression (and crime) and with withdrawal from interpersonal relationships in humans (Sundstrom, 1978). Also, density and crowding have a significant effect on human performance of complex tasks (for example, Aiello, Epstein, & Karlin, 1975; Evans 1979), but they have little affect on simple tasks (Freedman, Klevansky, & Ehrlich, 1971).

But are any health effects associated with density and crowding in humans? For ethical reasons, correlational studies must be relied on to answer to this question. Epidemiological research suggests that there is a direct relationship between high density and disease. Closer proximity is associated with the spread of contagious diseases (Paulus, 1988). Prison inmates and college students (no comparison implied!) who live in higher density conditions seek medical attention more frequently than those who live in lower density conditions (for example, Werner & Keys, 1988).

Beyond a direct relationship with contagious disease, might density and crowding have other health effects? Generally, people in high-density conditions have higher rates of physiological arousal like increased heart rate or blood pressure (for example, Aiello, Epstein, & Karlin, 1975; Baum & Paulus, 1987; Cox, Paulus, McCain, & Karlovac, 1982), suggesting that they are under stress. High density is also linked to changes in the brain and other organs (Myers, Hale, Mykytowycs, & Hughes, 1971) and to changes in endocrine system functioning (Christian, 1955). All of these changes suggest that density upsets homeostasis.

One field study has looked at the relationship between cardiovascular reactivity—a suspected risk factor for hypertension—and crowding (Fleming, Baum, Davidson, Rectanus, & McArdle, 1987). The blood pressure and heart rate of subjects similar in gender, age, and family income but from two different neighborhoods—one crowded and one not—were compared as they performed a stressful mental task. The subjects from the crowded neighborhood had greater cardiovascular reactivity, as demonstrated by higher increases in blood pressure and heart rate.

Of course, experimental research with humans can only examine the short-term effects of crowding on physiological responses, but it, too, demonstrates arousal linked to stress. One experiment randomly assigned mixed-sex study groups to two different environments—either a small or large room (Evans, 1979). Readings taken before and at three hours after the experiment revealed that the subjects in the high density (small room) condition had higher blood pressure and heart rates. Of course, whether or not these short-term changes affect health in the long term is open to question.

PERSONAL CONTROL   One of the most important variables that mediates the perception of crowding is personal control (Karlin, Epstein, & Aiello, 1978). In this context, personal control has to do with the extent to which an individual can cope with and control the effects of high density in his or her environment. If a person perceives control, he or she is less likely to experience the negative consequences of crowding. For example, you might experience stress in a crowded restaurant where strangers are seated so close to you that they can hear your private conversation. You could exercise personal control in a number of ways. You could ask to change to a private table or leave the restaurant.

Recently, a study was conducted in rural India among nearly 1,500 people in 6 villages where people live in conditions of high density (Ruback & Pandey, 1991). The perception of personal control was significantly related to physical health. However, *current* household density was only weakly related to it and not related at all if the effects of socioeconomic status and demographic factors were removed. But the density of the household where subjects had *grown up* was significantly related to health.

There tends to be a consensus among researchers that lack of personal control interacts with high density to threaten health (for example, Altman, 1978). Rodin (1976; see also Rodin & Baum, 1978) has proposed that this interaction can result in "learned helplessness" which may be related to poor coping responses to stress and depression (learned helplessness is discussed in Module 6.2). Rodin has found that children from higher density living situations are less likely to attempt to control the administration of their rewards and will give up more easily than will children from lower density situations.

SUMMARY   It does appear that there is an association between high density and the spread of contagious illness. Also, evidence is strong that high density and crowding results in short-term physiological changes, some of which are associated with cardiovascular problems, but whether or not these changes result in disease in the long term is not known. In general, the health effects of density and crowding seem to be mediated by perceptions of personal control.

Some enterprising researchers have attempted to treat the effects of crowding by placing subjects into a laboratory analog of a crowded transportation situation (Karlin, Rosen, & Epstein, 1979). The subjects were also randomly assigned to one of three treatments—cognitive reappraisal, progressive muscle relaxation, or imagery—or to a placebo group that received instructions to relax at the beginning but no other treatment. Subjects in the cognitive reappraisal group had the best results in reducing anxiety and arousal to the crowded situation compared to subjects in the other two treatment groups. The fact that cognitive reappraisal was most effective in treating the effects of crowding is consistent with the suspected interaction between personal control and crowding.

DISASTERS AND TECHNOLOGICAL CATASTROPHES

A *natural disaster* is usually defined as natural phenomena—for example, tornados, tidal waves, earthquakes, or fires—that cause death or extensive damage (Bell et al., 1990). You might expect people to panic after a natural disaster, but often they are subdued and withdrawn (Quarantelli & Dynes, 1972). The delayed effects are often consistent with *post traumatic stress disorder*, defined in the *Diagnostic and Statistical Manual III—Revised* (American Psychiatric Association, 1987) as anxiety, depression, insomnia, nightmares, and flashbacks. Studies show that only about one-quarter of people who survive a natural disaster experience psychological symptoms several months later. Those who do have usually lost the most as a result of the disaster (Parker, 1977). This suggests that symptoms are more related to the disruption of community institutions and personal loss than to the experience of the disaster itself (Erikson, 1976).

A nuclear power plant similar to Three Mile Island.

If human beings are responsible for disasters that result in death or extensive damage—for example, airplane crashes, nuclear accidents, toxic waste contamination—the term *technological catastrophe* is usually used. Everything from a temporary blackout to long-term contamination from a nuclear reactor can be a technological catastrophe. Effects from long-term catastrophes can be expected to be long term themselves, and they often stem from uncertainty. Large surveys taken following the Chernobyl nuclear power plant catastrophe revealed that West Germans were uncertain about the danger that remained up to three years after, perhaps with good cause (Peters et al., 1990).

An earlier accident occurred in 1979 at the Three Mile Island Nuclear Power Plant and allowed researchers to study people's reactions to a relatively long-lasting problem. When a combination of equipment failures and human errors caused the core of one of the nuclear reactors to become exposed, very high temperatures were generated, and hundreds of gallons of radioactive water accumulated on the floor of the containment building, which also trapped radioactive gases. The immediate crisis lasted several days, with recurrent rumors and scares, and officials ultimately advised evacuation. Nearby residents lived with the threat of a leak for more than a year before the radioactive gas could be safely released in small amounts.

Over the years since the accident, the residents of Three Mile Island have become a much-researched group. For the purposes of research they are usually compared to other groups—people who live near intact nuclear power plants, alternative fuel power plants, or those who do not live near a power plant. Nearby residents experienced significant distress immediately following the accident (for example, Houts et al., 1980), and longitudinal studies found that the effects of stress continued up to five years after the accident (Davidson, Fleming, & Baum, 1987), even though any threat from the accident had long since been resolved. The people who lived near Three Mile Island tended to have consistently high levels of physiological arousal while awake *and* asleep. Consistent with other research on stress, people who had better social support (Collins, Baum, & Singer, 1983) or who had a greater sense of personal control (Davidson, Baum, & Collins, 1982) tended to have fewer symptoms of stress.

The experience of chronic stress is capable of impairing immune functioning (see Chapter 10), and this is, in fact, what studies of people living near Three Mile Island have found. Some time after the disaster, residents were compared with people from a similar geographic area, and the effects of diet, smoking, and health were controlled. The residents of Three Mile Island had significantly lower concentrations of lymphocytes and lower salivary concentrations of an immunoglobulin, both of which protect the body against infection, and evidence of higher presence of viruses (McKinnon, Weisse, Reynolds, Bowles, & Baum, 1989; Schaeffer et al., 1985).

ENVIRONMENTAL SENSITIVITY

Some concerns about the environment and health do not have to do with disasters and catastrophes. They involve exposure to relatively low levels of supposed allergenic or toxic substances.

SICK BUILDING SYNDROME   Imagine that you are working in a newly constructed or remodeled "tight" building. These buildings are well insulated and sealed from the environment in order to increase their energy efficiency, but their internal environments contain a host of substances, some of which may be toxic or irritating. You are "trapped" inside for eight hours a day with the potential toxins and irritants. Some, but by no means all, workers in so-called tight or "sick" buildings experience three core symptoms of "sick building syndrome" (SBS)—headache, fatigue, and eye irritation—presumably due to substances in the environment (Burge, Hedge, Wilson, Bass, & Robertson, 1987).

One study of 2,369 office workers in 14 buildings found that organic floor dust and the type of carpeting were related to SBS (Skov et al., 1990).

However, another study of 55 sick buildings found that the symptoms people experienced were caused by many factors (Norback, Michel, & Widstrom, 1990). Among these were environmental factors such as the presence of high levels of hydrocarbons, but there were also individual factors. Some of the individual factors were physiological, such as a predisposition to allergies, and some were behavioral, such as whether or not a person smoked cigarettes. A history of cigarette smoking is significantly related to the development of SBS (Bauer et al., 1992), suggesting that smokers may have become sensitized to other substances in the environment. Some researchers have also suggested that SBS may be due to personality factors or a mass somatoform disorder (for example, Bardana & Montanaro, 1986), but others have found no evidence to support this suggestion (Bauer et al., 1992).

From a biopsychosocial perspective, there does not actually have to be a direct physiological effect of toxic exposure for it to affect well-being and possibly health. Just a perceived threat to health is associated with psychological distress (for example, Markowitz & Gutterman, 1986), and the belief that one works in a sick building may be sufficient to cause psychological distress (Ryan & Morrow, 1992).

"ALLERGIC TO EVERYTHING" Recently, a small number of physicians and attorneys have proposed that some people are "environmentally sensitive" and are made medically ill by the general environment. Environmental sensitivity is assumed to be an adverse reaction to commonly encountered foods and substances in the environment (Bell, 1987). Physicians interested in this phenomenon call it "clinical ecology." Patients usually present a variety of symptoms: headaches, fatigue, nausea, aches and pains, numbness, sneezing, coughing, insomnia, anxiety, and irritability brought on by any number of different environments (their workplace, a restaurant, their home, outdoors). They are diagnosed as environmentally ill or "allergic" to the environment, which is broadly defined and includes the indoors, the outdoors, and even additives in food.

People with this diagnosis are subjected to a variety of unconventional medical treatments that are unusual or bizarre (Ferguson, 1991). The treatments can include deliberate "neutralizing" injections of the substance that supposedly caused the symptoms in the first place, similar to the standard treatment for allergy. The treatments can also include the elimination of virtually every presumed toxic substance from the person's environment, including the avoidance of whole environments (Brodsky, 1983). Some patients are told to live in special hypoallergenic homes in isolated communities in the desert. Often, people's lives are so constricted by these special living conditions that they cannot work, so they claim disability. One study of eight people who had filed worker's compensation claims for illness caused by the environment, but who had no evidence of physical injury, found that they had adopted the identity of a disabled person and had developed lifestyles engineered to avoid supposed noxious substances (Brodsky, 1983).

Advocates of clinical ecology maintain that, because of the proliferation of chemicals in the environment, more and more people are environmentally ill. However, typically, classical medicine can find no physical basis for the environmental illness and no physiological abnormalities in people diagnosed as environmentally ill (Ferguson, 1990).

Some researchers suspect that the power of suggestion and the placebo effect are operating to produce many of these symptoms and that the symptoms would not stand up to experimental scrutiny. A recent experiment tested this suspicion (Jewett, Fein, & Greenberg, 1991). Several physicians who identify themselves as clinical ecologists selected 18 subjects who had consistently reported sensitivities to food. Before the experiment, when the clinical ecologists injected them with food extracts, these subjects had responded with various symptoms—nasal stuffiness, dry mouth, nausea, fatigue, headache, disorientation, and depression—and they did not react when they received placebo injections under these single-blind conditions. This would seem to provide support for the clinical ecology hypothesis.

However, when the experiment was conducted in these same physicians' offices under double-blind conditions, the results were quite different. Each subject participated in 20 sessions and received a series of random injections consisting of either food extracts or placebo. The subjects' rates of symptom response to the extracts or placebo were the same: They experienced symptoms with 27% of the injections that contained extracts, but they also reported symptoms with 24% of the placebo injections. Furthermore, neutralizing doses given to treat the supposed symptoms worked equally well, relieving symptoms whether they had been in response to a real extract or placebo.

These results suggest that, at least for these subjects, sensitivity to food extracts was all in their minds. Apparently, when the physicians injected the patients previously, they had somehow communicated which was the extract and which was the placebo. Results such as these have led researchers and medical authorities to go so far as to call clinical ecology a cult, and the treatments used "pseudo-allergic medicine hiding behind . . . fringe approaches" (Stevenson, 1991, p. 9).

The clinical ecology debate presents important issues for psychology (Edwards & Owens, 1984). First, the symptoms of environmental illness resemble those in somatization disorder, suggesting a psychological basis. Yet, from a biopsychosocial perspective, there is also the recognition that the environment may play a role in psychological disorders (Krop, 1986). Therefore, on one hand, food and chemical sensitivities may be another factor to be considered with those that are related to health and disease (Bell, 1987), whereas on the other hand, being "allergic to everything" may be the result of an individual's psychological makeup, perhaps a sign of somatization. Psychological research may be helpful in resolving questions about environmental sensitivity (Edwards & Owens, 1984).

THE WORK ENVIRONMENT

The classical approach to health in the work environment is concerned with direct physical hazards from contaminants and accidents. In contrast, this section involves a more contemporary approach by focusing on psychosocial factors in the work environment that are related to health.

RISKY BUSINESS

Some environments expose workers to a variety of physical, chemical, and biological hazards that are direct risks in disease (House & Smith, 1989), and in U.S. private industry, 1 in 10 workers experiences an injury every year, and 4 in every 100 of these workers will remain disabled from their injury (Hatfield, 1990). The 10 leading work-related diseases and injuries identified by the National Institute for Occupational Safety and Health (1988) are listed in Table 5.2-1.

The rate of work-related diseases and injuries is not the same across all types of jobs; people who work in different occupations have different rates of

---

Table 5.2.1   TEN LEADING WORK-RELATED DISEASES AND INJURIES

Occupational lung disease

Musculoskeletal injuries

Occupational cancers

Severe occupational traumatic injuries

Cardiovascular diseases

Disorders of reproduction

Neurotoxic disorders

Noise-induced loss of hearing

Dermatologic conditions

Psychological disorders (neuroses, personality disorders, and alcohol and drug dependency)

illness and death. For example, the California Occupational Mortality Survey recently reported that the suicide rate among European American male dentists and doctors is 121% above the average for European American males in other occupational groups; the death rate from breast cancer in secretaries and typists is 33% above the average for European Americans and 74% above the average for African Americans; and the death rate from hypertension in roofers is about 200% above the average for African and European Americans (Roan, 1990).

Many elements may contribute to these variations in mortality. One may be the diversity of the work environment: an executive in an office, an assembly worker in a manufacturing plant, or a U.S. ranger in a national park. However, we cannot simply compare illness, injury, or death rates in various *occupations* or *environments* to determine which are hazardous to health because other factors are also involved. For example, although secretaries and typists both have above average mortality rates from breast cancer, the rate for African Americans is more than twice that of European Americans. Also, occupations are directly related to socioeconomic status, which itself has a role in health.

Therefore, environmental psychologists have developed a contemporary approach to health in the work environment that also focuses on psychosocial factors. Psychosocial factors are related to general well-being and, through it, they may affect job performance and safety as well as health. Many environmental features—air quality, noise, heat, ergonomic conditions (engineering of the work station), and privacy—affect worker satisfaction and mental health (Enander & Hygge, 1990; Klitzman & Stellman, 1989), and environmental psychologists take these variables and others into account in an attempt to maximize productivity, satisfaction, and well-being on the job. One of the most researched environmental factors is occupational stress, which is related to health in a variety of different occupations (Levi, 1990).

OCCUPATIONAL STRESS

Job stress is associated with psychological and medical problems (Levi, 1990; Mackay & Cooper, 1987; Revicki & May, 1985), and job stress may erode a worker's ability to resist other health risks such as accidents (for example, Guastello, 1992), thereby acting as an indirect factor in some illnesses. Consider the "workaholic" corporate executive and an air traffic controller. Both have high levels of responsibility and high work loads. No doubt executives can have high job stress, but other jobs can also be stressful (Smith, Colligan, Horning, & Hurrel, 1978). For example, think of the air traffic controller in a busy airport. Within a hundred miles of the airport are dozens of planes. The controller must keep track of all of the planes, juggling arrivals and takeoffs which occur every three minutes, and integrating new arrivals into the holding pattern. One miscalculation and disaster could result. The executive may spend a lot of time away from work preoccupied with decisions that have to be made, but all of the controller's decisions are immediate and "on-the-job." However, the consequences of the controller's decisions are also immediate, while the consequences of the executive's decisions may not be known for a long time. Who has the more stressful job?

Jobs characterized by *high demand* (high work loads) and *low control* (low decision-making latitude) have a higher incidence of stress-related illnesses. Chronic high demand/low control work produces *job strain*. Therefore, an executive in a high demand/high control job may not have as much strain as someone in a moderate demand/low control job, and executives tend to have high control.

Secretaries, construction workers, farm workers, painters, laboratory technicians, machine operators, and waiters/waitresses are among the high job strain occupations (Smith et al., 1978). Why waiters/waitresses? Because job demands are high (they must satisfy the boss, cook, and customers) and control is low (they do not determine the menu or the prices, prepare the food, or govern how fast it is prepared). In a recent comparison of six occupations (from freight handlers to air traffic controllers to physicians), waiters reported the most unfavorable working conditions *and* they had the most cardiovascular risk factors (Theorell et al., 1990).

Not all work-related stress is a direct result of the job, however (Keita & Jones, 1990). Stress is mediated by other factors, such as a worker's family environment and the availability of adequate child care (for example, Bhagat & Ford, 1990; Zedeck & Mosier, 1990). Job strain may also vary as a function of economic status or race. Lower socioeconomic groups experience greater levels of job stress than higher socioeconomic groups (for example, Green, 1989), and some racial groups may experience stress at work differently than other groups (for example, Myers, 1982). For example, for African Americans, job stress may be compounded by actual or perceived racial discrimination.

HEALTH EFFECTS Job strain is related to several health problems. Among them are an increased risk of heart attack (Krantz, Contrada, Hill, & Friedler, 1988). High demand/low control jobs, particularly if they are combined with low social support, carry twice the risk of heart attack than jobs with low demand/high control and high social support (Johnson & Hall, 1988). One study of 215 men, 30 to 60 years of age, at 7 urban worksites (ranging from a newspaper typography department to a stock brokerage firm) found that job strain is directly related to underlying causes of heart attack: hypertension and structural changes in the heart (Schnall et al., 1990). In addition, pregnant women who experience job strain are twice as likely to deliver low-birth-weight, preterm infants as those who do not (Homer, James, & Siegel, 1990).

PSYCHOLOGICAL INTERVENTION IN THE WORKPLACE Research by environmental psychologists, industrial/organizational psychologists, and, more recently, health psychologists has helped to advance the cause of worker well-being by sufficiently increasing knowledge about job strain to make specific recommendations (Keita & Jones, 1990). Applied psychologists primarily take consultative roles in business and government, working to implement programs on an institutional level (Gregory & Burroughs, 1989). They find ways to make companywide changes that reduce job stress.

New roles for clinical and counseling psychologists in the workplace have also been envisioned (Timpe, 1990). They provide direct clinical services to workers experiencing stress (Keita & Jones, 1990). Cognitive stress management techniques have already been implemented in the workplace (Henrich, 1989). Physical fitness programs have also been used at the worksite and have reduced health care costs, absenteeism, and turnover (Gebhardt & Crump, 1990).

Job stress reduction offers obvious advantages to employers. Healthier employees are more likely to be fit, at work, and productive and less likely to be utilizing costly health insurance programs. In addition, job stress has other disadvantages besides illness that may be undesirable to an employer. For example, workers who do *not* have control—who cannot participate in decisions about their jobs—have higher rates of absenteeism, job turnover, and dissatisfaction, and lower rates of performance (Cooper & Marshall, 1976).

The implementation of health-promoting programs in the workplace has met with some resistance (Scofield & Frank, 1989). Barriers arise from managers' lack of awareness of environmental and job stress issues and their relationship to health, managers' own myths and misperceptions about stress and health, a general business orientation toward short-term results, and previous misguided behavioral interventions that have failed. Because of the failure of prior misguided interventions, psychologists must accept part of the blame for resistance to workplace health-promotion programs.

■■■■■

THE URBAN ENVIRONMENT

Cities are usually thought of as unhealthful environments offering too much of everything: too many people, too much dirt, and too much stimulation. Many of the environmental factors related to illness are found to a greater degree in urban areas. Yet, cities have come to dominate life in the industrialized world, so they must offer some benefits. There are, in fact, positive aspects to urban living, at least for some people (Bell et al., 1990). The stimulation that cities provide, although undesirable to some, may be just right for others (Krupat, 1985). Cities provide concentrations of services and cultural and recreational activities, and they can have an effect on how people relate. For example, the concentration of an ethnic group in a city can strengthen interrelationships and support (Fischer, 1976). However, there are negative health consequences of urban living, at least for some people.

The stress/adaptational model can be applied to the urban environment to help explain the benefits as well as its negative health effects. Some individuals may find the high level of stimulation that cities provide optimal for internal homeostasis. Only when environmental conditions are outside the perceived range of optimal stimulation do they lead to arousal, stress, and attempts at coping. Also, some individuals may have sufficient coping abilities to adapt to the conditions of urban living. Only in the absence of successful coping would urban living lead to continued arousal, strain, and possibly ill effects on health.

HEALTH EFFECTS

Psychologically, people who live in rural areas seem to be better off. They report that they are happier, more optimistic, and have higher levels of interpersonal trust than people who live in urban areas (Gallup Opinion Index, 1973; National Opinion Research Center, 1987). Research suggests that people who live in cities have more illness, but not uniformly so. Respiratory diseases linked to pollution (for example, emphysema, bronchitis) are more prevalent in urban areas (Ford, 1976). Also, hypertension and heart disease are more common in urban areas, but primarily in cities where the pace of life is faster (Levine, Lynch, Miyake, & Lucia, 1989).

When we are considering health in relation to urban and rural living, it is necessary to take into account several differences that may affect the reporting and incidence of illness. Cities have a higher concentration of medical specialists and medical facilities and they tend to be better (Dillman & Tremblay, 1977). Also, people may become ill in a rural area, then move to an urban area for the higher level of care (Srole, 1972). However, overall, urban living does appear to be more stressful than rural living and living in urban areas does seem to contribute to illness (Burton, 1990).

COMMUTING

Some people hope to have the best of both worlds by living outside urban areas and commuting to work. However, commuting can also be hazardous to health. Most of the research on commuting stress involves automobile drivers, although commuting long distances on a daily basis in a crowded environment (carpool, bus, or train) can be stressful regardless of the method of transportation (for example, Singer, Lundberg, & Frankenhaeuser, 1978).

Research has demonstrated that while drivers are exposed to rush hour traffic, they undergo a variety of physiological stress responses (Aronow et al., 1972; Bellet, Roman, & Kastis, 1969; Hunt & May, 1968, as cited in Bell et al., 1990). These include increased heart rate, blood pressure, and secretion of catecholamine. Even more ominously, exposure to rush hour traffic causes chest pain and cardiac arrhythmia (Aronow et al., 1972; Taggart, Gibbons, & Sommerville, 1969). This occurs more commonly in people with coronary artery disease, but also in others.

Commuters impeded by slowed, constrained traffic.

A series of studies on the behavioral effects of commuting has resulted in the notion of "impedance"—the extent to which commuters are slowed or constrained during their trip to work (Novaco, Stokols, Campbell, & Stokols, 1979; Stokols & Novaco, 1981). Distance and time are good objective indicators of impedance. Low impedance commuters spend fewer than 12.5 minutes and travel fewer than 7.5 miles either way to work, while high impedance commuters spend between 30 and 75 minutes and travel between 18 and 50 miles each way.

These studies find that people's appraisal of their commute as inconvenient and congested is related to their satisfaction level. The more they perceive their commute as congested, the less satisfied they are and the tenser they feel when they arrive at work. Interestingly, the highest level of stress-linked physiological arousal is found in people with high impedance who had an internal locus of control. However, this does not mean that these "internals" actually suffered the effects of stress because they also coped better with it and were better able to master it. (Arousal, locus of control, and stress are described in more detail in Module 6.2.)

COUNTERACTING THE URBAN ENVIRONMENT

Recently, experimental research has suggested that experience in the natural environment (backpacking in the wilderness) has restorative effects on psychological well-being and improves cognitive performance in urban dwellers

(Hartig, Mang, & Evans, 1991). The restorative effect of natural wilderness environments was greater than either nonwilderness environmental exposure or passive relaxation. It has also been suggested that natural environmental stimuli might reduce stress and blood pressure and increase relaxation if they were incorporated into our work and housing environments (Ornstein & Sobel, 1989).

MODULE SUMMARY

Environmental psychologists have identified a number of factors that are part of the built and natural environment and have a direct and indirect influence on health. The environmental stress/adaptational model helps integrate these factors conceptually with health psychology. Read this point-by-point summary of environmental health psychology before continuing to Part III:

1. The environmental stress/adaptational model holds that individual differences in perception of the objective physical environment can lead to a state of optimal stimulation, well-being, and homeostasis or to arousal. Arousal then leads to coping attempts that can result in either adaptation and positive after effects or continued arousal and stress.

2. Density is objective and has to do with the number of people in a given space. Crowding is a psychological state dependent on a perception of high density and the subjective experience of confinement. High density is linked to the spread of infectious disease. High density and crowding are associated with short-term physiological changes. The lack of feelings of personal control interacts with high density and can lead to poor coping responses.

3. Natural disasters produce psychological problems such as post traumatic stress disorder, but symptoms seem to be related to the disruption of community institutions as much as to the disaster itself. Human beings are responsible for technological catastrophes, which can produce significant stress for those affected. When the stress is long term, it can affect immune system functioning.

4. Exposure to some toxic chemicals can cause psychological symptoms, but whether this is through direct damage to the central nervous system or a subjective psychological reaction is difficult to sort out.

5. "Sick building syndrome" causes three symptoms—headache, fatigue, and eye irritation—in "tight," well-insulated buildings. It appears to be a physical reaction to environmental substances and not related to personality factors or psychopathology. Cigarette smoking is positively correlated with sick building syndrome.

6. People who are environmentally sensitive or "allergic to everything" report a variety of symptoms and have been subjected to unconventional and bizarre treatments such as living in specially constructed, isolated homes. Placebo-controlled research suggests that being allergic to everything may be the result of people's psychological makeup or a sign of somatization. Nevertheless, psychological research can be particularly helpful in resolving these issues.

7. In addition to direct physical hazards, environmental psychologists focus on psychosocial factors in the workplace that are related to health, safety, and job performance.

8. Job strain is produced by high demand/low control jobs. It is linked to increased risk of heart attack in men and low birth weight infants.

9. Urban living offers some benefits, but many of the environmental factors related to illness are found in cities. The stress/adaptational model helps explain how individual differences in perception and coping account for the positive and negative effects of urban living. People who live in rural areas are generally healthier psychologically and have fewer illnesses. Excursions into the natural wilderness appears to have restorative effects on the psychological well-being of city dwellers.

10. Commuting is stressful, and the more impedance (in terms of time and distance traveled), the greater the stress level. Commuting stress is linked to increases in heart rate, blood pressure, and secretion of catecholamine.

BIOPSYCHOSOCIAL FACTORS IN ILLNESS

How do biopsychosocial factors affect illness? In Part III, we explore this question by discussing how psychosocial factors relate to problems in the body's physiological systems. To accomplish this, Part III is organized around five physiological systems. Each system's function and organization  *is introduced with respect to the role it has in maintaining overall health and well-being. The psycho-social aspects of specific health problems pertaining to that sys– tem are then covered in modules.*

Part III is divided into two sections. Because of the importance of the nervous and endocrine systems in health psychology, each of the four chapters in Section 1 focuses on health problems related to them. The nervous and endocrine systems should be familiar territory to students of psychology and interesting to anyone because they involve the brain, which is the organ of the mind. The first three chapters in Section 1 are devoted to some of the most far-reaching health problems facing medical psychologists: stress (Chapter 6), pain (Chapter 7), and addiction (Chapter 8). The last chapter in Section 1 covers disability and rehabilitation (Chapter 9).

In Section 2, our exploration of the biopsychosocial factors in illness broadens to encompass four additional physiological systems, each covered in its own chapter.

Chapter 10 deals with the immune system and health topics that are very much in the news today—infectious disease, cancer, and AIDS. The cardiovascular and respiratory systems are covered in Chapter 11, which includes health problems that are responsible for more adult deaths than any other cause—heart disease and stroke. The digestive system is covered in Chapter 12, along with nutrition, appetite, eating behavior, weight control, and eating disorders—concerns with which many people in our society seem to be preoccupied. Finally, the reproductive system is the topic of Chapter 13, which includes a discussion of the human sexual response and sexual dysfunctions.

NERVOUS AND ENDOCRINE SYSTEMS: FUNCTION AND ORGANIZATION

Did you ever wonder how the many complex organ systems of the body are coordinated for the well-being of the whole? How is it that respiration and heart rate speed up when we need extra energy to run a race but slow down when we are resting? What accounts for the regulation of the cycles of sleeping and waking, of eating, and of reproduction? How does psychological stress affect physical health? How do we become conscious of an injury to the body? As these questions indicate, the body is a complex system.

Two important ingredients help any system to survive and thrive: (a) effective decision making that involves goal determination, planning, and efficient allocation of resources; and (b) effective communication within the system. In many ways, the body is organized, survives, and thrives on the basis of these two ingredients. In the body, communication is handled by the nervous and endocrine systems, and the brain is the processing center and decision maker. As suggested in Chapter 1, the brain is the executive homeostatic coordinator.

Information can be transmitted as fast, but short-lasting messages through the nervous system, or it can be transmitted as slow, but long-lasting messages through the endocrine system. Think of the nervous system as a telephone network and the endocrine system as a postal service. Neural fibers run throughout the body linking the various organs, much like telephone lines run throughout a community linking the homes and businesses. These neural fibers converge in the brain like telephone lines converge in a central switching facility.

In contrast, the endocrine system is made up of glands located throughout the brain and body. It has no rigid wiring, so it is more like a postal service. The endocrine system communicates through hormones released into the bloodstream, and these chemical messengers are "addressed" to different organs. Let us examine how these two important systems function.

■

NERVOUS SYSTEM

We begin our discussion of the nervous system by describing its basic elements, the neurons and neurotransmitters. We then describe the nervous system's important divisions responsible for relaying information within the body, ending with a detailed look at the brain.

NEURONS AND NEUROTRANSMITTERS

The basic unit of the nervous system is the **neuron**, a single cell that is specialized to receive, process, and transmit information electrochemically. Neurons consist of three parts: soma, dendrites, and axon. Figure I-1 shows the basic structure of a neuron. The **soma** or cell body contains the nucleus and is where most of the cell's chemical processes are carried on. Tree-like structures called **dendrites** project from the soma and receive messages from other neurons. The **axon** is the longer projection from the soma. It carries messages and can be thought of as the wire strung along telephone poles. The axons of some neurons are covered with a waxy, white substance called *myelin*, which speeds up transmission. When axons reach the dendrites and soma of other neurons, they split into branches that end in small knobs called **terminal buttons**. The terminal buttons do not actually touch other neurons; in between them is a microscopic, fluid-filled gap called a **synapse**.

Communication originates in the soma as an electrical impulse that travels along the axon ending at the terminal buttons. The electrical impulse causes the release of neurotransmitters that flow across the synapse to the next neuron. **Neurotransmitters** are molecules that either *excite* the receiving neuron, *increasing* its potential to transmit a new impulse, or *inhibit* the receiving neuron, *decreasing* its potential to transmit a new impulse. Table I-1 lists some of the neurotransmitters that may be important in illness and health.

The nervous system also has other cells. One type, called *neuroglia* or simply *glia*, provide a structural framework for neurons and are involved in important supportive metabolic functions for them. Glia cells appear to pass nutrients from the blood to the neurons and to return waste products from the neurons to the blood. In this capacity, glia cells probably function as a **blood-brain barrier**, protecting the delicate neurons from toxins and infectious agents that may be present in the blood (Marieb, 1989).

Neurons are grouped into several divisions, depending on their location and function within the body. Figure I-2 depicts the organizational divisions of the nervous system. The most important division is between the central nervous system and the peripheral nervous system. The *central nervous system* consists of the brain and spinal cord—it is where information *processing* takes place. The **peripheral nervous system** consists of all of the neural pathways that lie outside the brain and spinal cord—it is most like a network of tele-phone lines carrying messages to and from distant locations.

PERIPHERAL NERVOUS SYSTEM

The peripheral nervous system is subdivided into the somatic nervous system and the autonomic nervous system. The **somatic nervous system (SNS)** is made up of neural pathways, called *afferent* pathways, that carry information *from* the periphery of the body *to* the spinal cord and neural pathways, called *efferent pathways*, that carry information *from* the spinal cord *to* the skeletal

---

Figure I-1   **STRUCTURE OF A NEURON**

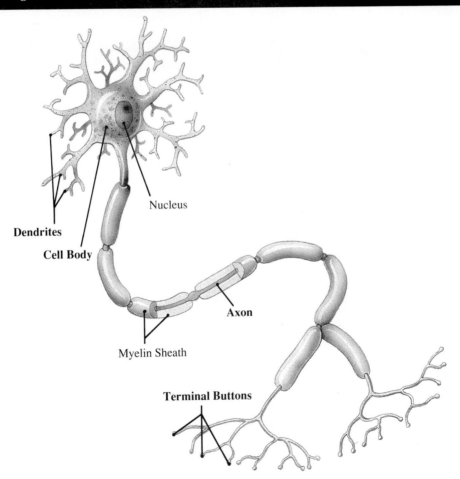

Nucleus

Dendrites

Cell Body

Axon

Myelin Sheath

Terminal Buttons

muscles. The afferent pathways transmit sensory information to the spinal cord, where it travels to the brain—for example, the pressure and warmth of someone holding your hand. The efferent pathways transmit commands down the spinal cord to the muscles—for example, to squeeze that person's hand. The brain is wholly dependent on the somatic nervous system for sensory information regarding touch, pressure, movement, external temperature, and pain, and to move the muscles of the body.

The **autonomic nervous system (ANS)** also consists of a network of neural pathways running throughout the body. However, it is entirely separate from the SNS. Like the efferent somatic nervous system pathways, ANS pathways carry information *from* the brain and spinal cord *to* various organs. The difference is that the ANS has a specialized role in maintaining survival. Through the ANS, the brain is able to exert control over the activities of various organs, either to promote a relaxed state of homeostasis in the body or to

Table I.1   NEUROTRANSMITTERS AND THEIR IMPLICATIONS FOR HEALTH

NEUROTRANSMITTER	AREA SECRETED	ROLE IN HEALTH	COMMENTS
Acetylcholine	Motor cortex	Decreased in Alzheimer's disease	Insecticides increase disease
Norepinephrine	Brain stem, limbic system, cortex	Autonomic arousal, stress response	Release enhanced by amphetamines; removal blocked by cocaine
Dopamine	Midbrain, hypothalamus	Deficit in Parkinson's disease, linked with schizophrenia	Release enhanced by amphetamines; uptake blocked by cocaine
Serotonin	Brain stem, limbic system, cerebellum, hypothalamus, pineal gland, spinal cord	May have a role in sleep	Blocked by LSD
Endorphins	Hypothalamus, limbic system, pituitary, spinal cord	Reduces perception of pain	Effects mimicked by morphine, heroin and methadone
Substance P	Midbrain, cortex, hypothalamus	Pain transmission	

immediately arouse it to prepare for a threat. Figure I-3 shows the divisions and pathways of the autonomic nervous system.

There are also two subdivisions of the ANS, one corresponding to the relaxed homeostatic state and one corresponding to the aroused state. The *sympathetic division mobilizes* the body for action by concentrating energy resources for muscle activity. This produces a state of high arousal: digestion slows; heart rate, respiration, and blood pressure increase; blood is shunted away from the periphery to lessen bleeding in case of injury and toward the muscles for activity; and the pupils dilate for far vision. The *parasympathetic division demobilizes* the body and promotes energy conservation: digestion increases; heart rate, respiration, and blood pressure decrease; and the pupils constrict to improve near vision.

One of the first researchers to study the ANS was Walter Cannon (1932). The sympathetic response, which Cannon called "fight-or-flight," is triggered by a threat. Imagine you are in the wild being stalked by a ferocious animal and that you fear you might end up as its dinner. Fighting or fleeing are the two options open to you, and the rush of nervous energy that you would feel in this situation is evidence of sympathetic nervous system activity preparing your body for either course of action.

Figure I-2   **ORGANIZATIONAL DIVISIONS OF THE NERVOUS SYSTEM**

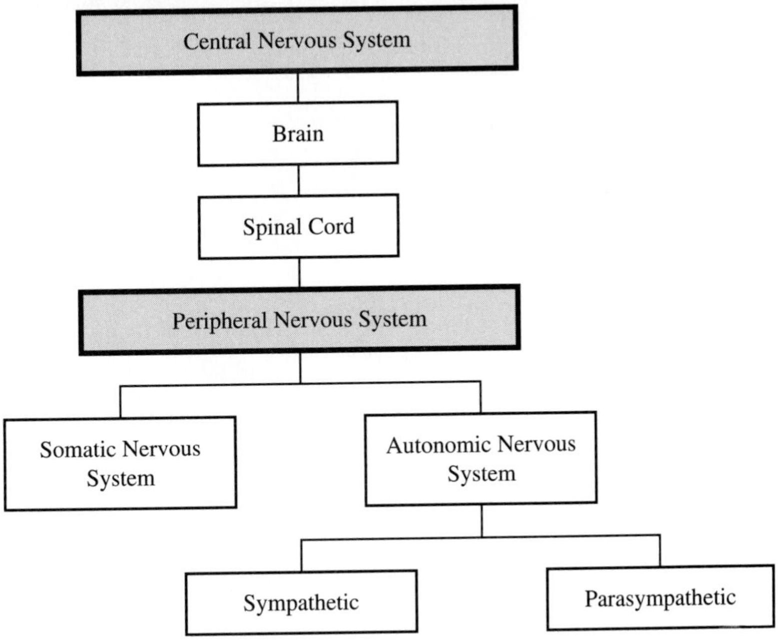

Figure I-3 DIVISIONS AND PATHWAYS OF THE
AUTOMATIC NERVOUS SYSTEM

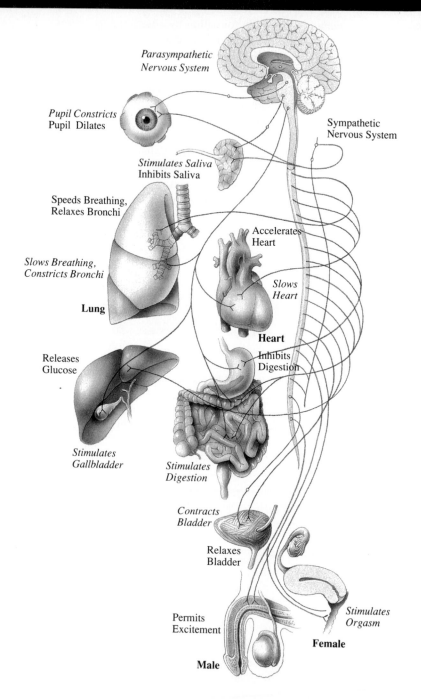

Parasympathetic
Nervous System

Pupil Constricts
Pupil Dilates

Sympathetic
Nervous System

Stimulates Saliva
Inhibits Saliva

Speeds Breathing,
Relaxes Bronchi

Accelerates
Heart

Slows Breathing,
Constricts Bronchi

Slows
Heart

Lung

Heart

Releases
Glucose

Inhibits
Digestion

Stimulates
Gallbladder

Stimulates
Digestion

Contracts
Bladder

Relaxes
Bladder

Stimulates
Orgasm

Permits
Excitement

Female

Male

CENTRAL NERVOUS SYSTEM

The **central nervous system (CNS)** is the control center for communication within the nervous system. The CNS (a) receives information about the world through the sensory organs and the somatic nervous system; (b) determines goals, makes plans, and allocates physical resources; and (c) controls muscle activity through the somatic and arousal through the autonomic nervous systems.

The CNS contains two subdivisions—the brain and spinal cord—which are encased in the skull and spinal vertebrae. The **spinal cord** is the major pathway between the brain and the peripheral nervous system. However, more than just a pathway, the spinal cord is actually an extension of the brain itself and simple information processing takes place there, such as controlling reflexive muscle movement like the knee-jerk reflex.

The spinal cord runs from the base of the brain to the tail bone. Peripheral nervous system pathways enter and exit between the vertebrae, and each level of the spinal cord is linked to different areas of the body in a hierarchical order. That is why damage to the cord in the lower back results in **paraplegia**, loss of function of the lower part of the body, usually the legs, whereas damage at the shoulders results in **quadriplegia**, loss of function in the lower and upper body, involving the legs, arms, and other functions.

Our exploration of the nervous system is now nearly complete, with the exception of its decision-making and control center, the **brain**. The philosophical debate between mind/body dualism and holism described in Chapter 1 may actually be easy to resolve when the role of the brain is considered.

The brain is unarguably part of the body, and it is the center for control of homeostasis and most other body systems. It exercises control over behavior by communicating with the muscles through the SNS, and it exercises control over other organs by communicating through the ANS and the endocrine system. At the same time, the brain is the organ of the mind and consciousness. On the one hand, the mind and consciousness are the products of brain activity. When there is little or no brain-wave activity in the cortex, a person is said to be in a *coma*—that is, without consciousness (and may even be "brain dead"). On the other hand, by consciously directing and controlling our thoughts (our minds), we can alter the activity of our brains, as demonstrated through biofeedback. At that point, we are, in a sense, "using consciousness" to affect the brain. The mind can be said to be acting on the brain and, through it, the body. Let us examine in more detail this most interesting of organs, the brain, which consists of several divisions (Figure I-4).

HINDBRAIN   Due to its importance in regulating basic bodily functions, the *hindbrain* is believed to have evolved before the other parts of the brain. It consists of the **brainstem**, a bulge in the spinal cord where it enters the skull. The brainstem contains two recognizable structures. The **medulla** regulates non-conscious processes such as breathing and circulation of the blood, and the

Figure I-4 DIVISIONS AND STRUCTURES OF THE BRAIN

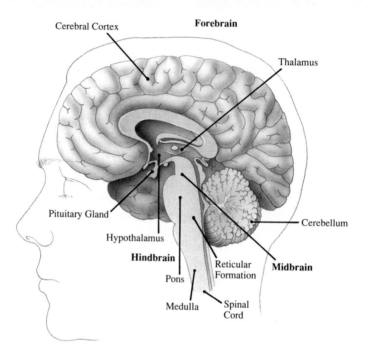

Forebrain, Midbrain, and Hindbrain with Some Associated Structures

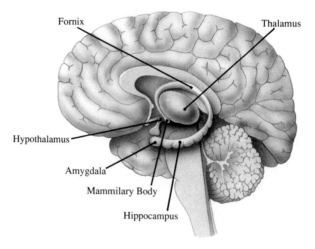

Some Limbic System Structures

pons regulates sleep and arousal. The pons also contains a bridge of fibers that connect the brain stem with the cerebellum, the other major structure of the hindbrain. The **cerebellum** or "little brain" is a large and distinctive structure attached to the back surface of the brainstem. It is involved in the coordination of movement, equilibrium, and balance, and it mediates commands for voluntary muscle movements that originate from other brain centers. Damage to the medulla and pons critically affects survival and is often fatal because respiration and circulation are disrupted, whereas damage to the cerebellum is not usually fatal but disrupts fine motor activities such as writing or playing sports.

MIDBRAIN The *midbrain* is a small region located above the brainstem. Several midbrain structures are concerned with relaying sensory (afferent) and motor (efferent) transmissions between the spinal cord and the forebrain. Lying in the center of the brainstem and running from the hindbrain through the midbrain is a group of cells called the reticular formation. The **reticular formation** is a major center for the sleep–wake cycle. During the waking state it maintains alertness in the forebrain by providing stimulation through its ascending fibers. Damage to the midbrain may not be fatal, but if the reticular formation is involved, it may result in **coma**, a state in which the "vegetative" processes necessary for life proceed but the normal sleep–wake cycle is disrupted and there is no conscious mental activity. Damage to the midbrain that does not involve the reticular formation can result in involuntary movements, muscular rigidity, and spastic paralysis.

FOREBRAIN The *forebrain* is a complex region of the brain filling most of the skull's volume. It consists of the *cerebral cortex* or simply **cortex,** the convoluted outer folding of tissue visible when the skull is removed. The cortex is where most high level, abstract information processing takes place. The forebrain also consists of two important structures—the thalamus and the hypothalamus—which are located deep within the cortex in the center of the brain.

The **thalamus** is the major relay center through which all incoming sensory information (with the exception of smell) passes on its way to the cortex. Far from passive, the thalamus appears to have a role in integrating information from different senses. Through connections with the reticular formation, the thalamus is involved in maintaining cortical alertness, and because it also receives pathways from the cerebellum, it plays a role in integrating sensory-motor functioning. Damage to the thalamus alters sensory experience and may result in the inability to experience touch, pain, heat, and cold; also, limbs may be neglected and motor movements may be disrupted, leading to difficulty standing or sitting.

The **hypothalamus** is a smaller structure located under the thalamus. It organizes and propels the goal-seeking behavior found in such basic biological drives as drinking, eating, sexuality, and aggression, sometimes called "the four F's"—fighting, fleeing, feeding, and mating. The hypothalamus is also the interface between the brain and three very important functions: maintenance of homeostasis, control of the autonomic nervous system, and regulation of the endocrine system.

In maintaining homeostasis, for example, the hypothalamus monitors the temperature of blood and controls heat regulation by either inducing sweating when the body is too hot or shivering when it is too cold. Another example of homeostatic control is the hypothalamus's role in eating behavior. If a certain hypothalamic area is destroyed, an animal will refuse to eat, while destruction of another area will result in insatiable eating, either condition of which will lead to death (Nelson, 1984).

The second function of the hypothalamus is control of the autonomic nervous system. By activating the sympathetic division, it produces a state of heightened arousal and makes energy readily available for fight-or-flight.

Third, the hypothalamus is the direct communications link between the nervous and endocrine systems through connections to the pituitary gland. The pituitary activates and coordinates the release of hormones by other glands in the endocrine system. Damage to the hypothalamus can result in disruption of homeostasis, dysregulation of arousal and basic biological drives, and hormonal imbalances.

The **limbic system**, a group of interconnected structures surrounding the thalamus and hypothalamus, is also part of the cortex. The limbic system is involved in the control of emotion, motivation, and memory, although its role in these functions is not entirely understood (Pribram, 1981). The limbic system has connections with the thalamus and hypothalamus, and it includes such structures as the hippocampus, which is involved with the formation of memories (Berger, 1984b). Alzheimer's disease affects the hippocampus (Hyman, Van Hoesen, Damasio, & Barnes, 1984).

Animal researchers discovered quite by accident that regions of the limbic system appear to be "pleasure centers" (Olds & Milner, 1954; Olds & Fobes, 1981). If unrestrained, rats and monkeys will press a lever in order to stimulate these pleasure centers with a mild electrical charge thousands of times, even to the point of exhaustion, ignoring other basic biological drives such as thirst and hunger. Research on human subjects undergoing brain surgery has also revealed the existence of pleasure centers in the human brain, although human reactions to stimulation appear to be milder and the relationship between these pleasure centers and emotions in humans is unclear (Bindra, 1985; Valenstein, 1973).

The outer layer of the cortex is divided into two halves or **hemispheres**, in which are located several specialized areas (Figure I-5). The sensory and motor strips are located on top of the hemispheres about at the center and run roughly vertically down the outside surface. They receive sensory (afferent) input and control motor (efferent) output for the *opposite* side of the body. For example, when you move your *left* arm, the command originates in the motor strip of your *right* hemisphere. This same opposite side arrangement, called

contralateral, is found in vision and hearing, with the *left* hemisphere receiving input primarily from the right ear and the right visual field.

In addition, in about 90% of people, the *left hemisphere* processes information more sequentially and linearly and is responsible for logical language processes such as speaking or writing, whereas the *right hemisphere* processes visual-spatial imagery, complex patterns, and emotions (Gazzaniga, 1970; Geschwind, 1979).

Four areas or "lobes" are located in each hemisphere. The **occipital lobes** are located at the back of each hemisphere and process visual material. The **temporal lobes** are along the outer sides in front of the occipital lobes. They are involved in the processing of auditory signals and play a role in memory. The **parietal lobes** are located above the temporal lobes. They contain the sensory strips and process physical sensations from the body. The parietal lobes also play a role in integrating sensory information from the temporal and

Figure I-5   CORTICAL FUNCTIONS

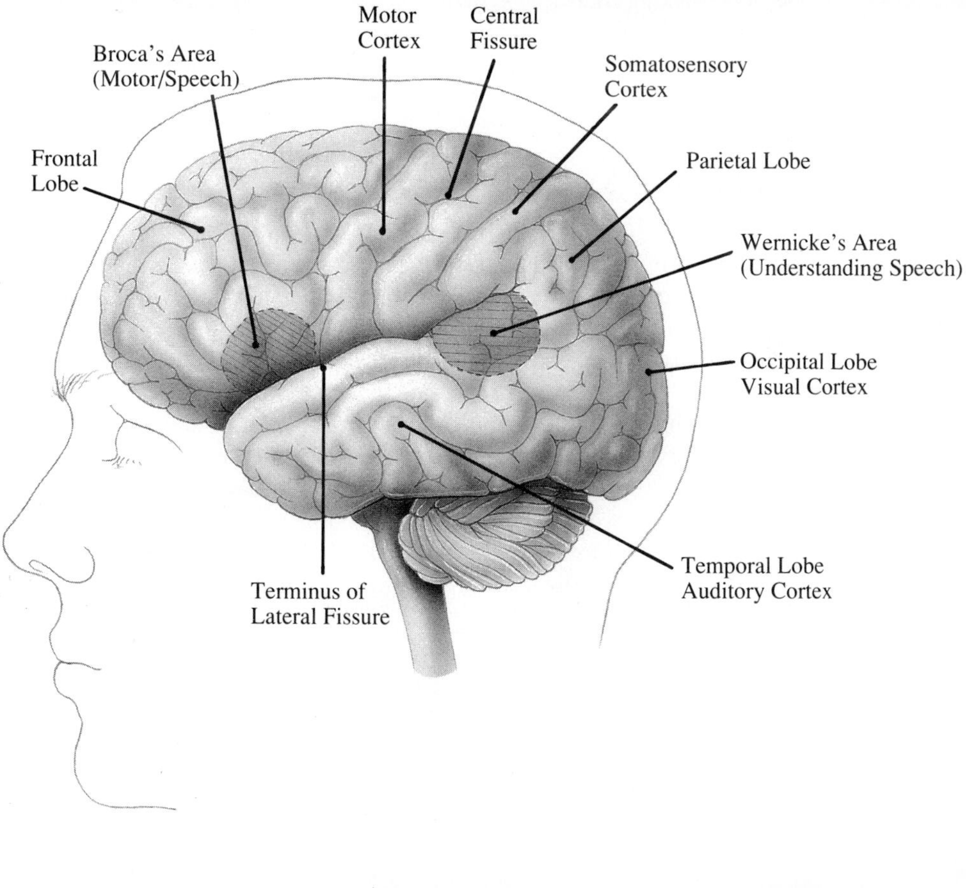

Broca's Area (Motor/Speech)

Motor Cortex

Central Fissure

Somatosensory Cortex

Frontal Lobe

Parietal Lobe

Wernicke's Area (Understanding Speech)

Occipital Lobe Visual Cortex

Temporal Lobe Auditory Cortex

Terminus of Lateral Fissure

occipital lobes and monitor the body's position in space. Finally, the **frontal lobes** are the largest areas in the human forebrain. The motor strip is located in the frontal lobes, which are involved in planning, organizing, initiating, and monitoring behavior. Personality and attention are greatly affected by damage to the frontal lobes, but the frontal lobes are not the sole focus for intelligence or memories (Luria, 1973).

Damage to the forebrain is rarely fatal unless it involves extensive areas or affects the brainstem as well. Usually, the effects are limited to specific aspects of behavior, thought, memory, emotion, or personality, depending on which area is destroyed. For example, damage to an area of the left temporal lobe known as *Wernicke's area* will result in problems *comprehending* language but not in speaking or in appreciating melodies. People with "Wernicke's aphasia" have what is called *word deafness*—they can hear, but they cannot interpret the meaning of sounds (Geschwind, 1979). They no longer know what words mean. In contrast, damage to *Broca's area* in the frontal lobe impairs fluent motor speech. People with "Broca's aphasia" can understand language but have difficulty speaking.

Although the brain can quickly control bodily activity through the somatic and autonomic nervous systems, it can also exercise control through the slower-acting endocrine system.

■■■■

ENDOCRINE SYSTEM

The **endocrine system** consists of glands that communicate with each other and with other organs by secreting hormones directly into the bloodstream. **Hormones** are chemical messengers that are analogous to neurotransmitters, except they are usually involved in the long-term regulation of ongoing functions of the body, like reproduction, growth, and metabolism. Endocrine glands are capable of maintaining homeostasis by responding independently to fluctuations of hormones in the bloodstream, increasing or decreasing their production in order to maintain normal body functions. However, the endocrine glands would act as simple thermostats, turning on or off, were it not for modulation by the brain (Marieb, 1989). The brain coordinates hormone release, integrating it with other processes in the body.

ENDOCRINE GLANDS

The distribution of endocrine glands is depicted in Figure I-6, along with some of the major hormones and their effects.

The **pituitary** is sometimes referred to as the "master gland" because it produces a number of hormones that affect the other endocrine glands. Through the hypothalamic-pituitary connection, endocrine system activity can be coordinated with nervous system activity. For example, when a threat is perceived by the cortex, the hypothalamus prepares the body for fight-or-flight by activating both the ANS and the pituitary. The pituitary responds by releasing adrenocorticotropic hormone (ACTH) into the bloodstream.

Figure I-6 THE ENDOCRINE SYSTEM

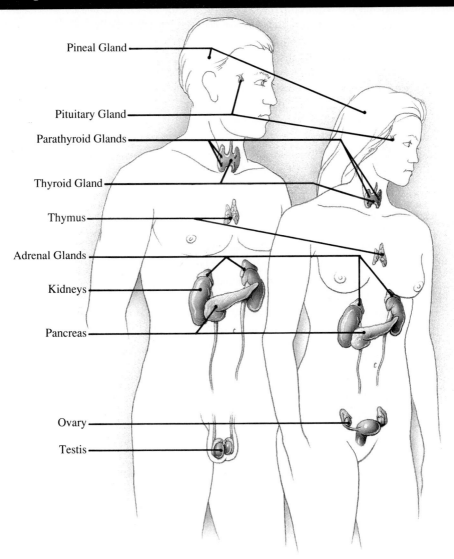

Pineal Gland

Pituitary Gland

Parathyroid Glands

Thyroid Gland

Thymus

Adrenal Glands

Kidneys

Pancreas

Ovary

Testis

When ACTH reaches another part of the endocrine system, the **adrenal glands**, which are located on top of each kidney, it causes them to release hormones called corticosteroids, which affect processes throughout the body. **Corticosteroids** regulate metabolism and the production of energy, and they are antiinflammatory, suppressing part of the immune system. One type of corticosteroid, glucocorticoids, increases blood sugar levels far above normal, providing energy for fight-or-flight.

As further illustration of the coordination between the autonomic and endocrine systems, ANS pathways also travel directly to the adrenal glands, where they cause the release of two additional hormones: epinephrine and norepinephrine. **Epinephrine** and **norepinephrine** remain in the bloodstream and prolong the fight-or-flight response even after the hypothalamus stops stimulating the ANS. Epinephrine is manufactured exclusively by the adrenal glands and is often used by doctors and researchers as a specific biological measure of stress. However, norepinephrine, which doubles as a neurotransmitter, is also manufactured by the brain.

Three endocrine glands are not directly involved in the fight-or-flight response, but they also have important functions. The **thyroid** gland is located in the throat near the larynx. It produces hormones that regulate physical growth and metabolism. Insufficient thyroid hormone, or *hypothyroidism,* results in low activity levels, lethargy, and weight gain, whereas abnormally high thyroid secretion, or *hyperthyroidism,* results in high activity levels, nervousness and tremors, insomnia, and weight loss (Marieb, 1989).

The **thymus** is located in the chest behind the sternum and produces hormones that are essential for normal immune system development. It is relatively large and active in infancy but decreases in size and function in adulthood.

The **gonads** are the only endocrine glands that differ in the two sexes. In females, the **ovaries** are located in the lower abdominal cavity and produce the ova, or eggs, as well as two hormones: estrogen and progesterone. In males, the **testes** are located in the scrotum and produce sperm, as well as several hormones including testosterone. Hormones produced by the gonads regulate maturation of the reproductive organs and appearance of the secondary sex characteristics such as breast development in females and facial hair in males.

Finally, the **pancreas** is located in the abdomen near the stomach. It is a "mixed organ" with several endocrine and nonendocrine functions. A portion of the pancreas, the islet cells, are endocrine. They produce two hormones required for metabolism: glucagon and insulin. **Glucagon** causes the release of glucose—a simple carbohydrate or sugar—into the bloodstream. **Insulin** decreases blood sugar by causing cell membranes to open, permitting glucose to be absorbed. If the amount of insulin produced is not sufficient, then glucose cannot be moved from the blood into the cells for use, and blood sugar rises. This condition is known as *diabetes mellitus* and, if untreated, it can result in coma or death.

DIABETES: A COMMON ENDOCRINE SYSTEM PROBLEM

In Chapter 1, diabetes was used as an example of what happens when one of the body's homeostatic mechanisms fails to work. If untreated or poorly managed, it can have serious health consequences. Diabetes causes about 38,000 deaths a year and may contribute to hundreds of thousands more (American Diabetes Association, 1986). About 5 million Americans have diagnosed diabetes and perhaps an equal number are undiagnosed. However, diabetes is manageable, and many of its consequences need not occur if people take control of their health. There are two types of diabetes: insulin-dependent and noninsulin-dependent.

Type I or insulin-dependent diabetes develops suddenly in childhood or adolescence, usually before 13 years of age, when *islet* cells lose their ability to produce insulin. It accounts for about 10% of all cases of diabetes (Marieb, 1989). There is not strong evidence of family history or twin concordance in Type I diabetes (Berkow & Fletcher, 1987).

To control Type I diabetes, people must receive several daily injections of insulin. They are vulnerable to many complications primarily resulting from vascular problems: arteriosclerosis, atherosclerosis, heart attacks, strokes, gangrene, and blindness. They are also subject to neuropathies that cause a loss of sensation in parts of the body and may result in sexual dysfunction. Without insulin injections, a person with Type I would enter a coma and die.

Table 1.2	CHARACTERISTICS OF INSULIN-DEPENDENT (TYPE I) AND NONINSULIN-DEPENDENT (TYPE II) DIABETES	
	TYPE I	**TYPE II**
Age	Onset before age 30	Onset after age 30
Body weight	Lean	90% are obese
Insulin production	None	Variable
Family history	Minor	Very high
Twin concordance	Low	High
Insulin injection	Required	Rarely required
Gender	No differences	More women
Socioeconomic status	No relationship	Lower socioeconomic status

Source: Berkow, R., & Fletcher, A. J., 1987, The Merck manual of diagnosis and therapy, *Rahway, NJ: Merck & Co.*

Type II: noninsulin-dependent diabetes develops later in life, usually after 40 years of age, and accounts for 90% of all cases. It is more common in women, European Americans, and people from low socioeconomic status (American Diabetes Association, 1986). In Type II diabetes, the ability of islet cells to produce insulin or the insulin sensitivity of other cells is reduced. There is strong evidence of a genetic component in Type II diabetes, and if one identical twin has it, the probability that the other will have it is 100% (Marieb, 1989).

Because there is some insulin production, injections are usually not required. Weight control, however, is a major problem. About 90% of Type II diabetics are overweight. Losing weight can often improve the sensitivity of insulin receptors and bring the disease under control (Marieb, 1989). Table I-2 summarizes the different characteristics of Type I and Type II diabetes.

CAUSES   It appears that both hereditary and environmental factors interact to reduce the effectiveness of insulin or its production by the pancreas (Berkow & Fletcher, 1987). Psychological factors do not have a causal role in diabetes, but stress is an important cofactor that increases diabetic symptoms (Berkow & Fletcher, 1987; Brand, Johnson, & Johnson, 1986; Hanson, Henggeler, & Burghen, 1987), regardless of insulin level, diet, or exercise (Hanson & Pichert, 1986).

In Type II diabetics, glucose levels fluctuate with stress, which increases hyperglycemia (Surwit & Feinglos, 1988). Also, Type A (see Module 11.1) diabetics are particularly prone to hyperglycemic episodes when under stress (Rhodewalt & Marcroft, 1988).

MANAGEMENT   Because stress is a cofactor in diabetes, stress reduction is a promising intervention (Surwit, Feinglos, & Scovern, 1983). Research has demonstrated that relaxation training helps people with diabetes reduce the effects of stress and, most importantly, control their blood glucose level (Surwit & Feinglos, 1988; Wing, Epstein, Nowalk, & Lamparski, 1986a). However, relaxation training is more helpful in Type II than Type I diabetes (Feinglos & Surwit, 1988), probably because there is some level of insulin function in Type II diabetes.

In addition to stress reduction, health psychologists are also interested in helping people achieve better management of their overall treatment regimen. About one-third of the deaths attributed to diabetes could be prevented with better management (Wing, Nowalk, & Guare, 1988). Patients must learn how to maintain a balance between glucose and insulin that would otherwise be maintained automatically by the endocrine system. This requires a rigid treatment regimen involving four elements: *monitoring* of glucose levels, *medication* with injectable insulin (if required) or oral medicine, *diet,* and *exercise.*

Despite the life-threatening effects of diabetes, adherence is a major problem—most people simply do not follow doctor's orders. Research has revealed that 77% of patients tested their glucose level incorrectly or misinterpreted the results, 75% did not follow the dietary regimen, and 58% administered the wrong dose of insulin (Wing et al., 1986b). Most people try to estimate their blood glucose levels based on perceived symptoms, which is not accurate (Diamond, Massey, & Covey, 1989; Gonder-Frederick, Cox, Bobbitt, & Pennebaker, 1989).

Because diabetes has no outward signs or symptoms, children do not appear any different, and because they do not usually undergo hospitalization or other painful procedures, they do not see themselves as ill (Eiser, 1985). As a result, they do not understand diabetes and its long-term consequences. Children in particular wonder why the rigid attention to diet, exercise, and insulin injections is necessary. As children mature cognitively, they are able to assume more responsibility for their treatment regimen, so by 12 years of age they are handling their own glucose testing and injections.

During adolescence, people have increased difficulty with adherence (Ingersoll, Orr, Herrold, & Golden, 1986; Jacobson et al., 1987; Johnson, 1980). Hormonal changes can affect glucose levels and may contribute to adherence problems, but emotional reactions may also play a role. Adolescents experience anger and feel cheated (Holmes, 1986). Feeling different because of their rigid health regimen, adolescents may attempt to avoid rejection by their peers and may neglect careful management (Turk & Speers, 1983). Adherence is positively correlated with self-esteem, parental support, and feelings of social competence (Hanson, Henggeler, & Burghen, 1987; Jacobson et al., 1987).

Health psychologists have attempted to understand the psychosocial factors that interfere with adherence and have studied ways of increasing it. The contiguity of reinforcement (see Module 2.2, page 50) does not work in favor of diabetic management, because the extreme health complications of diabetes take up to 20 years to develop, and since diabetes is not painful (except for its complications), patients are not highly motivated to follow the regimen closely (Kilo & Williamson, 1987). Also, in the past, medical personnel did a poor job of educating patients. They were given little or no information about diabetes, glucose, or metabolism (Hauenstein et al., 1987).

Health beliefs and goals also affect adherence in diabetes (Brownlee-Duffeck et al., 1987). Physicians' goals are to balance blood glucose levels and avoid long-term complications, but the goals of parents and children are the short-term avoidance of symptoms. These conflicting goals can also lead to misunderstandings and poor adherence (Marteau et al., 1987).

Social support contributes to adherence, but it appears to have a curvilinear relationship with adherence in diabetes, particularly in men. Men who have an extensive social network seem to have more norm conflicts that interfere with adherence. Perhaps they are more active and that interferes with their regimen. Therefore, a moderately extensive network seems to be related to greater adherence (Kaplan & Hartwell, 1987).

A variety of behavioral techniques have been applied to the problem of adherence with good success. Both glucose monitoring (Wing et al., 1986a) and self-injection behaviors (Wing et al., 1986b) can be improved through behavioral treatment. In a case study of three teenagers with adherence problems, an eight-week behavioral training program improved adherence in two, while the third did not improve (but there were marital and family problems in that case; Schafer, Glasgow, & McCaul, 1982). Behavioral weight reduction for diabetes also has met with success (Wing et al., 1986a).

The most promising behavioral programs utilize a multicomponent approach (Wing et al., 1986a). These programs include several elements. First, patients are thoroughly educated and provided with a complete understanding of diabetes and glucose metabolism. Second, a self-reinforcement behavioral approach is used to improve monitoring and foster better use of medication. Third, comprehensive diet control and exercise helps maintain desirable weight. Finally, stress management rounds out the approach. Such programs have as their goal the long-term management of diabetes.

Research has shown that people who have better long-term adherence and control over their blood glucose levels do have fewer health complications and that, when complications do occur, they occur much later than in those who have poor control (Santiago, 1984). Given the serious and life threatening complications of diabetes, the potential to relieve suffering for many thousands of people makes it a rewarding condition for health psychologists to work with.

■■■

SUMMARY

This introduction to the nervous and endocrine systems serves as a general foundation to several primary areas of interest in health psychology. Because of the importance of these two systems in the maintenance of health and well-being, the next four chapters are devoted to their related health problems. These chapters explore what happens to health when biopsychosocial factors interfere with the brain's ability to determine goals, to plan, to allocate resources, to direct communications through the nervous and endocrine systems, and to act as the executive homeostatic coordinator. Before continuing, however, review this summary of the function and organization of these two important systems:

1. The nervous and endocrine systems are the body's communications networks.
2. The nervous system provides rapid, short-lasting communication between the brain and the body through electrochemical neural impulses.

3. Single-celled neurons are the basic units of the nervous system, having the capability to transmit impulses to other neurons.
4. The peripheral nervous system relays information between the spinal cord and the body but does not process it. It has two divisions. The somatic nervous system transmits sensory impulses to the brain and motor impulses to the muscles. The autonomic nervous system mobilizes the body through a sympathetic response in times of threat and relaxes the body through a parasympathetic response at other times.
5. The central nervous system consists of the brain and spinal cord. The spinal cord is capable of controlling some reflexive behaviors, but all voluntary and most involuntary behavior originates in the brain, which coordinates activity in the nervous and endocrine systems.
6. The hypothalamus, a forebrain structure, links the brain with the endocrine system through connections with the pituitary gland.
7. The endocrine system provides slow, long-lasting communication between the brain and the body through the release of hormones.
8. A major health problem related of the endocrine system is diabetes, which is directly responsible for thousands of deaths and indirectly responsible for hundreds of thousands of deaths each year.
9. Diabetes is caused by an endocrine disorder affecting the pancreas. A reduction or cessation of insulin production by the pancreas is the primary cause of diabetes.
10. There are two types of diabetes: Type I or insulin-dependent, which develops at a young age, and is probably caused by an autoimmune disorder; and Type II or noninsulin-dependent, which develops after age 40, and is probably caused by obesity and genetic factors.
11. Both stress and Type A behavior can cause fluctuation in blood glucose levels.
12. The treatment regimen for diabetes involves four elements: monitoring of glucose levels, medication with injectable insulin or oral medicine, diet, and exercise.
13. Adherence is a problem in diabetes, with most people not following their treatment regimen. Adherence is better with monitoring and medication than with diet and exercise.
14. Behavioral and stress management treatments are successful in improving adherence.

6

STRESS

6.1 A Biopsychosocial Model
6.2 Illness and Management

Dave and Alex met for the first time when they moved into their dorm room the week before classes began. They both were new arrivals at a large, midwestern state university, and they both had similar backgrounds. Both grew up in small towns and this was the first time each had lived away from home, both showed academic promise, both enjoyed intramural sports, and both were pre-med majors. The housing office's computer apparently had made a good match of their backgrounds and interests.

However, some differences in the way each handled stress became apparent by the time their first semester finals approached. For example, after talking to his parents one night, Dave slammed down the phone and growled, "I don't need this stress!" Alex, having heard this and having seen Dave upset before, asked him what was up. Dave responded, "All my parents talk about is how expensive my education is, yet they go on about how proud they are of me and how they just know I'll do well on my finals." Alex wondered why Dave was taking the conversation so hard, recognizing it as standard "parent talk." "After all," Alex thought, "I look forward to my parents' calls, and they seem to say exactly the same things." However, when Alex's parents mentioned the expense of college, his response was, "It's great that they're able to afford it and that they enjoy helping me."

Both students were taking the same classes, facing the same finals, and doing B+ work. Yet with finals approaching, Dave was near panic, while Alex felt fairly confident. For a moment, Dave's stress and his mounting fears about finals captured Alex's own thoughts. He wondered, "Am I too complacent? Maybe I could fail." Then Alex bounced back, thinking, "Sure finals will be a challenge, but I'm doing B+ work and I'm not going to suddenly forget everything and fail."

Alex noticed that Dave was still talking. "And on top of that, I think I'm coming down with another cold. That will really screw up my studying and with finals coming too! That's my second cold this semester—and you haven't had any! I've just had the worst luck since I started college." Alex, wanting to *be supportive, added "Yeah, and you've had a rough time in intramural foot-ball, too, with all of those injuries that kept you sidelined so much of the time."*

Dave and Alex's experiences pose some interesting questions about stress. How can two people from similar backgrounds who perform the same quality of work experience the same events—a phone call from home or the approach of finals—and react so differently? Dave felt stressed, while Alex felt supported and challenged. Is stress in the event, or is it in the way the person responds to it? Also, could Dave's frequent illnesses and injuries be related in some way to his stress?

These questions will be addressed later in this chapter when we return to Dave and Alex's situation. In order to answer them, it is necessary first to understand the components of stress. In Module 6.1, a comprehensive biopsychosocial model of stress that includes these components is described and illustrated. This biopsychosocial model forms the basis for understanding the relationship between stress and illness and how stress can be managed, which is discussed in Module 6.2.

A BIOPSYCHOSOCIAL MODEL

THE THREE COMPONENTS OF STRESS

Stress can be caused by external components, internal components, or an interaction of both. The *external* component of stress is represented by **stressors**, the environmental events that precede the recognition of stress. Walter Cannon (1915/1929, 1932) was one of the first to take an interest in stressors and he viewed them as external events—either physiological or emotionally threatening stimuli—that disrupt homeostasis. Such threatening stimuli can include environmental circumstances (for example, natural disasters), changing life events (for example, losing a job), or chronic conditions (for example, crowding or poverty). Looked at this way, Dave's stressors include his upcoming finals and the phone calls from his parents.

Hans Selye (1956, 1976, 1985), another pioneer in stress research, was also concerned about disruptions of homeostasis but focused on the *internal* component of stress—the emotional and physical response of the body to stressors. Selye (1979) preferred the term **strain,** which describes the psychological and physiological reactions of an individual to *ongoing* stress. From this viewpoint, Dave's stressors were producing internal strain.

The third component of stress focuses on the *interaction* between these external and internal factors, between the environment and the internal world of the individual. The interaction takes place cognitively when external stimuli are perceived as stressors and results in an internal physiological response. We will discuss each component of stress separately.

THE EXTERNAL COMPONENT: STRESSORS

AWARENESS OF STRESSORS

We are usually aware of stressors when we feel either conflicted, frustrated, or pressured. A *conflict* occurs when there are two desires, motives, or goals that are more or less incompatible—for example, wanting to go out the night before an exam, but also wanting to do well on the exam. *Frustration* arises when we are in pursuit of a goal but are hampered or blocked—such as wanting to ask a certain person out but never having an opportunity to do so. Finally, we feel *pressure* when we must act according to the demands dictated by a person or situation, whether it be a life change requiring adjustment (such as divorce) or the rules we must conform to in the workplace.

SOURCES OF STRESSORS

Stressors can be categorized according to their source or context. Most of the common stressors fall within four broad categories: personal, social/familial, work, and the environment.

PERSONAL Psychologists have long recognized the role that conflict plays as a personal stressor (Lewin, 1935; Miller, 1944, 1959). Recently, Robert Emmons of the University of California, Davis, and Laura King of Michigan State University, have proposed that conflict among personal strivings can affect psychological and physical well-being.

Personal strivings are "what a person is characteristically trying to do" (Emmons, 1986, p. 1,059). They can be positive—something that is approached or sought after, such as "trying to be physically attractive"—or negative—something that is avoided or prevented, such as "trying to avoid maliciously gossiping about others." An example of a conflict in personal strivings is to keep "relationships on a 50-50 basis" *and* "to dominate, control, and manipulate people" (Emmons & King, 1988, p. 1,042). High conflict in personal strivings is associated with negative emotions, depression, anxiety, and psychosomatic complaints, and it can predict psychosomatic complaints a year later (Emmons & King, 1988). Therefore, inconsistencies in personal goals can result in stress.

SOCIAL/FAMILIAL People are embedded in social networks that include friends and relations, and sometimes social and familial relationships cause conflict, pressure, and frustration. Major life events, which often involve social beginnings and endings such as marriage, divorce, or death, have been implicated as an important source of stress (Holmes & Rahe, 1967). In addition to major life events, there are also the minor social/familial hassles experienced on a regular basis—for example, social obligations, poor health of a family member, unexpected company, loneliness. These are also correlated with psychological and somatic health status (Holahan, Holahan, & Belk, 1984; Lazarus, 1984; Lazarus & Folkman, 1989).

Several sources of social/familial stress have been investigated. Serious illness and disability of a family member can be stressors requiring major adjustments of a long-term nature for the caregiver (Johnson, 1985; Kosten, Jacobs, & Kasl, 1985; Leventhal, Leventhal, & Van Nguyen, 1985). Illness and disability restrict the caregiver's freedom and time availability for other activities, which can lead to pressure and frustration. As the caregiver's irritability increases, this may present resentment and guilt feelings that can cause additional personal conflict. For example, parents may love and want to care for a disabled child, but they may also feel irritated and resent the work involved, which can lead to guilt and additional stress.

Bereavement can be a particularly difficult stressor. This stressor provided some of the first systematic evidence of a link between stress and immune function (Zakowski, Hall, & Baum, 1992). The death of a spouse or child is a deeply felt loss (Kosten, Jacobs, & Kasl, 1985). The consequences of bereavement are usually felt for at least one year (Joyce, 1984; Silver & Wortman, 1980), and the death of a child can affect parents for many years (Knapp, 1987) as, presumably, the death of a parent might affect a child. Research generally supports a relationship between a sense of loss and changes in immune system functioning (Zakowski, Hall, & Baum, 1992).

WORK Another source of pressure, frustration, and conflict can be one's job. Changes in job responsibilities (being promoted or demoted) or being fired are counted among the life events adding to one's total stress (Holmes & Rahe, 1967). Also, work hassles that do not involve major changes but are nevertheless present are also among the stressors associated with illness (Lazarus, 1984; Lazarus & Folkman, 1989). These include problems getting along with fellow workers, hassles from the boss or supervisor, and even non-challenging work.

Work probably involves more of most people's time than any other single activity besides sleeping, and in addition to being a source of income, a job is also an important source of meaning and identity. Is it any wonder that there are a host of identified work-related stressors? Some of these include job insecurity, unemployment, retirement, task demands, responsibility for others' lives, and performance evaluation.

Job insecurity—the belief that one is likely to be laid-off or fired—becomes a stressor depending on one's likelihood of finding another job (Cottington et al., 1986; Quick & Quick, 1984). *Unemployment* is itself a stressor that can result in loss of self-esteem, and it is linked to hypertension (Olafsson & Svensson, 1986). In contrast to popular belief, research has not consistently found that *retirement* is related to poor health (Kasl & Berkman, 1981), although it may lead to feelings of loss of routine and influence in some people (Bradford, 1986).

Task demands, that is the work itself, can also be a source of pressure. Health problems and increased accidents are related to excessive work loads

These stock brokers work under pressure in a hectic environment without privacy and with little personal space.

(Quick & Quick, 1984). *Responsibility for others' lives* has been recognized as a specific source of "burnout" among health professionals (Maslach & Jackson, 1982). *Performance evaluation* is stressful, and people feel stress when they feel they are not receiving the recognition or advancement they deserve (Cottington, Matthews, Talbott, & Kuller, 1986; Quick & Quick, 1984). Occupational stress is also discussed in Module 5.2.

ENVIRONMENT As discussed in Module 5.2, the physical environment can be a source of stress if it involves extremes of density, temperature, noise, or illumination, among other factors (Quick & Quick, 1984). Recently, the American Psychiatric Association added the category of "post traumatic stress disorder" or PTSD to its *Diagnostic and Statistical Manual of Mental Disorders III-R* (American Psychiatric Association [APA], 1987). PTSD is used for persons who have "experienced an event outside the range of usual human experience" (APA, 1987, p. 250) and who are reexperiencing the event with symptoms of increased arousal. PTSD was intended to be used only for extraordinary environmental events such as war.

PTSD symptoms can include flashbacks, nightmares, irritability, and difficulty concentrating, among others. One common example of PTSD is "shell shock," experienced by some soldiers who have been in battle conditions. They may become hypervigilant (that is, on constant guard) and have an exaggerated startle response if they hear loud sounds similar to those experienced during battle. They also may relive their experiences through unwanted and intrusive memories or dreams, lose interest in activities they once enjoyed, and withdraw from others.

THE INTERNAL COMPONENT: PHYSIOLOGICAL AROUSAL

PHYSIOLOGY OF THE STRESS RESPONSE

Imagine you are in your car, stopped at a traffic signal. You glance into your rearview mirror and see a car heading toward you at full speed despite a red light. At the last minute the driver slams on the brakes and begins to skid, but it may be too late. If this has ever happened to you, then you are aware of the body's physiological response to threat. You probably noticed a flood of sensations as your heart beat stronger and faster, your breathing rate increased, your limbs began to tremble, and your skin tingled. You were aroused and you felt anxious.

If you analyze this situation carefully, you will realize that your arousal was automatic, that is, the physiological reactions occurred *before* you had time to think about the danger you were in. You will recognize that these reactions are part of the fight-or-flight response of the sympathetic nervous system. In anticipation of the need to take action for survival, your body had become physically and emotionally aroused, with energy made immediately available to respond to the threat. After the threat was over, your state of arousal gradually returned to normal. In order to understand the body's responses to stress, researchers have developed several ways to measure physiological arousal.

MEASUREMENT OF PHYSIOLOGICAL AROUSAL There are two methods of assessing the physiological reactions to stressors: (a) the assaying of hormones, and (b) polygraphic monitoring. The secretion of hormones involved in the stress response can be assayed or measured. Usually a *hormone assay* involves taking a urine or blood sample, which is then subjected to laboratory analysis. Corticosteroids—particularly cortisol—and the catecholamines—epinephrine and norepinephrine—are the most widely measured indexes of physiological arousal.

In **polygraphic monitoring,** noninvasive electrical devices are attached to the body to measure blood pressure, heart rate, respiration, and perspiration, all indicators of the sympathetic response. Polygraphic monitors are similar to

Polygraphs monitor the same physiological functions as biofeedback, but information is not provided to the person being monitored. Here a person's heart and respiration are being monitored.

biofeedback equipment (see Module 2.2, page 56), except that the results are not fed back to the subject (which would affect the ongoing measurement).

There are some advantages to measuring physiological arousal as an indicator of stress (Baum, Grunberg, & Singer, 1982; Cacioppo, Petty, & Marshall-Goodell, 1985). It tends to be reliable and objective, and it directly reflects the activity of the neuroendocrine responses to stress. However, there are some drawbacks, too. The hardware involved in polygraphic monitoring, as well as the taking of urine and blood samples, can be stressful in themselves, causing inaccurate readings. Also, measurement of physiological arousal is affected by such factors as gender, body weight, and whether or not one exercises regularly, extraneous variables that need to be taken into account. Finally, and most importantly, physiological measurements provide only part of the story—they miss the *subjective* cognitive and emotional aspects of stress. Therefore, a complete understanding of stress depends on combining physiological and psychological measurements. Nevertheless, the physiological measurement of arousal was instrumental in developing one of the earliest theories relating stress to illness—the general adaptation syndrome.

GENERAL ADAPTATION SYNDROME   Hans Selye, a medical doctor with an interest in organic chemistry, was a pioneer in stress research and one of the first to examine the physiological reaction of the body (Selye, 1956, 1976, 1979, 1985). Selye was particularly interested in the effects of chronic stressors. He called their effects strain and attempted to explain them with the general adaptation syndrome (GAS). There are three stages in the GAS: alarm, resistance, and exhaustion. They are described in Box 6.1-1.

Since Selye first proposed the GAS, a broad consensus has developed among researchers confirming the role of the hypothalamic-pituitary-adrenal connection in stress (for example, Watson, 1989). The nervous and endocrine systems, in general, appear to be extremely sensitive to psychosocial factors. Pituitary-adrenal hormones are released in conditions of high novelty and uncertainty, particularly when there is little control (Dantzer, 1982).

Selye (1979) described the stress response as "nonspecific." By *nonspecific*, he did not mean that the response itself was inexact; in fact, he believed that all stressors produce the very same physiological response. He meant that

---

Box 6.1-1   THREE STAGES IN GENERAL ADAPTATION SYNDROME

Stage 1:   Alarm
The alarm stage is equivalent to the fight-or-flight response. It occurs when the body's resources are mobilized in response to a threat. When a threat is first perceived, the hypothalamus signals both the sympathetic nervous system and the pituitary. The sympathetic nervous system stimulates the adrenal glands. They respond by releasing corticosteroids to increase metabolism, to provide access to energy reserves, and to decrease inflammation. The pituitary gland releases adrenocorticotrophic hormone (ACTH), which also affects the adrenal glands. They respond by releasing catecholamines—epinephrine and norepinephrine—which prolong the fight-or-flight response.

Stage 2:   Resistance
The physiological reactions of the alarm stage provide energy to deal with the threat, and resistance begins. If the threat is brief, there usually will be sufficient resources to adapt to it. However, a continued state of arousal is a strain in itself. The high level of hormones during the resistance phase may upset homeostasis and harm internal organs. Selye believed that this would leave the organism vulnerable to disease.

Stage 3:   Exhaustion
This final stage occurs after prolonged resistance. The body's energy reserves are finally exhausted and breakdown occurs. However, the body does not return to normal homeostasis. Instead, negative feedback involving the parasympathetic division of the ANS produces abnormally low arousal. Selye believed that this results in even more serious complications—disease, depression, and even possibly death.

the stress response can result from many different kinds of stressors. Selye predicted that the physiological responses of the GAS would occur in spite of the type of stressor, whether it were physical exertion or worrying about an exam, and research has indeed demonstrated an increase in adrenal hormones with a wide variety of stressors (Baum, Grunberg, & Singer, 1982; Ciaranello, 1983).

However, nonspecificity of the stress response has been challenged because it fails to take psychosocial factors into account. First, as we will discover in the next section, not all stressors are equivalent, and cognitive processes can influence whether or not a stimulus is perceived as a stressor in the first place (Scherer, 1986). Second, different stressors elicit different emotional responses, and strong emotional responses tend to trigger heavier secretions of cortisol, epinephrine, and norepinephrine (Mason, 1975). This suggests that there are different patterns of hormone secretion to different stressors. Also, different patterns of hormones are secreted, depending on the specific psychosocial context involved in the arousal (Henry, 1990). For example, anger is related to an increase in norepinephrine, and fear is related to an increase in epinephrine. In contrast, feelings of comfort and serenity are related to lowered epinephrine levels and decreased sympathetic nervous system activity.

By emphasizing the difference in acute versus chronic stressors, Selye made a major contribution to early research. He suggested how stress and illness might be linked, thus generating testable hypotheses. However, a more recent theory introduces a new idea with respect to stress—the duration of the stressor.

PHYSIOLOGICAL TOUGHENING   Richard Dienstbier (1989), of the University of Nebraska-Lincoln, introduced a theory called **physiological toughening**, which questions the emphasis the GAS places on the role of chronic stress. In order to understand Dienstbier's theory, we must begin with a consideration of the duration of stressors.

Stressors occur in varying durations. *Acute stressors* are the briefest, lasting a few seconds to a couple of days. They often present as a tangible threat and are usually readily identified as stressors. Our nervous and endocrine systems evolved in an environment where life was basic and most stressors were probably acute, such as a predatory lion, a fierce storm, or a neighboring clan that covets your cave (Carruthers, 1981). Today, there are few lions in the civilized world, but there are still some acute stressors. A tornado or a menacing stranger coming toward you on a dark street are examples of acute stressors. Acute stressors are not considered to be a health risk because they are limited by time.

What if the stressor is not acute? *Nonacute* or *chronic stressors*—those with which the GAS is concerned—are of the longest duration, lasting from weeks to years. They are not readily identified as stressors because they are often ambiguous and intangible. Chronic stressors are such a part of modern life that they may be taken for granted. Working on a night shift or a rotating shift, regular commuting through heavy traffic, or urban violence may not be viewed with the same sense of urgency as acute stressors. Nevertheless, they can pose a serious health risk. The stress that Dave experienced adjusting to college might be considered chronic, but only if it lasted beyond his first semester; otherwise, it would simply be acute.

Physiological toughening is concerned with the third category of stressors, called *intermittent*. *Intermittent stressors* are the most variable in duration, occurring periodically and alternating with periods of calm. When an intermittent stressor is viewed as a challenge, it may actually *improve* one's physiological resistance to stress by causing repeated, periodic *increases* in sympathetic arousal. These increases in arousal condition the body to better withstand subsequent stressors—hence, the name *physiological toughening*, which we will return to shortly.

So far we have examined the external environmental and the internal, physiological components of stress. Now we are ready to return to Dave and Alex's very different reactions to the same event—starting college. It seems that one person's stressor may be another person's welcome challenge, and the specific reaction one has lies in the cognitive *appraisal* of potentially stressful events.

The Interaction: Cognitive Appraisal of Transactions

Richard Lazarus and his colleagues at the University of California Berkeley Stress and Coping Project are interested in the interaction of the *external*—the stressor—and the *internal*—cognitive processes (Folkman & Lazarus, 1985; Cohen & Lazarus, 1983; Lazarus & Folkman, 1984b; Lazarus & Launier, 1978). They call this interaction a *transaction*, taking into account the ongoing relationship between the individual and the environment, and they use the concept of cognitive appraisal to explain the psychological processes involved in stress transactions (Cox, 1978; Lazarus & Folkman, 1984a, 1984b; Lazarus & Launier, 1978; Mechanic, 1976b). According to this theory, emphasis is placed on the *meaning* an event has for the person, rather than on the stressor or the strain. Lazarus believes that one's view of a situation determines whether it is stressful. This makes stress the consequence of appraisal, not its antecedent. External stimuli are not inherently stressful; they become so through the process of appraisal. Cognitive appraisal helps to account for the individual variability in people's responses to stressors.

COGNITIVE APPRAISAL

Cognitive appraisal is a two-part mental process during which decisions are made about potentially stressful stimuli. One part, primary appraisal, deals with determination of an event as stressful, and the other part, secondary appraisal, deals with determination of one's abilities to cope with the event. During *primary appraisal* an event or situation is categorized as follows.

1. *Irrelevant*—an event or change appraised to be of little or no consequence.
2. *Beneficial*—Lazarus called this "benign-positive."
3. *Stressful*—an event or change that is appraised as follows:
   a. *Potentially harmful or creating a loss*—usually having to do with illness or injury that has already occurred, such as having had your car stolen (and you didn't pay your last insurance premium!) or losing your job.
   b. *Potentially threatening*—an expectation of future harm (physical as well as psychological), such as living in a violent neighborhood or facing a difficult exam.
   c. *Potentially challenging*—stressful events or circumstances that can also provide an opportunity for gain or growth.

These categorizations are based mostly on one's own prior experiences and learning, but they may also derive from vicarious learning, through observing and empathizing with the transactions of others (Speisman, Lazarus, Mordkoff, & Davison, 1964). According to the theory, each of these evaluations generates different emotional responses. *Harmful* stressors can produce anger, disgust, sadness, or disappointment; *threatening* stressors can produce anxiety; and *challenging* stressors can produce excitement. Dave evaluated college, particularly during finals, as stressful and threatening, while Alex evaluated them as beneficial ("benign positive"). However, there is also another level of appraisal.

Secondary appraisal is an ongoing evaluation of one's ability and resources to cope with events judged to be harmful, threatening, or challenging. In secondary appraisal, one is concerned with several questions that relate to self-efficacy (Bandura, 1982): "What options do I have? Can I successfully apply these options? Will they work?" When we believe we can do something that will make a difference, the experience of stress is reduced.

In a way, people's emotional states can be "catching." For a moment, Alex "caught" Dave's anxiety about finals and thought, "Am I too complacent? Maybe I could fail." This was a primary appraisal of finals as a threat. However, in his secondary appraisal, Alex evaluated his abilities to cope and concluded he would do at least as well as he had done in the past.

Usually, primary appraisal precedes secondary appraisal, but this is not necessary because the two are interrelated. Secondary appraisals of limited coping abilities can also cause one to make primary appraisals of events as stressful that would not otherwise be evaluated so (Coyne & Holroyd, 1982; Cohen & Lazarus, 1983). As an illustration, imagine you have to take a class in a subject that you have never done well in—math, for example. You have no options; it's required. You've tried to cope with math classes before by extra studying and tutoring, but still did poorly. In this case, you would make a secondary appraisal that you had limited ability to cope with math, which is likely to increase your primary appraisal of the math class as a threat (it's a vicious cycle).

Lazarus and Folkman (1984b) also identified another type of appraisal, called reappraisal. *Reappraisal* is an acknowledgment that we are constantly reevaluating and changing our appraisals in the face of new information. Reappraisal can result in changes in previously made primary or secondary appraisals, so it can result in increased or decreased stress. For example, a situation originally determined to be benign—your coworker taking a vacation—is reappraised to be threatening when you find out that the boss expects you to do his or her work, too.

Two final concepts are important in this cognitive approach to stress: vulnerability and coping (Lazarus and Folkman, 1984). **Vulnerability** refers to an individual's lack of actual resources—physical or social—to cope with a particular situation. An example of a physical vulnerability would be not having adequate transportation to get to a worksite that is moved farther from home, whereas an example of social vulnerability would be not having the necessary skills for a good job interview. Vulnerability is a recognition that not all people are equally prepared to meet situations. In keeping with the cognitive nature of this theory, vulnerability represents a *potential,* for it only operates within the context of a situation that is personally relevant.

Coping is any cognitive or behavioral effort that one uses to manage specific demands appraised as exceeding one's resources. Coping is not an automatic process; it requires effort, and it involves past learned behavior. Interestingly, successful coping does *not* require that one overcome a situation, only that the situation be managed, that one strives to come to terms with it. Finally, in this theory of transactions, stress arises only when a particular transaction is appraised by the person as relevant to his or her well-being (Folkman & Lazarus, 1985).

So how do we answer the question, "Why do people seem to react differently to the same event?" In order for an event to be appraised as a stressor, it must be personally relevant, and very importantly, there must be a *perceived* mismatch between a situation's demands and one's resources to cope with it. This last point emphasizes that stress occurs only when one *believes* he or she cannot cope with a stressor. So, except for some major traumatic stressors (for example, war or natural disasters), it is best not to call some events "stressful" and others "nonstressful." Stress occurs in the interaction between the event and the individual's appraisal of two things: (a) whether it is a harm/loss, a threat, or a challenge, and (b) whether he or she has the ability to cope with it.

Reformulating Primary Appraisal Categories

Dienstbier (1989) has slightly reformulated Folkman and Lazarus's (1985) transactional stress categories to fit his theory that intermittent stress is beneficial. He asserts that, when an event is appraised as a challenge, it leads to different physiological consequences than when it is appraised as a harm/loss or threat. Acknowledging the role that strong emotions play in the stress response (Mason, 1975), Dienstbier uses "stress" to refer to transactions that lead *only* to negative emotions (harm/loss and threat), and he uses "challenge" to describe a transaction that *could* lead to positive (nonstress) *or* negative emotions (stress).

Support for Dienstbier's position that challenge should be viewed more positively than harm/loss or threat comes from an earlier series of studies by Marianne Frankenhaeuser and her associates, which evaluated the different patterns of physiological response—primarily hormonal—to different stressors (for example, Collins & Frankenhaeuser, 1978). Frankenhaeuser (1986) found that physiological reactions to stressors depended on *effort,* which she defined as interest, striving, and determination, and *distress,* which she defined as anxiety, boredom, and dissatisfaction. Based on this, she has identified three categories of physiological responses to stress:

1. *Effort* with *distress,* which leads to *increases* of both catecholamine and cortisol secretion and results from daily hassles. Distress is experienced as negative emotions, and this category corresponds to Dienstbier's characterization of the negative emotions present in harm/loss and threat.
2. *Effort* without *distress,* which leads to an *increase* of catecholamine and *suppression* of cortisol secretion. Frankenhaeuser defined this state as joyous, characterized by active and successful coping. Here there is still effort, but the emotions are positive, so this category corresponds to Dienstbier's characterization of challenge.
3. *Distress without effort,* which leads to *increased* cortisol secretion and possibly, but not necessarily, catecholamine secretion, is the pattern typically found in depressed persons; she defines this state as helplessness.

Alex's experience of college as a challenge exemplifies effort without distress, whereas Dave's experience of college as a threat exemplifies effort with distress (if he continues to try to succeed) or distress without effort (if he gives up trying).

This reformulation of the primary appraisal categories is useful because it links Lazarus's cognitive theory to physiological responses. From it, we can infer that Alex and Dave are experiencing different hormone secretion patterns and that their health will be differentially affected. This reformulation is also in keeping with the notion that some stressors, notably those defined as a challenge, may be beneficial.

CONCLUSION   Cognitive appraisal can explain the variability in peoples' reactions to stressors and how one person's stressor can be another person's welcome challenge. However, the study of cognitive processes is extremely complex, for they cannot be divorced from the whole person. Cognitive processes take place in a context such as one's mood. Research indicates that mood affects health-relevant cognitions (Salovey & Birnbaum, 1989) and that daily stressors (hassles) and physical symptoms are direct determinants of mood (Eckenrode, 1984). If this seems circular, that is because it is. Mood influences: (a) perceptions of physical symptoms, (b) beliefs about one's ability to take action to reduce the symptoms, and (c) perceptions of vulnerability (Salovey & Birnbaum, 1989). In turn, physical symptoms influence mood. This serves only to highlight some of the complexities that researchers face, but it does not negate transactional theory.

Cognitive appraisal theory is probably best applied to situations where a potential stressor is chronic rather than acute or where there is a consistently high level of daily hassles. Some emergency situations may provoke a state of shock, not even allowing time for cognitive appraisal. In such situations, the physiological stress response should be instantaneous, only to be followed later by an appraisal of the situation (Trumbull & Appley, 1986). As long as the situation is acute, it should not have any long-term health consequences.

A BIOPSYCHOSOCIAL MODEL OF STRESS

We have been leading up to a comprehensive model of stress that includes all of the biopsychosocial factors that have been examined. Figure 6.1-1 depicts such a model. The physiological processes involved in stress are represented in the center of the model. They include the endocrine and sympathetic nervous system pathways resulting in arousal and preparation for fight-or-flight, and these pathways are depicted as leading to the general adaptation syndrome on the right side of the model. Presumably, acute and intermittent stressors lead to resistance and physiological toughening, whereas chronic stressors lead to strain and illness.

The psychosocial processes involved in stress are represented on the left side of the model. They include the transactions between the environmental event and the central nervous system. A transaction can initiate physiological arousal if an event is appraised as a stressor and if coping abilities are appraised as insufficient. The psychosocial (left side) and physiological processes (center) of the model are linked by the hypothalamus.

There may also be different emotions attached to the appraisal of a stressor that may result in a different pattern of hormones released by the endocrine system. Positive emotions (stress resistance efforts without distress as in the case of a challenge) are associated primarily with the release of catecholamines, whereas negative emotions (stress resistance efforts with distress

Figure 6.1-1   A Biopsychosocial Model of Stress

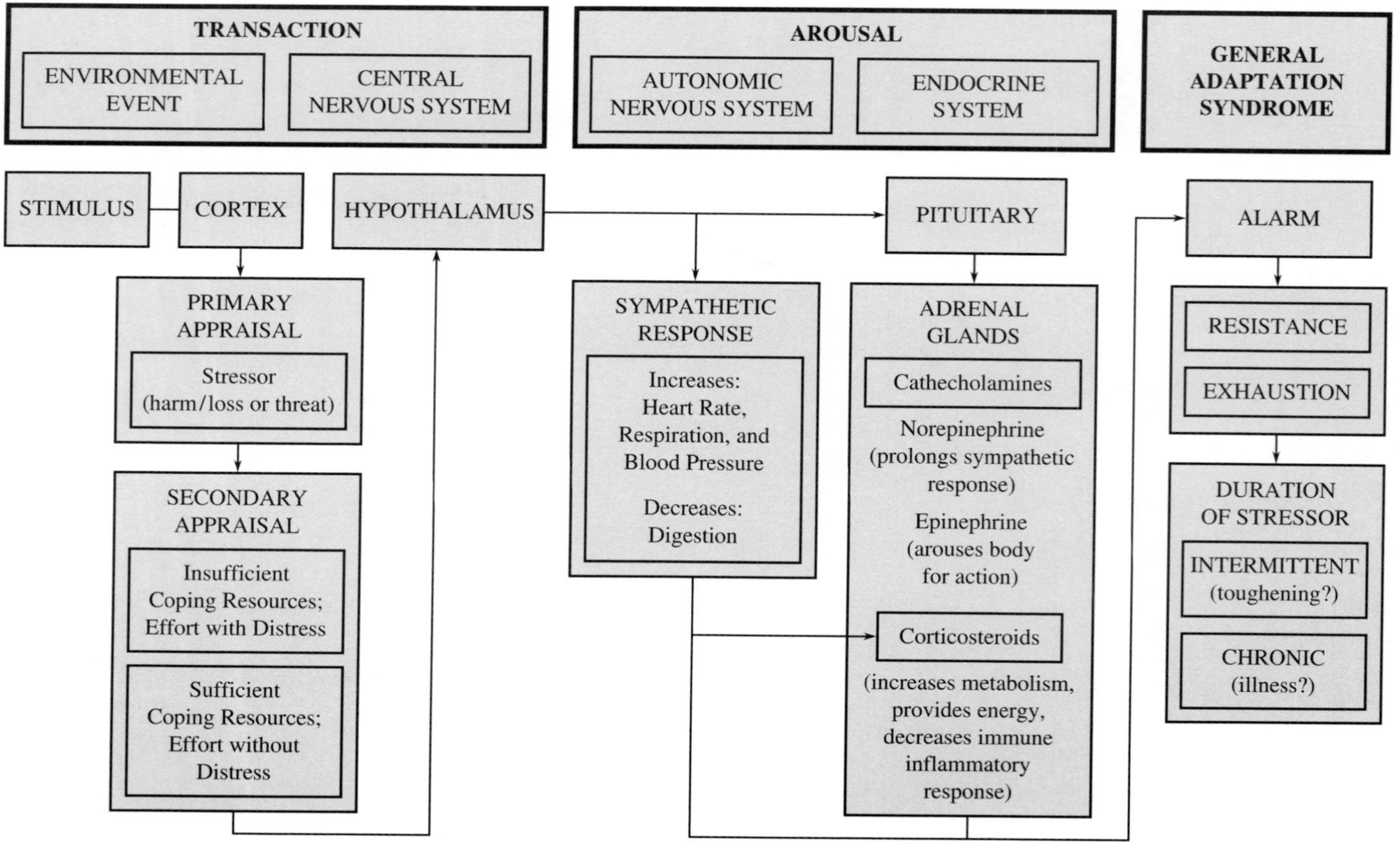

TRANSACTION

ENVIRONMENTAL EVENT   CENTRAL NERVOUS SYSTEM

STIMULUS → CORTEX — HYPOTHALAMUS

PRIMARY APPRAISAL
Stressor (harm/loss or threat)

SECONDARY APPRAISAL
Insufficient Coping Resources; Effort with Distress
Sufficient Coping Resources; Effort without Distress

AROUSAL

AUTONOMIC NERVOUS SYSTEM   ENDOCRINE SYSTEM

PITUITARY

SYMPATHETIC RESPONSE
Increases: Heart Rate, Respiration, and Blood Pressure
Decreases: Digestion

ADRENAL GLANDS
Catecholamines
Norepinephrine (prolongs sympathetic response)
Epinephrine (arouses body for action)
Corticosteroids (increases metabolism, provides energy, decreases immune inflammatory response)

GENERAL ADAPTATION SYNDROME

ALARM

RESISTANCE
EXHAUSTION

DURATION OF STRESSOR
INTERMITTENT (toughening?)
CHRONIC (illness?)

248

as in the case of harm/loss or threat) are associated with release of both cate-cholamines *and* corticosteroids. Corticosteroids—although initially beneficial in preparing the body to resist a threat—are anti-inflammatory and suppress the immune system, so they may be a crucial factor in the long-term stress–illness relationship (Zakowski, Hall, & Baum, 1992).

MODULE SUMMARY

This biopsychosocial model of stress is only speculative, but it is offered as an attempt to integrate the psychosocial and physiological theories and research on stress. The study of stress has advanced because of evidence that it has a role in illness. But does stress *cause* illness, and, if so, what can be done about it? These are the subjects of the next module. First, however, review this summary of Module 6.1:

1. There are three components of stress: the external, represented by the environmental stressor; the internal, represented by the emotional and physiological responses of the body; and the interaction of these two.
2. Conflict, frustration, and pressure make us aware of stress.
3. The internal component of stress can be measured by hormonal assay or polygraphic monitoring, although both miss the subjective experience of stress.
4. The general adaptation syndrome describes how the internal response to stress passes through three stages: alarm, resistance, and exhaustion. Chronic stress, or strain, can lead to exhaustion and possibly to illness.
5. The timing of the stressor may have an effect on the stress–illness relationship. Acute stress is not harmful, whereas chronic stress is. Intermittent stress may be beneficial by providing physiological toughening.
6. Transactions are interactions of the internal and external components of stress. The cognitive appraisal of stress determines its meaning and whether or not a physiological response is triggered.
7. During primary appraisal, events are categorized as either irrelevant, good, or stressful. Stressful events can be either harmful, a loss, threatening, or challenging. Secondary appraisal takes place after primary appraisal if an event is harmful, a loss, or threatening. During secondary appraisal, one's ability to cope is appraised. A stressful stimulus does not trigger a physiological response unless there are also insufficient coping abilities.

8. Different patterns of physiological response and hormonal secretions occur with different types of stress. Effort with distress, or a harm/loss, or threat, leads to negative emotions and potentially unhealthy physiological responses. Effort without distress, or a challenge, leads to positive emotions and potentially healthy physiological responses.

Illness and Management

Is There "Good" Stress?

Although primarily interested in the relationship between stress and illness, Selye (1974, 1985) proposed that certain stressors might have a beneficial effect. He used the term **eustress** (from the Greek word "eu," for good) to differentiate them from harmful stressors. Others have also suggested that some stress can be good (Seliger, 1986). What characteristics define "good stress"? In Module 6.1, we found that a stressor perceived as a challenge is accompanied by positive emotions and produces different patterns of hormonal secretion than a stressor perceived as a harm/loss or threat. We also found that the duration of a stressor may determine whether it has a good or bad effect. An intermittent stressor may be beneficial because of its ability to increase resistance to chronic stress.

The beneficial effects of stress probably come from its ability to produce arousal. Psychologists have long observed that there is an optimal level of arousal for task performance (Hebb, 1955; Malmo, 1975). For example, a test—if perceived as a threat—arouses the central nervous system, producing anxiety. It also triggers the general adaptation syndrome's alarm and resistance stages, producing energy for coping. One coping strategy would be to study, which should result in improved performance on the test. In fact, Alex, who viewed his finals as a challenge, did slightly better on them than his $B+$ average up to that time.

In contrast, too much of a threat (too much "test anxiety") results in deterioration of performance on a test (Wine, 1982). This would occur if the test were appraised as more of a threat than a challenge. Unfortunately, Dave, who viewed finals as a threat, did much poorer on them than his $B+$ average up to that time. In fact, this relationship between arousal (in the form of anxiety) and performance can be represented by an inverted "U"-shaped curve as illustrated in Figure 6.2-1.

As arousal increases, performance increases—up to a point. But if arousal continues to rise even higher, performance begins to deteriorate. You've probably experienced this when you were anxious and tried to recall someone's name or something you've learned for a test. The more anxious you became, the harder it was to remember. Then, later, when you were relaxed, the answer suddenly came to mind. The complexity of the task also has an effect on the relationship between arousal and performance. The simpler the task is, the higher the level of arousal necessary for optimal performance, whereas complex tasks are best met with lower levels of arousal.

So stress is a necessary and even beneficial part of life, and it can be good when it arouses us to deal with the challenges we face. When health psychologists speak of a relationship between stress and illness, then, they are referring only to stress that is appraised as a harm/loss or threat—stress that is *not* optimal for arousal, but that exceeds a person's ability to cope. Moderate levels of arousal are generally considered healthful because they facilitate coping.

THE RELATIONSHIP BETWEEN STRESS AND ILLNESS

MEASUREMENT OF STRESSORS

Researchers have used two methods to measure stressors: major life events and daily hassles. A **life event** is any major occurrence that requires a person

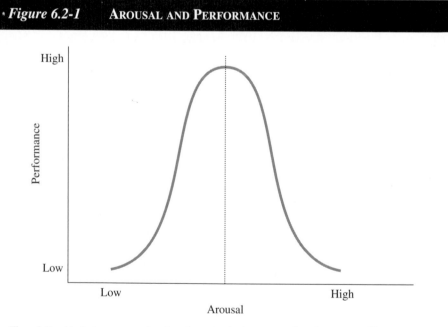

• *Figure 6.2-1*   AROUSAL AND PERFORMANCE

The relationship between arousal and performance is demonstrated in this inverted U-shaped curve. For tasks of moderate complexity, as arousal increases, so does performance; however, as arousal becomes higher, performance begins to decrease.

to adjust or adapt to it. The most widely used instrument to assess life events is the Social Readjustment Rating Scale (SRRS) developed by Holmes and Rahe (1967). They submitted a list of events, based on their own clinical experience, to hundreds of people from a variety of ages and backgrounds and asked them to rank the events based on the amount of readjustment, or coping effort, each would require (Holmes & Masuda, 1974). This produced a version of the SRRS consisting of 43 life events ranked from most to least stressful by their average readjustment value. Table 6.2-1 contains items from the SRRS and their mean values, which range from 11 to 100.

The SRRS is self-administered. People are given a list of the items and asked to indicate which events have happened to them over a recent period of time, usually the last 6 to 24 months. The mean values of each event checked are then summed to produce a total stress score.

Holmes and Rahe assumed that the crucial element in stressors is *change*, or the amount of psychological adjustment or coping an event requires. Therefore, as can be seen in Table 6.2-1, not all of the SRRS items are undesirable. For example, holidays, marriage, and being promoted may be stressful for some people. In one study, about 15% of people reported having experienced none of the SRRS events in the previous year, whereas 18% reported 5 or more (Goldberg & Comstock, 1980). Older people reported *fewer* SRRS events than younger people, and single, separated, or divorced people reported more events than married and widowed people.

The SRRS has been used primarily to study the relationship between stressors and illness. Early studies were retrospective, asking subjects to recall past illnesses and to complete the SRRS at the same time. This method confounds people's recall of illness and their recall of stressors, because people tend to remember negative events together.

The best studies have been prospective, first determining subjects' SRRS scores *before* they are ill, then checking their actual medical records over the next several months. Prospective studies have found a significant correlation of about .30 between stressful events and subsequent illness and accidents—those with the highest SRRS scores are more likely to become ill in the near future (Holmes & Masuda, 1974; Johnson, 1986; Rahe, 1974). However, overall, the correlation between the total SRRS score and illness is not very strong (Dohrenwend & Dohrenwend, 1981; Holmes & Rahe, 1967).

Dave and Alex's situation helps explain why this correlation is weak. Notice that "school" is one of the stressful life events on the SRRS. This suggests that a relationship exists between the experience of stress in adjusting to college and illness. Even though they both had to adjust to college, Dave experienced illness and injury, whereas Alex remained well. That is why there is only a weak correlation between SRRS scores and illness—not everyone who experiences these major life events becomes ill.

The SRRS benefits from sampling a wide variety of events that people experience in the course of their lives, and the items do relate significantly, if only weakly, to illness. Yet, the SRRS has been criticized for vague or ambiguous items (Hough, Fairbank, & Garcia, 1976) and for not taking into

	Table 6.2-1 STRESSFUL EVENTS AND THEIR MEAN VALUE FROM THE SOCIAL READJUSTMENT RATING SCALE	
RANK	LIFE EVENT	MEAN VALUE
1	Death of spouse	100
2	Divorce	73
3	Marital separation	65
4	Jail term	63
5	Death of close family member	63
6	Personal injury or illness	53
7	Marriage	50
8	Fired at work	47
9	Marital reconciliation	45
10	Retirement	45
11	Change in health of family member	44
12	Pregnancy	40
13	Sex difficulties	39
14	Gain of new family member	39
15	Business readjustment	39
16	Change in financial state	38
17	Death of close friend	37
18	Change to different line of work	36
19	Change in number of arguments with spouse	35
20	Mortgage over $10,000	31
21	Foreclosure of mortgage or loan	30
22	Change in responsibilities at work	29
23	Son or daughter leaving home	29
24	Trouble with in-laws	29
25	Outstanding personal achievement	28
26	Wife begins or stops work	26
27	Begin or end school	26
28	Change in living conditions	25
29	Revision of personal habits	24
30	Trouble with boss	23
31	Change in work hours or conditions	20
32	Change in residence	20
33	Change in schools	20
34	Change in recreation	19
35	Change in church activities	19
36	Change in social activities	18
37	Mortgage or loan less than $10,000	17
38	Change in sleeping habits	16
39	Change in number of family get-togethers	15
40	Change in eating habits	15
41	Vacation	13
42	Christmas	12
43	Minor violations of the law	11

Source: Holmes, T. H., and Rahe, R. H., 1967, The Social Readjustment Rating Scale, Journal of Psychosomatic Research, 11, *213–218.*

account the specific meaning an event has for the individual (Cohen, Karmarck, & Mermelstein, 1983; Lazarus & Folkman, 1984b). We can see the different meaning events have in the way Dave and Alex react to the same event—the phone calls from their parents.

The investigation of major life stressors continues to be a fruitful area of research activity. Newer life events scales have been developed to try to correct shortcomings of the SRRS (for example, Lewinsohn, Mermelstein, Alexander, & MacPhillamy, 1985). These new scales correct some the shortcomings of the original SRRS and should improve our understanding of the relationship between stress and illness in the future.

Measurement of Transactions

In keeping with their emphasis on the role of cognitive appraisal in stress and coping, Lazarus and Folkman (1989) have developed a dual self-report inventory that is an alternative to the SRRS: *the Hassles and Uplifts Scales.* These scales assess life's relatively minor irritations (such as losing your keys or getting caught in traffic) and pleasures (such as relating well to one's spouse or lover or satisfactorily completing a task), rather than major life events.

Hassles are defined as "experiences and conditions of daily living that have been appraised as salient *and* harmful or threatening," and **uplifts** are defined "as experiences and conditions of daily living that have appraised as salient *and* positive or favorable" (emphasis added; Lazarus, 1984, p. 376). Hassles are conceived of as potential stressors, while uplifts are conceived of as possible health promoters, or at least as being capable of counteracting hassles. This is quite different from the life events approach, which has emphasized only the potentially harmful role of stressors and which has viewed both good and bad changes as potentially stressful. Some of the most frequently checked items from the Hassles and Uplifts Scales are listed in Table 6.2-2.

There are two important questions with respect to the validity of the Hassles and Uplifts Scales: Do they measure a different aspect of stress than the life events scales? Are they related to health? The answer to the first question would appear to be "yes." In one study, hassles and life events were uncorrelated for men and were significantly, but only weakly, correlated at .36 for women (Kanner, Coyne, Schaefer, & Lazarus, 1981). Because of these correlations, Lazarus and Folkman (1989) concluded that major life events may cause some daily hassles for women, but a large proportion of hassles are independent of life events and arise from everyday living. There are also moderate correlations of about .43 to .60 between the Hassles and Uplifts Scales themselves, but they remain substantially independent (Lazarus & Folkman, 1989). However, it does appear that uplifts are of limited additional predictive value, adding little to hassles alone when predicting somatic health (Zarski, 1984).

The second question concerns the relationship between the Hassles and Uplifts Scales and health. Hassles are correlated with persistent symptoms of poor psychological adjustment in college students (Blankstein, Flett, & Koledin, 1991). In a study of college students, there was no causal pathway between major life events and psychological symptoms, but hassles were strongly and independently associated with psychological symptoms (Wagner, Compas, & Howell, 1988). There is also some preliminary research support for a relationship between hassles and physical health (DeLongis, Coyne, Dakof, Folkman, & Lazarus, 1982; Weinberger, Hiner, & Tierney,

Table 6.2-2 MOST FREQUENTLY CHECKED ITEMS FROM THE HASSLES AND UPLIFTS SCALES

DAILY HASSLES SCALE: TEN MOST FREQUENT HASSLES (*N* = 100)

	Item	% Endorsing*
1.	Concerns about weight	52.4
2.	Health of a family member	48.1
3.	Rising prices of common goods	43.7
4.	Home maintenance, inside	42.8
5.	Too many things to do	38.6
6.	Misplacing or losing things	38.1
7.	Yardwork or outside home maintenance	38.1
8.	Property, investments, or taxes	37.6
9.	Crime	37.1
10.	Physical appearance	35.9

UPLIFTS SCALE: TEN MOST FREQUENT UPLIFTS

	Item	% Endorsing
1.	Relating well with your spouse or lover	76.3
2.	Relating well with friends	74.4
3.	Completing a task	73.3
4.	Feeling healthy	72.7
5.	Getting enough sleep	69.7
6.	Eating out	68.4
7.	Meeting your responsibilities	68.1
8.	Visiting, phoning, or writing someone	67.7
9.	Spending time with family	66.7
10.	Home (inside) pleasing to you	65.6

The "% Endorsing" represents the mean percentage of people checking the item each month averaged over the nine monthly administrations.

Source: Lazarus, R. S., and Folkman, S., 1989, Manual for the hassles and uplifts scales, Palo Alto, CA: Consulting Psychologists Press.

1987; Zarski, 1984). Usually, the correlation between scores on the Hassles Scale and illness is slightly higher than that found with the SRRS, ranging from .30 to .40 (Lazarus & Folkman, 1989).

It is important to realize that, if one is prone to experiencing psychological symptoms, one's ongoing appraisal of events might also be effected, so daily occurrences would be more likely to be appraised as hassles. In other words, the appraisal of events is, of course, subjective, and so is one's self-report of psychological or physical symptoms. Lazarus and Folkman (1990) do not argue otherwise. In fact, they believe that there is "no satisfactory way to assess the environment as an objective set of conditions except through subjective consensual judgment" (p. 23). Of course, this makes the specification of causal pathways difficult.

Prospective designs help to overcome these problems, but there have not been many conducted yet. In one prospective study of 682 junior and senior high school students, daily hassles predicted life adjustment—as measured by both self-report *and* independent ratings of physical and emotional problems—better than life events (Rowlison & Felner, 1988). In fact, even when the effects of life events were removed, hassles scores continued to be good predictors of adjustment.

The Hassles and Uplifts Scales appear to be useful and meaningful additions to the measurement of stress, although, at this time, more evidence supports the role of hassles. In the relationship between stress and health, hassles appear to contribute significantly to the variance in health, over and above major life events.

STRESS-RELATED ILLNESSES

Stress has been suspected of having at least some role in many illnesses. Table 6.2-3 depicts many of the health problems and diseases with which stress has been linked. For each disease or problem listed, one or two representative examples of research supporting its relationship with stress is provided. (Some of these diseases are covered later in the modules related to the primary system involved.)

This fairly extensive list is impressive for the breadth of illnesses and problems in which stress has been implicated as a factor. Nevertheless, these examples should be considered cautiously, because in some cases, other studies have not found a correlation with stress. Also, in many cases, these supportive findings are based on retrospective data, so they suffer from the interpretational problems typical of correlational research.

Another reason for caution is that, as we have seen, the relationship between stress and illness is relatively weak (Dohrenwend & Dohrenwend, 1984; Gentry & Kobasa, 1984; Sarason & Sarason, 1984). A few critics of the correlational method used in some of these studies believe that the link between stress and illness may actually be even weaker, because some subjects may have a tendency to recall both more stress and more illness than others (Schroeder & Costa, 1984). Even so, most researchers continue to accept at least a modest relationship between stress and illness.

There are two ways that this relationship could occur. One is directly through stress-induced physiological changes and the other is indirectly through behavioral changes that then affect health status. **Psychoneuroimmunology** (discussed in Chapter 10) is the field most involved with the study of connections between psychosocial factors and the nervous, endocrine, and immune systems (Ader & Cohen, 1985; Pelletier & Herzing, 1988; Solomon, 1985). Although there generally is more evidence from animal studies than from human studies, research suggests that stress is related to immune suppression, which subsequently would leave the body more vulnerable to disease (Jemmott & Locke, 1984; Palmblad, 1981; Zakowski, McAllister, Deal, & Baum, 1992). Specifically, bereavement, marital discord, job loss, examinations, and chronic environmental or caretaker stress have all been associated with increases in catecholamines and corticosteroids and corresponding immune system changes (Zakowski, McAllister et al., 1992).

Table 6.2-3   SUSPECTED STRESS-RELATED DISEASES

DISEASE OR HEALTH PROBLEM	RESEARCH EVIDENCE[*]
Arthritis (rheumatoid)	Weiner (1977)
Asthma	Long et al. (1958)
Back pain	Holmes (1979)
Cancer	Sklar & Anisman (1981)
Cardiovascular disease	Garrity & Marx (1979); Theorell & Rahe (1975)
Diabetes	Bradley (1979)
Glaucoma	Cohen & Hajioff (1972)
Headaches	Andrasik, Blake, & McCarran (1986); Howarth (1965)
Hemophilia	Buxton et al. (1981)
Hernias	Rahe & Holmes (1965)
Herpes	Watson (1983)
Hypertension	Cottington et al., (1986)
Hyperthyroidism	Weiner (1978)
Leukemia	Greene & Swisher (1969)
Menstrual discomfort	Siegel, Johnson, & Sarason (1979)
Pregnancy (complications)	Georgas et al. (1984)
Reproductive problems (female)	Fries, Nillius, & Peterson (1974)
Stroke	Stevens et al. (1984)
Ulcers	Tennant (1988)

Examples of research evidence are given for reference only. Findings are tentative in many cases, are based largely on retrospective data, and suffer from the interpretational problems of all correlational research.

There is also research support for an indirect behavioral pathway between stress and illness. Wiebe and McCallum (1986) found that behaviors that increase the likelihood of one's becoming ill or injured are higher in people who are experiencing high levels of stress. This is corroborated by other studies that suggest that accident rates go up in highly stressed people (Johnson, 1986) and that the use of alcohol and cigarettes is also higher in people who experience high levels of stress (Baer, Garmezy, McLaughlin, Pokorny, & Wernick, 1987; Conway, Vickers, Ward, & Rahe, 1981). Therefore, people under stress are more likely to engage in disease-prone or accident-prone behaviors, which is why we need to view studies that find a correlation between stress and illness with caution.

From a biopsychosocial perspective, a variety of factors would be expected to be involved in any physical or psychological symptom. Therefore, when a single one of these factors—stress, for example—is correlated with illness, it should have only a modest relationship. Most people who are under stress do not become ill, and the effects of life event stressors are usually temporary anyway, with risk rarely remaining high for more than a year or two after a major change (Rahe, 1984). Another explanation for the weak correlation between stress and illness is that some stress may be good. Finally, other variables might mediate the stress–illness relationship. Mediators could act like a volume control on an amplifier, turning stress up or down. Stress mediators might account for why one person gets ill and another does not, even though they both experience the same stressor.

■■■■

STRESS MEDIATORS

Several factors may be capable of increasing or decreasing the effects of stress. When a mediator protects a person from the unhealthful effects of stress, it is called a buffer. By analogy, *buffers* "turn the stress-volume down." They are usually presumed to be influential only under conditions of high stress. Reducing an already low stress level would be superfluous. There is support for the role of buffers in reducing the stress–illness link (for example, Cohen & Willis, 1985; Kobasa, Maddi, & Courington, 1981). However, there is also evidence that some mediators may work directly and influence health status even under low stress conditions (Wortman & Dunkel-Schetter, 1987). Stress mediators, then, may act both directly or indirectly as buffers.

Buffers influence transactions (the left side of the biopsychosocial model in Figure 6.1-1), affecting primary and secondary appraisal in such a way that evaluations of harm/loss or threat would be reduced and beliefs in coping abilities would be strengthened. A stressor would then be less likely to produce a physiological response in the first place. On the other hand, *direct mediators* would counter the effects of the physiological response itself (the center of the model) through actions that prevent or ameliorate the physical effects of stress. Type A and B behavior patterns, social support, personal control, hardiness, exercise/activity level, sense of humor, and spiritual support have all been investigated as potential buffers or direct mediators of stress.

TYPE A AND B BEHAVIORS

Type A and Type B behaviors were first described by two cardiologists who were studying heart disease and are discussed in more detail in Module 11.1. Briefly, Type A is a behavioral and personality pattern characterized by the following: (a) competitive achievement orientation—goal striving without a sense of accomplishment and joy; (b) time urgency—constantly racing the clock, impatience, over scheduling; and, (c) anger and hostility—which may or may not be expressed (and which turned out to be the most important factor). In contrast, Type B is noncompetitive, enjoys the process as much as the goal, is patient, and has little anger and hostility.

Type A may mediate stress in at least two specific ways, one physiological, the other behavioral. First, Type A's have higher reactivity than Type B's. **Reactivity** is the speed and extent of the physiological changes involved in arousal. For example, a highly reactive person's heart rate would respond quickly and become very rapid in response to a threat. Most studies support the higher reactivity of Type A's in general, with Type A males even more reactive than Type A females (Contrada & Krantz, 1988; Houston, 1986). Second, Type A's thrive on activity and work, so they actually may take on more activities, thus *increasing* the number of stressors that they encounter in life (Byrne & Rosenman, 1986).

SOCIAL SUPPORT

People who have social support are part of a social network (such as family, friends, or community) on whom they can count in times of need, and they believe that they are loved, needed, and valued as part of that network (Cobb, 1976; Cohen & McKay, 1984; Wills, 1984). Social support may come in several forms:

- *Emotional support*   Verbal and nonverbal expressions of encouragement, reassurance, comfort, and caring.
- *Esteem support*   Verbal and nonverbal expressions that specifically build one's sense of self-worth, value, and competence.
- *Informational support*   Advice, guidance, and even directions from others.
- *Tangible support*   Direct material assistance in the form of services or resources.
- *Network support*   Membership in groups that share common interests and concerns.

Whether or not one receives social support and whether it is helpful is dependent on the circumstances in which it and stress occur. Some types of support, also called *optimal matching*, are better suited to particular needs (Cutrona, 1990; see Figure 6.2-2). For example, information or emotional support are

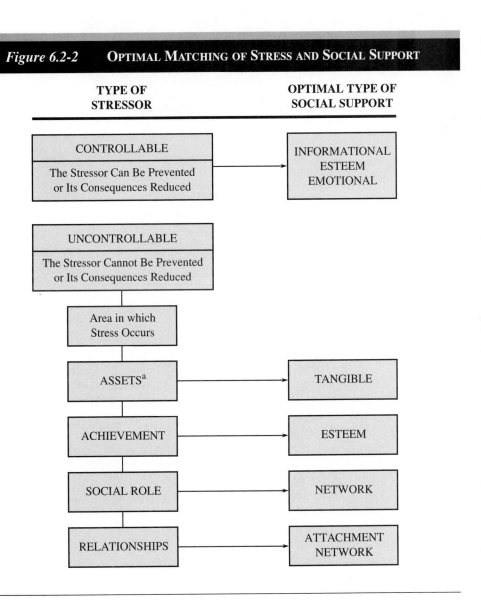

Figure 6.2-2   OPTIMAL MATCHING OF STRESS AND SOCIAL SUPPORT

Source: Adapted from Cutrona, C., 1990, Stress and social support—In search of optimal matching, Journal of Social and Clinical Psychology, *9, 3–14.*

[a]*Includes tangible resources and physical ability*

Warm, supportive relationships may help mediate the effects of stress.

better for the seriously ill (Wortman & Dunkel-Schetter, 1987). The manner in which support is asked for, such as pestering or not asking at all, can hinder its delivery. Of course, the extent of one's social network, the quality of the relationships one has with others, how often people are in contact, and the level of intimacy all affect how one receives social support (Mitchell, 1969; Schaefer, Coyne, & Lazarus, 1981).

Social support is probably a stress buffer, becoming more important in times of increasing strain. This appears to be particularly true for persons with Type A behavior (Kamarck, 1990). Cohen (1988) reviewed the research on social support and concluded that there is a clear link with mortality. The greater the number of family and friends and the greater the number of group activities and social affiliations, the longer one is likely to live. There is also evidence from animal experiments that social affiliation buffers the pathogenic effects of stress on immune system functioning (Cohen, Kaplan, Cunnick, Manuck, & Rabin, 1992). However, when it comes to links between social support and specific diseases, research support is not consistent, although the strongest evidence suggests that it plays a role in coronary artery disease. Interestingly, social support does appear to act as a buffer for distress resulting from physical illness itself (Bloom, 1982).

Personal Control

Julian Rotter (1966, 1975), was among the first to investigate locus of control. **Locus of control** refers to where a person locates the responsibility for her or his successes and failures. People with an *internal* locus believe they are in control of their lives, and they take responsibility for what happens to them. People with an *external* locus believe that outside forces or chance circumstances control their lives. Given these definitions, "internals" should have an advantage because they believe they are in control of their own health. They should be more sensitive to health messages and have more knowledge about health matters, and they should make more attempts to improve physical functioning.

Research suggests that internals are less susceptible to psychological and medical problems (Strickland, 1978). One study found that, in 2,090 middle-aged males, an internal locus of control had a buffering role against the effects of job and economic stress on health (Krause & Stryker, 1984). Other studies have generally supported the role of personal control in buffering health against the results of stress (Matheny & Cupp, 1983; Suls & Mullen, 1981).

Another personal control mediator is Albert Bandura's (1977, 1982, 1986) concept of **self-efficacy**, a person's belief in his or own ability to succeed at a task—to cope. Self-efficacy is not identical with an internal locus of control. While an internal locus of control would reflect a sense of efficacy, in Bandura's formulation, self-efficacy is a *prediction* of one's likelihood of success in a *specific situation.* Bandura emphasizes that self-efficacy is based on prior learning and reinforcement in similar situations. Evidence has shown that people with self-efficacy are better able to cope psychologically and physically with pain (Bandura, Reese, & Adams, 1982; Holahan, Holahan, & Belk, 1984), and self-efficacy has been linked to performing a variety of healthy behaviors (O'Leary, 1985).

What happens to people who do not have a sense of personal control? Martin Seligman's (1975) theory of learned helplessness, which he first proposed as a cause of depression, may answer this question. **Learned helplessness** develops when people repeatedly fail in situations they are unable to control (Hiroto & Seligman, 1975). People with learned helplessness give up easily. Even if they are presented with a new situation, they may not try to succeed.

However, uncontrollable failures do not always result in learned helplessness and depression. Therefore, a revision of the theory has invoked the cognitive process of attribution to help explain under what circumstances learned helplessness occurs (Abramson, Seligman, & Teasdale, 1978). In this revised theory of learned helplessness, a person in an uncontrollable situation assesses it on three dimensions:

1. *Internal-external* Whether the situation is caused by one's own limitations (internal) or by outside factors that would be beyond anyone's abilities (external).

2. *Stable-unstable* Whether the situation is long standing (stable) or temporary (unstable).
3. *Global-specific* Whether the situation is attributed to a broad, general failing on one's part (global) or is just a narrow, confined problem (specific).

Therefore, a person who is in a negative situation and attributes it to *global, stable, and internal* factors is more likely to develop learned helplessness. For example, imagine you do not get a date with a person you are attracted to—a situation you cannot control. If you attribute this to your own internal limitations ("I'm not attractive enough"), and you view these limitations as stable ("I'll never be attractive") and global ("I have *no* attractive qualities"), you may give up dating altogether.

Learned helplessness has generated a lot of research interest, which has supported the relationship between personal control, learned helplessness, and depression (Abramson, Garber, & Seligman, 1980; Alloy & Abramson, 1980). But critics have pointed out that much of this research was conducted in the laboratory with animals as subjects (Peterson, 1982). However, a few studies point to a relationship between learned helplessness and health in humans (for example, Langer & Rodin, 1976; Sklar & Anisman, 1981), but until there has been more naturalistic research with humans, it is best not to overstate the role of learned helplessness in illness.

HARDINESS

Hardiness is a personality characteristic proposed by Suzanne Kobasa (1979) as a mediator of the stress–illness relationship. Hardiness combines three characteristics (Kobasa, Maddi, & Kahn, 1982):

1. *Commitment* This develops when one approaches life with a sense of meaning and active involvement in one's work.
2. *Control* This is a feeling of being able to influence events.
3. *Challenge* This is a view of change as an opportunity for growth rather than a threat.

It has been proposed that people who demonstrate these characteristics, those with a "hardy personality," would be less likely to become ill when under stress (Gentry & Kobasa, 1984). Presumably, they are less likely to perceive stress as harmful and they are better equipped to cope with it if they do. Hardiness has been the subject of much research interest, but early studies suffered from methodological and measurement problems, and contradictory results have been reported (see Funk & Houston, 1987; Hull, Van Treuren, & Virnelli, 1987; and Rhodewalt & Zone, 1989).

Hardiness does appear to be a direct mediator of illness in some studies (for example, Kobasa, Maddi, & Kahn, 1982; Kobasa, Maddi, Puccetti, & Zola,

1985; Wiebe & McCallum, 1986), but other studies have failed to find any relationship between hardiness and illness (Bernard & Belinsky, 1992; Funk & Houston, 1987; Hull et al., 1987; Roth, Wiebe, Fillingim, & Shay, 1990). Nevertheless, hardiness is an interesting concept that has generated renewed interest in the relationship between personality and health (Suls & Rittenhouse, 1987), so research will probably continue. However, at present, the proposed link between hardiness and health should be viewed with caution.

EXERCISE/ACTIVITY LEVEL

Exercise can help reduce anxiety and depression and increase feelings of well-being (for example, Sime, 1984), and it can reduce physiological arousal after acute stress (Dienstbier, 1989), so exercise might be expected to mediate the stress–illness relationship. In a study of adults aged 24 to 65 who volunteered because they wanted help coping with stress, an aerobic conditioning treatment was found to be superior to no treatment and equal to a cognitive treatment in reducing self-reported anxiety and in increasing self-efficacy at a three-month follow-up (Long, 1984).

If stress and illness are related and if exercise is a buffer to stress, then exercise should be negatively related to the development of illness. In fact, a correlational study of 373 college students did find that exercise and illness were negatively related (Roth et al., 1990). Three other studies provide additional evidence of such a relationship. One retrospective study found that men who reported higher exercise levels also reported fewer illnesses over a three-year period, with greater benefits from exercise evident in higher stress subjects (Kobasa, Maddi, & Puccetti, 1982). A second study provided stronger evidence due to its longitudinal design (Roth & Holmes, 1985). Over a nine-week period, stress did not affect the health of fit subjects, but subjects who were not fit had higher levels of stress and poorer health. Finally, a longitudinal study of 212 adolescent girls indicated that exercise significantly buffered the effects of high stress on illness (Brown & Siegel, 1988), again indicating that the beneficial effects of exercise may be more important when stress is high. Together, these studies support the role of exercise as a stress buffer.

HUMOR

It has been proposed that humor is a cognitive strategy that evolved to handle stress in human beings (Dixon, 1980). This position received popular attention through Norman Cousins' (1979) recovery from a crippling and often fatal type of arthritis, which he attributed partially to laughter, a result of viewing Marx Brothers movies and episodes of *Candid Camera*. However, research has not consistently supported this proposition. In one study, neither humor nor the appreciation of humor affected the relationship between stressful life events and depression or anxiety (Safranek & Schill, 1982).

Nevertheless, a subsequent series of experiments (Lefcourt & Martin, 1986) did find support for humor as a buffer for the effects of stress on *psychological* well-being, specifically mood, and other research has suggested that humor used as a coping strategy is related to psychological and physical health (Anderson & Arnoult, 1989).

One experiment found that humor affected a physiological measure of immune system functioning, supporting its potential relationship to physical health (Dillon, Minchoff, & Baker, 1985). After viewing a humorous videotape, subjects' salivary immunoglobulin A (part of the defense against infection) increased significantly, but there was no increase after viewing a nonhumorous videotape. Yet, despite these promising indications, a later study was not able to find evidence that humor could affect the relationship between stress and physical illness, although it did find a relationship between humor and mood (Porterfield, 1987).

Are those who lack a sense of humor destined for ill health? Not according to a recent study. Those with a well-developed sense of humor (humorists and comics) *do not* live as long as serious writers and entertainers, although the *experience* of humor—positive emotions linked to amusing stimuli—may buffer stress (Rotton, 1992). More research will be needed before a conclusion can be reached about the role of humor in health.

SPIRITUAL SUPPORT

One intriguing area of stress-buffering research is spiritual support, which is defined here as perceived support from God. Some research has found a relationship between spiritual support and health status. For example, in 71 patients with cancer, self-reported church membership and attendance, as well as a feeling of closeness to God, were related to less pain (Yates, Chalmer, St. James, Follansbee, & McKegney, 1981). Among 400 elderly people, spiritual support—specifically viewing religion as a source of strength and comfort— was related to a lower rate of mortality for those who were poor in health (Zuckerman, Kasl, & Ostfeld, 1984).

One prospective study directly evaluated the stress-buffering role of spiritual support and found that, among college students who had experienced high life stress, spiritual support was predictive of later psychological well-being (Maton, 1989). This research provides an indication that spiritual support might buffer stress, but its role in health needs further study.

CONCLUSION

In conclusion, some of these potential stress mediators have received more research support than others. Generally, exercise, social support, and personal control have the most promise, while more data are needed before a judgment

Laughter and humor are possible stress mediators.

can be made about the role of hardiness, humor, and spiritual support. Studies of stress mediators have provided health psychologists with knowledge that can be applied to the development of stress management techniques. In the next section, we describe how stress can be managed.

MANAGING STRESS

Stress is an inextricable part of living, particularly in our fast-paced, technological world. It cannot be removed from our lives, and it may not be advantageous to do so, given that some stress is necessary for arousal and may actually be good. Therefore, our objective must be to learn how to live with stress while minimizing its unhealthful consequences. That is the goal of stress management, not to eliminate stress, but to learn to live compatibly with it.

APPLYING THE BIOPSYCHOSOCIAL MODEL

Theoretically, stress management should restore homeostasis disrupted by chronic stress. The biopsychosocial model offers two ways of approaching stress management. "Arousal management" attempts to affect physiological responses to stress (the center of Figure 6.1-1) by targeting the endocrine and autonomic nervous systems. It seeks to reestablish homeostasis by reducing arousal *after* encountering stress. On the other hand, "transaction management" attempts to affect the appraisal of stressors (the left side of Figure 6.1-1) by targeting the environment and the central nervous system (cognitions) in order to maintain homeostasis when facing stress. It seeks to reduce the *potential* for arousal to occur in the first place. Arousal management techniques will be examined first, followed by transaction management techniques.

AROUSAL MANAGEMENT

Arousal management consists of both pharmacological and behavioral techniques that prevent or reduce the physiological responses that occur when homeostasis is upset after a stressful transaction. As we have seen, some researchers believe stress is a problem of too much arousal, leading to exhaustion. Therefore, various therapies that lower arousal by promoting a parasympathetic response have been used to manage stress. These therapies include medication, relaxation training, and exercise.

MEDICATION   While this form of intervention is medical and not psychological, the widespread use of medication to help manage stress, particularly if anxiety is present, necessitates its mention. No medication can treat the *cause* of stress and medication might even prolong the problem by preventing physiological toughening from occurring (Dienstbier, 1989). However, medication is sometimes prescribed as a temporary means of reducing the acute symptoms of stress that interfere with normal functioning.

There are several categories of drugs with antianxiety or tranquilizing effects (Table 6.2-4). Nonpsychiatrists—usually family physicians, general practitioners, and gynecologists—write most of the prescriptions for benzodiazepines and the other "stress-reducing" medications (Lasagna, 1977). Because of the potential dangers of unwanted side effects, including dependency, and the fact that drugs do not treat the cause of the stress, the decision to use medication should be a joint one on the part of the patient and the physician and it must be determined that the short-term benefits exceed the risks.

When acute symptoms are clearly linked to a cause that is *temporary*, medication may be helpful (Berkow & Fletcher, 1987). However, medication is by no means required even in temporary situations, for research has shown that medication use can be reduced or discontinued in a majority of subjects undergoing an eight-session treatment consisting of relaxation training and cognitive-behavioral therapy (Richards et al., 1989). If stress is not temporary, then medication still leaves the problem of how the stress will be treated in the long term. If the stressful circumstances are chronic, or if the symptoms are not linked to a specific condition or event, then medication should gradually be replaced with a long-term stress management approach that includes both relaxation training and exercise.

R ELAXATION TRAINING   Relaxation is the goal of muscle relaxation techniques, meditation, and biofeedback (Silver & Blanchard, 1978), and all of these attempt to decrease sympathetic arousal (Gelhorn & Kiely, 1972). Relaxation training is believed to increase parasympathetic and to decrease sympathetic activity in the ANS (Borkovec, Johnson, and Block, 1984). It has been judged generally effective for anxiety and stress-related problems (Rachman & Wilson, 1980). It reduces arousal and increases the functioning of various parts of the immune system, although these changes are not long-lasting (Zakowski, Hall, & Baum, 1992).

Muscle relaxation is among the most widely used and simplest stress-reduction techniques to employ. It also requires no expensive equipment (unlike biofeedback), which probably explains why it is so popular. Two types of muscle relaxation were introduced in Module 2.2: (a) Jacobson's (1938) *progressive muscle relaxation* and (b) Benson's (1975) *progressive muscle relaxation with controlled breathing*. Both types have been used for stress management (Lavey & Taylor, 1985), but the effectiveness of progressive muscle relaxation with controlled breathing is better established (for example, Borkovec & Sides, 1979; Bradley & McCanne, 1981; Hoffman et al., 1982).

Table 6.2-4   TYPES OF MEDICATION PRESCRIBED FOR STRESS MANAGEMENT

CATEGORY	DESCRIPTION
Barbiturates (for example, Seconal) induce tranquilization, but there are many side effects: drowsiness, dependency, psychological impairment, and a potential for overdose.	
Benzodiazepines (for example, Valium) are considered safer than barbiturates, because the side effects are less frequent and less extreme (Lader, 1984). Nevertheless, the same side effects do occur with some frequency, and atypical behaviors such as excessive emotionality and criminal activities have been reported in people on benzodiazepines (Gaind & Jacoby, 1978).	
Beta-blockers are a newer category of drugs that is being prescribed with growing frequency. The Beta-adrenoceptor antagonists (or beta-blockers) reduce sympathetic responses of the autonomic nervous system without affecting the central nervous system. They were primarily used to treat cardiac arrhythmias when it was discovered that, by reducing the symptoms of sympathetic arousal such as rapid heart rate and palpitations, they also reduced the *feelings* of uneasiness and anxiety associated with them. Their anti-anxiety effects have been studied in a variety of situations, and they are frequently prescribed for stage fright (Frishman, Razin, Swencionis, & Sonnenblick, 1981).	

Meditation is another technique used to promote relaxation. Two versions of meditation were also discussed in Module 2.2: (a) *nonstructured meditation* (Carrington, 1978) and (b) *structured meditation* (Benson, 1975). As a method of promoting relaxation, there is more evidence for the efficacy of structured meditation. However, meditation appears to offer no specific benefits over muscle relaxation (Shapiro, 1985) or just plain rest (Holmes, 1984), so more research is needed before it can be prescribed for stress management, although it probably does no harm.

Biofeedback has also been used to increase relaxation. Overall, biofeedback does appear to be effective as a stress management technique; however, it has not been shown to have any advantage over relaxation training, which is simpler and less costly (for example, Achterberg, Kenner, & Casey, 1989; Andrasik, Blanchard, & Edlund, 1985; Nigl, 1984; Turner & Chapman, 1982a).

Of the forms described in Module 2.2, EMG, temperature, and EEG biofeedback are the most commonly used in stress management. EEG is used to train "alpha" brain waves, which are associated with a generally relaxed state of consciousness. EMG and temperature biofeedback are used to induce a parasympathetic response through muscle relaxation and vasodilation, respectively.

Biofeedback would probably be most effective for specific, treatable symptoms that accompany stress, such as migraine headache, back pain, or hypertension. A consensus appears to be developing among researchers, however, that even though biofeedback has been demonstrated to be an effective treatment for some stress-related problems, muscle relaxation training (which usually occurs as a side effect of biofeedback anyway) is just as effective on its own (for example, Blanchard et al., 1982; O'Leary & Wilson, 1987; Reed, Katkin, & Goldband, 1986).

EXERCISE Since research tends to support the stress-buffering role of exercise, it is not surprising that it is frequently prescribed as a stress-management technique (Zakowski, Hall, & Baum, 1992). The basis for its use has been its apparent "tranquilizing" effect (DeVries, Wiswell, Bulbulin, & Moritani, 1981). Research suggests that it alters mood, modestly reducing stress, anxiety, tension, and depression, with greater immediate than long-term effects (for example, Rodin & Plante, 1989). However, the effects of exercise are not that simple. It also increases metabolism and triggers the release of some of the very same hormones that are part of the stress response. How can this reduce the effects of stress? One possible explanation is discussed in the next section.

PHYSIOLOGICAL TOUGHNESS REVISITED: AROUSAL, RELAXATION, AND STRESS How does exercise promote stress reduction if it causes the release of stress-related hormones? In the first place, not all researchers view arousal management as a simple matter of inducing relaxation. In fact, in a critical review of the effects of relaxation techniques, Holmes (1984) concluded that such techniques may not result in decreased sympathetic arousal at all. Holmes found that there was no measure of physiological arousal (for example, heart rate, respiration, electrodermal response) on which there was a reliably *lower* arousal level produced by meditation than when subjects were in a resting state. In fact, there was about as much evidence that meditating subjects had a *higher* arousal level, particularly in response to stress.

One problem with Holmes's conclusions is that he only reviewed studies that used meditation. He believes meditation is generally equivalent to other forms of relaxation therapy, but as we have seen, it may not be as effective a method of inducing relaxation as some others. Another problem is that Holmes only reviewed studies of "normal" subjects, so his conclusions may not apply to clinical subjects.

Nevertheless, if arousal management is not a simple matter of inducing relaxation, could deliberately increasing tension and stress play a role? Richard Dienstbier's (1989) theory of physiological toughening (introduced in Module 6.1), which contradicts the notion that less arousal (that is, relaxation) leads to better stress coping abilities, may provide the answer.

Dienstbier (1989) maintains that the past emphasis on chronic stressors has led to a clinical focus on "stress control," in which any reduction of sympathetic arousal in response to a stressor is considered beneficial. Instead, he suggests that some stress, depending on the duration, may actually *strengthen* one's resistance to stress by temporarily and regularly *increasing* arousal. It sounds paradoxical, but think of this as a form of conditioning like the gradually longer distances that a person might run to prepare for a marathon race. Intermittent exposure to longer distances increases the runner's ability to withstand the strain of a marathon.

Elements of Dienstbier's theory have been suggested by others in the past (see Miller, 1980), and support for it has recently come unexpectedly from a study of major life events stress. Intermittent exposure to major life events was found to have strengthened later stress resistance (Boyce & Chesterman, 1990). Apparently, the experience of intermittent stressful events had an "inoculating effect" against subsequent stressors. Cognitively, this could happen if people learn effective coping strategies for the future from past stressful experiences.

Dienstbier, calls this a "positive spiral." It occurs when physiological toughness interacts with one's appraisal of one's ability to cope. Having more coping energy available (that is, physiological toughness, which is the same as the marathon runner being in better condition) produces a more positive appraisal of one's coping abilities and thus a greater expectation of success in coping with stress in the future. Deinstbier (1989) has demonstrated that people who are physiologically tough and have a positive appraisal of their coping skills perform better on complex tasks, have more emotional stability, and also have enhanced immune system functioning.

These enthusiasts, swimming in a lake on a cold winter's day, practiced physiological toughening long before its potential benefits came to the notice of psychologists.

If physiological toughening increases the ability to resist strain, it will have important implications for clinical stress management. Rather than emphasizing stress control and arousal reduction, stress management in the future might actually encourage intermittent exposure to stressors. So far, two potential physiological tougheners have been identified: cold temperature and aerobic exercise (Dienstbier et al., 1981; Dienstbier et al., 1987; Dienstbier, LaGuardia, & Wilcox, 1987). Dienstbier recognizes that people will probably not deliberately subject themselves to the cold, so he advocates the use of aerobic exercise, believing that even a modest level of physical training may produce results.

While the treatment implications of Dienstbier's theory have yet to be adequately researched, they do suggest that the optimum strategy for arousal management would be to combine relaxation strategies for short-term stress with physiological toughening for long-term stress. Even so, some psychologists would argue that arousal management might be unnecessary if transactions were successfully managed in the first place.

Transaction Management

One way to manage a stressful transaction is to change or remove the stimulus being perceived as a stressor. Such interventions target the environment and are considered **problem-focused coping**. People tend to use it when they believe the problem is changeable (Lazarus & Folkman, 1984b). For example, difficulties in a class may be dealt with by dropping it.

Unfortunately, many stressful stimuli cannot be dealt with as easily. When a situation is perceived as unchangeable, transactions can be managed by a cognitive intervention. Recall from Module 6.1 that in Lazarus's cognitive theory of stress, a stimulus provokes an arousal only when a mismatch occurs between one's perceived coping resources and a perceived stressor. It is important to keep in mind that successful coping does *not* require that a stressful situation be changed or eliminated, instead the cognitive aspects of stressful transactions can be altered (Lazarus & Folkman, 1984b). This is called **emotion-focused coping**, and there are two types:

1. *Distracting oneself* from the stressful situation, for example through the use of alcohol or drugs, by reading, or by engaging in recreation.
2. *Changing cognitive appraisals*, such as altering the perception of stress or learning to tolerate or accept it (Lazarus & Folkman, 1984b).

Both problem-focused and emotion-focused coping are useful, depending on the circumstances (Auerbach, 1989). Problem-focused coping includes any attempts to *approach* and alter the environmental stressor, whereas emotion-focused coping includes any attempts to *avoid* actually changing the stressor. Therefore, emotion-focused coping includes cognitive redefinition and arousal management, both of which do not take any action to change the stressor itself.

Roth and Cohen (1986) introduced a distinction between approach and avoidant strategies that can serve as a framework to help determine when to use these different coping methods:

> *Avoidant strategies seem useful in that they may reduce stress and prevent anxiety from becoming crippling. Approach strategies, on the other hand, allow for appropriate action and/or the possibility for noticing and taking advantage of changes in a situation that might make it more controllable (p. 813).*

In other words, there are costs and benefits associated with both strategies. Approach is best when the stressor is controllable and there is a chance it can be changed. There is a cost in terms of increased distress in facing the stressor, but this is offset by the possibility of changing it. Avoidance is best when the stressor is uncontrollable and there is no chance of changing it, because then an approach strategy would lead to increased distress without productive change (Roth & Cohen, 1986).

USING EMOTION-FOCUSED COPING   Distraction is probably one of the most widely used coping strategies and therefore the easiest to understand, although we sometimes call it by other names like "leisure activities." People distract themselves in many ways, and some are more beneficial than others. Again, consider the example of a difficult class that is a requirement and cannot be dropped. Drinking to cope with the class would be distracting, but clearly such a solution would be counterproductive because it interferes with memory, whereas regular recreation might provide an escape from the pressure and a return to the books with renewed energy. However, distraction is not always possible.

Sometimes it is more effective to change one's cognitive appraisal of a situation. **Cognitive redefinition** is a method people seem to use naturally to change their perception of stress (Taylor, 1983). It includes looking for the positive aspects of a situation, comparing it to even worse situations, or finding some good that can come out of it. This might seem like nothing more than a "Polyanna" attitude, but it does reduce stress.

For those who cannot simply adopt such a rosy outlook, Donald Meichenbaum and Roy Cameron have developed a strategy called stress inoculation or SI (Meichenbaum 1985; Meichenbaum & Cameron, 1983). SI is a cognitive-behavioral therapy that teaches people how to cope with stress. Although the therapy itself may seem artificial, it is believed to utilize inherent cognitive abilities (Epstein, 1982; Janis, 1983). Stress inoculation therapy has begun to generate a considerable amount of research, and it is worth examining further. The three-step process of SI therapy is described in Box 6.2-1.

Although SI therapy has yet to be fully evaluated, there is evidence that many of its components do work (Hamberger & Lohr, 1984). It has been used successfully to cope with the anxiety of dating (Jaremko, 1983) and of test-taking (Smith & Nye, 1989), and SI has been used to help adolescents control their anger (Feindler & Fremouw, 1983). The success of SI supports the theory that cognitive redefinition can successfully alter the *appraisal* of stress. Thus, people can manage transactions in any of three ways: (a) by changing the environmental stimulus, (b) by distracting themselves from it, or (c) by altering their appraisal of the stimulus.

Cognitive stress reduction may improve some aspects of immune system functioning and may reduce the incidence of disease. In two 2-hour sessions, researchers were able to enhance perceptions of self-efficacy in people who were severely snake phobic, counter their phobic thoughts, and reduce anticipatory stress (Wiedenfeld et al., 1990). Importantly, the rate of self-efficacy enhancement was correlated with improved immune system functioning. In another study, people with recurrent genital herpes lesions were randomly assigned to either a cognitive-behavioral treatment or placebo group (McLarnon & Kaloupek, 1988). The treatment group received cognitive restructuring, role playing, and homework, while the placebo group met for discussions only. Over a 12-week follow-up period, the lesion recurrence rate dropped significantly for the cognitive-behavioral group, but remained virtually unchanged for the placebo group.

CONCLUSION

Long-term stress management can be achieved through cognitive techniques that target transactions or physiological toughening (exercise) that targets

---

Box 6.2-1   STEPS IN STRESS INOCULATION THERAPY

Step 1: Conceptualization

This step is an exploratory process during which stress transactions are examined. Using both interview and more active data-gathering techniques such as guided imagery, role-playing, and behavioral observation, the therapist attempts to identify both stressful environmental stimuli and cognitive evaluations of them, with an emphasis on understanding the latter.

Step 2: Skills Acquisition Rehearsal

In this step, new coping skills are learned and practiced. This is when cognitive redefinition takes place. The client's self-statements are monitored and the therapist develops a new set of self-statements that redefine, replace, or counteract the preexisting, automatic self-statements. Self-statements are the ongoing internal monologue in which one thinks or "talks" to oneself. Meichenbaum and Cameron (1983) have found that self-statements influence the cognitive appraisal of stressors, such that the appraisal of a stressor can actually be changed by changing the self-statements about it. With the therapist's help, the client develops specific self-statements for each important stressful transaction in his or her life. Here are some general examples of the kinds of self-statements utilized by Meichenbaum (1977) in SI therapy:

Preparing for a Stressor
I can develop a plan to deal with the situation.
Don't worry, worry won't help anything.
Confronting and Handling a Stressor
One step at a time: you can handle the situation.
Relax; you're in control. Take a slow deep breath.
Coping with the Feeling of Being Overwhelmed
Keep the focus on the present; what is it I have to do?
Don't try to eliminate the fear totally; just keep it manageable.
Reinforcing Self-Statements
It worked; I did it.
I can be pleased with the progress I'm making.

Step 3: Application and Follow-through

This step involves behavioral therapy in this otherwise cognitive approach and is considered essential for successful completion of the therapy. During this stage the client applies the newly acquired skills, first in simulated situations and then in actual situations with gradually increasing demands.

arousal. One study compared the effectiveness of both of these approaches in reducing stress by randomly assigning 48 women and 25 men to one of three groups: (a) aerobic exercise (jogging), (b) stress-inoculation training, or (c) no treatment (Long, 1984). Both exercise and stress-inoculation were effective in significantly reducing anxiety and increasing self-efficacy at a 15-month follow-up (Long, 1985). Unfortunately, this experiment did not investigate whether a combination of the two would produce even greater change, nor did it examine subsequent health outcomes, but both treatments were effective psychologically.

Since there was no possibility of changing the stressors inherent in college, Dave ultimately benefited from an avoidant or emotion-focused strategy. Such a strategy was suggested by Alex, who had learned about stress in his health psychology class. Alex encouraged Dave to talk to his professor who referred Dave to the student counseling service for stress management. Therefore, social support helped to buffer Dave's stress: Alex provided emotional support in the form of caring, and the professor provided informational support in the form of guidance and direction.

Dave's counselor recommended a program of aerobic exercise three times per week, which served as a distraction, improved Dave's general mood, and may have resulted in physiological toughening. The counselor also used a cognitive redefinition program like SI to help Dave learn to view his stressors as challenges, more like Alex. As a result of the counseling, Dave's second-semester grades were better than his first-semester grades, and he continued to progress toward his ultimate goal of medical school. In the meantime, Alex changed his major to psychology.

MODULE SUMMARY

This completes our evaluation of stress, its relationship to illness, and ways it can be managed. The next module takes up the subject of pain, but before continuing on, make sure you understand these important concepts presented in this module:

1. Eustress is a form of "good" stress. Stress is beneficial if it leads to arousal that facilitates performance. Some stress is, therefore, necessary for survival, but it is harmful if it results in a deterioration of performance.

2. The overall correlation between stress and illness is weak, although other factors may offer a partial explanation for this. Stress mediators that may increase or decrease the effects of stress are: Type A or Type B behavior, social support, personal control, hardiness, exercise, humor, and spiritual support.

3. The biopsychosocial model of stress offers two ways of approaching stress management: Arousal management attempts to affect physiological responses, while transaction management attempts to affect the cognitive appraisal of stress.

4. Arousal management consists of medication, relaxation training, and exercise. Medication can treat the effects of acute stress but does not treat the cause and may be counterproductive in chronic stress. Relaxation training is beneficial, but meditation and biofeedback appear to offer no advantages beyond relaxation training. Exercise appears to be beneficial, but it may operate by physiological toughening rather than by promoting relaxation.

5. Transaction management involves problem-focused coping, which involves removing the environmental stressor, or emotion-focused coping, which involves distracting oneself from the stress or changing the cognitive appraisal of it.

6. Approach strategies, or problem-focused coping, probably works best when a stressor is controllable and when there is a potential to affect it, whereas, avoidant coping strategies—changing cognitions—would be better when there is no chance to change the stressor.

7. Stress inoculation therapy—a means of cognitive restructuring— appears to be an effective method of changing the cognitive appraisal of stress.

7

Pain

7.1 *Theory and Measurement*
7.2 *Syndrome and Management*

We cannot live without pain. That is a statement of fact, not the inspiration for a Shakespearean tragedy. Certainly pain hurts, but would we be better off without it? There are some people, fortunately few, with *congenital insensitivity to pain*; they experience little or no sensation to what would ordinarily be a painful stimulus (Chapman, 1984; Manfredi et al., 1981). Even scalding hot water, freezing cold, or strong electric shock can fail to elicit any sensation (Bakal, 1979). This condition is present from birth, but people who suffer from it rarely live to become adults. They die young from injuries and illnesses that often go unnoticed. For example, self-protection is partly learned through the punishment of pain, so it is difficult for children who are insensitive to pain to learn to avoid burning themselves. Such children often suffer repeated third-degree burns to the point of disfigurement and infection.

Insensitivity would have greatly delighted Jennifer the day that she felt an excruciatingly sharp stab of pain through her lower back. She had just bent over to remove an Open House sign from a property she was showing, something she had done a hundred times since becoming a real estate broker. Her parents had raised her to be independent and had expected her to have a career, just as they both had had. Jennifer had gone straight from high school to community college and finally into real estate classes.

Now, at the age of 27, she worked long hours, including weekends. She did pause long enough to marry another broker, but both she and her husband worked long hours and had little energy left over for their relationship. They were in the prime of their productive years and wanted to be successful.

Jennifer had never felt pain as intense as she did that day. She was used to getting through difficulties by sheer willpower, but it did no good; she could not straighten up and was taken to the doctor's office doubled over. All she wanted was for the pain to end. As she waited for the doctor, she thought, "How could this happen to me? I can't believe anything hurts this much. Will

I be able to show houses this weekend? I have to be at the escrow office first thing tomorrow. What will mom and dad think of me?"

At that moment, how could Jennifer appreciate that pain has survival value and that acute pain is an adaptive sensation? Acute pain is essential to survival for two very important reasons:

1. *It contributes to learning* by motivating us to avoid harm so gradually we learn to protect ourselves from environmental hazards such as a hot stove.
2. *It alerts us to danger* by motivating us to seek help when there is a potential for injury, such as when the acute pain of appendicitis causes someone to call the doctor or to go to the emergency room, avoiding its lethal complications.

Even though the survival value of pain is straightforward, the experience of pain is not. Jennifer's pain was caused by a ligament rupture. Although this condition would normally heal in a matter of weeks, her pain would continue much longer and take on important psychological dimensions in her life. That is because the experience of pain is partly psychological—it is different for different people and under different circumstances.

Jennifer's circumstances were that she had always tried to meet the high expectations of her parents and herself. As she sat in pain, she kept thinking, "This couldn't happen at a worse time." Sales had been down recently, and although she had been thinking about having children, she and her husband were not getting along well. She had gained 25 pounds in the past year and thought of herself as fat and ugly for the first time in her life. What she could not know was that, even though the initial injury would heal, the pain would continue for several years. How could Jennifer's pain contribute to learning or be a sign of danger?

Health psychologists usually answer such questions by looking for the meaning or function of pain within the whole context of a person's life. This requires an understanding of current biopsychosocial theories of pain, which are discussed in Module 7.1. In Module 7.2 we return to Jennifer's situation and find out how her pain was managed psychosocially.

THEORY AND MEASUREMENT

▀ THE EXPERIENCE AND MEANING OF PAIN

For 100 years, pain has been recognized as both a physiological and a psychological phenomenon. An early hypothesis held that pain is an experience resulting from a physical sensation and a psychological *reaction* to that sensation (Strong, 1895). If so, pain is a subjective experience, one that is affected by each individual's unique psychological makeup. Evidence supporting the subjectivity of the pain experience comes from two sources, studies of hypnotized subjects and soldiers who suffered injuries during battle.

Almost from the time of its initial discovery, hypnosis has been used as an analgesic for surgery, which makes it one of the first nonmedical treatments for pain (Hilgard, 1975; Hilgard & Hilgard, 1983). Interestingly, even when they are undergoing pain and *report no discomfort*, hypnotized subjects have physiological responses consistent with pain—increases in respiration, heart rate, and blood pressure (Orne, 1980). This suggests that hypnosis does not eliminate the physiological response to pain but alters the psychological experience of it.

It appears that what is happening to the pain experience under hypnosis is similar to the philosophical question, If a tree falls in the forest and nobody is there to hear it, does it make a sound? The answer is *yes*, if sound is defined as a vibration of air at a certain frequency and intensity, and *no*, if the definition of sound requires a person actually to be present to hear it. Likewise, one might ask, If there is a painful stimulus but a person does not experience it, is it pain? It can be demonstrated in the laboratory that experimental pain (for example, heat, pressure, or cold temperature) causes sensory receptors to send impulses to the brain and that the physiological responses that typically accompany pain occur. But if the person does not experience the pain, is it real, or rather, does it matter? The answer again is *yes*, if pain is defined simply as neural impulses that warn of impending tissue damage, and *no* if the person is not conscious of the impulses and does not experience them.

The other source of data supporting the subjectivity of pain is a comparison of the experiences of soldiers and civilians by Beecher (1946, 1956). Beecher interviewed soldiers in the battlefield during World War II. He found that, even though they had received serious wounds and had just undergone surgery, they experienced relatively little pain: 49% reported "moderate" or "severe" pain, and 32% requested medication when it was offered. The soldiers were generally cheerful, but Beecher noted their special circumstances: They were in the relative security of the hospital and out of further danger.

Ten years later, Beecher (1956) interviewed civilian patients who had undergone similar surgeries. Although their wounds were in the same body regions as the soldiers', they were *not* as extensive. Despite this, the civilians experienced far more pain: 75% reported "moderate" or "severe" pain and 83% requested medication. Why did the civilians experience more pain even though their surgery was less extensive? For the civilians, the surgery marked the beginning of their ordeal of recovery, whereas for the soldiers, who had been in a continuous battle for five weeks, the surgery was the end of the war for them and they knew they soon would be sent home. Beecher (1956) concluded that the different circumstances altered the *meaning* and thus the perception of pain. If the experience of pain can be altered both in the laboratory under hypnosis and naturalistically by the circumstances a person is in, such as war, then pain must be at least partly subjective.

■

Measuring Pain

Pain has been called the most frequent reason people claim disability, the strongest force that compels people to seek or avoid medical care, and the most pervasive medical symptom (Karoly, 1985). It should come as no surprise, then, that a variety of techniques have been devised to assess pain. These techniques can be divided into three types: (a) physiological, (b) behavioral, and (c) self-report (Syrjala & Chapman, 1984). Some of these techniques are used more often in research and some are used more often in clinical practice; the fact so many exist reflects the complexity and multidimensionality of the pain experience.

Physiological Measures

It has long been assumed that the experience of pain should correlate with physiological responses (Nigl, 1984). The reasons for this assumed correlation are the strong emotional response, typically anxiety, that often accompanies pain and the neurophysiological substraits of pain (for example, various diffuse cortical pathways on which pain impulses travel). Three psychophysiological variables have been studied in an attempt to measure pain: muscle tension, evoked potentials, and responses of the autonomic nervous system.

MUSCLE TENSION   The electromyograph (EMG) is the principal means of assessing electrical activity in the muscles (see Module 2.2, page 56). Muscle tension is found in several painful conditions such as headaches and low back pain, so it is reasonable to assume that it could be used as a reliable measure of pain. However, studies have found contradictory results (Wolf, Nacht, & Kelly, 1982). EMG levels in low back pain patients are sometimes higher and sometimes lower than patients without pain. Furthermore, EMG comparisons of headache and nonheadache patients when not in pain show no reliable differences (Blanchard & Andrasik, 1985), although there may be differences when under tension (Chapman et al., 1985).

EVOKED POTENTIALS   Evoked potentials are changes in brain wave activity (for example, sharp spikes) on recordings made by an electroencephalogram (see Module 2.2) in response to a specific stimulus. In this case, the stimulus would be pain. Chapman (1980) and his colleagues (Chapman et al., 1985) have found that evoked potentials can be elicited in response to painful stimuli, that they increase and decrease with the intensity of the painful stimulation, that analgesics decrease them, and that they tend to correlate with subjects' reports of pain. Evoked potentials can even differentiate people with chronic pain from people without it (Syrjala & Chapman, 1984). One problem, however, is that there may be some imprecision in evoked potentials because they can increase even when subjects' reports of the perception of pain remain the same (Syrjala & Chapman, 1984). Again, this demonstrates the subjectivity of pain.

AUTONOMIC RESPONSES   Autonomic nervous system responses—changes in heart rate, respiration, skin conductance, and so on—have also been investigated as potential physiological indices of pain. There is some evidence that chronic pain patients tend to hyperventilate (rapid, uncontrolled respiration) more than ex-pain patients (Glynn, Lloyd, & Folkard, 1981) and that changes in skin temperature relate to some types of pain (Syrjala & Chapman, 1984). For the most part, however, research has failed to support the use of autonomic measures of pain.

   This should not be too surprising. Recall that the peripheral nervous system is comprised of two divisions and that the pathways involved in the transmission of pain impulses are part of the somatic and not the autonomic division. Therefore, there is no anatomical basis to assume a direct relationship between the sensation of pain and autonomic activity (although the brain could activate the autonomic nervous system after receiving pain impulses). Also, recall from Module 6.1 that Selye (1979) called the sympathetic nervous system "non-specific" because it responds to many different stressful stimuli (which do not usually cause a physical sensation of pain). Therefore, autonomic responses often occur when there is no painful stimulus (Dowling,

1983). Also, the measurement of autonomic responses is affected by a variety of unrelated factors like diet, alcohol consumption, and infection (Nigl, 1984). It seems likely that researchers probably will remain interested in autonomic responses as emotional correlates or as a reflection of the strain of the pain experience but probably not as direct indices of pain (Chapman et al., 1985).

BEHAVIORAL MEASURES

Behavioral measures are derived from the learning theory approach to pain. They attempt to measure the *observable* behaviors related to the pain experience. Usually, they rely on ratings of a pain sufferer's behaviors made by others. The ratings can take place in a structured clinical setting or in a naturalistic setting, and each has its advantages and disadvantages.

STRUCTURED CLINICAL RATINGS   Health care workers are trained to observe pain patients in structured situations, checking various pain behaviors as they occur (Follick, Ahern, & Aberger, 1985; Keefe, 1982; Keefe & Block, 1982). Patients' routine behaviors can be observed and rated during various time samples, or a standardized set of tasks can be carried out in a laboratory (Follick, Ahern, & Aberger, 1985; Keefe & Block, 1982). Reliabilities of such structured rating scales are typically very high (for example, Keefe & Block, 1982; Richards, Nepomuceno, Riles, & Suer, 1982). Structural clinical ratings can distinguish between pain patients and patients without pain, and they correlate with patients' subjective reports of pain (Keefe & Block, 1982; Kleinke & Spangler, 1988). Their excellent psychometric properties make them a highly reliable means of measuring people's pain.

NATURALISTIC PAIN RATINGS   Because the "artificial" environment of a hospital or laboratory setting may not accurately reflect patients' pain behaviors in their own environments, techniques have been developed for use in naturalistic settings (Fordyce, 1976; Turk, Meichenbaum, & Genest, 1983). Naturalistic ratings evaluate patients as they go through their normal routines and rely on people close to the pain patient who act as raters (for example, a spouse). They are given formal training in how to rate the patient and then keep track of pain behaviors. Sometimes raters utilize a diary in which they also record their own responses to the patient's pain behavior, thereby taking interpersonal factors into account (Turk, Meichenbaum, & Genest, 1983).

SELF-REPORT MEASURES

Figure 7.1-1 depicts two types of self-rating scales (Chapman et al., 1985; Karoly, 1985). With the visual analog scale (Feuerstein, Labbe, & Kucz-mierczyk, 1986), patients merely mark a continuum of severity from "No

Pain behaviors are easy to identify.

Pain" to "Very Severe Pain," and with a category scale, patients mark categories in which they experience problems.

Self-rating scales have several advantages. They are simple and quick to use, so they can be filled out repeatedly (Turk, Meichenbaum, & Genest, 1983). Therefore, they can track the experience of pain as it changes, perhaps revealing patterns such as certain situations or times of the day when it is better or worse, and the visual analog scale can even be used by children as young as five years of age (Karoly, 1985). Self-rating scales also have adequate reliability (Kremer, Atkinson, & Ignelzi, 1981), but they have one serious shortcoming because they are limited to the single dimension of pain intensity alone (Syrjala & Chapman, 1984).

Another type of self-report measure grew out of the work of Ronald Melzack at Canada's McGill University. Melzack was able to demonstrate that the pain experience is multidimensional (Melzack & Torgerson, 1971), and others have confirmed this (Brennan, Barrett, & Garretson, 1987). The work of Melzack and his colleagues led to the development of the McGill Pain Questionnaire (MPQ) (Melzack, 1975). The MPQ is reproduced in Figure 7.1-2. It consists of three broad dimensions: affective, sensory, and evaluative. Within each dimension are subclasses, and these subclasses are in turn defined by specific terms. People are asked to circle the word that best describes the pain within each subclass. The terms are used to determine intensity within each subclass. For example, in the "Dullness" subclass of the "Sensory" dimension, "Dull" is rated "1" along the margin, whereas "Heavy" is assigned a rating of "3." The sum of all of the subclass ratings is the pain rating index.

Figure 7.1-1   SELF-RATING PAIN SCALES

(a) Visual Analog Scale

DATE: _____

UPON AWAKINING	4:00 P.M.	BEFORE BED
TIME: _____ (rate pain experienced during sleep up to now)	(rate pain experienced since morning)	**TIME:** _____ (rate pain experienced since 4:00 p.m.)

PAIN PRESENT: (circle)
   YES   NO
	PAIN PRESENT: (circle)
	   YES NO
		PAIN PRESENT: (circle)
		   YES NO

DURATION in hours: (circle one) 1 2 3 4 5 6 7 8 9 10 Other: _____	**DURATION** in hours: (circle one) 1 2 3 4 5 6 7 8 9 10 Other: _____	**DURATION** in hours: (circle one) 1 2 3 4 5 6 7 8 9 10 Other: _____

SEVERITY:
 No pain   Pain as bad
                     as could be
	SEVERITY:
	 No pain Pain as bad
	                     as could be
		SEVERITY:
		 No pain Pain as bad
		                     as could be

INTERFERENCE: No interference Could not with daily continue daily activities activities	**INTERFERENCE:** No interference Could not with daily continue daily activities activities	**INTERFERENCE:** No interference Could not with daily continue daily activities activities

MEDICATION: # OF
   TYPE   TABLETS
 1. _____ _____
 2. _____ _____
 3. _____ _____
	MEDICATION: # OF
	   TYPE TABLETS
	 1. _____ _____
	 2. _____ _____
	 3. _____ _____
		MEDICATION: # OF
		   TYPE TABLETS
		 1. _____ _____
		 2. _____ _____
		 3. _____ _____

LOCATION: (shade area where
             you currently
             experience pain) 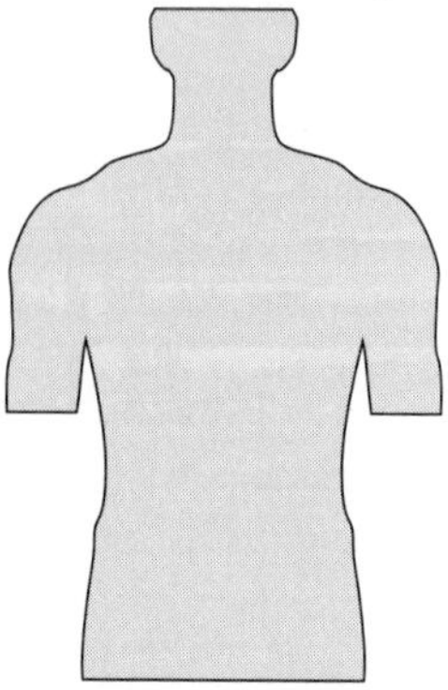
	LOCATION: (shade area where
	             you currently
	             experience pain) 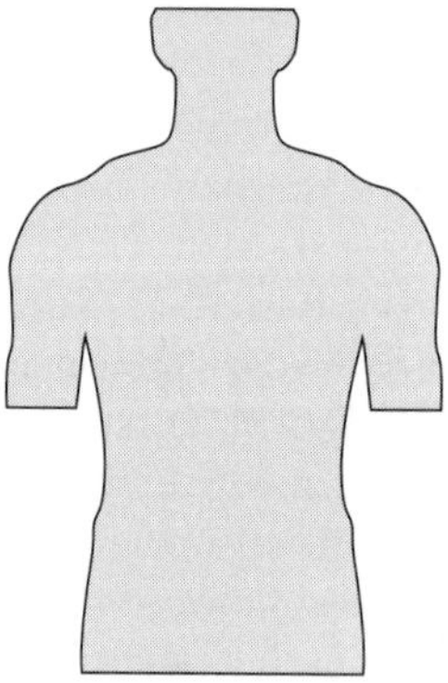
		LOCATION: (shade area where
		             you currently
		             experience pain) 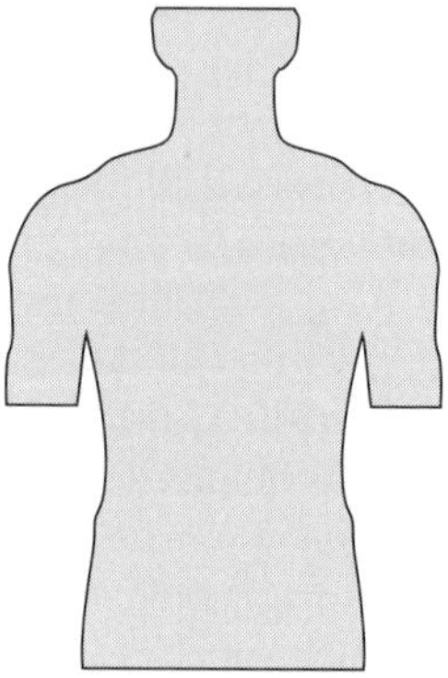

(b) Category Scale

		M	T	W	T	F	S	S
DATE								
*1. **Vocal Complaints: Verbal**	None	0	0	0	0	0	0	0
	Occasional	$\frac{1}{2}$	$\frac{1}{2}$	$\frac{1}{2}$	$\frac{1}{2}$	$\frac{1}{2}$	$\frac{1}{2}$	$\frac{1}{2}$
	Frequent	1	1	1	1	1	1	1
*2. **Vocal Complaints: Nonverbal** (moans, groans, gasps, etc.)	None	0	0	0	0	0	0	0
	Occasional	$\frac{1}{2}$	$\frac{1}{2}$	$\frac{1}{2}$	$\frac{1}{2}$	$\frac{1}{2}$	$\frac{1}{2}$	$\frac{1}{2}$
	Frequent	1	1	1	1	1	1	1
3. **Downtime** (time spent lying down per day because of pain)	None	0	0	0	0	0	0	0
	0–60 min.	$\frac{1}{2}$	$\frac{1}{2}$	$\frac{1}{2}$	$\frac{1}{2}$	$\frac{1}{2}$	$\frac{1}{2}$	$\frac{1}{2}$
	> 60 min.	1	1	1	1	1	1	1
*4. **Facial Grimaces**	None	0	0	0	0	0	0	0
	Mild and/or infrequent	$\frac{1}{2}$	$\frac{1}{2}$	$\frac{1}{2}$	$\frac{1}{2}$	$\frac{1}{2}$	$\frac{1}{2}$	$\frac{1}{2}$
	Severe and/or frequent	1	1	1	1	1	1	1
*5. **Standing Posture**	Normal	0	0	0	0	0	0	0
	Mildly impaired	$\frac{1}{2}$	$\frac{1}{2}$	$\frac{1}{2}$	$\frac{1}{2}$	$\frac{1}{2}$	$\frac{1}{2}$	$\frac{1}{2}$
	Distorted	1	1	1	1	1	1	1
*6. **Mobility**	No visible impairment	0	0	0	0	0	0	0
	Mild limp and/or mildly impaired walking	$\frac{1}{2}$	$\frac{1}{2}$	$\frac{1}{2}$	$\frac{1}{2}$	$\frac{1}{2}$	$\frac{1}{2}$	$\frac{1}{2}$
	Marked limp and/or labored walking	1	1	1	1	1	1	1
*7. **Body Language** (clutching, rubbing site of pain)	None	0	0	0	0	0	0	0
	Occasional	$\frac{1}{2}$	$\frac{1}{2}$	$\frac{1}{2}$	$\frac{1}{2}$	$\frac{1}{2}$	$\frac{1}{2}$	$\frac{1}{2}$
	Frequent	1	1	1	1	1	1	1
*8. **Use of Visible, Supportive Equipment** (braces, crutches, cane, leaning on furniture, TENS, etc.) DO NOT score if equipment prescribed.	None	0	0	0	0	0	0	0
	Occasional	$\frac{1}{2}$	$\frac{1}{2}$	$\frac{1}{2}$	$\frac{1}{2}$	$\frac{1}{2}$	$\frac{1}{2}$	$\frac{1}{2}$
	Dependent, constant use	1	1	1	1	1	1	1
*9. **Stationary Movement**	Sits or stands still	0	0	0	0	0	0	0
	Occasional shifts of position	$\frac{1}{2}$	$\frac{1}{2}$	$\frac{1}{2}$	$\frac{1}{2}$	$\frac{1}{2}$	$\frac{1}{2}$	$\frac{1}{2}$
	Constant movement, position shifts	1	1	1	1	1	1	1
10. **Medication**	None	0	0	0	0	0	0	0
	Nonnarcotic analgesic and/or psychogenic medications as prescribed	$\frac{1}{2}$	$\frac{1}{2}$	$\frac{1}{2}$	$\frac{1}{2}$	$\frac{1}{2}$	$\frac{1}{2}$	$\frac{1}{2}$
	Demands for increasing dosage or frequency and/or narcotics, and/or medication abuse	1	1	1	1	1	1	1
TOTAL BEHAVIOR (1, 2, 3, 4, 5, 6, 7, 8, 9)								
TOTAL DOWNTIME AND MEDICATION								

Source: Richards, J. S., Nepomuceno, C., Riles, M., & Suer, Z., 1982, Assessing pain behavior: The UAB Pain Behavior Scale, Pain, 14, 395.

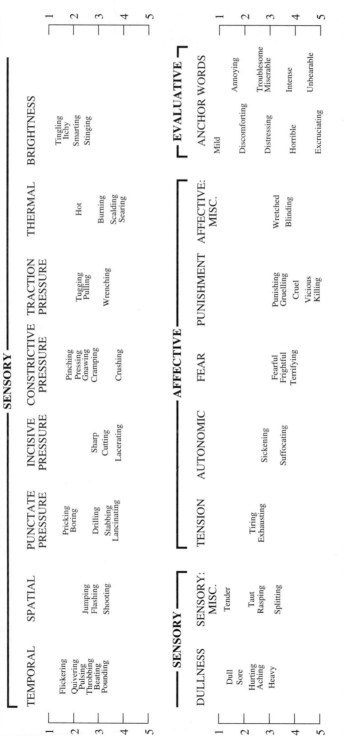

Figure 7.1-2   THE McGILL PAIN QUESTIONNAIRE

─── SENSORY ───

TEMPORAL	SPATIAL	PUNCTATE PRESSURE	INCISIVE PRESSURE	CONSTRICTIVE PRESSURE	TRACTION PRESSURE	THERMAL	BRIGHTNESS	
Flickering							Tingling	1
Quivering Pulsing Throbbing	Jumping Flashing	Pricking Boring		Pinching Pressing Gnawing Cramping	Tugging Pulling	Hot	Itchy Smarting Stinging	2
Beating Pounding	Shooting	Drilling	Sharp Cutting		Wrenching	Burning Scalding Searing		3
		Stabbing Lancinating	Lacerating	Crushing				4
								5

─── SENSORY ───   ─── AFFECTIVE ───   ─── EVALUATIVE ───

DULLNESS	SENSORY: MISC.	TENSION	AUTONOMIC	FEAR	PUNISHMENT	AFFECTIVE: MISC.	ANCHOR WORDS	
Dull Sore	Tender						Mild	1
Hurting Aching	Taut Rasping	Tiring Exhausting	Sickening				Discomforting	2
Heavy	Splitting		Suffocating	Fearful Frightful Terrifying	Punishing Gruelling	Wretched Blinding	Distressing	3
					Cruel		Horrible	4
					Vicious Killing		Excruciating	5

The multiple dimensions of the McGill Pain Questionnaire (sensory, affective, and evaluative), their subcategories, and descriptors used by pain patients to indicate the intensity level of the pain experience within each subcategory. The intensity levels range from 1 (mild) to 5 (excruciating).

Source: From Melzack, R., and Torgerson, W. S., 1971, On the language of pain, Anesthesiology, 23, 50.

The MPQ is probably the most widely used self-report pain scale. It has been used to treat a variety of types of pain, and has demonstrated reasonable validity (Dubuisson & Melzack, 1976; Hunter & Philips, 1981; Kremer, Atkinson, & Ignelzi, 1981). The MPQ has been criticized primarily for its vocabulary requiring fairly extensive knowledge of English, particularly in making fine discriminations between words such as "taut" and "rasping" (Chapman et al., 1985; Karoly, 1985; Syrjala & Chapman, 1984).

The final self-report measure that we will examine is the Minnesota Multiphasic Personality Inventory (MMPI) (Hathaway & McKinley, 1967). Although designed as a general measure of psychopathology, some researchers have used it to evaluate pain. Most notably, a series of studies (Bradley, Prokop, Gentry, Van der Heide, & Prieto, 1981; Bradley, Prokop, Margolis, & Gentry, 1978; Bradley, & Van der Heide, 1984) has found that several MMPI scales are consistently related to reports of pain: hypochondriasis, depression, and hysteria. These scales are also known as the "neurotic triad" and are implicated in the less severe forms of psychopathology. One caution in making interpretations based on these scales is that they contain many items having to do with somatic complaints or the lack thereof (for example, "I have a good appetite" or "I wake up fresh and rested most mornings"). It is, therefore, possible that pain patients obtain elevations on the scales primarily because they have somatic complaints and not necessarily because there is related psychopathology.

Certain clusters of elevated MMPI scales have been able to predict successful treatment outcomes for surgery to correct low back pain (Long, 1981; Turner, Herron, & Pheasant, 1981), but they have been unable to predict response to other pain treatments (McGill, Lawlis, Selby, Mooney, & McCoy, 1983; Moore, Armentrout, Parker, & Kivilan, 1986). The MMPI will probably continue to be used with pain patients, but caution is advised in drawing conclusions from it. Perhaps the best use of the MMPI with pain patients is to help understand other aspects of their personalities that may affect their experience of pain.

Conclusion

The variety of pain measurement techniques reflects the fact that pain is a complex and multidimensional experience. Only the most reliable of these assessment procedures are appropriate for laboratory research. However, in the clinical treatment of pain, where the individual's own unique lifestyle and subjective experience of pain must be taken into account, a wider variety of assessment procedures are likely to be used. Because of the complexity of pain, adequate measurement must rely on a combination of several assessment techniques simultaneously (Kanner, 1986).

■

Description and Categories of Pain

Researchers and clinicians use several categories to distinguish pain. The first distinction to be made is between acute and chronic pain. *Acute pain* is a relatively brief sensation, usually defined as lasting less than six months, and it is related to the potential for or extent of injury (Turk, Meichenbaum, & Genest, 1983). It is accompanied by arousal of the sympathetic nervous system and by feelings of anxiety (Fordyce & Steger, 1979). Acute pain is adaptive—usually a response to a specific trauma—and forms the basis for danger warnings and subsequent learning.

Chronic pain is pain that lasts more than six months (Keefe, 1982; Turk et al., 1983). At this length of time, the pain has often existed beyond the time for normal organic healing. With pain of this duration, the adaptive benefits of acute pain no longer operate, and the pain begins to impair other functions. Psychological factors can become more important than the organic condition that caused the initial sensation of pain. The anxiety of acute pain remains, but chronic pain patients may also begin to experience learned helplessness and hopelessness. Therefore, chronic pain can be accompanied by the classic signs of depression, such as lethargy, sleep disturbance, and weight loss. People with chronic pain sometimes quit work and adopt a self-imposed invalid lifestyle. A transition period between acute and chronic pain, called *prechronic*, during which pain is either overcome or the psychological factors, particularly hopelessness, begin to develop, has also been identified (Keefe, 1982).

Categories of Chronic Pain

Turk et al. (1983) have identified factors that characterize the chronic pain experience: (a) whether the pain is experienced continuously or episodically, and (b) whether it is caused by a benign or progressive (worsening) organic condition. Using these factors, Turk et al. have developed the following three subcategories of chronic pain.

1. *Chronic recurrent pain* arises from a benign condition and consists of periods of intense pain alternating with pain-free periods. Migraine and tension headaches are examples of this category.
2. *Chronic intractable-benign pain* is also not related to a malignant condition. It is persistent and does not alternate with pain-free periods, although the pain may vary in intensity. Low back pain is a classic example of this category.
3. *Chronic Progressive pain* originates from an organic condition that is malignant. Like intractable-benign pain, it is continuous, but it

increases in intensity as the underlying organic condition worsens. Cancer and rheumatoid arthritis are two examples of this category.

———————

At first, Jennifer's doctor diagnosed an acute back strain, put her on several medications—one to relieve pain, one to reduce inflammation, and one to relax her muscles—and confined her to bed. Unexpectedly, Jennifer found her parents and her husband to be quite supportive of her "sick role." As she began to feel less pain, her time off seemed like a relief to her because she did not have to work for the first time in her life.

Within a week, Jennifer's pain was nearly gone and she was able to be more active. However, the pain never really went away. In fact, after several weeks it started to worsen again. Her doctor was baffled because medical tests revealed no underlying organic condition. How could she get better and then get worse again if no additional trauma occurred? As the months dragged on, Jennifer would confine herself to bed on and off because of the pain and request refills of her medications. Finally, after eight months, her doctor referred her to a psychologist. Jennifer believed that her pain was "real" and not "in her mind," but she was receptive to the referral because she had not been happy with her life even before the injury. Together, the psychologist and physician determined that Jennifer had a chronic intractable-benign pain syndrome. Was it psychological or was it organic?

ETIOLOGY: PSYCHOLOGICAL VERSUS ORGANIC   An additional distinction can be made in chronic pain syndromes based on the extent of psychological versus organic factors involved. It is helpful to conceptualize these factors on a continuum from those instances that are wholly psychological to those that are wholly organic. The etiology of each pain experience lies somewhere on this continuum, combining psychological and organic factors to different degrees.

When chronic pain is due entirely to psychological factors and there is no organic pathology, it is classified as *psychogenic*, one of the *somatoform* disorders discussed in Chapter 1. Chronic progressive pain, associated with a worsening organic condition, falls at the other end of the continuum. Chronic recurrent and chronic intractable-benign pain are more likely to be somewhere in the middle of the continuum.

This conceptualization overcomes the need of some health care workers to place pain patients into one of two separate categories of psychological versus organic pain (Karoly, 1985). A tension headache is not, so to speak, all in the patient's head (or mind). There is also measurable contraction of muscles of the head that produces the sensation of pain. So, too, low back pain often begins with a muscular strain or sprain, but the pain, influenced by psychosocial factors, may continue long after the initial organic insult has healed, as in Jennifer's case.

███████

The Physiology of Pain

Now we will explore the organic side of the pain continuum, which involves some insult to the body's pain receptors and transmission of information about the insult to the brain through special neural pathways.

Pain Receptors

Unlike our other senses (for example, hearing), no specialized receptor cells respond to a specific type of painful stimulus (Melzcak & Wall, 1982). Instead, the body's receptors for pain are several million bare sensory nerve endings that thread through all tissues and organs of the body except the brain (Marieb, 1989).

These free nerve endings are part of the somatic division of the peripheral nervous system. They respond to many types of noxious stimuli ultimately perceived as painful: pressure, extremes of temperature, bruises, or lacerations. In short, they respond to anything that is potentially damaging to the tissues. Whenever there is injury or impending injury of body tissue, local free nerve endings are stimulated.

When there is actual tissue injury, enzymes from damaged cells at the injury site trigger the formation of bradykinin. **Bradykinin** is "the most potent pain-producing chemical known" (Marieb, 1989, p. 468), and it attaches to free nerve endings, causing them to transmit pain impulses. So, the difference in the intensity and duration of pain between impending injury and actual injury appears to be the presence of bradykinin. In the next section, we follow these impulses on their way to the central nervous system.

Neural Pathways in Pain

Free nerve ending impulses travel to the CNS through two types of afferent somatic nervous system fibers (Chapman, 1984; Melzack & Wall, 1982; Marieb, 1989):

- **A-delta fibers** carry the localized, sharp, and pricking but brief pain sensations. They are myelinated, so they transmit impulses quickly.
- **C fibers** carry the diffuse, dull, burning, aching, and longer-lasting pain sensations. They are not myelinated, so they transmit impulses more slowly.

Neurons in the A-delta fibers and C fibers send impulses by releasing a neurotransmitter called **substance P**. The A-delta and C fibers follow a similar pathway up the spinal cord, but they diverge once they reach the brain

(Marieb, 1989). C fibers mainly terminate in the lower regions of the fore-brain, at the limbic system, thalamus, and hypothalamus, although some C fibers terminate in other brain regions in a diffuse pattern. On the other hand, A-delta fibers pass through the thalamus but then go directly on to the motor and sensory areas of the cortex. This suggests that the sharp, localized pain signals of the A-delta fibers "take the shortcut" to the cortex, where they can obtain our immediate attention and be consciously analyzed, whereas the diffuse, aching pain signals of the C fibers exert more influence on our general motivational and emotional state.

■

A BIOPSYCHOSOCIAL THEORY OF PAIN

Historically, three theories of pain have been proposed by researchers probing its mysteries: *specificity theory, sensory decision theory,* and *gate control theory.*

SPECIFICITY THEORY

Specificity theory is biological and does not take psychological factors into account (Melzack & Wall, 1965; Weisenberg, 1977). Pain receptors transmit pain sensations directly to the brain. Any emotions that accompany the pain experience are viewed as *reactions* to the initial pain sensation; neither emotions nor any cognitive processes are believed to affect the pain itself.

Some successful medical treatments for pain such as neurosurgery and nerve blocks rely on this dualistic approach of specificity theory. How is it dualistic? Because it completely separates the biological and psychological aspects of the pain experience. Therefore, it is not surprising that specificity theory cannot adequately explain chronic pain syndromes like Jennifer's, for it does not account for pain experienced even when no organic basis for it exists. Once a lower-back injury has healed, there should be no pain. Furthermore, specificity theory cannot account for the athlete who suffers an ankle injury but plays on, completely unaware of it until after the excitement of the competition is over.

SENSORY DECISION THEORY

In contrast, sensory decision theory (Chapman, 1978, 1980) relies heavily on the psychology of perception. Cognitive processes such as perceptual habits, beliefs, expectations, costs and rewards, and memory all control how *any* sensory input, painful or otherwise, is perceived. This allows for the variance seen in how individual and situational factors affect pain.

Sensory decision theory emphasizes attentional processes. In that way, it explains how the athlete with an injured ankle, whose attention is directed toward the competition, is not aware of pain signals from the injured ankle. The experience of pain is increased by attention that is drawn to a specific, painful, area of the body, or by a conscious decision to focus attention on it. The focusing of attention may cause even weak or transient sensations to become more noticeable, heightening the experience of pain.

In a chronic pain syndrome, the attention directed to pain would "take on a life of its own," with the patient constantly focused on the painful area and sensitive to any sensations there. This can explain how Jennifer's lower-back pain could continue long after the initial injury healed—by becoming the focus of her attention. However, neither specificity theory nor sensory decision theory integrates biological and psychosocial factors.

GATE CONTROL THEORY

Gate control theory was introduced by Melzack and Wall (1965; 1982). It is closest to a biopsychosocial model of pain and is the leading theory at this time. In gate control theory, whether or not sensory impulses from free nerve endings reach the brain depends on the modulation effects of three variables: (a) the A-delta fibers that carry messages of sharp pain, (b) the C fibers that carry messages of dull pain, and (c) A-beta fibers that carry messages of light touch.

A potentially painful stimulus can cause messages to be sent through all three types of fibers simultaneously. However, certain neurons located in the grey matter of the spinal cord—the *gate*—have the ability to block or facilitate the transmission of pain impulses up the A-delta and C fibers; they can influence whether impulses get through to the brain. (Figure 7.1-3).

The gateway neurons are *inhibitory*; that is, they usually keep the gate closed by suppressing the flow of pain messages to the brain. They manufacture the pain-blocking neurotransmitter **enkephalin** (an endorphin), which is similar to opiates like heroin, and can block substance P. Enkephalins can also be released through electrical stimulation of the brain and acupuncture (Marieb, 1989), which may explain its pain reduction abilities as well.

The gate would remain perpetually closed, and we would feel little pain, were it not for the next part of the theory. The C fibers are *inhibitory* to the gate neurons, so impulses traveling along them tend to open the gate, whereas the A-beta fibers are *excitatory* to the gate neurons, so impulses traveling along them tend to close the gate. If the impulses in the C fibers are stronger than those in the A-beta fibers, the gate opens.

In addition, Melzack & Wall (1965) posit the existence of specialized nerve impulses that arise in the brain itself and travel down the spinal cord to influence the gate. This **central control trigger** transmits impulses through

Figure 7.1-3 GATE CONTROL THEORY

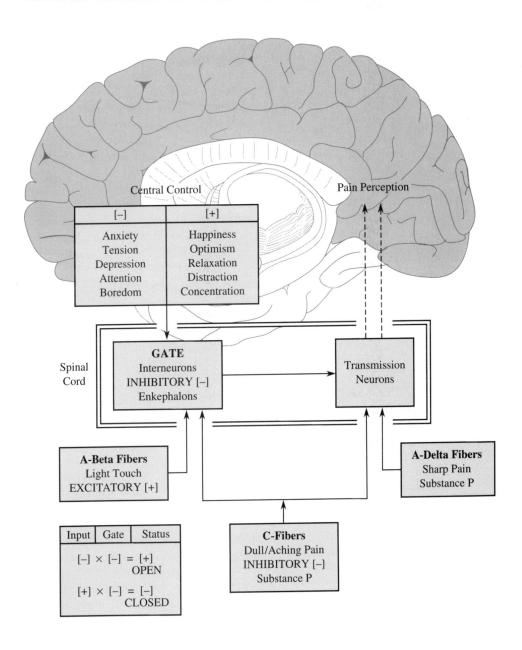

Central Control

Pain Perception

[−]	[+]
Anxiety	Happiness
Tension	Optimism
Depression	Relaxation
Attention	Distraction
Boredom	Concentration

Spinal Cord

GATE
Interneurons
INHIBITORY [−]
Enkephalons

Transmission Neurons

A-Beta Fibers
Light Touch
EXCITATORY [+]

A-Delta Fibers
Sharp Pain
Substance **P**

Input	Gate	Status
[−] × [−] = [+]		
	OPEN	
[+] × [−] = [−]		
	CLOSED	

C-Fibers
Dull/Aching Pain
INHIBITORY [−]
Substance P

large, rapidly conducting efferent fibers to the gate in the spinal cord. (Actually there are many gates located along the spinal cord.) The central control trigger can send either inhibitory or excitatory impulses to the gate and sensitize it to either C fiber or A-beta fiber inputs. If the brain sensitizes the gate to C fiber impulses, then it is more likely to open. If it sensitizes the gate to A-beta fiber inputs, then it is more likely to close. This incorporates sensory decision theory, providing a mechanism through which cognitive processes—emotions and thoughts—are able to influence the transmission of pain impulses *before* they are transmitted to the brain.

Gate control theory is another example of homeostasis. Positive feedback opens the gate, while negative feedback closes it. This allows the brain to influence pain impulses *before* it receives them. Presumably this mechanism has developed to allow the brain to control its own homeostasis, protecting it against overstimulation. Its survival value can be seen in the example of the athlete with an injured ankle who feels no pain during competition. Although athletic competition is not usually a life and death matter, in primitive times, the ability of the brain to block out pain sensations probably increased human survival by allowing people to ignore the pain and concentrate on the immediate threat.

To summarize, whether or not pain impulses are received by the brain is dependent on the *combination* of the following three factors:

1. The strength of C fiber impulses (opening the gate).
2. The strength of A-beta fiber impulses (closing the gate).
3. The central control trigger's sensitization of the gate to C or A-beta fiber impulses (to either open or close the gate).

This is a bit tricky, because the C and A-beta fibers each have two roles. One role is to open or close the gate, and the other role is to transmit impulses. But gate control theory has the advantage of integrating what is known about the anatomy and physiology of pain sensation with the subjective psychological nature of pain perception. It can also explain why some activities such as massage or rubbing a bumped "funny bone" in the elbow reduce the intensity of pain (Marieb, 1989). Theoretically, these activities reduce pain by stimulating the light touch A-beta fibers, which closes the gate.

Despite its ability to integrate physiological and psychological aspects of the pain experience, gate control theory is relatively new and has not been thoroughly researched. Furthermore, it has not been accepted unanimously (Bonica, 1980b). Nevertheless, research has supported some, if not all, of its features. Specifically, the central control trigger has received support from animal research suggesting that the brain does send impulses down the spinal cord that inhibit pain (Chapman, 1984; Melzack & Wall, 1982; Reynolds, 1969; Winters, 1985). Research with human subjects has also supported a CNS role in pain modulation (Willer & Albe-Fessard, 1980). At present, gate control theory is the most comprehensive and widely accepted theory of pain

(Marieb, 1989; Weisenberg, 1977) and allows us to take into account the operation of a wide range of biopsychosocial factors in the pain experience, which we will examine next.

OTHER FACTORS IN THE PAIN EXPERIENCE

A variety of physical and psychological factors are involved in the experience of pain. Some act as modulators, affecting the opening and closing of the gate, and some are reflected in the behaviors of people with pain.

BIOPSYCHOSOCIAL MODULATORS OF PAIN

A pain modulator is any factor that can increase or decrease the experience of pain. These factors could act psychologically, through the central control trigger, or at a physiological level. For ethical reasons, much of the research on pain modulators has taken place in the laboratory using induced, reversible pain. One laboratory method of inducing pain is to immerse a subject's hand and/or forearm in a tub of cold water kept at about 2°C (34°F), which people can rarely withstand for more than a few minutes. This produces intense pain but it does not result in tissue damage.

Laboratory experiments can be helpful in determining which factors have the *potential* to affect pain, but laboratory-induced pain can be very different from the pain experienced by chronic pain patients. To begin with, subjects in a laboratory experiment know at the outset that the pain will end relatively soon, whereas people with chronic pain often believe the pain is permanent. Also, people with chronic pain often have a strong conviction (true or not) that the pain is due to an underlying organic disease process. Recall that Jennifer still thought that her pain was real, even after eight months. In contrast, laboratory pain is not due to disease but has an obvious physical cause.

Table 7.1-1 depicts some of the factors that can modulate the experience of pain. From this list, we can hypothesize that, in general, the gate is opened by tension, anxiety, and focusing on pain, whereas the gate is closed by relaxing and distracting conditions.

A LEARNING THEORY APPROACH TO PAIN

Behaviorally oriented psychologists have contributed a more objective approach to the study of pain. Behaviorists, or learning theorists, have argued that, since the subjectivity of the pain experience cannot be observed or measured directly, pain research should focus on specific behaviors that can be observed and measured (Fordyce, 1976, 1978). This has led to the identification of certain *pain behaviors* such as distorted posture, irritability, moaning, grimacing, and limping that occur when a person is in pain (Turk, Wack, & Kearns, 1985). Pain behaviors are part of the "sick role" (see Module 3.3, page 109). Behaviorists tend to view pain as a functional phenomenon and are interested in the degree to which an individual's function is impaired. They also believe that pain behaviors are influenced by the environment regardless of the subjective experience of pain. In other words, the major learning mechanisms discussed in Module 2.2—classical conditioning, operant conditioning, and modeling—also affect pain behaviors. Most of this line of research has focused on the role that caregivers, particularly family, have on maintaining, increasing, or reducing pain behaviors.

This approach is limited to external, observable behavior, and it does not attempt to take into account the physiological or cognitive factors in pain. In spite of this limitation, behavioral research has made some important contributions. Because pain takes place in a social context (Fordyce, 1976), some of this research has looked at the role of family members. People in pain are affected by their spouse's reactions (Keefe, Dunsmore, & Burnett, 1992). Concern and support are natural responses to the sick role and to pain; how-

Table 7.1-1 POTENTIAL BIOPSYCHOSOCIAL MODULATORS OF THE PAIN GATEWAY

POTENTIAL MODULATOR	EFFECT ON THE GATE	
	Open	**Close**
Physical	Extent of injury	Medication Counterstimulation (e.g., massage)
Psychological		
Emotional	Anxiety Tension Depression	Positive emotions (e.g., optimism) Relaxation, rest
Cognitive	Attention/Vigilance Boredom	Distraction Involvement/Interest

Source: Adapted from Turk, Meichenbaum, & Genest, 1983, Pain and behavioral medicine: A cognitive-behavioral perspective, *New York: Guilford.*

ever, overly solicitous responses tend to promote increases in pain behaviors and less alternative activity (Block, Kremer, & Gaylor, 1980a; Flor, Kerns, & Turk, 1987). Jennifer's surprise at her husband's and parents' support when she was in pain indicates how rarely she must have felt supported before, and their behavior could have contributed to her maintaining a sick role.

Children's pain behavior is also responsive to the attention of their parents. In an example of operant conditioning, the scratching behavior of children with atopic dermatitis (a painful, itching skin condition) increased when parents paid attention to it (Gil et al., 1988). Conversely, scratching decreased when parents paid attention to their children when they were *not* scratching.

Other research has looked at the role that broader institutions have in influencing pain behavior. Of course pain is uncomfortable, but it also has its compensations. Psychologists call these compensations *secondary gains*. **Secondary gains** are situational rewards that sometimes occur with the sick role. They might include not having to go to work or relief from doing unpleasant chores. During the eight months that she was in chronic pain, Jennifer could not work effectively and was relieved not to have to continue working.

Our social and legal systems might unintentionally reward pain behaviors through disability payments, workers' compensation, or personal injury awards. These programs are absolutely necessary for legitimate injuries, but an unintended consequence may be the reinforcement of chronic pain behaviors through secondary gains. Patients who receive disability payments are hospitalized longer and are out of work longer than those who do not receive disability (Block, Kremer, & Gaylor, 1980; Chapman & Brena, 1985). One study did find that being involved in litigation is not associated with an increase in pain behavior (Peck, Fordyce, & Black, 1978), but it did not use an adequate nonlitigating chronic pain comparison group. The role of secondary gains in pain behavior is complex and not fully appreciated. For example, people who receive more compensation may simply take advantage of a longer recovery period in order to prevent a relapse. Although it is quite difficult to conduct, more research is warranted into learning theory and pain behavior.

MODULE SUMMARY

That completes our discussion of the theory and measurement of pain. The next module describes the various types of pain syndromes and how pain is managed clinically. Before continuing, review the major points in Module 7.1:

1. The experience of pain is necessary for survival. It contributes to learning and alerts us to danger.

2. Pain is a subjective experience, part physiological and part psychological.
3. Pain can be categorized by its duration—acute versus chronic.
4. Separate neural pathways relay pain impulses to the brain: A-delta fibers carry sharp, localized sensations, while C fibers carry diffuse, dull sensations.
5. Specificity theory is highly physiological and proposes that the experience of pain is directly related to sensation; any emotional features are merely a reaction to the pain sensation.
6. Sensory decision theory is highly subjective, and the pain experience is affected by either the attention paid to pain sensations or by conscious decisions to focus attention on pain.
7. Gate control theory is closest to the biopsychosocial model. A "gate" in the spinal cord can be opened or closed to the transmission of pain sensations to the brain. Whether or not the brain receives pain sensations is dependent on the strength of C fiber impulses that open the gate, the strength of A-beta fiber impulses that close the gate, and input from the brain itself that can sensitize the gate to either C fiber or A-beta impulses.
8. Pain is increased when it is focused on and when tension and anxiety are experienced. Pain is reduced when attention is diverted from it and when relaxation is experienced.
9. Pain behaviors are learned through the process of secondary gains or reinforcement.
10. Physiological measurement of pain is reliable but leaves out the subjective experience.
11. Behavioral measures of pain, particularly structured clinical ratings, are reliable and correlate with subjective pain ratings.
12. The experience of pain is multidimensional. Therefore, self-report measures of pain that rely on the single dimension of intensity are quite limited, whereas multidimensional measures have good reliability and validity. The MMPI may be helpful in understanding other aspects of personality, but is not useful for measuring pain itself.

SYNDROMES AND MANAGEMENT

Like stress, pain is one of the most pervasive phenomena dealt with by health psychologists. The primary focus of this module is how to manage it. What makes pain interesting to health psychologists is the subjective nature of the pain experience. However, pain is not a disease. Remember that it functions as the body's warning system of actual or impending tissue damage. Therefore, pain is usually described in relation to a syndrome named for its suspected origin (for example, cancer, headache, or lower-back pain). This module reviews several of the common pain syndromes and their management.

COMMON PAIN SYNDROMES

A variety of pain syndromes are described in this section. Some remain mysterious with no known causes, while the causes of others like headache, arthritis pain, and lower-back pain are fairly well understood.

PAIN SYNDROMES WITHOUT KNOWN CAUSES

Neurologists recognize several disorders that have either eluded attempts to find any pathological changes in the nerves or, if there is nerve damage, cause pain symptoms only in very few individuals. Despite the fact that they have a psychosocial component, these painful syndromes have historically been considered to be neurological rather than somatoform disorders (Berkow & Fletcher, 1987).

Myofascial pain is the most common of all pain syndromes, and almost everyone experiences it at one time or another (Fricton, 1982). The term refers to pain in the muscles or connective tissues usually experienced as diffuse and "achy" and is often located in the lower back, shoulders, neck, and head (Travell, 1976). Myofascial pain is benign, and although it may result from mild muscular trauma or strain, there is often no abnormality or inflammation present (Berkow & Fletcher, 1987). It can have either a gradual or rapid onset, and in most cases it subsides on its own. However, it can become chronic or recurrent. It has been hypothesized that chronic myofascial pain syndrome results from a self-perpetuating cycle (Fricton, 1982; Stroebel & Glueck, 1976). The cycle begins with muscle tension, which produces pain. Then, by focusing more attention on the pain, more muscle tension occurs, causing more pain. Not all researchers have been able to find evidence of this pain cycle, however (Bush, Ditto, & Feuerstein, 1985).

Another syndrome, *neuralgia*, also seems to have no basis in actual tissue damage. Nevertheless, people do experience the primary sign of neuralgia, a severe lancing pain along a nerve pathway (Berkow & Fletcher, 1987; Chapman, 1984; Melzack & Wall, 1982). The trigeminal nerve, which projects through the jaw and serves the mouth and face, is particularly susceptible to neuralgia. Pain can occur suddenly without an apparent stimulus, or it can be brought on by a normally inoffensive stimulus such as brushing the teeth or a light touch of the cheek. Although transient and brief, the pain recurs and may be incapacitating.

Phantom limb pain usually begins with amputation, which damages the somatic nervous system. However, even though the nerves are no longer there, many amputees continue to feel sensations and pain that seem to be coming from the nonexistent limb (Chapman, 1984; Melzack & Wall, 1982). In up to 10% of those who continue to experience sensation from the damaged or lost limb, pain can be severe and actually worsen over time. This is difficult to explain on a purely physiological basis, so psychosocial factors are probably involved. These patients closely resemble those with a chronic pain syndrome (Berkow & Fletcher, 1987).

Headache

The first of the common pain syndromes is headache, which is suffered by millions of Americans and is responsible for billions of dollars in lost work days and medication costs. Although headache can sometimes accompany a cold or the flu or signal a more serious medical problem, it is most often benign. Two types of headaches can produce chronic pain: migraine and tension headaches (Andrasik, Blake, & McCarran, 1986; Blanchard & Andrasik, 1982; Levor, Cohen, Naliboff, McArthur, & Heuser, 1986).

Migraine headache probably originates in the vascular system that supplies blood to the brain. It is considered to be a two-phase process, beginning with constriction of the arteries in the preheadache phase. This is followed by dilation of the arteries, which pressures the free nerve endings surrounding them, causing pain. The pain is usually confined to one side of the head, and it is experienced as a sharp throbbing that can last for hours or days.

In those who have "classic migraine," an "aura" or set of symptoms precedes the pain that may be due to the vasoconstriction in the preheadache phase. The aura usually consists of sensory phenomena such as strange visual abnormalities—patterns or spots in the visual field. Laboratory-induced stress can cause migraine attacks in susceptible individuals (Gannon, Haynes, Cuevas, & Chavez, 1987), and prospective research indicates that stress occurring the day before or the day of a migraine attack probably has a causal role (Kohler & Haimerl, 1990).

Tension headaches are far more common than migraine headaches. They are caused by contraction of the muscles in the head, shoulder, or neck. If the contraction persists, a dull, aching pain often felt as a band around the head may follow. Tension headaches may produce pain on both sides of the head and can last from hours to days.

Some headaches are brought on by sensitivities or allergies to certain foods such as chocolate, but stress plays an important role in both migraine and tension headaches (Andrasik, Blake, & McCarran, 1986; Levor et al., 1986). However, stress is not always associated with headache even in chronic headache sufferers (Bakal, 1979).

ARTHRITIS PAIN

Arthritis is a general term for more than 100 different conditions. Common to them all is pain, stiffness, and swelling in the joints (Achterberg-Lawlis, 1988; Kelsey & Hochberg, 1988). Arthritis affects at least 30 million Americans, more females than males, and tends to get worse as people age. About one-half of Americans over the age of 65 are afflicted (USDHHS, 1986a). A specific type, *juvenile rheumatoid arthritis*, affects many thousands of children and, like the adult types, affects more females. However, it rarely leads to serious impairment later in life, with complete remission in up to 75% of cases (Berkow & Fletcher, 1987).

There are two common types of arthritis in adults:

1. *Osteoarthritis* is the more degenerative form. It results from wear and tear, and it is associated with increasing age, with being overweight, and with repetitive motions (Kelsey & Hochberg, 1988).
2. *Rheumatoid arthritis* is due to inflammation of the joints, although often it is more widespread, affecting the heart and lungs. Abnormal immune system functioning is implicated in this type of arthritis, which also tends to be the most painful and disabling (Achterberg-Lawlis, 1988; Kelsey & Hochberg, 1988).

In both types of arthritis, the precise etiology is unknown, but hereditary factors are implicated along with others (Berkow & Fletcher, 1987). Stress has also been implicated as a potential psychosocial risk factor in rheumatoid arthritis. Stressful life events often occur immediately before the onset or worsening of symptoms (Achterberg-Lawlis, 1988; Anderson, Bradley, Young, McDaniel, & Wise, 1985).

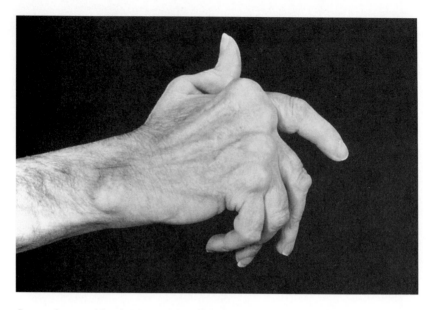

Severe rheumatoid arthritis can cause deformities of the bones and limbs.

Arthritis results in the greatest curtailment of normal activities (including work) of any chronic condition. It results in more bed rest than any condition, with the exception of heart disease (USDHHS, 1986a), so the importance of the successful management of arthritis is obvious. Medical treatments are directed at pain reduction through mild forms of daily medication (such as aspirin or ibuprofen that also reduce inflammation), and stronger medication in severe cases (such as steroids that can more dramatically lessen inflammation). Sometimes surgery is recommended for joint replacement in advanced cases. Behavioral treatments often include lifestyle changes such as weight control, participation in physical therapy, and exercise. However, adherence (see Module 4.2, page 136) to behavioral and lifestyle changes are often a problem, and arthritis is no exception (Anderson et al., 1985).

Research indicates that the severity of the condition is related to depression, helplessness, and stress (Anderson et al., 1985; Nicassio, Wallston, Callahan, Herbert, & Pincus, 1985). Therefore, personal control would appear to be a promising variable to explore as a potential mediator of successful adjustment, both psychologically and behaviorally. In fact, one study found that patients who believed they were partners with medical professionals in the decision making about their treatment—in other words those who felt more in control—adjusted better to their illness (Affleck, Tennen, Pfeiffer, & Fifield, 1987). Those who feel better would then be more likely to adhere to other parts of the treatment regimen such as physical therapy.

LOWER-BACK PAIN

Lower-back pain, although it affects only half as many people, is more debilitating than headache in terms of workdays lost. It accounts for higher overall medical costs (Bonica, 1980a). Lower-back pain has a complex etiology. It is most often initiated by an acute strain or sprain, as in Jennifer's case, but it can also be a symptom of infection, cancer, and degenerative diseases of the spine (Carron, 1984). Therefore, a careful medical evaluation is required to determine its etiology.

Chronic lower-back pain, though, presents a difficult course for medical treatments, and it serves as a model of biopsychosocial factors in illness (Feuerstein et al., 1986). Chronic lower-back pain can be aggravated by disease (for example, arthritis), physical factors related to lifestyle (for example, obesity or weak muscle tone), psychosocial factors (for example, premorbid anxiety, depression), and secondary gains (for example, workers' compensation; Berkow & Fletcher, 1987). Since so many factors can be involved in chronic lower-back pain, it provides a good illustration of pain management techniques (Loeser, 1980).

After careful evaluation, the health psychologist determined that Jennifer's lower-back pain was caused by these factors: (a) the intense experience of pain caused by the initial strain; (b) the relief from work and the support she obtained from her husband and parents for the sick role, which conditioned her to focus attention on pain sensations in her lower back; (c) premorbid anxiety and depression concerning her relationship with her husband and conflicts between her career and her role as a potential mother; and (d) gaining weight the year prior to the injury coupled with poor physical conditioning.

MANAGING ACUTE PAIN

Because pain serves a survival function, it would make no sense to discuss a "cure" for it. Instead, pain is managed in an attempt to reestablish homeostasis. The goal of management is to reduce sufficiently the experience of pain to allow a return to one's premorbid activity level. There may still be some pain, but of course we cannot live without it.

The first thing that health care workers must do in order to help people manage their pain is to make several determinations based on the acute and chronic categories of pain. There are different optimum pain management strategies, depending on whether the pain is acute, chronic, progressive, or intractable-recurrent (Holmes, 1990). These determinations suggest which medical and psychological treatments would be appropriate (Figure 7.2-1).

Acute pain is adaptive, but it has little value beyond its ability to warn of danger (Chapman, 1984). Medical management of acute pain usually involves medications, one of the most common being aspirin. Sometimes stronger pain medications such as narcotics or opioids like morphine are prescribed. Usually these are used when the benefits of pain relief are believed to outweigh the potential for addiction. In fact, it has been charged that in situations of acute pain, opioids may actually be underused, resulting in unnecessary suffering because concerns of addiction are overestimated (Berkow & Fletcher, 1987). Undue pain following surgery can lead to psychological reactions that actually complicate recovery, so adequate reduction of pain through medication is an important consideration (Chapman, 1984).

"Avoidant" coping strategies—those that divert or distract attention from pain—work best for acute pain (Holmes, 1990). Such techniques would tend to utilize briefer approaches and would include *hypnosis* for distraction and with a suggestion for pain reduction (Barber, 1986; Hilgard & Hilgard, 1983), *relaxation training* that might reduce sympathetic arousal and feelings of anxiety that accompany acute pain (Fordyce & Steger, 1979), or *attention-diversion.*

Attention-diversion is a cognitive technique in which the patient focuses on an alternative stimulus (Fernandez, 1986). This technique tends to work best with milder forms of pain (McCaul & Malott, 1984). Therapists help patients focus on a variety of stimuli that can be visual (for example, looking at a relaxing picture or view), auditory (for example, listening to music), or mental (singing a song or doing mental problems). Attention-diversion can produce a reduction in laboratory-induced pain, but not all types of attention-diverting activities are effective. Recent research suggests that distraction only works when it also arouses positive emotions (McCaul, Monson, & Maki, 1992).

The effectiveness of attention-diversion also appears to be influenced by other variables. A sense of personal control and a belief in the effectiveness of attention-diversion seem to enhance its results (Thompson, 1981). Belief in effectiveness can be increased when therapists provide an explanation for how it works.

Lower-back pain would be considered acute if its onset were recent, sudden, and, particularly, if the patient had not experienced it previously (Berkow & Fletcher, 1987). Acute lower-back pain is usually treated with rest and mild manipulation (physical therapy). As in Jennifer's case, pain relievers and muscle relaxant medications are often prescribed. Hypnosis and relaxation training are also effective in treating acute lower-back pain. However they would take several sessions to learn, and since acute lower-back pain is self-limiting, they would probably only be recommended if medication could not be used (for example, in cases where there was a probability of addiction). On the other hand, attention-diversion is relatively easy to learn and could reduce the amount of necessary medication, so it is the treatment of choice.

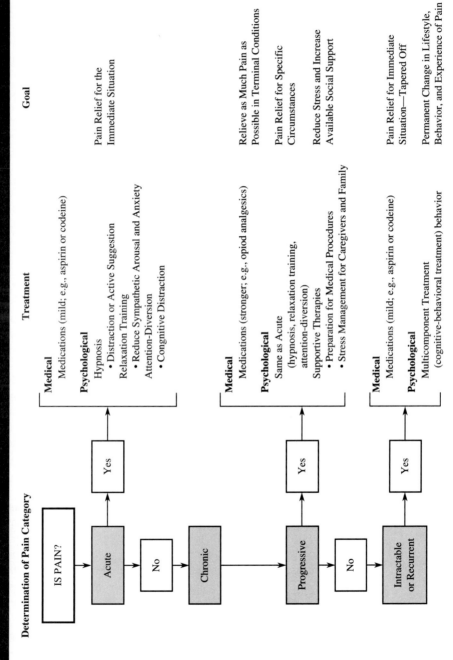

Figure 7.2-1 **PAIN CATEGORIES AND TREATMENT IMPLICATIONS**

Determination of Pain Category

Treatment

Goal

IS PAIN?

Acute — Yes →

Medical
Medications (mild; e.g., aspirin or codeine)

Psychological
Hypnosis
• Distraction or Active Suggestion
Relaxation Training
• Reduce Sympathetic Arousal and Anxiety
Attention-Diversion
• Cognitive Distraction

Pain Relief for the Immediate Situation

No → Chronic → Progressive — Yes →

Medical
Medications (stronger; e.g., opiod analgesics)

Psychological
Same as Acute
(hypnosis, relaxation training, attention-diversion)
Supportive Therapies
• Preparation for Medical Procedures
• Stress Management for Caregivers and Family

Relieve as Much Pain as Possible in Terminal Conditions

Pain Relief for Specific Circumstances

Reduce Stress and Increase Available Social Support

No → Intractable or Recurrent — Yes →

Medical
Medications (mild; e.g., aspirin or codeine)

Psychological
Multicomponent Treatment
(cognitive-behavioral treatment) behavior

Pain Relief for Immediate Situation—Tapered Off

Permanent Change in Lifestyle, Behavior, and Experience of Pain

Managing Chronic Pain

When pain is chronic, it usually presents a variety of symptoms. These symptoms include an underlying organic condition with actual tissue damage, characteristic pain behaviors, and complaints. In addition, there will be at least one of the following (Sanders, 1985):

1. Disruptions in activities of daily living, often a reduction from prior activity levels.
2. Problems in interpersonal relationships.
3. Changes in employment or recreational activities.
4. Increased use of drugs or medical treatments to relieve pain.
5. Sleep disturbance.
6. Anxiety and depression.

Self-Coping with Chronic Pain

Rosensteil and Keefe (1983) are interested in determining how people cope naturally with chronic lower-back pain. They asked patients to report various coping strategies they actually used and their ability to control or decrease pain. An analysis of the reported coping strategies revealed that three broad factors accounted for 68% of the variance in coping:

1. *Cognitive coping and suppression*, which included reinterpreting the sensations of pain; using self-statements about one's coping abilities; and ignoring pain sensations.
2. *Helplessness*, which included such coping methods as catastrophizing or increasing one's activity level.
3. *Diverting attention and praying.*

Importantly, the patients did *not* believe that their ability to control pain or decrease it was very good. In spite of this perception on the part of the patients, these three factors did predict 22% of the variance in average pain ratings, 14% of the variance in anxiety state, 12% of the variance in functional capacity, and 11% of the variance in depression. This suggests that these factors are related to some dimensions of chronic pain syndrome. However, these three factors were not related to three other variables: pain duration, number of back surgeries, or disability status.

More surprising was the finding that certain supposed effective "avoidant" coping strategies, such as cognitive coping and diverting attention, were related to *more* functional impairment. It appears from subsequent research that chronic pain patients do better with "approach" strategies that require them to pay more attention to the pain (Holmes, 1990). (See Module 6.2, page 273, for a discussion of approach and avoidant coping strategies.) It is important to remember that these are correlational data, and that they suffer from the problem of directionality. For example, we cannot know whether diverting attention leads to more functional impairment or whether people with more functional impairment divert their attention more.

Can we conclude that people are successful in their attempts to relieve the symptoms of chronic pain on their own? Perhaps only in a small way. However, this study does point up the intricate and sometimes perplexing interrelationships among the variables in chronic pain. This study gives us an idea of what people attempt to do on their own to cope with pain.

As we have seen, the symptoms of chronic pain can be quite disruptive and protracted and might require psychosocial intervention. A determination of the specific chronic pain category has important implications for pain management and must precede treatment. The most important distinction is between progressive and benign pain.

CHRONIC PROGRESSIVE PAIN

Because chronic progressive pain is caused by an underlying organic condition that is worsening, patients can be expected to experience increasing pain levels. For example, lower-back pain would be classified chronic progressive *if* it were caused by cancer of the spinal cord. Pain could also be caused by invasive cancer treatments (for example, a spinal tap, surgery, chemotherapy, or radiation).

Management of chronic progressive pain usually involves the stronger pain relief medications. Opioid analgesics are commonly prescribed in life threatening diseases such as cancer (Dugan, 1984; Foley, 1985) but rarely in nonterminal progressive conditions such as rheumatoid arthritis. One interesting trend with cancer is patient-controlled analgesia, in which patients self-administer preset doses of morphine when they feel the need for it. Results from one study indicated that patient use of morphine actually declined when they had control over its administration (Citron et al., 1986). So, again we see the importance of personal control in health.

Psychological management of chronic progressive pain usually includes supportive approaches that treat specific symptoms as they arise. The same techniques that are effective in acute pain—hypnosis, relaxation training, and attention-diversion—could be used on a symptomatic basis, and in terminal disease, counseling for death and dying might be appropriate, depending on the patient.

In addition, patients with chronic progressive pain usually must endure many stressful medical procedures. With lower-back pain this might include surgery to remove a tumor. Is it possible that psychological preparation for medical procedures can reduce suffering and hasten recovery? This question was first addressed more than 30 years ago. In a pioneering study, one group of patients who received psychological preparation (information about what would happen before, during, and after surgery) were compared to another group who received the routine hospital procedure (Janis, 1958). The preparation group needed less pain medication; demanded less of the hospital staff; and, most importantly, were discharged from the hospital sooner.

Since then, many studies have investigated psychological preparation for medical procedures and subsequent pain. A meta-analysis of these studies by Suls and Wan (1989) concluded that, despite the early success, procedural information preparation alone is not generally beneficial. In some cases it causes patients to focus attention more on the pain. However, in combination, sensory information (which describes the sensations that the patient will experience) and procedural information (which describes the sequence of events) do produce significant reductions in negative affect, stress, and pain reports.

Another area that often requires psychosocial intervention in progressive pain is stress in the patient's family and caregivers. A person with lower-back pain might be confined to bed and need to be waited on 24 hours a day. Much of the research on caregiver stress has involved the effects of chronic illness in children (for example, Barbarin, Hughes, & Chesler, 1985; Mattsson, 1977) and older adults with debilitating, but not necessarily painful, illnesses (such as Alzheimer's disease). From these studies, we can conclude that caring for a chronically ill family member, whether pain is significant or not, is highly stressful (Zakowski, Hall, & Baum, 1992).

Relationships between spouses are severely strained when caring for a sick child, but the risk of divorce may actually decline. This apparently contradictory result suggests that families are under stress but that they tend to pull together. When a variety of coping styles were examined in families of sick children, two were significantly related to better health: (a) maintaining family integration ("pulling together"); and (b) maintaining external sources of social support (obtaining additional outside help; McCubbin et al., 1983).

In one study, two types of tasks were singled out as particularly stressful for family members of older chronically ill patients: (a) nursing-type care (for example, bathing and dressing); and (b) errands and transportation (Montgomery, Gonyea, & Hooyman, 1985). These caregiving tasks take an inordinate amount of time, which may be the reason they contributed most to the objective burden of family members. The authors concluded that the subjective burden of the caregiver (the emotional reaction to the family member's distress) is not particularly responsive to intervention, so intervention should be directed toward giving caregivers "time off" from responsibilities to reduce the objective burden.

CHRONIC BENIGN PAIN: INTRACTABLE AND RECURRENT

This category encompasses symptoms that are not linked to a worsening underlying organic condition but are more related to psychosocial factors.

Although chronic benign pain often begins with some organic pathology, physicians tend to be cautious in treating it medically, because its continuation is suspected to be largely psychological (Berkow & Fletcher, 1987). Therefore, medical treatments for this category of pain often rely on a variety of nonnarcotic medications (for example, aspirin for arthritis).

The use of opioids is controversial because of the potential for addiction. However, one study suggested that this potential may be overemphasized (Urban, France, Steinberger, Scott, & Maltbie, 1986). Hospitalized chronic phantom-limb pain patients were given minimal doses of methadone (an opioid analgesic) and an antidepressant during hospitalization and for two years following their hospitalization. At discharge, subjects reported significantly reduced pain levels which continued throughout the two-year study period, even though drug levels were kept very low.

This suggests that small doses of opioid analgesics may be effective in relieving pain without the need to increase them to potentially addictive or dangerous levels. But it is not clear from this study if the effect is due to the opioid, to the antidepressant, or to a combination of both, and antidepressants alone can be used to treat chronic pain with some success (Berkow & Fletcher, 1987). Additional research is needed to sort out these factors. Because of its importance for these chronic pain syndromes, psychological treatments will be covered in detail in a later section on pain clinics. We now turn our attention to some specific psychological and behavioral approaches that have been used with chronic pain.

TECHNIQUES FOR MANAGING PAIN

Psychological and behavioral techniques were described in Module 2.2. Here we are concerned only with the effectiveness of such techniques when used to manage chronic pain.

BEHAVIOR MODIFICATION   The natural consequences of pain behavior—attention and sympathy, time away from work or other responsibilities, and financial compensation—can sometimes reward its continuation (Fordyce, 1974). In a behavior modification program, patients are ignored when they display pain behaviors and rewarded and praised when they comply with treatment, for example, exercising or reducing their pain medication. Behavior modification has been used to achieve several goals: (a) to reduce specific pain behaviors, (b) to decrease reliance on medication, and (c) to increase activity levels.

Usually the entire multidisciplinary team of a pain clinic are involved in the behavior modification program (for example, Varni, Jay, Masek, & Thompson, 1986; Varni & Thompson, 1986), and sometimes patients' spouses are included as well (Fordyce et al., 1973). For example, as Jennifer gradually became less active because of her pain, her muscles became weaker and this increased her back problems. The danger is that patients like her will require continuous medication because of this vicious cycle. In such cases, patients are reinforced for attending physical therapy exercise classes and for increasing daily physical activity such as walking to the store. Treatment team members verbally reinforce the patient, and family members reinforce the patient perhaps by going along on the activity.

Is behavior modification effective? Many studies have addressed this question with the general conclusion that it can reduce reliance on medication and increase activity level (Brownell, 1984a; Roberts, 1986; Turk et al., 1983; Turner & Romano, 1984). However, very few of the available studies compared behavioral treatment to nontreatment or placebo treatment.

Comparisons with other forms of treatment can provide a measure of relative effectiveness. In one study that compared behavior modification (including cognitive therapy) with traditional physical therapy, both treatments produced improvements in pain and psychological and psychosocial functioning (Heinrich, Cohen, Naliboff, Collins, & Bonnebakker, 1985). In another study comparing behavior modification with "traditional" medical management (that is, pain medication as needed), there was little difference between them at six-week follow-up, but the behavior modification group was doing significantly better one year later (Fordyce, Brockway, Bergman, & Spengler, 1986). Together, these studies suggest that behavior modification is at least as effective as some traditional approaches to pain management, although better studies are still needed.

COGNITIVE THERAPY   The gate control theory suggests that cognitive control over pain impulses might reduce the perception of pain. Consistent with this, Bandura (1986) hypothesized that perceived self-efficacy might affect the release of endorphins, thereby closing the gate. In general, cognitive therapy attempts to change beliefs, thoughts, and feelings such that self-efficacy is increased. There is a specific cognitive program for pain management developed by Donald Meichenbaum and Dennis Turk (Meichenbaum & Jaremko, 1982; Meichenbaum & Turk, 1976; Turk, 1978; Turk et al., 1983). The program uses a three-step process similar to Meichenbaum's stress inoculation therapy described in Module 6.2, except that it is adapted specifically to pain (see Box 7.2-1).

Also, some specific cognitive techniques have been used for pain. They include attention-diversion, guided imagery, and redefinition (Fernandez, 1986; McCaul & Malott, 1984; Turk et al., 1983). Attention-diversion was described earlier. *Guided imagery* is similar to attention-diversion, except the patient's imagination is relied on rather than some environmental stimulus. Patients are taught to create a pleasant, involving, and distracting image in their mind. They are encouraged to focus on as many sensory features of the image as possible—the sights, as well as the smells, sounds, and tactile sensations. Like attention-diversion, guided imagery helps reduce acute pain and mild to moderate pain better than stronger pain (McCaul & Malott, 1984; Turk et al.,

1983). There is, unfortunately, little evidence of its utility with long-lasting pain, but the biggest weakness is that some people just have difficulty creating mental images (Melzack & Wall, 1982).

Cognitive redefinition occurs when a patient either uses self-statements to control the experience of pain or is assisted by a therapist to evaluate the logic of their reactions to, and thoughts about, pain (Fernandez, 1986). We do know that the beliefs that chronic pain patients have about pain are predictive of subjective pain intensity and other pain dimensions (Williams & Thorn, 1989), suggesting the importance of cognitions in the pain experience. Self-statements include the positive coping statements patients make about their ability to tolerate pain and the reinterpretive statements they make to counter the unpleasant aspects of the pain. Patients may use such self-statements as, "It isn't so bad. I can stand and walk around. I know I'll be able to walk to the store. I'll feel good if I do."

Is cognitive therapy an effective treatment? Although research tends to be favorable, again most of it lacks adequate placebo comparisons (Turner & Chapman, 1982b; Turner & Romano, 1984). One of the best controlled studies randomly assigned people with tension headaches to either a nontreatment group, cognitive therapy, or EMG biofeedback therapy and followed them up two years later (Holroyd & Andrasik, 1982; Holroyd, Andrasik, & Westbrook, 1977). Cognitive therapy produced the only significant reduction in headaches during the treatment and subjects in that group continued to have significantly less pain two years later.

Another study compared lower-back pain patients randomly assigned to a nontreatment waiting list or one of two treatment groups: cognitive-behavior therapy with relaxation training or relaxation training alone (Turner, 1982).

> ***Box 7.2-1***   **THREE STEPS IN MEICHANBAUM AND TURK'S COGNITIVE PAIN MANAGEMENT PROGRAM**

1. *Reconceptualization.* Patients are provided with a psychological explanation for pain, which they are encouraged to accept at least partly as an explanation for their own pain; gate control theory can be used to explain to the patient how lower-back pain can occur in the absence of an organic cause or after one has healed.

2. *Acquisition and Skills Rehearsal.* This active part of the treatment consists of learning relaxation training, controlled breathing, and imagery techniques to direct attention away from the pain.

3. *Follow-through.* In this step, the skills are applied to the natural environment as patients learn to use them outside therapy. This step also includes increasing physical activity and exercise, components that are not strictly cognitive, although they may result in increased self-efficacy. Attention is also paid to the possibility of a relapse, and a plan for coping with future pain is devised with the therapist's help.

Both treatment groups were significantly improved over the nontreatment group at the end of treatment and not significantly different from one another. Both groups also maintained their improvements up to two years later; however, only the cognitive-behavior group had also significantly increased hours spent at work.

Other studies have indicated that combined cognitive-behavioral therapy is effective in reducing abdominal pain in children aged 6 to 12 (Sanders et al., 1989), and that it can be equally effective in reducing work-related upper limb pain in adults whether treatment is given individually or in a group (Spence, 1989). In addition, cognitive-behavioral therapy appears to be equal to relaxation training in treating migraine headache pain and in reducing subjects' use of medication and superior because it also appears to improve assertiveness and active problem solving and reduce depression, whereas relaxation training does not (Sorbi, Tellegen, & du Long, 1989). Cognitive-behavioral therapy is also an effective method of reducing the problems and pain of people with chronic headaches (Holroyd, Nash, & Pingel, 1991).

Two experiments used relatively large subject samples and followed them for up to 12 months after treatment. The first compared operant and cognitive-behavioral treatments for lower-back pain (Turner & Clancy, 1988). Although the operant group had greater initial improvement, the cognitive-behavioral group had steady improvement that resulted in equal decreases in psychosocial and physical disability at 12 months posttreatment. The second experiment randomly assigned lower-back pain patients to aerobic exercise treatment, behavioral treatment, aerobic plus behavioral treatment, and a no-treatment group (Turner, Clancy, McQuade, & Cardenas, 1990). Initially, only the aerobic plus behavioral treatment group had improved significantly, but at 12 months posttreatment, all three treatment groups had improved. Therefore, behavioral, cognitive, and cognitive-behavioral therapy all appear to be effective treatments for chronic pain syndromes.

BIOFEEDBACK AND RELAXATION TRAINING   Biofeedback and relaxation training are both considered effective for pain management, although relaxation training has the advantage of not requiring the additional complication and expense of equipment (Turk, Meichenbaum, & Berman, 1979). Many reviews have concluded that both biofeedback and relaxation training are effective in reducing headache pain, in particular (for example, Andrasik et al., 1986; Belar & Kibrick, 1986; Blanchard, 1987; Holroyd & Penzien, 1985; Turk et al., 1979).

Another way to gauge the effectiveness of treatment is its cost benefit. One such analysis looked at self-reported medical costs for headache patients who received various combinations of relaxation training and biofeedback (Blanchard, Jaccard, Andrasik, Guarnieri, & Jurish, 1985). The average medical costs associated with the headaches for the 2 years prior to treatment were $955, compared to $52 for the 2 years following treatment.

There is one difference between biofeedback and relaxation training for headache pain. Biofeedback appears to be more effective with tension headaches, whereas relaxation training is more effective with migraine (Andrasik et al., 1986; Holroyd & Penzien, 1985). There are also slight differences over time. Four years after treatment, tension headache patients still had good maintenance of headache reduction, while migraine headache patients showed a gradual, but not significant, deterioration of treatment effectiveness (Blanchard, Andrasik, Guarnieri, Neff, & Rodichok, 1987).

Although the majority of studies of biofeedback and relaxation training have dealt with headache pain, a few studies have addressed other types of pain. In patients with chronic pain caused by ulcerative colitis, relaxation training produced significant gains compared to an attention placebo (Shaw & Ehrlich, 1987). At six-week follow-up, patients receiving relaxation training rated their pain as less frequent and less intense than those receiving the placebo, and importantly, the relaxation training group was taking significantly less antiinflammatory medication on follow-up. Some research suggests that biofeedback is superior to relaxation training for lower-back pain (Strong, Cramond, & Maas, 1989), while other research indicates that they are equivalent in treating pain resulting from orthopedic trauma (Achterberg, Kenner, & Casey, 1989). In summary, research supports the use of both biofeedback and relaxation training for headache and possibly for other types of pain as well.

HYPNOSIS AND PLACEBO Many physicians and patients are skeptical about hypnosis as a pain treatment. This skepticism is understandable, given hypnosis's origins as a sideshow entertainment and the inability of researchers to define precisely what it is (see Module 2.2, page 57). Yet, hypnosis can reduce the subjective experience of pain. Several experiments have looked at pain and hypnosis, and people actually do experience less pain when hypnotized (Hilgard & Hilgard, 1983).

Interestingly, when people are hypnotized and subjected to laboratory-induced pain (described in Module 7.1, page 281), highly hypnotizable subjects do not verbalize discomfort or present any observable behavioral signs of undergoing pain, although if asked, some rate the pain as substantial (Hilgard & Hilgard, 1983). In other words, they are aware that it is painful but are somehow cut off from the full experience of the pain.

Hilgard (1978) compared highly hypnotizable subjects to nonhypnotizable subjects. The highly hypnotizable subjects were randomly assigned to receive or not receive a suggestion for analgesia. While undergoing pain, the highly hypnotizable subjects, without a suggestion for analgesia, reported nearly as much pain as waking subjects, while those with a suggestion for analgesia reported no pain. Therefore, it is not hypnosis alone but the specific suggestion of analgesia that results in diminished pain. Somehow, highly hypnotizable subjects are able to "decouple" the psychological experience of pain from the physiological experience of it.

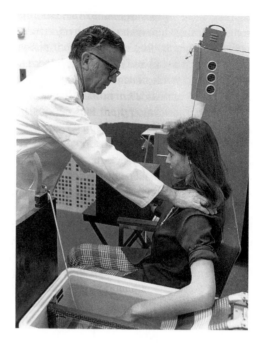

Immersing the hand in frigid water, which is otherwise painful, is one method of testing the depth of hypnosis.

There are some problems with the study of hypnosis. Experts do not agree on what hypnosis is, so the underlying mechanism for pain relief remains a mystery (Barber, 1986). It was once thought that hypnosis might trigger the release of endorphins, but research has not supported this hypothesis (Barber, 1986). In the laboratory, hypnosis does reduce pain, but it tends to work best in those who are highly hypnotizable. Also, subjects who achieve pain relief are apparently using their own spontaneous cognitive strategies, so hypnosis alone may not be responsible (Barber, 1982, 1986; Turk, Meichenbaum, & Genest, 1983).

To make matters worse, most of the research on the use of hypnosis with pain patients has not used adequate comparison and placebo groups (Barber, 1982; Melzack & Wall, 1982). One study did examine the relative effectiveness of hypnosis and cognitive-behavioral therapy in a group of patients with chronic pain over a one-month follow-up period (Edelson & Fitzpatrick, 1989). Both treatments reduced the subjects' self-reports of pain, but only those subjects receiving cognitive-behavioral therapy also had significant reductions in pain intensity and increases in activity level. This suggests that cognitive-behavioral therapy is superior. However, patients in the hypnosis group were not screened for hypnotizability. Because of the inclusion of subjects in the hypnosis group who might not be hypnotizable, it is likely that pain reduction is more successful with highly hypnotizable patients than these results indicate. Nevertheless, cognitive-behavioral therapy would still be effective for more people. Because of this, we must conclude that, unless a patient were highly hypnotizable, it would be better to use cognitive-behavioral therapy for lower-back pain.

Turner and Chapman (1982b) have argued that the placebo effect (see Module 2.2) could account for the experience of analgesia under hypnosis. This argument would seem plausible and offers an alternative explanation for Hilgard's (1978) results. However, other studies have cast doubt on the placebo argument by first assessing the pain reactions of groups of high and low hypnotizable subjects to a placebo presumed by the groups to be pain medication (McGlashan, Evans, & Orne, 1969; Orne, 1976). When given the placebo, the groups did not differ significantly in their pain tolerance. However, when under hypnosis, the highly hypnotizable subjects experienced significantly greater pain tolerance than the low hypnotizable subjects. Therefore, hypnosis is more effective than placebo for some people, but it is not an effective analgesic for everyone.

■■■■

MULTICOMPONENT PAIN TREATMENT

As we have seen, psychosocial factors play a prominent role in chronic pain syndromes. Even so, we should also take into consideration that patients' *experiences* of chronic pain are "real," not just "in their head" (Hendler, 1984; Karoly, 1985), and that most chronic pain syndromes begin with some tissue injury. Therefore, a comprehensive approach to therapy probably offers the greatest likelihood of success for chronic pain syndromes. In fact, single modality pain treatments should probably be avoided (Kanner, 1986).

"Pain clinics" were begun by an anesthesiologist at the University of Washington Medical School, John Bonica, who was searching for a better way to help patients who did not seem to respond to traditional methods of pain control (Bonica, 1976; Melzack & Wall, 1982). Referred to as interdisciplinary or multicomponent treatment centers, pain clinics have multiplied until there are now more than 1,000 nationwide (Newman & Seres, 1986).

There are detailed descriptions of pain clinics available (for example, Bonica, 1976; Zlutnick & Taylor, 1982). They usually employ multidisciplinary teams of professionals (such as physicians, psychologists, physical therapists, social workers) whose work reflects the variety of biopsychosocial factors involved in chronic pain. Ideally, the team does a thorough and *integrated* assessment, meeting together to take into account as many of the biopsychosocial factors in pain as possible and to formulate a comprehensive treatment plan (Follick, Ahern, Attanasio, & Riley, 1985). The goals of pain clinics typically include most, if not all, of those given in Table 7.2-1, and the psychological and behavioral treatments used to help accomplish these goals draw on most of the techniques just described.

EFFECTIVENESS AND CONCLUSION

Despite the large number of pain clinics in the United States, there have been only a handful of studies of their effectiveness. One study, conducted at the University of Nebraska Pain Management Center, did include a control group (Guck, Skultety, Meilman, and Dowd, 1985). Twenty treated patients were compared to 20 patients who met the criteria for admission to the program but could not receive treatment because they were denied insurance coverage by their insurance companies. The groups were similar in many important characteristics such as age, employment status, pain history, and medication usage. The 4-week multicomponent treatment program involved planned withdrawal from medication, cognitive-behavioral therapy, self-monitoring, physical therapy, relaxation training, and family participation.

Patients were followed for 1 to 5 years after completion of the program. At these follow-ups, 60% of treated patients reported improvements in level of pain, subsequent hospitalizations, performance of physical activities, use of medication, and depression. One of the most impressive results was that nearly two-thirds of the treatment group were employed at follow-up, compared to only one-fifth of those who were not treated.

These results suggest that the passage of time does little to improve the condition of patients with chronic pain syndrome. The old adage "time heals all wounds" does not seem to apply to chronic pain. However, we still do not know if treatment is significantly better than a placebo, and we do not know which aspects of the treatment are the "active ingredients" actually causing the improvement. So additional research is warranted.

Table 7.2-1   TYPICAL PAIN CLINIC GOALS

TO REDUCE	TO INCREASE

1. The experience of pain and related emotions:
  a. Anxiety
  b. Depression
  c. Helplessness
2. The use of pain medications and medical services
3. Pain behaviors
4. Secondary gains
	5. Mental well-being
	  a. Self-efficacy
	  b. Personal control
	6. Physical functioning
	  a. Strength
	  b. Mobility
	  c. Endurance
	7. Social supports and family relationships

In an unintended way, the design of this study also points up one of the main problems with our health insurance system. The nontreatment group was able to be formed because some patients had been denied access to treatment by their insurance companies. By denying treatment, the insurance companies saved the cost of the four-week treatment program. However, the follow-up years later revealed that the control subjects continued to use more pain medication and to require more hospitalizations, adding to the insurance companies' costs. Also, far fewer of the nontreatment group were employed, meaning they could not contribute as much to society and could not continue to pay health insurance premiums.

Another study at Boulder, Colorado's, Memorial Hospital Pain Control Center specifically evaluated the cost effectiveness of pain clinics (Steig & Williams, 1983). It analyzed patients' anticipated total amount of medical costs, disability payments, and lost potential earnings through age 72 (the average age of the patients was 41), if they had not been treated. These figures were compared to the costs of the pain program itself and to the patients' potential earnings based on their observed improvement on follow-up 1 year later. The pain treatment resulted in a net estimated lifetime savings of more than $250,000 *per patient*. This figure represents potential earned income, less medical and disability costs, and is in early 1980s dollars.

Our optimism about these dramatic savings must be restrained somewhat because of the results of a recent study (Jensen & Karoly, 1991). A survey of 118 people who completed a hospital-based multicomponent pain program over a 7-year period found a significant relationship between cognitive coping strategies—belief that the patient has control over pain, attention-diversion, ignoring, and coping self-statements—and low levels of pain severity. However, this relationship was not significant for people with medium or high levels of pain severity, and surprisingly, it was not related to lower levels of medical services utilization. The correlational nature of this study precludes causal conclusions, and the types of patients receiving treatment differ in various treatment programs (Holzman et al., 1985). Yet, the results of this study do suggest that multicomponent treatment may not be effective for all patients, particularly those with higher levels of pain severity.

Jennifer did not attend a pain clinic, but she received individual multicomponent treatment. The first part of her treatment was to assess the function and meaning of pain in Jennifer's life. As much as the initial injury hurt, the pain came to symbolize relief from pre-existing anxiety and depression over conflicts and concerns about her role as a wife, potential mother, and even a daughter. Therefore, her pain and incapacitation were maintained by her escape from these conflicts and concerns. Furthermore, her pain behaviors were reinforced by the support and concern of her family and the relief from working. Finally, being overweight and out of condition put additional strain on her lower back, occasionally aggravating the injury. Because she had learned to attend to her lower back from the first painful experience, she was constantly aware of sensations in her lower back and immediately noticed even slight discomfort there.

Jennifer's treatment had three steps. The first was cognitive-behavioral. It involved relaxation training and guided imagery to divert her attention and cognitive redefinition to help her control the experience of pain. The second step was to improve her general physical condition and help her lose weight through an aerobic exercise program. This took the strain off her lower back. The third step, a year after treatment started, consisted of involving her husband in treatment. By the time couple therapy began, she was feeling better about her appearance, and they agreed that her husband would no longer support her pain behaviors. Instead, he would show his support and caring for her in other ways when she was not emitting pain behaviors. The couple also went on to discuss their family plans and determined to share the parenting and career aspects of family. This helped relieve Jennifer's role conflicts.

At a follow-up a year later, Jennifer required no pain medication, was back at work, and was a month pregnant. To prevent relapse, Jennifer returned for a couple of booster sessions to prepare her for the potential pain and lower-back strain that often accompany pregnancy.

MODULE SUMMARY

1. Myofascial pain—an achiness that can affect many parts of the body—is the most common pain syndrome, although its origin is unknown and it resolves on its own.
2. Migraine headache originates in the vascular system of the head and is related to stress.
3. Tension headache is the most common form of headache and originates in tension of the muscles of the head, shoulder, and neck. Again, stress plays a role in tension headache.
4. Lower-back pain may originate from a strain or sprain. It can also be a symptom of serious diseases such as cancer. Chronic lower-back pain is related to many complex psychosocial factors.
5. Arthritis pain is very common, affecting ½ of people over 65 years of age. Hereditary factors play a role, as do stress and other emotional factors.
6. Pain syndromes without known causes are usually not treated as somatoform disorder but are puzzling to neurologists.
7. The type of pain syndrome—acute, chronic progressive, chronic intractable-benign, or chronic intermittent—determines what physiological and psychological treatments are used. Generally, psychological treatments are preferred for chronic intractable-benign and chronic intermittent pain syndromes.

8. Pain management includes a variety of techniques. Behavior modification is effective in reducing reliance on medication and includes increasing activity. Cognitive therapy, relaxation training, and biofeedback all seem to be effective, but cognitive therapy may result in additional benefits in increased problem solving and assertiveness. Hypnosis is effective, but it is limited because it works best for subjects who are highly hypnotizable.

9. Multicomponent pain clinics involve using a variety of health care professions and treatments simultaneously. They appear to have the greatest effectiveness, and they are especially successful in returning chronic pain patients to work. They also seem to result in significant cost savings.

8

Addiction

For several years, we have witnessed an endless parade of people, some well-known, some not, appearing on talk shows and writing books to confess their addiction to one substance or another and of course to tell how they are "recovering." But some of them, it seems, did not recover enough and are back to confess for their second or third time. If you've seen this parade you may have wondered, "What is going on? When does use become abuse? What is addiction—a behavior or an illness? Is it really that hard to recover from addiction? If addiction is a disease, why can't it be cured?" These same questions have also interested health psychologists.

Addiction is defined as devoting or surrendering oneself to a habit, appetite, or behavior. So, addiction is not limited to drugs. It was, in fact, only during this century that the term came to be applied specifically to substances like alcohol and other drugs (Peele, 1989). Also, the definition of addiction does not preclude choice, and people who use or even abuse a substance should not be thought of as mindless zombies ensnared by some evil power that could trap anyone.

There are many **psychoactive substances** capable of affecting the chemical environment of the brain and, therefore altering mood, perception, or behavior. They can also be overused and abused to the point that they seriously affect health. Two legal substances—alcohol and tobacco—account for a majority of premature deaths in this country, in numbers that run into the hundreds of thousands *per year,* and there are growing concerns about the abuse of illegal substances like "crack" cocaine. However, psychoactive substances are only part of the puzzle of addiction; they are not the sole "cause" of it.

Unfortunately, there is no comprehensive theory or model of substance addiction at this time. Instead, there are at least 40 distinct theories, each one taking a narrow view of addiction, entirely ignoring either the psychosocial or the biological factors (Galizio & Maisto, 1985). To complicate matters, several *treatment* models also exist, but they tend to be substance specific; that is, there are treatments for alcoholism, treatments for narcotics, and treatments for smoking tobacco (Roche, 1989).

It is a challenge to consolidate the separate biomedical and psychosocial models and treatments. Several are reviewed in Module 8.1 and a tentative biopsychosocial model is proposed to integrate them. This model is then used to explore the epidemiology, health effects, and treatments for smoking tobacco (Module 8.2) and abusing alcohol and drugs (Module 8.3) in more detail.

BACKGROUND AND THEORIES

MODELS OF ADDICTION

Most theories of substance abuse have one thing in common—the "biomedical model"—which holds that addiction is a disease. However, since there is no pathogen, addiction is assumed to be the result of some biological defect—either a genetic predisposition or the *result* of a physiological change in the brain *caused* by the psychoactive substance itself. (If this seems circular, that is because it is.)

The biomedical model has dominated addiction theory and treatment for many years and is described here along with its limitations. As an alternative, we introduce a more comprehensive biopsychosocial approach later in this section.

BIOMEDICAL MODEL OF ADDICTION

The biomedical model emphasizes **physical dependence**, which is a state of physiological adaptation to a substance that is characterized by tolerance and withdrawal. *Tolerance* occurs when the body accommodates to a certain level of a substance. In order to achieve the same effects, increased doses of the substance are required. In other words, the brain's natural homeostasis has been altered by the substance. *Withdrawal* consists of the uncomfortable physiological and psychological symptoms that occur when the substance is discontinued. Withdrawal symptoms vary depending on the substance but often include anxiety and paranoia, depression, nausea, irritability, headaches, body aches, sweating, tremors, hallucinations, and cravings for the substance.

The belief that addiction is a disease is not only held by many medical researchers and clinicians, but it is also promoted by self-help programs such as Alcoholics Anonymous. There are some compassionate reasons for considering addiction a disease. In the past, alcoholics and addicts had been demeaned for having no self-control. Labeling addiction a disease reduces "blaming the victim" (after all, we do not blame people for having diabetes). This may make substance abusers feel less guilty and stigmatized, thus increasing the likelihood that they will enter treatment.

LIMITATIONS OF THE BIOMEDICAL MODEL   There are several limitations of the biomedical model of addiction. First, there is no pathogen—addiction is neither contagious nor infectious—so there is a philosophical problem with calling it a disease (Peele, 1989). Of course there are other diseases that are not caused by a pathogen, so it might be more accurate to characterize addiction as a "lifestyle disease" like cancer and heart disease. However, lifestyle diseases are believed to be caused, as least in part, by behavioral factors like diet and stress. Of course, one of the important behavioral factors in addiction is the *use* of substances such as alcohol and tobacco, but it makes no sense to refer to the abuse of these substances as both the cause of a lifestyle disease and a lifestyle disease itself.

A second limitation is that the biomedical model is dualistic and focuses on the biological to the exclusion of psychosocial factors (Peele, 1981). This has led medical researchers to classify drug dependence based on the specific substance involved, rather than to attempt to find a single general definition for it (Berkow & Fletcher, 1987). This substance-specific approach does have advantages. It improves the medical management of treatment, particularly detoxification, because it takes into account the individual physiological mechanisms involved with a substance and helps predict the withdrawal symptoms. It also encourages investigation of the genetic factors that may contribute to the abuse of certain substances.

However, the subject-specific approach has disadvantages. It does not promote investigation of the psychosocial factors that may be common to all of the addictions, regardless of the substance involved. Also, treatment that focuses on detoxification is not a cure, for it leaves the person with the same lifestyle and behavioral patterns as before. Finally, while it is not appropriate to demean someone struggling with an addiction, the biomedical model permits little focus on individual responsibility. Stanton Peele, a social psychologist and researcher, has stated, "The label *addiction* does not obviate either the meaning of the addictive involvement within people's lives, or their responsibility for their misbehavior, or for their choices in continuing the addiction" (1989, p. 3). Labeling a behavior a disease removes one's personal responsibility for it, and *not* holding people responsible for addiction may ultimately work against treatment (Fingarette, 1988).

Here is a humorous anecdote that points out that "addiction" can occur in situations that we do not consider evidence of a disease:

> *Trousers are another example of the similarity between drug-oriented behavior and other relationships that we consider perfectly normal. We depend quite intensely on this substance (our trousers), both mentally and physically, its withdrawal causes discomfort, mental distress, and it is a well-known weapon in brain-washing (Laurie, 1967, p. 12).*

A final limitation of the biomedical model has been pointed out by several prominent researchers in the field of addiction:

> *One common myth in drug abuse is that drugs cause drug abuse and that, if a drug user has sufficient exposure to a drug of abuse, he or she will become dependent on the drug. Investigators have now shown that exposure to a drug of abuse is not sufficient for (physical) dependence to develop. In fact, there are numerous persons who use drugs of abuse over extended intervals who never experience the typical symptoms associated with dependence, such as withdrawal. (Epstein, Grunberg, Lichtenstein, & Evans, 1989, p. 714)*

This suggests that physical dependence is not the property of particular substances but rather results from a variety of factors, psychosocial as well as biological. That is why researchers and therapists are beginning to look for the *underlying* processes of addiction common to all conditions (Roche, 1989). In other words, addiction is not viewed as being caused solely by the substance; rather, it is viewed as being caused by an *interaction* between the person, the environment, and the substance. To illustrate this, some people who take a substance *do not* develop physical dependence, yet they may develop psychological dependence. This is not to say that physical dependence is unimportant; it is, and it requires competent medical treatment. However, psychological dependence turns out to be an even more widespread problem than physical dependence, so addiction theory and treatment must incorporate all of the relevant biopsychosocial factors involved in addiction.

BIOPSYCHOSOCIAL FACTORS IN ADDICTION

The first step in determining the biopsychosocial factors in addiction is to recognize the interplay of psychological dependence and physical dependence. **Psychological dependence** is a strong *desire* or *compulsion* to take a substance in order to produce feelings of pleasure or to avoid feelings of discomfort. Psychological dependence does not necessarily result in physical dependence, although it may lead to it after some time. Note that psychological dependence is an *internally experienced* state—a desire, compulsion, or craving.

On the other hand, **substance abuse** is defined only in terms of *external behavior*. As a behavior, when use becomes abuse is a matter of judgment, and it is not an easy determination to make. How much of a behavior is abuse? What about the widespread recreational use in our society of substances to which *some* people may become addicted but many others do not? Certainly we cannot call a person who has a glass of wine with dinner an abuser. When use becomes abuse is also culturally determined. Some abused substances are legal—for example, alcohol and tobacco. Then there are the illegal substances, such as marijuana, but national samples indicate such a high incidence of experimentation (National Institute on Drug Abuse, 1986) that "it cannot be considered deviant behavior for high school seniors in this culture at this time. In a statistical sense it is *not* trying marijuana that has become deviant" (Shedler & Block, 1990, p. 625).

Experimentation with illegal drugs is so widespread that newspaper reports cite government *encouragement* that the incidence of young people admitting to having tried any illegal substance *fell* to "only" 48% in 1990 (Cimons, 1991). Drug use is certainly a major social, economic, and health problem in our society, and some people have become so concerned that they advocate that *any* use of a substance is dangerous. However, as we will see later, there are young people who have experimented with illegal substances, did not go on to abuse them, and are in good psychological health, so substance abuse should only be diagnosed when there is impairment of normal functioning.

Although the field has not yet developed a comprehensive model that deals with addiction both in terms of development and treatment, we can explore some of the biopsychosocial factors that would probably be included in it. There are four categories of factors: (a) the *brain*—the hypothalamus, neurotransmitters, and genetic predisposition; (b) *motivation*—specifically drives and needs; (c) *learning*—conditioning and reinforcement; and (d) *social influences*—environmental cues and pressure.

THE BRAIN   If we are going to understand addiction, we must begin by looking at the brain and how it responds to and mediates pleasure and pain. The exact brain mechanisms involved in addiction are not completely known. There is evidence that a region known as the median forebrain bundle, an area involved with rewards and motivation (Lowinson, Ruiz, Millman, & Langrod, 1992) and a major pathway of the limbic system, runs through the hypothalamus. The hypothalamus mediates various drive states necessary for survival, including the *primary drives*: thirst, hunger, aggression, and sex (Marieb, 1989). These primary drives motivate a lot of our basic behavior. They generate a mild feeling of discomfort that "pushes" people to satisfy them. When a drive is satisfied, there is a reduction in discomfort, which is experienced as a feeling of pleasure or gratification and is a reward in itself (Dollard & Miller, 1950; Hull, 1943).

The hypothalamus is also part of the limbic system, which is involved in the regulation of emotional states such as pleasure and rage. A specific bundle of fibers deep within the hypothalamus has been labeled the "pleasure center" (Marieb, 1989). Two neurotransmitters are found in the hypothalamus: substance P, which transmits messages of pain, and endorphin, which blocks pain messages and produces feelings of pleasure. So the pleasure of drive reduction is built into the neurophysiology of the brain.

Coincidentally, opium (heroin, morphine, methadone) is chemically similar in important ways to endorphin. Of course, our brains did not evolve specific receptors for opium. They evolved a chemically mediated mechanism for controlling pleasure (endorphins) and pain (substance P), and other substances (such as heroin) just happen to resemble the brain's natural chemical mediators. Psychopharmacologist Candace Pert (1987) once remarked, "God did not put opiate receptors in our brains so that we would eventually discover opium."

But we clever humans have discovered natural psychoactive substances (and more recently created and synthesized substances) that fit into the already existing receptors of our brains or otherwise alter our brains' chemical environment. In that way, we can manipulate the brain's homeostasis to produce desired effects. Most addictive substances have stimulant properties that provide pleasure by activating certain neural mechanisms, while some substances suppress pain and distress (including withdrawal from the substance itself) by activating other neural mechanisms (Wise, 1988). Therefore, drugs have reinforcing properties similar to drive reduction.

In addition, some people may have a genetic predisposition that affects the sensitivity of their brains to certain psychoactive substances. The role of genetics has been of interest primarily with respect to alcoholism and will be explored in Module 8.3. A genetic predisposition may make addiction more probable, but other factors like motivation determine whether it will occur.

MOTIVATION   One recent theory holds that use of a substance may ultimately be a motivated choice, one that is both conscious and driven (Vuchinich & Tucker, 1988). This is known as "incentive motivation" (Hull, 1951). Similar to primary drives, but essentially learned and more complex, *incentive motivation* is "a motivational state or current concern that lasts from the time of the initial commitment until the incentive is either consummated or relinquished" (Cox & Klinger, 1988, p. 169). People *decide* to use a substance according to whether or not they expect the positive emotional consequences will outweigh the negative ones.

Like primary drives, incentives represent a potential source of manipulating one's emotional state to reduce discomfort and produce pleasure and gratification. The attractiveness of any substance is weighed against the other positive incentives that are currently available to the person (for example, productive work and accomplishment, intimacy, and social support), and a decision is made about whether to partake of the substance. However, people are not necessarily aware of having made the decision or of the process involved in it (Cox & Klinger, 1988).

Incentive motivation helps explain how some people can be susceptible to psychoactive substances. To the extent that an individual is unable to meet his or her needs and incentives and obtain pleasure in other ways, the pleasure increasing and pain blocking properties of a psychoactive substance will be relatively stronger. One shortcoming of incentive motivation is that it does not yet offer an adequate explanation for how the incentive to consume a substance (for example, alcohol) comes to dominate other valued activities (Vuchinich & Tucker, 1988).

It has even been suggested that the use of psychoactive substances is actually a form of coping behavior because it enables people to experience pleasure in the face of pain (Wills & Shiffman, 1985). Accordingly, the type of drug used should depend on the type of experiences a person is undergoing. People who experience few positively appraised events and little stimulation (relative to their need for it) should be vulnerable to a substance that improves mood through stimulation (for example, cocaine). Whereas people who have stress-related physiological reactions from too much stimulation (arousal) should be vulnerable to a substance that improves mood through relaxation (for example, marijuana or valium). This is known as "self-regulation" of the brain from a recent model of opiate addiction (Wilson, Passik, Faude, Abrams, & Gordon, 1989).

LEARNING   Patterns of tolerance and withdrawal symptoms are subject to classical conditioning (Lowinson et al., 1992). Classical conditioning helps explain how relapse can occur after long periods of abstinence. For example, when an alcoholic enters a bar (the conditioned stimulus) where he or she used to enjoy the pleasant responses brought on by alcohol (the conditioned response), the bar acts as a cue to begin drinking again. Classical conditioning can also explain some drug fatalities.

Clinicians have long observed that many people who die from apparent drug "overdoses" have taken no more than their usual dose but did so in an unfamiliar environment (Siegel & Ellsworth, 1986). An ingenious series of experiments with rats demonstrated that this is due to classical conditioning of the brain to the environment in which a drug is customarily taken (for example, MacRae & Siegel, 1987). When a drug upsets homeostasis, the brain "pushes back" (chemically) to restore it. The brain becomes conditioned to the familiar environment, which influences how much it pushes back. In the absence of the familiar environmental cues, the brain does not push back as much so that homeostasis is not restored, and death is more likely even though the dose is no more than what is typically used.

Two principles of operant learning theory help explain how use can become abuse. The first principle—**contiguity of reinforcement**—has to do with the timing of reinforcement. A reinforcement (or punishment) is more likely to increase or decrease a behavior the closer (in time) it follows it (Lett, 1975). Once one has begun to use a substance to self-regulate the brain, the contiguity of reinforcement takes over. The rewards of the drug are immediate, and the punishments—lung cancer, cardiac arrest, stroke, cirrhosis of the liver, loss of friends, loss of a job, loss of self-esteem, and even loss of the hypothalamus's ability to adequately regulate pleasure—all come much later.

Although the punishments of substance abuse can be significant, **avoidance conditioning** explains how the abuse is maintained. Use of the substance is now reinforced by its ability to allow one to *avoid* the punishments it has caused in the first place (Mowrer, 1947). Avoidance conditioning produces a simultaneous upward and downward spiral in one's life. As the quality of life and health spirals downward, use of the substance to escape this deterioration spirals upward.

SOCIAL INFLUENCES   Finally, social influences provide a context in which substance use and abuse take place. Social factors are important in the introduction to and experimentation with legal and illegal substances. People imitate models and are persuaded and pressured by peers. As we shall see, most people begin to use alcohol, tobacco, and drugs as teenagers, not because they expect the gratification of drives but because of social influences. People are also influenced by the environment in which they live, including whether or not a particular substance is available and how much it costs.

However, individuals also vary in the extent of the influence that social factors possess. Individual variation may be caused by differences in motivation, learning, and the reward value of one's lifestyle. For example, some people's lives are lived in such poverty and hopelessness that it seems impossible for them to meet their most basic needs.

CONCLUSION   The biopsychosocial factors we have examined apply to the phenomenon of addiction in general and not to a specific substance. Figure 8.1-1 is offered as a way of conceptualizing the relationships among these factors. The psychosocial factors are depicted in the top half of the figure, and the biological factors are depicted in the bottom half. Addictive behavior is placed at the center of the figure between the reward/punishment balance of reinforcement and the pleasure/pain balance of motivation, indicating that addiction is a partly learned and partly motivated behavior. Cognition serves as the broader context for reinforcement, which acknowledges that an individual's rewards and punishments are determined by his or her own goals, beliefs, and values. Likewise, the broader context for pleasure and pain are the physiologically mediated drive states. Social influences affect cognitions, as well as the availability of the various substances that can be involved in addictive behavior.

This is a dynamic and interactive model. A person can seek reward and pleasure and avoid punishment and pain through a substance *or* nonsubstance. The substances are "shortcuts" to manipulating the reward/punishment and pleasure/pain homeostasis of the brain. In this diagram, the "upward and downward spiral" of avoidance conditioning is represented by the circular "trap" that surrounds addictive behavior.

People engaging in addictive behavior usually also experience other serious psychological problems such as depression, anxiety, and personality disorders (Bukstein, Brent, & Kaminer, 1989; Goggins, Odgers, Luscombe, & Foust, 1989; Kosten, Kosten, & Rounsaville, 1989; Sternberg, 1989). Of course, these problems may be as much a result of addiction as they are the cause of it. Either way, these problems add power to avoidance conditioning because they contribute to the downward spiral, providing more punishment and pain to avoid.

One conclusion that can be derived from this biopsychosocial model is that treatment should not just focus on the substance; it must include the

Figure 8.1-1   A BIOPSYCHOSOCIAL MODEL OF ADDICTION

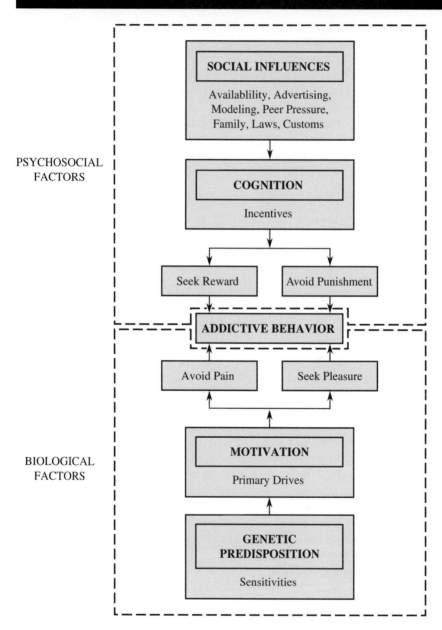

individual's entire lifestyle. Recognizing this, treatments are becoming sensitive to the necessity of helping substance abusers develop satisfying lives (for example, Cox & Klinger, 1988). To do this, treatments must address the following:

1. *Behavioral factors* Prior reinforcement history of the addictive behavior.
2. *Cognitive factors* The individual's incentives to seek reward and to avoid punishment.
3. *Biological factors* The motivation to seek pleasure and avoid pain, individual genetic sensitivities, and the physiological effects of a substance and how they interact with cognitive and motivational factors.
4. *Social influences* The context of the addictive behavior (for example, peer pressure, availability).

MODULE SUMMARY

A comprehensive biopsychosocial model that may be able to explain addictive behavior has been described in this module. In the next two modules, we examine three substances that are widely used and abused in our society with respect to this model: tobacco, alcohol, and drugs. Before continuing, however, here is a review of the major points covered in this module:

1. Addiction involves devoting oneself to a habit, appetite, or behavior, but it does not exclude choice and responsibility.
2. Addiction to psychoactive substances is based on their ability to affect the brain's homeostasis.
3. The biomedical model treats addiction as a disease and defines it as physical dependence, which is characterized by tolerance and withdrawal.
4. The biomedical model is limited because there is no pathogen in addiction, it excludes psychosocial factors, it is substance specific (not a general model), and some people do not develop physical dependence even though they develop psychological dependence.
5. A biopsychosocial model of addiction is comprehensive and takes into account the role of the brain, motivation, learning, and social influences. It recognizes that the same factors are involved with addiction to a variety of different substances and suggests that treatments must take a person's entire lifestyle into account.

SMOKING TOBACCO

HISTORICAL PERSPECTIVE

In the 1942 film *Now Voyager*, suave Paul Henreid lit two cigarettes in his mouth at the same time then put one in Bette Davis's mouth. During the 1930s and 1940s, movies and advertising often portrayed smoking as sophisticated, linking it to romance and sex. It had not been socially acceptable for women to smoke tobacco before that time, but images such as these probably aided the subsequent growth of cigarette smoking among both men and women.

In the 1950s, tobacco smoking began to attract the interest of researchers. About a decade later, the U.S. Surgeon General issued the first report concluding that smoking tobacco was hazardous to health (USPHS, 1964). This was followed in 1967 by a health warning that appears on every pack of cigarettes and in 1970 by a ban on TV advertising. At the time of the Surgeon General's first report, about 53% of men and 34% of women over age 18 smoked regularly (Shopland & Brown, 1985). This compares to about 33% of men and 28% of women who were smoking regularly two decades later in 1985 (McGinnis, Shopland, & Brown, 1987). This reduction in the percentage of people who smoke was probably due directly to the Surgeon General's report and other measures such as the ban on advertising. Unfortunately, over the same time, the total number of cigarettes consumed has increased. This has occurred for two reasons: First, the proportion of the population over age 18 has grown, and second, the proportion of heavy as opposed to moderate smokers has increased (McGinnis et al., 1987). This suggests that the health risks to those who continue to smoke are greater than ever.

HEALTH EFFECTS OF TOBACCO

Smoking is the single greatest preventable cause of death. Each year, almost 400,000 Americans die from tobacco-related illnesses—more than 1,000 people a day (USDHHS, 1992). The costs in health care, insurance, and lost

Scene from the 1942 film Now Voyager, *depicting cigarette smoking as suave and sophisticated.*

productivity from this carnage is the equivalent of a yearly tax on each individual of $221, which represents $52 billion annually.

Smoking is very strongly associated with a variety of serious diseases. It is a major risk factor in cardiovascular disease and cancer, the two biggest causes of death in the United States. For example, the probability that a 35-year-old man will die of lung cancer by age 65 rises 21 times if he smokes (from less than .003% to 6.3%), and the probability he will die of heart disease rises 1.5 times (from about 4% to nearly 7%; Mattson, Pollack, & Cullen, 1987). Smoking is also linked to chronic obstructive lung diseases, bronchitis and emphysema, ulcers, mouth diseases, and cancers. Furthermore, smokers experience more acute illnesses such as colds and flu and miss more days of work than nonsmokers (USDHEW, 1979b). A 30- to 35-year-old person who smokes 10 to 20 cigarettes a day will die, on average, 5 years sooner than a nonsmoker (Fisher & Rost, 1986). This adds up to 390,000 premature deaths in the United States every year as a direct result of smoking (USDHHS, 1989). About 170,000 of these deaths are from cardiovascular diseases and 125,000 are from cancer.

What accounts for the unhealthy effects of smoking tobacco? There are many components of tobacco smoke, but two are probably responsible for

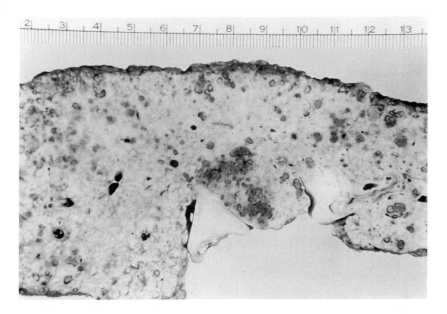

A lung damaged by cigarette smoking.

most of its ill effects. First, carbon monoxide is a likely contributor to cardio-vascular disease because it reduces the amount of oxygen available to the heart and brain. Second, "tar," which is a residue of tobacco smoke, contains a variety of compounds, several of which are carcinogenic. These carcinogens probably disrupt the normal activity of cells in the mouth, throat, and lungs, increasing the probability of cellular mutation and abnormal growth.

Those who smoke filtered or low-tar cigarettes have slightly reduced health risks (USDHEW, 1979b; USDHHS, 1981), but smokers who prefer these cigarettes may be different to begin with, adding confounding factors that are difficult to sort out. Unfortunately, concentrations of tar and nicotine, the psychoactive component of tobacco smoke, are found together, which means that low-tar cigarettes are also low in nicotine. Therefore, smokers who try to reduce the ill effects of tobacco by using low-tar cigarettes usually end up compensating for the low nicotine by smoking more or inhaling more deeply so they get more exposure to the tar as well (Herning, Jones, Bachman, & Mines, 1981; Maron & Fortmann, 1987; Schachter, 1980).

Passive smoking, which is breathing someone else's smoke secondhand, has recently become a health issue. Very strong evidence has accumulated that smoke inhaled involuntarily is a cause of disease, particularly lung cancer (USDHHS, 1986c). Furthermore, secondhand smoke can aggravate chronic diseases such as asthma and hay fever, and it can cause attacks of angina (chest pain) in persons with cardiovascular disease (Eriksen, LeMaistre, & Newell, 1988).

There is a relationship between the development of disease and (a) the total amount smoked, (b) the amount of tar and nicotine ingested, (c) the amount of inhalation, and (d) how long one has smoked (USDHEW, 1979b). Fortunately for smokers, the body begins to repair smoking damage soon after quitting. There is measurable improvement within five years after quitting, and by 15 years the mortality rate of smokers is the same as nonsmokers (Rogot, 1974).

PHYSIOLOGICAL ASPECTS OF SMOKING

Nicotine is the substance in tobacco that acts directly on the CNS. It fits brain receptors for the neurotransmitter acetylcholine, which causes the release of epinephrine and norepinephrine and arouses the sympathetic nervous system. This causes the blood vessels to constrict and may be a health hazard to people with circulatory problems. Nicotine also simulates and arouses the CNS and increases heart rate and blood pressure. It is able to be absorbed into the bloodstream directly through cell membranes in the mouth, nose, and lungs, so it quickly reaches the brain, but the body rids itself of nicotine very rapidly, reducing the level in the blood by half in about 30 minutes.

Nicotine is generally considered to be a stimulant, which may explain a recently described relationship between smoking and depression. During a 9-year follow-up period, smokers in a large national health study who were also diagnosed as depressed were 40% less likely to quit than nondepressed smokers (Anda et al., 1990). Furthermore, when depressed smokers do quit, depressive symptoms may increase (Glassman et al., 1990). This suggests that some depressed people may be self-regulating with nicotine in order to increase stimulation and that treatment programs will have to take into account psychological problems that may be related.

The role of nicotine as a stimulant has led to the *nicotine regulation model* of smoking addiction. In this model, smokers continue to smoke to maintain arousal at a certain level and to avoid the withdrawal symptoms associated with nicotine, thereby regulating the motivational pleasure/pain balance. Evidence for this model comes from the recognition that smokers of low-tar, low-nicotine cigarettes usually compensate, as noted above, by smoking and/or inhaling more.

A series of experiments strongly supports this model (Schachter et al., 1977). In one, using drugs researchers manipulated the ability of subjects' bodies to excrete nicotine in urine. When the excretion of nicotine was *increased* so it had less of an opportunity to affect the brain, the subjects compensated by increasing the number of cigarettes smoked by an average of four per day. In contrast, when the excretion of nicotine was *decreased* so it had more of an opportunity to affect the brain, the subjects continued to smoke at their usual rate.

While Schachter et al. (1977) have demonstrated that smokers do attempt to regulate the level of nicotine in their bodies, nicotine regulation is probably not the entire basis for smoking (Leventhal & Cleary, 1980). If it were, then long after smokers have quit and the nicotine has been eliminated from their bodies, they should not crave it; but they do, so cognitive factors must also be involved in the addiction. In addition, the nicotine regulation model cannot explain how people start to smoke, since they could not be aware of the effect of nicotine before starting to smoke. A comprehensive model of addiction would integrate the biological effects of nicotine with psychosocial factors (Galizio & Maisto, 1985), and smoking tobacco is now recognized as an addiction that involves a variety of biopsychosocial factors (Lichtenstein & Glasgow, 1992). Smoking is determined by an interplay of factors, no single one of which is necessary or sufficient to explain it (Fisher, Lichtenstein, & Haire-Joshu, in press).

STARTING AND CONTINUING TO SMOKE

STARTING

Even though more than 90% of teenagers are aware that smoking is harmful, most people begin smoking during adolescence (USDHEW, 1979b). Adolescence can be a difficult period of adjustment during which a transition is made from family centered to primarily peer-centered social reference. Psychosocial factors are probably important in starting to smoke at this time. These factors include social influences (for example, availability, peer pressure), modeling, rebelliousness, and independence, as well as dependence. The role of modeling and peer pressure is evident in studies indicating that adolescents are more likely to smoke if their parents and peers do (Hansen et al., 1987; Mittelmark et al., 1987; Murray, Swan, Johnson, & Bewley, 1983), and that they usually smoke when they are in the company of peers (Leventhal, Prohaska, & Hirschman, 1985). This reflects dependence on the group as well as peer pressure. In addition, adolescents believe that smoking represents independence from authority (Leventhal & Cleary, 1980), as well as a tough, attractive image (Barton, Chassin, Presson, & Sherman, 1982).

Most teenagers will try at least one cigarette, but few will smoke as many as four (Leventhal & Cleary, 1980). Those who do usually go on to become regular smokers. The development into a regular smoker takes as long as a year (Ary & Biglan, 1988) and depends on other factors.

CONTINUING

Continuing smoking probably depends on psychosocial and biological factors. In particular, cognitive factors may explain the early continuation of a behavior

Today, teenage smokers provide an updated image of the suave and sophisticated smoker from the 1940s films.

that teenagers know is unhealthy. Teenagers are present oriented. They do not believe that they will still be smoking five years later, so they do not believe that the health risks matter (Murray et al., 1983; USDHEW, 1979b). Another cognitive factor—**optimistic bias**—has also been identified in continuing to smoke. It is the belief that negative consequences affect others but not oneself (Weinstein, 1984).

In addition to the health risks, other irritations are mildly painful or punishing: shortness of breath, increased upper respiratory infections, coughing, and the smell of stale smoke on the person and their clothes. These might deter some beginning smokers during the first year. However, the contiguity of reinforcement promotes the continuation of smoking, because these irritations usually are delayed relative to the immediate pleasures of lighting up, belonging to a group, and feeling "tough, cool, and independent of authority" (Leventhal & Cleary, 1980, p. 384). These pleasures are particularly strong for teenagers who are not doing well in school, in other words, for those who do not receive rewards from their lifestyle.

Once smoking behavior has continued for awhile, other factors probably become important in its maintenance and resistance to extinction. Silvan Tomkins (1966, 1968) hypothesized that regular smokers fit into four categories (see Table 8.2-1).

Research has tended to support Tomkin's categorization of regular smokers. A series of studies used questionnaires to categorize smokers and then tested the validity of these categories (Ikard & Tomkins, 1973; Leventhal & Avis, 1976). For example, positive affect smokers should decrease their smoking if they are given bad-tasting cigarettes. Researchers dipped cigarettes in vinegar and repackaged them (with the explanation that they were testing a special ingredient to counteract the harmful effects of smoke). As predicted, the positive affect smokers smoked less, while the addictive smokers smoked just as much. Other researchers also looked at Tomkins' negative (tension-reduction) affect and positive (arousal-seeking) affect smokers (Myrsten, Andersson, Frankenhaeuser, & Elgerot, 1975). They had them perform monotonous (low tension) and complex (high tension) tasks. The arousal smokers did better on the monotonous task after smoking, and the tension-reduction smokers did better on the complex task after smoking, supporting predictions of how negative and positive affect smokers would perform.

Despite the apparent validity of Tomkins' categorizations, there may not be just four distinct categories (Ikard, Green, & Horn, 1969; Leventhal & Avis, 1977). Tomkins (1968) allowed that positive or negative affect smokers probably would become habitual or addictive smokers at some point, so the categories may overlap.

Other research has not categorized smokers in advance but found equally interesting results. Schachter (1980) found that smokers who are allowed to smoke do better on tasks requiring concentration, especially when under stress, but their performance deteriorates when they are not allowed to smoke. However, even though smokers do better when smoking, their overall performance is not better than nonsmokers. Apparently, smoking allows some smokers to perform *up to* the level of nonsmokers. Similar results were reported on tasks involving vigilance and motor coordination (Heimstra,

---

Table 8.2-1   FOUR CATEGORIES OF SMOKERS

1. *Positive affect* smokers smoke to increase stimulation, relaxation, or pleasure; also known as "pleasure-taste smokers."
2. *Negative affect* smokers smoke to reduce feelings of anxiety or tension.
3. *Habitual* smokers may have been positive or negative affect smokers at first, but they begin to smoke out of habit. They may not even be aware of having lit a cigarette and may smoke with little reward from it.
4. *Addictive* (psychological dependence) smokers may smoke to affect the CNS, and they are aware when they are *not* smoking. They may also have been negative or positive affect smokers at first.

Source: Adapted from Tomkins, S. S., 1966, Psychological model for smoking behavior, American Journal of Public Health, 56 *(Suppl. 12), 17–20; Tomkins, S. S., 1968, A modified model of smoking behavior. In E. F. Borgatta & R. R. Evans (Eds.),* Smoking, health and behavior, *Chicago: Aldine.*

1973). Another study assigned smokers to three groups: (a) a relaxation placebo, (b) a group in which tension anxiety was induced, and (c) a tension-concentration group that had to do a monotonous task (Rose, Ananda, & Jarvik, 1983). Smoking in the two tension groups increased significantly but not in the relaxation group.

Taken together, this research suggests that, as smokers continue, they learn that smoking influences their mental performance. For some, improvement may come on monotonous tasks (by arousal), and for others, improvement may come on more complex tasks (by tension reduction). Improvement in performance, then, serves as additional reinforcement for smoking. The fact that smoking can arouse some *and* reduce tension in others seems paradoxical because nicotine is considered a stimulant. However, at high levels, nicotine may sometimes act as sedative (USDHHS, 1988) and may be able to produce paradoxical tranquilizing effects so some smokers obtain arousal and others tension reduction (Gilbert, 1979).

Whether smoking produces arousal or tension reduction may also depend on the smoker's personality. Smokers who are high on extroversion may use nicotine as a stimulant, whereas those who are low on extroversion may smoke only for the motor sensory aspects of the habit. Interestingly, smokers have consistently been found to be more extroverted than nonsmokers (Eysenck, 1982; Smith, 1970), which suggests that most smokers are probably seeking stimulation.

STOPPING SMOKING

SELF-QUITTING

The Surgeon General reported in 1979 that about 29 million people had quit smoking over the 15 years since it had been declared a health hazard. Remarkably, about 95% had quit on their own. Surveys have tended to report a high rate of self-quitting, although long-term (more than 7 years) abstinence rates are typically just over 60% (Rzewnicki & Forgays, 1987; Schachter, 1982). In these surveys, about 50% of respondents who smoked more than three-fourths of a pack per day reported that they had severe withdrawal symptoms, including cold sweats, insomnia, cravings, and irritability, while, surprisingly, almost 30% had no withdrawal symptoms. Light smokers reported little trouble quitting.

Several factors are related to success in self-quitting. More men are more successful than women—about 70% versus 30% (Eisenger, 1971). Self-quitting is higher among smokers who know someone whose health has been impaired by it, about 27%, compared to smokers who know no one with health impaired by smoking, about 10% (Eisenger, 1972). Still others appear to quit because they see its benefits rather than fear the consequences of smoking (Mausner, 1973). How do self-quitters do it? They seem to employ a variety of different strategies (see Table 8.2-2).

Because of the high rate of self-quitting, Schachter (1982) believes that the majority of smokers quit on their own without professional treatment. He also believes that those who receive treatment are the smokers who have been unsuccessful on their own, which leads to the much poorer success rate of formal treatment programs.

Contradicting Schachter's contentions and the apparent high success rates of self-quitters is a recent review by Cohen et al. (1989) of 10 long-term prospective studies involving more than 5,000 subjects. Schachter turned out to be right—most participants in treatment programs are failed self-quitters (the median of relapsed self-quitters was 88% in these studies)—but the success rate of self-quitters was no better than smokers who participate in a formal treatment program. Abstinence, defined as not smoking at the point of assessment, was achieved by 13.2% of self-quitters at 6-month follow-up and by 13.9% at 12-month follow-up. However, when abstinence was defined as "not a puff" *since quitting,* it fell to 4.9% and 4.2% at six- and 12-month follow-ups. Overall, smokers who smoked less than 21 cigarettes per day were about twice as successful at self-quitting as those who smoked more. Cohen et al. (1989) concluded that smoking is a central part of a person's lifestyle and that quitting must be viewed as an ongoing, dynamic process rather than a discrete event.

Table 8.2-2 STRATEGIES USED BY SMOKERS WHO SELF-QUIT

1. Most quit *"cold turkey"* instead of gradually reducing their rate of smoking.
2. Many use *oral substitutes* such as cigars or pipes, candy or chewing gum (of course cigars and pipes carry their own, albeit less, health risks).
3. Males, in particular, *substitute eating* by increasing their consumption of food.
4. Many use *cognitive techniques* such as thinking about the health risks (to induce fear).
5. Some *reward themselves* for success.
6. Others *punish themselves* for mistakes.
7. Some use *social supports* such as involving others in bets.

Source: Adapted from Garvey, A. J., Heinold, J. W., & Rasner, B., 1989, Self-help approaches to smoking cessation: A report from the normative aging study, Addictive Behaviors, 14, 23–33; Glasgow, R. E., Klesges, R. C., Mizes, J. S., & Pechacek, T. F., 1985, Quitting Smoking: Strategies used and variables associated with success in a stop-smoking contest, Journal of Consulting and Clinical Psychology, 53, 905–912.

Prochaska and DiClemente (1983) have also proposed a theory of quitting in which quitters move through five consecutive stages (see Table 8.2-3). The first two stages take into account the large amount of time smokers spend thinking about quitting. Smokers progress through the stages in order, but the relapse stage is an important part of the theory, for it recognizes that most people cycle through these stages several times before they are successful. In effect, they are *learning how* to quit smoking.

Research has tended to support the theory for adults (DiClemente & Prochaska 1985; Prochaska, DiClemente, & Norcross 1992). Research with adolescents suggests that they spend less time than adults in the contemplation stage but cycle much more frequently between the active change and relapse stages (Pallonen, Murray, Schmid, Pirie, & Luepker, 1990). This research provides some consolation to quitters. They should not be demoralized by "slips" when they are trying to quit but rather accept them as part of the learning process. Although some people do eventually quit on their own, others will still turn to formal treatment programs.

TREATMENT FOR SMOKING

Is it really that hard to quit smoking? Apparently it is, according to a survey of people addicted to a variety of drugs, from alcohol to heroin (Kozlowski et al., 1989). Eighty-four percent were also regular smokers, and 91% had smoked at some time in the past. Overall, 74% said that tobacco would be *at least as hard* to quit as the drug for which they were receiving treatment. While about 58% of alcoholics and 96% of cocaine abusers reported that they got less pleasure from cigarettes than from their other drug, 50% of alcoholics and 44% of cocaine abusers reported that their urge for tobacco was as strong or stronger. This suggests that tobacco addiction can be as difficult to treat as any of the other substance addictions. Perhaps that is why there is such a variety of treatments.

MEDICATION   Many drugs have been tried to assist smokers in breaking the addiction (Blaney, 1985; Kozlowski, 1984). Given the characterization of

Table 8.2-3	PROCHASKA AND DiCLEMENTE'S (1983) FIVE STAGES OF QUITTING

1.	*Precontemplation*	Not seriously thinking about quitting.
2.	*Contemplation*	Aware of the problem, thinking about quitting.
3.	*Active change*	Changing behavior and the conditions that support it.
4.	*Maintenance*	Working at continuing the changes.
5.	*Relapse*	Returning to smoking.

people as arousal smokers or tension-reduction smokers, it should come as no surprise that both tranquilizers and stimulants have been tried. Until recently, most drugs that have been tried have been found to not help.

The newest drug treatment uses nicotine itself in the form of a gum that is chewed or as a patch that is placed on the skin. Nicotine in these forms provides the effects smokers find pleasurable without many of the health risks. Nicotine replacement therapy is a promising adjunct to other approaches to treatment, but it is no cure (Lichtenstein & Glasgow, 1992). By itself, it does not deal with the psychosocial factors in addiction and leaves the physical dependence on nicotine intact.

BEHAVIORAL AND COGNITIVE THERAPY   Behavioral and cognitive strategies are often used to help people stop smoking. The behavioral strategies consist primarily of aversion conditioning and cognitive self-management techniques.

Aversion therapy treats smoking addiction by pairing an unwanted, repugnant stimulus with smoking, such as one of the following:

1. *Electric shock* is administered at a predetermined uncomfortable or slightly painful (but not injurious) level as a smoker engages in normal smoking behavior (that is, takes out a cigarette, lights it, takes a drag; Rimm & Masters, 1979).
2. *Negative imagery* is usually used in a relaxed state during which smokers are guided by the therapist to create mental images of their smoking behavior (that is, taking out a cigarette), which is then paired with an aversive mental image (such as vomiting or excrement; Kamarck & Lichtenstein, 1985).
3. *Aversive smoking* includes several techniques that make smoking itself the aversive stimulus. These include "smoke holding," when the smoker holds the smoke in the mouth for an extended period of time; "focused smoking," when the smoker pays close attention to the unpleasant features of smoking as they are smoking (for example, the heat, the burning sensation, the smell); "satiation," which has the smoker double or triple their rate of smoking over a period of time; and "rapid smoking," during which the person smokes very rapidly and continuously (a puff every six seconds) until he or she cannot tolerate it any longer (Lichtenstein & Mermelstein, 1984).

Of these three aversion techniques, aversive smoking appears to be the most effective (Kamarck & Lichtenstein, 1985; Lichtenstein & Mermelstein, 1984). However, rapid smoking does pose health risks to people with cardiovascular or respiratory problems and should only be used with healthy individuals who have been screened medically.

Self-management techniques involve smokers more directly by teaching them to take control over situations and use stimuli that elicit or support smoking

(Blaney, 1985; Lichtenstein & Mermelstein, 1984). Behavior therapists who were treating a variety of problems recognized that when they asked people, as part of an assessment procedure, to record information about a target problem behavior as it occurred, the target behavior often decreased. This happened because people become more aware of when and under what circumstances they are engaging in the target behavior, giving them more conscious control over it. When this procedure is used for treatment, it is called *self-monitoring*, but it rarely produces lasting changes by itself. Three other self-management techniques have been used in treatment:

1. *Contingency contracting* involves a written agreement between the therapist and smoker that describes the behavior to be changed and how changes will be rewarded or punished. Often the smoker is asked to place a sum of money on deposit, which is returned if the goals are met.
2. *Stimulus control* involves determining what aspects of the environment trigger smoking behavior. Often, smokers report that they *have* to have a cigarette in certain situations, such as immediately following a meal. Then circumstances are altered so the stimulus, finishing a meal, is not followed by smoking. For example, the smoker will be taught not to linger at the table but to get up immediately when finished.
3. *Response substitution* partly addresses the problem with aversion techniques mentioned above, because it recognizes that alternative, desirable behaviors should be substituted for smoking (for example, taking a walk after a meal). Preferably, the alternative behaviors are incompatible with smoking.

These self-management techniques are helpful, but they do not seem to produce dramatic effects when used alone. They are, however, particularly valuable when combined with other methods in a multicomponent approach.

MULTICOMPONENT TREATMENT   As we have seen, this approach attempts to combine several successful techniques. One of the earliest attempts at multicomponent treatment combined rapid smoking with contingency contracting (Lando, 1977). This program also included group contacts and "booster" sessions, which are single follow-up sessions after the treatment is completed. The program achieved a success rate of 76% abstinence at 6-month follow-up. This rate is quite high, considering that most treatments only report about 20% to 30% abstinence after 6 months. Another successful multicomponent program combined behavioral and educational approaches to achieve 46% abstinence after 4 years (Hughes, Hymowitz, Ockene, Simon, & Vogt, 1981). Even though success rates vary considerably, multicomponent programs are the most promising of the formal approaches.

RELAPSE PREVENTION   One problem that affects success rates is relapse, which is estimated to be quite high, between 70% and 80%. It may be that smokers who have successfully quit but then slip and have just one cigarette *think* they are total failures, become demoralized, give up, and resume smoking regularly (Marlatt & Gordon, 1980). In fact, one study has confirmed that sense of failure due to a slip does lead to relapse (Curry, Marlatt, & Gordon, 1987). It is believed that, by anticipating relapses, people are able to feel in control and not resume regular smoking. However, research indicates that relapse prevention has had only mediocre impact in overall treatment effectiveness (Lichtenstein & Glasgow, 1992).

Researchers have identified other factors related to relapsing, however. One of the most important is weight gain. In fact, on the whole, smokers do weigh less than nonsmokers, and when they stop smoking, many do gain weight (Grunberg & Bowen, 1985; Hofstetter, Schutz, Jequier, & Wahren, 1986). This can be explained partly by the fact that nicotine is a stimulant and stimulants decrease appetite due to activation of the ANS. (In fact, potent stimulants like amphetamines were once prescribed for weight loss).

Smokers who quit do not have a higher overall calorie intake, but they do eat more sugar, and they are less physically active (Rodin, 1987). However, the primary reason smokers gain weight when they quit is that their metabolism slows and less energy is burned (Hofstetter et al., 1986). Nevertheless, weight gain is by no means a foregone conclusion. A recent study found that only a minority of smokers had gained weight a year after quitting (Williamson et al., 1991). Average gains were 2.7 kg (6 lbs) for men and 3.6 kg (8 lbs) for women. Only about 10% of men and 13% of women experienced a major weight gain of 13 kg (28.6 lbs). People over 55 years of age, those who had smoked 15 or more cigarettes a day, and African Americans were at the greatest risk for weight gain.

Another recent study also found that body weight did not differ significantly for those who never smoked and those who were long-term quitters (Klesges, Klesges, & Meyers, 1991). However, the body weight of current smokers was lower than nonsmokers, and this effect was greater for women than men. This means that some smokers who quit will notice a slight weight gain, but they will not end up weighing more, on average, than people who do not smoke. Some smokers may, therefore, be using smoking to self-regulate their weight, and they will have to learn to control their weight in other ways—for example, by exercising more and watching their diets. Research suggests, though, that most smokers can quit without concern about major weight gain.

Another factor in relapsing is social support, which can come in many forms and can discourage or encourage more smoking. Ex-smokers can be encouraged to smoke again by people who doubt their ability to remain abstinent and who offer them cigarettes (Sorensen, Pechacek, & Pallonen, 1986). On the other hand, support can prevent relapse if acquaintances actively encourage an ex-smoker to remain abstinent (Colletti & Brownell, 1983). People whose partners give more positive support statements (for example, express confidence in their ability to quit) than negative support statements (for example, comment that smoking is a dirty habit) are more likely to be successful at quitting (Cohen & Lichtenstein, 1990).

Finally, the role of motivation in the maintenance of quitting has recently been evaluated. It appears that the type of motivation, intrinsic or extrinsic, affects success (Curry, Wagner, & Grothaus, 1990). Intrinsic motivation involves personal health concerns and self-control (for example, concerns about illness and showing people you can quit), and extrinsic motivation involves immediate reinforcement and social factors (for example, to save money or to avoid disapproval from others). Successful quitters are more likely to be motivated by internal factors.

CONCLUSION   Much more needs to be learned about treatment to stop smoking. Although treatment may be generally effective, research has failed to distinguish the specific components related to treatment effectiveness (Lichtenstein & Glasgow, 1992). One consistent finding, however, is that interventions that maintain contact over a longer period of time produce better results (Baille, Mattick, & Webster 1990).

PREVENTING SMOKING

With the tremendous risks to health and the difficulty in stopping smoking, wouldn't it be better if people never started? That is the rationale behind many educational programs. In order to be successful, educational programs must reach children before they are likely to try smoking. High school is when most people try smoking, so programs usually begin before age 12 (Evans, 1984; Matarazzo, 1982). They typically take place in the school and use lectures, posters, pamphlets, and educational films, and they usually rely on raising fears about health hazards. These programs do help children form negative attitudes toward smoking, but they have been judged ineffective in preventing smoking (Flay, 1985; Thompson, 1978). It may seem contradictory that children can have negative attitudes toward smoking, be aware of the health risks, and yet not be prevented from smoking. However, remember the effect of optimistic bias, and that young people do not believe they need to worry about the health risks because they do not expect to continue smoking.

The reason educational programs are ineffective is that they do not take into account the complex psychosocial factors involved in smoking. Realizing this, researcher Richard Evans and his colleagues at the University of Houston (Evans, 1976, 1984; Evans, Smith, & Raines, 1984) developed a promising program to be used in the schools that would "inoculate" children against the multiple pressures to smoke. The program used teenagers who provided information about the harmful effects of smoking and about the pressures to smoke that the children were likely to encounter. It also used teenagers as models shown encountering and resisting pressure to smoke. A three-year follow-up on the program in the Houston schools indicated modest success (Evans et al., 1981).

Other psychosocial prevention programs have used similar components and some additional ones as well (Botvin & Wills, 1985; Flay et al., 1985; Johnson et al., 1990; Severson & Lichtenstein, 1986). Some of these added components have included rehearsal and role-playing of refusal skills, having students publicly declare their intention to smoke or not, teaching social skills and coping techniques for anxiety and stress, teaching parents positive parent–child communication skills, and mass media campaigns. In controlled studies, subjects who received these inoculation programs smoked less than control subjects who did not receive them, and they were still smoking less up to 18 months later (Flay et al., 1985). In one large study in Kansas City schools, a comprehensive intervention program given to students in grades 6 and 7 was found to have significantly reduced the prevalence of cigarette and marijuana smoking when the students reached grades 9 and 10 (Johnson et al., 1990).

These results suggest that children who are inoculated against the psychosocial pressures to smoke are better able to successfully resist smoking. Currently, researchers are not sure which are the effective components of these programs (McCaul & Glasgow, 1985; Severson & Lichtenstein, 1986), and quite a large number of subjects drop out of them (Biglan et al., 1987). Still, based on their success so far, the health risks of smoking, and the difficulty of stopping, they should be used in more schools (Best, Thomson, Santi, Smith, & Brown, 1988).

CONCLUSION: APPLYING THE BIOPSYCHOSOCIAL MODEL OF ADDICTION

The model in Figure 8.1-1, shows that social influences (for example, peer influence, availability) are involved in starting to smoke. So, too, are several cognitive factors—an incentive to be independent, to mature, or to be part of a group. Once having started, the biological factors become more important. Smokers may use nicotine to self-regulate the brain to avoid pain (for example, to improve cognitive performance or to decrease depression) and/or to produce pleasure (for example, stimulation). Smoking may also become a behavioral habit—a comforting and time-occupying ritual—maintained through reinforcement.

■

MODULE SUMMARY

This module used a biopsychosocial perspective to explore the use and abuse of tobacco. Before continuing to explore abuse of alcohol and drugs in Module 7.3, review the major points covered here:

1. An addictive behavior pattern is evident with each of the three substances discussed: tobacco, alcohol, and drugs.
2. The factors involved in starting to smoke cigarettes are different from those in continuing to smoke cigarettes.
3. People are introduced to smoking cigarettes very early in life, and social influences, primarily models and peer pressure, are responsible for experimentation with them.
4. Some smokers may smoke to increase stimulation, relaxation, or pleasure ("positive affect" smokers), while others may smoke to reduce feelings of anxiety or tension ("negative affect" smokers). Eventually, either may become habitual or addictive (psychologically dependent) smokers.
5. Many people who successfully quit smoking do so on their own. More self-quitters are men, and self-quitting is higher among smokers who know someone whose health has been impaired by it. Others appear to quit because they expect benefits rather than fear the consequences of smoking.
6. Quitting smoking seems to require moving through stages involving contemplation, active change, maintenance, and relapse. Relapse suggests that many people must "learn how" to quit by cycling through these stages more than once.
7. Treatment with nicotine is helpful but it is not a cure and does not address the psychosocial factors in addiction.
8. Cognitive-behavioral therapy is generally effective, but aversion therapy is the most effective treatment, and cognitive self-management works well when combined with other techniques.
9. Relapse prevention improves outcomes and is an important component of contemporary programs.
10. Prevention programs can be successful in helping children resist pressures to begin smoking.

ALCOHOL AND OTHER DRUGS

ALCOHOL

HISTORICAL PERSPECTIVE

People began to openly criticize drinking alcohol in the early nineteenth century. Known as the "temperance" movement, this group of activists advocated complete abstinence and prohibition—not for health reasons but on moral and religious grounds. Their activism culminated in 1919 with the passage of the Eighteenth Amendment to the U.S. Constitution, which outlawed the sale of alcoholic beverages.

Contrary to popular belief, prohibition was successful in reducing the amount of alcohol consumed. It dropped from approximately 2.5 gallons per capita annually in 1910 to less than 1 gallon per capita annually in 1920, a 60% reduction (NIAAA, 1983; Rorabaugh, 1979). After prohibition was repealed in 1934, consumption quickly rose to prior levels. The current rate is about where it was in 1910.

EPIDEMIOLOGY

GENERAL CHARACTERISTICS OF DRINKERS A relatively small number of people do most of the drinking—about one-tenth of the U.S. adult population drinks one-half of the alcohol consumed (NIAAA, 1983). In surveys of the general population, about one-third report that they abstain, one-third report that they are light drinkers, and one-third report that they are moderate or heavy drinkers (NIAAA, 1981).

Although it is illegal in every state for high school age people to purchase alcoholic beverages or drink them, they do it anyway. Surveys of high school students reveal that 90% had tried alcohol by the end of their senior year (NIAAA, 1983). Just as with adults, a small number do most of the drinking. In one survey, 29% of boys and 15% of girls reported consuming alcohol at least 40 times the preceding year but only about 8% of boys and 3% of girls reported daily use (Johnston, Bachman, & O'Malley, 1982). But when does drinking become a problem?

People often drink to relieve inhibitions and "let loose."

Researchers generally agree on the following regarding **problem drinkers**: (a) they drink heavily on a regular basis; (b) they become *psychologically* dependent; and (c) they have impaired social relationships and/or work performance (Mayer, 1983). Some other behavioral manifestations of problem drinking include drinking during the day, drinking at work, driving while under the influence of alcohol, and drinking alone. Problem drinkers are estimated to include about 18 million people (NIAAA, 1987). There are approximately 3 males to every female in this category (McCrady, 1988).

It is estimated that about one-half of problem drinkers are alcoholics. In addition to the characteristics of problem drinkers, **alcoholism** involves (a) the development of tolerance, (b) blacking out, (c) memory impairment, and (d) withdrawal symptoms. Alcoholic withdrawal symptoms are called **delirium tremens**, and they include gross disorientation, cognitive disruption, impaired motor coordination and tremor, and fleeting hallucinations. Therefore, alcoholism involves both psychological and physical dependence, while problem drinking involves only psychological dependence

ETHNICITY AND SOCIAL CLASS Ethnic and cultural background is related to drinking in the United States. One longitudinal study found that alcoholism rates were higher in young men of Native American, European (western and eastern), and Irish extraction, compared to those of southern European (Italian and Latin) extraction (McCord, McCord, & Gudeman, 1959, 1960). It was also found that more alcoholics were from the *middle* as opposed to the lower class. Drinking and alcoholism also varies by occupation (Fillmore & Caetano, 1980). Bartenders and waiters, who are constantly around alcohol, tend to drink more on average, but so do sailors and railroad workers.

GENDER   There are also gender differences in alcohol consumption (Lex, 1991). Women report using significantly less alcohol than men. Nevertheless, women do become problem drinkers and alcoholics. Typically, women's drinking problems begin at later ages than men's, but they progress more rapidly. Also, while men with drinking problems tend to receive a diagnosis of antisocial personality disorder, women with drinking problems tend to receive a diagnosis of mood disorder.

PERSONALITY   Researchers have attempted to define a particular "alcoholic personality," but these efforts have not been productive. Instead, several different personality types occur in alcoholics (Skinner, Jackson, & Hoffman, 1974). However, most studies suffer from the usual problems of correlational research. Better-controlled longitudinal studies have revealed two personality characteristics that were evident in alcoholics *before* they developed drinking problems: childhood hyperactivity (Hechtman, Weiss, & Perlman, 1984) and antisocial behavior (Jones, 1968, 1971). Interestingly, antisocial behavior may be generally predictive of both alcohol and drug abuse (Davison & Neale, 1990).

PHYSIOLOGICAL ASPECTS OF ALCOHOL CONSUMPTION

ETHANOL   Ethanol is the type of alcohol in beverages, and like all types of alcohol, it is toxic. However, very few people actually die directly from alcohol poisoning because it is hard to consume enough ethanol in a short enough time to cause death. People usually pass out before they are able to ingest enough to kill them. However, on occasion, inexperienced drinkers who quickly downed a bottle of distilled liquor on a dare have been poisoned.

Alcohol is absorbed directly into the bloodstream without being digested. A small amount is absorbed immediately through the lining of the stomach, while most is absorbed in the small intestine. Once in the bloodstream, alcohol is eliminated by the liver, which can break down about 1 ounce of 100-proof distilled liquor (about 50% alcohol) per hour.

MODERATE DRINKING AND HEALTH   While investigating the effects of alcohol, researchers discovered that drinking may actually have health *benefits* (Room & Day, 1974; Stason, Neff, Miettinen, & Jick, 1976). Early correlational studies suggested that light to moderate drinkers (defined as one to five drinks a day) had the best health, whereas nondrinkers and heavy drinkers had poorer health. This is known as a "U-shaped" relationship.

One retrospective study confirmed this U-shaped relationship between alcohol consumption and strokes in men, even after the effects of hypertension, smoking, and medication were removed (Gill, Zezulka, Shipley, Gill, & Beevers, 1986). It was the nondrinkers and heavy drinkers who had the most strokes. Of course, these studies are difficult to draw causal conclusions from because they are correlational. It is possible that people who feel ill drink less alcohol, so the nondrinker category has an overrepresentation of ill people to begin with.

Several longitudinal studies overcame these drawbacks and still found that moderate drinking can be beneficial. One well-known study involved more than 2,000 people who were first broken down into groups based on their drinking habits and then followed for 10 years (Klatsky, Friedman, & Siegelaub, 1981). The groups consisted of (a) *nondrinkers*, (b) *light drinkers* (fewer than 3 drinks per day); (c) *moderate drinkers* (three to five drinks per day); and (d) *heavy drinkers* (more than five drinks per day). The lowest mortality rate was in the light drinkers. Compared to them, the mortality rate of the nondrinkers and moderate drinkers was 50% higher, and the mortality rate of the heavy drinkers was 200% higher. Increased mortality was due largely to accidents, cancer, respiratory problems, and, of course, cirrhosis of the liver.

Subsequent community-based longitudinal studies, including the Alameda County study (Berkman, Breslow, & Wingard, 1983), the Framingham study (Friedman & Kimball, 1986; Gordon & Kannel, 1984), and the Albany study (Gordon & Doyle, 1987), have confirmed these results. These studies have also yielded additional information. The relationship between alcohol consumption and mortality appears to be stronger in men than it is in women and stronger in men under age 60 (Berkman et al., 1983). In the Framingham study, which looked specifically at coronary heart disease (CHD), the U-shaped relationship was observed to occur in smokers and nonsmokers alike. Mortality was 40% less in nonsmoking, moderate drinking men (defined as consuming 20 to 30 ounces of alcohol per week) and 50% less in smoking, moderate drinking men (Friedman & Kimball, 1986). Similar results were found for smoking women but not as clearly for nonsmoking women. Finally, the Albany study produced intriguing results with regard to *what* causes the increased mortality associated with abstention. Abstainers had a significantly greater likelihood than any category of drinkers to die from CHD, but the mortality rates from non-CHD causes did not differ much.

These studies suggest that differences in mortality rates between nondrinkers and moderate drinkers are largely due to cardiovascular problems, whereas heavy drinkers have additional health risks from accidents and cirrhosis of the liver. Moderate consumption of alcohol may confer protection against CHD by raising high density lipoprotein (HDL) cholesterol, which provides a protective function against arterial blockage and heart attacks (see Module 11.1). However, the evidence is not yet convincing. One study supported the role of alcohol in raising HDL cholesterol (Avogaro, Cazzolato, Belussi, & Bittolo Bon, 1982), but another study found that alcohol also increases total cholesterol, which would not be protective (Haskell et al., 1984).

As of now there is little understanding of the mechanism by which light-to-moderate drinking may produce health benefits. Before drinking could ever be recommended in place of abstinence, this mechanism would need to be fully understood, especially since some people are vulnerable to alcoholism, which most certainly affects health adversely. Furthermore, even moderate drinking during pregnancy can have undesirable effects on a fetus (see Table 5.1-1, page 168).

HEAVY DRINKING AND HEALTH Light-to-moderate social drinking does not appear to have deleterious effects on the brain, but the long-term consumption of alcohol in excess negatively affects the brain and neuropsychological functioning (Delin & Lee, 1992). Such consumption damages neurons, particularly those in the frontal lobes (Parsons, 1975; 1986). About 10% of alcoholics are affected by **Wernicke-Korsakoff syndrome**, which is caused by neuron damage as well as poor nutrition (Parsons, 1977). It consists of more or less permanent memory impairment, confusion, drowsiness, and gait disturbance.

However, most long-term alcoholics (ingesting for approximately 6 to 19 years) do not have such obvious and gross mental functioning impairments (Parsons & Farr, 1981), but they do have some degree of neuropsychological impairment even when sober (Butters & Brandt, 1985). For their age and education level, their verbal abilities are likely to be intact and their IQ scores within the normal range, but there is a significant relationship between years of heavy drinking and poor performance on tests of concept formation, cognitive flexibility, and perceptual-motor abilities (Svanum & Schladenhauffen, 1986). The neuropsychological performance of alcoholics who remain abstinent does improve, although the amount of improvement and the length of time it takes are variable.

Moderate-to-heavy drinking increases the risk of death, particularly from heart disease, stroke, cancer, and cirrhosis of the liver, but the primary health concern for the long-term, heavy drinker is liver damage (Eckhardt et al., 1981). Drinking more than five drinks a day causes fat to accumulate in the liver. Eventually, blood flow is blocked, cells die, and cirrhosis (the accumulation of nonfunctional scar tissue) develops. In addition, alcohol is suspected as a cofactor in many types of cancers (Levy, 1985; Schottenfeld, 1979), from cancer of the larynx (Flanders & Rothman, 1982) to pancreatic cancer (Heuch, Kvale, Jacobsen, & Bjelke, 1983). Finally, alcohol increases the risk of accidents of all kinds (Smith & Kraus, 1988).

When alcoholics seeking treatment were compared to nonalcoholics of similar age, education, and family history of alcoholism, the alcoholics had a higher incidence of concussion, automobile accidents, partial drownings, electrical shocks, and unconsciousness (Glenn, Parsons, & Stevens, 1989). The alcoholics also had a history of more use of many drugs, from major tranquilizers to amphetamines to opiates, and they had more communicable diseases; eye, ear, nose, and throat problems; high blood pressure; and gastrointestinal

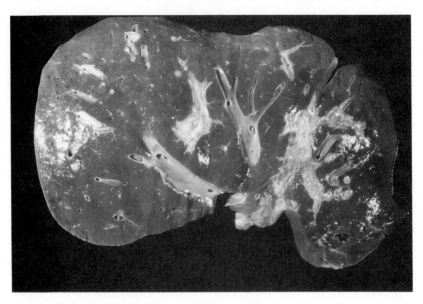

This liver has been damaged by alcohol. Note the lighter areas of nonfunctional fat and fibrotic tissues that have replaced normal liver tissue.

and kidney and bladder problems. Therefore, we can conclude that moderate-to-heavy consumption of alcohol is a very serious health risk indeed.

PSYCHOLOGICAL EFFECTS OF ALCOHOL CONSUMPTION

BENEFITS OF SOCIAL DRINKING

Much attention has been focused on the negative aspects of alcohol use (Neff & Husaini, 1982). However, light-to-moderate social drinking may have certain psychosocial benefits such as reduction in stress, increase in positive emotions, and improvement of certain geropsychiatric problems (Baum-Baicker, 1985). Alcohol seems to decrease anxiety in some phobics and to reduce the tremor of stress (Pohorecky, 1991).

Alcohol is a CNS depressant. Yet, paradoxically, the ingestion of small amounts usually has an initial stimulating effect on *behavior*. In many people, tensions and inhibitions are reduced, leading to a feeling of well-being and increased sociability. Therefore, alcohol consumption can be a reward in itself.

BEHAVIORAL EFFECTS OF HEAVY DRINKING

However, as greater amounts of alcohol are ingested, behavioral problems begin to occur. In some people, alcohol can increase suspiciousness and violence, and there is impairment of motor coordination, balance, speech, and vision, leading to increased accidents. Drunk driving is associated with about 25,000 deaths from automobile accidents each year in the United States, and alcohol is sometimes a factor in other accidents such as airplane and boating disasters (McGuire, 1982).

The behavioral effects are also evident in the fact that alcoholics comprise a large proportion of new admissions to psychiatric and general hospitals, and the suicide rate of alcoholics is higher than the general population, particularly for women. Alcohol is a factor in one-third of suicides and one-half of homicides in the United States, and sexual, spouse, elder, and child abuse are all typically committed under its influence (Brecher, 1972; NIAAA, 1986).

With even larger amounts, the depressant effects of alcohol become more obvious: pain is blunted, some people become depressed and withdrawn, and ultimately sedation and sleep occur. Interestingly, one behavioral effect alcohol can have is to increase people's smoking, which appears to be due to an attempt to use nicotine to stimulate the brain and counteract the sedating effects of alcohol (Michel & Battig, 1989). This tends to support the role that addiction may play in the self-regulation of brain processes.

COGNITIVE INFLUENCES   Interestingly, beliefs about the effects of alcohol influence its behavioral effects. Even the loss of control characteristic of intoxication appears to be as much related to cognitive factors—the expectancy that one will lose control—as to the pharmacological effects of alcohol.

Using an elaborate design, experimenters randomly assigned subjects to one of four groups that were given a beverage. These groups included those who (a) expected the beverage contained alcohol, and it did, (b) expected it contained alcohol, and it did not; (c) did not expect alcohol but it did contain it, and (d) did not expect alcohol, and it did not contain it. The people who expected to receive alcohol behaved as though they had, with more loss of control, *whether or not they had received it*; whereas the people who did not expect to receive alcohol behaved as though they had not, with normal self-control, whether or not they had received it (Marlatt, Deming, & Reid, 1973; Marlatt & Rohsenow, 1980).

There is a common belief that alcohol stimulates aggression and sexual responsiveness, but experiments have demonstrated that, when people believe that they are ingesting alcohol but are *not,* they still act more aggressively (Lang, Goeckner, Adessor, & Marlatt, 1975) and become more sexually aroused (Wilson & Lawson, 1976). This suggests that the behavioral effects of alcohol are due as much to cognitive factors as to the pharmacological action of alcohol on the CNS. Nevertheless, alcohol does have some direct physiological effects on behavior. It can reduce sexual performance in both women (Wilson & Lawson, 1976) and men (Farkas & Rosen, 1976).

The immediate cognitive effects of alcohol depend on whether one is becoming intoxicated or sobering up (Jones, 1973; Jones & Parsons, 1971). Abstract problem-solving and short-term memory performance are significantly better when a person is sobering up as when that same person is becoming intoxicated, even at identical blood alcohol levels.

STARTING AND CONTINUING TO DRINK

STARTING TO DRINK   With about two-thirds of adults in the United States drinking alcohol at least periodically and a preponderance of print and TV advertising for beer, wine, and spirits, drinking is a normative behavior in our society. Therefore, it should come as no surprise that social and cultural factors are of primary importance in explaining why people start to drink (Jessor, 1984).

Children and adolescents are often introduced to drinking at home in their families (NIAAA, 1974). Then, as social drinking continues, alcohol becomes associated with many pleasant expectations (Adesso, 1985). Teenagers see their parents drinking, and they are exposed to advertising that depicts young adults drinking and having fun, so through modeling they learn that drinking is sociable and it makes them feel more adult. Throughout adolescence, teenagers' drinking gradually increases. They report that they have more friends who drink often and that they need more alcohol to get the same effect (Schwartz, Hayden, Getson, & DiPaola, 1986).

Modeling plays a particularly influential role in how much people drink. When college males were exposed to a heavy drinking model, they drank more, although those with a prior history of heavy drinking increased their drinking more than those with a history of light drinking (Caudill & Marlatt, 1975; Lied & Marlatt, 1979). This suggests that peers influence drinking behavior, but there are also individual limits.

CONTINUING TO DRINK   While starting to drink depends on cultural factors and social learning, continuing to drink may depend more on reinforcement, incentive motivation, and the physiological effects of alcohol. *Future* decisions to drink are dependent on expectations about pleasurable consequences based on *past* reinforcing experiences (Adesso, 1985). Rewarding experiences may come from the company of friends or the exciting social occasions during which one drinks. In addition, pleasurable consequences come from reduction in reactions to stress, called *stress-response dampening* (Sher & Levinson, 1982), and reduction in negative thoughts and self-statements (such as, "I can't do anything well"; Hull, Young, & Jouriles, 1986). These provide incentives to drink again. Eventually, consuming alcohol may change people's evaluations of incentives and their emotional reactions to them (Cox & Klinger, 1988). People may learn to evaluate alcohol more positively than nonchemical incentives.

Curiously, research has *not* found anxiety reduction to be a reinforcing factor in drinking. In fact, in heavy social drinkers, the less anxious they were, the more they drank (Rohsenow, 1982). This is probably because tension is reduced and mood improved after a few drinks, but as drinking continues, anxiety and depression increase (Adesso, 1985; Hull & Bond, 1986).

The contiguity of reinforcement explains why people continue to drink in spite of the punishments associated with heavier levels of alcohol consumption. The rewards of drinking occur immediately, while the punishing consequences of heavy drinking such as hangovers or income lost by work absences come later. The ultimate punishments, brain damage or cirrhosis of the liver, come years later. Furthermore, as one's lifestyle and health deteriorate, a downward spiral based on avoidance conditioning takes hold. The deterioration occurring in one's life may be avoided by drinking more.

ROLE OF GENETICS   One additional factor, heredity, may predispose some people to develop problem drinking (Crabbe, McSwigan, & Belknap, 1985; Goodwin, 1986; Schuckit, 1985). If one twin is alcoholic, the likelihood that the other twin will be alcoholic is twice as high if they are identical than if they are fraternal. Furthermore, the children of alcoholics who are adopted are four times as likely to become problem drinkers than are the children of nonalcoholics who are adopted, regardless of the drinking behavior of the adoptive parents.

However, the influence of heredity appears to be demonstrated more reliably for men than for women (Goodwin, Schulsinger, Knop, Mednick, & Guze, 1977; Bohman, Sigvardsson, & Cloninger, 1981). Also, heredity should be viewed as one among many interdependent factors that contribute to the development of problem drinking (Zucker & Gomberg, 1986). Heredity, overall, probably accounts for no more than 20% of the variance in problem drinking (Moos, Cronkite, & Finney, 1982), and, unfortunately, much of the research into the genetic basis of alcoholism suffers from serious methodological problems (Searles, 1988).

Nevertheless, an interesting series of studies reveals how heredity may affect problem drinking. Marc Schuckit (1985) studies young males who have not yet developed a drinking problem. He first divides them into high and low risk groups for becoming alcoholic by evaluating their close relatives for alcoholic behavior. Then he matches the high and low risk groups on important variables (for example, age, race, religion, and education).

His subjects receive drinks that cannot be distinguished from those containing a placebo or those containing alcohol, and there are both subjective and performance differences between the high and low risk groups. When they receive alcohol, high risk subjects report significantly less intoxication, and they perform better on visual-motor coordination tasks than low risk subjects. The high risk subjects seem not to have the same feelings of intoxication that other people do at relatively high blood levels of alcohol, suggesting that they are *not sensitive* to the symptoms of intoxication early enough to prevent ingesting heavy amounts of alcohol.

What might account for this difference in sensitivity to alcohol? A series of studies has identified a specific gene that may be related to alcoholism—one that controls the development of receptor sites for dopamine on neurons in the CNS. A recent review of these studies concluded that the association between this gene and alcoholism is highly significant (Cloninger, 1991). The mean prevalence rate of the gene is about 45% in alcoholics, compared to only about 26% in nonalcoholics. However, because more than half of alcoholics do not have this gene, and one-quarter of nonalcoholics do, it is "neither a necessary nor a sufficient cause of alcoholism" (Cloninger, 1991, p. 1834). Therefore, this gene is *not the cause* of alcoholism but probably interacts with other causal factors to modify its clinical expression. Those with it would be more likely to develop problem drinking.

In summarizing the research on the role of genetics in alcoholism, Searles (1988) concluded that there may be one type of alcoholism that probably has this genetic basis and would be the most difficult to treat. The criteria for distinguishing this form of alcoholism are as follows: (a) it always occurs in men, (b) there is an early onset of problem drinking behavior, and (c) it is associated with antisocial personality disorder. Alcoholism that does not fit these criteria is probably not genetic and may be easier to treat.

Prevention of Alcohol Abuse

Legal barriers have been successful in reducing the consumption of alcohol. Prohibition is the best example, but since its repeal, other less drastic legal methods have been used. These have included high taxes that increase the cost of alcohol, prohibiting young people from buying alcoholic beverages, and strict control over the number of places where alcohol can be purchased (Ashley & Rankin, 1988). Despite these barriers, the drinking of alcohol is still a legal and popular behavior.

So, it remains important to prevent the abuse of alcohol, but as with smoking, education alone has not been successful (Nathan, 1985). Inoculation programs similar to those used with smokers hold promise when they target people early in the process of developing a drinking habit. They provide information and help people recognize the effects of alcohol and help them moderate their drinking behavior accordingly.

For example, early intervention programs can help reduce drunk driving, but they work best with people who are light drinkers to begin with (McGuire, 1982). Generally, if drinking is detected early, before a pattern of heavy drinking develops, people can control it (Ashley & Rankin, 1988; Engstrom, 1984). Today, many employers and unions have "employee assistance programs" or EAPs that help workers who have drinking or other problems that can affect health.

TREATMENT OF ALCOHOL ABUSE

Most people who drink alcohol in the United States are not problem drinkers, and, just as with smoking, many problem drinkers quit on their own. In addition, many problem drinkers vary from time-to-time in their alcohol intake and resulting problems (Clark & Cahalan, 1976). Self-quitting rates of problem drinkers have been found to range from 4% to 42% (Smart, 1976), with an average rate of about 19% (Imber et al., 1976; Miller & Hester, 1980). This suggests that about one-fifth of problem drinkers can successfully stop drinking on their own, while the remainder would benefit from a formal treatment program.

ABSTINENCE VERSUS CONTROLLED DRINKING   Should a treatment program have as its goal complete abstinence, or do alcoholics ever recover to the point that they can drink moderately? This has been one of the most controversial questions in the field. In the United States, where the biomedical model is dominant, treatment programs have traditionally been oriented toward abstinence, a position advocated by both the National Council on Alcoholism and Alcoholics Anonymous. However, Herbert Fingarette (1988), a consultant on addiction to the World Health Organization, has argued that the "disease" of alcoholism is a myth based on four propositions that have no scientific support:

1. Problem drinking is progressive, resulting in increasing mental and physical deprivation.
2. Craving is irresistible and drinking is uncontrollable once it has begun.
3. Medical expertise is needed to cure the symptoms.
4. Alcoholics are not responsible for their drinking.

If, as Fingarette claims, these propositions are false, then problem drinkers should not progress inevitably downhill, and they should be able to control their own drinking. In fact, research has indicated that a small number of problem drinkers and alcoholics, about 15% to 18%, do successfully drink in moderation after they complete a standard treatment program with abstinence as its goal (Armor, Polich, & Stambul, 1978; Davies, 1962; Kendall, 1965), and that they continue to control their drinking on follow-up years later (Helzer et al., 1985; Polich, Armor, & Braiker, 1980).

An early behavioral treatment was developed specifically to teach controlled drinking to alcoholics and was claimed to be effective (Sobell & Sobell, 1973, 1978). However, critics doubted the treatment's effectiveness, and it was strongly opposed (Block, 1976; Marlatt, 1983; Pendery, Maltzman, & West, 1982). They were concerned that it would lead alcoholics to relapse, but the treatment was found to be effective (Dickens, Doob, Warwick, & Winegard, 1982). This was recently confirmed in an experiment that randomly assigned 43 college student problem drinkers to 1 of 3 groups: (a) a cognitive-behavioral controlled drinking training group, (b) a placebo group that only received information about alcohol, and (c) a nontreatment group. Treatment for the controlled drinking and placebo groups consisted of 8 weekly meetings (Kivilan, Marlatt, Fromme, Coppel, & Williams, 1990).

Self-reported drinking was significantly reduced in all groups. Just being in the experiment helped the nontreatment group reduce their drinking, but the cognitive-behavioral group was twice as successful as the nontreatment group, and the placebo group was in-between. Consumption of alcohol in the cognitive-behavioral group was reduced to about 40% overall. However, a year later occasional episodes of heavy drinking continued in all groups, with 70% of subjects reporting at least 1 occasion of 10 or more drinks. Given the strong social influence factor of peer drinking in this college population, the researchers consider these results encouraging.

Controlled drinking may not be the appropriate treatment for all problem drinkers, however. Chronic alcoholics with long histories of problem drinking are poor prospects (Nathan, 1986). Those who seem to do best in controlled drinking programs include those that are (a) young (usually less than 40 years of age); (b) married, employed, and stable; (c) not personally committed to abstinence; (d) not prone to withdrawal symptoms; (e) otherwise healthy and have no alcohol-related diseases; and (f) not subject to long-term drinking problems (under 10 years duration; Miller & Hester, 1980; Peele, 1984).

Today, many prominent researchers accept controlled drinking as a viable alternative to abstinence (for example, Brownell, 1984b; Peele, 1984), but it still remains controversial in the United States. In contrast, in Britain controlled drinking is widely used at treatment centers (Fingarette, 1988; Robertson & Heather, 1982). Although controlled drinking is not an alternative for some problem drinkers, the fact that many can learn to control problem drinking supports Fingarette's (1988) criticism of the biomedical model of alcoholism. In spite of this, the treatment approaches that follow are typically based on the biomedical model and have abstinence as their goal.

ALCOHOLICS ANONYMOUS (AA) AA is the original "12-step program," and it fostered many other self-help groups. AA was founded around 1935 by several people in Akron, Ohio, who were able to remain sober by meeting together and sharing their problems and experiences with alcohol and attending the services of a local religious group (Robinson, 1979). Eventually, the process they used to keep sober was codified into the 12 steps (see Table 8.3-1). Inspection of the 12 steps reveals the religious and spiritual background of AA, as well as its self-help aspect. There are no membership or dues, and the only requirement is the desire to stop drinking. AA strongly promotes the disease model of alcoholism, and it urges complete abstinence. It has been estimated that more than 5 million people attend AA meetings throughout the world, but is the AA program effective?

This is a difficult question to answer because very little research has been done (Peele, 1984). There are, of course, no membership lists, so keeping track of members for research and follow-up is impossible. Also, AA is not a research enterprise—its members are more interested in dealing directly with the problem of alcoholism. AA does maintain that two-thirds of people who want to stop drinking have been successful in the program (Robinson, 1979), but this success rate needs to be examined closely because it is not as good as it seems:

> *The general applicability of AA as a treatment method is much more limited than has been supposed in the past. Available data do not support AA's claims of much higher success rates than clinic treatment. Indeed, when population differences are taken into account, the reverse seems to be true (Baekeland, Lundwall, & Kissin, 1975, p. 306).*

As many as 80% of people who join AA may drop out (Edwards, Hensman, Hawker, & Williamson, 1967). This high dropout rate is supported by a well-controlled experiment that compared an AA group to insight group therapy, behavior group therapy, and a nontreatment group (Brandsma, Maultsby, & Welsh, 1980). AA had the highest dropout rate at 68% (the other groups had dropout rates of 57%), and for those who did not drop out, AA was no more successful than any of the other group therapies.

Table 8.3-1   THE TWELVE STEPS OF ALCOHOLICS ANONYMOUS

1. We admitted we were powerless over alcohol—that our lives had become unmanageable.
2. Came to believe that a power greater than ourselves could restore us to sanity.
3. Made a decision to turn our will and our lives over to the care of God *as we understood Him.*
4. Made a searching and fearless oral inventory of ourselves.
5. Admitted to God, to ourselves, and to another human being the exact nature of our wrongs.
6. Were entirely ready to have God remove all these defects of character.
7. Humbly ask Him to remove our shortcomings.
8. Made a list of all persons we had harmed, and became willing to make amends to them all.
9. Made direct amends to such people wherever possible, except when to do so would injure them or others.
10. Continued to take personal inventory and, when we were wrong, promptly admitted it.
11. Sought through prayer and meditation to improve our conscious contact with God *as we understand Him,* praying only for knowledge of His will for us and the power to carry that out.
12. Having had a spiritual awakening as the result of these steps, we tried to carry this message to alcoholics and to practice these principles in all our affairs.

Source: The Twelve Steps and Twelve Traditions. *Copyright (c) 1952, by Alcoholics Anonymous World Services, Inc.*

A meeting of a 12-step group modeled after Alcoholics Anonymous.

Given the high dropout rate and doubts about its effectiveness, AA would not seem to be the answer for the overwhelming majority of alcoholics. For those who do stay in the program, however, AA appears to be about as successful as other approaches. Those who are more successful in AA are male; with lower educational levels (generally high school or below); and with a high need for authoritarianism, dependency, and sociability (Miller & Hester, 1980).

MEDICAL TREATMENT   Traditional medical treatment is hospital based and directed toward **detoxification**—treating the physical symptoms of withdrawal. The process usually takes a month, and it is sometimes a necessary step before other forms of treatment can begin. Tranquilizers can be prescribed for the anxiety and general discomfort of withdrawal, but alcoholics are prone to abuse tranquilizers too, so they must be tapered off. Sometimes, dietary supplements and anticonvulsants are also prescribed. But only about one-half of alcoholics need hospital-based detoxification; problem drinkers without a long history of drinking and without symptoms of withdrawal do not (Miller & Hester, 1986). Today, it is possible for such drinkers to receive detoxification at home under medical supervision.

Beyond detoxification, medical treatment consists of prescribing **emetics**, drugs that interact with alcohol to cause extremely unpleasant reactions if alcohol is ingested. Commonly used drugs are *disulfiram* (Antabuse) and *emetine*, which has fewer side effects. After taking these drugs, even a single drink causes extreme nausea, vomiting, and other uncomfortable symptoms. If an alcoholic takes the drug, it can be an effective deterrent (Bourne, Alford, & Bowcock, 1966). The problem, of course, is how to motivate people to continue taking a drug that makes them sick if they drink. Also, gradually, as people become sober, psychological problems begin to surface.

INSIGHT THERAPY   As mentioned earlier, personality problems accompany problem drinking. Although they are certainly not the sole cause of alcoholism, they may contribute to its continuing. Therefore, individual insight-oriented psychotherapy has been advocated because it may offer advantages over other approaches that do not address the personality (Zimberg, 1985a). Although group approaches such as AA offer certain advantages—models who have achieved abstinence, social support, and a chance to act therapeutically for someone else—individual therapy also has advantages. It can be adjusted to the specific needs of the person, and a trained professional may be better able to deal with difficult personality problems. However, psychotherapy cannot be successful with intoxicated people, so sobriety is often the first goal (Zimberg, 1985b). Often medical treatment and AA are used to achieve abstinence before psychotherapy begins.

Reports of success rates vary greatly. At the low end, one study reported a success rate of 26% abstinent or improved at 1-year follow-up (Miller & Hester, 1980), whereas some private treatment centers claim rates of 90% recovery (Hunter, 1982), although this is undoubtedly exaggerated. A review of several studies found that success rates varied from 65% to 82% at 1-year follow-up (Brownell, 1982a), but researchers have found that these higher success rates would be cut in half at 3-year follow-up (Armor, Polich, & Stambul, 1978; Wiens & Menustik, 1983).

Many factors influence the effectiveness of psychotherapy in treating alcoholism (Emrick & Hansen, 1983). Some of the variables that may account for the radically different reports of success include the demographic characteristics of who has been treated, how success is defined, and the length of follow-up. The best estimate of the success of psychotherapy 3 years after treatment is probably about 40%, which is about twice as high as the estimate of the self-quitting rate of 19%, and suggests that psychotherapy is effective treatment for problem drinking.

BEHAVIORAL AND COGNITIVE THERAPY   Two types of aversion therapy have been applied to help people stop drinking. Electric shock has been used in much the same manner as for smoking. Drinks containing alcohol are held, sniffed, and in some programs, drunk, while a shock is administered. There are two drawbacks to this technique, however. It requires the use of alcohol (substitutes and pictures do not work), and it has not achieved much success (Miller & Hester, 1980).

Emetics, the same drugs prescribed to make alcoholics sick whenever they ingest alcohol, have been used to *condition* an aversion to drinking. Usually treatment has begun in the hospital with several sessions during which the alcoholic receives an emetic and then deliberately drinks alcohol. He or she gets very nauseated and vomits immediately, eventually becoming conditioned to dislike the smell and taste of alcohol. There are periodic "booster" sessions after discharge, but the emetic is usually not taken in between.

In one study of 685 patients who received this treatment, 63% were not drinking on 1-year follow-up, but this success rate dropped in half to 31% at 3-year follow-up (Wiens & Menustik, 1983). Therefore, it appears that the rate of quitting with emetic aversion therapy is higher than the self-quitting rate, yet not as high as psychotherapy. The effectiveness of aversion therapy with emetics may be higher when controlled drinking is the goal of treatment (Miller & Hester, 1980).

Several cognitive methods have been used to help people stop and resist drinking. One teaches *social and problem-solving skills.* Problem drinkers are taught how to resist temptation, such as when they are out socially and friends order drinks. The skills are taught in therapy through imagination and rehearsal. In one study, at one-year follow-up, drinkers who underwent skills training were much more successful than those who did not receive the training (Chaney, O'Leary, & Marlatt, 1978).

Another cognitive method teaches *self-management techniques* similar to those used to help people stop smoking (Lang & Marlatt, 1982; Miller & Hester, 1980). These techniques also can involve family members who are taught to support drinkers in their self-management (Sisson & Azrin, 1986). Contingency contracts that determine rewards and punishments for drinking are used, and drinkers learn how to control the stimuli that encourage drinking (for example, talking out a problem with a friend instead of dealing with it alone and drinking). Finally, *systematic desensitization and relaxation* have been used to help drinkers cope with tension and anxiety, two possible reasons that someone may drink (Miller & Hester, 1980).

MOTIVATIONAL THERAPY   Recently, a new therapy has been developed that is based on incentive motivation (Cox & Klinger, 1988). It attempts to take a more comprehensive lifestyle approach. First, it carefully assesses the alcoholic's motivational structure. The individual's goals and interrelationships among them are determined. Each goal is paired with every other goal, and a decision is made about whether they facilitate, interfere with, or have no effect on each other. Second, goal conflicts are resolved, and the alcoholic is encouraged to pursue goals that will facilitate overall well-being through multicomponent counseling. In other words, the alcoholic is encouraged to develop a meaningful life without alcohol. With the exception, perhaps, of insight therapy, the other treatments have tended to overlook the broader context of a meaningful lifestyle. While motivational therapy holds promise, its effectiveness is yet to be investigated.

MULTICOMPONENT TREATMENT Research indicates that the best chance of long-term success is multicomponent treatment that combines elements from a variety of techniques (Costello, 1975; Costello, Baillargeon, Biever, & Bennett, 1980; Moos & Finney, 1983). Multicomponent treatment typically begins with several weeks of inpatient treatment and the use of aversion therapy. Then, treatment continues for another three to four weeks on an outpatient basis. All environmental factors that may help a person control drinking are taken into account. Self-management techniques are taught, and family are involved in aftercare.

There is some concern because of the costliness of the inpatient component, but it seems that, except for extremely impaired alcoholics, there is no advantage to it, and outpatient programs are just as successful (Holden, 1987). There is also no advantage to longer treatment programs (Miller & Hester, 1986). However, separate inpatient treatment programs for women appear to produce better results than mixed-sex treatments (Dahlgren & Willander, 1989).

TREATMENT DROPOUTS AND RELAPSE More than 50% of alcoholics drop out of treatment, and less than half of those who finish them are still successful on long-term follow-up (Stark, 1992). Those who are successful typically have the best adjustment at the start of treatment (Nathan, 1986). The people who are most likely to remain in treatment and be successful are older, have a higher socioeconomic status, have little or no history of abuse of other substances, have stable employment and social relationships, are free of psychopathology or are only depressed, have no history of other treatment failures, and are motivated (Holden, 1987; Stark, 1992).

Most relapse will occur within 90 days after treatment (Hunt, Barnett, & Branch, 1971). Research has found that "negative emotions" such as anxiety, depression, anger, and social pressure are related to relapse (Abrams, Niaura, Carey, Monti, & Binkoff, 1986; Marlatt & Gordon, 1980). This suggests that relapse needs to be anticipated in treatment, and that cognitive and behavioral therapy may help drinkers deal with these negative emotions so they do not lead to drinking.

Recently, Prochaska and DiClemente's stage theory of quitting smoking (see Table 8.2-3, page 344) has been applied to quitting drinking as well as using other substances (Prochaska, DiClemente, & Norcross, 1992). Substantial research evidence supports their observation that people cycle through the stages of quitting several times before finally quitting.

A recent review made several suggestions for reducing dropouts and increasing the success of treatment (Stark, 1992). These suggestions include the following: (a) decreasing the wait between the client's seeking treatment and entry into a program, (b) pretherapy training and education to let clients know what to expect from treatment, (c) phone calls to follow up after missed appointments, (d) individual attention in treatment, (e) smaller groups, and (f) clinicians who are committed to clients' treatment continuation.

SUMMARY   There is effective treatment for alcoholism and problem drinking. Long-term success rates of up to 40% can be achieved. Psychotherapy and multicomponent treatment are effective. Except when detoxification is necessary, treatment does not require hospitalization, and it may be relatively short term, up to about 8 weeks, as long as booster sessions are included. Unfortunately, alcoholism remains a major problem because about 85%, or 8 million, of the problem drinkers in the United States do not receive any formal treatment (USDHHS, 1981). It also remains a problem because, even when treatment is attempted, more than 50% of alcoholics drop out. In order to improve treatment, researcher Stanton Peele has made a number of specific suggestions (Table 8.3-2).

Table 8.3-2   RECOMMENDATIONS FOR IMPROVING ALCOHOLISM TREATMENT

1. *Broaden treatment services* by eliminating the dominance of the disease model and AA-based treatment.
2. *Emphasize cost effectiveness* by finding the most economical services and spending the most on them.
3. *Study people who quit or control drinking on their own.*
4. *Fund more research studies* that compare the outcome of various types of treatments.
5. *Consider drinking in context* by taking into account the person's overall functioning (work, family, etc.).
6. *Emphasize the teaching of skills* in treatment (for example, job training, problem solving, marital counseling).
7. *Match patients to treatments* by building on patient preferences (instead of telling those who refuse conventional treatment that they are "in denial").
8. *Use minimal intervention first,* especially for young people and other less severely impaired drinkers.
9. *Acknowledge controlled drinking* as an acceptable goal.

Source: Adapted from Peele, S., 1991, What we know about treating alcoholism and other addictions, The Harvard Mental Health Letter, 8, 5–7.

OTHER DRUGS

EPIDEMIOLOGICAL PERSPECTIVES

Even though the use of drugs seems to have peaked in the 1970s, it is still widespread (Pope, Ionescu-Pioggia, & Aizley, 1990). It is estimated that 22 million Americans have tried cocaine at least once; as many as 5 million use it with some regularity; and in its new, less expensive form called "*crack*," its use may even go up (Cohen, 1986a; NIDA, 1983).

In addition, about 20 million people use marijuana (Hingson et al., 1986). *Daily* marijuana use among high school students had dropped from a high of 10.7% in 1978, but it was still *6.3%* in 1982 (Miller & Cisin, 1983). A variety of other stimulants, hallucinogens, and depressants are also used and abused by high school students. Among college students, the proportion using marijuana at least once a week had been 18% in 1969, 29% in 1978, but had dropped to 6% in 1989 (Pope et al., 1990). From 1978 to 1989, the proportion of students who had ever used cocaine dropped from 30% to 20%, and the proportion who had ever used LSD dropped from 20% to 12%. Although the use of drugs has been declining, a substantial minority of people, especially teenagers and young adults, are still involved.

CLASSIFICATION OF DRUGS: HEALTH, BEHAVIORAL, AND PSYCHOLOGICAL EFFECTS

Drugs are classified into categories that primarily reflect their affect on the brain. **Depressants** reduce CNS arousal and promote relaxation. The narcotics (for example, morphine) have strong pain relieving properties, while the minor tranquilizers (for example, benzodiazepines) reduce anxiety. Those who use depressants risk developing physical and psychological dependence. Even the use of the minor tranquilizers over a long period of time is associated with neuropsychological impairment of visual-spatial abilities and sustained attention (Golombok, 1989).

Stimulants (for example, amphetamine) arouse the brain, leading to increased alertness and mood elevation. They also reduce fatigue and suppress the appetite. Although stimulant use can lead to moderate psychological dependence and tolerance does develop, physical withdrawal symptoms generally do not occur (Bardo & Risner, 1985).

Hallucinogens generally produce distortions of perception, with either sedative-like feelings of intoxication and relaxation (for example, marijuana) or stimulant-like feelings of exhilaration (for example, LSD). Their use does not lead to physical dependence, but it can lead to psychological dependence (Jaffe, 1985; Rice, 1990). One detailed review of the neuropsychological effects of long-term drug abuse found no impairments for marijuana and inconsistent findings for polydrug (including hallucinogen) users (Parsons & Farr, 1981). A more detailed classification of substances with a potential for psychological and physical dependence is depicted in Table 8.3-3.

EXPERIMENTATION AND STARTING

Like smoking and drinking, the use of drugs is likely to begin in adolescence. Marijuana, the most widely used drug, will have been tried by most people

Table 8.3-3   SUBSTANCES WITH POTENTIAL FOR DEPENDENCE

SUBSTANCE	PHYSICAL DEPENDENCE		PSYCHOLOGICAL DEPENDENCE
	Withdrawal	**Tolerance**	
Depressants			
Narcotics	High	High	High
Opioids (e.g., morphine)			
Synthetics (e.g., methadone)			
Nonnarcotics	Moderate	Mild	Moderate
Barbiturates			
Methaqualone			
Ethanol			
Minor Tranquilizers	Moderate	Slight	Moderate
Meprobamate			
Benzodiazepines			
Stimulants			
Amphetamine	?	High	Moderate
Methamphetamine	?	High	Moderate
Cocaine	None	None	Moderate
Hallucinogens			
LSD	None	Mild	Mild
Mescaline, peyote	None	Slight	Mild
Marijuana	None	?	Mild

Source: Based on Berkow, R., and Fletcher, A. J., 1987, The Merck manual of diagnosis and therapy, Rahway, NJ: Merck Sharp & Dohme Research Laboratories.

before they graduate from high school (Johnston, Bachman, & O'Malley, 1982). Much of this is experimentation, however, because 85% of teenagers disapprove of "regular use" of marijuana (Miller & Cisin, 1983).

Teenagers begin to use marijuana for much the same reasons that they begin to smoke or drink alcohol (Hansen et al., 1987; Stein, Newcomb, & Bentler, 1987). Social learning and modeling play a dominant role. The use of alcohol and marijuana by parents and peers is related to a teenager's own use (Brook, Whiteman, & Gordon, 1983; Stein et al., 1987), although their first introduction to marijuana is usually by a friend (Kandel, 1974).

Once teenagers have tried marijuana and enjoyed its pleasurable effects, it is understandable why some might experiment with other illegal substances in an attempt to self-regulate the experience of pleasure and pain during what can be a tumultuous and tense period of life. Generally, experimentation with other drugs begins several years later than marijuana, but does experimentation lead inevitably to drug abuse or addiction?

CONTINUING TO USE DRUGS: FROM USE TO ABUSE?

PROGRESSION THEORIES AND PERSONALITY It is said that the more a person has used marijuana the more likely that person is to use other drugs (for example, Kandel & Faust, 1975; Newcomb & Bentler, 1986). This has led some researchers to speculate that drug abuse involves a progression through predictable stages. One such progression theory, involving three stages, was proposed by Miller and Cisin (1983):

- ■ Stage 1   Use of two legal drugs—alcohol and cigarettes.
- ■ Stage 2   Use of an illegal drug—marijuana.
- ■ Stage 3   Use of other illegal drugs such as cocaine or heroin.

Supporters of progression theories point to the fact that about 95% of people who use marijuana have used alcohol or cigarettes, and that about 90% of people who use other illegal drugs have used marijuana. However, only a *minority* of adolescents who have used alcohol or cigarettes *ever* goes on to use marijuana regularly, and an even smaller minority of marijuana users ever goes on to use other illegal drugs. Also, progression should not be confused with causation. Just because people who use marijuana have used alcohol does not mean that alcohol use causes marijuana use—100% of marijuana users have also drunk water.

Certain personality characteristics may be related to drug use. Like alcoholics, people who abuse drugs are more antisocial. They are characterized as more impulsive, rebellious, and sensation seeking than people who either do not use drugs or just experiment with them (Brook, Whiteman, Gordon, & Cohen, 1986; Newcomb, Maddahian, & Bentler, 1986; Stein et al., 1987). Although these characterizations are reliable, they are based on relatively short-term longitudinal studies of adolescents.

Recently, Jonathan Shedler and Jack Block (1990) of the University of California, Berkeley, reported the results of a long-term study of the antecedents of adolescent drug use. Their subjects were 101 18-year-olds—49 boys and 52 girls—who had been part of a 13-year longitudinal study of ego and cognitive development beginning when they were 3 years old. At 18, the subjects were divided into 3 groups (that did not differ significantly in socio-economic status or intelligence) based on their use of drugs:

- *Abstainers*—those who had never tried marijuana or any other drug.
- *Experimenters*—those who had used marijuana as much as once a month and had tried no more than one other drug.
- *Frequent users*—those who had used marijuana once a week or more and had tried at least one other drug (81% had used cocaine, 67% had used hallucinogens, and 43% had used amphetamines).

When the subjects were five years of age, the quality of their interactions with their mothers or fathers were observed and videotaped in separate sessions. There were differences in parental interaction among the three groups. The mothers of both the *abstainers* and the *frequent users* were described as colder and more unresponsive than the mothers of the experimenters. If the laboratory observations can be generalized, these mothers probably interacted with their children in a manner that lacked joy—pressuring their children to perform, but offering little support and encouragement. An additional, perhaps critical factor, was that the *fathers* of the *abstainers* were described as impatient, hypercritical, authoritarian, and domineering.

Then, at 7, 11, and 18 years of age, personality data were gathered on each subject. There were distinct personality differences among these three groups. The *abstainers* were more rigid and overcontrolled; they were also more timid and less warm, curious, or cheerful. In contrast, the *frequent users* were under-controlled; they were insecure, impulsive, and had poor interpersonal relationships, with signs of emotional distress. The *experimenters* were the psychologically healthiest of the three groups. They were described as warm, responsive, active, and cheerful. It is important to remember that the personality differences were evident many years before subjects began using drugs. Therefore, drug use did not cause them.

Shedler and Block (1990) discussed the implications of their results for social policy. They believe that peer pressure does not fully explain drug abuse. Instead, parenting and personality antecedents may influence whether a person will later abstain, experiment, or become a frequent user. A recent model of developmental psychopathology also suggests that certain environmental factors and experiences beginning as early as birth are conducive to later drug use (Glantz, 1992). Finally, Shedler and Block also believe that people probably do not change groups once they are into late adolescence.

This contradicts both progression theories and the idea that addiction is a disease, because some people are able to experiment with drugs and *not* progress to drug abuse. The experimenters appear to have a "resistance" to frequent drug use regardless of social pressures or the potential pleasure a substance may provide. Shedler and Block also questioned current drug education efforts, because they may overly alarm parents and educators and use scarce resources for a whole group of people with "natural resistance"—the experimenters. Also, current efforts may oversimplify the underlying factors that lead to frequent drug use.

PREVENTING DRUG ABUSE

Children begin using drugs as early as the sixth grade (Johnston, Bachman, & O'Malley, 1982), so prevention has relied on education efforts aimed at children and adolescents and carried out in schools and the media. It has been argued that children at high risk for developing drug abuse should be targeted by these prevention programs (Jalali, Jalali, Crocetti, & Turner, 1980). High risk children (a) are dropouts from school, (b) usually come from a drug or alcohol abusing family, (c) may have psychological problems, and (d) have peers who use drugs (Kandel, 1982).

Prevention efforts have relied primarily on raising fears about drugs but have not had much success in preventing drug abuse (Des Jarlais, Friedman, Casriel, & Kott, 1987; Kaminer & Bukstein, 1989). Yet, there have been successful programs. The Midwestern Prevention Project is an example of a program that has experienced moderate success (MacKinnon et al., 1991). Conducted in 42 middle and junior high schools in Kansas and Missouri, it involves over 5,000 students. The program consists of 10 sessions. It provides information about drugs and their prevalence and teaches techniques to resist social pressure. Regular teachers are trained to use behavioral techniques such as role playing, assertiveness training, modeling, and rehearsal to teach resistance. There is also group feedback and homework.

A one-year progress report compared students in about half of the schools who had been through the program with students in schools without the program. The program did change students' perceptions of drug and alcohol use and their intentions to use them, and there were significant but only small decreases in the proportion of students reporting the use of cigarettes, alcohol, and marijuana in the previous month.

Programs such as this and the widely publicized "Just Say No" media campaign (Cohen, 1986b), which broadly target all children, may help parents, educators, and politicians feel they are doing something about drugs, but their effectiveness for *changing* behavior appears to be extremely limited. They may be too simplistic and uneconomical because they treat all young people the same. Shedler and Block's (1990) research suggests that abstainers do not need the "Just Say No" message, experimenters are already resistant and not likely to become frequent users, and frequent users are so alienated that they will not listen anyway. Perhaps that is why large-scale programs produce so little behavior change.

Other prevention programs have avoided fear messages about drugs, and they have attempted to help students resist drugs by building self-esteem and reducing alienation. However, they, too, have proven to be only moderately effective (Schaps, Moskowitz, Malvin, & Schaeffer, 1984). In fact, a review of 143 adolescent drug prevention programs found that, overall, they have had very little success (Tobler, 1986).

Apparently, a very careful analysis of drug prevention programs is needed. The concept of "targeting" may help (Mosbach & Leventhal, 1988). Because there may already be personality differences by 7 years of age, children at high risk to become frequent users should be targeted early. Since Shedler and Block's (1990) results suggest that parenting problems may precede drug abuse, family therapy might have the best chance of helping children resist frequent drug use later in life. Although relatively expensive, family therapy could be targeted just at those children who are at high risk.

TREATMENT FOR DRUG ABUSE

MEDICAL TREATMENT Like alcoholism, medical treatment for drug abuse has focused on inpatient detoxification. Attempts have also been made to find substitutes for some abused drugs, notably the narcotics, that will reduce the cravings after detoxification. For example, *methadone* was developed as a cure for heroin (which, ironically, was developed as a cure for morphine addiction). Methadone prevents withdrawal symptoms; it does not produce euphoria itself, and it blocks the euphoric feelings if heroin is taken. However, it is no cure for heroin addiction, for withdrawal returns if it is discontinued, so dependency is just transferred from heroin to methadone.

Heroin antagonists such as cyclazocine and naloxone have also been tried. They bind to the same postsynaptic receptor sites in the brain that heroin does, thus preventing euphoria if heroin is taken, but they do not otherwise stimulate the neurons. Unfortunately, the craving for the pleasure afforded by heroin continues. These treatments can only be successful in the most motivated addicts, because they must keep frequent appointments at clinics to receive the heroin antagonists and yet receive no rewarding high.

PSYCHOLOGICAL TREATMENT Medical treatments can only be viewed as a first step toward controlling drug addiction. After detoxification and even if a substitute is found that prevents withdrawal, the craving and the memory of the euphoria remains a powerful allure. Even more importantly, a detoxified drug addict's lifestyle is probably in shambles, meaning that interpersonal and work relationships are disrupted, and there is little left in life to provide pleasure. Complete environmental overhaul is necessary because stimuli associated with drugs—people, needles and drug apparatus, and places—can elicit the craving (Wikler, 1980). Although many forms of psychotherapy and behavior therapy have been used with drug addicts, shockingly little is known about their effectiveness (Kaminer & Bukstein, 1989; Liskow, 1982).

Success is related to the same factors as in treatment for alcohol abuse. The use of opioids or marijuana as the primary drug also is related to poor prognosis. For adolescents, more successful outcomes are possible if you are white, a nonopioid user, in an educational program, and older when the drug of abuse was first tried (Rush, 1979). The single most important variable for predicting success in adolescents, however, is absence of psychopathology (Kaminer & Bukstein, 1989).

Residential programs are the most widely used approach to treatment. They combine several features based on Synanon, which was founded in Santa Monica, California, in the late 1950s (it has since disbanded). These residential programs provide a drug free environment staffed by ex-addicts. Participants are kept from contact with former friends and places associated with their drug use. Group therapy is the primary method of treatment, and it is very confrontational. Participants are forced to take responsibility for their drug addiction and their life. Like AA, these residential programs may be beneficial for people who can remain in them, but only a small number of addicts ever elect to enter them (Jaffe, 1985). Unfortunately, there have been no scientific studies of their effectiveness.

At the present time, an effective comprehensive approach to treatment is lacking, although the same factors that may improve alcohol treatment (Stark, 1992) have been recommended for drug abuse treatment. Given recent formulations that contribute to a single biopsychosocial model in addiction (for example, Vuchinich & Tucker, 1988; Cox & Klinger, 1988), there is hope that what is learned about new multicomponent and motivational treatments for alcoholism may be successfully applied to other drugs as well.

■■■

MODULE SUMMARY

This completes Chapter 8. Chapter 9 looks at disability. Before continuing, however, review these major points about the use and abuse of alcohol and drugs:

1. About 90% of high school students report that they have tried alcohol, and about ⅓ of adults report that they are moderate or heavy drinkers.
2. Problem drinking is defined by heavy drinking, psychological dependence, and impaired relationships and/or work performance, while alcoholism is defined by the development of tolerance, blacking out, memory impairment, and withdrawal.
3. Not all alcohol consumption is bad. In fact, moderate drinking is related to *better* health outcomes. Moderate to heavy drinking increases the risk of death from heart disease, stroke, cancer, and liver disease.
4. "Alcoholic" behavior is due as much to the expectancy of its effects as to the pharmacological effects of the drug.

5. Children are introduced to drinking in the home, and modeling plays a role in how much people drink.

6. Continuing to drink seems to be due to its pleasurable consequences and the contiguity of reinforcement—the fact that its punishments come much later.

7. Genetics may play a role in some alcohol addiction. However, less than half of alcoholics have the suspect gene and about one-quarter of nonalcoholics do, so genetics cannot be the sole cause of alcoholism.

8. The factors involved in starting to use a substance are different from those in continuing to use it.

9. Substances may have different psychoactive effects, but each one can produce effects that *some* people experience as pleasurable.

10. Genetic predisposition may affect sensitivity to a substance, and individuals vary in what they experience as pleasure (stimulation or sedation or hallucination), but cognitive factors such as one's goals, beliefs, and values determine the pleasure an individual derives from a substance.

11. Although widely believed to be an effective treatment for alcoholism, too many problem drinkers drop out of AA for it to be considered generally successful. It works for some, but not the overwhelming majority of alcoholics.

12. Other approaches to treating alcoholism can achieve a success rate of up to 40% on follow-up. Psychotherapy and multimodal treatment—specifically including behavioral and cognitive therapy—are effective. Abstinence is not necessary for all problem drinkers; some are able to become controlled drinkers.

13. Drugs may be classified by their effects on the brain. Depressants reduce CNS arousal and promote relaxation, stimulants arouse the brain and promote increased alertness and heightened mood, and hallucinogens distort perception.

14. Drug use and experimentation does not progress inevitably to drug abuse. Some people may naturally resist becoming frequent users, and research has shown that some adolescents can experiment with drugs and not become frequent users.

15. Drug prevention programs have not proven to be particularly effective, whether or not they relied on fear messages. Early family based prevention may increase the likelihood that a child can resist drug addiction later in life.

16. Although detoxification is a necessary first step, medical treatments are not effective against the underlying psychosocial problems of drug abusers.

17. Surprisingly little is known about the effectiveness of psychological treatment for alcohol or drug abuse.

9

DISABILITY

9.1 The Nature of Disability
9.2 Rehabilitation

Disability is caused by a variety of conditions. People are born with certain impairments, and others are acquired through accident, illness, or aging. Disability can arise from a strictly physical impairment or an impairment of the central nervous system. In this chapter we explore the nature of disability and the role of psychologists in rehabilitation.

The Nature of Disability

Understanding Disability

Brian was a 23-year-old high school graduate and a rookie on the police force of a city of 65,000 people at the time of his injury. While on a weekend white water rafting trip with several buddies to celebrate his recent engagement, he dove into a quiet part of the river for a swim. Brian miscalculated the river's depth at that point—it was only five feet—and he struck his head on the bottom. The blow caused a compression of the spinal cord. Someone had to hike out to reach paramedics and it took some time to evacuate Brian by helicopter to an acute care hospital.

After two weeks, he was transferred to a rehabilitation hospital near his hometown where he spent five weeks. Part of the spinal cord was damaged, resulting in a lasting impairment of his ability to stand and to walk, but fortunately there was no permanent brain damage. Eventually, Brian would learn to use a wheelchair for mobility, but first his fiancée would leave him, and his career plans would change.

Maricela was an 11-year-old girl from a large, close-knit family. Her parents emphasized education and they sacrificed to keep her in private, parochial schools, where she was an excellent student. One morning while preparing for school, she experienced a severe headache and nausea. Maricela was not one to miss school, so her mother took the symptoms seriously. She thought that Maricela was coming down with the flu, but there was no fever. When Maricela's breathing became harsh and gasping, her mother became alarmed and called the paramedics. They arrived just as she lost consciousness.

Fortunately, Maricela was on the operating table within one hour, where the congenital vascular malformation that was bleeding into her brain near the cerebellum was diagnosed and surgical repair begun. Many people have inherited these malformations, which cause no problems but occasionally rupture and bleed.

Within 10 days Maricela was in a rehabilitation hospital where she remained for 6 weeks. During that time, she started to learn how to overcome her balance problems so she could stand and walk again, and she began cognitive and educational therapy so she could eventually return to school.

Brian and Maricela are two young people whose lives were dramatically changed by damage to the central nervous system, one due to trauma and one due to a vascular malformation. The effects of trauma and disease can be limited to the peripheral nervous system, bones, or muscle tissue, where it results only in physical impairment, but our primary interest here is with impairments that result from damage to the central nervous system.

TERMINOLOGY

Certain words like "handicapped" and "disabled" deserve some clarification because they are often perceived negatively (Smyer, McHale, Birkel, & Madle, 1988). For our purposes, **impairment** refers to limitations of specific organs or functions, for example, "impaired eyesight" or "impaired verbal abilities"; **handicap** refers to limitations of environments such as architectural barriers, for example, the absence of a wheelchair ramp, rather than people; and **disability** refers to the interaction between an individual with a specific impairment and a specific handicapping environment (Gliedman & Roth, 1980). These are regarded as more than just semantic distinctions. Consider this example of how these terms are used:

> . . . *a person is disabled when, due to impaired heart functioning, she is unable to climb stairs. If all stairs were replaced with elevators, it would not be useful to refer to this person as disabled any longer (Smyer et al., 1988, p. 10).*

These distinctions remind us that, even though a person may have an impairment of a specific function, many other functions may remain unimpaired. Therefore, an impairment may be disabling only in relation to a specific environment. The term "disability" is sometimes used here because of convention, but it is necessary to keep in mind its relationship to environments. Finally, **habilitation** refers to *acquiring* a function or ability, and **rehabilitation** refers to *restoring* a former function or ability.

EPIDEMIOLOGY

The total number of Americans with impairing conditions is between 34 and 43 million (USDHHS, 1992). The prevalence of disability increases with age.

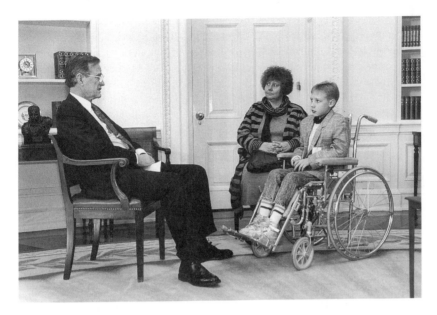

Developmental and acquired impairments in childhood can make a wheelchair a necessity for mobility.

Only 7% of people 15 to 44 years of age have an impairment of a major activity (for example, their ability to attend school or work) compared to 17% of people 45 to 64 years of age and 25% of people older than 74 years of age (USDHHS, 1992). Disability also varies by race. About 8% of European Americans have a limitation of a major activity compared to about 13% of African Americans.

The economic impact of disabilities to society is considerable. Lifetime medical treatment and rehabilitation for a single person with quadriplegia is $570,000, while the first-year cost of treating a person with a severe head injury is $310,000. There is also a substantial loss of income from their reduced capacity to work, so state and federal programs are necessary to support many people with disabilities. A 1977 estimate put total government disability payments at more than $60 billion (DeJong & Lifchez, 1983).

ASSESSMENT OF DISABILITY

Impairment is assessed with respect to function. *Functions* are usually thought of as skills, abilities, and activities necessary for survival in society. They are sometimes called "adaptive abilities," because they allow individuals to adapt to and survive in their society, and health psychologists refer to them as "coping abilities." Within a given area, for example arithmetic abilities, functions can be classified as *high level* (for example, filling out your income tax forms or balancing your checkbook), *intermediate* (for example, checking your restaurant bill and figuring the tip), or *low level* (for example, making sure you get the correct change back for a dollar when you buy a pack of gum). Usually, an intermediate level of functioning is considered sufficient for survival in our technological society. Below that, a person may have a disability. Of course, such determinations are relative. A person with average ability in math and science would be disabled in a seminar on nuclear physics, just as a person who cannot read American Sign Language would be disabled in a conversation among hearing-impaired people.

How is the level of functioning determined? This is usually a two-step process. First, the extent of the impairment is assessed—that is, quantified in some manner and compared to normative values. Second, functioning is evaluated by determining how much the assessed impairment affects adaptive abilities. For example, if it were suspected that a man's mathematical abilities were affected by a stroke, they would first be assessed. Is he able to add, subtract, multiply, and divide? Can he carry out these processes with only two-digit numbers, or can he process larger ones? Can he do them with decimal numbers? Then, it would be necessary to determine how the impairment affects his functioning. If he could add and subtract, but only with two- or three-digit numbers, then he could get the correct change for a pack of gum, but he could no longer figure a tip.

Functioning is usually assessed in four broad categories: physical, intellectual, personality, and social. Typically, physicians specializing in disability and physical and occupational therapists evaluate physical functioning, while psychologists evaluate intellectual and personality functioning.

PHYSICAL FUNCTIONING   Physical functioning encompasses what are called the **activities of daily living** or **ADLs**. ADLs involve the most basic human activities in our society such as driving a car or taking public transportation, engaging in personal hygiene, shopping in a store or market, making simple meals, and feeding oneself. Impairments of strength, endurance, flexibility, or mobility will affect ADLs and can be caused by muscle or nerve damage to a limb or damage to the brain. Damage to the sensory or motor areas of the cortex or to the frontal lobes can produce what appears to be a purely physical impairment.

Of course, people vary widely in their basic physical abilities, but impairment is considered only when a person does not have *average* ability for their age, height, and weight. If a woman had impaired mobility due to the loss of her legs, this *could* profoundly affect her functioning in ADLs. However, if she used a wheelchair, there would be little or no reduction in functioning, although she would still have her impairment. Physical impairments are often obvious, but ADLs can also be affected by the next two functional categories.

INTELLECTUAL FUNCTIONING   Most conditions that affect the brain also impair intellectual functioning to some degree. It is possible to obtain an assessment of global functioning such as an IQ score; however, it is of little use for the purposes of rehabilitation. Instead, psychologists assess performance on many specific components of cognitive functioning. These include the higher level abilities involved with thought, judgment and reasoning, memory, and communication. These are further broken down into subcomponents, such as memory for past learned information versus the ability to learn new information or memory for visual versus auditory stimuli. The assessment of intellectual functioning is a complex process because damage to the cortex may disrupt only certain abilities, leaving others intact.

EMOTIONAL AND PERSONALITY FUNCTIONING   Emotional and personality functioning can be affected in any of three ways: (a) in reaction to one's own impairment, (b) in reaction to the reaction of others, or (c) as the result of damage to the areas of the brain that mediate emotion and personality—the frontal lobes and limbic system. With regard to one's own reaction, a large and representative community sample of 22,000 people 18 years of age and older in Canada revealed that people with disabilities are at a significantly greater risk for anxiety and depression (Turner & McLean, 1989). The prevalence of major depressive disorder was almost four times higher for disabled people than for a comparison sample, and more symptoms of anxiety and depression were reported by people with disabilities regardless of sex or age.

Another study obtained a statewide random sample of 4,745 disabled and nondisabled adults over 17 years of age residing in Colorado and divided them into 5 categories based on the level of dependency and its invasiveness (in the person's life): (a) no disability; (b) disability but no dependency; (c) mildly invasive disability, some dependency; (d) moderately invasive disability, moderate dependency; and (e) severely invasive disability, high dependency (Tweed, Shern, & Ciarlo, 1988). Subjects completed the Center for Epidemiological Studies Depression Scale (Radloff, 1977), which was used to assess demoralization, and their suicidal ideation was assessed by the question "Has there ever been a period of two weeks or more when you felt like you *wanted to die?*"

The results are presented in Table 9.1-1. There is a clear relationship between the degree of disability/invasiveness and both demoralization—low self-esteem, helplessness, hopelessness, and sadness—and suicidal ideation. In short, the more dependent people are, the more demoralized they are. Just having an impairment raises one's risk for emotional and personality problems and can result in demoralization and even the wish to die.

Emotional and personality functioning can also be affected by a reaction to the reactions of others. Asch (1984) reviewed the research on people's reactions toward people with disabilities and concluded:

> *The presence of someone who actually is or is thought to be disabled arouses in the nonhandicapped person a variety of emotions that, at the very least, hinder ordinary social interaction. Nonhandicapped people prefer to avoid social contact with the disabled or behave more formally and in distorted ways if they are forced to interact with handicapped persons (p. 532).*

Disabled people would, of course, be aware of such distortions in social contact. So they have to deal not only with their own emotional response to their disability but also to the distorted reactions of others.

The third way that emotional and personality functioning can be affected is through direct injury to the CNS. Damage to the limbic system or hypothalamus impairs the mediation of emotional states, whereas damage to the frontal lobes often alters personality. In limbic system damage, emotions may be poorly integrated with reality, erratic, and inconsistent. Damage to the frontal lobes can lead to either **deregulation of behavior**, with spontaneous and not-well-coordinated responses and outbursts of emotion and behavior, or to **deactivation of behavior**, with little emotional responsiveness and lethargy. In either case, the ability to engage in social relationships will be impaired.

Table 9.1-1 THE RELATIONSHIP BETWEEN DISABILITY, DEPENDENCY, DEMORALIZATION, AND SUICIDAL IDEATION IN BOTH MALES AND FEMALES*

	MEAN DEMORALIZATION SCORE	EXPERIENCED PERIOD WHEN WANTED TO DIE	EVER ATTEMPTED SUICIDE
No disability	5.6	6.6%	3.5%
Disability with			
No dependency	9.2	10.8%	5.6%
Mild dependency	11.7	12.3%	7.5%
Moderate dependency	13.3	16.1%	2.4%
Severe dependency	17.8	25.0%	4.7%

Females had consistently and significantly higher demoralization scores than males.

Source: Adapted from Tweed, D. L., Shern, D. L., and Ciarlo, J. A., 1988, Disability, dependency, and demoralization, Rehabilitation Psychology, 33, 143–154.

Table 9.1-2   CATEGORIZATION OF PHYSICAL DEFECTS AND THEIR EMOTIONAL SIGNIFICANCE

Minor impairments such as scoliosis (curvature of the spine), hairlip, protruding ears, or poor eyesight, which can usually be corrected or compensated for, may affect self-concept in a minor way.

Moderate impairments include visible defects that continue as impairments such as the absence or malformation of a limb, paraplegia (loss of the use of the lower limbs), and neuromuscular diseases. People in this category may actually have fewer emotional problems than those with minor impairments, presumably due to the fact that the limits of the impairment are known and that there is maintenance of functioning in other areas. Individuals who overcome their impairment to make extraordinary achievements, such as Lord Byron, who swam the Hellespont with a club foot, or Sam Millsap, who held the national 75-yard dash record even though he was blind, are found in this category (Krueger, 1984).

Severe Impairments like quadriplegia (loss of the use of the lower and upper limbs), extensive brain damage, or extensive burns usually require major rehabilitation efforts, despite which only limited recovery is possible. The impairment becomes a major defining characteristic of life, and few ever rise to make extraordinary achievements.

Source: From Castelnuovo-Tedesco, P., 1981, The psychological consequences of physical trauma and defects, International Review of Psychoanalysis, 8, 145–154.

Physical defects can be categorized according to their emotional significance (see Table 9.1-2). Generally, the more severe the impairment, the more significant the emotional response. However, people with moderate impairments may actually have *fewer* emotional problems and be motivated by their difficulties to go on and have extraordinary accomplishments in life.

The recovery of emotional functioning and adjustment to a new limitation may depend on several factors, including the stage of development at the time of the impairment, the extent of physical disfigurement, and pre-existing personality adjustment (see Table 9.1-3). Generally, individuals who are older, have more emotional stability, and have more developmental maturity cope better with the emotional reactions (Krueger, 1984).

SOCIAL FUNCTIONING   Given the important role of social support in health, and the possibility that it buffers stress, social functioning is of special importance for people with disabilities. An individual's ability to function socially is affected by his or her physical mobility, intellect, emotionality, and personality, any of which may be impaired. Therefore, careful assessment of

Table 9.1-3 **Factors that Affect the Recovery of Emotional Functioning and Adjustment to a New Limitation**

Time of acquisition relative to the place in the developmental cycle (see below).

Size and location of impairment, relating to the categories of minor, moderate, and severe.

Effect on general health because the more organ systems there are involved, the more difficult the adjustment.

Internal/external location, which has to do with whether damage is visible or not and the loss or addition of body parts. Generally, the more physically disfiguring, the more difficult the emotional adjustment.

Predictability/unpredictability of the cause or process. Predictability is generally more favorable in outcome.

Nature and recall of the trauma, whether or not it is remembered and to whom blame is attributed.

Pre-existing personality psychopathology, emotional stability, maturity, and adjustment all affect outcome.

Preceding loses that may compound the new loss.

Source: Identified by Castelnuovo-Tedesco, 1981, and condensed here.

these three categories helps predict future social functioning and suggests possible intervention strategies.

A recent study of 100 men and 40 women with spinal cord injuries found that the amount of social support was positively related to life satisfaction and physical well-being (Rintala, Young, Hart, Clearman, & Fuhrer, 1992). Social support was defined as the individual's judgment about the availability or actual provision of resources—whether tangible, informational, or emotional—through interactions with other people.

A Life Span Perspective on Disabling Conditions

Impairments occur within the context of life span development and may have different affects, depending on the particular stage of development (Smyer et al., 1988).

CHILDHOOD

DEVELOPMENTAL IMPAIRMENTS   A developmental impairment is one that is evident very early in childhood, and it often has an identifiable genetic or environmental cause. An example of a genetic developmental impairment is phenylketonuria, in which the absence of an enzyme allows the build-up of toxic levels of an amino acid that damages the CNS and causes mental retardation. While the mental retardation cannot be cured, it can be prevented by a special diet that is low in phenylalanine, but this requires swift medical diagnosis and intervention.

Examples of environmental causes of developmental impairments are fetal alcohol syndrome and malnutrition. There is usually no cure for the underlying cause of the impairment, and resulting physical and brain abnormalities can affect the individual's future growth and development (see Table 5.1-1, page 168). The range and diversity of developmentally impairing conditions is quite extensive. They include asthma, autism, cerebral palsy, epilepsy, sensory impairments, attention deficit disorder with hyperactivity, learning disabilities, mental retardation, and musculoskeletal disorders.

The issue with developmental impairments is how to help the individual achieve the maximal level of functioning. The primary goal is habilitation, rather than rehabilitation. One physically impairing condition is *cerebral palsy*, a nonprogressive disorder of motion and posture resulting from early brain damage (prenatal to 5 years of age; Vining, Accardo, Rubenstein, Farrell, & Roizen, 1976). The frequency of mental retardation may be as high as 50% to 70% in individuals with cerebral palsy. However, there is some doubt as to the accuracy of these estimates (Alexander & Bauer, 1988), and probably the majority of people with cerebral palsy are *not* retarded. There are language and cognitive deficits, but these may be due to basic motor problems and difficulty coping in a classroom. Although many are not retarded, all people with cerebral palsy have motor and postural problems.

Habilitation in cerebral palsy primarily focuses on promoting mobility. Some medications, physical therapy, and early surgical interventions are beneficial, and assistive devices usually allow successful movement through space. An important component involves the child's educational and social development. Special services such as occupational and speech therapy are sometimes necessary adjuncts to the academic program. In particular, individual and family counseling are recommended. Family therapy may be beneficial when the child is as young as three years of age, with individual counseling becoming important during adolescence (Alexander & Bauer, 1988). Family therapy helps people deal with their guilt and learn how to cope with an impaired family member.

An example of a condition that primarily affects intellectual functioning is *mental retardation*. A standard definition of mental retardation has been difficult to establish, which should not be surprising since intelligence is partly socially and culturally defined to begin with (Tyson & Favell, 1988). However, the American Association on Mental Deficiency has provided a definition that is widely used:

> *Mental retardation refers to significantly subaverage general intellectual functioning resulting in or associated with impairments in adaptive behavior and manifested during the developmental period (Grossman, 1983, p. 1)*

This definition involves three criteria that must be considered together to reach a diagnosis: (a) a low level of intelligence, usually defined as an IQ below 70 points; (b) impairment of adaptive behavior, usually moderate to severe limitations in ADLs; and (c) impairment beginning before 18 years of age. Only when all of these conditions are met is a diagnosis of mental retardation made (Sattler, 1988). Based on this definition, the prevalence rate of mental retardation is about 1% of the population, or about 2½ million people (Tyson & Favell, 1988).

Intervention in mental retardation involves early detection and an intensive focus on education. With the passage of The Education for All Handicapped Children Act in 1975, it was mandated that even the most mentally impaired children receive a free and appropriate education in the least restrictive environment. Bricker and Bricker (1971) first proposed that mentally impaired and nonimpaired children should be educated in the same setting, an idea called *mainstreaming*. It was suspected that educational expectations, and thus ultimately performance, might be lowered if mentally retarded children were segregated.

Others worry that mainstreaming might be harmful to both groups, but some research suggests that it is not harmful (Peck & Cooke, 1983). There are very few adequately conducted studies available on which to judge whether or not mentally impaired children do better when they are mainstreamed. But there are some drawbacks to mainstreaming. First, regular classroom teachers are not as favorably inclined toward mentally retarded children as special education teachers are (Tyson & Favell, 1988). Second, mentally retarded children usually require education in ADLs (self-help, grooming, socialization, language), which are not taught in mainstream classrooms. Third, most regular classroom teachers lack the expertise, resources, and time to handle mentally retarded children. Therefore, mainstreaming may be appropriate for only the most mildly retarded children.

ACQUIRED IMPAIRMENTS   Acquired impairments usually result from injury or infection. As mentioned in Module 5.1, accidents are the primary cause of death in children under 15 years of age, and children are involved in numerous poisonings, falls, and auto accidents that can cause permanent impairments. Also, child abuse may account for 10% to 15% of all trauma cases in children under the age of 3 who are seen in emergency rooms (Kempe, 1971). Child abuse can cause fractures of the bones of the limbs and skull, and it can result in permanent brain damage (Cone, 1988).

It was estimated in the 1960s that more than 1 million U.S. children sustained a head injury each year, and there is no reason to doubt the same rate now (Boll & Barth, 1981). Head injury often results in brain damage and epilepsy (Boll & Barth, 1981). In addition to accidents, infection and brain tumors can occur at any age and result in the loss of physical or intellectual functioning. Tumors do occur in children; however, in contrast to adults, two-thirds of them are located at the base of the brain rather than in the cortex (Boll & Barth, 1981).

The age of onset is a particularly critical variable. When acquired impairments occur in childhood, they affect the individual's future growth and development by exerting an organizing influence on development (Niederland, 1965). Physical impairments that are acquired early may give rise to unresolved conflicts and distortions of body image and self-image (Krueger, 1984).

The goal is to help the child acquire function, both physically and emotionally. However, in contrast to developmental impairments, the older a child is and the more normal development and learning has occurred before the impairment is acquired, the more the goal becomes to help the child *maintain* function—that is, rehabilitation instead of habilitation. One of the most important influences on the child's perception of an impairment is the attitude of his or her parents, especially the mother, toward the impairment (Lussier, 1980). Maricela's mother was initially highly anxious, which made Maricela anxious about her future, too.

An impairment occurring early in life allows more time to learn how to cope with it. By adulthood the individual would have had many experiences to help build a repertoire of coping behaviors and self-efficacy. In fact, people whose impairment occurs before the age of 20 report greater satisfaction with their lives than those whose impairment occurs during middle age (Mehnert, Kraus, Nadler, & Boyd, 1990). This suggests that, because she is young, Maricela's prognosis for adjustment is good.

ADULTHOOD

Accidental injuries, heart disease, cancer, and stroke are all causes of brain damage and physical impairments in adults. In addition, adults are vulnerable to some of the same infections of the brain as children and to other infections, such as sexually transmitted diseases like syphilis and AIDS, that can also affect the brain. Adult rehabilitation always involves the maintenance of acquired functioning; otherwise, it differs little from rehabilitation in childhood. An impairment that occurs at 30 or 40 years of age will probably have a more extensive impact on the course of one's career and lifestyle than if it occurs at 60 years of age.

LATER ADULTHOOD

ACQUIRED IMPAIRMENTS   A major developmental issue in older adult-hood is separating the changes that occur with normal aging from acquired impairments and degenerative conditions (the subject of the next section). After age 30, people loose as many as 100,000 neurons a day. That can add up, but it is still a minuscule loss when estimates of the number of neurons in the CNS run to 180 billion. Whether the loss of neurons has any functional signif-icance is not clearly established (Larue & Jarvik, 1982). However, there are normal aging processes (described in Module 5.1) that must be taken into con-sideration in any assessment of a newly acquired impairment.

When older adults acquire an impairment, the goals of rehabilitation are often more limited than in children or younger adults. For example, there is no need to prepare someone for re-entry to the work force if they are already retired. Sometimes older people were already semidependent, perhaps living in special retirement communities or living independently with some assis-tance from family members. They may already have accepted a certain level of dependency, so it may not be a major rehabilitation issue.

DEGENERATIVE CONDITIONS   People often think of degenerative con-ditions as occurring later in life, but some actually occur quite early. For example, muscular dystrophy, a progressive muscle disorder, begins in child-hood, and multiple sclerosis, a slowly progressive disease in which the myelin sheath of neurons in the CNS is gradually destroyed, usually begins during the decades of the 20s and 30s.

For those over 40 years of age, there are two degenerative conditions that occur with some frequency. The first and most widespread is osteoarthritis, which results in physical but not intellectual impairment (see Module 5.1). Physical therapy can be effective in slowing the progression of osteoarthritis.

The second degenerative condition is **dementia**, which is one of the most fear provoking of all problems related to aging, primarily because it represents a serious impairment of intellectual functioning. Two of the most common types are Alzheimer's disease and multi-infarct dementia. *Alzheimer's disease* results from an extensive loss of neurons from the cortex and other brain areas. Its cause is unknown. It usually begins between 50 and 70 years of age, and the earliest symptom is memory loss. Deterioration is usually rapid, with the per-son becoming totally incapacitated within two to three years. *Multi-infarct dementia* refers to the occurrence of numerous small strokes over a period of years. Some may have gone unnoticed; however, the accumulation of brain damage leads to a gradual deterioration of intellectual functioning. Multi-infarct dementia usually is not evident until the decade of the 70s. It is associ-ated with hypertension, although it can also occur in its absence.

Rehabilitation goals in dementia are usually limited because of its pro-gressive nature. Most of the attention is focused on family members who must provide the care. In the case of dementia, attending to the well-being of the patient also includes the well-being of the family. The stress involved in caring for a disabled person is enormous, especially when the person may not even be aware of the efforts involved, as in Alzheimer's disease (Kiecolt-Glaser, Dyar, & Shuttleworth, 1988; Schulz, Tompkins, Wood, & Decker, 1987; Zarski, West, DePompei, & Hall, 1988).

LIVING WITH DISABILITY

ATTITUDES TOWARD PEOPLE WITH DISABILITIES

People believe that someone who has an impairment in one area is probably inadequate in other areas, too, so disability is perceived as related to global intellectual and psychological dysfunction (Wright, 1960). This view was substantiated in a series of studies of the general public's attitudes toward disabled people (Siller, Chipman, Ferguson, & Vann, 1967). Disability was found to negatively affect people's appraisals of the emotional status and the *character* of disabled people.

People also have unpleasant feelings and anxiety about their own vulnerability, which causes them to reject interpersonal interactions with disabled people. In 1984, the American Psychological Association's Task Force on Psychology and the Handicapped reported that discrimination resulting from nondisabled people's attitudes, "particularly with respect to expected but imaginary problems" (p. 548), creates more difficulties for disabled people than their physical impairment. That statement is worth pondering.

One study found that college students hold similar negative appraisals of disabled people but added an interesting twist (Fichten, Robillard, Judd, & Amsel, 1989). This study also examined the appraisals of two groups of people with disabilities—visually impaired students and wheelchair-using students—toward people with disabilities. The two disabled groups were comfortable with both nondisabled students and students with their own disability. However, they were just as uncomfortable as nondisabled students with students who had a *different* disability. This is consistent with another study that found that people with disabilities who felt a strong identity with others who had disabling conditions were *less* satisfied with their lives than people with disabilities who did not (Mehnert et al., 1990).

Traditionally, studies of attitudes toward people with disabilities relied on a unidimensional approach with a single dimension of acceptance or rejection (for example, Yuker, Block, & Young, 1966). Other studies have used a multidimensional approach that holds that attitudes toward disabled people are composed of more than one underlying dimension (for example, Siller et al., 1967). Using this multidimensional approach, Gordon, Minnes, and Holden (1990) examined the attitudes of 259 university students in various health-related fields on the *Disability Social Relationship* scale (Grand, Bernier, & Strohmer, 1982). They found that attitudes about disabled people varied depending on the type of impairment (amputee, visually impaired, cerebral palsy, and epilepsy) *and* the specific social situation (work, dating, and marriage).

Their results are depicted in Figure 9.1-1. Overall, epilepsy had the highest mean acceptance, followed by visual impairment, amputation, and cerebral palsy, which had the lowest. However, as Figure 9.1-1 reveals, the social situation also had an effect. All types of impairment had higher mean acceptance scores in the work setting. People are more uncomfortable with disability in more intimate relationships.

Although federal legislation mandates that hiring decisions must be based on qualifications and not on other factors such as race, gender, or disability, negative appraisals of disabled people might produce hiring bias. A study by Bordieri and Drehmer (1988) evaluated the hiring recommendations of 125 subjects, all of whom were undergraduate seniors majoring in business. The subjects were given similar cover letters and identical resumes from a hypo-

Figure 9.1-1   **MEAN ACCEPTANCE OF TYPE OF DISABILITY IN DIFFERENT SETTINGS**

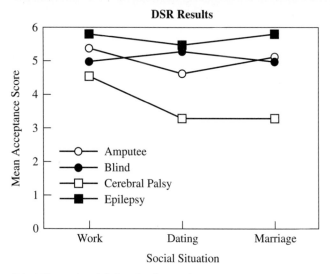

Disability and social situation interaction
on the mean acceptance ratings.

Source: Gordon, E. D., Minnes, P. M., & Holden, A. R., 1990, The structure of attitudes toward persons with a disability when specific disability and context are considered, Rehabilitation Psychology, 35, 79-90.

thetical male applicant for a position as a system analyst with a management consulting firm. The cover letters were manipulated only to briefly mention a specific impairment without providing information about functioning. The following impairments were used: Kidney disease, learning disability, colon cancer, cerebral palsy, paraplegia, auditory impairment, arm amputation, drug dependency, and emotional disorder. The subjects' hiring recommendations were then analyzed.

First, the applicants' qualifications did significantly influence hiring recommendations—better qualified individuals were more likely to be hired. However, another factor also significantly influenced hiring recommendations, but it was not just based on the type of disability. Instead, judgments concerning the *blame* for the impairment affected hiring recommendations. The more the applicant was seen as personally responsible for his or her disability, the lower the hiring recommendation. The subjects attributed the highest personal responsibility to emotional disorder and drug dependency and the lowest to cerebral palsy, paraplegia, and auditory impairment. The only disability type that had a consistently negative impact on hiring was cancer, which was probably because subjects did not expect people with cancer to live long.

DISABILITY AND LIFE SATISFACTION

Recently, a stratified random sample of 675 working age (16 to 64) Americans with disabling conditions was surveyed to determine the relationship between several variables and their satisfaction with life (Mehnert et al., 1990). The respondents were classified according to type of impairment: Physical (45%), sensory (13%), mental (9%), or other health problem such as heart disease, cancer, and so on (20%). Because of the careful sampling methods employed by the researchers, these percentages probably reflect the relative prevalence of these four impairment categories among people of working age who have a disability. On the whole, life satisfaction was self-rated as quite high; 68% of the respondents reported that they were somewhat or very satisfied. However, life satisfaction also varied significantly in relation to several variables.

Younger respondents reported the most satisfaction with their lives, and those between 45 and 54 years of age reported the least. People with sensory impairments reported much greater satisfaction, while those with physical and health impairments or those with multiple impairments reported the least. Life satisfaction also varied according to the degree of functional limitation, economic status, and social relationships. Eighty-six percent of those who felt they had minor functional limitations were satisfied compared with only 49% of those who felt they had a severe functional limitation. Both being employed and having a higher household income were associated with greater satisfaction. Finally, fewer of the widowed, separated, or divorced people rated their life as satisfying.

These results suggest that the overwhelming majority of people with disabilities can lead satisfying lives, but that there is a greater chance of being satisfied with life if the impairment occurs earlier rather than later in life. They also suggest that the degree of independence and one's general attitude toward disability affect satisfaction.

MODULE SUMMARY

Here is a quick review of the major points concerning the nature of disability:

1. A disability is an interaction between a person with an impaired function and a handicapping environment.
2. Disability determination involves assessment of physical, intellectual, emotional/personality, and social functioning.
3. Purely physical defects can be categorized in terms of their emotional significance as either minor, moderate, or severe. Individuals with moderate impairments are capable of extraordinary achievements, whereas severe impairments can become a defining characteristic of life.
4. Children are subject to both developmental and acquired impairments. Developmentally impairing conditions include cerebral palsy and mental retardation. Accidents are largely to blame for acquired impairments in children. Intervention during childhood is concerned with habilitation, or the acquisition of abilities.
5. Adults over 45 years of age are primarily vulnerable to acquired impairments from heart disease, cancer, and stroke, which can all result in brain damage.
6. Physical impairments are quite common in adults over 65 years of age. Assessment must take into account the normal changes related to age in determining the extent of impairment from newly acquired conditions. Although degenerative conditions can occur at younger ages, they are usually associated with advanced age. They include osteoarthritis, a physical condition, and dementia, a mental impairment.
7. Attitudes toward people with impairments are generally negative, and even people who are impaired themselves hold negative attitudes toward others with different impairments.
8. Although affected by a variety of variables, a large percentage of people with impairments rate their life satisfaction quite high.

Rehabilitation

Rehabilitation and the Role of Psychologists

The role of psychologists in rehabilitation has been recognized in two landmark federal initiatives: The Rehabilitation Act of 1973 and The Education for All Handicapped Children Act of 1983 (DeLeon et al., 1986). These acts mandate and provide funding for rehabilitation and educational programs for disabled people of all ages. They are important because they specifically include psychological services and because they include provision for comprehensive counseling and social, vocational, educational and mental services.

Rehabilitation itself is one of the fastest growing areas of health care, and psychologists have become well-established providers of rehabilitation services (Frank, Gluck, & Buckelew, 1990). Three types of psychologists are involved in treating people with disabilities: health psychologists, rehabilitation psychologists, and neuropsychologists.

Health Psychology

Health psychologists are involved with research that affects people with disabilities. Many of the diseases and traumas that cause disabling conditions have been a focus of health psychology research for a long time. Health enhancement and disease prevention, two very important areas of current research, are particularly important to people with disabilities who may be more vulnerable to illness or injury (USDHHS, 1992).

Rehabilitation Psychology

Rehabilitation psychologists research attitudes toward disability, as well as ways in which people with a disability adjust, but they are primarily concerned with intervention. Their goal is to facilitate the impaired person's adjustment by learning how to maximize functioning within new limitations. In the clinic and hospital, rehabilitation psychologists assess and treat the psychological—

largely emotional—consequences of impairment. Most rehabilitation psychologists—about 60%—were trained as clinical psychologists (Parker & Chan, 1990). Rehabilitation represents a particularly challenging clinical arena. The emotions felt over the loss of a limb or motor function have been likened to grief over the death of a loved one (Krueger, 1984).

STAGES OF PSYCHOLOGICAL RECOVERY Krueger (1981–1982) has defined the stages involved in the process of making a healthy psychological adjustment to physical trauma and disability. He maintains that the typical patient will go through them all, although not necessarily in order. These stages provide a framework for understanding the process of recovery and the role of the rehabilitation psychologist when assessing or treating a patient. Krueger's five stages are shock, denial, depression, reaction against independence, and adaptation.

Shock is an overwhelming time when the patient is not usually integrating incoming stimuli and may be in a state of numbness. This is followed by *denial*. It is difficult for the person to accept that a physical impairment may be permanent. This is often expressed in the belief that recovery will be complete, and patients may hang on to anecdotes about how doctors underestimated a similar patient's full recovery. They sometimes take a doctor's statements apart word-by-word, looking for anything that will support their belief in a complete recovery. The fact that most diagnoses and prognoses are phrased in probabilistic terms can unintentionally support denial and false hopes. Nevertheless, denial is actually a necessary and healthy defense mechanism during the early stages of recovery. The more people believe in their recovery, the harder they tend to work at rehabilitation. Denial may last up to several weeks, but eventually reality begins to intrude. Rather than a major breakthrough, however, periods of reality begin to alternate with denial (Horowitz & Kaltreider, 1977). Because denial can be beneficial and reality will eventually assert itself anyway, denial is not usually treated unless it interferes with rehabilitation itself (Krueger, 1984).

Brian's denial was shattered by his fiancée's reassessment of their pending marriage on hearing that he would probably not walk again without assistance. She had been attracted to Brian's vigorous and active lifestyle and could not bear to imagine him as an "invalid, stuck in a wheelchair." Also, his financial stability was in doubt for his career as a police officer, which depends on physical mobility, was probably over, too.

Depression follows denial as reality takes hold. It certainly did for Brian, and it also did for Maricela. Maricela and her family were most concerned about her cognitive abilities and future education. Depression signals the recognition, but not acceptance, of the loss. It is a normal grief process that may, for a time, slow rehabilitation. This is the stage at which psychological intervention becomes more active. The absence of even a brief depression may be a warning that the person is not recognizing the loss emotionally (Krueger, 1984). However, it is necessary to recognize that the depression and feelings of anxiety, sadness, and anger of people with disabilities are reality based and not psychological disorders (Steiger, 1976). A feeling of helplessness is realistic, at least for a time. This may lead to inappropriate expressions of hostility toward caregivers and family, or it may be appropriately channeled into rehabilitation. As the depression is dealt with and the new limitations are accepted, rehabilitation can proceed toward achieving maximal functioning.

Eventually, as gains are made in rehabilitation, the patient approaches independence. That is when *reaction against independence* is likely to occur. This may be expressed only as ambivalence about leaving the sheltered rehabilitation environment, or there may actually be attempts to slow one's progress in rehabilitation. Finally, as discharge approaches and, even beyond that, as more independent living begins, *adaptation* takes place. Adaptation depends on resolution of the depression and helplessness, realistic expectations about one's limitations, and the development of new coping strategies (Krueger, 1984). Wright (1984) suggests that caregivers must recognize the individuality of people with disabilities, but that the consistent emphasis must be on an active as opposed to a passive patient role.

TREATMENT In rehabilitation, the intervention depends on the extent of impairment: whether it affects only the body, only the CNS, or both. Strictly physical impairments will primarily affect activities of daily living. Rehabilitation goals will include recovery and maintenance of physical functioning and dealing with the emotional reactions. Physical and occupational therapy along with psychotherapy are typically involved. Impairments that result from brain or spinal cord injury pose a more complex challenge for rehabilitation. Physical, intellectual, and personality functioning may be affected, and the goals will involve rehabilitation and maintenance of all three functions. Physical and occupational therapy, psychotherapy, and cognitive therapy may all be involved. Prognosis for recovery is very much determined by the extent of neuropsychological impairment and the highest level of premorbid functioning—that is, functioning before the illness or injury. These topics will be covered in the section on "Neuropsychology." First let's return to Brian's case, in which the spinal cord injury did not affect his brain.

People with spinal cord injuries have a significantly higher rate of death compared to members of the general population of the same age, and research suggests that better self-care could prevent many of these deaths. About 8% to 18% of all deaths in spinal-cord injured people might be due to suicide, and an additional 16% of deaths might be due to substance abuse or personal neglect (Nyquist & Bors, 1967; Wilcox & Stauffer, 1972).

An 11-year longitudinal study of the survival of people with spinal cord injury examined the high level of deaths, called "psychological suicides" (Krause & Crewe, 1987). Several variables were related to long-term survival: psychosocial and vocational adjustment, being socially active, having a greater tolerance for sitting, and working or attending school. The researchers concluded that there is a need for intensive psychological rehabilitation for spinal-cord injured people, with a particular emphasis on social skills training.

Brian's case illustrates the importance of these variables. Psychological intervention was focused on two goals: social adjustment and vocational adjustment. The former was attained by encouraging his friends and cowork-ers to visit the hospital and become involved with his rehabilitation from the beginning. Of course, there was a self-selection process, and those who could best deal with his disability became most actively involved. Fortunately, Brian had a large social support network, so many friends remained involved. He worked out his reactions to this social reintegration, the ups and downs, in individual counseling. Additional individual counseling with his friends helped them learn to interact with him on a realistic basis that took into account his issues with dependence and independence.

Brian's vocational adjustment involved assessing what he could do as well as what he wanted to do. Obviously, he could not return to field work as a police officer. However, as he accepted his limitations and became active in his rehabilitation, his coworkers began to lobby for his retention on the police force. Eventually, he was offered a desk job in the station where he could be productive and remain in the same supportive social network. This required some effort on the part of the department to overcome architectural barriers, but the work was done, and Brian returned to work about six months after the injury.

Emotionally, physical impairments are more traumatic for people whose esteem and lifestyle are focused on physical activities, whereas intellectual impairments are more traumatic for people like Maricela whose esteem and lifestyle are oriented toward intellectual functioning (Krueger, 1984). The next section on neuropsychology focuses on the rehabilitation of intellectually impaired individuals.

NEUROPSYCHOLOGY

Neuropsychology is the study of brain behavior relationships. Neuropsychologists research normal brain development and function from the level of the individual neuron to the level of the whole brain. Clinical neuropsychologists

Clinical neuropsychologists use standardized psychological measures of cognitive functions to help plan a rehabilitation strategy.

research what happens if there is a disruption of normal development or function and how to rehabilitate people with brain impairments. In the clinic, neuropsychologists work primarily with individuals who have suffered some degree of damage to the brain and spinal cord. They assess impairments, evaluate how impairments affect an individual's functioning, and plan habilitation and rehabilitation programs (Barry & O'Leary, 1989). With improved emergency medical care, more people are surviving major traumatic accidents with brain damage (Kreutzer, Gordon, & Wehman, 1989). However, these survivors often face long-term unemployment and dependency after the accident.

Therefore, there is great interest in the new field of cognitive rehabilitation. **Cognitive rehabilitation** is a diverse set of interventions designed to remediate the effects of brain damage on intellectual, behavioral, and personality functioning (Kreutzer et al., 1989). Neuropsychologists typically provide the leadership role in planning and evaluating cognitive rehabilitation programs. They are usually carried out by a multidisciplinary team consisting of physical therapists, occupational therapists, speech/language therapists, and neuropsychologists. Although cognitive rehabilitation is a promising approach to reduce the effects of brain damage on future functioning, there is currently little evidence that it is effective (Kreutzer et al., 1989).

Researchers are looking for ways to stimulate regrowth of damaged CNS neurons which do not regenerate. In the absence of regeneration, there remains only the natural processes of recovery of function and what might be gained from cognitive rehabilitation.

The natural recovery of intellectual functioning after brain damage is related to several variables: location, extent, and type of injury, as well as the age of onset and premorbid personality (see Table 9.2-1). Neuropsychologists use these variables to assess each individual and determine a prognosis.

Table 9.2-1	VARIABLES AFFECTING THE RECOVERY OF INTELLECTUAL FUNCTIONING AFTER BRAIN DAMAGE

Location of the lesion has to do with what area of the brain is damaged. The specific intellectual processes that are impaired depend on the area of the brain involved and whether or not other areas can substitute.

Extent of the lesion has to do with how much of the brain is damaged. Some insults produce limited damage, whereas others can cause diffuse damage. Generally, the more diffuse the damage, the poorer the prognosis.

Type of insult/injury refers to the difference between a discrete event or an ongoing, progressive process. Traumas are categorized as discrete events, whereas infections and tumors of the brain may remain from days to years and either progress or remain static.

Age at onset is a very important variable affecting neuropsychological prognosis and rehabilitation. Generally, the end of the primary grades, which is about 12 years of age and the beginning of puberty, is a crucial dividing line. The primary grades are the period of acquisition. During acquisition, the basic skills such as language, communication, and math are developed, and factual knowledge, such as the months of the year and how to tell time, is learned. The major issue for rehabilitation before the age of 13 is disruption in the acquisition of skills and knowledge. However, although acquisition may be disrupted if injury occurs during that time, the brain has more "plasticity" then, too. **Plasticity**, which refers to the ability of one area of the brain to substitute for another, is assumed to be greatest before the age of 13 (Boll & Barth, 1981; Filskov, Grimm, & Lewis, 1981). After the period of acquisition, the issue becomes one of maintaining past learned skills and knowledge. There is less plasticity to aid in the process of substitution, but there is also a foundation from prior learning that may be built upon.

Personality before the injury is the last variable related to recovery. Changes in emotional functioning are imposed on a pre-existing personality. For example, if disinhibition is a result of the damage, then we might expect that the person's pre-existing personality traits will be amplified.

Source: Reitan, R. M., Davison, L. A., 1974, Clinical neuropsychology: Current status and applications, *Washington, DC: V. H. Winston & Sons; Smith, A., 1981, Principles underlying human brain functions in neuropsychological sequelae of different neuropathological processes. In S. B. Filskov & T. J. Boll (Eds.), Handbook of clinical neuropsychology, pp. 175–226, New York: John Wiley & Sons.*

Cognitive rehabilitation depends on two neuropsychological principles: *substitution* and *compensation*. **Substitution of function** has a basis in the structure of the brain itself. It occurs when an adjacent or similar area of the cortex substitutes for a damaged area, enabling a prior learned skill or ability controlled by the damaged area still to be carried out. Substitution of function is not possible for the so-called "hard-wired" brain areas. Hard-wiring refers to the fact that the neurons in some areas of the brain are dedicated to a specific activity. The most hard-wired areas include: (a) the motor strip, (b) the somatosensory strip, and (c) the midbrain and hindbrain. There is usually no substitution for a skill or ability lost because of damage to one of these areas. For example, if paralysis of the left arm results from damage to the right motor strip, even though the arm is in perfect physical condition, the paralysis will be permanent.

Substitution is more likely to occur for the soft-wired areas of the brain. These include the prefrontal lobes and the juncture of the parietal, occipital, and temporal lobes sometimes referred to as "association cortex." Substitution is also more likely to occur in a younger as opposed to an older brain.

Compensation is a conscious process in which a new sequence is learned to replace an old one. It relies on regaining a previous function by developing new *skills* to replace those that the impaired individual is no longer capable of performing. Functions are broken down into a set of specific skills or abilities. If a person is no longer able to perform a certain function, the skills that comprise it are analyzed to determine which are impaired. Then alternate skills that allow the person to reach the same functional goal are substituted for the impaired ones. The functional goal remains the same, but the route taken to reach the goal is different. Usually, the new route and the new skills are not as efficient as the impaired ones, but they do work. For example, quadriplegics may not be able to type with their hands, but they can, and do, type with a mouth stick. It is slower, but the finished product looks the same.

———

For Maricela, neuropsychological assessment, in addition to determining her impairments and planning her rehabilitation, fulfilled an important treatment function. Her intellectual strengths and her improvements, even from week to week, were emphasized. This helped to relieve her mother's and her own concern about her academic future.

Because the area of the brain damaged by the bleeding was largely subcortical, neuropsychological impairments were limited to some attentional deficits (which were also due to anxiety) and to motor coordination problems. Rehabilitation consisted of cognitive therapy for the attentional deficit (but were also designed to demonstrate her successes and relieve her anxiety). It also consisted of physical therapy for standing and walking and occupational and language therapy for drawing and writing, which were affected by a tremor.

Because of her age, an additional goal in Maricela's treatment was to maintain as normal a process of habilitation as possible. This meant facilitating the acquisition of knowledge that would be taking place during the semester she would miss at school. As part of her therapy, a tutor was engaged to help her maintain normal academic progress.

INDEPENDENCE: THE ONLY GOAL?

How do you think you would have reacted in Brian's or Maricela's situation? Or, how would you react if you were suddenly impaired and could no longer see, speak, or think clearly? At first, you would be more dependent on others. Then, as you adapted and learned new compensatory skills, your independence would once again increase. Traditionally, the ultimate goal of rehabilitation programs has been to increase independence to reach the highest level of independent functioning that a person with an impairment could obtain (Mathews & Seekins, 1987).

However, recently Nancy Kerr and Lee Meyerson (1987) of Arizona State University have questioned such single-mindedness. They caution that rehabilitation efforts sometimes stress independence to such an extent that dependency becomes stigmatized, and they suggest that some degree of dependency may actually be adaptive. They believe that individuals, and not just people with disabilities, participate in a variety of roles and situations with a variety of people, and that sometimes independence is advantageous, and sometimes it is not. Instead, they propose that the ultimate goal of rehabilitation should be flexibility.

Kerr and Meyerson propose that there are four possible behavioral styles, each of which has a healthy aspect and each of which may be advantageous depending on the circumstances. These behavioral styles are dependent, interdependent, dependable, and independent. Dependency may be healthy if it reflects the recognition of one's realistic limits and if the person acknowledges that sometimes relationships with other people who can meet one's needs are necessary.

The behavioral style of interdependence is reflected in mutual cooperation and sharing. It allows for tasks to be divided according to ability so group goals can be met.

As a behavioral style, dependability is highly prized in our culture because dependable people are responsible and can be counted on. Certainly, people with disabilities can be dependable.

Finally, independence involves being in charge of one's life—making decisions and taking responsibility for them. Independent people know they can "go it alone" if necessary. Kerr and Meyerson believe that this behavioral style is a reasonable goal for rehabilitation; however, it has a negative side if it results in a disregard for the needs of others or leads people with disabilities to reject legitimate assistance. Kerr and Meyerson's stress on flexibility reflects a new approach for rehabilitation psychologists.

MODULE SUMMARY

Here is a quick review of the major points concerning rehabilitation:

1. Psychologists are involved with rehabilitation in three capacities—as health psychologists, rehabilitation psychologists, or neuropsychologists. Health psychologists are primarily concerned with research, while rehabilitation and neuropsychologists often provide clinical services.

2. The process of making a healthy psychological adjustment to a newly acquired physical defect involves the stages of shock, denial, depression, reaction against independence, and adaptation.

3. Impairments may be categorized depending on whether they affect only the physical body, only the CNS, or both. The most difficult rehabilitation challenges occur when both are involved.

4. Neuropsychologists are concerned with conditions that affect the functioning of the brain. Recovery of function from brain damage depends on several variables, including the location and extent of the lesion, cause, age, and personality of the patient.

5. Brain damage is permanent, although the resulting impairment of intellectual functions can improve through substitution of function or compensation. Cognitive rehabilitation is an attempt to directly improve intellectual function, although its effectiveness is not proven.

6. Independence should not be the only goal of rehabilitation. In some situations, interdependence and even dependence are desirable.

OTHER PHYSIOLOGICAL SYSTEMS

Health psychologists are also involved with problems that are related to other physiological systems: In Section 2, we examine those that involve the immune, cardiovascular, respiratory, digestive, and reproductive/sexual systems.

10

THE IMMUNE SYSTEM: FUNCTION AND ORGANIZATION

INTRODUCTION

David is a 27-year-old single man who had always thought that he was in per-fect health. A track man in college, he excelled in the hurdles and middle-distance events, and he continued to run just for pleasure. In the past year, however, David's health changed. He noticed that for periods of time he was more tired than usual, and he awoke some nights with profuse sweating that could not be explained. When he got the flu, he was ill weeks longer than he could ever remember. He did not trouble his doctor with any of these symptoms, however, until he broke out with a painful rash of blistering sores on his back.

David had herpes zoster, commonly known as "shingles." Not related to any other form of herpes, it is caused by the same virus that causes chicken pox. Any person who has had chicken pox can develop herpes zoster, but it usually occurs in people with weak immune systems. The virus, which remains dormant in nerve roots for years after the initial disease, is believed to become reacti-vated during a temporary suppression of the immune system. In healthy individ-uals, the outbreak usually lasts less than a week as the immune system quickly answers the threat and subdues its old foe. However, when it persists for two weeks or more in people of David's age, an immunologic defect is suspected.

When David's doctor heard of his other symptoms, he advised the blood test for human immunosuppressive virus (HIV). David had just begun to have some success at work, receiving a promotion to a middle-management posi-tion in a health care firm. He had also just found out that he is infected with

HIV, which inevitably results in Acquired Immune Deficiency Syndrome or AIDS. Never having used drugs, David believes that he contracted HIV through sexual contact.

Initially, he was devastated by the news—he was ready to quit his job and stop living. Fortunately, however, David lives in a large city with a well-established support system for people with HIV infection, and his doctor was able to offer a referral for HIV counseling. Through counseling, an HIV support group, and knowledgeable medical care, David has learned how to live with HIV. He kept his job, and he has remained symptom-free for more than two years. Nevertheless, having a potentially fatal disease has caused him to change his plans, and he now lives his life quite differently.

The immune system is the only one of the body's organ systems that is entirely devoted to its health, well-being, and integrity. AIDS has made us all aware of the fact that we cannot live long without a well-functioning immune system. As David has learned, HIV cripples the immune system, leaving it unable to fight infection. AIDS is presently incurable, although many people do live with it for years.

This introduction to Chapter 10 explains the function and organization of the immune system, which is necessary for an understanding of the biopsychosocial factors in infectious disease (Module 10.1), cancer (Module 10.2) and AIDS (Module 10.3). David's experiences with HIV are described more fully in Module 10.3.

███████

IMMUNE SYSTEM FUNCTIONING

The immune system has several functions. It *recognizes, responds to,* and *remembers* any substance that threatens health, either *foreign* matter (chemical or cellular substances from outside the body) or *malignancies* (from mutations of the body's own cells).

Think of the immune system as a country's armed forces, which protect it against invasion and destruction. The first task of the armed forces is to detect foreign invaders. The immune system also detects foreign invaders, but in order to do this, it must be able to recognize the "self" (the healthy tissues of the body) so as not to destroy them. The immune system is powerful, and it could do irreparable harm if it attacked the body. Occasionally, there is a breakdown in the immune system's ability to recognize the self. This can result in an **autoimmune disorder**, which is like the "friendly fire" that sometimes kills a country's own soldiers during a battle. Lupus, rheumatoid arthritis, and some forms of diabetes and anemia are believed to be autoimmune disorders (Berkow & Fletcher, 1987).

How does the immune system recognize "self"? The surface of every cell has specific physical features that mark it as part of the body—as the "self." Every one of an organism's cells has the same surface features, the same "identity." Any substance with different surface features is recognized as "not self," a foreigner, and triggers an immune response.

Such substances are called **antigens**, and they are often *pathogenic* (cause disease). There are also hundreds of other harmless agents in the environment that sometimes enter the body and trigger an immune response. These are called **allergens** rather than antigens or pathogens. Unfortunately, about 20% of people react with an immunologic response and discomfort to allergens too (Berkow & Fletcher, 1987). Ordinarily, the other 80% of people have no response to allergens, so an allergic response is an overreaction of the immune system. The most common forms of allergy are urticaria (hives), hay fever, and asthma.

THE IMMUNE SYSTEM IN ACTION: RESPONSE TO INJURY OR INFECTION

In this section, we will follow the immune system through a typical response to an antigen, pointing out as we go the components of the body's armed forces and how they operate. Refer to Figure 10.1 for a diagram of the immune system's response to invasion.

INFLAMMATION

Tissue damage or invasion by an antigen triggers the body's first line of defense—a local response called **inflammation.** First there is constriction of blood vessels. This serves to limit invasion of microorganisms and, in the case of injury, to preserve blood and permit a clot to form. Then there is dilation of blood vessels, which results in warmth, redness, and swelling. Meanwhile, damaged cells release enzymes that can destroy some microorganisms, protecting intact cells. These enzymes also help digest any damaged or dysfunctional cells.

CELLULAR RESPONSE

Enzymes are not enough to protect against many antigens. Complete protection involves the body's full armed forces, which are divided into two branches—the cellular and the humoral—that function like an army and navy,

Figure 10.1 THE IMMUNE SYSTEM'S RESPONSE TO INVASION

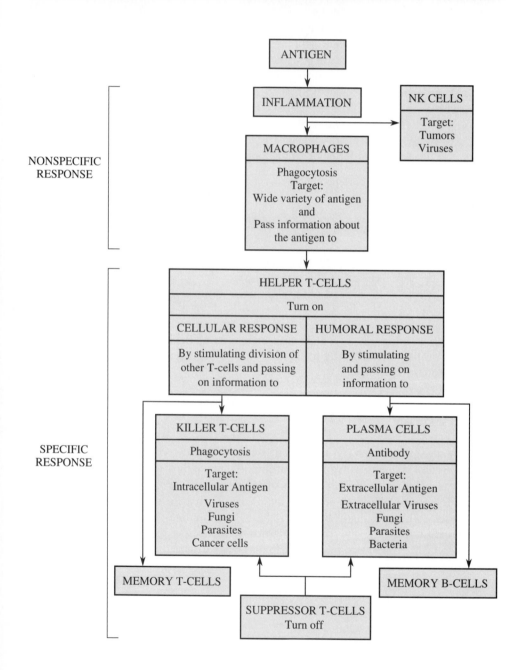

respectively. The **cellular response** involves white blood cells or **leukocytes**. Think of leukocytes as active, mobile soldiers. They can migrate almost anywhere in the body, pass through capillary walls into body tissue, and engulf and destroy invaders through the process known as **phagocytosis**, in which they literally digest the invading cells. One type of leukocyte is the **lymphocyte**, from which lymph derives its name. Lymphocytes can be either nonspecific or specific. Specific lymphocytes target specific invaders, whereas nonspecific lymphocytes attack more general targets.

N O N S P E C I F I C   L Y M P H O C Y T E S   Nonspecific lymphocytes are the foot soldiers in the body's army. They are the frontline troops deployed throughout the body, and they work day in and day out. One type of nonspecific lymphocyte is the **natural killer** (NK) **cell**. NK cells make up about 10% of white cells. They specialize in destroying tumors and viruses, and they will attack any that they encounter. **Macrophages** are another type of nonspecific lymphocyte that specializes in attacking bacteria and cellular debris of any type. NK cells and macrophages are usually the first troops to challenge an invading antigen.

S P E C I F I C   L Y M P H O C Y T E S   Specific lymphocytes are the "elite" troops, which have highly specialized duties. **T-lymphocyte** or T-cells (named for the thymus where they mature) are the primary soldiers in the elite troops. There are several types of T-cells. **Helper T-cells** are part of the army's intelligence corps, and they are the crucial link in the immune response. As the cellular response begins, macrophages that have ingested the antigen offer information about its surface markers, its "identity," to helper T-cells. They use this information to alert the army and to stimulate production of **killer T-cells**—the attack soldiers that destroy the invading antigen. Killer T-cells are the bulk of the army's elite troops. They target specific fungi, parasites, cancer cells, and viruses, even *intracellularly*—that is, after they have invaded other cells in the body.

H U M O R A L   R E S P O N S E

Meanwhile, the **B-lymphocyte** or B-cells (called that because they mature in the **bone marrow**) are involved in the **humoral response**. Think of B-cells as the body's navy, a flotilla of ships that indirectly attack invaders. Also alerted by T-helper cells, B-cells become **plasma cells** and begin to secrete antibody. **Antibody** is a chemical specially made to match the surface features of a particular antigen. Therefore, antibodies might be likened to the guided missiles a ship fires at an enemy. Antibody circulates in the bloodstream and binds to the antigen. When antibody attaches to an antigen, it slows it down and marks it as a target for destruction. Antibody targets *extracellular* antigens such as

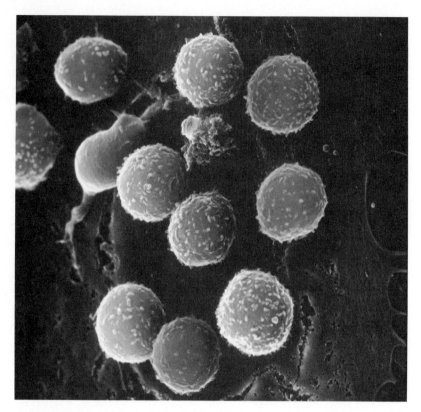

T-lymphocytes attacking a cancer cell

bacteria, fungi, parasites, and viruses (when they are outside a cell). When the antigen is a virus, B-cells also produce **interferon**, a chemical that travels to other cells helping them to better resist viral infection.

As the battle progresses, the action of T-cells helps to attract more macrophages into the fray. Macrophages provide support for the killer T-cells and are involved in the "mopping up" operations, ingesting the debris left after the battle.

SUPPRESSION OF THE IMMUNE RESPONSE

Another part of the army's intelligence corps—**suppressor T-cells**—keeps track of the activity of the antigen and helper T-cells during the battle. When it is won, suppressor T-cells signal the killer T-cells and B-cells to stop the fighting.

THE LYMPHATIC SYSTEM

The lymphatic system may be thought of as the sewer system of the body. Fluid secreted by cells during their normal functioning, as well as debris from damaged cells left after a battle, drain into this vessel network, which is nearly as extensive as the cardiovascular system, reaching every part of the body. Once the fluid and debris enters the vessels, it is called **lymph**.

Ultimately, lymph is returned to the bloodstream. Before it is returned, however, it passes through at least one lymph node. **Lymph nodes** are thickenings of lymph vessels that contain concentrations of leukocytes, which filter foreign material from the lymph. The nodes are concentrated in certain areas of the body such as the neck, armpits, and groin.

OTHER COMPONENTS OF THE IMMUNE SYSTEM

Other components of the immune system include the thymus, the spleen, and the tonsils (see Figure 10.2). The **thymus** is an endocrine gland that lies behind the sternum in the center of the chest cavity. It secrets hormones that help train the T-cells to function against specific pathogens. The function of the thymus is not fully understood, although it is known to have direct neural connections to the brain (Bulloch, 1985), and its removal severely impairs immune system functioning (Marieb, 1989). The **spleen** is located in the left side of the abdominal cavity beneath the diaphragm. The spleen serves as a reservoir for leukocytes while they mature, and blood flowing through the spleen is constantly cleansed of debris and bacteria by macrophages. The **tonsils** are a ring of lymphatic tissue that surrounds the entrance to the pharynx. Its role in the immune system is not well understood, although lymphocytes are known to migrate to the oral cavity from the tonsils.

THE SECONDARY IMMUNE RESPONSE AND IMMUNITY

The immune system response described above is a **primary immune response**—one in which the body has had no prior experience with the antigen. During a primary response, some leukocytes are kept out of the battle, like reserve troops. They become *memory B-cells* instead of plasma cells and *memory T-cells* instead of killer T-cells. Memory T- and B-cells are committed to react to the same antigen in the future. If there is ever reinfection, they are available for an immediate response to it, which would be called a **secondary immune response**. Memory T- and B-cells may remain in circulation for many years and provide the basis for immunity from diseases such as mumps, measles, and chicken pox.

Figure 10.2 COMPONENTS OF THE IMMUNE SYSTEM

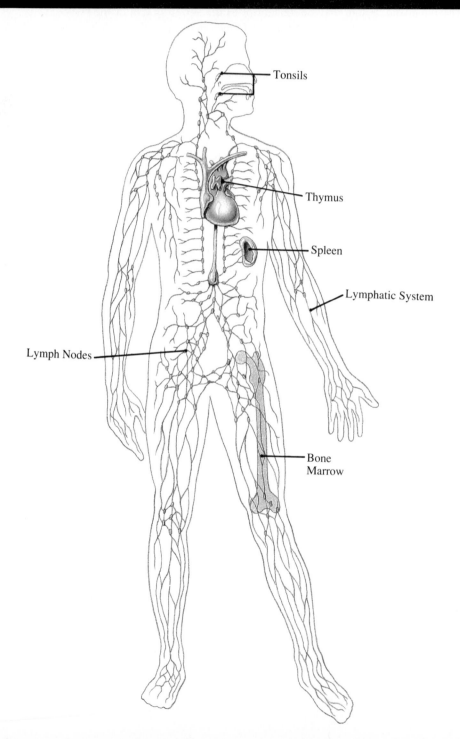

Tonsils

Thymus

Spleen

Lymphatic System

Lymph Nodes

Bone
Marrow

Immunity may also be obtained through inoculation, when a weakened form of a virus is introduced into the body. It cannot cause a complete infection and illness, but the immune system recognizes it as an antigen, and memory cells are manufactured that prevent future disease. This is the process that has been successfully used in polio vaccinations.

PSYCHONEUROIMMUNOLOGY

Current research suggests that psychosocial factors, through their effect on the immune system, may influence immunity and disease processes (Pelletier & Herzing, 1988). **Psychoneuroimmunology** is an interdisciplinary field on the forefront of research into the mind/body relationship as it affects the immune system (Ader, Felton, & Cohen, 1991). It is concerned with relationships among the mind ("psycho"), the nervous and endocrine systems ("neuro"), and the immune system ("immunology"; Vollhardt, 1991). The central hypothesis of psychoneuroimmunology is that the brain coordinates the immune system and that psychosocial factors, through the brain, can influence immune responses.

At first, this might seem farfetched. However, you may have wondered how the complex immune responses we just examined are coordinated. A nation would never send its armed forces into battle without a leader. The people would want to know who is in command, who is the general of the army, who is the admiral of the navy. The brain is the master regulator for most other bodily systems and may fulfill this role for the immune system as well (Schwartz, 1984).

THE ROLE OF THE BRAIN

Connections between the brain and the immune system have been well-demonstrated experimentally in both animals and humans (for example, Blalock, 1989). Surgical damage or removal of tissue in certain areas of the brain results in changes in immune system functioning (Bosedovsky, Sorkin, Felix, & Haas, 1977; Brooks, Cross, Roszman, & Markesbery, 1982; Cross, Brooks, Roszman, & Markesbery, 1982). The hypothalamus, locus ceruleus, and the limbic system are areas of the brain that are most related to immune function. Lesions in certain regions (for example, anterior hypothalamus) result in reductions in the number and function of leukocytes, while lesions to other regions (for example, posterior hypothalamus or hippocampus) result in increases. This suggests that activity in different brain regions can regulate the homeostasis of the immune system by either enhancing or inhibiting it.

The brain can also communicate directly with individual lymphocytes. Lymphocytes have receptor sites on their surfaces for certain hormones and the neurotransmitter catecholamine. Why should lymphocytes, which are not neurons, have receptor sites for a neurotransmitter if not to respond to what is happening in the brain? Furthermore, immunity to infectious agents can be increased or decreased by hormones and neurotransmitters circulating in the bloodstream (Boranic, 1980).

Communication between the brain and the immune system also takes place through the autonomic nervous system. Animal studies have demonstrated that sympathetic nervous system fibers provide a direct link between the brain and the lymph nodes, spleen, and thymus (Felten & Felten, 1991). In rats, the sympathetic nervous system can suppress the immune response through these neural pathways and also by the release of norepinephrine (Bosedovsky, Del Rey, Sorkin, Da Prada, & Keller, 1979; Williams, Peterson, Shea, Schmedtje, Bauer, & Felten, 1981).

Communication between the brain and immune system seems to go in both directions (Blalock, 1989). This communication has been described as "a complete regulatory loop" (Blalock & Smith, 1985, p. 108), which is assumed to take place through activation of hypothalamic-pituitary-adrenal connections (Figure 10.3a). Importantly, this is the same general pathway for the physiological response to stress (see Chapter 6).

The brain receives feedback from hormones and other chemicals produced by lymphocytes and macrophages (Figure 10.3b). When T-cells are active they produce a chemical called interleukin. **Interleukin** helps other T-cells mature into killer T-cells, but it also travels through the bloodstream to the brain, where it affects neurotransmitters and neuroendocrine functions, perhaps providing feedback about T-cell activity. Interferon has also been found to increase the firing rate of neurons in the brain (Hall, 1988).

If the brain is the regulator of immune system function, then what affects the brain might also affect the immune system. In fact, a series of experiments suggests that the immune system is subject to classical conditioning (Kusnecov, King, & Husband, 1989). In the typical animal experiment, rats are randomly assigned either to a conditioned immunosuppression treatment or a placebo group. Both groups are offered a sweet-tasting solution that rats prefer. This is paired with an injection: The immunosuppression group receives a chemical that suppresses part of the cellular immune response, while the control group receives a placebo. Later, when the rats in the immunosuppression group taste the sweet-tasting solution alone, there is a drop in the same cellular immune response, and when they are injected with an antigen, they produce significantly less antibody to it.

Similar experiments have also demonstrated classical conditioning of the cellular branch of the immune system, and more recent experiments have demonstrated that immune system functioning can be enhanced as well as suppressed by conditioning. Classical conditioning is one mechanism whereby

Figure 10.3 **HYPOTHALAMIC-PITUITARY-ADRENAL PATHWAYS FOR IMMUNOLOGIC ACTIVATION**

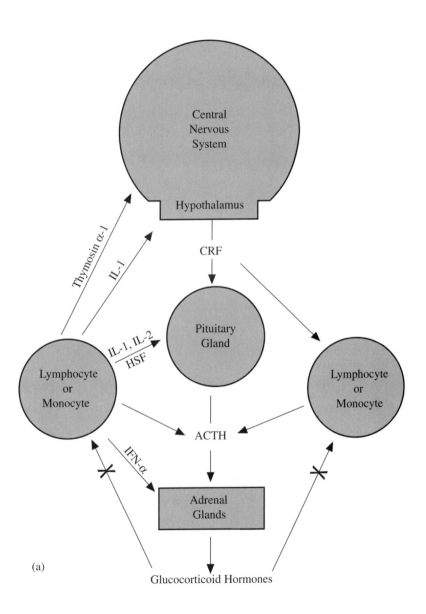

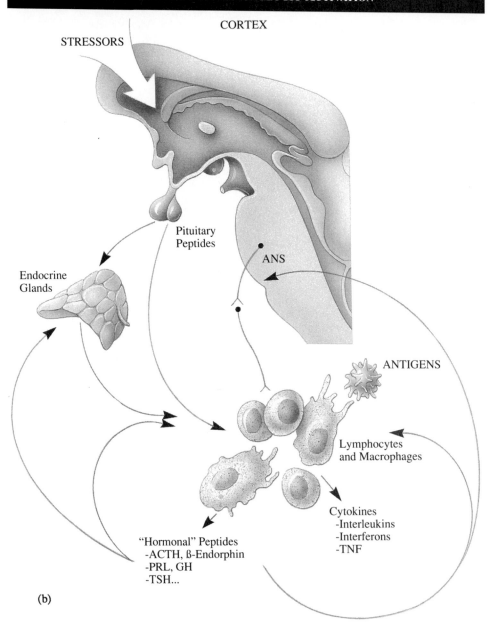

(b)

Source: Adapted from Blalock, J. E., 1988, Immunologically-mediated pituitary-adrenal activation. In G. P. Chrousos, D. Lynn Loriaux, & P. W. Gold, Mechanisms of physical and emotional stress, pp. 217–222, New York: Plenum; Dantzer, R., & Kelley, K. W., 1989, Stress and immunity: An integrated view of relationships between the brain and the immune system, Life Sciences, 44, 1995–2008.

psychosocial factors might affect the immune system. There is now adequate evidence that various psychosocial factors, through the brain, adversely affect immunologic functioning (Kiecolt-Glaser & Glaser, 1992; Zakowski, McAllister et al., 1992). The remainder of this module looks at several of them: stress and personal control, bereavement and depression, and personality and mood.

Stress and Personal Control

Many studies suggest that stress produces a "down-regulation" in a range of immune system responses (Kiecolt-Glaser & Glaser, 1992). For example, the immune system of rats is suppressed when they are exposed to electric shock (Laudenslager et al., 1983). However, the suppression occurs *only* when the shock is inescapable (that is, uncontrollable) and not when the shock is escapable (that is, controllable). Consistent with this, cancerous tumor growth is heightened by exposing rats to inescapable shock but not by exposing them to escapable shock (Visintainer, Volpicelli, & Selisman, 1982).

Another experiment that uses a different type of stress demonstrates how this research is conducted (Kandil & Borysenko, 1987). Mice that live in identical conditions are randomly assigned to either a treatment or nontreatment group. Those in the treatment group are subjected to "rotation stress" by placing their cages in an enclosed isolator unit and rotating them on a turntable at 45 rpm for intermittent periods of 10 minutes per hour for 6 days. Periodic assays of NK cells from both the treatment and nontreatment mice are made.

For up to 10 days following the stress, there is no difference in NK cell activity. However, from 13 to 27 days following the stress, significant differences emerge, with the NK cells from the stressed mice exhibiting decreased ability to kill tumor cells. The researchers report that, "rotation stress-induced impairment of NK cells . . . may account at least in part, for the progressive growth of lymphosarcoma tumors. . . ." (Kandil & Borysenko, 1987, p. 97).

Can stress affect the human immune system in the same way? Stressful events do depress the reactivity of the human immune system to infectious disease (Jemmott & Locke, 1984). Research with college students has demonstrated that the activity of NK and T-cells is decreased when students undergo stress during examinations (Glaser, Rice, Speicher, Stout, & Kiecolt-Glaser, 1986; Stein, Schiavi, & Camerino, 1976), and that the manufacture of antibodies to hepatitis B inoculation is temporarily suppressed in medical students undergoing examinations (Glaser, Kiecolt-Glaser, Bonneau, Malarkey, & Hughes, 1992). Other studies have found that life change and reported distress are correlated with low NK cell activity (Locke, Hurst, Williams, & Heisel, 1978). One mechanism through which stress can affect the immune system is through the release of corticosteroids, which interfere with leukocyte function and antibody production (Levy, 1982).

Is stress-related down-regulation of the human immune system related to an increase in disease? Again, there is generally good evidence from animal experiments (for example, Cohen et al., 1992). Also, in humans, there is a higher incidence of respiratory infections following stress (Boyce, Jensen, Cassell, Collier, Smith, & Ramey, 1977; Hinkle, 1974), and outbreaks of genital herpes occur when stress and emotional factors depress the immune system, although this relationship appears to be stronger when there is a lack of social support, too (VanderPlate & Aral, 1987; VanderPlate, Aral, & Magder, 1988).

A recent quasi-experiment demonstrated a link between the chronic stress of taking care of someone with progressive dementia and increased illness (Kiecolt-Glaser et al., 1991). It involved 2 groups of 69 subjects each. One was comprised of the spousal caregivers of people with dementia; the other group was matched sociodemographically with them. Both groups were followed for 13 months. The caregivers had already been providing care for an average of 5 years before the study, so presumably any adaptation to stress would have already occurred. Still, over the 13-month study period, there was evidence of a significant down-regulation on 3 measures of cellular immunity in the caregivers, and they also reported significantly more upper respiratory infections.

Would it be possible to counteract the effects of stress and improve immune system functioning? Two experiments by Kiecolt-Glaser and colleagues suggest that the answer is yes. In one, medical students who used relaxation training to reduce stress had higher levels of T-cells during stressful periods than those who did not (Kiecolt-Glaser et al., 1986). In another, old-age home residents were randomly assigned to one of three groups: (a) relaxation training, (b) enhanced social contact, and (c) nontreatment (Kiecolt-Glaser et al., 1985). Those taught relaxation techniques reported significantly fewer stress-related symptoms *and* they experienced a significant increase in NK cell activity. The other groups did not.

DISREGULATION THEORY   **Disregulation theory** has been proposed to explain the relationship between personal control and immune functioning (Schwartz, 1984). The theory includes a role for stress *and* pain. It maintains that healthful regulation of the immune system is achieved by gaining control over a stressful situation. In contrast, the psychological experience of losing control causes disregulation of the immune response.

However, if pain is at too low a level, then no health-enhancing behaviors may be generated, with or without control. For example, if you do not feel achy and feverish with the flu, you are not likely to stay in bed.

Disregulation is not caused by pain alone. It occurs when a *high level of pain* is experienced in the *absence* of control, and this, theoretically, results in disease. Therefore, moderate levels of pain and control are necessary for regulation and health (homeostasis). Pain alerts the individual to a threatening situation and permits control to be established. Finally, the theory holds that there is an inverted U-shaped relationship between pain and health, because extreme pain, even with control, would arouse the sympathetic nervous system, causing strain and reduced immune system functioning.

There is experimental evidence that supports disregulation theory by demonstrating the inverted U-shaped relationship between pain and health (Zagon & McLaughlin, 1983). The experience of pain in mice that had cancerous tumor growths was manipulated by the administration of either morphine, which reduces it, or naltrexone, which increases it. The mice were randomly assigned to three groups: (a) those allowed to experience moderate pain, (b) those who had pain removed by morphine injection, or (c) those whose pain was allowed to become extreme by naltrexone injection. The group allowed to experience moderate pain lived significantly longer than either the no pain or extreme pain groups.

Disregulation theory has received some support in human research as well. One experiment first assessed the extent of the physiological response to mental stress in 25 healthy males between 18 and 30 years of age (Manuck, Cohen, Rabin, Muldoon, & Bachen, 1991). On that basis, subjects were divided into high and low reactors to stress. They were placed in environmentally controlled chambers where autonomic and immune system functions could be monitored, and they were again subjected to mental stress. The monitoring revealed that the functioning of T-cells was altered under acute stress, but only for the high stress-reactors. The subjects that responded with high levels of catecholamine had *increases* in suppressor T-cells and *decreases* in helper T-cells. Together, these experiments suggest that stress and pain (or discomfort) interact to down-regulate the immune system, but other factors may also affect immune system functioning adversely.

Depression and Bereavement

Several studies have focused on the immunological effects of depression but have produced contradictory findings. Certainly not all depressed people will become ill, but emerging from this research is a picture of emotional influences on immunity that are more complicated than originally hypothesized. Age, severity of depression, and whether or not people are hospitalized for depression interact to determine the extent to which depression affects immune system functioning (Geiser, 1989).

The effects of bereavement, however, seem more clear-cut. A recent study assessed major life event stress, depression, NK cell activity, and T-cell percentages during bereavement (Irwin, Daniels, Bloom, Smith, & Weiner, 1987). The subjects were 37 women whose husbands had either recently died from lung cancer, had recently been diagnosed with lung cancer, or were in good health. Those whose husbands had cancer were more stressed and depressed and had significantly lower NK cell activity. These results have been replicated in other samples (for example, Irwin, Daniels, Risch, Bloom, & Weiner, 1988), and research has also demonstrated the effects of bereavement on T-cells (Bartrop, Luckhurst, Lazarus, and Kiloh, 1977). Together, these studies strongly suggest that bereavement decreases immune system functioning, at least temporarily.

The effects of bereavement on immune function might be explained by disregulation theory. A significant reduction of lymphocyte response has been found during the first two months following the death of a spouse, with a return to normal by five months postbereavement (Stein, 1982a). In the loss of a loved one, there is usually no control over the event itself—which accounts for the initial reduction in immune system functioning—although there may be varying degrees of control exerted over subsequent events. Eventually, over time, as the widowed begin to exert more control, their immune systems return to normal.

PERSONALITY AND MOOD

Correlational studies have found a relationship among personality, mood, and immune functioning. One hundred eleven physically healthy college students had the activity level of their NK cells assessed and completed a standardized personality questionnaire. Students with the highest and lowest levels of NK cell activity were then compared. Those with low NK cell activity had a significant elevation in several personality scales, including one measuring college maladjustment, and were characterized as dissatisfied, sad, lonely, and anxious (Heisel, Locke, Kraus, & Williams, 1986). Another study found that the amount of antibody in college students fluctuates *daily* with changes in mood (Stone, 1987). Immune functioning was better on days characterized by more positive mood.

In a quasi-experimental study, saliva samples were taken from 46 college students after an important midterm examination (McClelland, Ross, & Patel, 1985). The samples were assayed for norepinephrine and an antibody that reflects B-cell functioning. Six days later saliva samples were taken again, and the students were given a projective personality test to determine their "need for power"—a desire to have power over others—and "need for affiliation"—a desire to be socially related to others.

Those students with need for power greater than need for affiliation had higher concentrations of norepinephrine immediately after the examination, suggesting a more pronounced sympathetic response (presumably due to the challenge of the examination interacting with their power need). More importantly, six days later, their antibody production had dropped below normal, suggesting that sympathetic arousal during the examination inhibited immune functioning later. This effect was not present in students who had higher need for affiliation than need for power, suggesting that there is a relationship between motivational traits and response to stressful situations.

Studies like these provide strong *correlational* evidence of a psychosocial effect on immune functioning, but they cannot establish that mood and personality cause changes in the level of immune function. Stronger evidence of a causal relationship has come from an experiment demonstrating that psychological treatment can influence the immune system (Pennebaker, Kiecolt-Glaser, & Glaser, 1988). The researchers began with the hypothesis that psychotherapy allows people to express stressful and traumatic experiences, and that this might improve health.

They randomly assigned 50 college students to one of 2 groups: (a) a *traumatic events* group which, in a condition similar to psychotherapy, was required to write essays revealing personally traumatic events; or (2) a *trivial events* placebo group, which was required to write essays about noninvolving topics (see Figure 10.4). Both groups engaged in essay-writing sessions of 20 minutes in length on each of 4 consecutive days. Blood was drawn from the students and assayed for the ability of their lymphocytes to respond to an antigen. In addition, the students' health center records were examined, and the activity of their autonomic nervous systems was monitored.

The group disclosing traumatic personal events had significantly better T-cell functioning, less sympathetic arousal, less subjective distress, and fewer health center visits for illnesses up to six weeks after the treatment. Although this study needs to be replicated, it is highly suggestive of a relationship between one's psychological state, immune system functioning, and health. In particular, it demonstrates that psychotherapy might have a positive effect on immune function.

CONCLUSION

Down-regulation of immune functioning is caused by several psychosocial factors and appears to be related to changes in health status as well. It may also be possible to reverse the down-regulation through psychosocial means. However, not all changes in immune functioning relate to changes in health, and it would not be desirable to increase immune functioning in someone who is healthy and not subject to chronic stress (Kiecolt-Glaser & Glaser, 1992). First, it may not be possible to boost immune functioning above normal. Second, overactive immune functioning is related to autoimmune disorders. In other words, optimal health requires respect for the homeostasis of the body.

SUMMARY

The remainder of this chapter looks at three disease processes or disorders related to immune system function: infectious disease, discussed in Module 10.1; cancer, discussed in Module 10.2; and acquired immune deficiency syndrome, discussed in Module 10.3. However, before continuing, here is a review of the function and organization of the immune system:

Figure 10.4   EXPERIMENT DEMONSTRATING THE EFFECTS OF A PSYCHOTHERAPY ANALOG ON IMMUNE SYSTEM FUNCTIONING AND ILLNESS

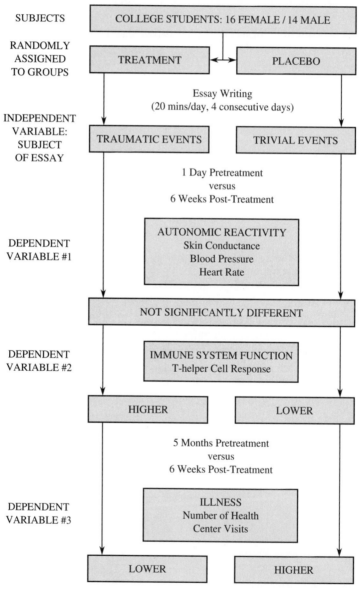

HYPOTHESIS: Writing about tramatic experiences heightens T-helper cell response and decreases health center visits.

SUBJECTS — COLLEGE STUDENTS: 16 FEMALE / 14 MALE

RANDOMLY ASSIGNED TO GROUPS — TREATMENT ↔ PLACEBO

Essay Writing
(20 mins/day, 4 consecutive days)

INDEPENDENT VARIABLE: SUBJECT OF ESSAY — TRAUMATIC EVENTS / TRIVIAL EVENTS

1 Day Pretreatment
versus
6 Weeks Post-Treatment

DEPENDENT VARIABLE #1 — AUTONOMIC REACTIVITY
Skin Conductance
Blood Pressure
Heart Rate

NOT SIGNIFICANTLY DIFFERENT

DEPENDENT VARIABLE #2 — IMMUNE SYSTEM FUNCTION
T-helper Cell Response

HIGHER / LOWER

5 Months Pretreatment
versus
6 Weeks Post-Treatment

DEPENDENT VARIABLE #3 — ILLNESS
Number of Health
Center Visits

LOWER / HIGHER

Source: Pennebaker, J. W., Kiecolt-Glaser, J. K., & Glaser, R., 1988, Disclosure of traumas and immune func-tion: Health implications for psychotherapy, Journal of Consulting and Clinical Psychology, 56, *239-245.*

1. The immune system recognizes, responds to, and remembers substances that threaten health.
2. It can detect foreign substances because their identity, expressed by the surface features of all cells, is different.
3. An antigen is any potentially pathogenic foreign material that triggers an immune response.
4. Inflammation is a local immune response to any injury or infection.
5. The immune system has two branches. The humoral branch can be likened to a navy because it operates through B-cells that circulate in the blood. The cellular branch can be likened to an army because it operates through T-cells that can leave the bloodstream and move through the tissues. There are also nonspecific lymphocytes, or white cells, that attack any virus (NK cells) or bacterium (macrophages).
6. Specific lymphocytes include B-cells that create antibody, chemicals that attach to the surface of invaders and mark them for destruction, and T-cells.
7. Helper T-cells signal B-cells and killer T-cells to attack a specific invader.
8. Memory B-cells and T-cells remain after infection to provide immunity. They can immediately defend the body if an infection reoccurs.
9. The lymphatic system drains fluid and debris from the body and cleanses it.
10. Psychoneuroimmunology is an interdisciplinary field of research into mind/body relationship and the immune system.
11. Research suggests that there is two-way communication between the brain and the immune system and that the brain probably exerts control over the immune system.
12. Stress depresses immune functioning and disregulation theory suggests that stress and pain interact. Uncontrollable stress with pain is unhealthful, while controllable stress is not. Moderate pain is healthful because it motivates healthy behavior.
13. Research also links personality and mood to the functioning of the immune system. Sadness, depression, a lonely mood, maladjustment, and a high need for power are associated with poor immune function.
14. At least one study demonstrates that psychotherapy can have a positive affect on health by increasing immune system function.

Infectious Disease

We are in contact with numerous pathogens each day. They may enter our bodies through a cut, in the food we eat, or in the air we breathe. Normally, the immune system is capable of dealing with these invaders. NK cells and macrophages are constantly on patrol, and they can eliminate newly invading pathogens if their numbers are not too large.

Interestingly, the symptoms of infectious disease result partly from a pathogen and partly from the immune system's response to it. For example, the pain that accompanies a bruise or cut is partly due to pressure on surrounding tissue from the swelling of the inflammatory response itself. Also, fever is the result of macrophages releasing a substance called "pyrogen" when they detect bacteria or other foreign substances. Pyrogen travels through the bloodstream to the hypothalamus and causes it to reset core temperature upward (Marieb, 1989). Although high fevers can be dangerous, fever is beneficial because it disrupts the normal functioning of bacteria and increases cellular metabolism, resulting in quicker defensive and repair functions. Therefore, the uncomfortable symptoms of disease are indicative of our immune system's resistance to an antigen.

Viral Infection and Disease

The common cold and flu are examples of viral infections that can cause disease. Infectious disease usually follows a predictable course: A pathogen is detected, humoral and cellular responses are initiated, the pathogen is neutralized and destroyed, and the immune system response winds down.

Viral infection of the respiratory tract is the cause of that all-too-frequent experience known as the "common cold" as well as the "flu." The **incubation period**, the time between infection with an antigen and symptoms, is short, one to three days. Again, much of the nasal and throat discomfort, mucous secretions, sneezing, coughing, and general malaise associated with a cold—the "illness"—is actually due to the *responses* of the immune system itself and not to the virus. The major features distinguishing flu from a cold are the chills, fever, and severe aches that accompany the flu.

About 100 different cold viruses have been identified and many more remain unidentified. In contrast, relatively few types of influenza virus have been identified. There is no cure for the cold or flu; rest is the only treatment, but symptoms rarely last beyond two weeks in healthy individuals. Flu can be life threatening and kills thousands of children and older adults with immature or weakened immune systems each year, often by allowing secondary infections such as pneumonia to develop.

THE COFACTOR THEORY OF INFECTIOUS DISEASE

Normally, the immune system keeps pathogens under control, and there is a wide margin of protection, with each liter of blood containing up to 4 billion leukocytes. The immune system's nonspecific responders to infection maintain homeostasis and the integrity of the body. Even if they are initially overwhelmed by an invader, it will usually be dealt with swiftly by the engagement of B-cells and T-cells, and even faster if it is a secondary immune response.

That is part of the reason why, even though exposure to cold and flu viruses is very common, a relatively small proportion of infected people actually develop clinical symptoms. For example, of 1,400 cadets studied after exposure to infectious mononucleosis, only 20% actually became infected (Kasl, Evans, & Niederman, 1979). Interestingly, only 25% of those infected developed symptoms. One reason is that a pathogen is only a single factor in disease, and that *cofactors*—other circumstances either in the person or the environment—are necessary for the clinical expression of disease.

One of the most important cofactors is stress. The introduction to this chapter described the evidence for the effect of stress on immune system functioning, and there is additional evidence for the role of stress in infectious disease. An early prospective study followed 100 members of 16 families for a year (Meyer & Haggerty, 1962). Subjects recorded stressful life events in family diaries on a daily basis, their blood was drawn every four months and assayed for antibody levels, and throat cultures were taken every three weeks. Chronic family stress was related to increased infections, higher streptococcal illness, and elevated antibody to streptococcus. Importantly, stressful life events were four times more likely to precede than to follow new infections and symptoms, strongly suggesting that stress has a causal role in the development of infection.

A more recent study investigated this relationship experimentally (Cohen, Tyrrell, & Smith, 1991). Four hundred twenty healthy adult volunteers completed a questionnaire that assessed life events stress. Groups of subjects were then given nasal drops containing 1 of 5 respiratory viruses or a placebo. The viral doses were similar to those commonly transmitted person-to-person. The subjects were quarantined beginning 2 days before receiving the nasal drops and continuing for 7 days after. Each subject was examined daily by a clinician who completed a standard checklist of respiratory infection symptoms. Blood samples were also drawn 28 days after receiving the nasal drops.

The rates of both respiratory infection and clinical colds increased in relationship to the stress level before the experiment began. The incidence of infection ranged from 74% to 90%, and the incidence of clinical colds ranged from 27% to 47% (see Figure 10.1-1). The higher the stress level before exposure to the virus, the higher the incidence of infection and colds. This relationship was not affected by age, gender, education, allergic status, weight, the season, or the number of subjects housed together.

Another experiment found a similar relationship among stress, other psychological factors, and colds (Totman, Kiff, Reed, & Craig, 1980). Fifty-two volunteers aged 18 to 49 were assessed on a variety of psychological measures, then received nasal inoculation with cold viruses and were monitored over a 10-day controlled residential stay. Major life events stress was significantly related to the degree of viral infection. In addition, introverts had significantly worse symptoms and infections than extroverts, and the level of social activity and extraversion were independently predictive of the extent of

Figure 10.1-1   RELATIONSHIP BETWEEN STRESS AND THE RATE OF CLINICAL COLDS

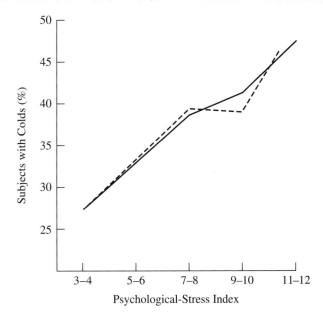

Observed association between the Psychological-Stress Index and the rate of clinical colds (solid line) and the association adjusted for standard control variables (dashed line).

Source: Cohen, S., Tyrrell, D. A. J., & Smith, A. P., 1991, Psychological stress and susceptibility to the common cold, The New England Journal of Medicine, 325, 606–612.

viral infection. This suggests that stress, social activity, and personality are related to the expression of infectious disease. One explanation for the introverts' worse symptoms could be that they are more withdrawn and lack external stimulation and diversion, so their attention may be more focused on their cold symptoms.

Finally, one study also explored the relationship between daily events, both desirable and undesirable, and upper respiratory tract infections (Evans, Pitts, & Smith, 1988). Daily events were tracked for 9 weeks in 30 undergraduate subjects. Undesirable events were *not* related to an increase in infection, but, intriguingly, episodes of infection were preceded by a significant *decrease* in *desirable* events during the 4 days prior to symptom onset. These studies and others provide substantial evidence for an association between stress and increased illness behavior and somewhat less, but still provocative, evidence for an association between stress and infectious pathology (Cohen & Williamson, 1991).

Why a stronger relationship between stress and illness *behavior* than between stress and infectious *pathology*? The answer to this question points out the difficulty in researching psychological variables and health. There can be laboratory evidence of an active pathogen in the body without any symptoms of disease. This is called a "subclinical" infection, but can we say that people with subclinical infections are "dis-eased?" This situation is evident in experiments, where infection rates can be up to 90%, but the incidence of clinical colds is only up to 47% (Cohen et al., 1991). Infection and cofactors may both be required for a disease to manifest itself clinically. As described in Module 3.3, illness behavior is not so much dependent on actually having a disease as it is on the *belief* that one has a disease. People who perceive a lot of stress in their lives may also be more likely to believe that they are ill, or perhaps they are more sensitive to illness symptoms and thus engage in more illness behavior. Therefore, researchers cannot rely solely on laboratory evidence of pathology.

Cohen and Williamson (1991) suggested a model for the pathways between stress and infectious disease (see Figure 10.1-2). Although the pathways in this model are only shown in one direction, the relationship could be bidirectional, and infectious disease could itself be a stressor. In this model, stress is not the primary cause of infectious disease; that role is reserved for the infectious agent itself and whether or not there is any prior immunity to it. Stress and other psychological variables are cofactors. Other possible psychological cofactors have also been investigated. Currently, however, the research on cofactors other than stress is sketchy and primarily correlational.

Behavioral Factors in the Transmission of the Common Cold Virus

Susceptibility to the common cold is *not* affected by a person's health or nutrition, and chilling of the body's surface will not, by itself, induce a cold

(Berkow & Fletcher, 1987). So, folk wisdom about "catching cold" from exposure to cold temperature, drafts, or dampness is a fallacy.

The exact method of transmission of the viruses that cause the common cold is not entirely understood, although there are two likely possibilities. The first is *airborne* transmission on mist expelled by sneezing or coughing. The second is by *direct contact.* A virus is picked up by contacting contaminated surfaces such as door knobs and desks or by shaking hands. It is allowed entry to the body when the eye, mouth, or nose is touched. This mode of transmission is believed to be the most common.

Remember, however, that exposure to a cold virus does not mean that cold symptoms will develop. Clinical symptoms seem to occur in slightly less than half of people directly exposed to a variety of cold viruses (Cohen et al., 1991). According to the cofactor theory, *if* a person has recently been exposed to a cold virus, the likelihood of illness symptoms developing may be increased if he or she has been undergoing stress (Berkow & Fletcher, 1987).

Several behavioral measures can be taken to prevent viral infection. One—the use of facial tissues (rather than handkerchiefs) to cover sneezes and coughs—is the responsibility of those with a cold. Another is to avoid touching eyes, nose, or mouth with the hands and to wash the hands frequently and

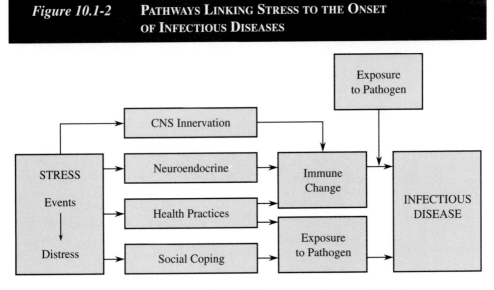

Figure 10.1-2   PATHWAYS LINKING STRESS TO THE ONSET OF INFECTIOUS DISEASES

Behavioral and biological pathways linking stress to the onset of infectious diseases. (CNS = central nervous system. For brevity, this indicates paths moving in only one causal direction, from stress to disease.)

Source: Cohen, S., & Williamson, G. M., 1991, Stress and infectious disease in humans, Psychological Bulletin, 109, 5–24.

particularly after exposure (to prevent transmission by absentmindedly touching oneself). This will reduce the rate of infection. Finally, reduction and management of chronic stress may also reduce illness.

■■■■

MODULE SUMMARY

Infections are only one type of challenge dealt with by the immune system. The next module examines the role of the immune system in cancer, which presents an entirely different challenge. Before continuing, review these points:

1. Infections are frequent, but the nonspecific aspects of the immune system—on constant alert—are capable of dealing with many invaders without our knowledge; part of the reason we become aware of infection is the response of the immune system itself.
2. The fact that only a small percentage of people actually develop clinical symptoms, despite exposure to pathogens, suggests that cofactors may be involved in the development of clinical symptoms.
3. Research strongly suggests that stress is a cofactor in the development of colds, although it is more strongly related to illness behavior than to infectious pathology.
4. Common colds are not caused by exposure to cold temperatures, drafts, or damp environments. Transmission is either airborne or, more likely, through touching one's eyes, mouth, or nose.
5. Infection with cold viruses can be avoided behaviorally by refraining from touching one's eyes, mouth, or nose and by washing one's hands after exposure.
6. Reduction of stress and avoiding fatigue may help one avoid clinical symptoms of infection with cold viruses.

CANCER

EPIDEMIOLOGY

Currently, about 1 million Americans develop cancer annually, and about 500,000 die of it each year (USDHHS, 1992). The incidence varies greatly among the more than 100 types of cancer. Overall, mortality rates for cancer are holding steady, with the exception of lung cancer (National Institutes of Health, NIH, 1985; USDHHS, 1992). The death rate from lung cancer for men has risen by a factor of 10 from 1930 to 1980, and the death rate for women has also risen dramatically, although it did not begin to rise rapidly until after 1950.

What might account for the increase in lung cancer deaths, while the death rates for other cancers hold steady or decline? Undoubtedly, the most important factor is smoking. Smoking became fashionable for men in the 1930s but was not as widespread for women until the 1950s, both dates corresponding to the rise in lung cancer deaths. This was first noticed in the 1950s (Doll & Hill, 1956; Hammond & Horn, 1954; Wynder & Graham, 1950), but the relationship was correlational, not causal, and did not exclude other factors in the lives of smokers that could have contributed to death from lung cancer. However, later studies found that smoking is a separate risk factor independent of age, sex, alcohol consumption, race, occupation, or other variables (Fielding, 1985).

In 1983, the U.S. Surgeon General estimated that smoking contributed to the premature deaths of 340,000 people a year. Many of these deaths are from lung cancer, but smoking is also implicated in other forms of cancer. Smoking is a **behavioral risk factor**. More recently, researchers have become interested in determining what other risk factors might be involved in cancer.

IMMUNE SURVEILLANCE THEORY: A BIOPSYCHOSOCIAL PERSPECTIVE ON CANCER

British psychologist Hans Eysenck (1984) has proposed a multifactor model of cancer. Eysenck (1987) argues that dualism has restricted researchers' study of cancer to look for a single factor in the disease. Instead, he proposes that several psychological cofactors—stress, personality, and coping—in addition to genetic and behavioral factors interact to produce cancer. A similar notion, immune surveillance theory, has emerged from cancer research and provides a model by which psychological cofactors may influence the disease processes of cancer. It begins with a consideration of the *primary* causes of cancer.

SUSPECTED PRIMARY CAUSES OF CANCER

The primary cause of cancer is biological—uncontrolled cell growth—without which cancer would not occur. Cell growth and replication is a very complex and little understood phenomenon. Cells in the central nervous system do not grow or regenerate if damaged, whereas skin cells do replicate at a constant rate but will speed up and replace damaged tissue, only to slow again after the repair is completed. New cells must also have the same identity as all other cells in the body so the immune system does not attack them (which can happen in organ transplants and foreign skin grafts).

Cancer begins with a dysfunction that causes cells to lose normal control over their growth. They grow in an unregulated fashion, lack differentiation (that is, they no longer do their specialized task), and sometimes have the ability to invade other normal tissue. When cells grow in an unregulated manner they are called **neoplastic**, and when they spread to other parts of the body through the lymph or blood they are said to have **metastasized**. Cancer can develop at any age and in any organ of the body.

Medical researchers have focused on four primary factors in the etiology of cancer because of their ability to affect cell growth: random mutation, genetic susceptibility, viruses, and environmental factors.

RANDOM MUTATION   When new cells develop, occasionally something goes wrong and a mutation occurs, perhaps due to a breakdown in copying the DNA. A new cell's DNA might be abnormal in any number of ways, some of which would be no threat whatsoever to the cell's or the body's functioning. However, if the mutation affects the regulation of the cell's growth, it may become cancerous.

GENETIC SUSCEPTIBILITY   Genetic susceptibility is an inherited predisposition to develop a disease. Cancer itself is not inherited, but there is an inherited susceptibility to some types of cancer (Moolgavkar, 1983). These types of cancer appear to be linked to certain **genes** believed to regulate cellular growth and development. One way an inherited disorder may be linked to cancer is through chromosome breakage, which occurs in some congenital diseases.

Extensive exposure to the sun is a behavioral risk factor in skin cancer.

VIRUSES   Viruses may alter DNA and thereby cause a cell to grow in an unregulated manner. Viruses are known to cause some cancers in animals—for example, feline leukemia—and some viruses are associated with cancer in humans. However, most cancers have not been linked to a virus.

ENVIRONMENTAL FACTORS   The third cause of cancer may be exposure to known **carcinogens**, chemicals that are suspected to cause cancer by damaging DNA and interfering with normal growth regulation. Suspected carcinogens are tobacco, nickel, asbestos, and radiation (either ultraviolet radiation from the sun, which causes skin cancer, or radioactive nuclear energy).

CONCLUSION   These four primary factors account for the fact that among the billions of cells that comprise a human body, some will become damaged, destroyed, or mutate in the normal process of living. Still, the body has several ways to protect itself against the development of cancer. Chemical carcinogens may be eliminated by enzymes, and cells with damaged DNA may be able to repair it themselves in some cases, thereby avoiding cancerous mutations (Fox, 1981). However, these processes may not be sufficient to eliminate all potentially cancerous cells from the body.

IMMUNE SURVEILLANCE

Once a cell becomes cancerous, responsibility for its detection and destruction resides with the immune system. Mutation is likely to alter the identity of cells, so their surface markers will be slightly different from the other cells in the body. NK cells specialize in recognizing mutant cells as "non-self" and engage in an ongoing mission to search for and destroy them. This process is known as "immune surveillance." Because there normally are some mutant cells present, immune surveillance theory holds that cancer develops only when the immune system is deficient or dysfunctional and fails to detect or destroy these cells when they mutate.

According to immune surveillance theory, down-regulation of the immune system, particularly if it affects the surveillance of mutations, provides an opportunity for unchecked growth of cancerous tissue. Anything that affects normal immune surveillance is considered a secondary, or cofactor, in cancer.

SUSPECTED COFACTORS IN CANCER

Some have gone so far as to suggest that there might be a "cancer-prone personality," but there is no evidence that such a personality style exists or that it could cause cancer (Wolman, 1988). There are, however, a number of suspected cofactors that have received varying degrees of research support. Some of these are behavioral—smoking cigarettes, diet, drinking alcohol, and sexual behavior—and some are psychosocial—stress, depression, and suppression of emotion.

SMOKING CIGARETTES   Most researchers agree that smoking is a strong independent risk factor. Recent research has focused on determining the extent of risk, and it appears that the risk of lung cancer developing in smokers is generally *nine times higher* than for nonsmokers. Filters may reduce the risk by half, and pipe and cigar smokers are still at risk, but "only" *two and one-half to three time higher* than nonsmokers (Lubin, Richter, & Blot, 1984).

DIET   Nutritional factors may be involved in 40% of cancer in men and 60% of cancer in women (Simone, 1983). Poor diet is a cofactor in breast, stomach, and intestinal cancer, among others. It may be related to the development of cancer in one of two ways: (a) some foods may contain carcinogenic substances, and (b) other foods may contain substances that are protective against cancer.

Carcinogens may either be a natural constituent of food or an additive. For example, a diet high in animal fat has been implicated in various types of cancers, and **nitrites** (food additives in processed meats such as hot dogs) may become carcinogenic after ingestion (Winick, Morgan, Rozovski, & Marks-Kaufman, 1988).

In contrast, some diets may provide protective factors. People with a diet high in vitamin A (found in tomatoes, carrots, and sweet potatoes) have a relative risk factor *one and one-half to two times lower* than those with a diet low in vitamin A (Hinds, Kolonel, Hankin, & Lee, 1984; Peto, Doll, Buckley, & Spron, 1981). Ascorbic acid (vitamin C) has been proposed as an anticancer dietary supplement (Pauling, 1980); however, the evidence in support of this hypothesis is not strong (Newberne & Supharkarn, 1983). More recently, researchers have been recommending increasing fiber and vegetables in the cabbage family, such as broccoli and cauliflower, as a cancer preventive (Roan, 1991).

DRINKING ALCOHOL Alone, alcohol is not as high a risk factor as smoking or nutrition, perhaps accounting for only about three percent of cancer deaths (Doll & Peto, 1981). However, in combination with other factors, it appears to magnify the risk. This synergistic effect is particularly pronounced with tobacco. Smokers who are nondrinkers or light drinkers have a risk factor for laryngeal cancer of about 3:1 over nonsmokers, and drinkers who are nonsmokers or light smokers have a risk factor of about 4:1 over nondrinkers. However, heavy smokers who are also heavy drinkers have a *risk factor of 14:1 over people who neither smoke nor drink* (Herity, Moriarty, Daly, Dunn, & Bourke, 1982). Large amounts of alcohol are associated with poor nutrition and also suppress the immune system, so it may be that alcohol magnifies risk through other cancer risk factors (Schottenfeld, 1979). As a single factor, alcohol is particularly associated with pancreatic cancer and heavy drinkers may be 5 times more likely to develop it (Heuch, Kvale, Jacobsen, & Bjelke, 1983).

SEXUAL BEHAVIOR Certain cancers appear to be related to sexual activities and reproduction (Doll & Peto, 1981; Levy, 1985). Pregnancy early in life seems to reduce the incidence of breast and ovarian cancer, as opposed to late pregnancy or none at all. On the other hand, cancer of the cervix is higher among women who have had very early pregnancy, whose first sexual intercourse was at an early age, who have had many sexual partners, or whose male partners have had many sexual partners, especially prostitutes.

STRESS The introduction to Chapter 10 described how stress can affect immune system functioning. However, the relationship between stress and cancer has not been consistently supported by research (Cox & Mackay, 1982). In humans, stress does not appear to be related to cancer of the cervix, while it does appear to be related to lung and gastric cancer (Graham, Snell,

Graham, & Ford, 1971; Horne & Picard, 1979; Lehrer, 1980). If stress were a general cofactor in cancer, according to immune surveillance theory, it should be related more consistently to a variety of cancers.

One problem may be the methodology of the research. Much of it has relied on self-report, and it has been criticized for relying on people's imperfect memories of past events (Fox, 1978; Greer & Morris, 1978). Also, research should combine both biological and psychological factors in cancer. One study did attempt to predict disease outcome from psychological factors in 126 people age 15 to 71 years old with incurable cancer (Achterberg, Lawlis, Simonton, & Matthews-Simonton, 1977). Psychological factors were related to blood chemistries and were also predictive of future cancer status. Although Achterberg and colleagues were cautious about drawing conclusions, they did call the role of psychological factors "impressive" (p. 107).

Animal research has also contributed important knowledge about cancer. Yet, scientific research on animals is opposed by some people. See Box 10.2-1 for a discussion of the ethics of using animals in cancer research and an example of a worthwhile research design that could only be conducted on animals.

Animal research has tended to support a link between stress and cancer (Schwartz, 1984). For example, direct administration of hormones involved in the sympathetic nervous system's response to stress enhances cancer growth in mice (Santisteban, Riley, & Spackman, 1977). Tumor growth is also accelerated when stress is induced by the way animals are treated, either by inescapable shock (Visintainer, Volpicelli, & Selisman, 1982) or crowded housing conditions (Sklar & Anisman, 1981). It has been suggested that corticosteroids, which rise during stress, inhibit the cellular immune response, allowing cancer to develop and spread (Weinstock, 1984).

However, the results of animal research are sometimes contradictory (Riley, 1979). It appears that stress sometimes enhances tumor growth and sometimes inhibits it. Interestingly, stress does not seem to be neutral in relation to cancer. It would appear that another variable—the degree of personal control over the stressful situation—is the reason for inconsistent results (Visintainer et al., 1982). When an animal has control and can escape the stressor, tumor growth is inhibited, whereas when it has no control and cannot escape the stressor, tumor growth is enhanced. As researchers begin to focus on mediating variables such as control, the relationship between stress and cancer should become clearer.

DEPRESSION   It is understandable that people with cancer usually score higher than people without cancer on any measure of depression. Therefore, depression is correlated with cancer, but this does not prove that it causes it. The type of research that would demonstrate causality would be prospective, beginning *before* people develop cancer and following them until they do.

When 2,082 men aged 40 to 55 were randomly selected from workers at a Western Electric Company plant for a large study of coronary heart disease begun in 1957, they were also diagnosed as either depressed or nondepressed and evaluated for cancer. Seventeen years later, their mortality rate from cancer was compared, and those who were depressed in 1957 had twice the rate of several types of cancers, even after smoking, alcohol use, age, occupational status, and family history of cancer were taken into account (Bieliauskas, Shekelle, Garron, Maliza, Ostfield, & Raynor, 1979; Shekelle et al., 1981). A similar study confirmed these results for men but not for women (Whitlock & Siskind, 1979), but another 5-year study of breast cancer in women found that recurrence was significantly related to feelings of helplessness and hopelessness, which are linked to depression (Greer, Morris, & Pettingale, 1979).

If depression were related to cancer, it should also affect the course of the disease. In fact, depressed adult patients have lower survival rates than patients who are angry or hostile (Krantz & Glass, 1984), but in a long-term

---

Box 10.2-1   **ETHICS AND ANIMALS IN CANCER RESEARCH**

Much of the research that attempts to establish a relationship between psychological factors and cancer is correlational. Correlational research can be conducted with a minimum of inconvenience and risk to participants, so it is used frequently with humans, but it cannot establish cause and effect relationships between variables. Would you agree that if psychological variables are cofactors in cancer, it would be worthwhile to know this so treatments could be developed?

Here is a simple type of experimental design that could establish a cause-and-effect relationship between psychological factors and cancer. First, participants would be randomly assigned to a treatment or nontreatment group. The treatment group would receive stress while the nontreatment group would not. Before the treatment, both groups would be exposed to a carcinogen, such as a strong dose of nuclear radiation—not enough to kill quickly, just enough to cause leukemia. Then both groups would be followed after the stress/no stress treatment to see if the stress group had a significantly higher incidence of leukemia. If they did, then this would provide strong evidence that stress is a causal cofactor in cancer.

Of course, it is doubtful that there would be any volunteers for this experiment. Also, this experiment would violate the Ethical Principles of the American Psychological Association because it would submit human subjects to unreasonable and irreversible harm. In short, it could never be carried out.

This is one important instance where animal research is substituted for research on human beings. The APA's Ethical Principles do permit the use of animals for research if three criteria are met: (a) they are otherwise treated humanely, (b) they may not be subjected to any undue suffering, and (c) the research question is considered important. In this case, the possibility of preventing or treating cancer in human beings would probably be considered important enough so a *well-designed* study producing *useful* results could be performed with animals. Of course, the animals would not be permitted to suffer the full consequences of leukemia. Many lifesaving advances in the treatment of cancer and other life threatening illnesses have come from animal research.

study of children and adolescents with cancer, depression was unrelated to the course of the disease (Kaplan, Busner, Weinhold, & Lenon, 1987). Another study examined the reports of 272 medical school students concerning childhood events that are linked with depression and followed them for a number of years (Duszynski, Shaffer, & Thomas, 1981). There was no difference in the occurrence of these events among those who developed cancer or remained cancer free. So the data, while suggestive, are not conclusive with respect to depression as a cofactor in cancer.

SUPPRESSION OF EMOTION A lifelong pattern of suppressing emotional expression, particularly when one feels angry and hostile, has also been investigated as a cancer cofactor. Psychological interviews and test data were collected on 160 women admitted for breast tumor biopsy before they underwent the operation (Greer & Morris, 1978). As a result of the procedure, 69 were diagnosed with breast cancer. The remaining 91, diagnosed with benign breast disease, served as a comparison group. The women with breast cancer were found to have had abnormal release of anger and extreme suppression of emotion before biopsy. Even when stress levels were held constant, suppression of anger continued to be significantly related to cancer.

A replication of this study also found a significant correlation between breast cancer and a chronic behavioral pattern of concealing emotions and bottling up anger (Bageley, 1979). A similar study used ratings (based on recordings made before surgery or the results of biopsy were known) of women with breast cancer or benign tumors (Wirsching, Stierlin, Hoffmann, Weber, & Wirsching, 1982). The rater was unaware of the cancer status of these women but was able to correctly classify 94% of people with cancer and 68% of people with benign tumors on the basis of emotional suppression and other psychological factors.

There are fewer studies with men. In one study, men who were free of diagnosed medical or psychological symptoms were followed for 10 years, at which time medical records were used to divide them into cancer and noncancer groups (Dattore, Shontz, & Coyne, 1980). At that time, psychological test data from before the study were examined, and the cancer group was found to have been suppressing emotion before the onset of cancer.

Another study matched three groups of 20 people each—one with malignant skin cancer, one with cardiovascular disease, and one disease free—on ethnic origin, gender, and age (Kneier & Temoshok, 1984). The cancer and cardiovascular groups were also matched on disease severity. Suppression of emotion was significantly greater in the cancer group than in either of the other groups. There was not a difference in suppression as a function of severity of illness in either the cancer or cardiovascular groups, so cancer does not appear to cause suppression of emotion. These skin cancer patients may have suppressed emotion before they developed the disease, and that may have aided the development of cancer.

CONCLUSION

In conclusion, among the behavioral cofactors, the role of cigarette smoking has received substantial research support, drinking alcohol is more of a synergistic factor increasing the consequences of other cofactors, and sexual behavior may be a cofactor in certain types of cancer such as cancer of the cervix. A recent study looked at the relationship of a combination of behavioral health practices to the development of cancer (Enstrom, 1989). The subjects were 5,231 men and 4,613 women who were religiously active Mormons and refrained from smoking and drinking alcohol. Their mortality rate from cancer over an 8-year period was only one-half that of the general U.S. population for men and about three-fourths for women. The cancer mortality rate for a subset of the male subjects who reported engaging in three health practices—never smoking cigarettes, regular physical activity, and getting proper sleep—was even lower, only about one-third of males in the general population. Although correlational, this study does suggest that a meaningful reduction in cancer death is related to health behaviors.

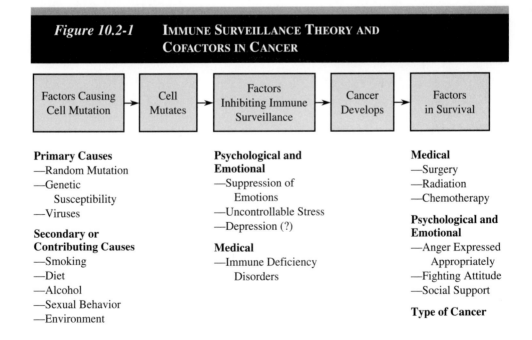

Figure 10.2-1   IMMUNE SURVEILLANCE THEORY AND COFACTORS IN CANCER

| Factors Causing Cell Mutation | → | Cell Mutates | → | Factors Inhibiting Immune Surveillance | → | Cancer Develops | → | Factors in Survival |

Primary Causes
—Random Mutation
—Genetic Susceptibility
—Viruses

Secondary or Contributing Causes
—Smoking
—Diet
—Alcohol
—Sexual Behavior
—Environment

Psychological and Emotional
—Suppression of Emotions
—Uncontrollable Stress
—Depression (?)

Medical
—Immune Deficiency Disorders

Medical
—Surgery
—Radiation
—Chemotherapy

Psychological and Emotional
—Anger Expressed Appropriately
—Fighting Attitude
—Social Support

Type of Cancer

Among psychosocial cofactors, stress has received fairly good research support, but its effects are mediated by personal control. The role of depression as a cofactor has not been consistently supported. However, suppression of emotion has received good research support and may even be a better predictor of the course of cancer than stress.

Figure 10.2-1 depicts the immune surveillance model and some of the cofactors reviewed here. This model demonstrates how, theoretically, the full expression of cancer requires a primary causal factor and additional cofactors. It would require a mutation of cells *and* poor surveillance by the immune system, and the theory itself has received some limited experimental support (for example, Dorian, Keystone, Garfinkel, & Brown, 1982; Riley, 1981).

PSYCHOLOGICAL INTERVENTION AND FACTORS IN SURVIVAL

Because of its inclusion of behavioral and psychological factors, the immune surveillance model provides psychologists with an important role in the prevention and treatment of cancer. While psychosocial interventions are no substitute for appropriate medical treatment, behavioral risk reduction may help prevent the development of some cancers, and recent experiments suggest that group psychotherapy may improve the quality of life of people with cancer and help them live significantly longer.

CANCER PREVENTION

One important role for psychologists is the prevention of behaviors that put people at risk for cancer. This involves interventions that help people change risky behaviors like smoking, alcohol abuse, and poor diet. The effectiveness of interventions for these risk behaviors is discussed in Modules 8.2, 8.3, and 12.1, respectively.

Because early detection increases the likelihood of a successful outcome with cancer (Battista & Fletcher, 1988), health psychologists have also been involved in developing programs to encourage more self-examination. A regular breast self-examination is strongly recommended for women, but only about 35% do it, and many do not do it correctly (National Cancer Institute, NCI, 1980). Fear of what might be found probably accounts for more women not checking themselves regularly (Trotta, 1980). Even so, almost 90% of breast lumps are first discovered by women themselves, and there is a very high survival rate if tumors are found when they are small (Craun & Deffenbacher, 1987). Young men, too, should check for testicular cancer regularly, because it is the leading cause of death from tumors in men 15 to 34 years of age, and it can be detected by self-examination (Frame, 1986). Likewise, both men and women should check their skin for abnormal growths or changes that can indicate skin cancer.

CANCER TREATMENT AND QUALITY OF LIFE

Another role for psychologists has been helping people cope with the disease itself, including the severe pain that often accompanies the disease and its treatment (Daut & Cleeland, 1982). Chemotherapy to treat cancer—which often causes appetite loss, nausea, and vomiting—can result in aversive conditioning that contributes to people's discomfort and may make them less likely to pursue treatment (Bernstein, 1991), but a variety of behavioral techniques can reduce the aversive conditioning. These techniques include relaxation training, systematic desensitization, and biofeedback, and all are equally effective in reducing some of the side effects of chemotherapy (Redd & Andrykowski, 1982).

Not all people with cancer have difficulty dealing with the psychological and emotional problems, but a sizeable minority would benefit from psychological counseling (Telch & Telch, 1985). Individual therapy that teaches coping and problem-solving skills as well as pain management is effective. The use of groups has also been proposed because of the added social support (Wellisch, 1981). While the involvement of significant others in groups may have some benefits, it is not necessary to achieve gains (Andersen, 1992).

Although the role of psychosocial factors in the etiology of cancer is still controversial, there appears to be a stronger relationship between adjustment to the disease and prognosis. Poor prognosis is related to depression, rigidity, and defenses such as denial, whereas a better prognosis is related to a strong self-concept, flexibility, social competence, and emotional stability (Fox, 1983).

One study did not find a relationship between survival and several variables, including helplessness, subjective view about health, or adjustment to the diagnosis (Cassileth, Lusk, Miller, Brown, & Miller, 1985). However, these were patients with newly diagnosed advanced stage cancer, so perhaps the advanced state of the disease affected the results.

Another study followed up breast cancer patients after 10 years (Pettingale, Morris, Greer, & Haybittle, 1985). Long-term survivors either did not accept the disease or they were "fighters." They were not severely depressed by the diagnosis, they did feel angry and hostile, they did not lose control, and they had a sense of well-being. Those who did not survive long either felt helpless or were unemotional in their acceptance of the disease. A recent study also found that patients who had a "fighting spirit" and felt that they had more control over the course of cancer had better psychological and medical outcomes (Watson, Greer, Pruyn, & van den Borne, 1990).

The relationship between psychosocial factors and survival rates has led several researchers to investigate the effects of group therapy on cancer. One study involved patients who had undergone surgery for early-stage malignant melanoma (skin cancer). Thirty-eight of them received 6 weeks of group psychotherapy, while 28 did not (Fawzy et al., 1990a; Fawzy et al., 1990b). The group treatment consisted of health education, training in problem solving, and stress management. At 6-month follow-up, the patients who had received group psychotherapy had less anxiety and depression, and they considered themselves to be more active and satisfied and less avoidant. Importantly, they also had increased immune system activity.

Another experiment investigated the possibility that group psychotherapy might extend the length of survival of women with breast cancer (Spiegel, Bloom, Kraemer, & Gottheil, 1989). Eighty-six women were randomly assigned to a treatment group or a nontreatment group. The treatment consisted of 1 year of weekly supportive group therapy. The therapy encouraged mutual support, dealing with issues about dying, development of a life project, realignment of social networks, working through problems communicating with their doctors, monthly meetings that included family members to enhance social support, and self-hypnosis for pain control (Spiegel, 1991). The nontreatment group lived an average of only 19 months, while the treatment group lived an average of nearly 37 months, or almost twice as long. At 4 years post treatment, all of the nontreatment patients were dead, whereas ⅓ of the treatment patients were still alive, and at 12 years post treatment, 3 of the treatment patients were still alive. These results are quite startling and other researchers are currently attempting to replicate them.

Although this experiment demonstrates a strong effect of group psychotherapy on survival, it is a small sample and will need to be replicated. Nevertheless, it demonstrates the potential importance of health psychology's role in future cancer treatment (Andersen, 1989). A recent review (Andersen, 1992) suggested that the primary mechanism for increasing cancer survival in this experiment and others like it appears to be immune enhancement from learning to cope with chronic stress. However, the group treatments were lengthy and multifaceted, requiring hard work on the part of subjects. Group support alone did not produce these benefits; effective therapy required learning about the disease, learning cognitive-behavioral coping strategies, and learning relaxation training.

There is no magical cure for cancer, medically or psychologically. We must avoid falling into the trap of "media hype about patients being able to wish away their cancers" (Spiegel, 1991, p. 15). The unfortunate result of such simplistic notions is that some patients blame themselves for having cancer and feel guilty for having it and not being able to cure it.

Long-term group therapy may prolong the lives of people with cancer.

MODULE SUMMARY

Although still a major killer and likely to remain so for a long time, cancer is one of the most active research areas in health psychology. Progress is being made in understanding the behavioral and psychosocial cofactors and in prevention and treatment. Before continuing, here is a review of the major points in this module:

1. Almost 1 million Americans develop cancer and half a million die of it each year.
2. Different cancers have different incidences; some have decreased while others have increased. Lung cancer has increased largely due to an increase of cigarette smoking until the 1980s.
3. The primary cause of cancer is biological—uncontrolled cell growth. Several causal factors are involved: random mutation, genetic susceptibility, viruses, and environmental factors.
4. Immune surveillance theory holds that abnormal cells occur constantly in the body and that the immune system is able to eliminate them under normal conditions. However, immune dysfunction can allow cells to grow unchecked and become cancerous.

5. Psychosocial cofactors can disrupt immune system function. The behavioral factors include smoking tobacco, diet, drinking alcohol, and sexual behavior. The psychosocial factors include stress, depression, and suppression of emotion.

6. Cancer prevention largely involves early detection efforts. Other psychological treatments (for example, to help stop smoking cigarettes) can also help prevent cancer.

7. There is no cancer-prone personality, but longer-term survival of cancer seems to be related to certain personality characteristics, notably a "fighting spirit" and a sense of control.

8. Cancer treatment involves helping people cope with the pain of medical procedures and the disease process.

9. The latest advances in cancer treatment involve group psychotherapy. At least one study has demonstrated that group psychotherapy can increase the survival of women with breast cancer.

ACQUIRED IMMUNE DEFICIENCY SYNDROME

BACKGROUND

What is now the AIDS epidemic began quietly on June 5, 1981, when the U.S. Centers for Disease Control's (CDC) *Morbidity and Mortality Weekly Report* (*MMWR*; Gottlieb, Schanker, Fan, Saxon, & Weisman, 1981) reported that five gay men in Los Angeles had acquired an immune deficiency. Its origins were at once mysterious and devastating. Despite this, it took a scant two years to isolate in 1983 the virus that causes AIDS and just two years more to produce a blood test for it in 1985. Few knew about the disease or what precautions to take during those early years, but with the development of the test, the nature of the epidemic became apparent.

David was diagnosed with the virus in 1991. By then, he knew what he faced: An estimated 1–2 million Americans were infected with HIV, more than 250,000 had AIDS, and more than 112,000 had died of it (CDC, 1992). In people aged 24 to 45, AIDS had become the second leading cause of death in men and the sixth in women (*MMWR*, 1991). However, like most people, when his diagnosis was made, David was unaware of the immune system, its functioning, and its importance in maintaining life.

If there is a deficiency in immune system functioning, it is unable to protect the body from invaders. People with immune deficiency have frequent infections and diseases that correspond to the specific part of the immune system that is involved. These **opportunistic infections** are caused by common pathogens that are easily controlled by a healthy immune system. Only in persons with compromised immune systems do they grow out of control.

Immune deficiencies may be acute and temporary or chronic. There are two types of chronic immune deficiency: primary and secondary. **Primary immune deficiency** is usually the result of a genetic defect that becomes evident at a young age. There are many types of primary immune dysfunctions, and any part of the immune system may be affected. People with primary immune deficiency are usually brought up in germ-free enclosures, but they still rarely live to adulthood.

Secondary immune deficiency is more common and occurs in people who had previously normal immune function. Hospitalized patients and the

447

very old sometimes experience secondary immune deficiency as a result of serious prolonged illness that overburdens the immune system, but in such cases it is reversible. However, when an immune deficiency remains chronic, the person is often mortally weakened in both body and mind, eventually worn down by recurrent opportunistic infections, and dies.

David learned that he is infected with HIV, the major cause of secondary immune deficiency in the world today. He became aware of his situation when an opportunistic infection, herpes zoster—the chicken pox virus that he had been infected with as a child—reactivated and caused painful blisters that did not go away. This prompted him to go to his doctor.

Although the American Medical Association steadfastly maintains that it is the responsibility of all physicians to treat AIDS patients, nearly one-third of primary care physicians in the United States say that they would not (Gerbert, Maguire, Bleecker, Coates, & McPhee, 1991). Fortunately for David, this was not the attitude of his physician, and he had supportive and knowledgeable medical care and counseling from the beginning. Because of that, he has since learned a lot about AIDS, and that has helped him adjust to living with it.

David learned that HIV is a retrovirus and the underlying cause of AIDS. The nature and action of HIV is well-known (Hall, 1988). Like all retroviruses, HIV is nothing much more than a tiny protein-coated capsule containing an enzyme (RNA) that can alter the DNA of the cells it enters. This allows the HIV's genes to integrate with the cell's genes and take it over, using the cell to produce more HIV. The infected cells may become dysfunctional, cancerous, or die. When a cell dies, HIV is freed to infect additional cells, and the cycle continues.

Ordinarily, a virus and viral-infected cells would be identified as "nonself" and destroyed by the immune system. However, HIV infects the cells of the immune system itself, where it hides undetected. It shows a particular affinity for helper T-cells, apparently penetrating them by mimicking their identifying surface features, which it uses like a key to gain entry.

Once inside, HIV uses helper T-cells to replicate itself, severely disrupting their activities. Eventually so many virus particles are created in the T-cell that it dies and they escape to infect other cells. Also, any other infection that triggers growth and reproduction of HIV-infected T-cells also causes the virus to multiply. HIV also infects macrophages, although it does not appear to replicate within and destroy them. Macrophages migrate throughout the body and may be an important method of transport of HIV, even into the brain.

Epidemiology

AIDS has been perceived as a disease of European American gay males and intravenous (IV) drug users exclusively, but this is simply not the case (Mays & Cochran, 1988). A disproportionate rate of infection exists in U.S. minorities, particularly among African Americans and Latin Americans, and heterosexual transmission is on the rise (Mays & Cochran, 1988; Peterson & Marin, 1988). HIV infection has been reported on every continent, with the most widespread infections in Africa, Europe, and North America (Piot et al., 1988). Outside of the United States and northern Europe, AIDS is found almost exclusively in heterosexuals (CDC, 1988). In Central and East Africa, the HIV infection rate may be as high as 8% to 10% of the urban population (Ungar, 1989). In contrast, the U.S. infection rate is believed to be less than 1%.

It is difficult to determine the infection rate for the entire population. However, during 1989 and 1990, two large community-based, randomly selected samples were interviewed under the auspices of the Los Angeles County Department of Health Services (Kanouse et al., 1991a; Kanouse et al., 1991b). One involved 300 homosexual and bisexual men and one involved more than 1,300 heterosexual men and women, all residing in Los Angeles County. This is one of the most representative community studies of AIDS.

Among the homosexual and bisexual men, 66% reported that they had been tested once or more for HIV infection, and 16% reported that they were positive. In the general population, 23% reported that they had been tested for HIV, and about $\frac{1}{2}$ of 1% reported that they were positive. Although collected in relative anonymity, these data are based on self-report and may be subject to underreporting.

In the United States, the rate of *increase* of new infections grew rapidly and then peaked in the mid-1980s, so the infection rate may have plateaued (Brookmeyer, 1991). Unless the rate of new infections declines, however, AIDS will remain a significant problem for many years. With the rate of HIV infection plateauing, the incidence of AIDS may also plateau, although for the near future, the number of AIDS cases may continue to rise because of the delayed onset of disease. Worldwide, however, the situation is much worse. The World Health Organization recently had to revise its infection estimates upward to between 15 and 20 million people infected by the mid- or late 1990s, and 30 to 40 million by the turn of the century (Brookmeyer, 1991).

TRANSMISSION OF HIV

Despite the high infection rate, HIV is a relatively "weak" virus that is not very contagious. It is difficult to transmit HIV from person to person, and it does not easily survive in the body once it is transmitted (Batchelor, 1988). HIV is killed by heat, drying, bleach, hand soap, detergent, and alcohol and does not survive outside the body for any length of time. Therefore, HIV is not transmitted by casual contact (CDC, 1985). Even close, nonsexual contact such as that which occurs in a household, at work, or at school cannot transmit it. In people who have had close household contact with persons with AIDS (for example, bathing, dressing, and eating together), there have been no reported cases of HIV transmission (Koop, 1986). Also, in the most physically intimate relationship possible, that between a woman and her fetus, most studies show that transmission of HIV is only about 30% (Oxtoby, 1990).

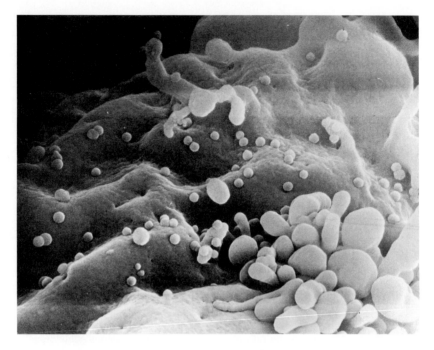

A close-up of the surface of a dead T-lymphocyte infected by dozens of smaller, round-appearing HIV particles, some of which are escaping from the cell's interior.

HIV is transmitted by direct contact with fluid that contains HIV infected helper T-lymphocytes. They are present in blood, saliva, tears, semen, mucous, breast milk, and vaginal secretions. However, there is no report of transmission by saliva, tears, or air (through expelled mucous). That is because, although HIV has been detected in all of these fluids, it is in such a low concentration in some of them that it poses almost no danger of infection. One of the codiscoverers of HIV calculated that it would take one quart of fluid (tears, sweat, saliva, or urine) injected directly into the bloodstream for there to be any likelihood of infection (Batchelor, 1988). The only confirmed means of transmission is from direct blood-to-blood contact through hypodermic needles and blood transfusions or sexually through semen and vaginal secretions (CDC, 1985). In the United States and Europe, the majority of infections have occurred through sharing of hypodermic needles or male–male sexual contact, whereas in Africa the majority of infections have occurred through male–female sexual contact.

When HIV enters the body, the immune system reacts toward it the way that it does toward any other antigen. Antibody is manufactured by B-cells, and it is attacked by the nonspecific cellular components of the immune system. However, if the virus enters in sufficiently large numbers, it may not be eliminated before it infects macrophages and helper T-cells. The immune system is not able to detect or react to HIV once it is inside these cells (Batchelor, 1988) because they are recognized as self. HIV multiplies unchecked from that protected position.

TESTING FOR HIV

The two most widely used tests, the enzyme-linked immunosorbent assay (ELISA) and the Western Blot, detect the presence of antibody to HIV. Usually, the presence of antibody indicates a past infection with a pathogen. However, because HIV infects helper T-cells, where it remains unaffected by the immune system, the presence of HIV antibody indicates a *current* infection.

The CDC has issued recommendations for those who should take the HIV antibody test (see Box 10.3-1). These are considered "high risk groups." There is usually a great deal of anxiety surrounding the decision as to whether or not to take the test, and counseling before and after is recommended. Just trying to get up the courage to take the test is often anxiety provoking, and taking the test is usually a traumatic experience. Many people underestimate the extent of anxiety they will have while waiting for results, which can take from one day to two weeks, depending on the setting. Those with positive results especially need follow-up counseling because many people misunderstand the meaning of medical tests and the progression of HIV infection.

A "positive" result means that the test has detected antibody to HIV in a sample of a person's blood. This means that the virus is *probably* present in infected helper T-cells. How accurate is a positive result? If you are in a "high risk group" (see Box 10.3-1), a positive result is more accurate than if you are not. The reason for that is simply the mathematics involved in determining the

---

Box 10.3-1   WHO SHOULD TAKE THE HIV ANTIBODY TEST?

This question is very much on people's minds today. The National Center for Disease Control recommends that the following "high risk groups" take the test:

1. Persons who have shared a needle with an intravenous drug user since 1977.
2. Men who have had sex with another man since 1977, except in a strictly and mutually monogamous relationship.
3. Men or women who have had sex in an area where heterosexual transmission is known to be high such as central Africa.
4. People exposed to blood or blood products between 1977 and 1985, through transfusions or by accident.
5. Prostitutes.
6. People who have been a sexual partner with anyone in the preceding categories.

accuracy of medical tests. See Box 10.3-2 for a surprising explanation of the accuracy of the HIV antibody test and medical tests in general.

■■■■

HIV INFECTION AND THE DEVELOPMENT OF AIDS

HEALTH EFFECTS

An infection with HIV does not lead immediately or even shortly to AIDS. HIV does not destroy the entire immune system; it damages one part of the cellular branch. The humoral branch is relatively untouched, so adults do not contract the same diseases that affect people with humoral deficiencies

---

Box 10.3-2 ACCURACY OF MEDICAL TESTING

What does it mean if a medical test is considered 99% accurate? If you take the HIV test, and it is positive (indicating that you have antibodies to HIV), what is the probability that you do, in fact, have antibodies to HIV? It is *not* 99%. To understand why, you must realize that the probability of infection is related to three factors:

1. *False positives*—finding infection in someone who is *not* infected.
2. *False negatives*—not finding infection in someone who *is* infected.
3. *The base rate*—of infection in the population.

Here is how a person's probability of infection can be figured, using relatively accurate estimates of the base rate of HIV infection in the United States:

■ A 99% accurate test—such as ELISA or Western Blot—will produce 1% false positives (Sloand, Pitt, Chiarello, & Nemo, 1991).
■ It is believed that 1 out of 200 people in the U.S. population actually has an HIV infection, so the base rate is equal to 1/2 of 1 percent (0.5%).
■ So, if you took the test and were told it was positive, how worried should you be? To answer this, it must be assumed that a large number of tests—perhaps 10,000—have been administered to the general population; given the base rate of 0.5%, approximately 50 would actually be infected—"true positives"—and 9,950 would *not* be infected—"true negatives."
■ Since 99% of those who are infected would test positive, 50 positive test results would result from them (50 true positives x .99 accuracy = 49.5).
■ From the remaining 9,950 people who are *not* infected, 1% can be expected to be false positives; that is, 100 people are told that they have a positive test result, even though they are *not infected* (9,950 true negatives x .01 inaccuracy = 99.5).

(McCutchan, 1990). A classification system with four categories has been proposed for HIV infection (see Table 10.3-1). Generally, one progresses through these categories, so they may cautiously be considered as stages; however, the progression is not always uniform. Some, particularly those with undetected infections, may experience few or no symptoms before a devastating opportunistic infection and death occur.

David's outbreak of shingles meant that he was classified with ARC. He could have been asymptomatic for up to 10 years before this happened. This caused him to reflect on any and all sexual contacts that he had had over those years. He had been practicing "safer sex" the last 2 years and this somewhat relieved his concern, but he felt anxious about the possibility that he may have passed the virus on to others before that and angry at how he may have contracted it.

- Therefore, a total of 150 people have been told that they are positive (50 true positives + 100 false positives = 150), but 100 out of the 150 or *2 out of 3* who are told they are positive are *not*.
- So, the probability that *you* have the disease, if you have a positive result, is the number of true positives, 50, divided by the number of total positive test results, 150, or 33%—*if* you are in the *general population* and *not* in a high risk group.

However, if you are a member of a high risk group (see Box 10.3-1) and test positive, then the probability that you are infected approaches the overall accuracy of the test (99%), because the *base rate* in a high risk group is much higher. For example, if you are in a high risk group where the base rate is 50%, and you test positive, then the probability that you have antibodies to HIV is 99% (which you can prove by recalculating this example by starting with a base rate of 50% instead of 0.5%). For those testing positive, laboratories usually repeat the test automatically, thereby increasing its accuracy.

The first six to eight weeks following exposure to HIV is referred to as the "window period" (Sloand et al., 1991). During this period, the immune system is beginning production of antibody, so it does not show up in a positive test result until after the eighth week. For this reason, in those people with known exposure to HIV, a single negative test result is usually not considered conclusive (even though it has been repeated by the lab). Medical authorities recommend that the test be repeated approximately six months later, after a period of sexual abstinence, when the window period is completely over. This provides the immune system more opportunity to produce antibodies. A second negative result under these conditions is considered truly negative.

Table 10.3-1 CATEGORIES OF **HIV** INFECTION

CATEGORY	DESCRIPTION
Acute Infection	Within a few weeks of infection, many (perhaps half of) people develop a self-limited, 3-to-10-day illness with fever, sore throat, headache, and other symptoms. Unfortunately, the symptoms are hard to distinguish from flu or mononucleosis and are almost never diagnosed as HIV related.
Asymptomatic	At the beginning of this period, an HIV antibody test will be negative, and the virus can only be detected by a culture. However, virtually all people will test positive 6 months after infection. The length of the asymptomatic period is unknown but it may last up to 10 years; during this time, the functioning of the cellular branch of the immune system gradually deteriorates. There are usually no physical or medical abnormalities during this period, and yet asymptomatic people can infect others through sexual contact.
AIDS-Related Complex (ARC)	Approximately 5 to 10 years after infection, the deterioration of cellular immunity often becomes evident with a variety of nonlethal symptoms such as chronic enlarged lymph nodes, weight loss, intermittent fever, fatigue, thrush (an oral infection of candida, a fungus), and chronic diarrhea. Women may have a different constellation of symptoms than men (for example, recurrent yeast infections). Symptoms may remit and people can be otherwise healthy for long periods of time; medical treatment may also slow the progression of the disease.
AIDS	Without intervention, a diagnosis of full-blown AIDS often occurs in the next 12–18 months following a diagnosis of ARC. AIDS consists of a continuation of ARC symptoms, along with either the development of *at least one* of several characteristic opportunistic infections, cancer, or a T-helper cell count of less than 200 per cubic millimeter of blood. The most common opportunistic infection is *Pneumocystis carinii* pneumonia (a fungal infection of the lung leading to fluid buildup and suffocation if untreated), and the most common cancer is Kaposi's sarcoma (a cancer of the capillaries that may occur in many locations internally and on the surface of the skin, where it causes purple-brown blotches). AIDS appears to express itself differently in women. They may have none of these symptoms of full-blown AIDS but may have gynecological problems such as pelvic inflammatory disease instead. Multiple opportunistic infections involving the lung, gastrointestinal tract, and brain usually result in death.

Source: Adapted from McCutchan, J. A., 1990, Virology, immunology, and clinical course of HIV infection, Journal of Consulting and Clinical Psychology, 58, 5–12.

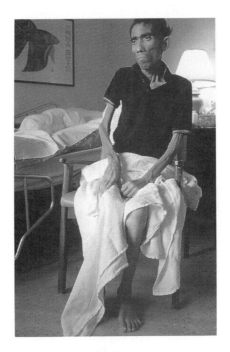

The ravages of acquired immune deficiency syndrome take their toll.

He asked himself, "Why didn't I protect others? And, why didn't I protect myself?" These were issues that he worked on with his AIDS support group, since many others were dealing with them, too. When he learned that HIV can also infect the brain, however, David's concerns turned to his mental status.

NEUROPSYCHOLOGICAL EFFECTS

HIV is often found in brain cells (McCutchan, 1990). A global deterioration in mental functioning due to HIV infection of the brain and known as **AIDS dementia complex** can occur, but typically only at the end stage of the disease (Navia, Jordan, & Price, 1986). Because of this, there have been numerous neuropsychological studies of people with HIV infection and AIDS, but these have produced conflicting results as to the severity of impairment, perhaps due to methodological differences (Grant & Heaton, 1990). Most studies have compared groups of subjects who were either HIV negative, HIV positive but asymptomatic, or had ARC or AIDS. All of these studies have found some degree of neuropsychological impairment in most, but not all, people with advanced AIDS (Grant & Heaton, 1990).

However, in comparisons of people who are HIV positive but asymptomatic with people who are HIV negative, some studies have found only slight to moderate impairment (for example, Lunn, et al., 1991; Skoraszewski, Ball, & Mikulka, 1991), while other studies have found no significant impairment at all (for example, Swanson, Bieliauskas, Kessler, Zeller, & Cronin-Stubbs, 1991; van Gorp et al., 1991). Currently, the most likely conclusion is that some HIV positive but asymptomatic people, but not a majority, may have slight neuropsychological impairments. This information, given to David during a neuropsychological consultation, helped to ease his concern, especially since he had no neurological symptoms.

MEDICAL MANAGEMENT

Although there is active research on both fronts, there is currently no vaccine and no cure for HIV infection. Therefore, AIDS remains as nearly 100% fatal as any disease in history. There are, however, many long-term survivors (people living over 5 years after a diagnosis of AIDS), and as specific treatments for each of the opportunistic infections become available, longevity is expected to increase. It is currently projected that AIDS may become a chronic disease in which previously lethal opportunistic infections are manageable indefinitely.

At this time, only two agents have been demonstrated to be effective against HIV: azidothymidine (AZT) and dideoxyinosine (DDI). Both AZT and DDI appear to interfere with the ability of HIV to replicate, stopping its proliferation. However, both often produce side effects, the most dangerous of which are anemia (reduction and damage of red blood cells) with AZT and damage to the peripheral nervous system with DDI.

AZT is now prescribed for persons with ARC because it may delay the onset of AIDS. Even asymptomatic carriers may receive AZT if there is a significant drop in their helper T-cells. These medications may lengthen the latency period, with people remaining longer at an earlier stage of the disease. In one experiment, survival from the time of diagnosis with AIDS was only 190 days for people who did not receive AZT, compared to 770 days for those who did receive it (Moore, Hidalgo, Sugland, & Chaisson, 1991).

Healthy individuals have about 1,000 helper T-cells per cubic millimeter of blood, and they typically outnumber suppressor T-cells by a ratio of 2 to 1 (Berkow & Fletcher, 1987). At the time AIDS is diagnosed, most people have 200 or less helper T-cells and a reversal of the helper to suppressor T-cell ratio. When David found out he was HIV positive, his doctor did another test to find out the numbers of helper and suppressor T-cells. David had 400 helper T-cells and a ratio of 1 to 1. He was on the way to developing AIDS but was not there yet. His doctor prescribed AZT, which he has been taking for a year, and recent tests indicate a rise in helper T-cells to near 600, which is usually sufficient to keep opportunistic infections in check.

HEALTH PSYCHOLOGY AND AIDS

Although there are currently tremendous research efforts directed at developing a vaccine or finding a cure for AIDS, without them, prevention programs are of the utmost urgency and behavioral scientists have taken a central role in the prevention of AIDS and HIV infection (Baum & Nesselhof, 1988). Prevention of AIDS has two focuses: (a) preventing additional people from contracting HIV, and (b) preventing those who have HIV from progressing to full-blown AIDS. Health psychologists are active in both.

PREVENTION

EDUCATION EFFORTS   The primary method of preventing new infections of HIV has been large-scale community education. Supported by the U.S. Surgeon General, education has concentrated on describing the methods of transmission and ways to prevent it (Koop, 1986). Unfortunately, health education efforts alone usually do not produce significant behavioral change (Haynes, 1976).

However, the two large-scale community studies in Los Angeles County do suggest some self-reported change in behavior that may have resulted from education efforts (Kanouse et al., 1991a, 1991b). Twenty-nine percent of randomly selected heterosexuals said that they made at least one change in their behavior in the past 10 years as a result of AIDS awareness. The biggest categories of change were becoming more selective in choosing a partner (24%), reducing the number of sexual partners or casual partners (21%), or using condoms more (16%). Even if these self-reported changes were made, these data still suggest that 71% of heterosexuals have made no change in their behavior. One possible reason might be that they are in monogamous relationships and believe that their sexual behavior is safe; however, about 30% of the sample were not in a monogamous relationship.

In contrast, it does appear that education efforts have had a profound effect among homosexual males (Joseph, Montgomery, Emmons, & Kessler, 1987). In the Los Angeles County survey, the principal modes of transmission of HIV were nearly universally known among males who engage in sex with males (Kanouse et al., 1991a). One in ten reported becoming celibate, a third of those who were having anal intercourse stopped, half used condoms more often, and four out of five reduced the number of sexual partners.

These dramatic changes in behavior may not have resulted solely from knowledge about HIV. The health belief model (described in Module 3.1) predicts that perceived threat, susceptibility, and severity are related to health behavior. People who have heard of AIDS only through media accounts, who perceive of AIDS as being remote and not affecting their community or

Education efforts to fight the spread of acquired immune deficiency syndrome often require taking to the streets.

acquaintances, are less likely to perceive it as a threat. In contrast, the more personal involvement one has with people who have AIDS, the greater the perceived threat, susceptibility, and severity will be. Eighty-six percent of homosexual and bisexual males in the Los Angeles County study reported personally knowing someone, either living or dead, with AIDS. Therefore, the perception of one's own risk is very real to them and probably contributed, along with education efforts, to behavior change.

Consistent with these self-reported changes in behavior, the rate of new HIV infections among gay men in Los Angeles, San Francisco, and New York has fallen dramatically (Glasner & Kaslow, 1990; Steinbrook, 1988). There has been a steady drop in new infections among subjects in longitudinal study groups in San Francisco, from a high of 10% to 18% becoming HIV positive per year in 1982–1984 to a low of 1% to 4% becoming HIV positive per year by 1986. This reduction in the infection rate among gay men has been called one of "the most profound modifications of personal health-related behaviors ever recorded" (Stall, Coates, & Hoff, 1988, p. 878).

In contrast, education efforts do not appear to have had any effect on the rate of transmission among IV drug users, whose rate of new infections from 1984 to 1987 appears to have ranged from as high as 60% in New York City to 10% in other parts of the country. Nor have these prevention efforts had any effect in minority communities, among homosexual and bisexual men in rural areas, or among heterosexual adolescents and adults in general (Kelly & Murphy, 1992). From 1988 to 1990, the incidence of AIDS increased 40% in adolescents (Blake, 1990). Therefore, the factors related to behavioral risk reduction in urban gay men may provide a starting point but only a starting point for understanding AIDS risk prevention in general. In addition, since many IV drug users also know people with AIDS, personal knowledge of someone with AIDS apparently does not always lead to behavior change, so researchers have been investigating other factors.

FACTORS RELATED TO RISK REDUCTION   Stall, Coates, and Hoff (1988) reviewed 24 studies of factors related to behavioral risk reduction in homosexual and bisexual men. Knowledge about AIDS risk was the variable most strongly associated with risk reduction in the short term; however, it was not related to risk reduction in the long term. This confirms that educational programs may reduce risk briefly, but more is required for long-term risk reduction. Stall et al. recommended targeting specific groups with behavioral intervention programs, and they suggested that two variables found to relate to risk reduction in homosexual and bisexual men may be especially important: (a) separating sex from drug and alcohol use and (b) increasing self-efficacy.

The use of drugs and alcohol during sex seems to promote high-risk sexual activity (Stall, Wiley, McKusick, Coates, & Ostrow, 1986; Siegel, Mesagno, Chen, & Christ, 1987). Drugs and alcohol increase impulsivity in "the heat of passion," leading to unsafe behavior. So, behavioral interventions that teach people to separate sexual activity and the use of alcohol and drugs might also result in a reduction of unsafe sex activities.

Since self-efficacy is a belief in one's ability to make the behavioral changes necessary to reduce risk and improve health, it should result in less risky behavior. Research has shown that self-efficacy is strongly related to risk reduction in gay men (Stall et al., 1988), and it may be one of the few variables related to reduced risk over time (Joseph, Montgomery, Kirscht, Kessler, Ostrow, Emmons, & Phair, 1987). In a recent study of AIDS risk-reduction behavior in 389 gay men, self-efficacy, along with several other variables from the health belief model (for example, perceived risk and barriers to change), accounted for 70% of the variance in the total number of sexual partners and anonymous partners over a 6-month period (Aspinwall, Kemeny, Taylor, Schneider, & Dudley, 1991).

Social psychological research has uncovered another variable related to low risk behavior in gay men. Homosexuals are a stigmatized group, and individuals can be isolated from social support, their family, and the community (Coates et al., 1987). Correlational research has indicated that the more comfortable gay men are with being gay (the higher their self-acceptance), the more likely they are to be involved in social networks where AIDS-preventive behavior is supported and the safer their behavior (Fischer, 1988). Data from a study of protective condom use in 529 gay men also supports this conclusion (Catania et al., 1991). Among the variables most related to the increased use of condoms is informal support (from friends, parents, siblings, and so on).

Two other variables—learning one's HIV status and expecting condoms to have a positive effect on health—are also related to increased condom use.

In summary, research has supported a number of psychosocial factors related to risk reduction: separating sex from alcohol and drug use, self-efficacy, social support, knowing one's HIV status. Unfortunately, recent research suggests that up to 45% of men who have initiated safer sex practices may relapse (Kelly & Murphy, 1992). Relapsing is related to two factors: (a) intoxicant use; and (b) the development of affectionate, committed relationships as opposed to casual partnerships for sex. This second factor is ironic. Apparently being in a committed relationship (which, if monogamous, is a recommended safe sex practice) lends to a false sense of safety. Unprotected sex is safe *only* when both monogamous partners are known to be HIV negative.

PSYCHOSOCIAL EFFECTS OF HIV ANTIBODY TESTING   Several studies have evaluated the effects of being tested for HIV and subsequent risk behaviors in homosexual and bisexual men (reviewed by Jacobsen, Perry, & Hirsch, 1990). Generally, when people are tested and notified of their results, risky behaviors decrease. Notification of a positive result has the greatest risk-reduction effect, while notification of a negative result has a weaker effect, perhaps because receiving a negative result reduces pretesting anxiety about AIDS. As might be expected, being tested, but choosing not to be notified of the results, has little effect on risk reduction.

A recent experiment evaluated the effect of HIV testing and education on 186 heterosexual subjects, two-thirds of whom were men (Wenger, Linn, Epstein, & Shapiro, 1991). Subjects were randomly assigned to receive either: (a) AIDS education alone (the placebo group); or (b) AIDS education, an HIV antibody test, and the test results. All of the subjects who were tested turned out to be negative. Nevertheless, upon follow-up at the end of 8 weeks, 40% of the subjects who received the education and the test were either using condoms, avoiding genital intercourse, or aware that their partner had also tested negative. Only 20% of those in the placebo group had made these behavior changes. So, it appears that just undergoing the test for HIV antibody *and* learning the result significantly increases risk-reduction behavior, compared to AIDS education alone.

HONESTY AND SEX   Other research suggests that people frequently lie about their sexual history and the results of the HIV antibody test (whether or not they have been tested). In a study of 138 mostly low income HIV positive men (83% of whom were Spanish speaking and 91% of whom were homosexual or bisexual), 45% reported that they had been sexually active since learning of their HIV status, and 52% reported that they had kept their infection secret from one or more partners (Marks, Richardson, & Maldonado, 1991).

Another survey conducted among 442 college students at a large state university in California also investigated sexual dishonesty (Kalechstein, Triplett, Rolfe, Rotstein, & Cochran, 1988). The students' responses had menacing implications for health (see Table 10.3-2), because a large number of them admitted that they would lie to a potential sexual partner about their own HIV risk status. Most ominously, 20% of men said they would lie and say they had a negative HIV antibody test even if they had never taken it, while 40% of women said they would rely on the men's answers to such questions. This situation undoubtedly facilitates the transmission of HIV.

BIOPSYCHOSOCIAL FACTORS AND AIDS: IMPLICATIONS FOR TREATMENT

SLOWING AIDS PROGRESSION The development of AIDS may require more than just infection by HIV. The wide variance in the course of the disease, from those who deteriorate rapidly shortly after infection to those who live many years with few symptoms, suggests that cofactors are involved. Genetic inheritance plays a role in primary immune deficiency disorders, and it may be that there is some genetic variance in the ability of the immune system to withstand HIV infection. Also, lifestyle and behavior factors that suppress immune system functioning may play a role in susceptibility to or progression of the infection.

In order to prevent the progression of AIDS, it has been suggested that researchers take psychoneuroimmunological cofactors such as stress into

Table 10.3-2   WOULD COLLEGE STUDENTS LIE ABOUT SEX?

QUESTION	MEN	WOMEN
Would report *fewer* sexual partners than they really had.	47%	42%
Would *never* admit a one-time impulsive sexual affair.	42%	33%
Would say they had a negative HIV test result even if never had taken it.	20%	>1%

Source: Based on Kalechstein, A., Triplett, J., Rolfe, E., Rotstein, K., & Cochran, S. D., April 1988, Little white lies: Sexual dishonesty among college students. *Paper presented at the meeting of the Western Psychological Association, Bulingame, Calif.*

account (Baum & Nesselhof, 1988; Livingston, 1988; Solomon & Temoshok, 1987). As noted, stress can cause immune suppression. This, in turn, can activate latent viruses in the body and perhaps HIV (Kiecolt-Glaser & Glaser, 1987). Also, future research should examine the effects of classical conditioning on immune responsiveness, because conditioning procedures may be an effective way of dealing with side effects of HIV medication (Kiecolt-Glaser & Glaser, 1988). The use of conditioning techniques in the treatment of cancer has also been suggested (Cautela, 1977).

Antoni et al. (1990) recently proposed a psychoneuroimmunological model outlining how HIV disease may be accelerated or decelerated (see Figure 10.3-1). In a test of this model, Antoni et al. reported a study in which 45 minutes of aerobic exercise 3 times a week resulted in a significant boost in the immune system functioning of HIV positive men as measured by the number of helper T-cells. A correlational study also found support for the application of psychoneuroimmunological principles to AIDS (Temoshok, Zich, Solomon, & Stites, 1987). There was a significant relationship between psychological variables and immunological measures, but the sample size of 12 limits conclusions that can be drawn from this study.

A more recent experiment randomly assigned 50 gay men to an exercise group or a nontreatment group (Schneiderman, Antoni, Ironson, Laperriere, & Fletcher, 1992). Exercise helped buffer the psychological impact of learning one is HIV positive *and* produced some immunologic benefits. The magnitude of the increase in helper T-cells was about the same as that found with AZT.

It also appears that cognitive-behavioral stress management might affect immune system functioning. Forty-seven healthy gay men who were unaware of their HIV status were randomly assigned to either a nontreatment group or a cognitive-behavioral group that met twice weekly for 10 weeks (Antoni et al., 1991). Measures of psychological distress and immune system functioning were taken at the beginning, 5 weeks into the cognitive-behavioral training, which was just before they were notified of their HIV status (17 were HIV positive), and at 1 week after the conclusion of the training. Cognitive-behavioral stress management did significantly buffer the psychological distress encountered in learning about HIV test results and, most importantly, it also increased helper T-cell and NK cell counts.

The results of these studies hold promise for future patient care, and they certainly deserve replication. The use of exercise and cognitive-behavioral stress management to delay the onset of AIDS symptoms is both inexpensive and noninvasive with few, if any, side effects. Pending further study, they might become safe and effective methods of slowing the progression of AIDS.

SUPPORTIVE PSYCHOTHERAPY   AIDS is devastating to mental and physical well-being. There is disease, weakness, and pain, coupled with social stigma and the high likelihood of disability and death. About half of people with AIDS have significant psychological problems, but even more, 75%, of

Figure 10.3-1 A PSYCHONEUROIMMUNOLOGICAL MODEL FOR ACCELERATING OR DECELERATING HIV DISEASE PROGRESSION

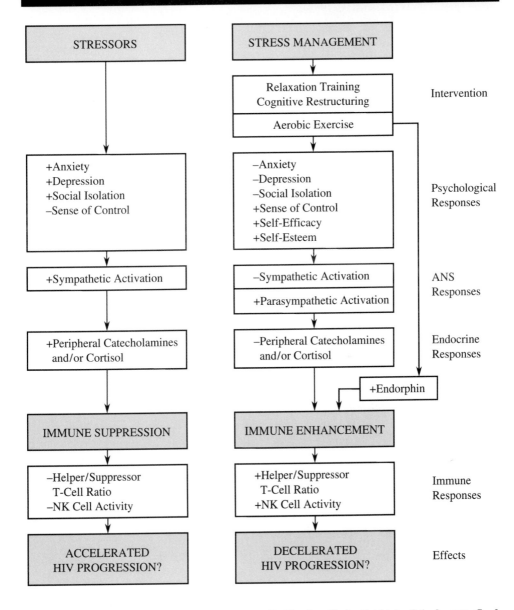

Source: Adapted from Antoni, M. H., Schneiderman, N., Fletcher, M. A., Goldstein, D.A., Ironson, G., & Laperriere, A., 1990, Psychoneuroimmunology and HIV-1, Journal of Consulting and Clinical Psychology, 58, 38–49.

people with ARC do (Holland & Tross, 1985; Selwyn, 1986). This probably reflects additional stress among ARC patients due to the uncertainty of their status. Just a positive HIV antibody status can result in anxiety, fear, depression, psychosomatic preoccupation, loss of sexual drive, and relationship conflicts (McKusick, 1988).

With his diagnosis of ARC, David went through all of these reactions at first. His psychotherapy group eventually helped him to realize that he was not dying and that he was still in relatively good health. He could still work and remain a productive member of society. He also found the support he needed to explain his medical condition to his mother and stepfather, who proved steadfast in his time of need. His anxiety and depression eventually subsided. David decided that the best he could do about his guilt was to tell his sexual partners of the last 10 years about his situation and ask them to be tested—this was the most difficult thing of all to do, but at least he might be preventing them from infecting anyone else.

David remained symptom-free for more than a year, and gradually his sex drive returned, posing a dilemma. He had heard that the only "safe sex" is no sex with a partner, yet he craved physical contact and affection. He began to have nightmares about accidentally infecting someone else when a condom ruptured during "safer sex." He had been meeting other HIV positive people through support groups and supposed that if he only had sex with someone with HIV, he could not be responsible for infecting anyone new. However, David's doctor quickly pointed out the risk involved. An accidental re-inoculation with the virus might overwhelm his already weakened immune system. Furthermore, reports indicate that HIV may be mutating into different strains (Hall, 1988), each one of which might produce a separate infection and an additional challenge to the immune system. David learned that he could have close physical contact—touching and hugging with someone—but absolutely no exchange of bodily fluids of any kind in order to be entirely "safe." This could meet his need for physical contact and affection, but he would have to forgo forever his desire for other types of sexual contact. He reasoned he could do this; after all, he was glad just to be alive and feeling good.

David's health care is exceptional. Those who treat him, from the physicians to the counselors, are all knowledgeable, supportive, and professional. Eventually, however, they may need to help David prepare for his death and their own feelings of loss for a patient they have come to respect and care for.

The U.S. Department of Health and Human Services (1986b) has made several recommendations that health care providers should consider in treating people with AIDS. These guidelines suggest that professionals should be aware of their own anxieties about AIDS and working with fatally ill people. They should closely monitor patients' changing psychological reactions to the disease process and their neuropsychological status. Finally, they should encourage strong social support networks as part of treatment. For the most part, treatment issues are similar to other debilitating and fatal diseases, such as cancer, with the important exception that AIDS in the United States currently affects groups that carry an additional heavy burden of social stigma. People with AIDS are viewed less favorably than cancer patients and are rated as more sick, sinful, untrustworthy, and dislikable (Hart, 1990).

Despite the human tragedy of this modern plague, AIDS presents health psychology with an opportunity to play a significant role in understanding biopsychosocial cofactors in immunity, as well as to provide educational, preventive, and supportive care to people with HIV infection. Perhaps David's situation and what he learned has made you more aware of the immune system and its vital importance in maintaining life.

MODULE SUMMARY

The next chapter deals with the cardiovascular and respiratory systems. However, before continuing, make use of this quick review of AIDS:

1. People with immune deficiency are unable to fight off opportunistic infections.
2. In contrast to primary immune deficiencies, which are inherited, AIDS is a secondary immune deficiency, which occurs in people with previously healthy immune functioning.
3. HIV is a retrovirus that infects helper T-cells and uses them to reproduce.
4. HIV infects people worldwide. Less than 1% of the U.S. population is infected with HIV, but this amounts to between 1 and 2 million people; 112,000 people have died of AIDS in the United States.
5. The incidence of new HIV infection has dropped dramatically in homosexual and bisexual men in the United States, but it is rising among minorities, IV drug users, and heterosexuals.
6. HIV is a "weak" virus that is difficult to transmit; it can be transmitted by direct exchange of certain bodily fluids such as blood and semen.
7. HIV tests detect the presence of antibody in the blood with about 99% accuracy; however, the probability that a positive result indicates a true HIV infection is a function of whether or not a person is in a high risk group.

8. HIV infection does not immediately result in AIDS. There are several categories of disease: acute infection, asymptomatic, ARC, and AIDS. People may be infected but asymptomatic for up to 10 years, during which time they can transmit the virus to others. HIV gradually reduces the number of helper T-cells. A diagnosis of AIDS is made when opportunistic diseases are present.

9. HIV enters the brain and may infect neurons. At the end stage of AIDS, dementia and neuropsychological impairment are more common. Research suggests that some HIV positive but asymptomatic people, but not a majority, may have slight neuropsychological impairments.

10. There is no cure for AIDS, although two medications—AZT and DDI—prolong the asymptomatic period and perhaps prolong life. It is currently projected that AIDS may become a chronic disease in which previously lethal opportunistic infections are manageable indefinitely.

11. Education may increase HIV-preventive behaviors. In gay men, it appears that education and personal acquaintance with someone who has AIDS combine to produce significant health behavior change.

12. Separating sex from drug and alcohol use and increasing personal efficacy appear to be cofactors that decrease risk of HIV infection.

13. Taking the HIV antibody test and receiving a positive result are linked to a subsequent reduction in risky behavior.

14. Research suggests that people would lie to sexual partners about whether they have been tested for HIV and what the results are.

15. Cognitive-behavioral stress management and aerobic exercise may help reduce stress and enhance immune system functioning, possibly slowing the progression of AIDS.

16. People with HIV infection often have many profound psychological problems and concerns to deal with, including death. Supportive psychotherapy is a helpful adjunct to medical treatment.

11

CARDIOVASCULAR AND RESPIRATORY SYSTEMS: FUNCTION AND ORGANIZATION

11.1 Coronary Heart Disease
11.2 Cerebral Vascular Disease

While rushing from the parking lot to the office one day, Richard, a 47-year-old wholesale salesman for a home appliance manufacturer, noticed tightness and pressure in the center of his chest, just beneath the sternum. It passed in a couple of minutes after he was seated at his desk. A week later, he noticed a similar sensation while finishing the 18th hole on the golf course, except this time there was also pain in his left arm. It persisted for about 10 minutes. He thought it might have been something he ate for lunch and promptly forgot about it. If he had not had his annual physical examination the next day, he might not have mentioned it to his doctor. The fact that he did probably saved him from a heart attack and may have saved his life.

All life requires energy in some form to maintain, grow, and reproduce. Energy for the body is produced when cells combine glucose with oxygen—a process called *metabolism*. Three organ systems are involved in providing glucose and oxygen to the cells. The digestive system provides glucose. The cardiovascular and respiratory systems provide oxygen and transport it and glucose to every cell in the body. The nervous system monitors the cells' use of glucose and oxygen, and with the endocrine system, it can speed up or slow down heart rate and respiration, depending on either the *perceived* need for energy (as in a threat) or the body's *actual level* of exertion.

THE CARDIOVASCULAR SYSTEM

Richard's pressure and chest pain—known as *angina pectoris*—occurred when the demand he placed on his heart exceeded the ability of his cardiovascular and respiratory systems to supply oxygenated blood. What he felt was his heart literally starving for oxygen. The cardiovascular and respiratory systems are normally able to meet the physical demands placed on them, and even some extraordinary ones if you consider marathon running. How, then, can Richard have experienced angina pectoris with such minimal physical exertion? That question is answered in the next module. First, we will follow the blood through a complete circuit of the cardiovascular and respiratory systems, pausing along the way to describe their essential parts.

THE HEART AND VASCULAR SYSTEM

The cardiovascular system is pictured in Figure 11.1. It consists of the heart—the system's central pump—and the blood vessels. The circuit begins as oxygenated blood from the lungs flows into the heart's left upper chamber, or *atrium*, then into the left lower chamber, or *ventricle*. Contraction of the heart forces the blood out of the ventricle through the *aorta*, the main artery leaving the heart. This bright red, oxygenated blood is dispersed throughout the body in gradually smaller vessels, the *arteries*, *arterioles*, and finally the capillaries. The *capillaries* are thin vessels through which nutrients and oxygen are delivered to individual cells. Waste products and carbon dioxide also enter the blood through the capillaries, causing it to turn dark blue. The blood returns to the heart through gradually larger vessels, beginning with the *venules* and then the *veins*. The veins enter the right atrium and then ventricle, which contracts to force it out through the pulmonary artery to the lungs.

THE CARDIAC CYCLE

At rest, it takes about 20 seconds for blood, driven by the regular beating of the heart, to make a complete cycle through the cardiovascular and respiratory systems (Davis & Park, 1981). The *cardiac cycle* is a 2-phase process. In the first phase, called *systole*, blood is pumped out of the ventricles into the body and lungs simultaneously, causing a rise in blood pressure. In the second phase, called *diastole*, the heart muscle relaxes and blood rushes into the atria. Valves between the atria and ventricles and between the ventricles and the aorta and pulmonary artery ensure that blood flows in the proper direction. Diastole is the crucial period during which the heart rests, and it is the only rest the heart muscle ever gets.

Figure 11.1   THE CIRCULATORY SYSTEM

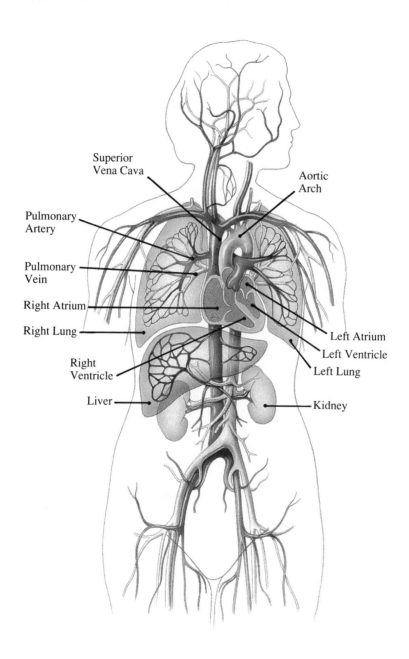

Superior
Vena Cava

Aortic
Arch

Pulmonary
Artery

Pulmonary
Vein

Right Atrium

Right Lung

Right
Ventricle

Liver

Left Atrium

Left Ventricle

Left Lung

Kidney

The normal heart rate in infants in about 110 beats per minute, but it declines gradually throughout the life span. In adults, the heart normally beats between 72 and 78 times a minute (Berkow & Fletcher, 1987). People in poorer physical condition have a higher heart rate, while well-conditioned athletes can have a heart rate in the low 50s. Stress and exercise increase the heart rate at the expense of the *diastolic* phase, so the heart has less time to rest. Temporarily, this is of little consequence, but chronically, this lack of rest can compromise the heart's strength, reducing the volume of blood pumped.

Blood Pressure

The force of the blood against the vascular walls creates *blood pressure*, which results from three factors: (a) the force of the beating of the heart; (b) the volume of the blood; and (c) the resistance of the blood vessels (Marieb, 1989). Blood pressure increases with more forceful beating of the heart, a higher volume of blood, and more resistance in the blood vessels.

Blood pressure is monitored and regulated by the *medulla oblongata* at the base of the brain stem. It can adjust the force and rate of the heart's contractions and act on muscles in the walls of blood vessels to constrict or dilate them, causing a rise or drop in blood pressure. The medulla regulates blood pressure without the involvement of higher brain centers, but the cortex (particularly the hypothalamus) and the sympathetic nervous system have direct connections to the medulla and can affect its function (Marieb, 1989).

Blood pressure is usually given in two measurements related to how many millimeters (mm) it can raise mercury in a glass column. One measurement is taken during systole, when the heart contracts and the pressure is greatest. *Systolic pressure* is the first measurement given and the higher of the two numbers. The second measurement of blood pressure is taken during diastole, when the heart is at rest. Called *diastolic pressure* it is the lower of the two. Normal blood pressure is less than 140/85 mm (USDHHS, 1984).

The Respiratory System

The lungs are part of the respiratory system, which also consists of the nose, mouth, pharynx, trachea, and diaphragm. The respiratory system (see Figure 11.2) provides a mechanism for oxygen and carbon dioxide to be exchanged between the blood and the air.

Respiration has two phases: inhalation and expiration. Inhalation is an active process that occurs when the muscles of the diaphragm and ribs contract,

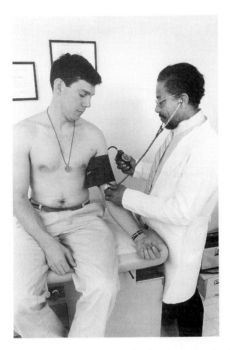

Blood pressure readings are a familiar part of a physical examination.

expanding the chest and inflating the lungs. Oxygenated air is drawn through the nose, pharynx, larynx, trachea, and bronchus, which warm and humidify it, facilitating the exchange of gases. These structures also filter foreign matter and infectious agents from the air. Sneezing and coughing expel some more, while those that get through are ultimately trapped by mucous excreted from membranes lining the airway.

As the air moves toward the lungs, it enters a large tube called the *bronchus*, which separates into two smaller tubes entering the left and right lung. The bronchus branches off into smaller tubes, the *bronchioles*, that end within each lung in millions of *alveoli*—small, thin bubblelike membranes that give the lungs their spongy appearance (see Figure 11.3). The cardiovascular and respiratory systems interface at the alveoli. Each alveolus is only one cell thick and is surrounded by tiny capillaries. Oxygen passes through this thin membrane into the blood, and carbon dioxide passes in the other direction.

Exhalation is a passive process. The muscles of the diaphragm and ribs relax, and the chest cavity shrinks to normal. This expels most, but not all, of the air from the alveoli. The reoxygenated blood then returns to the left atrium and ventricle of the heart, completing the circuit of the blood through the cardiovascular and respiratory systems.

Chronic Obstructive Pulmonary Disease

Even if the cardiovascular system is healthy, problems in the respiratory system can impair health by reducing the supply of available oxygen. **Chronic obstructive pulmonary disease** or COPD is a relatively new diagnostic category. People with COPD have frequent pulmonary infections and **dyspnea**—a

---

Figure 11.2   The Respiratory System

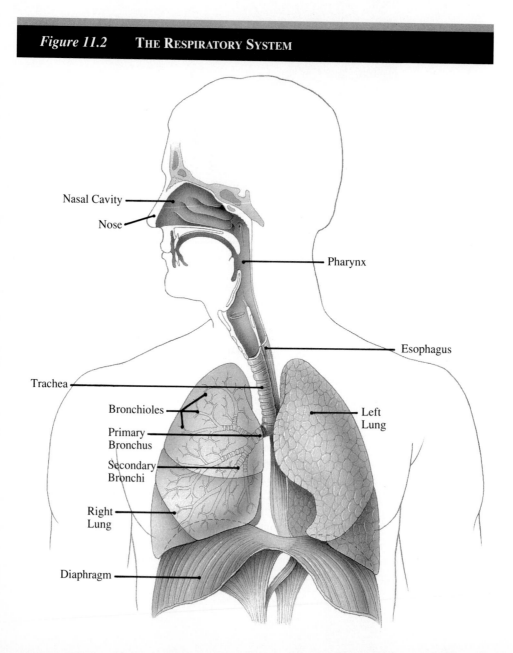

breathing difficult sometimes referred to as "air hunger." They may also develop respiratory failure, which can cause death. COPD places an additional burden on the health of people who already have a reduced supply of blood to the heart and brain, as in coronary heart disease (CHD) or stroke, and those who also have arteriosclerosis can least tolerate the reduction of oxygen. COPD is a major contributor to disability and death in the United States, accounting for more deaths per year than lung cancer and second only to heart disease as a cause of disability (Berkow & Fletcher, 1987).

CONDITIONS RELATED TO COPD The term "COPD" was introduced to acknowledge the fact that three respiratory disorders—asthma, emphysema, and chronic bronchitis—often coexist (Berkow & Fletcher, 1987). Figure 11.4 depicts the interrelationship among these conditions.

Figure 11.3   ALVEOLI

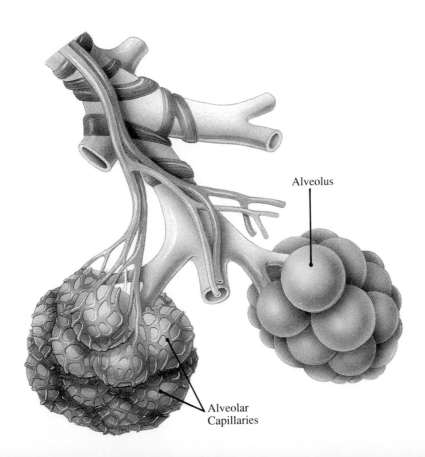

Alveolus

Alveolar Capillaries

Actor Dick York died from chronic obstructive pulmonary disease, related to emphysema, from smoking multiple packs of cigarettes a day for many years.

Although bronchitis, emphysema, and asthma all have milder forms, when they are chronic and severe, they usually result in COPD.

Bronchitis is characterized by an oversecretion of mucous in the lower respiratory system, a mucous-producing cough, and structural changes in the bronchi (Berkow & Fletcher, 1987). Acute bronchitis is usually the result of inflammation of the lower respiratory tract and often accompanies or follows a cold. Chronic bronchitis is a behavioral disease because it is almost always caused by cigarette smoking, with environmental pollution a minor causative factor (Marieb, 1989).

Emphysema is distinguished by destructive changes in the alveolar walls that cause their degeneration. There is loss of elasticity in the lungs and also the destruction of pulmonary capillaries (Berkow & Fletcher, 1987). The airways collapse during expiration and become obstructed. Cigarette smoking is also a major factor in the development of emphysema, although hereditary factors may play a small role (Marieb, 1989).

Asthma is characterized by heightened sensitivity of the immune response—particularly inflammation—in the respiratory system. During an attack, there is a sudden spasm of the bronchi and increased mucus production. This makes it difficult to expel air from the lungs, and less oxygen is able to enter the blood. There is a feeling of suffocation that is sometimes accompanied, understandably, by extreme anxiety. In an attempt to compensate for reduced airflow there may be **hyperventilation**—shallow, rapid breathing that increases oxygen intake but upsets the balance of carbon dioxide in the blood.

A precise definition of asthma has proved difficult. Intermittence and reversibility of the attacks are the hallmark of episodic or *acute asthma* (Creer, 1988). People with episodic asthma experience long symptom-free periods punctuated by acute attacks. On the other hand, those with persistent or *chronic asthma* suffer more or less continuous coughing and wheezing that worsens in response to irritation. The persistent form resists antiasthmatic medications, and it is this type that can lead to COPD.

Asthma, alone, is one of the major causes of disability in the United States (USDHHS, 1986a). Just among children, it is estimated that asthma results in 28 million days of restricted activity and more than 2 million visits to the doctor a year (Gergen, Mullally, & Evans, 1988). About 9 million children and adults have asthma in the United States (Cluss & Fireman, 1985; Gergen et al., 1988), and every year, 5,000 people die during an asthma attack (McFadden & Austen, 1980).

Figure 11.4 INTERRELATIONSHIP OF ASTHMA, EMPHYSEMA, AND CHRONIC BRONCHITIS

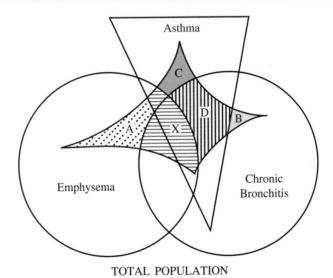

TOTAL POPULATION

Source: Berkow, R., & Fletcher, A. J., 1987, The Merck manual of diagnosis and therapy, *Rahway, NJ: Merck Sharp & Dohme Research Laboratories.*

PSYCHOSOCIAL FACTORS IN ASTHMA   French and Alexander (1941) were among the earliest theorists to propose a role for emotional factors in asthma. They correctly observed that children with asthma avoid crying, but they incorrectly provided a psychoanalytic explanation for this. They theorized that asthma resulted from an unexpressed conflict deep in the psyche. However, there has never been any evidence to support this theory (Creer, 1988).

Instead, it may be the physical behavior of crying, laughing, yelling, and so on that acts as an irritant to the airways, much as exercise does (Creer, 1979). Exercise can induce an asthma attack in some people due to the irritation of the lung tissue caused by deep inhalation of cold, dry air (McFadden, 1984; Rees, 1984). The same deep inhalation can occur during emotional outbursts, so emotional *behavior* may trigger an attack (Creer, 1988). Therefore, it could be that children learn to avoid crying through conditioning so they do not trigger an attack.

Although there may be no emotional problem per se, an initial sensitizing event (an asthma attack) can lead a person to *believe* that he or she has a sensitivity to an allergen, so adverse reaction to an allergen is likely to occur in its presence, even if there is no current physiological basis for it (Spear, 1987). This suggestion that asthma may be the result of *conditioning* is one of the oldest theories in psychosomatic medicine (French & Alexander, 1941); however, conclusive evidence is still lacking (Wolman, 1988). Therefore, more research is necessary to determine the role of conditioning in asthma.

Psychological conflicts may also be a contributing factor in asthma, and they appear to be especially relevant when asthma develops in childhood. Some asthmatic children experience remission as soon as they are removed from a troubled home environment, and some have attacks at home but not when they are in school, even when they are exposed to the same allergens (Weiner, 1985). This suggests that something about the home's emotional environment may trigger the attacks. Stein (1982b) has suggested indicators that may be used to determine the extent of psychological factors in a child's asthma. These indicators measure (a) if acute asthma episodes are associated with environmental stress, (b) if wheezing clears with separation from the family, or (c) if parents have difficulty recognizing improvement in the child. This last indicator may reveal the parents' needs for a dependent child. In conclusion, research suggests that psychosocial factors do not cause asthma but they may precipitate attacks (Teshima, Nagata, Kinara, & Sogawa, 1986; Williams, Lewis-Faning, Rees, Jacobs, & Thomas, 1958; Wistuba, 1986).

PSYCHOLOGICAL MANAGEMENT OF ASTHMA   A variety of psychological treatments for asthma have been investigated, including psychotherapy, hypnosis, relaxation training, biofeedback, and family therapy (DePiano & Salzberg, 1979; Gustafsson, Kjellman, & Cederblad, 1986; Pinkerton, Hughes, & Wenrich, 1982; Rainwater & Alexander, 1982). There has been little evidence of a direct and robust effect of these treatments on respiratory function, and the methodology of some of the research has been seriously questioned (for example, Alexander & Smith, 1979). Nevertheless, these treatments provide some relief, but it seems to be limited to the reduction of the anxiety related to an attack. They are simply not a cure for asthma (Pinkerton et al., 1982).

Self-management programs, which are rooted firmly in cognitive-behavioral psychology, have received great interest (see Creer & Winder, 1986; NIAID, 1981; Thoreson & Kirmil-Gray, 1983). These programs turn the traditional model of health care on its head. They employ education, relaxation training, biofeedback, and family therapy, and, most importantly, they teach self-management so the person with asthma assumes responsibility for controlling it (see Table 11.1; Lehrer, Sargunaraj, & Hochron, 1992). Health care is not given over to someone else but is managed by the patient (Creer, 1988). To accomplish this goal, children with asthma and their families are educated about respiration and asthma and taught specific skills to control it.

Table 11.1   ELEMENTS OF COGNITIVE-BEHAVIORAL SELF-MANAGEMENT OF ASTHMA PROGRAMS

PHASE 1: EDUCATION

1. *Mechanics of breathing* teaches physical mechanism of breathing and the possible triggers of asthma attacks.
2. *Treatment of asthma* teaches ways to control the attacks.
3. *Self-management skills training* presents the skills to the participants.
4. *Self-management skills application* teaches participants how to prevent attacks by adhering to the medication protocol, what sequence of steps to take during an attack to gain control, and how to manage the consequences of asthma.

PHASE 2: SKILLS PRACTICE

1. *Self-monitoring* includes observation and monitoring of physical sensations such as wheezing and tightening in the chest.
2. *Self-recording* of attacks, respiratory flow capacity, adherence to medication protocols, expenses due to asthma in special asthma diaries.
3. *Information processing* has the participants analyze, detect potential problems, and evaluate problems using the data from self-monitoring and recording.
4. *Decision making* requires the participants to take potential problems that had been identified, consider solutions for them, and choose the most appropriate solution.
5. *Self-instruction* is used at every phase of the program; participants are taught how to make statements to themselves in order to prompt, direct, or maintain the desired behavior.

With such programs, participants have significantly increased their total activity level and significantly decreased their health care visits. In one study, hospital admissions decreased by 44%, emergency visits by 24%, medication use by 10%, and school absenteeism by 50% (Hindi-Alexander & Cropp, 1984). In another study, health care costs were reduced by 66% (Creer, 1988). This would translate to a combined savings for people with asthma and their families of $5 billion annually, quite impressive support for cognitive-behavioral intervention.

In conclusion, psychological approaches appear to be a cost-effective means of providing relief to people with asthma. They improve adjustment, increase adherence to medication regimens, enhance self-competence, and decrease the utilization of medical services (Lehrer, Sargunaraj, & Hochron, 1992).

PREVENTION AND TREATMENT OF COPD   Smoking is implicated most strongly as a risk factor in COPD, specifically for bronchitis and emphysema, although it can aggravate asthma too. At any age, the mortality rate from COPD is much higher in smokers. Between the ages of 65 and 75, for every 100,000 Americans, 180 smokers die of bronchitis and emphysema, compared to only 16 nonsmokers (USDHHS, 1986a). Because of this strong relationship between smoking and COPD, it has been suggested that bronchitis and emphysema would not be major health problems if cigarette smoking were eliminated. (The prevention and treatment of smoking is discussed in Module 8.2, page 342).

There is no medical treatment for COPD. Instead, treatment consists of relieving the symptoms and controlling any potentially fatal complications (Berkow & Fletcher, 1987). Exercise is an important treatment measure and can be tolerated as long as an individual does not have severe CHD. People with COPD who become inactive can compound their problems by also developing a physical impairment, but exercise prevents this. Depression and anxiety are also often present in COPD, and exercise can help to reduce them by providing a sense of control.

■■■

SUMMARY

Normal functioning of the cardiovascular and respiratory systems are essential for a healthy life. The remaining modules deal with some of the primary causes of premature death at this time. These include coronary heart disease, discussed in Module 11.1, and cerebral vascular disease, discussed in Module 11.2.

However, before continuing, review the following major concepts from this introduction to the function and organization of the cardiovascular and respiratory systems:

1. The cardiovascular and respiratory systems are responsible for providing nutrients and oxygen to cells and for removing waste products and carbon dioxide.
2. Glucose and oxygen usage is monitored by the nervous system, which, along with the endocrine system, can speed up or slow down heart rate and respiration, depending on either the *perceived* need for energy (as in a threat) or the body's *actual level* of exertion.
3. The nervous and endocrine systems, through the autonomic nervous system, can direct blood flow either to the muscles for fight or flight or to the internal organs for maintenance during relaxation.
4. The myocardium, or heart muscle, is the pump for the cardiovascular system.
5. Arteries carry the oxygenated blood from the heart to the body, while veins return the deoxygenated blood containing carbon dioxide to the heart.
6. The atrium and ventricle of the *left* side of the heart pump oxygenated blood to the body. The blood returns to the atrium and ventricle of the *right* side of the heart, where it is pumped to the lungs.
7. The tiny alveoli of the lungs permit the exchange of oxygen and carbon dioxide between the blood and the air.
8. Systole is the contraction phase of the heart's pumping cycle when the blood pressure is highest, and diastole is the rest phase of the cycle when the blood pressure is lower.
9. Blood pressure results from the force of the beating of the heart, the volume of the blood, and the resistance of the blood vessels.
10. The medulla usually regulates blood pressure without the involvement of higher brain centers. However, the cortex (particularly the hypothalamus) and the sympathetic nervous system can affect the medulla and increase or decrease blood pressure.
11. Chronic obstructive pulmonary disease is a new diagnostic category that includes three related disorders: asthma, emphysema, and chronic bronchitis.
12. COPD reduces the exchange of oxygen and carbon dioxide between the blood and the air. It results in reduced oxygen supply to the internal organs, aggravating other chronic health problems such as coronary heart disease.
13. Among psychosocial factors in asthma, emotionality and conditioning are questionable.
14. Although a variety of traditional psychological interventions such as psychotherapy or relaxation training have been tried, there is serious doubt that they are effective beyond reducing the anxiety surrounding attacks. Family therapy may help reduce family conflicts and thereby result in symptomatic relief. There is good evidence that cognitive-behavioral self-management programs result in significant improvements in self-efficacy and reductions in the symptoms of asthma. Self-management also promise impressive economic savings.

CORONARY HEART DISEASE

INTRODUCTION

Richard's experience of angina pectoris is a clear indication of cardiovascular disease, the leading cause of death in the United States today. Approximately 38% of deaths are attributable to heart disease and another 8% to stroke. There are about 500,000 deaths annually from heart disease, and another 1,250,000 people have nonfatal heart attacks every year (USDHHS, 1992). Most of the deaths are premature, occurring before 75 years of age (American Heart Association, 1984). Nevertheless, these death rates represent a *decline* of 40% since 1970 (USDHHS, 1992).

Research among males has shown that not only is heart attack recovery better today, but also fewer are experiencing first heart attacks compared to 1957 (Pell & Fayerweather, 1985). This decline is probably due both to better medical care, which improves recovery from a heart attack, and to changes in lifestyle and behavior, which reduce the occurrence of first heart attacks (Stamler 1985a, 1985b). People, especially men, are smoking less, and they are more aware of the relationship between diet and exercise and health. Nevertheless, heart attacks remain a major killer, and behavioral and lifestyle changes have been far from universal.

Take Richard for example. He thought he was in good health. After all, he played baseball in high school, still played golf almost every weekend, and had never had any signs of cardiovascular disease before. However, he smoked and was about 15% overweight. His doctor had been concerned about his blood pressure and cholesterol and had tried to get Richard to stop smoking, exercise more, and reduce the fat in his diet, but he had not made these changes. Richard figured he smoked less than a pack a day, thought of weekend golf as exercise, and intended to change his diet "sometime." Meanwhile, he was building up to a potentially fatal heart attack.

HEART ATTACKS

The heart, like all other organs, must itself be supplied with nutrients and oxygen from the blood. A special vascular system surrounds the heart near the top, somewhat like a crown, which is where the name coronary (from corona or crown) heart disease or CHD derives. This crown has several major arteries with downward branches on the outside of the *myocardium* or heart muscle. If one of these arteries is blocked, blood cannot reach the part of the heart that it serves, and, after several minutes, the cells begin to die from lack of oxygen.

The primary cause of blockage is the narrowing of the coronary arteries. *Arterio*sclerosis is the general term for arteries that become thick and loose their elasticity, sometimes called "hardening of the arteries." It is assumed to be a normal process of aging, although it does not necessarily have to lead to premature death. A related process, called *athero*sclerosis, occurs when fat—primarily cholesterol—is deposited along artery walls. Atherosclerotic deposits are evident in all children from about 3 years of age and occur in all races and geographic locations (Berkow & Fletcher, 1987). They are assumed to be a normal part of the body's response to injuries within the arteries. However, large atherosclerotic deposits reduce the flow of blood. Furthermore, partially obstructed arteries are more prone to sudden, complete blockage if a piece of an atherosclerotic deposit or clot breaks away and lodges in them.

A local decrease in blood supply is called **ischemia**, and any resulting area of dead cells is called an **infarct**—hence, the term "myocardial infarction" or "MI" for heart attack. MIs can occur at any time, but they are least likely to happen during sleep and most likely to happen in the morning between 7 A.M. and 11 A.M., presumably due to increasing blood pressure and biochemical changes associated with rising (Muller et al., 1987). One of Richard's coronary arteries was partially, but not completely, blocked. He did not have an MI, but he did have ischemia, which caused the symptoms of angina. If a clot had lodged in Richard's blocked artery, he would surely have had a heart attack. Usually, arteriosclerosis and atherosclerosis develop gradually over many years, and a heart attack may be the first indication of the disease (Kannel & Abbott, 1984). Fortunately for Richard, he only received a warning.

RISK FACTOR RESEARCH

In an attempt to prevent what eventually happened to Richard, his doctor had tried to warn him of the potential danger and help him to modify his lifestyle. He based his warning on community studies that helped determine the risk factors in CHD.

Several large, long-term community studies have been conducted over the past 30 years. These are excellent examples of the prospective or longitudinal research design (see Module 2.1, page 40), and they demonstrate how epidemiologists, studying and comparing communities of individuals, can contribute in a very useful way to medical treatment and health. Because of such studies, even before the underlying causes of a disease are understood, risk factors can be identified and interventions begun. Richard *might* have benefitted from these studies and reduced his probability of CHD had he listened to his doctor's advice. One of these large risk factor identification studies—the Alameda County study—was described in Module 3.1 (see page 65).

The Framingham study (Dawber, 1980) established that, regardless of age or sex, high blood pressure increases the risk of cardiovascular disease, and that the higher the blood pressure, the higher the risk of disease. Also, very importantly, the Framingham study provided some of the earliest evidence that **hypercholesterolemia**, abnormally high levels of cholesterol in the blood, was an additional risk factor in CHD in men (too few women developed CHD during the study to establish a reliable statistical relationship).

Jenkins (1988) reviewed the community studies and other epidemiological research on the risk factors in cardiovascular disease. He concluded that, although it is a biological condition, many of the risk factors are behavioral. In general, people who have two or more of these risk factors are at greater jeopardy for CHD, and their health should be monitored closely (see Table 11.1-1). Jenkins divided these risk factors into two types: modifiable and nonmodifiable. This distinction is important because nonmodifiable risk factors are genetic or physical factors that cannot be altered. Because of that, we will discuss this category only briefly. On the other hand, the modifiable risk factors—hypertension, cholesterol, diet, obesity, smoking, physical inactivity, diabetes, and Type A behavior—are subject to behavioral and psychological interventions. We will discuss each of these in more detail.

NONMODIFIABLE RISK FACTORS

AGE   Arteriosclerosis is related to aging, so the longer one lives, the thicker and less elastic the arteries become (Berkow & Fletcher, 1987). However, arteriosclerosis will not necessarily lead to CHD. It is atherosclerosis that is the major culprit in CHD. Again, the longer one lives, the more time there is for atherosclerotic deposits to build up, too. Yet, even with some build-up of deposits (which occur, to some extent, universally), CHD is not inevitable—other factors are involved.

SEX   Throughout the life span males are more prone to develop CHD, although the difference is greater between males and females at younger ages. Female hormones appear to be responsible for the reduced risk of CHD in women, so risk increases after menopause (Lerner & Kannel, 1986).

FAMILY HISTORY   Hypercholesterolemia, another CHD risk factor, runs in families, and a family history of CHD and/or elevated cholesterol is, by itself, sufficient cause to prompt close monitoring. In addition, African Americans are at a higher risk for CHD than European Americans. This is presumed to be related to the higher rates of hypertension among African Americans.

HYPERTENSION

Hypertension is diagnosed only when blood pressure is found to be consistently above 160/105. Systolic readings between 140 and 159 and diastolic readings between 85 and 104 are considered "borderline hypertension." Because the diastolic reading is taken during the heart's rest period, it is a reflection of the elasticity of the arteries and a method of determining the extent of arteriosclerosis. Richard did not realize that he had high blood pressure when his doctor first told him several years earlier. At 145/95, medication was not indicated, and his doctor believed it could be reduced by dietary control. His doctor did, however, remain concerned about the possibility that early arteriosclerosis might be developing.

Table 11.1-1   RISK FACTORS IN CORONARY HEART DISEASE

NONMODIFIABLE

Age
Sex
Family history of CHD

MODIFIABLE

Hypertension (both systolic and diastolic blood pressure)
Dietary habits (consumption of fat related to obesity and cholesterol; salt related to hypertension)
Obesity (related to hypertension)
Cigarette smoking (not pipes or cigars)
Physical inactivity
Diabetes
Type A behavior

OTHER POSSIBLE RISK FACTORS IN CHD

Socioeconomic status (SES; may be related to the other modifiable risk factors)
Occupational stress (work overload)
Chronic negative emotions (anxiety, depression)

Richard did not adhere to the low sodium diet prescribed by his doctor because he thought if his blood pressure were really high, he would feel it. Would you know if your blood pressure was abnormally high? If you are like most people, you answered "yes," but you would be mistaken (Bauman & Leventhal, 1985; Meyer et al., 1985). Hypertension is sometimes called the "silent killer" because it produces *no* symptoms. Yet, it is the most important single risk factor in cardiovascular disease (Dawber, 1980).

PREVALENCE   About 35 million Americans are estimated to have hypertension and, if those with borderline hypertension are included, the figure totals 60 million (Horan, 1988). Blood pressure tends to increase with age and weight. Approximately 10% to 15% of hypertension is due to other medical problems, the most common ones being diabetes and kidney disease. The cause of the remaining 90% of cases—called **essential hypertension**—is unknown. There are important racial differences in the development of hypertension. The rate of hypertension among African Americans is 37%, twice as high as the rate of 18% among European Americans. Therefore, the fact that Richard is African American is an important factor.

DEVELOPMENT   Although the specific causes of essential hypertension are unknown, it does appear to have a genetic basis, and high blood pressure in a child is predictive of the development of hypertension as an adult (Herd & Weiss, 1984; Sallis, Dimsdale, & Caine, 1988; Smith et al., 1987). Dietary factors may also contribute to the development of hypertension. Hypertensives are more likely to be overweight, but sodium seems to be the crucial dietary factor in hypertension (Winick, Morgan, Rozovski, & Marks-Kaufman, 1988). The water content of the body is regulated by controlling the balance of sodium. The average adult requires only about ½ gram of sodium per day, but the daily diet of the average American contains about 3½ teaspoons of salt (Winick et al., 1988). An excess of dietary sodium can cause water retention and increase blood pressure (Falkner & Light, 1986; Kaplan, 1986).

The development of hypertension may also be related to stress (Henry & Cassel, 1969). As mentioned in Module 5.2, naturally occurring environmental stressors such as crowding result in increases in blood pressure. It is well established that laboratory-induced stress (for example, electric shock, loud noise, being asked emotionally disturbing questions, or taking mental arithmetic tests) results in blood pressure increases in both African Americans and European Americans (Anderson et al., 1986; Shapiro & Goldstein, 1982). However, this does not establish that stress causes a *chronic* elevation in blood pressure.

Recently, Fredrickson and Matthews (1990) reviewed the existing well-controlled studies of stress, blood pressure, and heart rate. Hypertension seems to occur in people who are abnormally sensitive to stress. The blood pressure of hypertensives takes longer to return to homeostasis after exposure to stress, suggesting that they have inherited a heightened sensitivity to it (Harrell, 1980). An excessive sympathetic nervous system response is implicated in the development of hypertension (Fredrickson & Matthews, 1990; Jorgensen & Houston, 1981).

The sympathetic nervous system's delayed return to normal after chronic stress suggests that a dysfunction in the homeostatic abilities of the hypothalamus, which regulates blood pressure, may be partly responsible for hypertension. This dysfunction may be caused by poor regulation of the circulatory and neuroendocrine responses to stress (McCubbin, Surwit, & Williams, 1985, 1988).

Exposure to chronic stress, combined with a high sodium and low potassium diet, can produce hypertension in dogs that have no genetic predisposition toward it (Anderson, 1987). It might be that when chronic stress occurs in a person with heightened stress sensitivity, the resulting blood pressure changes eventually cause arteriosclerosis, and in a circular manner, arteriosclerosis eventually results in chronic hypertension.

Another factor in hypertension may be anger. It is commonly believed that people who are tense and angry but who try to control it might "blow a fuse"—that is, burst a blood vessel because of their presumed heightened blood pressure. In fact, there is evidence to support a relationship between suppressed rage and hypertension (Dimsdale et al., 1986; James, Strogatz, Wing, & Ramsey, 1987; Sommers-Flanagan & Greenberg, 1989). In particular, this might explain why African Americans have twice the rate of hypertension of European Americans (see Box 11.1-1).

It is doubtful that personality factors are the sole cause of hypertension, but they may be part of a complex interaction with other biopsychosocial factors (Harrell, 1980). Richard was under a lot of stress as he tried to get ahead on the job, but he was successful and certainly not poor. He never felt that he had experienced overt racism, but he did believe that he needed to work harder than others in his company just to prove himself.

TREATMENT   Typically, treatment for hypertension includes changes in diet and behavior. Reducing sodium intake and controlling weight (with exercise sometimes prescribed for those who are overweight) may be sufficient to control borderline hypertension in most patients (Berkow & Fletcher, 1987).

Although medications—**diuretics** that cause the excretion of sodium or *beta-blockers* that reduce cardiac output and increase kidney function—are often prescribed for moderate to severe hypertension, they do have side effects (Berkow & Fletcher, 1987), which can even include raising blood pressure (Lee et al., 1988).

These side effects and the evidence that psychological factors play a role in the development of hypertension have led health psychologists to use cognitive-behavioral techniques to manage it (Glasgow & Engel, 1987). In one study of the effectiveness of behavior modification, people who had been hypertensive for at least five years and were maintained within normal blood pressure limits on medication were taken off of their medication and randomly assigned to one of three groups: (a) a sodium-restricted diet, (b) a weight loss diet, or (c) no treatment (Langford et al., 1985). Of those who were successful in the two diet groups, 78% of the sodium and 72% of the weight loss groups were able to maintain their blood pressure within normal limits without resuming medication. This suggests that behavior therapy can produce behavior changes sufficient to cause a reduction in the need for antihypertensive medication.

Research also indicates that procedures that reduce sympathetic arousal, particularly biofeedback and relaxation training, are effective in reducing blood pressure (for example, Aivazyan, Zaitsev, Salenko, Yurenev, &

Box 11.1-1   HYPERTENSION IN AFRICAN AMERICANS: STRESS, POVERTY, ANGER, AND "JOHN HENRYISM"

A significantly higher rate of hypertension arises in African Americans compared to other groups. Genes do appear to play some role in this difference. There are racial differences in physiological responses to various situations related to *changes* in blood pressure (Anderson, Lane, Taguchi, & Williams, 1989; Durel et al., 1989; McNeilly & Zeichner, 1989; Tischenkel et al., 1989). However, the incidence of hypertension is also related to socioeconomic status (SES). Among all races, low-SES men are four times as likely to become hypertensive as high-SES men (Keil, Tyroler, Sandifer, & Boyle, 1977), and consistent with this, hypertension is more likely to occur in low-income than middle- and upper-income African Americans.

Some researchers suspect that stress may be an important factor related to hypertension in African Americans. Poverty is a chronic stressor, and chronic stress prolongs the recovery of the sympathetic nervous system (Pardine & Napoli, 1983), leading to exhaustion (see General Adaptation Syndrome in Module 6.1, page 241). Harburg et al. (1973) compared African American men living in higher stress (poorer) and lower stress areas of Detroit and found that those living in the higher stress areas had significantly higher blood pressure. Harburg et al. (1973) suggested that the experience of anger without expression is also related to elevations in blood pressure. This coincides with other data suggesting that the experience of racism can cause blood pressure elevations (Armstead, Lawler, Gordon, Cross, & Gibbons, 1989).

The Harburg et al. (1973) study found that African American men living in higher stress areas of Detroit had higher blood pressure, and also that the highest blood pressure readings were in those individuals with suppressed anger. This combination of high stress and suppressed anger has come to be called "John Henryism," after a legendary black laborer. John Henry was reputed to have won a competition against a mechanical drill only to die from exhaustion (James, Hartnett, & Kalsbeek, 1983). Psychologists refer to "John Henryism" as a personality trait of active coping efforts expended in what is ultimately a "no-win" situation (see Effort with Distress in Module 6.2). Research has shown that those with a high level of John Henryism are at a particularly greater risk for hypertension, especially in the presence of other variables such as lower levels of education, lower socioeconomic status, or racism (James et al., 1983; James, Strogatz, Wing, & Ramsey, 1987).

Patrusheva, 1988; Blanchard, Khramelashvili et al., 1988; Blanchard, McCoy et al., 1988). There are, however, some studies that do not support the effectiveness of biofeedback and relaxation training (for example, Jacob, Forman, Kraemer, Farquhar, & Agras, 1985). This contradiction appears to result from the fact that patients cannot simply be told to relax in order to reduce their blood pressure without being taught step-by-step procedures. Just telling patients to relax can produce the *opposite* result—blood pressure actually goes up, perhaps because they focus on and worry about it (Suls, Sanders, & Lebrecque, 1986). Instead, patients must receive thorough instruction in relaxation training.

Cognitive stress management programs (see Module 6.2, page 274) have been also adapted to treat high blood pressure (Weiss, 1988). There is no clearly superior treatment among the various cognitive-behavioral methods (Hoelscher, Lichstein, & Rosenthal, 1986). Although they have had some success in reducing blood pressure, they produce only modest reductions at best (Schneiderman, Chesney, & Krantz, 1989), and they tend to work better with borderline rather than full-blown hypertension (Richter-Heinrich et al., 1988). In one placebo-controlled study of stress management with African American men, those who received cognitive self-management training had significant reductions in systolic but only slight reductions in diastolic blood pressure (Bosley & Allen, 1989).

In cases of severe hypertension, medication reduces blood pressure much more consistently and effectively than cognitive-behavioral treatments, and medication is still preferred in these cases because of the immediate health risks such as stroke (Wadden, Luborsky, Greer, & Crits-Christoph, 1984). Yet, even for severe cases of hypertension, cognitive-behavioral treatments may enable the amount of medication to be lowered, reducing unwanted side effects. Since cognitive-behavioral treatments have no adverse side effects, they are a good adjunct to medication even for cases of severe hypertension.

CHOLESTEROL, DIET, AND OBESITY

Imagine that it is several decades ago, before high-technology diagnostic techniques, and you are a physician performing autopsies. Some of the people died of heart attacks, but they were otherwise healthy and had no prior symptoms. As you dissect their hearts, you find their coronary arteries clogged by waxy deposits. You find that the deposits consist primarily of cholesterol and suspect a link between it and heart attacks. That is, in fact, one way that medical researchers learned of the role of cholesterol in coronary artery disease.

Cholesterol is an oily yellowish substance that is essential for life. It is a constituent of vitamin D, all cell membranes, myelin, and the steroid hormones. In fact, if the body is deprived of two steroids derived from cholesterol, cortisol or aldosterone, then death results (Marieb, 1989). However, cholesterol is also the primary ingredient in the fatty deposits or plaque that forms along artery walls.

The liver and intestines manufacture sufficient cholesterol for all of the body's needs, about .5 to 1 gm per day, and heredity determines how much cholesterol is manufactured by the body (Rona et al., 1985). Otherwise, blood levels of cholesterol are related to diet. In most people, the body maintains homeostasis well by lowering cholesterol production with dietary intakes of up to 300 mg per day. However, the body cannot keep up with higher dietary levels, homeostasis is upset, and serum cholesterol rises. Typically, men consume about 450 mg and women about 266 mg of cholesterol per day, so men tend to consistently exceed what their bodies can adjust to (Winick et al., 1988).

Cholesterol is found in all animal cell membranes, so it permeates all meat, not just the fat. It is also found dissolved in fat in dairy products and in the yolk of eggs. Oils account for only a small proportion of cholesterol in the American diet, but they contain other fats that affect the body's manufacture of cholesterol. Saturated fats, which are found in meat, dairy products, and coconut and palm oils, are the so-called "hard" fats because they tend to congeal at room temperature and are readily converted to cholesterol by the body. In contrast, polyunsaturated fats, which are obtained primarily from vegetable sources such as corn or soybeans, and monosaturated fats, found in fish, peanuts, and olives, are liquids at room temperature and are believed to have a cholesterol lowering effect.

Cholesterol is measured in milligrams per 100 milliliters of blood. It rises with age, and adult Americans under 45 years of age average about 200 mg. Not all researchers agree on what constitutes too much cholesterol in adults, but a convenient method is to consider any level above 180 mg (190 mg in post-menopausal women)—plus the person's age—as abnormal (Berkow & Fletcher, 1987). Under 10 years of age, boys usually have a level of 125–190 mg and girls have a level of 130–195 mg. However, the upper limits of these levels in adults and children may still be too high to eliminate the risk of CHD (Berkow & Fletcher, 1987).

The Multiple Risk Factor Intervention Trial (MRFIT) study described in Module 3.2 confirmed the relationship between cholesterol and CHD (Caggiula et al., 1981; Dolecek et al., 1986; Gorder et al., 1986). The risk of mortality from CHD or stroke was 3.4 times higher for those participants with blood cholesterol levels above 245 mg than for those with levels below 180 mg. Furthermore, the relationship between cholesterol and mortality held regardless of age.

Nevertheless, some people in the MRFIT study with cholesterol levels below 180 mg also had heart attacks, although at a much lower rate. What can account for this? The explanation may be found in the way cholesterol is transported in the blood by two proteins: *High density lipoprotein (HDL)* and *low density lipoprotein (LDL)*. LDL carries cholesterol from the liver to the arteries, while HDL carries it from the arteries back to the liver. LDL is positively correlated with CHD, while HDL is negatively correlated with CHD (Castelli et al., 1986; Gordon, Castelli, Hjortland, Kannel, & Dawber, 1977). This suggests that the level of total cholesterol may not be the best risk indicator. Even when total cholesterol is low, high levels of LDL are related to CHD, which probably accounts for the heart attacks that occur in people with total cholesterol levels below 180 mg. Also, people with 60 mg of HDL have less than half the risk of CHD than those with 30 mg (Berkow & Fletcher, 1987).

For this reason, the *ratio* of total cholesterol to HDL, called the *risk ratio*, is now considered to be the best predictor of a future heart attack (Winick et al., 1988). A ratio of more than 4.5 to 1 is considered at least as important a risk factor as a total cholesterol above 300 mg. A ratio of 3.8 to 1 in men or 2.9 to 1 in women is associated with only half the average risk of heart disease. This means that a person with a total cholesterol of 250 mg and an HDL of 75 mg is at lower risk than a person with a total cholesterol of 200 mg and an HDL of 40 mg. In fact, in patients with low HDL and high LDL, for every 1% increase in HDL cholesterol, there is a 3% *reduction* in heart disease (Frick et al., 1987).

C O N C L U S I O N   Obesity, hypertension, blood cholesterol, and heart disease are all interrelated. Overweight people are more likely to have CHD, but obesity is probably not an independent risk factor. It is hypertension and cholesterol that are the direct risk factors for CHD (Keys, 1979). Obesity may just be linked to hypertension and cholesterol level through poor dietary habits and through them to CHD.

When Richard was tested about 14 months prior to his angina attack, he was slightly overweight, his total cholesterol level was 246, and his ratio was 4 to 1. This represents a moderate risk, but it is not severe enough to treat with medication, so his doctor prescribed a cholesterol-lowering diet (see Table 11.1-2). Richard followed this diet for about a week, but since he did not feel that his cholesterol was "real high," he was not motivated to continue it, and his children complained about the "boring food." He decided just to wait until next year's physical and see if his cholesterol was still elevated. He did, however, resolve to loose the extra weight.

T R E A T M E N T   The MRFIT study discussed in Module 3.2 was actually designed to find out whether behavioral intervention to reduce dietary cholesterol resulted in a lower risk of CHD.

Recall that both the treatment and nontreatment groups had an average daily intake of about 450 mg of cholesterol at the start of the study. By the end, the average daily cholesterol intake of the treatment group had dropped to 267 mg, whereas the controls' intake was 425 mg. Most importantly, the level of serum cholesterol had also dropped in the treatment group, and the men who were at the highest risk achieved the largest reduction, because they had the highest initial levels of total cholesterol. Participants with an initial total cholesterol >300 mg obtained an average reduction of nearly 15%, whereas those with an initial level between 220 to 239 mg obtained an average reduction of only about 4%.

Subsequent research has confirmed that adherence to a low cholesterol diet reduces serum cholesterol (for a review, see Carmody, Matarazzo, & Istvan, 1987). Furthermore, the combination of anticholesterol medication and dietary changes can stop and may even reverse the progression of atherosclerosis (Blankenhorn et al., 1987). However, as Richard's case demonstrates, adherence is difficult to achieve, particularly with dietary modifications, whether or not the modifications are made at the instruction of a physician because of medical necessity (Hjermann, Velve, Holme, & Leren, 1981; Rose, Tunstall-Pedoe, & Heller, 1983).

Cognitive-behavioral strategies that teach people self-monitoring, that focus on stimulus control, that use contingency contracting, and that include relapse prevention have tended to produce better results than just education and counseling alone (Carmody, Fey, Pierce, Connor, & Mararazzo, 1982).

New approaches to intervention attempt to improve adherence by involving the entire family. An example is the Family Heart Study (Carmody et al., 1986), which begins with a standard educational program about cholesterol and diet. This is followed by meetings with a dietary counselor who helps the family overcome any difficulties in making the necessary changes and by monthly meetings of families where problems are shared and information such as recipes are exchanged. These sessions also serve a social function, providing group support and reinforcement.

Table 11.1-2   **DIETARY RECOMMENDATIONS TO LOWER HIGH CHOLESTEROL**

	PERCENT OF TOTAL CALORIES
Fat	
Total	<30%
Saturated	<10%
Polyunsaturated	Increase, up to 10%
Monounsaturated	Reduce to 10% to 15%
Carbohydrates	Increase to 50% to 60%
	MILLIGRAMS PER DAY
Cholesterol	<300

Source: Lecos, C. W., 1989, Planning a diet for a healthy heart, HHS Publication No. FDA 89-2220, Rockville, MD: Department of Health and Human Services.

Family involvement might have improved Richard's adherence to the dietary changes, but dietary changes can usually reduce total serum cholesterol by only about 20% to 25% (Lipid Research Clinics Program, 1984). This might have been sufficient to bring Richard's total cholesterol below 200 mg, but some people—particularly those above 300 mg—may not achieve sufficient cholesterol reduction to reduce their risk of CHD. Also, those in the moderately elevated range, like Richard, usually do not achieve more than a 10% reduction. Therefore, other interventions may be necessary.

One of these is exercise. People engaged in regular aerobic sports such as running and skiing tend to have much higher than average levels of HDL (Winick et al., 1988). So, it may be possible to raise the level of HDL through strenuous aerobic exercise (at least 20 minutes a day 4 times a week; see Physical Inactivity, below).

In addition, certain types of fiber that appear to lower LDL levels and raise HDL levels may be added to the diet. The daily addition of oat bran, psyllium hydrophilic mucilloid, or pectin may be able to reduce LDL by an additional 10%. Most people can tolerate this additional fiber, but it can cause gastric upset and diarrhea in some.

When dietary changes do not produce a sufficient reduction in total cholesterol or a more favorable risk ratio, medication is often prescribed. Anticholesterol medications, when coupled with reductions in dietary intake of cholesterol, can lower LDL levels by 25% to 50% (Berkow & Fletcher, 1987). The most commonly prescribed medications are cholestyramine, cholestipol, and niacin. Unfortunately, they sometimes have severe side effects that limit their use such as constipation; gastric irritability; "hot flashes"; and, ironically, cardiac problems. So, currently, dietary reduction of cholesterol, vigorous exercise, and the daily intake of additional fiber are the most effective and best tolerated means of treating moderate levels of hypercholesterolemia.

Smoking

Although there was evidence linking cigarette smoking to cancer when the Framingham Study began, there was very little linking it to CHD. Nevertheless, the researchers who designed the Framingham Study included cigarette smoking as a possible risk factor. By the end of the study, they found a relationship between smoking and CHD in men but not in women. The lack of a significant relationship for women, remember, may be due to their lower overall incidence of CHD.

Whether smoking is an *independent* risk factor for CHD is unclear, because it may actually be related to CHD through hypertension. As discussed above, hypertension may develop in people who have a heightened sensitivity to stress and excessive sympathetic nervous system responses. This predisposition may be aggravated by nicotine's ability to stimulate the sympathetic nervous system. Given Richard's borderline hypertension, his doctor had recommended that he stop smoking several years earlier, which was especially good advice considering that Richard also experienced job stress. But Richard rationalized that he smoked less than a pack a day anyway, and he received no formal help in stopping smoking, so he continued. See Module 8.2 (page 344) for a discussion of effective treatments for smoking.

PHYSICAL INACTIVITY

People who have sedentary lifestyles are more likely to die from CHD than people who engage in physical activity (Powell, Thompson, Caspersen, & Kendrick, 1987), and recently accumulating evidence suggests that physical inactivity is an important independent risk factor in CHD (Dubbert, 1992). One prospective study followed 93 boys and 107 girls from 13 to 21 years of age (Kemper, Snel, Verschuur, & Storm-van Essen, 1990). A strong relationship was found between physical activity level and CHD risk factors. Increased physical activity was related to higher HDLs and a lower percentage of body fat.

It has been proposed that exercise may reduce CHD by slowing or reversing atherosclerosis, reducing the incidence of arrhythmia (erratic heartbeats), and/or reducing hypertension (Haskell, 1984, 1985). Of these three potential mechanisms, the reduction of blood pressure through exercise is the best established. There is a lot of correlational evidence that indicates that people who are physically active have lower blood pressure (Hofman, Walter, Connelly, & Vaughn, 1987; Panico et al., 1987). In addition, experimental research has found that vigorous aerobic exercise three times per week lowers blood pressure (Jennings et al., 1986).

DIABETES

Diabetes was discussed in the introduction to Part III, Section 1, and is probably indirectly related to as many as 300,000 deaths from heart and kidney disease annually (American Diabetes Association, 1986). It contributes to CHD because it can cause changes in the walls of capillaries and arteries, promoting the development of arteriosclerosis and hypertension. The incidence of atherosclerosis is also abnormally high in diabetics, although the reasons for this are unknown (Berkow & Fletcher, 1987). Diabetes can be well-controlled medically, but the primary health issue is adherence to treatment.

TYPE A BEHAVIOR

Beginning in the 1950s, two physicians, Meyer Friedman and Ray Rosenman, began to study a specific behavioral pattern they believed might be linked to

CHD (Friedman & Rosenman, 1974; Friedman & Ulmer, 1984; see also Friedman, 1990, for an overview). They hypothesized that people could be divided into two types: Type A and Type B. **Type A** is as an aggressive, hard-driving, and competitive behavior style, believed to be a risk factor for CHD. Type A individuals are achievement oriented, with easily aroused hostility and an exaggerated sense of time urgency. **Type B** is a relaxed "stop and smell the roses" style, believed to be related to a lower incidence of CHD. Type B individuals are lacking in competitiveness, hostility, and a sense of time urgency.

RESEARCH SUPPORT   Scores of studies have investigated the Type A/Type B pattern. The earliest tended to support the description of Type A individuals as achievement oriented (Burnam, Pennebaker, & Glass, 1975; Fekken & Jakubowski, 1990; Glass, 1977; Sorensen et al., 1987), hostile (Carver & Glass, 1978; Van Egerer, Sniderman, & Roggelin, 1982), and having an urgent sense of time (Bortner & Rosenman, 1967; Glass, Snyder, & Hollis, 1974). Type A's also react differently to stress. In moderately stressful situations, Type A's are significantly more physiologically reactive (Contrada, Wright, & Glass, 1985; Ward et al., 1986). The differences are most apparent when a situation requires slow, careful work, endurance, broad attention, and they cannot control it (Matthews, 1982). Controllability appears to be important to Type A's, who fare poorly when situations are unpredictable and work harder to maintain control when it is threatened (Carver & Humphries, 1982). Many, but not all, studies have found that stress and competition causes more changes in blood pressure and heart rate in Type A's (Dembroski et al., 1983).

When socioeconomic factors are controlled, the incidence of Type A is similar in men and women (Baker, Dearborn, Hastings, & Hamberger, 1984). Although many of the early studies used men, recent research supports the same characterizations of Type A women. Type A women express more anger and hostility and have a more masculine gender role orientation than Type B's (Baker et al., 1984).

One difference between Type A's and Type B's has important implications for research: Type A's seem to experience and report physical symptoms differently than Type B's (Offutt & La Croix, 1988). Type A's report fewer physical symptoms when under stress (Carver, DeGregorio, & Gillis, 1981). Yet, Type A's are just as aware of their arousal (Essau & Jamieson, 1987) and do not have higher rates of general physical illness (Suls & Wan, 1989). This suggests that Type A's may be able to work harder because they suppress their physical symptoms. Self-report, then, would probably not be a valid method of assessing the relationship between Type A and CHD, which has implications that are discussed in the next section.

MEASUREMENT OF TYPE A   There have been two primary methods for measuring Type A: personal interviews and paper-and-pencil questionnaires.

Friedman and Rosenman developed the Structured Interview (SI) method (Friedman & Ulmer, 1984; Rosenman, 1978). The SI asks people how they respond to a variety of naturally occurring situations (for example, waiting in line).

More important than the actual answer people give is the *style* of their vocal responses. The questions are deliberately asked in a way that would elicit Type A behavior (for example, questions are asked slowly or responses are challenged). As a result, Type A's show their annoyance at being challenged and try to complete an interviewer's slowly asked questions for them. This method of scoring the vocal style of interviewees is so reliable that a voice analysis machine can do as well as trained interviewers in determining Type A's (Glass, Ross, Isecke, & Rosenman, 1982). People are categorized by the SI as either Type A, partial Type A, balanced Type A/Type B, or Type B.

The most widely used Type A questionnaire is the Jenkins Activity Survey (JAS), which is based on the SI (Jenkins, Zyzanski, & Rosenman, 1979). The JAS is a reliable instrument (Abbott, Peters, & Vogel, 1988; Yarnold, Mueser, Grau, & Grimm, 1986), and as scores go up, so does the risk of CHD (Jenkins, Rosenman, & Zyzansky, 1974). The Framingham Study researchers also developed a Type A questionnaire, similar to the JAS but much shorter, called the Framingham Type A Scale (FTA; Haynes et al., 1980).

Unfortunately, the SI, JAS, and FTA only partially overlap, which means that they may measure different aspects of Type A personality (Kittle, Kornitzer, DeBacker, & Dramaix, 1982; MacDougall, Dembroski, & Musante, 1979; Matthews, 1988; Mayes, Sime, & Ganster, 1984). The SI is related to a wider variety of physiological and psychological correlates of Type A (for example, Allen, Lawler, Matthews, Rakaczky, & Jamison, 1987; Contrada, 1989; Friedman & Booth-Kewley, 1988; Matthews, 1988), and it is a better predictor of CHD than the JAS (Dembroski, MacDougall, Herd, & Shields, 1983). Therefore, researchers concerned specifically with predicting CHD have begun to rely increasingly on the SI, even though it is more time consuming than the JAS (Evans, 1990).

TYPE A AND CHD   In 1981, a panel of the National Heart, Lung, and Blood Institute reviewed the research on Type A and determined that it should be added to the official list of risk factors for CHD (Review Panel on Coronary-Prone Behavior and Coronary Heart Disease, 1981). The panel based its determination partly on an 8½-year prospective study called the Western Collaborative Group Study (WCGS; Rosenman et al., 1975). The WCGS classified 3,524 men between 39 and 59 years of age as either Type A or Type B. By the end of the study period, 257 men had developed CHD. Even though there were about the same number of Type A's as Type B's at the outset, of the subjects who developed CHD, 69% had been classified as Type A compared to only 31% classified as Type B. This suggests that the risk of CHD in middle-aged men is 2 to 1 for Type A compared to Type B.

The Framingham study found a similar relationship between Type A and CHD for men between 55 and 64 years of age (Haynes, Feinleib, & Kannel,

1980; Haynes, Feinleib, & Eaker, 1983), but this relationship was evident only in white-collar workers, not in blue-collar workers. However, it held for women as well as men. Type A is also related to angina and heart attack in African American men and women (Sprafka, Folsom, Burke, Hahn, & Pirie, 1990).

There have been other studies that failed to find a relationship between Type A and CHD (Case, Heller, Case, & Moss, 1985; Shekelle, Gale, & Norusis, 1985). There are two possible explanations for these failures (Evans, 1990). First, they may be due to the different ways of measuring Type A. Those reaching negative conclusions usually employed the JAS, whereas those that have supported Type A as risk factor have tended to use the SI (Evans, 1990). The second explanation is that the studies that did not support Type A as a risk factor tended to be "high risk" studies with subjects who were already at risk for CHD or had an MI (Evans, 1990). High risk subjects may be different from the general population, and they may respond differently to self-report measures such as the JAS.

RECONCEPTUALIZATION OF TYPE A: CYNICAL HOSTILITY, ANGER, AND HEART DISEASE

Type A, as initially conceptualized, is a broad behavioral and emotional syndrome, but hostility and irritability are more strongly correlated with CHD than other aspects of Type A (Dembroski & Costa, 1988; Matthews, Glass, Rosenman, & Bortner, 1977; Weinstein, Davison, DeQuattro, & Allen, 1987; Williams & Barefoot, 1988). Hostility is also related to atherosclerosis independently of Type A (Williams et al., 1980).

In one prospective study, 192 men who later had a fatal or nonfatal heart attack were matched with 384 who did not. Hostility, rather than global Type A, was the single most significant predictor of CHD, even after the effects of age, blood cholesterol, blood pressure, and cigarette smoking were removed (Dembroski, MacDougall, Costa, & Grandits, 1989). This finding only held for men under 47 years of age, but it suggests that hostility in younger men is a major, independent risk factor for CHD.

Again, researchers have used different measures of hostility, and, again, some studies have failed to find a relationship between hostility and CHD (for example, McCranie, Watkins, Brandsma, & Sisson, 1986), causing some researchers to question the relationship (Friedman & Booth-Kewley, 1988). However, **cynical hostility**, a specific type described as resentful, suspicious, and angry distrust of others, seems to be consistently and strongly related to CHD. Even the Type B's who have heart attacks score higher on measures related to cynical hostility (for example, Dembroski & Costa, 1988; Siegman, Dembroski, & Ringel, 1987; Smith & Frohm, 1985). Currently, a consensus is building that cynical hostility is the lethal risk factor in Type A (Evans, 1990; Schneiderman et al., 1989).

Other research has implicated anger, usually suppressed, as an additional risk factor in CHD (MacDougall, Dembroski, Dimsdale, & Hackett, 1985;

Siegel, 1992). One study used the SI and rated subjects on 12 separate components of global Type A (Dembroski, MacDougall, Williams, Haney, & Blumenthal, 1985). Only hostility and suppressed anger ("anger-in") significantly predicted atherosclerosis. Importantly, hostility and anger interacted such that people high on both had the highest levels of atherosclerosis. A joint relationship among anger and hostility and CHD is also found in adolescents (Siegel, 1984) and children (Woodall & Matthews, 1989).

In summary, it appears that a general negative emotional state characterized by anger and cynical hostility, rather than the competitive, achievement-oriented, and impatient behavioral aspects of Type A, is the lethal pattern related to CHD (Booth-Kewley & Friedman, 1987). Currently, there is some disagreement over whether "anger-out," which is *expressed* anger, or "anger-in," which is *suppressed* anger, both result in higher blood pressure and heart rate (Dembroski et al., 1985; Diamond et al., 1984; Holroyd & Gorkin, 1983; MacDougall, Dembroski, & Krantz, 1981). Research is continuing in an attempt to resolve such questions and in the hope of improving treatment. In the meantime, it appears that hard-driving "workaholics" may *not* be at any greater risk for CHD as long as they are not angry and hostile.

Some researchers caution that anger and cynical hostility may not be the only two pathogenic factors in Type A and that, even if they are, they should not be viewed as enduring personality traits (Thoresen & Powell, 1992). Instead, they propose a cognitive approach that views Type A as a multidimensional, interactional concept in which emotions, behaviors, perception, thoughts, and physiological processes function together over time in relation to environments to produce Type A. Like the transactional view of stress, a Type A style would take place in the transaction between the individual and the environment.

Richard might be characterized as hard-driving. However, his feeling that he had to work harder than some others in order to be successful possibly betrays suppressed anger and hostility. His doctor did not consider this aspect of Richard's health, but a psychological evaluation did evaluate his transactions with the environment, revealing a relationship between his emotional state and his health.

THE PHYSIOLOGICAL CONNECTION   It is not yet clear how Type A is linked to the development of CHD, but research has concentrated on understanding the differences in the physiological responses of Type A's and Type B's. Excessive neuroendocrine activity is the suspected link between stress and the development of CHD, although there is probably no simple mechanism (Evans, 1990). Type A's do have more sympathetic activity and catecholamine secretion during stress (Dembroski, MacDougall, Shields, Petitto, & Lushene, 1987; DeQuattro, Loo, Yamada, & Foti, 1985; Manuck, Craft, & Gold, 1978), and they have greater physiological reactivity to stress in general (Contrada, Wright, & Glass, 1985; Krantz & Manuck, 1984; McKinney, Hofshire, Buell, & Eliot, 1984). In contrast, Type B's have more parasympathetic activation, which could buffer the effects of stress (Muranaka, Lane et al., 1988; Muranaka, Monou et al., 1988).

Over time, the heightened sympathetic activation in response to stress and/or hostility of Type A's may produce harmful changes in the cardiovascular system (Schneiderman et al., 1989). This could occur through the actions of the catecholamines—epinephrine and norepinephrine. One theory holds that a combination of increased heart rate and vasoconstriction, brought on by the catecholamines, causes the heart to work harder, resulting in small lesions in the artery walls and the build-up of atherosclerotic deposits (Eliot & Buell, 1983). Catecholamines also affect platelet aggregation, which is involved in the formation of artery-blocking clots (Ardlie, Glew, & Schwartz, 1966).

A second theory proposes that changes in the level of the catecholamines causes fluctuations in the constriction of blood vessels, gradually reducing their elasticity (Glass, 1977; Herd, 1978). Neither of these theories is mutually exclusive, and both mechanisms might be occurring simultaneously to produce CHD.

Another consideration is that Type A's may have a genetic predisposition toward heightened neuroendocrine reactivity to stress, and that they then may develop Type A behavior in *response* to it. If there is a genetic basis, Type A behavior may not be linked *causally* to CHD at all (Carmelli, Chesney, Ward, & Rosenman, 1985; Carmelli, Rosenman, & Chesney, 1987; Carmelli, et al., 1988; Smith et al., 1987). Type A behavior would then be an attempt to cope with genetically heightened reactivity to stress (Krantz & Deckel, 1983; Krantz & Durel, 1983), and it would be more likely to occur in an environment that presented more stressors (Krantz, Arabian, Davis, & Parker, 1982). Consistent with this, research suggests that Type A's generate their own stressful situations and actually create more difficult situations for themselves (Byrne & Rosenman, 1986; Smith, 1989; Suls & Sanders, 1989). Type A's may be less mindful of stressful symptoms, so they may be inclined to overdo some risky behaviors (Cohen & Matthews, 1987; Suls & Sanders, 1989).

MODIFYING TYPE A   There has long been interest in modifying Type A behaviors (Schneiderman et al., 1989). One of the first attempts to modify Type A took place in a group of more than 1,000 people who had already had an MI (Friedman & Ulmer, 1984; Friedman et al., 1986). Those who were willing to participate in cardiac rehabilitation were randomly assigned to one of two groups: (a) standard cardiac rehabilitation under the care of a cardiologist, or (b) standard cardiac rehabilitation and group therapy to change Type A behavior.

At the end of 3 years, those who received group therapy had significantly reduced their scores on the SI. More importantly, they had half the annual MI recurrence rate (3%), compared to the standard cardiac rehabilitation group (6%). These results continued to hold at 4½-year follow-up as well (Friedman et al., 1986). However, this group might have been highly motivated to change because they had a previous MI. Would Type A's who have not had a heart attack be as motivated to change their behavior?

Results from the Montreal Type A Intervention Project (Roskies et al., 1986) suggest that Type A's who have not had a heart attack can also change their behavior. Participants were randomly assigned to one of three groups: (a) aerobic exercise, (b) weight training exercise, and (c) cognitive-behavioral stress management. Those in the cognitive-behavioral group were able to significantly reduce their Type A *behavior* compared to both exercise groups. Other studies have also found that cognitive-behavioral therapies successfully modify Type A behavior (for example, Levenkron & Moore, 1988) and reduce blood cholesterol (Gill et al., 1985).

Surprisingly, in the Montreal Project, exercise was not sufficient to reduce the behavioral symptoms of Type A, and *physiological* reactivity was not changed significantly in any of the groups, which contradicts the expected stress-reducing effects of exercise (see Module 6.2) and suggests that exercise does not affect cardiovascular reactivity. However, this is only one study, and there are others that contradict it.

As mentioned, people who are more physically active are less likely to have CHD, so exercise may also be an effective way to modify the physiological *effects* of Type A behavior. In one study, Type A men who had not had a heart attack were randomly assigned to one of two groups for 12 weeks of training in: (a) aerobic exercise or (b) strength and flexibility (Blumenthal et al., 1988). The aerobic exercise group had significant declines in blood pressure, heart rate, and an estimate of myocardial oxygen consumption. This ability of aerobic exercise to reduce these sympathetic responses to stress, thereby reducing physiological arousal, is consistent with Dientsbier's (1989) theory of physiological toughening of the sympathetic nervous system (discussed in Module 6.1). In this study, Type A was modified in both groups. But exercise has failed to modify Type A behavior in other studies (Abbott, Peters, & Vogel, 1990). Whether or not exercise modifies Type A behavior itself, however, it may buffer its effects on health. Interventions that reduce sympathetic nervous system reactivity should also reduce heart attacks. Consistent with this, relaxation training has also been a regular feature of such interventions and shows some promise (English & Baker, 1983; Roskies, Spevack, Surkis, Cohen, & Gilman, 1978).

Generally, attempts to modify Type A behavior have produced encouraging results (Levenkron & Moore, 1988; Thoresen & Powell, 1992), but many of these attempts have been short term, and the changes may not last. More research is needed to determine the best treatment and its long-term effectiveness, not just in modifying Type A behavior, but on the development of CHD. Until then, it appears that relaxation training, cognitive-behavioral therapy, and exercise may lower the incidence of CHD, although they may not directly modify Type A.

■■■■

HEART ATTACK PREVENTION

Prevention efforts target modifiable risk factors. Because the effects of these risk factors are cumulative and delayed, prevention must start early in life. People between the ages of 35 and 65 are the primary targets for current preventive efforts, but some even advocate targeting children, because otherwise healthy young men who died in battle already showed signs of atherosclerosis on autopsy (Enos, Holmes, & Beyer, 1953; McNamara, Molot, Stremple, & Cutting, 1971). The development of CHD is a slow process, becoming a major threat to life only after 65 years of age, when $^3/_4$ of all CHD deaths occur, so it is difficult to get people to change their behavior when it takes many years to benefit from the results. Nevertheless, with CHD the major cause of death in the United States, many preventive efforts have been undertaken.

Not all prevention efforts are effective. Individual counseling for risk factor reduction in a large study of Australian government workers was not (Edye, Mandryk, Frommer, Healey, & Ferguson, 1989). This long-term study utilized trained professional counselors and followed almost 2,000 subjects for three years. Systolic blood pressure was the only risk factor that was reduced during the program, and the reduction was judged to be clinically insignificant.

In contrast, a recent review of cognitive stress management techniques found that they are effective in reducing serum cholesterol, hypertension, and Type A behavior (Bennett & Carroll, 1990). Not only does stress management reduce individual risk factors, but it also appears to reduce mortality and morbidity.

A recent experiment used an intensive multicomponent lifestyle treatment program to reduce coronary atherosclerosis (Ornish, et al., 1990). Subjects were randomly assigned to either (a) an intensive treatment program consisting of a low fat vegetarian diet, aerobic exercise (walking for either a half-hour per day or for an hour three times per week), an hour per day of various stress management techniques (for example, yoga, breathing, meditation, or progressive muscle relaxation), and supportive group therapy; or (b) a conventional program consisting of a diet recommended by the American Heart Association and moderate exercise.

All subjects had high cholesterol levels and were at risk for MI. After a year, those in the intensive program had a significant reduction of coronary atherosclerosis, while those on the conventional program had a significant increase. This is the first experimental evidence of behavioral and psychological treatment actually *reversing* the development of heart disease. No other medical intervention, including cholesterol-lowering medication, has produced better results (Dienstfrey, 1992).

Because all behavioral and psychological treatments are not equally effective, they must be specifically targeted to CHD risk factors (Johnston, 1989). For this reason, a multicomponent approach seems to have the most promise as a preventive for CHD (Dienstfrey, 1992). Programs also need to take into account the complexities of human nature. For example, when patients were told their blood cholesterol level was low initially, it was found to have *increased* two to four months later (Gorman, 1988). Presumably, they took the results of a low cholesterol test as a license to indulge. But carefully designed prevention efforts hold much promise for the future.

Large-Scale Prevention Studies

Winkelstein and Marmot (1981) reviewed many large-scale prevention studies and found that there were three general types of prevention efforts: ecological models, screening and targeting programs, and community programs. *Ecological Models* work indirectly by changing environmental factors such as traffic and pollution that contribute to stress. Although correlational research does support a connection between the pace of life and CHD in 36 U.S. cities (Levine, Lynch, Miyake, & Lucia, 1989), as an intervention, ecological models are only theoretical because they would involve major expenditures and a long time frame to evaluate. Imagine trying to change the pace of life in an entire city.

Screening and targeting programs screen large numbers of individuals for known risk factors and target *only* those who are at high risk, primarily with special counseling and behavioral modification efforts. In the Chicago Coronary Prevention Evaluation Program (Stamler et al., 1980), 500 men between 40 and 59 years of age and judged to be at risk for CHD were followed for 15 years. The intervention included monthly counseling sessions for 6 months, followed by counseling sessions every 3 months. These were aimed at improving diet (reducing fat and salt), stopping smoking, and supervision of antihypertensive medication (when indicated). Sixty-five percent of the participants completed the entire program. Serum cholesterol was lowered about 10%, the proportion of smokers was reduced from 37% to 28%, and blood pressure fell to within normal limits. Importantly, mortality from CHD was about 25% lower than in a group matched for age and risk factors.

Community programs employ mass education and organization efforts and target an entire community. One very good example of a community-based program is the Stanford Heart Disease Prevention Project in several California communities (Leventhal, Safer, Cleary, & Gutmann, 1980; Maccoby & Alexander, 1979; see Module 3.2, page 92). The treatment produced a significant reduction in serum cholesterol, smoking, consumption of saturated fat, and blood pressure. Both education alone and education with group counseling were effective in producing a decline of 17% in the overall level of CHD risk factors compared to the control community, which experienced a 6% increase.

These results suggest that educational media programs may be just as effective as group counseling programs or group counseling combined with educational programs. Educational programs are less expensive and may reach people who would not attend group counseling, so they may be best for large-scale efforts at risk reduction. However, the results produced by education efforts alone are modest at best, probably because some people need more intensive encouragement. Those people would probably benefit from interventions such as behavior modification to change their lifestyle. Unfortunately, for the many hundreds of thousands of people each year who have a heart attack, prevention is too little or too late.

RECOVERY FROM HEART ATTACK

About 1.5 million people will have a heart attack this year in the United States (USDHHS, 1992). Those who do not die immediately or within a few weeks—about half—will return home to begin the long road to recovery (Krantz & Deckel, 1983). Although as many as 20% of MIs may go unnoticed, it is usually a painful and frightening experience as the heart muscle struggles to survive while starving for oxygen.

An MI usually requires hospitalization in a special coronary care unit. Because the risk of another MI is high during the first few days, vital signs are continuously monitored through electrodes on the skin while an intravenous drip administers medication through a needle in a vein.

Some patients will be anxious as they lie there contemplating their brush with death and wondering how it will turn out, whereas others may be in a state of denial and may not appear anxious (Doehrman, 1977; Froese, Hackett, Cassem, & Silverberg, 1974). In a study of 367 post MI patients followed for 3 to 5 years, a low level of denial was associated with more problems readjusting to work, sex, and physical activities, whereas a high level of denial was associated with *better* emotional adjustment but also weakly associated with increased mortality (Havik & Maeland, 1988). So, a certain amount of denial may be beneficial to recovery if not to survival. Denial also serves as an adaptive mechanism during the recovery from **coronary bypass** surgery (Folks, Freeman, Sokol, & Thurstin, 1988).

After a few days in the hospital, those with high anxiety experience some reduction in it, although the anxiety levels of patients, regardless of whether they are in denial, remain above normal (Cay, Vetter, Philip, & Dugard, 1972; Froese et al., 1974). Those who have the hardest time adjusting psychologically are not necessarily those with the most damage to the heart. Rather, people who were experiencing stress or social or work problems before the MI have the most difficult time adjusting. Angina pectoris may occur and persist for many years. Even though this can be frightening because it reminds patients of the heart attack, it is usually well controlled with medication. After about 7 to 10 days of acute care, patients are transferred to a unit where rehabilitation can begin.

REHABILITATION

The quality and comprehensiveness of cardiac rehabilitation vary greatly. The elements described here are not necessarily part of every rehabilitation program, although they should be. The goal of cardiac rehabilitation is to help patients reach their optimal physical, medical, psychological, social, emotional, vocational, and economic status (Dracup, 1985). Education is usually the first element of rehabilitation and is carried out by physicians (usually cardiologists), nurses, and nutritionists. Patients are told what to expect in the future, what symptoms might occur, what medications they will be taking, and what risk factors may contribute to another heart attack. Patients are usually placed on low salt and low cholesterol diets and told to stop smoking, lose weight, and reduce alcohol consumption.

Beginning with short walks in the hospital, most patients are gradually given training and supervision in an exercise program that typically consists of walking, jogging, bicycling, or calisthenics for 30 minutes three times a week (DeBusk, Haskell, Miller, Berra, & Taylor, 1985). Exercise may reduce heart attack risk, and it also helps patients cope psychologically with CHD (for example, Rovario, Holmes, & Holmstein, 1984; Thompson & Thompson, 1987). Exercise tends to improve self-concept, sexual activity, involvement in other leisure activities, and perceived health—in short, the quality of life. However, adherence with this aspect of rehabilitation is a problem, and half of the people will usually quit exercising within the first 6 months (Dishman, 1982; Dishman, Sallis, & Orenstein, 1985). Adherence improves if patients are closely supervised, rather than exercise by themselves.

After the acute period, additional medical procedures may be recommended, but ultimately the extent of damage to the heart muscle and the condition of the coronary arteries and the ventricles determine prognosis (Langosch, 1984). The 10-year survival rates after MI with good ventricular functioning are 97% with one artery damaged, 79% with two damaged, and 66% with three damaged. These rates drop to 85%, 58%, and 40% if ventricular functioning is also impaired (Berkow & Fletcher, 1987).

PSYCHOSOCIAL REACTIONS AND LONG-TERM CONSIDERATIONS

As rehabilitation begins to focus on the long term, it tends to be more individually tailored, and psychologists become more involved. There is a need for careful individual assessment and follow-up of cardiac patients. Initial levels of anxiety and depression resolve somewhat over the first year or two following MI (Doehrman, 1977). Those with a high level of emotional upset need to be identified and treated, because emotional upset is related to failure to resume work and an increased likelihood of rehospitalization (Havik & Maeland, 1990).

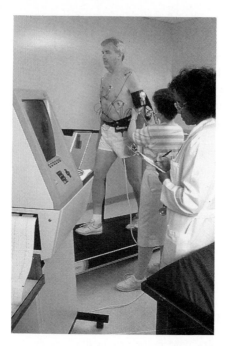

This cardiac patient on a treadmill is undergoing physical stress to determine the extent of exercise that can be tolerated and if there are any irregularities on an electrocardiogram.

One study evaluated a comprehensive psychological intervention program that began while patients were still in the hospital (Oldenberg, Perkins, & Andrews, 1985). They received information about their physical status, relaxation training, and counseling. Patients who received the treatment made a significantly better adjustment over the next year than those who did not, but counseling may not be equally effective for all patients. In a study of 862 non-smoking post-MI patients, counseling to reduce Type A significantly reduced mortality over a 4½-year period, but only for patients with mild heart attacks (Powell & Thoresen, 1988). It had no effect on those who had severe heart attacks, perhaps because the heart was too extensively damaged.

WORK   Patients often see their return to work as an important milestone indicating that they are getting better (Croog, 1983). Those who are recovering well and do not require additional medical procedures are encouraged to return to work after about two months, although some may be able to return to work even sooner (Dennis et al., 1988).

About 85% return to work within a year, although it may be in a reduced capacity (Doehrman, 1977). Sometimes it is necessary to advise cardiac patients with high-stress jobs to change them or cut back. Those who do not go back to work or put it off tend to have more emotional distress and depression

(Krantz & Deckel, 1983). Although, more severe MIs decrease the likelihood of return to work, psychosocial factors are more strongly related to work outcome. Women, blue-collar workers with strenuous jobs, and people with emotional problems are the least likely to return to work post-MI (Shanfield, 1990).

STRESS   Stress is an important consideration in cardiac rehabilitation. Half of patients report difficulty controlling the stress in their lives, and many find their lives even more stressful after a heart attack (Croog & Levine, 1977). Therefore, stress management is an important component of long-term rehabilitation (Langosch, 1984). The most effective stress management programs for CHD are cognitive-behavioral, involving relaxation training and cognitive restructuring (Friedman et al., 1986; Powell, Friedman, Thoresen, Gill, & Ulmer, 1984; Razin, 1984).

SOCIAL SUPPORT   Relationships and social support have a strong effect on cardiac rehabilitation. Changes in lifestyle and dependency can provoke conflict in a marriage, and pre-existing family problems can become worse after a heart attack (Croog & Fitzgerald, 1978; Michela, 1987; Swan, Carmelli, & Rosenman, 1986). Despite this, divorce or separation are not related to subsequent heart attacks (Case, Moss, Case, McDermott, & Eberly, 1992). Even though many of the risk factors for CHD are *not* modifiable, the patient and family members may engage in a cycle of guilt and blame for the heart attack (Croog, 1983). In these cases, family counseling may help all members of the family to adjust. Furthermore, living alone after an MI is related to an increased risk of another MI (Case et al., 1992), suggesting that social support is an important factor in subsequent heart attacks.

SEXUAL FUNCTIONING   One of the most common problems that arises after a heart attack is sex—that is, whether or not to have it. An MI rarely, if ever, affects sexual functioning at a physiological level, but patients and their partners are afraid that sexual activity might cause another heart attack. Given the role of the autonomic nervous system in the sexual response (see Module 13.1), and the effects of sex on the cardiovascular system, this fear is not entirely unfounded. As a consequence, sexual activity rarely returns to the same level as before the attack (Krantz, & Deckel, 1983; Michela, 1987). However, many people are capable of enjoying sexual activity after a MI without jeopardizing their health. Sexual satisfaction can be improved by *gradually* increasing the frequency of sex from very little or none initially (Michela, 1987).

PHYSICAL IMPAIRMENT   People's physical abilities and endurance are usually more limited after a heart attack, often surprising patients and sometimes resulting in feelings of shame and low self-esteem (Finlayson &

McEwen, 1977). After MI, wives tend to believe their husbands are more dependent and irritable (Skelton & Dominian, 1973), whereas husbands tend to believe their wives are more intrusive and overprotective (Croog & Levine, 1977). Wives are undergoing their own psychological reactions to their husband's heart attack, and their behavior may be a response to anxieties about their spouse's survival (Skelton & Dominian, 1973).

These may be realistic reactions to real physical impairment. Patients may actually *be* more physically dependent, but a situation known as **cardiac invalidism** can also develop, in which patients become dependent and helpless and believe that they are less able than they actually are (Krantz & Deckel, 1983). Research suggests that social support can reduce the distress of the cardiac patient and reduce physical and psychological symptoms (Fontana, Kerns, Rosenberg, & Colonese, 1989). Counseling for the wives of MI patients also significantly reduces their anxiety (Thompson & Meddis, 1990).

Having a realistic sense of the patient's physical abilities seems to help the couple adjust. One study either just gave wives information about their husband's abilities, had them observe their husbands undergoing a treadmill stress test (a walk on a treadmill that gradually increases in speed while the heart is being monitored by electrocardiogram), or had the wives actually try the treadmill themselves after observing their husbands (Taylor, Bandura, Ewart, Miller, & DeBusk, 1985). The wives who experienced the treadmill themselves *increased* their perceptions of their husbands' physical abilities, while those wives who only received information or observed continued to perceive their husbands as impaired.

Even though patients' initial heightened levels of anxiety and depression tend to be reduced with time, they are vulnerable to becoming more anxious or depressed at any time as they come to terms with the lifestyle changes caused by CHD and the threat of another heart attack. Out of fear, they may deny future symptoms of MI, postponing seeking treatment (Matthews, Siegel, Kuller, Thompson, & Varat, 1983). That could be lethal, so patients and family members should be prepared for the recurrence of symptoms in a gentle and comfortable manner. First, they should be taught how to distinguish heart attack symptoms from other types of symptoms, and second, the patient's family should learn cardiopulmonary resuscitation or CPR and how to reach emergency services.

■

CONCLUSION

Richard is one of the lucky ones. His angina was a warning before any permanent damage was done to his heart. The angina reflected an underlying insufficiency of oxygen to the heart muscle, which was confirmed by an angiogram that revealed a 50% restriction in blood flow in one coronary artery. The reason for the restriction was probably underlying mild arteriosclerosis, caused by borderline hypertension, in combination with the build up of artery-narrowing atherosclerotic deposits, caused by high cholesterol. Family history is probably the most important nonmodifiable cause of Richard's condition. His father died of a heart attack at the age of 57, and his mother, still alive at 68, has a cholesterol level of 310. The modifiable causes are Richard's lack of physical activity, smoking, diet, stress, and perhaps suppressed anger and hostility, all of which can be treated.

After experiencing angina and viewing the blockage during his angiogram, Richard was highly motivated to change his poor health habits. He stopped smoking, modified his diet, and began a regular exercise program. He also began to see a psychologist who taught him stress management and relaxation techniques. He appreciated the changes these brought to his life so much that he began to explore potential sources for suppressed anger and hostility. Within 6 months, Richard's cholesterol fell to 185, his total cholesterol to HDL ratio fell to 3.1 to 1.0, and his blood pressure fell to 145/82. His doctor was fully prepared to prescribe antihypertensive and anticholesterol medication if the lifestyle changes had failed to produce sufficient improvement, but they were not necessary. Of course, Richard remains at risk for a heart attack and also for cerebral artery disease, the subject of the next module.

MODULE SUMMARY

Before continuing, here is a review of the major aspects of coronary heart disease covered in this module:

1. Cardiovascular disease, including heart attacks and stroke, is the leading cause of death in the United States today.
2. The heart receives blood through a special vascular system surrounding it at the top. Several major arteries with downward branches cover the outside of the heart. If one of these is blocked, blood cannot reach the part of the heart muscle that it serves, and after several minutes, the cells begin to die from lack of oxygen.
3. Ischemic heart disease is caused by insufficient blood flow, and any resulting area of dead cells is called an infarct.
4. The two basic processes in cardiovascular disease are arteriosclerosis, when arteries become thick and lose their elasticity, and atherosclerosis, when fat is deposited along artery walls. Both reduce blood flow through the arteries.

5. Large-scale community studies have identified risk factors in heart disease.

6. Nonmodifiable risk factors include age, sex, and family history.

7. Modifiable risk factors include hypertension; cholesterol, diet, and obesity; smoking; physical inactivity; diabetes; and Type A behavior.

8. Hypertension is affected by heredity, salt intake, stress, and suppressed anger and hostility. African Americans have double the hypertension rate of European Americans. Cognitive-behavioral methods can reduce moderate hypertension somewhat and are a useful adjunct to medication, but medication is often required for large reductions in blood pressure.

9. Total cholesterol above 300 mg/ml of blood and a ratio of total cholesterol to HDL above 4.5 to 1 are considered major risk factors in heart disease. Obesity is correlated with heart disease, but probably only because obese people also ingest high levels of cholesterol. Dietary control through behavior modification can reduce cholesterol levels.

10. Smoking is probably related to coronary heart disease because it raises blood pressure.

11. Physical inactivity is a risk factor in coronary heart disease. Exercise may slow or reverse atherosclerosis.

12. Diabetes is related indirectly to heart disease because it contributes to arteriosclerosis.

13. Type A's have about twice the risk of heart attack compared to Type B's. The lethal components of Type A behavior appears to be hostility and anger. Type A can be successfully modified and heart attacks reduced by group therapy and by cognitive-behavioral stress management, but more research is needed.

14. Research shows that population screening and targeting programs and community-based programs can reduce heart disease by changing people's lifestyle. Education alone does not appear to be effective in these programs, but some individuals will need more intensive intervention.

15. About half of people survive a heart attack. Recovery and rehabilitation are long-term processes, usually beginning with hospital care. Psychosocial consequences include initial anxiety, possibly denial, family problems, work problems, and sexual dysfunction. Psychosocial intervention can improve outcome and even reduce health complications and the recurrence of attacks.

CEREBRAL VASCULAR DISEASE

█████

INTRODUCTION

The underlying causes of cerebral vascular disease and coronary heart disease are, for the most part, the same—arteriosclerosis and atherosclerosis. Therefore, people who have one are at risk for the other. The difference is that cerebral vascular disease affects the brain, while coronary heart disease affects the heart.

Cerebral vascular disease is the third leading cause of death in the United States. There are 600,000 cerebral vascular accidents, or "strokes," per year, and about 150,000 people die as a result (USDHHS, 1992). Just as with heart attacks—and for the same reasons—the mortality rate has been declining for several decades (Acheson & Williams, 1980; Glick & Cerullo, 1986; Newman, 1984b). However, the death rate for stroke is about twice as high for African Americans than for European Americans (USDHHS, 1992). Also, a substantial number of people survive strokes each year, many of them with physical and cognitive impairments, which presents a substantial challenge to rehabilitation psychologists and neuropsychologists.

CEREBRAL VASCULAR ACCIDENTS

Cerebral vascular disease often results in cerebral vascular accidents or strokes. The three most common types are cerebral infarction, transient ischemic attacks, and cerebral hemorrhage. The first two are the result of blockage of arterial blood flow, while the latter results from the rupture of an artery that bleeds into the brain.

CEREBRAL INFARCTION   Just like a myocardial infarction, a **cerebral infarction** occurs when blood flow to the brain is obstructed, resulting in a loss of the supply of oxygen and nutrients to brain cells. Neurons cannot survive longer than a few minutes without oxygen, and since CNS neurons do not regenerate, strokes usually result in permanent brain damage.

The obstruction begins with the build up of atherosclerotic deposits in the arteries serving the brain. Some time later, either a thrombus or an embolus

This woman has had a stroke of the left hemisphere frontal region, which interferes with her ability to walk. The effects are also evident in the drooping of the right side of her face and her immobile right arm.

blocks the narrowed artery, cutting off blood to the area of brain tissue served. A **thrombus** is a clot of blood that forms on the atherosclerotic tissue, while an **embolus** is either a piece of a thrombus that breaks loose from another part of the vascular system, a clump of foreign matter, or a gas bubble. The embolus is carried by the blood until it lodges in the narrowed artery.

When an embolus is the cause of the obstruction, physical and cognitive symptoms generally appear very rapidly, usually within minutes. When a thrombus obstructs blood flow, symptoms usually develop more slowly, perhaps over a half hour. In both cases, there frequently is loss of consciousness (Reitan & Wolfson, 1985). Neurons supplied by the obstructed artery die, leaving a permanent, focal lesion. Although an embolus typically gives no warning, in the case of a thrombus, there may be warnings in the form of transient ischemic attacks.

Some people do not experience a single, major cerebral infarction but instead have numerous small ones over many years. By definition, *multi-infarct dementia* is applied to people with cardiovascular disease who become progressively demented. Although there is often a problem differentiating it from Alzheimer's disease (see Module 9.1, page 390), the two result from entirely different causes. In multi-infarct dementia, atherosclerotic changes in the arteries of the brain lead to many small blockages. The result is separate infarcts widely scattered in the brain. Many, if not all, of these produce such small effects that they go unnoticed. However, the cumulative effect causes deterioration in intellectual functioning (Reitan & Wolfson, 1985). Eventually, like Alzheimer's patients, people become unable to care for themselves.

TRANSIENT ISCHEMIC ATTACKS **Transient ischemic attacks (TIAs)** are episodes of *temporary* obstruction of the arteries that supply the brain (Lezak, 1983; Reitan & Wolfson, 1985). They may last only a few moments or up to 24 hours but, by definition, no longer. If they persist beyond 24 hours they are called cerebral infarcts, and there is irreversible brain damage. TIA episodes may vary in occurrence from several times a day to once every few months. TIAs are caused by the same underlying factors that cause cerebral infarction, and about 80% of cerebral infarctions are preceded by TIAs (Lezak, 1983).

TIAs are sometimes present with a headache but always with various brief symptoms that are similar to, but milder than, those that result from a cerebral infarction. The patient may experience only dimness of vision or a brief period of complete blindness affecting only one eye, partial paralysis of one side of the body, difficulties in receptive or expressive language abilities, or visual-spatial orientation problems. The precise symptoms depend on which area of the brain is involved.

It is commonly believed that patients make a complete recovery between episodes and suffer no permanent impairment, perhaps because the symptoms of TIAs clear, and physical functioning generally returns to normal. However, careful neuropsychological testing has revealed that some mild cognitive impairments are present between episodes (Lezak, 1983). This may be due to the continuing diminished blood supply, even though the obstruction itself has cleared. TIAs are considered a warning, since many people with TIA go on to experience a cerebral infarction.

CEREBRAL HEMORRHAGE Neurons receive oxygen and nutrients through the blood–brain barrier. Direct contact with blood damages the delicate neurons, which is why hemorrhaging in the brain is dangerous.

Brain hemorrhaging can result from the rupture of an **aneurysm**, a weak vessel wall that blows out like a balloon and can burst under pressure. Aneurysms can occur in many parts of the vascular system; about 2% of people have them and most cause no problems (Adams, Corsellis, & Duchen, 1984). However, if an aneurysm bursts in the brain, there is a sudden, dramatic onset of symptoms. The symptoms often include nausea and vomiting with severe headache 60% of the time (Reitan & Wolfson, 1985). Within a few hours, a stiff neck may develop, and there will be neuropsychological impairments. About 20% of patients will lose consciousness immediately, with another 50% losing consciousness in 6 to 12 hours. There are no warning signs, and the effects of cerebral hemorrhage can range widely from death to mild brain damage.

A second cause of hemorrhaging in the brain is hypertension. High blood pressure can cause ruptures in blood vessels, usually those at the base of the brain that supply the thalamus and brain stem. Because these brain areas serve vital functions, there is a relatively high mortality rate of 50% associated with hypertensive hemorrhages (Raichle et al., 1978). Damage to these critical subcortical areas can leave the patient in a near vegetative state (unconscious), but if it is a very limited stroke, patients can survive with just some minor attention and memory problems.

CEREBRAL INFARCTION AND TIA

RISK FACTORS AND PREVENTION

The primary risk factors for stroke are the same as those for coronary heart disease: hypertension, arteriosclerosis, atherosclerosis, and diabetes. Therefore, reduction of blood pressure and dietary restrictions are the most effective long-term treatments. A direct role for Type A behavior in stroke has not been established. However, since coronary heart disease is itself contributory to stroke, reduction of Type A behavior may have an indirect effect in reducing stroke.

TREATMENT

During the acute phase of a stroke or hemorrhage, medical care is directed at treating complications such as heart failure or respiratory infection. After that, the underlying causes are assessed and treated, and rehabilitation then begins. Occasionally, when indicated, angioplasty or surgery is undertaken to reduce or bypass blockage of the major arteries that supply blood to the brain from the aorta. Because of the sensitivity of surrounding neural tissue, such procedures are not usually undertaken for blocked arteries within the brain itself. Sometimes anticoagulant medications are prescribed for TIA, although their use is controversial. Instead, the most commonly prescribed medication is aspirin, which thins the blood (Berkow & Fletcher, 1987).

EFFECTS

Strokes have widespread repercussions, affecting people socially and physically and, depending on whether or not they have reached retirement, also affecting them vocationally (Thompson et al., 1989). The acute effects of a stroke can appear quite pronounced, but these quickly resolve to leave more limited impairments related to the area of the brain involved. Impairments can affect a person physically, neuropsychologically, and psychosocially.

PHYSICAL   Motor impairments are the most immediate and common result of a stroke (Gordon & Diller, 1983; Newman, 1984b). Typically, a stroke affects only a portion of one hemisphere. Therefore, most strokes produce lateralized physical effects—that is, they usually occur on only one side of the body and contralateral to the hemisphere in which the stroke occurred. Even so, the physical effects can be quite disruptive of a patient's activities of daily living (discussed in Module 9.1). If the preferred hand is involved, writing and eating will be effected. If either leg is involved, a person may have to learn to walk with an assistive device like a cane or walker.

NEUROPSYCHOLOGICAL   The effects of a lesion on motor and cognitive abilities depends on a number of factors, the major ones being the location of the lesion, the cause of the lesion, the extent of the lesion, and the patient's age and personality (see Module 9.1, page 383). Even so, distinctive patterns of impairment occur in strokes. The most characteristic feature of cerebral infarction is that the resulting neuropsychological impairments are **focal**, meaning they affect a limited number specific cognitive abilities, leaving many others intact. In contrast, head injuries, multi-infarct dementia, and cerebral hemorrhage tend to produce **diffuse impairments** affecting many cognitive abilities. Another distinguishing characteristic of multi-infarct dementia is that it is progressive, leading to a gradual decline in intellectual functioning.

Because there is swelling and disruption of function in the area adjacent to any brain lesion, cognitive symptoms may seem more diffuse at first. As these resolve, usually in several weeks, focal cognitive impairments become more obvious. With left hemisphere damage, many stroke patients experience **aphasia**, which is a broad term for many types of language problems (Kertez, 1983). Those with *expressive aphasia* typically have difficulty producing fluent, coherent speech, although they can make the basic sounds of speech and understand language. Those with *receptive aphasia* can speak fluently but have difficulty understanding language (so they may also make no sense when speaking).

With right hemisphere damage, there is a disruption in processing visual-spatial information and patterns. One common visual disorder in right hemisphere lesions is **neglect syndrome**, in which a patient may fail to recognize or process stimuli on the left side of the visual field (Gordon & Diller, 1983). People with neglect syndrome may have more accidents because they are not aware of objects on the left. They also do not eat food on the left side of their plate and fail to dress the left side of their body.

Sometimes brain damage from a stroke results in major neuropsychological impairments affecting important areas of intellectual functioning (Horton

& Wedding, 1984). This can be so profound that an employed person who has a stroke may be unable to return to work at all (Gordon & Diller, 1983; Krantz & Deckel, 1983).

PSYCHOSOCIAL   Emotional disorders are quite common after a stroke. Not only does a stroke present major adjustment problems physically and undermine one's belief in one's own intellectual abilities, but lesions can disrupt the brain's ability to process emotions. Changes in a patient's emotionality after a stroke may be due to brain damage itself (Gordon & Diller, 1983; Newman, 1984b; Robinson & Benson, 1981). Stroke patients may have **emotional lability,** which is the expression of dramatic emotionality such as laughing or crying, either without provocation or with minimal provocation (Bleiberg, 1986). Sometimes their emotional expression is the opposite of what they are thinking about or reacting to. For example, they may laugh when they are talking about a tragedy. The pattern of emotional effects after a stroke also appears to be lateralized. People with right hemisphere lesions tend to have difficulty understanding, interpreting, and expressing emotions, whereas people with left hemisphere lesions are typically depressed (Ross, 1981, 1982).

Depression can affect progress in rehabilitation. A two-year longitudinal study of post-stroke patients revealed that "depressions, once they develop, are sustained by severe (physical and cognitive) impairments, and impairments, once they develop, are sustained by severe depressions" (Parikh, Lipsey, Robinson, & Price, 1988, p. 45). Even though there may be a neuropathological basis for emotional responses to stroke, psychosocial factors are also involved. The quality of the relationship with the caregiver is related to depression after a stroke (Thompson, 1989).

Caregivers themselves are not immune to depression. Depression in caregivers is related to a prior history of depression, more concern about the patient's future, a closer relationship with the patient, and poorer financial status (Tompkins, 1988). Some families simply do not adjust well to a member's stroke. Although a severe impairment of mobility or speech, for example, will limit social activities, many patients with relatively minor impairments dramatically limit their social and leisure activities. Some of the physical and cognitive changes may also socially stigmatize patients so others avoid or reject them (Newman, 1984b). See Module 9.1 (page 391) for a discussion of the issues that many people with disabilities must deal with.

Denial appears to be more common in stroke patients than in those with CHD (Krantz & Deckel, 1983). Part of the reason may be that stroke patients often recover very rapidly in the first few weeks (Dahlberg, 1977). However, this rapid recovery eventually gives way to very slow gains, and patients may find it difficult to accept their remaining impairments. Another reason for denial may be resultant brain damage, which could affect the ability of patients to appreciate their situation. Denial is related to better prognosis in post-MI patients, but it creates problems for post-stroke patients because recognition of one's problems is necessary for progress in rehabilitation, especially in cognitive rehabilitation.

REHABILITATION

Rehabilitation usually focuses on three areas: psychosocial adjustment, cognitive impairments, and motor impairments. Physical and occupational therapy are directed at a patient's motor impairments. Generally, physical therapists use education and exercises aimed at building strength and endurance. For example, a person with impaired use of the left side of the body will need to build up the strength of the right to compensate. Occupational therapy is more directed at integrating newly learned or strengthened physical abilities into a community context. This may involve relearning how to drive or use public transportation.

Although in many ways every brain is similar, every brain is different in the precise manner in which cognitive functioning will be affected by damage. For that reason, a careful neuropsychological assessment can provide valuable information about prognosis. The importance of neuropsychological assessment was demonstrated in a recent study of stroke patients after discharge from the hospital (Sundet, Finset, & Reinvang, 1988). The ability to predict later dependency was significantly improved by the use of neuropsychological test results.

Neuropsychological testing is also used to guide cognitive retraining. *Cognitive retraining* attempts to help patients regain basic cognitive abilities (also see Module 9.2, page 399). Speech and language specialists use a variety of exercises to help patients regain abilities to read, write, speak, and understand language. Clinical neuropsychologists and cognitive therapists attempt to restore patients' higher-level intellectual abilities involved with memory, learning, and thinking (Diller & Gordon, 1981; Gordon & Diller, 1983). Higher-level abilities, however, are dependent on a number of more basic cognitive functions, which is where rehabilitation efforts typically begin. One technique helps patients with right hemisphere strokes overcome neglect syndrome. They are taught to follow a moving stimulus by turning their heads to the left (Gordon & Diller, 1983). This compensates for the loss of attention to the left visual field by bringing the left visual field into the right visual field as the head is turned. Cognitive retraining is a relatively new and emerging field. Therefore, there is little evidence to support its effectiveness, although there is much hope for the future.

Psychological and psychosocial rehabilitation efforts have been around much longer than cognitive retraining. The primary modality for therapy is group rather than individual (see Krantz & Deckel, 1983, for a review). One goal of therapy with stroke patients is to overcome denial if it is present and to help them fully engage in rehabilitation. Therapy for the patient's family and primary caregiver is also becoming more frequent. See Module 9.1 for a complete discussion of therapy issues related to rehabilitation.

Module Summary

Here is a review of the major points concerning cerebral vascular disease:

1. Cerebral vascular disease and coronary artery disease usually have the same underlying causes—arteriosclerosis and atherosclerosis.
2. There are three types of cerebral vascular disease: cerebral infarction, transient ischemic attacks, and cerebral hemorrhage.
3. Cerebral infarction occurs when an artery serving the brain is narrowed by atherosclerotic deposits and then becomes blocked by a thrombus or embolus.
4. A transient ischemic attack is similar to a cerebral infarction, but the obstruction lasts only temporarily, from a few minutes up to 24 hours.
5. A cerebral hemorrhage is bleeding into the brain tissue. Aneurysms are the cause of most hemorrhages, although hypertension can cause bleeding from ruptured blood vessels in the base of the brain.
6. Multi-infarct dementia is a progressive disease resulting from many small infarcts in the brain. The cumulative effects of the infarcts causes deterioration of intellectual functioning.
7. The primary risk factors in stroke are the same as for coronary heart disease: arteriosclerosis, atherosclerosis, hypertension, and diabetes.
8. Strokes affect people's physical, neuropsychological, and psychosocial functioning.
9. Physical effects are usually lateralized to one side of the body.
10. Neuropsychological impairments are usually focal in cerebral infarcts and more diffuse in multi-infarct dementia and hemorrhagic strokes. Left hemisphere damage often results in language impairment, or aphasia, whereas right hemisphere can result in neglect syndrome.
11. Psychosocial effects include emotional lability, which is the expression of emotions such as laughing or crying with minimal provocation. Left hemisphere lesions typically produce depression, while right hemisphere lesions typically cause difficulty understanding, interpreting, or expressing emotions.
12. Rehabilitation focuses on psychological and psychosocial adjustment, cognitive impairments, and motor impairments.
13. Neuropsychological assessment can predict later dependency and guide cognitive retraining.
14. There is hope that cognitive retraining may improve intellectual functioning, but there is little evidence yet to show that it does.

12

DISGESTIVE SYSTEM: FUNCTION AND ORGANIZATION

12.1 Nutrition, Appetite, and Eating Behavior
12.2 Weight Control and Eating Disorders

INTRODUCTION

S*ome people eat to live and others live to eat. Alice, a 35-year-old Japanese American woman, never could make up her mind about that, but she knew that eating was important to her, even too much so. A third-generation American, Alice considers herself fully acculturated and speaks little Japanese, although her parents do, and she has been exposed to both cultures. Larger in stature than most of her female relatives, she remembers believing she was "bulkier" most of her life. In spite of this, Alice has never weighed more than 144 pounds, scarcely 10% more than the desirable weight for her height of 5' 4".*

Alice ate heavily and was depressed often during adolescence. Being overweight, she did not socialize or date much. Sensing her concern about her body, her parents encouraged her to diet, but when she did, she would lose a few pounds, find it difficult to lose more, give up, and become more depressed.

In college, Alice concentrated on her studies. Feeling fat and unattractive, she discouraged men who found her attractive and claimed that she was too devoted to her studies to socialize. When her roommate had dates, Alice went to the market and bought three or four bags of potato chips, several half gallons of ice cream, and soda pop. She ate all of this in one sitting, alone in her room, being careful to dispose of the trash where it would not be noticed. While she did this she felt out of control. Immediately afterwards she felt guilty and resolved to diet. Occasionally, her diets were successful, but she always gained the weight back in a short time.

Since graduating, her loss of eating control has taken a new, troublesome direction. Alice has been working for a financial services company, and as she has become successful, she has attended more social functions involving food.

After these rich meals, she began to feel bad. She could not concentrate on the business agenda and wished that she had controlled what she had eaten. Her mind was occupied with thoughts of how bad she had been. Then, one time it occurred to her to go to the ladies room and trigger her gag reflex in order to vomit. She felt relieved afterwards and has been doing this to control her weight for some time, although she weighs no less than she did before.

*Recently her vomiting has been increasing almost on its own and she is scared that it is now getting out of control. Alice has **bulimia nervosa**, a threat to physical and psychological well-being. Is there something wrong with her physiologically? With her appetite? Can anything be done about it? These questions will be answered in Module 12.2, but it is first necessary to understand the digestive system and the relationship among nutrition, appetite, and eating behavior.*

The digestive system converts food into a form that the body can use for growth, basic physiological functions, and energy. It also provides the mechanism by which nutrients are absorbed into the bloodstream and solid waste products are excreted from the body. Food consists of various complex, highly organized plant and animal tissues. **Digestion** is the process in which food is broken down into its constituent nutrients, and **absorption** is the process in which the nutrients pass out of the digestive system into the bloodstream.

The brain influences digestion, appetite, and energy consumption. It can affect the rate of digestion through the autonomic nervous system by speeding it up (parasympathetic response) or slowing it down (sympathetic response). The hypothalamus—not the digestive system—controls appetite.

DIGESTION

Digestion is a complex chemical process, during which the digestive system acts on the various constituents of food in order to prepare them for absorption.

THE CONSTITUENTS OF FOOD

Animal and plant tissues contain the basic nutrients of life, which are a combination of protein, carbohydrate, and fat, as well as compounds, such as vitamins and minerals, that are required in small amounts for the maintenance of many of the body's chemical processes.

Protein consists of amino acids that are the basic building material for bones, muscles, and organs. It is also the basis of many hormones and enzymes (molecules that act as catalysts in biochemical reactions and are responsible for the process of digestion itself).

Carbohydrate is metabolized (combined with oxygen) by individual cells to provide energy. It is found in plant and animal tissue in two forms: *Simple* carbohydrate such as sucrose (common table sugar) is used for energy, while *complex* carbohydrate such as starch (found in grains, potatoes, beans, and peas) is an important source of indigestible fiber. Fiber provides bulk (which exercises the muscles of the digestive tract), draws water into the digestive tract (which softens the stool and speeds its passage), and binds cholesterol (decreasing its absorption and carrying it out of the body).

Fat is the term for a variety of compounds that cannot be dissolved in water. Fat is the primary means the body has of storing reserve energy, but it cannot be metabolized. It must first be converted into simple carbohydrates.

THE DIGESTIVE TRACT

In order to illustrate the function and organization of the digestive system, consider how a grilled chicken breast sandwich on whole wheat bread with lettuce and tomato is digested and absorbed. The digestive system consists of several distinct but coordinated structures strung together into a long tube called the alimentary canal. The **alimentary canal** is a coiled, hollow, muscular tube approximately 10 meters (30 feet) in length, beginning at the mouth and ending at the rectum (see Figure 12.1). Digestion is largely a chemical process of decomposition aided by a number of digestive juices containing enzymes that break food down to its constituents.

The alimentary canal starts at the mouth, where the teeth tear the chicken sandwich apart and grind it into small pieces. The **salivary glands** release saliva, a watery fluid that contains enzymes that digest carbohydrate. Saliva mixes with the small pieces of the sandwich providing additional moisture. The moisture helps hold the sandwich pieces together for compaction into a ball for swallowing. By the time the sandwich ball is swallowed, digestion of the primarily carbohydrate wheat flour in the bread has already begun.

The compacted sandwich-saliva ball passes to the **pharynx**, a common passageway for food, fluids, and air. The pharynx is lined with glands that produce mucous, further facilitating the movement of the sandwich ball. The pharynx is also circled by a set of muscles that can contract in an alternating fashion. This produces a wave-like motion called **peristalsis** that propels food throughout the alimentary canal. Peristalsis moves the sandwich ball into the esophagus.

The **esophagus** is a mucus-lined, muscular, collapsed tube about 25 cm (10 inches) long that routes food to the stomach. At the junction between the esophagus and the stomach is a circular band of muscle called a **sphincter** that acts as a valve. It opens as the sandwich mixture passes through the esophagus, but then quickly closes to keep the gastric juices in the stomach from entering the esophagus.

The **stomach** is an expandable cavity about 25 cm (10 inches) long that can hold between 1.5 and 4.0 L (1 to 2 quarts). It temporarily holds food,

Figure 12.1 **THE DIGESTIVE TRACT**

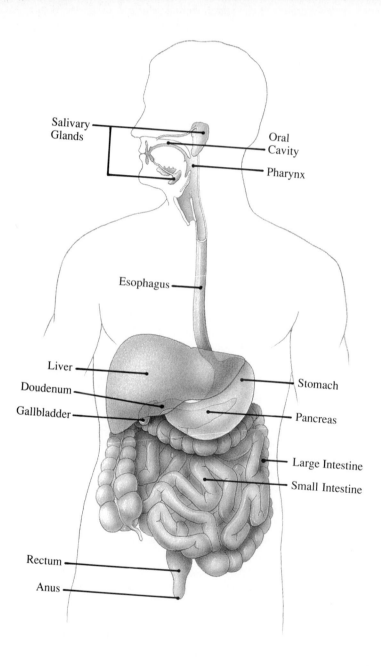

breaks it down, and mixes it into a creamy consistency. Very strong gastric juices that are highly corrosively acidic are excreted by glands into the stomach to begin the digestion of protein. These acidic juices also kill some of the bacteria that have hitched a ride on the chicken sandwich, providing protecting from infection.

Another sphincter at the base of the stomach controls the emptying of its contents into the small intestine. Fluids pass out of the stomach relatively quickly, while solids remain to become well mixed with gastric juices. Depending on the amount of solid content, it takes about four hours for the stomach to empty completely after a meal. At the end of that time, the carbohydrates and proteins have begun to break down to their molecular components, and the chicken sandwich is nearly unrecognizable, having the consistency of a creamy semifluid mass mixed with gastric juices.

As the creamy mass moves from the stomach to the small intestine, it passes through the **duodenum**, where it encounters additional enzymes. **Bile**—a yellow-green, watery solution produced by the liver—breaks down the relatively large fat globules in the chicken breast into small fatty droplets that can be acted on by enzymes. At the same time, the **pancreas**, which is also part of the endocrine system, excretes pancreatic juice into the duodenum. It is an alkaline fluid that contains a variety of enzymes, and it reduces the acidity of stomach contents before they enter the small intestine.

The **small intestine**, at approximately 6 m (20 feet), is the longest section of the alimentary canal, hanging in coils from the abdominal wall. It is only about 2.5 cm (1 inch) in diameter, yet it is the site of nearly all nutrient absorption (Marieb, 1989). As the sandwich puree enters the small intestine, the bulk of chemical digestion is yet to take place. In the three to six hours that the puree spends in the small intestine, the digestion of fat will begin and most of the protein and carbohydrate will be completely absorbed.

About seven hours after the chicken sandwich was eaten, the carbohydrates are transported across the wall of the small intestine as simple sugars (glucose), where they directly enter the blood through capillaries. Protein is broken down into individual amino acid compounds, which also enter the blood directly. Other enzymes break down the small fatty droplets into smaller "free fatty acids." A few of these free fatty acids enter the bloodstream directly through capillaries, but most are still too large. They will enter the blood in a more complicated process that takes them through the lymphatic system (see Chapter 10). Water is 95% reabsorbed into the bloodstream by the time the end of the small intestine is reached. What entered as sandwich puree is now no longer recognizable. Amino acids, carbohydrates, water-soluble vitamins, and minerals have been absorbed into the bloodstream; fat is on its way through the lymph system; and water has been reabsorbed, leaving only a residue of damp fiber.

Another sphincter controls the movement of this residue into the large intestine. The residue will spend an additional 12 to 24 hours in the **large**

intestine, which is about 1.5 m (5 feet) in length, and consists of several regions, including the colon, rectum, and anus. The large intestine does not produce any enzymes or have an active role in digestion. It primarily absorbs more water from the residue and controls defecation. Eventually, what remains of the chicken sandwich will collect in the rectum, finally exiting the anus as a semidry fiber residue with most of its nutrients gone about 24 to 48 hours after it was first ingested.

SUMMARY

The remainder of this chapter explores the importance of nutrition and appetite and their relationship with eating behavior (Module 12.1). It also examines the biopsychosocial factors involved in weight control and eating disorders (Module 12.2).

Before continuing, here is a review of the function and organization of the digestive system:

1. During digestion, animal and plant tissue are broken down into their nutrient constituents—protein, carbohydrate, fat, vitamins, and minerals. Absorption is the process during which these nutrients enter the bloodstream. Cellulose and other complex carbohydrates are indigestible and pass out of the body.

2. Protein provides the basic building material of the body, simple carbohydrates (sugar or glucose) provide the energy, and fat stores potential energy for later needs.

3. The digestive tract is also known as the alimentary canal. It is a tube that begins at the mouth and becomes the pharynx, esophagus, stomach, small intestine, duodenum, large intestine, rectum, and anus.

4. Digestion of carbohydrate begins in the mouth with the enzymes in saliva. Carbohydrate digestion continues and protein digestion begins in the stomach. Absorption of carbohydrate and protein takes place primarily in the small intestine. Fat digestion takes longer, and fat enters the bloodstream indirectly by traveling through the lymph system from the small intestine. The large intestine absorbs most of whatever water has not been absorbed through the small intestine, and bacteria there digest the residue and produce small amounts of vitamins that are absorbed.

NUTRITION, APPETITE, AND EATING BEHAVIOR

INTRODUCTION

Eating is a complex behavior, both psychologically and physiologically. It serves a purely biological need—to provide nutrients to maintain the body and its energy supply—but it can fulfill purely psychosocial needs, too. To many people, eating functions as a source of taste stimulation and pleasure; to some, it is a creative art form; and to others, it has important social meaning. It is this variety of functions that makes eating such a complex phenomenon.

How, then, can we determine what "healthy" eating behavior is? Healthy eating fulfills two goals: (a) it provides adequate nutrition for physical growth, development, and maintenance of the body; and (b) it provides sufficient, but not excessive, calories to meet the body's needs for energy while maintaining a desirable weight (described in Module 12.2).

Alice's eating behavior may have met the first goal, but it did not meet the second. As she lost control and binged, she was only aware of the desire for the taste and stimulation of eating. Also, her eating took on a social function, because she perceived her being overweight as a rationale for not dating. But, returning to the first goal, what kind of nutrition was Alice getting?

NUTRITION

It has been proposed that total health is a result of genetics, environmental factors, and nutrition (Lonsdale, 1986). The idea of an interplay among these factors and physical health is supported by an interesting review of tumor research that concluded that tumor growth may be *facilitated* by environmental stress but *hindered* by good nutrition (Seifter, Rettura, Padawer, & Fryburg, 1983). There is also a growing awareness of the importance nutrition may play in mental health (Sperry, 1984). A number of psychological problems, including depression, fatigue, insomnia, irritability, poor memory, and sexual dysfunction, are related to poor nutrition (Cassel, 1987). For most people, nutrition for optimum health can be obtained by following the Recommended Daily Allowances (RDA) set by the Federal Government. The RDA provides the average person with sufficient nutrition for growth, development, and maintenance of body functions and sufficient calories for energy.

CALORIES

A *calorie* is the amount of heat (energy) necessary to raise the temperature of 1 g of water from 14.5º to 15.5º C, so it represents the amount of *potential* energy a substance contains. One pound of body weight is equal to 3,500 calories. As a point of comparison, that chicken sandwich in the introduction to this chapter contained about 320 calories.

The body utilizes only simple carbohydrates to produce energy, but protein and fat can be converted to simple carbohydrates to produce energy if necessary. A gram of carbohydrate and a gram of protein each contain four calories, while a gram of fat contains nine calories, over twice as many.

The amount of calories used per hour to maintain vital bodily functions at rest is known as the *resting metabolic rate* (RMR). For males, a crude estimate of RMR is given by weight in kilograms (1 kg = 2.2 pounds); for women, multiplying weight in kilograms by 0.9 provides an estimate of RMR (Marieb, 1989). Estimated RMR for a man of 150 pounds and a woman of 120 pounds is about 68 [150 ÷ 2.2] and 50 [(120 ÷ 2.2) × 0.9], respectively. People with low RMRs gain weight more easily (Ravussin et al., 1988).

Because calories are a uniform measure of energy potential, it might seem that "all calories are equal," but recent research suggests their *effect* on the body differs. In a study of 141 women aged 34 to 59 who were monitored over a year, there was no correlation between obesity and the amount of *total* calories consumed, but there was a significant correlation between obesity and the amount of *fat* calories consumed (Romieu et al., 1988). This relationship remained significant even after adjusting for the effects of age and physical activity level.

The body may react to the ingestion of fat calories differently. Because fat is used to store energy, the ingestion of fat may signal the body to be less wasteful of energy, and metabolism may be reduced. This could result in fewer calories being burned and more calories being stored. Therefore, fat presents one definite and one potential handicap in a healthy diet. Gram for gram, it contains twice the calories of protein and carbohydrate, and, adding insult to injury, it may signal the body to use less and store more calories.

DIET AND OPTIMUM NUTRITION

In 1989, based on a review of 5,000 research studies, the National Research Council (NRC) made specific dietary recommendations that it claimed could lead to a 20% reduction in coronary heart disease in the United States. and also substantially reduce cancer, stroke, high blood pressure, obesity, osteoporosis, and liver disease.

The NRC determined that the average American is getting twice the amount of protein necessary and recommended that daily protein intake should be 0.8 g per kilogram of body weight, which is about 48 g (or 192 calories) of protein for a 150-pound person. Excessive amounts of protein have been linked to colon and breast cancer, although this may result from the fact that, in this country, most protein is consumed in the form of meat. Meat has a high percentage of fat, and excess fat appears to be the primary dietary factor in these cancers.

The average American is also getting more fat than necessary—about 40% of total calories. This compares to the average Asian, who obtains only 10% of total calories from fat (Winick et al., 1988). The NRC recommended that fat be kept to no more than 30% of total calories, or 80 to 100 g (720 to 900 calories) per day. In addition, saturated fats should be limited to 10% or less of total fat intake, and cholesterol should be no more than 250 mg per day (the amount in one egg yolk).

Finally, the average American obtains about 46% of total calories, 200 to 300 g per day, from carbohydrates. Although the minimum requirement for carbohydrates is unknown, it is believed that 100 g per day is sufficient to maintain adequate blood glucose levels. Nevertheless, the human body appears to be able to tolerate wide variations in daily carbohydrate intake, from the low carbohydrate diet of Eskimos to the high carbohydrate diet of the Far East (Marieb, 1989).

The body compensates for too low of a carbohydrate intake by converting protein and fat to carbohydrate to meet energy needs. While the conversion of fat may seem to be a potential benefit of a low carbohydrate diet, protein from muscles and other body tissues is also converted in the process. Therefore, the NRC recommended a carbohydrate intake between 125 and 175 g (500 to 700 calories) per day.

Remember the "four food groups"? It placed equal emphasis on eating from four categories of food: grains, dairy, meat, and vegetables/fruits. Based partly on the 1989 NRC report, the U.S. Department of Agriculture (USDA) recently developed a replacement for that outmoded nutritional approach called the "Eating Right Pyramid" (Consumer Reports, 1991). The "food groups" were increased to six, and a pyramid shape was adopted to help people conceptualize the *relative* amounts to eat from each (see Figure 12.1-1).

The Eating Right Pyramid contains important nutritional suggestions, but according to the NRC report, just holding calories from fat to 30% per day will produce health benefits, and for those who typically exceed that target, it should also result in weight reduction. However, many diet, but when it comes to maintained weight loss, few succeed. Why? The answer lies in the complex interplay of biopsychosocial factors that influence appetite and eating behavior, which most diets have failed to take into account.

Figure 12.1-1   THE EATING RIGHT PYRAMID

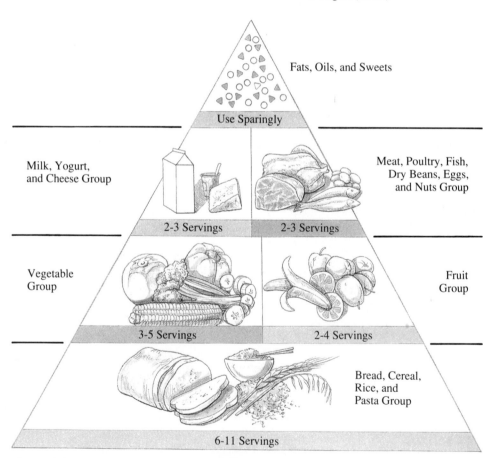

○ Fat (naturally occurring and added)

▽ Sugars (added)

Fats, Oils, and Sweets

Use Sparingly

Milk, Yogurt, and Cheese Group

Meat, Poultry, Fish, Dry Beans, Eggs, and Nuts Group

2-3 Servings

2-3 Servings

Vegetable Group

Fruit Group

3-5 Servings

2-4 Servings

Bread, Cereal, Rice, and Pasta Group

6-11 Servings

Source: U.S. Department of Agriculture as described in Consumer Reports, October 1991, A pyramid topples at the USDA, *Yonkers, NY: Author.*

Biopsychosocial Factors in Appetite and Eating Behavior

Appetite is the term for the general motivational state that influences eating behavior. *Hunger* is the specific term for the cognitive and emotional state associated with the *initiation* of eating behavior, that conscious feeling of being "empty." *Satiety* is the specific term for the cognitive and emotional state associated with the *termination* of eating behavior, that conscious feeling of being "full."

However, the *behavior* of eating is a multidetermined activity bound up with a variety of biopsychosocial factors. Thus, people may engage in continued eating when they are satiated, eat when they are not hungry, or not eat when they are hungry. Because of this and because many of the biopsychosocial factors involved with eating behavior are incompletely understood at this time, comprehensive theories are scarce. Nevertheless, many of the individual biopsychosocial factors involved in eating are understood.

Overeating and Starvation

Early experiments examined forced over- and undereating in order to demonstrate their effects on psychological and physiological well-being. During World War II, 36 conscientious objectors volunteered for a study of starvation in lieu of service in the armed forces (Keys, Brozek, Henschel, Mickelsen, & Taylor, 1950). After first determining their normal diet and weight, subjects were placed on one-half of their normal daily caloric intake (but one that provided adequate nutrients) until body weight was reduced to a target of 75% of normal.

Weight loss was rapid at first, and the subjects' mood remained good despite feelings of constant hunger. However, after an initial loss, further weight loss slowed stubbornly. For many of the subjects, it became necessary to reduce caloric intake to less than one-half of their normal level to reach the target. As subjects neared the target, profound psychological and behavioral changes took place. If you think that subjects were constantly hungry and preoccupied with food, you are right. Yet, the most striking behavioral change was that these pacifists became physically aggressive and got into fights.

Both hunger and aggression are mediated by the hypothalamus, so there could be a neural basis to the increased aggression. Perhaps this was adaptive in more primitive times when hunger induced people to fight for food. Eventually, the starving pacifists became apathetic, began to avoid physical activity, and lost interest in sex (another behavior mediated by the hypothalamus). Again, this could be adaptive because it conserves energy.

Another experiment involved prison inmates who volunteered to overeat until they gained 20 to 30 pounds over their normal weight (Sims, 1974, 1976; Sims & Horton, 1968). They were given special treatment, improved living conditions, delicious and ample food, and they were less physically active than normal. Of course, they gained weight rapidly, but after an initial gain, further increases slowed. Subjects had to increase their intake even more, in some cases up to double their normal calorie intake, and some could not reach their target even at that.

Finally, psychological changes began to take place. Subjects became repulsed by food and had to force themselves to eat. In the final phase, requirements to overeat were removed, and the subjects voluntarily reduced their food intake radically, with the result that they lost weight and almost all returned to their normal weight.

Although these experiments on starvation and overeating push the limits, they demonstrate just how firm those limits are. But it is not necessary to engage in such extreme alterations in diet to find this out. Have you ever observed that people who lose weight on a diet seem to gain it right back, while other people have to work hard to gain any weight at all? That common observation and the starvation and overeating experiments led to an interesting notion called "setpoint theory."

SETPOINT THEORY

Setpoint theory maintains that an internal homeostatic mechanism regulates body weight so it remains near a certain predetermined level (Bennett & Gurin, 1982; Keesey, 1980; Nisbett, 1972). Some people's setpoint may be higher or lower than what is considered normal by an individual or society (Kolata, 1985). Theoretically, in order to maintain the setpoint, the brain monitors fat stores, RMR, appetite, and activity level, increasing or decreasing them accordingly (Keesey & Powley, 1975, 1986).

"How is the setpoint set?" Theorists believe that setpoint is determined by the *number* of fat cells in the body. Each person has a genetically determined number of fat cells and, although weight changes somewhat over time, the number of fat cells does not change much. People of average weight have 23 to 35 billion fat cells (Leibel, Berry, & Hirsch, 1983). Mildly obese people have about the same numbers, but in people whose weight is more than 100% above normal, the number of fat cells can be 100 to 125 billion. Weight is gained or lost through the storage of fat *within* the fat cells, and the more fat cells, the more readily the body stores fat.

Fat cells enlarge as they store more and more fat. When fewer calories are ingested than needed, fat cells shrink (Salans, Knittle, & Hirsch, 1968), but the overall number of fat cells does not decrease. Also, the amount of deposited fat in the body is correlated with the overall number of fat cells (Gurr et al., 1982). This suggests that the setpoint of overweight people may be adjusted up but not down. People whose weights are above their setpoint may be able to lose weight easily until they reach their lower weight limit, but their weight at this limit would depend on the number of fat cells they have (Brownell, 1986b). Children and adolescents are particularly vulnerable to this upward but not downward change in the number of fat cells, because their fat cells proliferate much more readily than adults (Brownell, 1986b).

The number of fat cells multiply and then stabilize in childhood, but it is possible to increase the number by consistent overeating in childhood (Knittle, 1975). In adults, overeating just seems to cause the fat cells to get larger, without increasing their number. This suggests that setpoint overrides other factors in determining adult weight, and that eating behavior and diet may have little affect.

Setpoint theory is supported by evidence that body weight has a substantial genetic component (Brownell & Wadden, 1992). A recent study used 247 pairs of identical and 426 pairs of fraternal twins, some reared together and some reared apart, to estimate the heritability of the body-mass index (Stunkard, Harris, Pedersen, & McClearn, 1990). **Heritability** is a computed numerical value that indicates the relative importance of genetic influences. The **body-mass index** is a ratio calculated by dividing the weight in kilograms (1 kg = 2.2 pounds) by the square of the height in meters (1 m = 39.4 inches). A person who is 5 feet 10 inches (1.78 m) tall and weighs 150 pounds (68.18 kg) would have a body-mass index of 21.5 [68.18 ÷ 1.78²]. Health authorities define a body-mass index of 20 to 25 as desirable. The body mass index was found to have a heritability of .70 for men and .66 for women, with environmental influences accounting for only about 30% of the index (Stunkard et al., 1990).

Another recent study attempted to determine the responses of pairs of identical male twins to overfeeding (Bouchard et al., 1990). Overfeeding resulted in weight gain, but the amount of weight gain and even the distribution of the fat added to different areas of the body was three times more consistent *within* pairs than between them. So even when people gain weight, genetic factors influence how much weight is gained and where it is distributed in the body.

Results like these demonstrate why setpoint theory is one of the leading physiological theories of obesity today (Brownell & Wadden, 1992). A recent comprehensive research review concluded: "Displacement of body weight usually results in 'homeostatic' metabolic adjustments designed to return the organism to the body weight normally maintained" (Garner & Wooley, 1991, p. 742). Could this have been Alice's problem when she dieted? After all, she was never more than 10% above her desirable weight. Was she just destined to gain the weight right back? Probably, and although this may be unwelcome news to those who struggle to reduce their weight, setpoint theorists believe that it is still possible to influence weight somewhat.

Remember the starvation and overeating experiments? People could lose and gain weight relatively easily initially, although at a certain point they ran into a barrier. This suggests that there is some range within which voluntary changes in eating behavior can control weight, although there may be a firm limit. As we have seen in other cases, behavioral and psychosocial factors affect many physiological processes, and probably also weight. For example, reducing fat calories in the diet can reduce the amount of fat stored in cells, and although one's setpoint may compensate by lowering metabolism to maintain weight, there is evidence that another behavioral change, increasing regular exercise, can increase metabolism.

Setpoint theory helps explain the difficulties that subjects in the overeating and starvation experiments encountered in reaching their goals after initial rapid weight gain or loss. However, it represents only a part of the picture, because there are other psychosocial and physiological factors with a role in appetite (the motivational state) and eating (the behavior).

PHYSIOLOGICAL FACTORS IN APPETITE AND EATING

The *primarily* physiological factors include the hypothalamus; setpoint, fat cells, and metabolism; blood glucose; temperature; and hormones.

HYPOTHALAMUS   The hypothalamus has received a lot of study for its relationship to hunger and eating. That is because animal research seemed to indicate that two hypothalamic areas were *directly* involved in eating behavior: (a) the *lateral hypothalamus*, which, when stimulated electrically, produces eating behavior and, when destroyed, causes animals to ignore food, resulting in the possibility of starvation; and (b) the *ventromedial nucleus of the hypothalamus*, which, when stimulated, causes eating behavior to stop and, when destroyed, causes animals to overeat, resulting in obesity. This suggests that one region of the hypothalamus mediates hunger, while another mediates satiation.

However, later research suggested that this connection with eating may not be as direct as first believed (Valenstein, 1973). The hypothalamus is not a simple "on-and-off" switch that controls eating directly. Its role is still considered important, but it is probably an indirect one (Grossman, 1979). The hypothalamus appears to be one, perhaps central, element in the mediation and control of appetite but one that may react to a variety of other factors.

SETPOINT, FAT CELLS, AND METABOLISM   For setpoint to work, fat storage has to be monitored. The mechanism that monitors fat stores is unknown, but a certain type of fat, called *"brown fat,"* may be involved in speeding or slowing metabolism, depending on whether or not there is an excess of caloric intake (Bennett & Gurin, 1982; Rothwell & Stock, 1979). As excess calories are stored, brown fat could signal the brain to reduce hunger (Faust, 1984; Nisbett, 1972).

The hypothalamus may receive information about fat stores, stimulating appetite and eating behavior when they fall and stopping it when they rise, thereby maintaining the setpoint. This feedback process may take place within a range (with a floor and ceiling) that determines how much body weight can be changed, except in extreme conditions of overeating or starvation.

When the floor or ceiling is reached, the hypothalamus could activate other mechanisms to maintain weight (for example, increasing RMR). The higher the RMR, the more fat is consumed as energy. Evidence for this comes from the finding that not all overweight people eat an excessive amount of calories once they have become obese. Furthermore, some lean people eat more than some overweight people. The difference may be the *level* of their RMR; lean people may have a higher RMR, thereby allowing them to maintain a leaner weight.

Finally, obese rats and humans both have elevated levels of lipase (the enzyme that digests fat), which facilitates the storage of calories as fat. This correlation might just be the consequence of being obese, except that research has shown that lipase activity *increases* in obese individuals who lose weight (Schwartz & Brunzell, 1981). This suggests that weight loss in an overweight person may actually provoke an increased tendency to store fat, maintaining a higher setpoint.

BLOOD GLUCOSE Glucose is metabolized by cells to produce energy. Because carbohydrate digestion begins in the mouth, glucose is absorbed early in the digestive process, and blood glucose begins to rise a few minutes after eating begins (Strubbe, Steffens, & deRuiter, 1975). When glucose is experimentally lowered by injecting insulin in nondiabetic people, hunger and appetite are increased, and when it is experimentally raised, satiation occurs (Rezek, 1976).

This suggests that satiation and appetite suppression occur as a response to blood glucose levels, and that glucose utilization is monitored by the brain (Mayer, 1955, 1968). Either the hypothalamus monitors serum glucose directly, the liver monitors it and relays the information to the hypothalamus through the vagus nerve (Mayer, 1955; Novin, Robinson, Culbreth, & Tordoff, 1983), or both. The specific mechanism remains undetermined.

TEMPERATURE Animals in a hot environment decrease their intake of food (Brobeck, 1948), and experimental warming of the hypothalamus also results in reduced food intake (Andersson & Larsson, 1961). Because body temperature rises while eating a meal (Brody, 1945), the hypothalamus, which monitors and regulates body temperature, may respond to the increase by reducing appetite, so this may be an additional feedback mechanism.

HORMONES *Cholecystokinin*, or CCK, is an intestinal hormone that stimulates gallbladder contraction and pancreatic juice release. Interestingly, CCK is also found in the hypothalamus, where it may play a primary role in signaling satiety (McCaleb & Meyers, 1981). When CCK is injected into starving rats and humans, it results in feelings of satiation and inhibits consumption of food (Smith, 1984). Perhaps CCK, when released by the gall bladder and pancreas, travels to the brain and signals the hypothalamus. Not much more is known about CCK and its role in satiation at this time (White & White, 1988).

CONCLUSION   A variety of physiological mechanisms affect appetite. Low levels of glucose or fat stores may increase appetite, whereas high levels of glucose, fat stores, or CCK, triggered by the presence of food in the digestive tract and rising body temperature during a meal, may decrease it. In each of these processes, it appears that the hypothalamus plays a coordinating role, triggering the psychological state of hunger or satiation in response to physiological status.

Appetite, however, is a motivational state, and although it may drive behavior, it is not equivalent to it. Some people do not eat when they are hungry, while others eat even though they are satiated. Thus, the physiological factors do not provide a complete picture of eating behavior. The next section examines some of the psychosocial factors in eating behavior.

PSYCHOSOCIAL FACTORS IN EATING BEHAVIOR

The psychosocial factors involved in eating include food availability, food preferences and conditioning, social factors, food cues, stress and emotion, and activity level. These also act through the brain to affect hunger, satiation, appetite, food cravings, and arousal.

FOOD AVAILABILITY   This is an environmental factor. Research with rats has shown that when food is made easier to obtain, when its fat content is increased, when it is made more palatable, or when its variety increases, intake goes up and the rats gain weight over the long term (White & White, 1988). Residents of affluent countries, especially the United States, live with these same conditions. Food is abundant, cheap, and easy to obtain, while food processing typically adds fat and simple carbohydrates, making it more palatable. Therefore, Americans, because of their success, both economically and in food production, are trapped in the same experimental conditions as rats. In fact, a higher percentage of the U.S. population is overweight than either the populations of Canada or Britain (Millar & Stephens, 1987). Availability, however, must be only one factor in poor weight control, otherwise being overweight would be far more common than it is in affluent countries.

FOOD PREFERENCES AND CONDITIONING   We do have some inherent food preferences, but these are very limited, including only the taste of

Supermarket shelves display the wide variety of abundant, cheap food available in the United States.

sugar and salt. The remainder of our food preferences depend on oral sensations, such as texture and temperature, and on olfactory sensations (the many subtle flavors of foods depend entirely on combinations of various odor molecules reaching the upper nasal passages). These oral and olfactory preferences are acquired through learning and tend to reflect our culture's and our family's tastes (Logue, 1986; Brownell, 1984b).

Stimulus–response conditioning can modify, strengthen, and add to the short list of food preferences that elicit eating behavior. The pleasurable aspects of eating, including the reduction in the motivational state of hunger, can serve as the reward in this conditioning process. After conditioning, the external stimulus alone can elicit approach and consumption in rats (Winegarten, 1983), and although difficult to observe, indirect measurements suggest that the same is true for humans (White & White, 1988).

People also learn how much to eat. In experimental conditions, but without subjects' knowledge, calories in subjects' diets were reduced by substituting artificial for real sugar in the foods they ate (Porikos, Hesser, & VanItallie, 1982). It took several days before subjects began to increase their food intake to compensate for the lower calorie level. At least two conclusions can be drawn from this experiment. First, if eating behavior were under direct control of a physiological mechanism, compensatory eating would be expected to increase immediately to replace the lost calories. Second, since it took several days before subjects increased their food intake, other factors such as learning may have been operating. In other words, subjects continued to eat at their conditioned or habitual level for a time before compensating.

Satiation, which has a physiological basis, may also become more psychological through experience and conditioning (Booth, 1977). It has been observed that most people actually stop eating before sufficient absorption could have taken place to provide a feedback signal to the hypothalamus to initiate satiation (White & White, 1988). This suggests that people have learned when to stop eating and stop out of habit. People become conditioned to be aware of how much of certain foods make them feel full and of how ingesting more can lead to an uncomfortably overfull feeling (Wooley, 1972; Wooley, Wooley, & Dunham, 1972).

SOCIAL FACTORS   Family environment may be an important social factor that contributes to a child's being overweight. About 7% of the offspring of normal weight parents are obese, compared to 40% of those with 1 obese parent, and 80% of those with 2 obese parents (Mayer, 1975, 1980). Although this supports a genetic basis, it can also support an environmental basis, because certain nongenetic aspects of family environment seem to be related to being overweight, too. Parental feeding practices during infancy appear to involve a higher risk of obesity (Striegel-Moore & Rodin, 1985). Obesity-related practices include overfeeding, bottle feeding, and irregularity or unpredictability of feeding.

As infants mature, the home environment continues to exert an influence. Children who are encouraged to overeat and whose exercise level is low are more likely to become overweight adults (Berkowitz, Agras, Korner, Kraemer, & Zeanah, 1985). Broader economic and cultural factors may also be related because a higher percentage of African American and Latin American adults are overweight than are European Americans (Forman, Trowbridge, Gentry, Marks, & Hogelin, 1986; USDHHS, 1986d), and obesity is associated with socioeconomic status.

Obesity is *less* frequent in developing countries, where it rises with increasing income, presumably because food is not as abundant. It is *more* common among low-SES compared to high-SES women in the United States, but not in men or children. This may be because there is more plentiful, inexpensive, high calorie food in the United States, and values of high-SES groups in developed countries have tended toward thinness in women (Sobal & Stunkard, 1989).

Finally, some researchers believe that the most important sociocultural factor in overeating is advertising (Jeffrey & Lemnitzer, 1981). The average child entering kindergarten will have been exposed to 70,000 food-related television commercials, two-thirds of which are for sugared products like cereal, candy, and gum. Advertising works as a food cue.

FOOD CUES   Cues are environmental events, or stimuli, that trigger psychological reactions. Seeing a clock at 12 noon is a food cue. Even if you are not hungry, you may stop and eat because you are used to the routine of a noon lunch, the clock being the stimulus. An ingenious experiment misled subjects about the time by turning a clock ahead while making food available (Schachter & Gross, 1968). Obese subjects, thinking that it was later in the afternoon and therefore longer since they ate lunch, ate more, whereas subjects who were not obese ate less, because, thinking it was later, they did not want to spoil their dinner. It was the subjects' perception of the time that influenced their eating behavior and not the internal state of hunger. This confirms that appetite is only one influence on eating behavior. Cues and perception can influence eating even in the absence of hunger.

Food cues can also arouse hunger, and commercials make use of this connection. The image of butter melting on top of a steaming, golden-brown biscuit fresh from the oven is meant to send us scrambling to the kitchen for that package of biscuit mix. The more food cues there are in the environment, the more hunger will be aroused.

STRESS AND EMOTION   Obese binge eaters report higher levels of distress and are more likely to have psychological disorders during their lifetimes than nonobese people (Brownell & Wadden, 1992). They are particularly prone to develop mood and personality disorders, but whether these disorders precede or follow abnormal eating behavior is unclear.

For many people, one of the symptoms of stress is an increase in eating behavior (Slochower, Kaplan, & Mann, 1981). However, this effect is not uniform—about half of people eat more, and half eat less (Willenbring, Levine, & Morley, 1986). In particular, anxiety seems to suppress hunger and eating behavior in nonobese and nondieting people, but it seems to increase eating behavior in dieters and obese people.

Could it be that the perception of stress is a psychological sign that a physiological process is under way to restore setpoint? One theorist believes so (Herman, 1987). In this case, unsuspecting dieters would become more prone to perceive stress, then go off their diets in order to restore weight to a higher level consistent with their setpoint.

ACTIVITY LEVEL   Once ingested, calories can be disposed of in one of three ways: They can be stored for later use, burned to generate heat, or used to provide energy for physical activity (White & White, 1988). Storage and heat generation involve the RMR, while activity level relates to one's lifestyle. The balance among these three factors influences whether calories are stored as fat (McMinn, 1984), but whether or not there is weight *gain* is related to activity level.

There is a consistent negative correlation between activity level and weight (Stern, 1984). Low levels of exercise are related to obesity in women (Romieu et al., 1988), and two studies suggest that differences in activity level *pre-exist* the development of overweight in both men and women (Bullen, Reed, & Mayer, 1964; Durnin, Lonergan, Good & Ewan, 1974). Physical activity increases metabolic rate during and for a period after exercise, which expends calories (Thompson, Jarvie, Lahey, & Cureton, 1982). Therefore, all things being equal, increasing activity level reduces weight.

CONCLUSION

Current thinking is that each individual inherits a certain number of fat cells and a setpoint. Perhaps the setpoint is best conceived of as a weight range; an individual may fluctuate somewhat within this range (perhaps 5% either way?). This range may also have upper and lower limits (perhaps a deviation of 25% in either direction?), which may only be exceeded with very drastic changes in food intake, requiring extremes of overeating or starvation. Consistent overeating causes the number of fat cells to increase, probably until late adolescence, but undereating will not decrease them. The higher the number of fat cells, the higher the setpoint may be; so it is easier to adjust a setpoint up than down.

It must be remembered that this is a theory, with limited evidence to support it at this time. There is, however, ample evidence for the role of individual biopsychosocial factors in appetite and eating behavior. Most have been reviewed in this section. Some are physiological and some are psychological, and it appears that they interact to produce the complex behavior of eating. Figure 12.1-2 summarizes these many factors.

There is reasonably good evidence for the role of the hypothalamus as the central mediator of appetite, although which physiological processes it monitors and their relative importance is not firmly established. In humans, the hypothalamus appears to induce a motivational state of either hunger or satiation, which is only indirectly related to eating behavior. Cues and habits (conditioning) also help to determine eating behavior. And, although they have been little explored experimentally, additional cognitive factors for controlling one's weight (for example, a desire to be healthy or more attractive) probably also play a role. Finally, stress affects eating behavior differentially, causing increases in some and decreases in others. With all of these factors—both physiological and psychological—is it any wonder why dieting is so difficult?

■■■

MODULE SUMMARY

The next module considers eating behavior specifically with regard to being overweight, to obesity, and to eating disorders. First review this module:

1. Healthy eating provides adequate nutrition for physical growth, development and maintenance of the body, and it provides sufficient calories to meet the body's needs for basic metabolism and energy.
2. Calories are the basic unit of measurement used to describe the energy content of foods; protein and carbohydrate both contain the same number of calories per gram, while fat contains twice as many. When ingested, fat calories may also signal the body to store fat.
3. The incidence of many diseases could be reduced if people followed the dietary recommendations of the NRC: no more than 30% of calories from fat (10% from saturated fat), 15% of calories from protein, and 55% of calories from carbohydrate.

Figure 12.1-2 **BIOPSYCHOSOCIAL FACTORS IN APPETITE AND EATING BEHAVIOR**

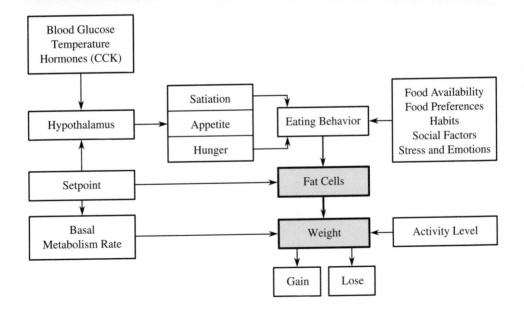

4. Experiments with volunteers who overeat or starve have demonstrated that there are natural limits to weight control through diet, supporting the theory of setpoint.

5. Setpoint theory holds that a physiological mechanism regulates body weight so it remains at a predetermined level.

6. The hypothalamus mediates appetite and controls the motivational states of hunger and satiation. It also monitors blood glucose, temperature, and probably hormones from the digestive track to determine food consumption and needs.

7. Fat cells may communicate with the brain regarding the amount of fat in storage. In keeping with setpoint theory, metabolism may, in turn, be altered to store or burn fat.

8. Psychosocial factors involved in eating behavior involve food availability, food preferences, habits, social factors, and food cues. Evidence for their importance comes from the fact that some people do not eat when they are hungry, and others eat even when satiated.

9. Additional psychosocial factors include stress and emotions, which can cause some people to eat more and some people to eat less, and activity level, which affects how calories are disposed of (higher activity levels are associated with lower weight).

WEIGHT CONTROL AND
EATING DISORDERS

WEIGHT CONTROL

Over time, weight should be consistently maintained through the homeostatic mechanisms that control appetite. Theoretically, if more calories are ingested than needed, physiological controls should decrease appetite and eating behavior, thereby leading to natural adjustment. However, it does not always work that smoothly. Some people—Alice for example—seem to be in a continuous "battle of the bulge," while others seem to have lost the war. What happens to the normal process of weight regulation to cause overweight and obesity, and why does it take so much effort for some people to maintain a "desirable" weight?

DESIRABLE WEIGHT

Any definition of "desirable" weight is to some extent arbitrary because it is related to society's prevailing concept of physical attractiveness, which changes over time (Bennett & Gurin, 1982). Therefore, researchers use a more objective criterion based on the relationship between height and weight and mortality. The height–weight charts published by Metropolitan Life Insurance Company are one widely accepted method of determining desirable weight (see Table 12.2-1). The charts reflect a careful statistical analysis of mortality rates in the United States, so the weight associated with the *lowest* mortality rate is given for each height category. Keep in mind that this chart is merely a guide to make the determination of desirable weight more objective. Also, remember that weight is only one of many other factors related to mortality.

OBESITY   Three categories have been used to determine overweight: *mild* (20% to 40% overweight), *moderate* (41% to 100% overweight), and *severe* (>100% overweight; Berkow & Fletcher, 1987). These categories are somewhat arbitrary, however, because they do not relate strictly to increasing health risk. An alternative method of determining desirable weight, the body mass

Table 12.2-1 **DESIRABLE WEIGHT FOR ADULTS**

HEIGHT	DESIRABLE WEIGHT	OVERWEIGHT THRESHOLDS		
		Mild +20%	Moderate +40%	Severe +100%
Men				
5'2"	136	163	190	272
5'3"	138	166	196	276
5'4"	140	168	199	280
5'5"	142	170	199	284
5'6"	145	174	203	290
5'7"	148	178	207	296
5'8"	151	181	211	302
5'9"	154	185	216	308
5'10"	157	188	220	314
5'11"	160	192	224	320
6'0"	163	196	229	326
6'1"	167	200	234	334
6'2"	171	205	239	342
6'3"	174	209	244	348
6'4"	179	215	251	358
Women				
4'10"	115	138	161	230
4'11"	117	140	164	234
5'0"	119	143	167	238
5'1"	122	146	171	244
5'2"	125	150	175	250
5'3"	128	154	179	256
5'4"	131	157	183	262
5'5"	134	161	188	268
5'6"	137	164	192	274
5'7"	138	166	193	276
5'8"	143	172	200	286
5'9"	146	175	204	292
5'10"	149	179	209	298
5'11"	152	182	213	304
6'0"	155	186	217	310

Source: Adapted from the Metropolitan Life Insurance Company Height and Weight Tables to show weights that are desirable, 20% over, 40% over, and 100% over by height for men & women of medium frame, without shoes or clothing. Metropolitan Life Insurance Company, 1983, Statistical Bulletin, New York: Author.

index, was introduced in Module 12.1. About 39% of men and 36% of women in the United States exceed their desirable body-mass index (NRC, 1989).

Except for major metabolic disorders, which are quite rare, most people probably inherit a setpoint that places them somewhere within a normal distribution of the body-mass index (Stunkard et al., 1990). It is unlikely that evolution would have led to a setpoint that would result naturally in obesity, because it can have dangerous health consequences (for example, it would have been more difficult for an obese person to escape a predatory animal). Of course, there would be some people at either end of the distribution; they inherit either a *tendency* to be at the low end or at the high end of desirable body mass (Brownell & Wadden, 1992). This is the subtle genetic push toward thinness or heaviness that may run in families. This tendency, however, would be affected by diet and exercise and interact with psychosocial influences. These influences might encourage ingestion of too many or the wrong type of calories, which if it were chronic, could lead to development of additional fat cells, a higher setpoint, and eventually a higher body-mass index.

ETIOLOGY OF OBESITY

Being overweight and obesity are *not* considered to be psychological disorders, and overweight people do not differ significantly from normal weight people in psychological functioning (Brownell & Wadden, 1992). There are, however, psychological as well as physiological explanations for it.

PSYCHODYNAMIC   According to the psychodynamic view, obesity is the acting out of unconscious conflicts representing a basic personality problem (Stunkard, 1988). However, since the effectiveness of psychodynamic treatment for obesity is doubtful, it also casts doubt on the psychodynamic explanation (Slochower, 1983). One study did find that obese people who had undergone psychoanalytic therapy lost weight and maintained it after therapy (Rand & Stunkard, 1983). But it is not clear why the patients lost weight, because it was only a therapeutic byproduct; the subjects did not start therapy to lose weight.

BEHAVIORAL   Another psychological explanation for obesity is based on the learning approach. Eating is a biologically rewarding activity (Brownell & Wadden, 1992). The pleasurable sensations that accompany it are rewarding, so too are some of the social activities that surround it, such as the company of friends and family at meals. Presumably, the rewards are balanced by the physiological discomfort of satiation triggered by overeating. However, these homeostatic mechanisms developed early in human evolutionary history when food was not plentiful, and today's availability of calorie-packed foods may too easily overwhelm them. It is possible to ingest hundreds or even thousands of calories before becoming aware of satiation. Alice was able to ingest many thousands of calories in a binge before becoming uncomfortable. Furthermore, there may be individual differences in physiological and psychological responsiveness to internal sensations. Overweight people may be less sensitive to unpleasant sensations related to satiety and more sensitive to pleasant sensations related to the taste of food (White & White, 1988).

Research has revealed behavioral differences between obese and nonobese people (Schachter, Goldman, & Gordon, 1968; Schachter, 1971). In obese people, physiological factors appear to be less important in triggering eating. Time cues are stronger, and obese people will eat at mealtimes whether or not they are physiologically hungry. They are also more likely to eat everything on their plate. Finally, obese people are more sensitive than nonobese people to the taste of food, making them more responsive to its rewarding qualities.

Interestingly, other research has found these same characteristics in *nonobese* people who diet (Polivy & Herman, 1983). Dieters can be differentiated as "restrained eaters," those who are constantly aware of restricting their food intake, and "unrestrained eaters," those who are not constantly aware. The restrained eaters resemble obese people, in that they are more sensitive to taste and eat by the clock.

FAMILY   The final psychological explanation for obesity is family based. One study has shown that extremely disrupted family environments are related to the development of obesity in children in the absence of any biological cause (Christoffel & Forsyth, 1989). Family disorganization, separation of mother and child, placing children under the care of others, and maternal depression are some of the features of these environments. Although this has been incompletely explored, it does suggest family disruption is related to obesity.

CONSEQUENCES OF OBESITY

HEALTH   Aside from the implications for attractiveness, does being overweight carry any health risks? The answer to this question must be a *qualified* "yes." Obesity is a major risk factor for many health problems, both directly and indirectly (Alexander, 1984; Bray, 1984; Brownell, 1982b; Dawber, 1980; Hubert, 1986). Obesity is linked to heart disease and contributes to diabetes, hypertension, and cholesterol levels. Obesity is also related to some cancers, gall bladder disease, and arthritis. Furthermore, obesity increases risks from childbearing, surgery, anesthesia, and **sleep apnea**, which is the occurrence of intermittent periods of decreased breathing during sleep that are occasionally life threatening. With so many health risks linked to obesity, why is the answer only a "qualified" yes?

There are two reasons. First, research indicates that whereas *moderate to severe* obesity is associated with an overall mortality rate up to 2.5 times the average, *mild* obesity carries only a small risk for increased mortality (Bray, 1976; VanItallie, 1979). Mildly overweight people are not much more likely than normal or underweight people to die (Sorlie, Gordon, & Kannel, 1980), and being overweight by up to 20% does not increase the risk of dying from heart disease or diabetes. However, a person who is more than 40% over their desirable weight is at much greater risk than someone who is only 20% over (Manson et al., 1990). Generally, the degree of risk rises with the amount of being overweight, but up to 20%, the risk is negligible (Bray, 1976; Sorlie, Gordon, & Kannel, 1980).

In addition, the degree of being overweight might not be as important as the distribution of fat in the body. Fat stored abdominally is more strongly related to the development of atherosclerosis in both men and women (Bouchard, Bray, & Hubbard, 1990; Depres et al., 1990). In particular, women with higher waist-to-hip measurement comparisons—the rounded middle or "apple figure" look—are at higher risk for diabetes, hypertension, and gall-bladder problems, than those with more weight on the hips—the "pear-shaped figure" look (Hartz, Rupley, & Rimm, 1984).

The second reason that being overweight must be qualified as a health risk is that the increased weight itself may not be the cause of health problems. Instead, it may be poor nutrition and a high intake of salt and calories, partic-ularly from fat, that is the culprit. This would mean that thin people could also eat poorly and compromise their health. A person who is thin may have a low setpoint and therefore be able to consume high quantities of cholesterol and saturated fat. Such a diet would compromise health and demonstrates the importance of keeping aware of the nutritional component of healthy eating behavior, and not just focusing on calories and weight.

Eating large quantities of food coupled with frequent weight fluctuations due to "on-again, off-again" diet cycles, known as **"yo-yo dieting,"** may be the reason for the association of obesity and poor health (Borkan, Sparrow, Wisniewski, & Vokonas, 1986; Polivy & Herman, 1983). One study looked at the effects of yo-yo dieting on the more than 5,000 men and women initially involved in the Framingham Study (see Module 3.2) over a 32-year followup period. Overall, yo-yo dieting raised the risk of mortality and morbidity from coronary heart disease between 25% and 100%, *whether or not people were actually obese.*

Some qualifications are necessary, however. First, the effect was more pronounced in people aged 30 to 44. Second, animal studies have provided only limited support for the health effects of diet cycles, although better designed animal research may support it in the future (Bouchard, 1991). However, a substantial body of research has supported the adverse health effects of weight variability (Brownell & Wadden, 1992).

Meals can be an important focus of family activity.

Yo-yo dieting may be a greater risk to health than mild obesity (Lissner et al., 1991). Optimum health is achieved by maintaining steady weight on a nutritionally balanced and fat-limited diet (Brownell & Wadden, 1992). Alice would have been considered a yo-yo dieter during her adolescence and, ironically, that would have been a greater threat to her health than being 10% overweight. Perhaps her poor health contributed to her depression, making it more difficult to diet and to interact socially.

Two practical, although tentative, conclusions can be drawn: (a) if one is up to 20% over one's desirable weight, it is probably *not* necessary to reduce, other than for cosmetic reasons and a sense of well-being; (b) in cases of moderate to severe obesity, weight reduction is necessary, but it should only be done gradually and for good. Cyclical dieting may raise the risk of heart disease over and above any risk from obesity itself, while in overweight people, even small weight losses can produce significant health benefits (Brownell & Wadden, 1992).

PSYCHOSOCIAL   There is a social stigma attached to obesity in our society. Other people blame obese people for their condition, and there is self-blame as well (Young & Powell, 1985). Obese people have more difficulty finding employment and earn less than nonobese people in comparable jobs, so they also face discrimination (Bray, 1984). Alice was not obese but she did engage in self-blame for her perceived "bulkiness." Her parents did not appear to mean any harm, but they probably encouraged this self-blaming by supporting Alice's repeated dieting when she was not substantially overweight. Instead, they might have encouraged her to accept her body type as reasonable and to seek counseling to reduce her self-blame. With the many health and psychosocial consequences of obesity, and its very high incidence in our society, it is clear that prevention is an important goal.

PREVENTION OF OBESITY

Since overweight children do not outgrow their problem and usually become overweight adults, prevention efforts must begin in childhood (Brownell, 1986a). Two risk factors are helpful in identifying which children require early prevention efforts: (a) a family history of obesity, and (b) children who are already overweight. Researchers believe that intervention efforts must be based in the family (Brownell, Kelman, & Stunkard, 1983).

There are also two primary targets for any intervention program: eating behavior and physical activity level. Parents can affect these by modeling, but a complete family-based program should consist of many elements (Striegel-Moore & Rodin, 1985). An example of such a program is depicted in Table 12.2-2. These elements are based on sound research, and there is evidence that

---

Table 12.2-2   **ELEMENTS IN A FAMILY-BASED OVERWEIGHT PREVENTION PROGRAM**

- Involve the entire family in the program together; modeling is a very important form of learning.
- Begin by taking everyone's weight and comparing it to a standard height–weight chart; monitor progress periodically.
- Eat a healthy breakfast, avoiding too many eggs and sugary cereals.
- Don't keep foods high in fat or sugar in the house.
- Rely on healthier foods such as fruit and nonfat yogurt for snacks and regular desserts.
- Avoid evening snacks that are high in calories.
- Prepare and serve nutritional meals, avoid most frozen and fast foods, and make sure fat content of all meals is below 30%.
- Do not bargain with food (that is, "You can have dessert if you eat your vegetables.").
- Use praise as a reward for healthy eating habits.
- Increase physical activity and decrease TV watching.

obesity in children can be reduced if parents are trained early to utilize meal planning to change eating habits (Kirscht, Becker, Haefner, & Maiman, 1978). Also, when children are taught about nutrition and diet, they respond by bringing healthier lunches to school (Striegel-Moore & Rodin, 1985; Wadden & Brownell, 1984). In addition to family-based prevention, school-based prevention has also been effective (Striegel-Moore & Rodin, 1985). School-based programs involve education and providing healthier snacks and cafeteria foods. They work best when parents, teachers, and cafeteria staff are all involved.

There is also evidence that programs targeted at adults can be effective. One study randomly assigned adults who were not overweight to: (a) a treatment group that received an education about weight control, additional informational newsletters, and a financial incentive for not gaining weight; or (b) a nontreatment group (Forster, Jeffrey, Schmid, & Kramer, 1988). The treatment group lost significantly more weight, almost two pounds on average, compared to the nontreatment group. However, since about 80% of people who were overweight as children become overweight adults (Abraham, Collins, & Nordsieck, 1971), prevention programs are most important for children whose eating behavior could be laying the physiological foundation for later weight control problems.

TREATMENT OF OBESITY

The NRC (1989) estimates that at any given time, between 25% and 50% of Americans are attempting to lose weight. A substantial number indeed and perhaps more than are attempting any other single change that affects health status. Are these people motivated by the health risks of obesity? Some are, but the majority are concerned with their attractiveness and the social consequences of obesity (Hayes & Ross, 1987). Researchers and clinicians would do well to keep this fact in mind when designing and evaluating treatments for obesity.

In a recent review of obesity treatment, Kelly Brownell and Thomas Wadden (1992) suggest that a new goal for weight loss treatment should be "reasonable weight" instead of ideal, desirable, or even healthy weight. Reasonable weight stresses the interrelationship of physiological (setpoint) and psychosocial factors in weight maintenance. Brownell and Wadden offer a series of questions to help determine this weight (see Table 12.2-3).

Brownell and Wadden also advocate individually tailored treatment, and they provide a three-step decision procedure to accomplish this (see Figure 12.2-1). The "classification decision" divides people according to their percentage of being overweight. The "stepped care decision" assigns the least intensive, costly, and risky treatments to the lower levels of being overweight. The "matching decision" tailors program factors to client factors. Among the program factors are psychological and behavioral treatments.

EFFECTIVENESS OF PSYCHOLOGICAL AND BEHAVIORAL TREATMENTS

BEHAVIOR MODIFICATION AND DIETING   Dieting does work for many people who do it on their own. In one study of people dieting on their own, over 62% reached their desired weight (Schachter, 1982). In contrast, some fad diets that recommend single foods or that drastically restrict either protein, fat, or carbohydrate, produce no lasting results and can be downright dangerous. People rarely maintain their weight loss from very low calorie diets unless it is combined with behavior modification (Wadden, Stunkard, Brownell, & Day, 1984). Health authorities and physicians do not recommend diet programs for those who are close to their desirable weight (Polivy & Herman, 1983), nor do they recommend them for those who are overweight unless they are combined with behavior modification. Today, behavior modification is included with many diet programs because it is the best means of changing eating habits and promoting maintenance.

Early research strongly supported behavior therapy for dieting. It used stimulus control principles to train people to change the stimuli in their environments that elicited and maintained eating behavior (Stuart, 1967). Overweight people were taught to control their food cues: (a) to not eat when doing other pleasurable activities (so as not to reward eating and to pay attention to the activity of eating when eating), (b) to toss out high calorie foods and replace them with low calorie ones, and (c) to restrict eating to certain places and times of the day. Behavior therapy achieves a success rate of 60%, nearly equivalent to that of people who successfully diet on their own, and weight loss has been maintained up to one year on follow-up (Stuart, 1967).

Table 12.2-3   QUESTIONS TO DETERMINE "REASONABLE WEIGHT"

1. Is there a history of excess weight in your parents or grandparents?
2. What is the lowest weight you have maintained as an adult for at least one year?
3. What is the largest size of clothes that you feel comfortable in, at the point you say, "I look pretty good considering where I have been?" At what weight would you wear these clothes?
4. Think of a friend or family member (with your age and body frame) who looks "normal" to you. What does the person weigh?
5. At what weight do you believe you can live with the required changes in eating and/or exercise?

Source: Brownell, K. D., and Wadden, T. A., 1992, Etiology and treatment of obesity: Understanding a serious, prevalent, and refractory disorder, Journal of Consulting and Clinical Psychology, 60, *505–517.*

Subsequent research has continued to support the effectiveness of behavior therapy; although perhaps due to more carefully conducted studies, rarely has success been as remarkable as in the earliest programs (White & White, 1988). It appears that simple behavior modification is most effective with those who are only moderately overweight (Foreyt, 1987; Wilson, 1980). For them, it may actually be superior to other forms of treatment (Stunkard & Mahoney, 1976).

Other research has looked at combinations of diet and behavior modification and also at length of treatment. In one comparison of dieting versus

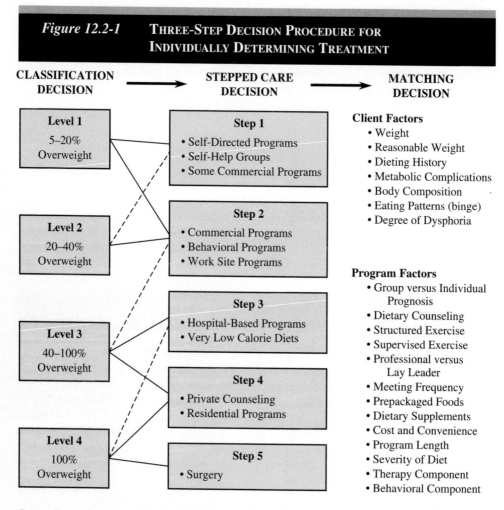

Figure 12.2-1 **THREE-STEP DECISION PROCEDURE FOR INDIVIDUALLY DETERMINING TREATMENT**

CLASSIFICATION DECISION → **STEPPED CARE DECISION** → **MATCHING DECISION**

Level 1 5–20% Overweight

Level 2 20–40% Overweight

Level 3 40–100% Overweight

Level 4 100% Overweight

Step 1
• Self-Directed Programs
• Self-Help Groups
• Some Commercial Programs

Step 2
• Commercial Programs
• Behavioral Programs
• Work Site Programs

Step 3
• Hospital-Based Programs
• Very Low Calorie Diets

Step 4
• Private Counseling
• Residential Programs

Step 5
• Surgery

Client Factors
• Weight
• Reasonable Weight
• Dieting History
• Metabolic Complications
• Body Composition
• Eating Patterns (binge)
• Degree of Dysphoria

Program Factors
• Group versus Individual Prognosis
• Dietary Counseling
• Structured Exercise
• Supervised Exercise
• Professional versus Lay Leader
• Meeting Frequency
• Prepackaged Foods
• Dietary Supplements
• Cost and Convenience
• Program Length
• Severity of Diet
• Therapy Component
• Behavioral Component

Source: Brownell, K. D., & Wadden, T. A., 1992, Etiology and treatment of obesity: Understanding a serious, prevalent, and refractory disorder, Journal of Consulting and Clinical Psychology, 60, 505–517.

behavior modification, 50 subjects were randomly assigned to 3 groups: (a) very low calorie diet, (b) behavior modification, and (c) very low calorie diet plus behavior modification (Wadden, Stunkard, & Liebschutz, 1988). After treatment, the first 2 groups had achieved equivalent weight loss results, 14.3 kg (6.5 lbs) for the diet compared to 14.1 kg (6.4 lbs) for behavior modification, suggesting that behavior modification can be as effective as a diet. The combination of the 2 produced more weight loss but it was not significantly more than either of the 2 solo treatments.

When subjects were contacted 3 years later for follow-up, weight loss had declined to 3.8 kg for diet, 4.8 kg for behavior modification, and 6.5 kg for the combination treatment. These differences were not significantly different from one another or from the subjects' original weights and suggest that for the long term, any of these treatments produce losses, but they are not major. These subjects did not receive booster sessions, although 40% reported seeking additional therapy on their own.

Another study evaluated behavior modification in combination with 2 diets, a very low intermittent 800 calories per day (used four days per week) and moderate continuous 1200 calories per day (Viegener et al., 1990). Although those receiving the very low intermittent diet achieved the fastest losses initially, both groups had similar losses at 6- and 12-month followups, indicating that behavior modification works with a variety of diets, and that long term, there is no need for the deprivation of a very low-calorie diet.

In conclusion, behavior modification is effective. The dropout rate is low (10% to 15%) and average weight loss is .5 kg (1.1 lb) per week maintained for up to a year (Brownell & Wadden, 1992). Nevertheless, there is marked variability in weight loss, with some participants loosing nothing at all (Foreyt, 1987; Wilson, 1980). One problem may be that strict behavior modification has focused only on changing eating behavior, mainly through reducing intake, rather than on any other element of weight control (LeBow, 1977). Treatment effectiveness might be improved, for example, by also increasing physical activity. More recently, treatment programs have become more comprehensive, adding other techniques to behavior modification. Also, while most behavior modification treatments last 12 to 26 weeks, longer treatment (up to 72 weeks) produces significantly better results (Perri, Nezu, Patti, & McCann, 1989).

MULTICOMPONENT PROGRAMS   More recent programs utilize a variety of cognitive and behavioral techniques (McReynolds, Green, & Fisher, 1983; Stunkard, 1979). Typically, multicomponent programs have six major elements: (a) self-monitoring, (b) self-control, (c) exercise, (d) cognitive restructuring, (e) social support, and (f) relapse prevention with booster sessions.

Self-monitoring techniques rely on people keeping detailed records of what, when, where, and how much they eat. Monitoring alone often causes some reduction in intake as people realize how much they eat without being aware. The records are carefully analyzed to determine the cues to eating so stimulus control can be made more effective. Research has suggested that self-monitoring is the single component most highly related to immediate success (Israel, Silverman, & Solotar, 1988).

Self-control training helps people take charge of eating behavior itself. They are taught to slow it down by putting down their utensils between each bite of food and counting each chew before swallowing (Stunkard, 1979). It is first introduced at the end of meals, when people are most likely to be satiated, then increasingly moved to the beginning of meals. Slowing down eating may help in two ways. First, it allows more time for the relatively slow physiological feedback process of satiation to occur. Second, by focusing on each bite of food as it is chewed, people may more fully appreciate the pleasurable sensations of taste.

Self-control is also cognitive and involves rewarding oneself for successes in the program. Rewards can be verbal praise, such as "I did great today, eating slowly and counting chews," or tangible, such as buying a new piece of clothing for keeping a detailed record for a month. Both self-monitoring and self-control techniques may produce additional benefits through increased feelings of self-efficacy.

The addition of exercise in multicomponent programs recognizes that physical activity raises metabolism and expends calories. People are encouraged to engage in any additional physical activities that they find enjoyable. They do not have to become long-distance runners; any increase in activity level is welcomed and will result in some extra expended calories as long as it is done consistently.

Cognitive restructuring is similar to self-control with verbal praise, except that it is used in relation to *specific* maladaptive thoughts. First, maladaptive thoughts regarding dieting and weight loss such as, "I can't stay on my diet; it's too hard," are identified. Then, they are replaced with more positive ones like, "Success comes in little steps; I am keeping a good record and eating less."

People who have the support of others are usually better able to maintain their weight loss (Brownell & Stunkard, 1981). Therefore, some multicomponent programs teach participants formally to ask for help and encouragement from their spouses, friends, and coworkers.

Finally, relapse prevention and booster sessions have become important additions. Just as with addiction (see Chapter 8), people are taught to anticipate difficulties after termination of the formal program so they are prepared for minor slips (Gintner, 1988). They are taught how to deal with future setbacks so they do not view them as catastrophic failures leading back to a pattern of overeating. People also return periodically for booster sessions for reviews of their progress and the basic principles of the program. Booster sessions significantly increase weight loss maintenance over behavior modification alone (Perri et al., 1988).

How successful are multicomponent programs? This is difficult to assess directly, because very few studies have included all of the components.

Generally, the average participant loses between 1 to 2 pounds a week for up to 20 weeks, and maintains the loss for up to 2 years if relapse prevention is included (Brownell, 1982b; Brownell & Kramer, 1989; Hall & Hall, 1982). Multicomponent programs are less effective for binge eaters, who tend to drop out (Marcus, Wing, & Hopkins, 1988), and, since they usually result in only modest weight loss, their effectiveness for severely obese people is questionable (Brownell & Jeffrey, 1987). Given the major health implications of severe obesity, medical treatments are probably best for this group.

One study has looked at the relative effectiveness of a multicomponent program compared to narrower behavior modification treatments (DeLucia & Kalodner, 1990). Sixty-three overweight subjects were randomly assigned to either behavior modification or to a treatment that combined cognitive and behavioral interventions. At a three-month follow-up, both approaches produced the same weight loss results, surprising the experimenters. However, follow-up was not long term and the treatment did not include all of the six major elements of multicomponent treatment.

For the mildly and moderately obese, multicomponent programs probably still offer advantages over behavior modification and commercial diet programs (Box 12.2-1). They have fewer dropouts overall, so more people will complete treatment, and they result in additional improvements in psychological functioning (Brownell, 1982b; Stunkard, 1979). This last advantage is important, since permanent weight loss requires changes in lifestyle that can only be achieved through increases in self-efficacy (Blair, Lewis, & Booth, 1989). However, there is certainly room for improvement. Perhaps Brownell and Wadden's (1992) individually tailored approach will improve treatment.

CONCLUSION

The effectiveness of dieting to reduce obesity has recently been questioned in a comprehensive review by Garner and Wooley (1991). When outcome data from long-term follow-up studies were analyzed, subjects almost always returned to their pretreatment weight, and they concluded that "It is difficult to find any scientific justification for the continued use of dietary treatments for obesity" (p. 767).

This failure was attributed to the setpoint mechanism. Because only moderate to severe obesity carries definite health risks and because yo-yo dieting may carry its own health risks, they recommend changing the emphasis of treatment from helping people lose weight through dieting to improving physical and psychological well-being. Brownell and Wadden (1992) also argue for a "compassionate treatment" that considers psychological well-being.

This new emphasis would combine cognitive-behavioral treatment with helping people to improve their nutrition and eating habits (for example, reducing fat) and to increase their physical activity level. These changes would be best for overall health, but without dieting they might not result in dramatic weight loss. The current cultural ideal of physical attractiveness, one "so gaunt as to represent virtually no women in the actual population," would have to be abandoned (Garner & Wooley, 1991, p. 731).

The new emphasis would focus on helping people accept their reasonable weight. Perhaps the reasonable weight criteria may have helped Alice accept herself and not become depressed each time she returned to her setpoint. Instead, she attempted to meet an unreasonable, ideal weight goal, and her pursuit of thinness developed into an eating disorder. In fact, Alice is not alone, 25% to 40% of overweight people have problems with binge eating (Brownell & Wadden, 1992).

EATING DISORDERS

THE PURSUIT OF THINNESS

From all of the focus on dieting, it might seem that one of our society's major health problems is that too many people weigh too much. They do—

Box 12.2-1   COMMERCIAL DIET PROGRAMS

It has been estimated that half a million people attend some form of commercial diet program, such as *Weight Watchers* or *Take Off Pounds Sensibly (TOPS)*, weekly (Brownell, 1986b; Stunkard, 1986). Commercial programs can vary in their content, from nutritional education to using group support (TOPS), to providing prepackaged meals. In one of the few comparative studies (Levitz & Stunkard, 1974), nearly 300 members of TOPS were given 1 of 4 treatments for 12 weeks: (a) behavior modification by psychiatrists; (b) behavior modification by TOPS group leaders; (c) nutrition information by TOPS group leaders (a standard TOPS approach at the time); or (d) social pressure, periodic weighing, and discussions of ways to lose weight (another standard TOPS approach at the time). Subjects in the two behavior modification groups dropped out at a significantly lower rate and lost significantly more weight.

Because research has demonstrated their effectiveness, some commercial programs have adopted behavioral modification techniques. However, commercial programs have also been resistant to research attempts to evaluate their overall effectiveness (Brownell, 1986b). What research there is indicates that the dropout rate in commercial programs is very high indeed. During the first 6 weeks, up to 50% of enrollees may leave at a rate far higher than typically occurs in research programs (Stunkard, 1987). Such a high dropout rate must be a serious concern, given the apparent health risks of repeated diet cycles.

The pursuit of thinness is evident in the ideal represented by fashion models.

Americans are among the most overweight populations on Earth. Yet, ironic as it is, we are also a culture in pursuit of thinness. Many people want to transform their bodies to meet ideal standards promoted by a multibillion dollar advertising and diet industry (Brownell, 1991). Sixty-three percent of high school aged girls and 16% of boys report that they are trying to reduce their weight, while almost all of these dieters are already at a desirable weight for their height (Rosen & Gross, 1987). What is going on? At least for the majority of young American women, and some young men, dieting has become "normal" eating behavior (Polivy & Herman, 1987). How can this pursuit of thinness be explained?

The most likely explanation is cultural pressure, particularly on women, to be thin. Women's sexual desirability is linked to beauty, and our notions of ideal beauty have undergone a change in recent decades (Polivy & Thomsen, 1988; Striegel-Moore, Silberstein, & Rodin, 1986). One study documented this changing notion of beauty specifically with regard to thinness (Garner, Garfinkel, Schwartz, & Thompson, 1980). Objective data about women in *Playboy* centerfolds and the "Miss America Pageant" indicate that for roughly two decades, from 1960 to 1980, there was significant movement toward a thinner standard and a significant increase in the number of diet articles appearing in popular women's magazines. Our popular culture has been telling women that thinness is beauty. Over the same period, two forms of disordered eating behavior have also come to the attention of health care professionals: anorexia nervosa and bulimia nervosa.

ANOREXIA NERVOSA

Anorexia nervosa, literally means "nervous loss of appetite." Although it has received more attention recently, it is not a new disorder (Sours, 1980). The term for this life-threatening disorder is misleading, for rather than a loss of appetite, anorexia is a *fear* of eating that results in self-starvation, sometimes to the point of death (Achenbach, 1982). Anorexia is intentional, it is not caused by any known physical disease. It is diagnosed on the basis of several characteristics, the most important of which is *refusal* (notice the intent) to maintain a desirable weight for age and height, such that weight drops 15% or more *below* normal (APA, 1987). The other diagnostic characteristics include: (a) intense fear of gaining weight; (b) disturbance in body image (for example, claiming to feel fat even when below desirable weight); and (c) in women, **amenorrhea**, the absence of menstruation, for at least two consecutive periods. Table 12.2-4 gives the major warning signs of anorexia. Among these, a major sign of anorexia is dissatisfaction with *successful* weight losses. Typically, dieters are pleased when they meet their goal. Some fail to meet their weight loss goals, but those who do usually celebrate (even by overeating!). They cannot wait to abandon their diet. When they have successfully met their goal, typical dieters do not usually lower it again, demanding that they lose even more, but anorexics do.

INCIDENCE   Anorexia primarily affects adolescent girls, the ratio being as high as 20 females to 1 male, but male anorexics are reported to resemble their female counterparts in background, characteristics, and symptoms (for example, Hamlett & Curry, 1990; Oyebode, Boodhoo, & Schapira, 1988). The incidence of anorexia probably rises during adolescence and falls in early

Table 12.2-4   WARNING SIGNS OF ANOREXIA NERVOSA

- Excessive weight loss (>15% below desirable weight)
- Dieting but dissatisfied with weight losses (changing weight loss goals)
- Preoccupation with food, calories, and weight
- Relentless exercise
- Avoiding food-related activities
- Mood swings
- Distorted body image (believe overweight when not)

adulthood (Polivy & Thomsen, 1988). Still, anorexia is considered to be rare. It is estimated that there is about 1 case per 100,000 people on a yearly basis (Sours, 1980). Some data suggest that more women may share the symptoms, if not the disorder, for about 1 woman for every 450 to 750 in the general population has at least 1 anorexic symptom over the life span (Schwartz, Thompson, & Johnson, 1982). Estimates for adolescent girls are higher, ranging from 1 in 200 in England (Crisp, Palmer, & Kalucy, 1976) to 1 in 250 in the United States (Lacey & Birtchnell, 1986; Polivy & Thomsen, 1988). Anorexics are usually from upper socioeconomic backgrounds, although the incidence among lower socioeconomic groups seems to be increasing (Garfinkel & Garner, 1982).

HEALTH EFFECTS   Anorexia is a serious health hazard. It causes changes in the heart (for example, enlargement) and sudden death from irregular heart beats can occur. Between 5% and 18% of anorexics die from it, a mortality rate higher than many infectious diseases (APA, 1987; Berkow & Fletcher, 1987).

ETIOLOGY   So far, with limited research, there is scant evidence for biological factors in the etiology of anorexia (Lacey & Birtchnell, 1986). Psychodynamic theorists propose that unconscious conflicts may be the cause of anorexia, based on Freud's theory that eating can be a substitute for sexual expression. In this conception, the anorexic's fear of eating actually represents fear of developing sexual desire (Ross, 1977). There is little research to support this conception; however, one recent review did conclude that anorexics have more sexual inhibitions and are less sexually active than either bulimics or people without an eating disorder (Kerr, Skok, & McLaughlin, 1991).

Learning theorists believe that anorexia may be a conditioned weight phobia (Crisp, 1967). They propose that our society's association of thinness with beauty forms the basis for this conditioning. Through modeling (the learning theory type as well as the commercial type), people learn that being thin is rewarded, which causes them to reject or fear eating. After all, fashion models are constantly presented to us as beautiful and thin, and they are portrayed as reaping the rewards of a rich, glamorous life. Although this makes sense, there is also little research evidence to support the explanation of learning theorists.

Some have looked for the etiology in the family (Garfinkel & Garner, 1983; Marcus, 1989; Rakoff, 1983). Externally, the family of an anorexic person can appear to be "normal" or even "high achieving," but internally, family members may not be able to communicate well emotionally, particularly when there is conflict. Hilde Bruch (1973, 1978, 1982), who has studied eating disorders for many years, reports that anorexic girls view their parents as overdemanding and controlling. So, anorexia may be an attempt to gain control by controlling eating behavior. It is also perceived as a culturally desirable goal—being thin.

Failure to adapt to environmental demands and a threat to personal control may trigger anorexia (Weiner, 1977). Certainly, the demands of adolescence are considerable and may serve as the trigger for girls who are growing up in a dysfunctional family. There is some research support for the role of family dynamics in the etiology of anorexia, although it is far from conclusive (Kog & Vandereycken, 1985). However, the fact that family therapy has resulted in one of the few successful, although limited, treatments lends indirect support.

Family therapist Salvador Minuchin has done considerable work with families of anorexics (Minuchin, Rosman, & Baker, 1978; Rosman, Minuchin, & Liebman, 1975, 1976). Minuchin believes that the problem is interpersonal, and that a troubled family makes a family member "sick" in a way that masks its own dysfunction. In these families, conflicts develop but are not dealt with. They are ignored as the "sick" family member becomes the center of focus, keeping the family together. Family members are typically rigid and overinvolved.

A research review of families of anorexics has provided support for this conceptualization (Kog & Vandereycken, 1985). The families were found to be overinvolved, focusing on the daughter and lacking adequate conflict resolution. Minuchin's family therapy attempts to restructure family relationships and to increase communication and conflict resolution. Theoretically, if the family dynamics improve, the anorexic will no longer need to be the "sick" family member.

TREATMENT   A variety of treatments, including psychoanalysis (Wilson, 1983), medication (Halmi, 1982), and behavior therapy (Garner, Garfinkel, & Bemis, 1982), have been used to treat anorexia (for a review, see Yager, 1989), but none is particularly effective. Ideally, treatment should involve a combination of both family therapy and some form of individual therapy (Bruch, 1978).

There is support for Minuchin's family therapy as a treatment for anorexia. One study of 50 anorexic daughters treated with their families found that 86% of them were functioning successfully up to 4 years after treatment (Minuchin et al., 1978; Rosman et al., 1976). One important limitation of family therapy for anorexia is that it is only appropriate for younger people, since they must be living with or still very involved with the family.

Cognitive-behavior therapy has been used increasingly to treat anorexia. If hospitalized, the anorexic person is isolated so eating behavior can be monitored and rewarded with such things as visits from friends, entertainments, and walks. Maladaptive cognitions about thinness and body image are also firmly attacked by a therapist who maintains a warm, accepting attitude. Although criticized as coercive (Bruch, 1973), cognitive-behavioral therapy has produced better short-term results than those reported with other techniques (for example, Agras, 1987; Channon et al., 1989; Eckert et al., 1979).

New approaches are becoming broader, involving multicomponent treatment and focusing on more than just weight gain (Vandereycken, 1989).

BULIMIA NERVOSA

The other form of disordered eating, **bulimia nervosa**, literally means "continuous nervous hunger." Bulimia was only recognized as a separate disorder from anorexia in the 1970s. Bulimia is a disorder of eating in which there are alternating cycles of binging on huge quantities of food (usually certain favorites) and of purging the ingested food primarily through self-induced vomiting and/or excessive use of laxatives and sometimes with drastic dieting or fasting or drug or alcohol abuse (Hamilton, Gelwick, & Meade, 1984).

Bulimia is diagnosed on the basis of two primary characteristics: (a) recurrent binge eating (a minimum average of two per week for at least three months) and (b) regular purging afterward. Other diagnostic characteristics include a feeling of loss of control over eating behavior during binges and persistent overconcern with body shape and weight (APA, 1987). Both bulimics and anorexics are preoccupied with weight and dieting; however, the major difference between them is that the anorexic is successful in reducing food intake and weight (Schlesier-Stropp, 1984). The bulimic's weight may fluctuate, but it does not drop low enough to be a serious health threat. Bulimics are actually more likely to be somewhat overweight (Telch, Agras, & Rossiter, 1988). Concerned about her weight, but unable to control her eating, Alice became caught in the binge-purge cycle of bulimia, which can happen to long-term dieters.

Table 12.2-5 gives the major warning signs of bulimia. The overwhelming majority of bulimics (who are not also anorexic) will not be able to be identified on sight, since they are within 15% either way of their desirable weight. Also, dissatisfaction with *successful* weight losses, a good indicator of

Table 12.2-5	**WARNING SIGNS OF BULIMIA**

- ■ Excessive concern about weight*
- ■ Dieting and binging
- ■ Absences and bathroom visits after meals; purging
- ■ Criticism of body
- ■ Depressed mood

Weight may be at a desirable level or somewhat below or above it; there is usually not excessive weight loss.

anorexia, is unlikely to be present since bulimics will rarely meet their weight-loss goals. Nevertheless, bulimics will express an excessive concern with their weight. Binges and purges are unlikely to be observed by casual relations, since they take place in private. However, more intimate relations may find the telltale signs (for example, cartons of ice cream stuffed in the garbage or stockpiled laxatives in the medicine chest). Absences and bathroom visits after meals are good indicators of bulimia, as are any changes in or avoidance of social or work activities that may be involved with binging and purging behavior.

Bulimics often have other serious problems. Alcohol abuse appears to be much higher than it is in the general population (Pope & Hudson, 1984), with an incidence perhaps as high as 40% of bulimics (Cauwells, 1983). There is also a high incidence of stealing among bulimics. One study found that ²/₃ of bulimics have stolen (Pyle, Mitchell, & Eckert, 1981), and another reported that 1 in 6 bulimics had stolen compared to only 1 in 100 anorexics (Garfinkel & Garner, 1984). Although some stealing involved food, many bulimics have stolen things they did not have any use for. This has led to speculation that many bulimics may also have *kleptomania*, a psychological disorder characterized by compulsive stealing.

Unlike anorexics, bulimics recognize that their eating behavior is abnormal. They believe that it is out of control, and it makes them feel guilty, disgusted, and helpless. They may even panic during a binge, experiencing a profound loss of control. It is no surprise then that most bulimics are clinically depressed, unlike most anorexics. There is a high correlation between depression and bulimia, far higher than with anorexia (Kerr et al., 1991). Up to one-third of bulimics in treatment reported having made at least one serious suicide attempt, and about half of women with bulimia were depressed for at least a year *before* they began binging and purging (Garfinkel & Garner, 1984; Piran, Kennedy, Garfinkel, & Owens, 1985; Pope & Hudson, 1984).

INCIDENCE The prevalence of bulimia is hard to estimate. Unlike anorexia, which eventually becomes evident due to obvious dramatic weight losses and illness, most bulimics are near their desirable weight or somewhat above, and their abnormal eating behavior takes place in private (Martin & Wollitzer, 1988).

Like anorexia, bulimia primarily affects young women. The full bulimic syndrome may occur at a somewhat later age than anorexia since it takes some time to evolve (Polivy & Thomsen, 1988). About 10% of 300 females aged 12 to 65 who were anonymously surveyed in a middle-class, suburban shopping mall met the criteria for bulimia at some point in their lives (Pope, Hudson, & Yurgelun-Todd, 1984). Studies have reported rates from 0% to 1.4% for male college students, and 8% to almost 19% for female college students (Pope & Hudson, 1984; Pyle et al., 1983). Among high school students, rates of 1.2% for males and 9.6% for females have been reported (Gross & Rosen, 1988). One survey at a family practice medical clinic found a history of bulimia in

21% of their female patients (Martin & Wollitzer, 1988). Although these estimates may not be completely reliable, they still suggest that bulimia affects many young women and some young men.

Eᴛɪᴏʟᴏɢʏ   Learning theory explains bulimia better than anorexia. Society's association of thinness with beauty forms the basis for conditioning (Crisp, 1967). Through modeling, people learn that being thin is rewarded, which may result in a fear of eating. However, in contrast to the anorexic, the bulimic is periodically overcome by hunger or otherwise loses control and binges, perhaps as a result of stress, depression, or inadequate coping resources (Cattanach & Rodin, 1988). Binging raises feelings of anxiety about gaining weight, so purging is a way of reducing the anxiety and regaining control (Rosen & Leitenberg, 1985). Ironically, vomiting is an escape response that *reduces* normal inhibitions against overeating. In other words, once a bulimic learns that the anxiety of binging can be relieved by purging, binging increases. This is somewhat speculative, but the health effects of bulimia are not.

Hᴇᴀʟᴛʜ Eꜰꜰᴇᴄᴛꜱ   Bulimia does not result in the same life-threatening consequences that anorexia does, and it is not considered fatal. However, bulimia does have harmful physical effects (Berkow & Fletcher, 1987). The intake of huge quantities of food (which can exceed 15,000 calories at once), followed by purging can disrupt the body's homeostatic control mechanisms. Bulimics are prone to hypoglycemia because, when a large amount of sugar is consumed, the pancreas releases huge amounts of insulin, precipitating a drop in blood sugar. Also, frequent purging can lead to nutritional deficiencies (of vitamins, minerals, and, ironically, fat because it is absorbed last), even though enough calories are being consumed. Binge eating can stretch the stomach and rupture is possible. The excessive use of laxatives can result in laxative dependence (with constipation in their absence), dehydration, and nutritional deficiencies. Frequent vomiting may cause tearing and bleeding of the esophagus and brings hydrochloric acid in contact with delicate oral tissues that are not able to withstand its corrosive effects. This can lead to erosion and loss of teeth and burning of the throat and mouth. Aspiration pneumonia can result from stomach contents flowing into the lungs as vomiting occurs, but this is more likely to happen if drugs or alcohol have been consumed in conjunction with a binge.

Bulimia is also not without harmful psychosocial effects. One study of 275 bulimics found that 70% had strained interpersonal relationships, 53% had family problems, and 50% had work problems (Mitchell, Hatsukami, Eckert, & Pyle, 1985).

Tʀᴇᴀᴛᴍᴇɴᴛ   Just as with anorexia, researchers have had little time to begin to explore ways of preventing bulimia. Again, the cultural value of thinness would be a likely target, but there is little that can be done to rectify this. Therefore, major prevention efforts are virtually nonexistent. In addition, although family-based intervention is promising in anorexia, the dysfunctional family has not received the same focus of attention in the etiology of bulimia.

Because of the relationship between depression and bulimia, antidepressant medication has been used in its treatment. In one double-blind study, 19 bulimic women were randomly assigned to receive either the antidepressant imipramine or a placebo (Pope, Hudson, Jonas, & Yurgelun-Todd, 1983). After 6 weeks on the treatment, those receiving imipramine experienced a 70% reduction in the frequency of binges, while the frequency of binges in those receiving the placebo were unchanged. Those receiving the antidepressant continued to do better up to 6 months later. Although encouraging, this study used very few subjects, and $^2/_3$ of those receiving imipramine still had occasional binges. Still, other studies have also demonstrated that antidepressants can be useful, if not a complete cure, for bulimia (for example, Gotestam & Agras, 1989; Hughes, Wells, Cunningham, & Ilstrup, 1986; Pope & Hudson, 1989).

The limited success of antidepressants indicates that other treatments are also necessary (Pope & Hudson, 1989). Cognitive-behavioral techniques have been used extensively with bulimia, producing results at least as effective as antidepressants (Gotestam & Agras, 1989). Typical approaches combine conditioning and cognitive restructuring. Conditioning attempts to change the reinforcement contingencies of the abnormal eating behavior (Agras, Schneider, Arnow, Raeburn, & Telch, 1989). A dietary record similar to that used to treat overeating is often employed (Fairburn, 1980). Research has shown that this technique alone can result in reductions of binging and purging, probably because it makes bulimics more aware of their behavior (Orleans & Barnett, 1984; Wilson, 1984).

Response prevention (Marlatt & Gordon, 1980), in which the bulimic is allowed to binge but is prevented from vomiting afterwards, has also been used with some success to break the reinforcement cycle (Agras et al., 1989). Habitual behaviors associated with the disordered eating cycle may also be attacked by changing the pattern of meals, increasing their regularity and the variety of foods eaten, eating in new surroundings not associated with the disordered behavior, and attempting to delay the desire to purge (Kirkley, Schneider, Agras, & Bachman, 1989). Cognitive restructuring involves changing beliefs that thinness and success are necessarily related and increasing beliefs in self-efficacy (Schneider, O'Leary, & Agras, 1987; White & White, 1988). Self-efficacy can be increased by helping bulimics to disconfirm their fears about losing control (Wilson, Rossiter, Kleifield, & Lindholm, 1986). A recent review of 31 studies concluded that group therapy (primarily cognitive) is an effective treatment for bulimia (Zimpfer, 1990). Compared to imipramine, cognitive group therapy was a more important factor in maintaining normal eating behavior after treatment (Pyle et al., 1990). Other research supports the effectiveness of cognitive-behavioral therapy (Agras et al., 1989;

Fairburn, 1988; Schneider, O'Leary, & Agras, 1987), although not all studies have reported impressive *rates* of success (for example, Cox & Merkel, 1989).

CONCLUSION

Anorexia and bulimia both involve exaggerated concerns about being overweight and a preoccupation with being thin. However, there are differences. Anorexia is less frequent, but more deadly, than bulimia. Family problems also appear to figure prominently in the etiology of anorexia, although not in bulimia. In contrast, depression is more related to bulimia. These differences have important implications for treatment. The cognitive-behavioral approach appears to be effective with bulimia, while family therapy is most promising as a treatment for anorexia.

Although depression was not new to her, Alice knew that her binging and purging was getting out of control, so she contacted a counselor through the employee assistance program at work. The counselor consulted a psychologist who specialized in eating disorders, and they developed a cognitive-behavioral treatment for Alice. She kept a dietary record for a month and noticed a downward trend in caloric intake, binging, and purging. This encouraged her because she realized for the first time that she had some control over her eating. She reasoned that if it could go down just by her being aware of it, she could probably control it. Next, cognitive restructuring was used to change her beliefs about thinness and her body image and to increase her self-efficacy.

Finally, the social patterns of Alice's life were investigated and altered. Following college, she tended to overeat while alone in the evenings, so she arranged a busier social schedule with friends and activities in the evenings. She also learned how to exert more control over where and when business events took place. She met business associates for meals less often, and, when she did, she chose restaurants where she could eat lightly. She also agreed that, if she overate, she would postpone any desire to purge as long as possible.

As Alice gained control over her eating behavior, in about six months she was able to use the counseling to explore her sense of herself and her interpersonal relationships. She realized that she had been lonely much of her life and that her shame from her own sense of herself as being overweight kept her from becoming involved with others, which increased her loneliness. Her counselor recommended that Alice join a social skills group of men and women. This was very traumatic for her, but with the counselor's support, she persevered. She became more confident and began to appreciate that others liked her as she is. About every other month or so, usually during a period of increased stress, she still had the desire to binge, but she was managing to control it.

■■■■

MODULE SUMMARY

Here is a review of weight control and eating disorders:

1. Desirable weight is determined objectively by standard weight to height charts that are related to mortality rates. The body-mass index is an alternative method of determining the relationship between weight and health.

2. Some overweight people may have inherited a setpoint above what is desirable for their height, while most overweight people probably inherited a desirable weight to height ratio but adjusted their setpoint up by continual overeating. Psychological explanations play an important role in the latter case.

3. Three psychological explanations for being overweight have been suggested. The psychodynamic model was dominant at one time but lacks controlled experimental research. Behavioral explanations suggest that some people learn to overeat because it is a biologically rewarding activity and because we ingest too many plentiful, calorie-packed foods before the internal primitive homeostatic mechanisms that signal satiation can react. The third explanation is family centered, in which disrupted family environments lead to the development of obesity in children.

4. Moderate to severe obesity is related to numerous health problems and carries a 2.5 times higher mortality rate. Mild obesity may only represent a small risk of increased mortality and presents very little health risk.

5. It may not be obesity itself that increase health problems but rather the high fat diets of obese people.

6. Dieting cycles (yo-yo dieting) may be a separate health risk factor.

7. Obesity is associated with psychosocial problems as well. People blame obese people for their condition, and they blame themselves.

8. Prevention efforts must begin with children. Family-based and school-based prevention programs that change eating behavior and increase physical activity levels are effective in reducing people's weight.

9. Many people diet on their own and achieve their desired weight loss. Behavior modification of eating habits is considered as effective for weight loss as dieting. However, some people do not lose weight on behavioral programs, so adding other techniques might improve its effectiveness.

10. Multicomponent approaches are cognitive-behavioral but also involve increasing physical activity. Multicomponent treatment offers advantages over behavior modification alone; in particular, it has fewer dropouts.

11. Commercial diet programs have adopted behavior modification techniques; however, their effectiveness has not been well researched, and they appear to have a high rate of dropouts.

12. Many people in our society are preoccupied with losing weight, probably because there is cultural pressure to be thin. Eating disorders represent extreme cases of people pursuing thinness to the point of endangering their health.

13. Anorexia involves extremes of self-starvation, whereas bulimia involves cycles of binging and purging. These disorders primarily affect women, but some men also have them. Anorexia is dangerous because it can be fatal. However, anorexics also do not cooperate with treatment and outcome is poor.

14. The etiology of anorexia is not well understood. Psychodynamic theory holds that it is caused by unconscious, probably sexual, conflicts. Family dysfunction and learning may play a role but more research is needed.

15. Treatment for anorexia may involve hospitalization and forced feeding. Overall, treatment effectiveness is not good, with symptoms returning in at least half of treated anorexics. Cognitive-behavioral and family-based treatments are both promising.

16. Bulimia is often accompanied by depression and stealing, but bulimics, who recognize that their behavior is abnormal, are more cooperative with treatment. Bulimia is not life threatening. Bulimics get sufficient calories and are usually average or slightly above average in weight.

17. The etiology of bulimia is unknown, but learning theory provides a useful approach.

18. Antidepressant medication has been helpful, but it is not a cure. Group therapy and cognitive-behavioral approaches have been used with some success. Much more research on etiology and treatment needs to be done on these two eating disorders.

13

REPRODUCTIVE SYSTEM:
FUNCTION AND ORGANIZATION

13.1 The Human Sexual Response
13.2 Sexual Dysfunction

Maria is a 29-year-old registered nurse whose parents immigrated to the United States from Cuba when she was an infant. She has been married for 2 years to Steve, a European American and an administrator at the hospital where she works. The couple decided to begin a family about a year ago but have not been able to conceive yet. Maria and Steve had been having sexual intercourse several times a week since they were married, but Maria has been avoiding it lately. They have only had intercourse once in the last couple of weeks, and Steve is beginning to become more insistent. Lately, when they do have intercourse, she finds it uncomfortable, almost painful. Maria and Steve's problem demonstrates how biopsychosocial factors affect the reproductive and sexual system.

The reproductive system contributes indirectly to mental well-being and does not have a direct role in maintaining physical well-being. Nevertheless, reproduction is one of the defining characteristics of living organisms, and the continuance of a species depends on it. The reproductive system is unique because (a) it is not completely functional until many years after birth, (b) its purpose is to produce another new individual, and (c) it produces another individual through interaction with the complementary reproductive system of another person (no other system depends on another person to fulfill its role).

In animals, reproduction is strongly influenced by a biologically determined drive. Animals are usually sexual only during limited periods of time, and their sexual activity and reproduction are strongly linked. The female's receptivity to sex and the male's drive are determined by hormones that govern the reproductive cycle.

For example, female dogs will come into "heat" only once or twice per year at 6-month intervals. Heat lasts about 21 days, and during that period a female will be highly attractive to males, who will make repeated attempts to get near her. At other times, the same males may be no more interested in her than in any other dog. During the second and third weeks of heat, when she is maximally fertile, she will be receptive to sexual activity (although as in most mammals, she may reject specific males).

In human beings, sexual behavior is not as strongly linked to reproduction. Biological drives and hormones govern sexuality and reproduction, but psychosocial factors greatly influence its expression (Marieb, 1989). Emotional, cultural, and social factors enhance or restrain human sexual activity to a great extent. These psychosocial factors supersede the biological control of sexual behavior found in animals. Human females can be receptive to sexual advances, and males can be attracted to females almost any time. In fact, William Masters and Virginia Johnson (1966), the first researchers to scientifically study the human sexual response, called human sexuality "a dimension and an expression of *personality* (not biology)" (p. 301; emphasis added).

This chapter actually has two topics—reproduction and sexual behavior—which both depend on the same organ system, but can function independently. Human sexual behavior is not strictly dependent on reproductive cycles.

THE MALE REPRODUCTIVE SYSTEM

The male reproductive system (see Figure 13.1) produces and delivers half of the genetic material necessary to create a new individual. It also determines the gender of this new individual.

STRUCTURE AND PHYSIOLOGY

The primary male sex organs are the **testes**, and without them a person would not be considered male (Marieb, 1989). From puberty on, the testes produce hormones called **androgens** and sperm. **Testosterone** is an androgen that initiates the maturation of the reproductive system, the development of secondary sex characteristics (for example, changes in voice and distribution and growth of hair during puberty), and the sex drive.

Sperm are small single cells with a head containing 23 chromosomes ($\frac{1}{2}$ of the normal complement of 46 necessary to produce a human being), a middle section that provides energy, and a tail that lashes to drive the sperm forward. From puberty, sperm cells are produced and divide in the testes through the process of *meiosis*. Meiosis has two important outcomes: (a) it reduces the chromosomal number by half in each sperm (from 46 to 23), and (b) it introduces genetic variability by randomly shuffling pairings of genes. It takes about 3 months for sperm to develop in the testes and then complete their journey through a system of narrow tubes a little over 6 m (21 feet) in length that deliver them to the prostate gland.

The **prostate gland** is about the size of a walnut and is located just below the bladder. Sperm accumulate in the prostate, where they await ejaculation, when they are mixed with various fluids to form **semen**. The fluids activate the mature sperm, provide energy, serve as a lubricant during sex, and maintain a hospitable medium for the delicate sperm.

During ejaculation, muscle contractions force semen out of the prostate and into the urethra. The **urethra** is a narrow tube that carries the ejaculate from the prostate through the length of the penis to its head, where it is ejected. The ejaculated semen totals only about 2 to 6 ml, each milliliter containing 50 to 100 million sperm. The urethra also has a branch from the bladder and carries urine, so it serves as part of both the reproductive and urinary systems.

The **penis** is composed of three cylindrical cavities of erectile tissue separated by bands of muscle tissue. In its flaccid state, it permits elimination of urine from the bladder. Increase of the arterial blood supply *to* the penis, coupled with restriction of venous blood flow *from* the penis, causes it to become erect during sexual arousal in preparation for ejaculation.

Figure 13.1   **MALE REPRODUCTIVE SYSTEM**

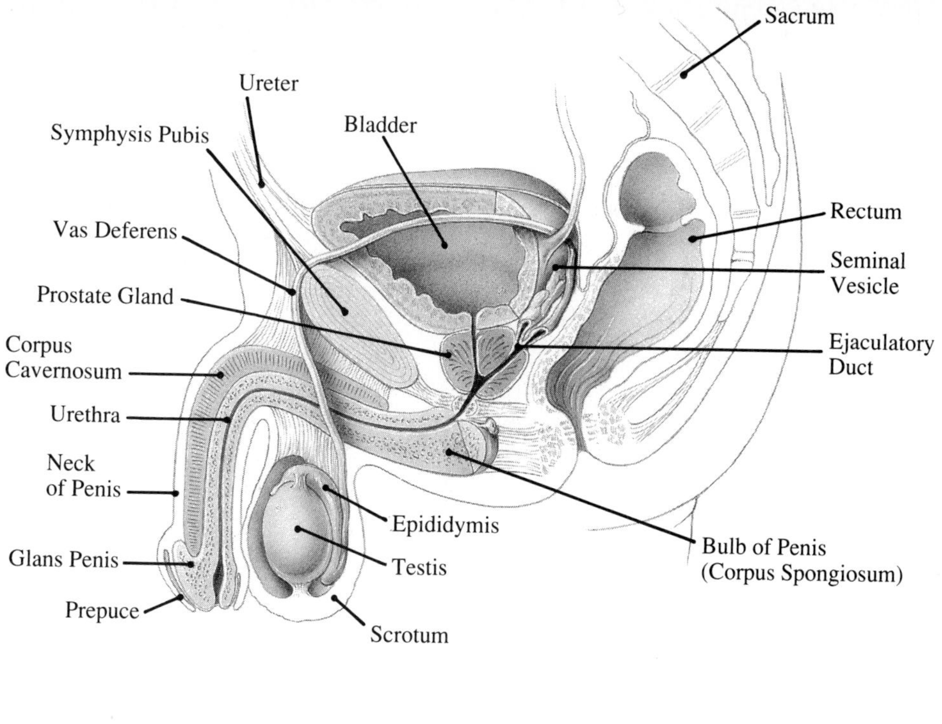

THE FEMALE REPRODUCTIVE SYSTEM

The female reproductive system (see Figure 13.2) has similar functions. Like the male, it produces and delivers the genetic material necessary to create a new individual in the form of an **ovum** or egg. However, unlike the male, should the ovum become fertilized, the female reproductive system also provides the environment and nourishment for the developing fetus during pregnancy.

STRUCTURE AND PHYSIOLOGY

The primary female sex organs are the ovaries. Like the testes, the **ovaries** serve two roles. First, they manufacture the sex hormones estrogen and progesterone. Together, these hormones initiate the maturation of the reproductive system and regulate the uterine cycle. In addition, **estrogen** promotes general physical development and the development of secondary sex characteristics (for example, breast development, widening of the pelvis), while **progesterone** promotes lactation.

Second, the ovaries are the repository for the **oocytes**, the immature eggs. In contrast to the male's continuous production of sperm, a woman's entire

Figure 13.2　　**FEMALE REPRODUCTIVE SYSTEM**

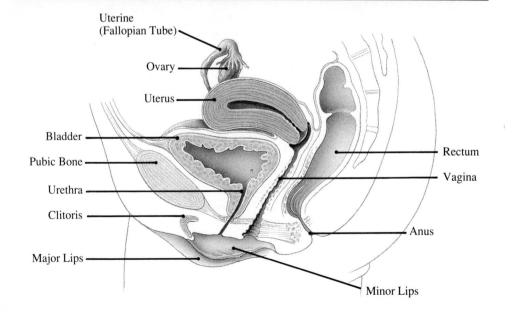

supply of oocytes, approximately 700,000, is in place at her own birth. Unlike sperm, each one contains a full complement of 46 chromosomes.

During the **ovarian cycle**, which usually lasts 28 days, several of the oocytes will grow, culminating in the *ovulation*, or release, in 11 to 14 days of a single oocyte. The best chance for conception is shortly after ovulation, and the reproductive cycle ends 14 days later. In 1% to 2% of cycles, more than 1 oocyte is ovulated and can result in nonidentical ("fraternal") twins if both are fertilized. Identical twins result from a single fertilized ovum that divides into 2 early in its development.

The oocyte takes about 7 days to pass through the **fallopian tubes**, which are approximately 10 cm (4 inches) long, to the uterus. Meanwhile, sperm travel up the vagina to the fallopian tubes where fertilization takes place. The oocyte accepts only one sperm, and then its membrane becomes impenetrable to others.

Upon fertilization, the oocyte divides, resulting in 2 cells, one large and one small. The large one, now technically the **ovum**, contains ½, that is 23, chromosomes of the 46 originally in the oocyte, and the 23 chromosomes from the sperm. The smaller cell contains the other half of the oocyte's chromosomes, and it will ultimately wither and die.

The fertilized ovum continues to travel down the fallopian tube until it becomes implanted in the wall of the uterus, where it remains and develops during pregnancy. The **uterus**, or womb, is an expandable muscular cavity located centrally in the pelvic area behind the bladder. The muscles of the uterus contract rhythmically to expel the baby at birth. These contractions force the baby through the **cervix**—a muscular tube approximately 8 to 10 cm (3 to 4 inches) in length—that connects the uterus to the **vagina**. Normally, the vagina is a "potential space" rather than an actual one (Masters & Johnson, 1966). That means that it expands and widens on sexual arousal to admit the penis and to channel the sperm toward the uterus. It also expands during birth.

Directly above the external opening to the vagina is the clitoris. The **clitoris** is a small rounded structure that extends slightly from the body. It is biologically homologous to the penis, which has led to some misunderstandings about its functions (Masters & Johnson, 1966). It enlarges slightly during stimulation through the same vascular mechanisms that cause the penis to become erect, but it responds more slowly than the penis, and it does not lengthen appreciably. It also retracts just before orgasm.

Functionally, the clitoris differs from the penis in important ways. Unlike the penis, the urinary and reproductive tracts do not run through the clitoris. It is also richly supplied with sensory nerves, making it the "unique organ in the total of human anatomy" (Masters & Johnson, 1966, p. 45). It is unique because it is the only organ in either gender whose sole function is to initiate and elevate sexual arousal; it has no other purpose. The clitoris and vaginal opening are enclosed by the **labia minor**, two delicate folds of skin, which, in turn, are enclosed by the **labia major**, two larger outer skin folds.

FERTILITY AND CONCEPTION

For human beings, sex is capable of providing much pleasure and has many functions beside procreation. It can be a means for people to achieve intimacy, develop communication skills, explore issues of vulnerability and trust, and express affection and love (Masters, Johnson, & Kolodny, 1986). However, sex is also the primary method of conceiving and reproducing. The likelihood of conception in fertile women varies by age (see Table 13.1), but even though the probability of conception within a year declines from the early 20s to the late 30s, it still remains quite high in later years.

INFERTILITY

A diagnosis of **infertility** is made only when a couple who are not using contraception has not been able to conceive after 1 year of trying. Under this definition, about 15% of couples in the United States—including Maria and Steve—are unable to conceive (Berkow & Fletcher, 1987). About 40% of the time, a couple's infertility is caused by a male reproductive problem, whereas about 55% of the time it is caused by a female reproductive problem (sometimes both male and female factors are involved). In the remaining 5% of cases, infertility is unexplained even after a complete evaluation.

Age and race can also be factors in infertility (Berkow & Fletcher, 1987). Women 34 to 44 years of age have twice the risk of being infertile than women 30 to 34 years of age. Also, African American women have $1\frac{1}{2}$ times the risk of being infertile compared to European American women.

Table 13.1	**LIKELIHOOD OF PREGNANCY IN FERTILE WOMEN**		
AGE	**PROBABILITY OF CONCEPTION PER MONTH**	**AVERAGE TIME TO CONCEPTION (MONTHS)**	**PROBABILITY OF CONCEPTION WITHIN A YEAR**
Late 30s	8% to 10%	12 to 10	65% to 72%
Early 30s	10% to 15%	10 to 6.7	72% to 86%
Late 20s	15% to 20%	6.7 to 5	86% to 93%
Early 20s	20% to 25%	5 to 4	93% to 97%

Source: Silber, S. J., 1980, How to get pregnant, *New York: Charles Scribner's Sons.*

Infertility can be psychogenic, although the precise mechanisms for this are not well understood (Berkow & Fletcher, 1987). One indication of a psychogenic effect on fertility is the relationship between amenorrhea and anorexia nervosa (see Module 12.2, page 554). Stress is also believed to be an important factor in infertility, and sperm count is believed to vary according to stress levels. However, there has been little well-controlled research on infertility, because infertile couples are understandably under stress, and infertility itself can have major psychological effects, making it difficult to separate cause-and-effect relationships in research.

Infertile couples are profoundly psychologically challenged. The assignment of blame is often an issue that couples must work through. In addition, infertility can affect one's self-image and self-esteem, and it can even be a causal factor in sexual dysfunction. Maria was afraid to tell Steve about her discomfort during intercourse and her worries that there might be something physically wrong with her, but she also realized that something had to be done about the problem before it jeopardized their marriage. Maria finally confided in a gynecologist on the hospital staff, who gave her a physical examination and referred her to an infertility specialist.

Because of the psychological impact of infertility, it is important for the couple trying to conceive to have a careful medical evaluation. The medical evaluation usually begins with the man, because it is less time consuming and less expensive. Therefore, the specialist Maria went to wanted to see them both to discuss the situation. With a lot of encouragement and support from the specialist, Maria was able to tell Steve about her concerns and her visit to the doctor. Steve, who wanted children very much, was willing to go along.

Male fertility depends on three factors: (a) adequate sperm production, (b) collection and transportation of the sperm through the seminal tract, and (c) the deposit of the sperm in the vagina. Each of these is checked in a physical and laboratory examination, and appropriate remedial action is taken when possible.

Sperm development can be impaired for a number of reasons, such as environmental heat or radiation, prolonged fever, and endocrine disorders. Among the behavioral causes of insufficient sperm production are alcohol abuse and long-term marijuana use (Berkow & Fletcher, 1987). These require referral to appropriate treatment programs, and, with time, sperm production may improve. Deposit of sperm in the vagina may be affected by sexual dysfunctions like premature ejaculation or inhibited orgasm. After evaluation, if the male is determined to be fertile, then an evaluation of the female takes place.

Part of the reason that evaluation of the female is more complicated is the number of potential factors that can be involved. There may be disorders or damage of the reproductive organs themselves, genetic or hormonal disorders, systemic disease such as diabetes, or immunologic causes such as antibodies to sperm. One important preventable behavioral cause of infertility in women is inflammation of the vagina, which can be caused by a history of STDs.

Unfortunately, treatment of infertility varies in its effectiveness, and it results in pregnancy in only about 40% of cases (Berkow & Fletcher, 1987). Therefore, many couples that desire pregnancy will remain infertile even after extensive evaluation and treatment.

Some infertility researchers have recently taken a new direction, by investigating the relationship between reproductive failure resistant to treatment and stress. There is heightened anxiety in these infertile couples compared to initially infertile (but later fertile) couples, and it may affect neuroendocrine functioning and the hormone balance that governs the reproductive cycle (Edelmann & Golombok, 1989). Much more research is needed, however.

Couples with irreversible infertility must deal with feelings of loss for the children they cannot conceive. There can be denial, guilt, and anger associated with this process and supportive couple therapy is often used. After dealing with the emotional aspects of infertility, the couple may move on to consider alternatives. A self-help support group, Resolve, is available for infertile couples. Even couples who are ultimately able to conceive are often strongly affected by the experience they have undergone. The evaluation and treatment can take years and can result in considerable financial hardship and stress. The couple or individual may feel "defective," and if only one partner is identified with the problem, there can be self-blame, anger, and resentment. Couples may be left with sexual problems, inhibition, and decreased communication.

Fortunately, nothing was physically wrong with Maria or Steve's reproductive systems. Most likely it just took a little longer than they expected to conceive. Then as the pressure mounted, stress interfered with their reproductive functioning, and Maria and Steve developed a sexual dysfunction. Therefore, the infertility specialist referred them to a psychologist.

SUMMARY

The remainder of Chapter 13 looks more closely at Maria and Steve's problem and the biopsychosocial factors in the human sexual response (Module 13.1) and sexual dysfunction (Module 13.2).

Take a moment before going on, however, to review these major points about the function and organization of the reproductive system:

1. Among the body's organ systems, the reproductive system is unique because it is not completely operative until many years after birth, it functions to produce another new individual, and this reproduction can only be accomplished by interacting with the complementary reproductive system.

2. In human beings, sexual behavior is not as strongly linked to reproduction as in animals. Psychosocial factors supersede biological control of sexual behavior, and humans can engage in sexual behavior at nearly any time. The human reproductive system fulfills two functions: reproduction and sexual behavior.

3. The male reproductive system functions to produce and deliver one-half of the genetic material necessary to create a new individual. The primary male sex organs are the testes, which produce sperm and hormones that affect secondary sex characteristics.

4. The female reproductive system produces and delivers one-half of the genetic material to produce a new individual, and it also provides the environment and nourishment for the developing fetus.

5. The primary female sex organs are the ovaries, which contain all of the woman's oocytes at her own birth. They also manufacture sex hormones that affect secondary sex characteristics.

6. The penis serves more than one purpose as the receptor of pleasure and the pathway for sperm and urine, while the clitoris serves only a single role as the sensory organ of pleasure.

7. In human beings, sex and reproduction have been decoupled. Human beings can engage in sex at almost any time, sex is capable of providing pleasure, and it has other relationship functions in addition to reproduction. However, propagation of the species depends on healthy reproduction.

8. Fertility declines with age, but most women remain fertile into their 40s. Infertility affects about 15% of couples in the United States. About 40% of the time it is traced to a male reproductive problem and about 55% to a female reproductive problem. It is believed that psychological factors such as stress may increase infertility, although there is very little research on this topic.

9. Infertility results in considerable psychological and emotional hardship for couples who may be left with sexual dysfunction, inhibition, and relationship problems.

THE HUMAN SEXUAL RESPONSE

THE SCIENTIFIC STUDY OF HUMAN SEXUALITY

Alfred Kinsey was the first researcher to study human sexual behavior in the laboratory, although some of his methods have been criticized. Because he feared public reaction to his work, he reported only the interview portion of his data and not the laboratory work (Kinsey, Pomeroy, & Martin, 1948; Kinsey, Pomeroy, Martin, & Gebhard, 1953). He was right to be cautious, because just the reports of the interviews caused substantial public shock on its own (Gagnon, 1977).

Researchers William Masters, a physician, and Virginia Johnson, a nurse, built on Kinsey's earlier research, obtaining detailed physiological measurements of people masturbating and having sex in the laboratory of their Reproductive Biology Research Institute in St. Louis, Missouri. Masters and Johnson realized that their work might also cause public shock, so, at first, it was only published in scholarly journals. They followed that with two books written for a professional audience: one book was titled the *Human Sexual Response* (1966), and the other book was titled *Human Sexual Inadequacy* (1970) and featured their pioneering therapy to treat it.

Masters and Johnson's (1966) research remains the most comprehensive study of the human sexual response. There were 694 subjects in the original study, 382 women and 312 men. The majority of these subjects were 276 married couples. They were predominantly European American, and they were purposely selected from above average socioeconomic backgrounds to increase the probability of healthy physical functioning. They also had above average intelligence and had to be willing to engage in sexual activity in a laboratory. All subjects had a physical examination to establish normal genital functioning, and they had to be fully sexually responsive. The women ranged in age from 18 to 78, with 48% in the 21- to 30-year-old age group. The men ranged in age from 21 to 89, with 38% in the 21- to 30-year-old age group. Data were collected on 10,000 complete sexual response cycles, 7,500 in females and 2,500 in males.

William Masters and Virginia Johnson, pioneer researchers in human sexuality

There are several inadequacies with Masters and Johnson's initial sample. Realizing that social taboos would make it difficult to obtain any sort of random sample of the population, they did not try. These above-average subjects were anatomically normal and were fully able to engage in sex under intrusive and difficult laboratory conditions. This included observation, videorecording, and electrodes and probes attached to various parts of their bodies. It is clear that their sample was not representative of the general population, because many people would find it difficult to function sexually under these conditions. Despite this, Masters and Johnson's research remains a landmark in the scientific study of human sexuality.

As research at the institute has continued beyond the initial sample, a broader cross-section of subjects in terms of ethnicity, socioeconomic status, and functioning has been studied. Subsequent research has also involved gay and bisexual men and women and found essentially the same sexual responses, and even some overlap in fantasies and sexual behaviors between them and heterosexual subjects (Masters & Johnson, 1979).

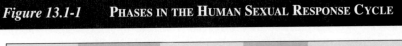

Figure 13.1-1   PHASES IN THE HUMAN SEXUAL RESPONSE CYCLE

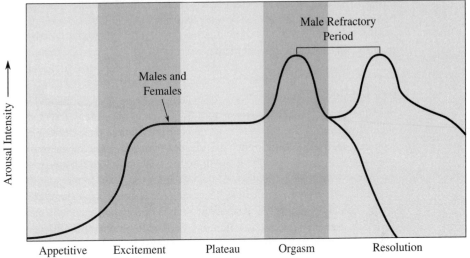

HUMAN SEXUAL RESPONSE

Masters and Johnson's pioneering research provided a detailed description of the phases in the human sexual response.

THE FIVE PHASES

There are five phases of the human sexual response: appetitive, excitement, plateau, orgasm, and resolution (Kaplan, 1974; Masters & Johnson, 1966). Males and females experience the same phases, although the specific aspects of the phases are somewhat different for each sex (see Figure 13.1-1). The human sexual response is, perhaps, one of the best understood examples of the complex interplay of biopsychosocial factors in human well-being.

APPETITIVE PHASE   This phase precedes sexual excitement and was added by Helen Kaplan (1974), a clinician who recognized that sexual interest and desire are important precursors to sexual responsiveness. Interestingly, nonhuman animals also have certain environmental factors or conditions that are necessary before they will readily engage in sex (Hediger, 1965). This phase is a recognition that there are minimal conditions that must be met before a person will initiate or be receptive to sexual activity. Of course, these conditions are thoroughly individualized, but they often involve comfort, security, and sexually arousing fantasies.

EXCITEMENT PHASE   The excitement phase is a physiological *reflex* mediated at the level of the spinal cord. It is usually initiated by direct stimuli such as physical contact with the genitals or other body parts. Other external stimuli—such as pleasing sights, sounds, or smells perceived by the brain—or even internal stimuli—such as the thought of an attractive person or sexual encounter—can cause impulses to be sent from the brain to the spinal cord, triggering the excitement reflex. These impulses are sent by the cortex via parasympathetic pathways, and, even though the parasympathetic nervous system is associated with relaxation in other organ systems (see Chapter 6), it produces arousal in the reproductive and sexual system.

There is a subjective awareness of increasing sexual pleasure. In males, the most obvious physiological change is penile erection. The testes also begin to elevate toward the base of the penis. In females, there is vasocongestion in the pelvis, the vagina lengthens and lubricates, and the clitoris and breasts swell. The excitement phase may be interrupted by exposure to noxious stimuli or by activation of the sympathetic nervous system (Masters & Johnson, 1966).

Individuals whose spinal cord is severed above the sacral plexus will still exhibit the physiological changes of the excitement phase in response to direct stimulation. However, in these individuals the excitement phase cannot be triggered by brain-mediated stimuli and the psychological experience of orgasm is attenuated (Whalen, 1977).

PLATEAU PHASE   If effective sexual stimulation continues, the plateau phase is entered. This phase is supported by continued parasympathetic nervous system activation, and it may vary in length depending on the intensity of sexual stimuli and the drive for culmination of sex. Some people can learn to prolong the plateau phase and may remain in it for long periods. If sexual stimuli or drive are inadequate or if the stimuli are withdrawn, the individual will not attain orgasm but will move to the resolution phase.

Physiological changes are not as dramatic as in the excitement phase. In males, the penis becomes somewhat more enlarged, and the testes become completely elevated and drawn toward the base of the penis. In females, vaginal lubrication reaches maximum, and there is extensive vasocongestion of the vagina. Also, the clitoris retracts from its normal overhanging position until it is almost unobservable.

ORGASM PHASE This is the briefest phase, lasting only seconds. For most people, if stimulation has continued to build during the plateau phase, orgasm is inevitable. It is triggered by a sudden activation of the sympathetic nervous system. Animal research has demonstrated that electrical stimulation of various cortical regions alone can cause such activation and ejaculation (Whalen, 1977).

As orgasm approaches, awareness focuses on the pelvic region, and there is a sense of impending release. Males experience a feeling of "ejaculatory inevitability," followed by involuntary contractions of the entire urethra and expulsive penile contractions at intervals of 0.8 seconds. The average duration of orgasm in males is about 25 seconds (Bohlen et al., 1980). Females experience a feeling of "suspension of tension," then the outer third of the vagina contracts involuntarily, also at intervals of 0.8 seconds. There is no known clitoral response during orgasm. There are other extragenital physiological responses in both sexes, which are generally related to sympathetic activation (for example, rapid breathing and heart rate).

RESOLUTION PHASE This is a period of reduced tension, usually characterized by a subjective sense of well-being and a general reduction of vasoconstriction. During the resolution phase, males enter the **refractory period** when no further sexual excitement or erection is possible. The refractory period varies in length; depending on the individual, it can last from several minutes to a day or so, and it tends to lengthen with age. As the resolution phase progresses, the penis becomes flaccid and the testes descend.

In contrast, many women are able to respond to sexual excitement again almost immediately. They may return to the plateau phase and attain orgasm with no refractory period. They are called "multiorgasmic." There have not been good representative samples taken, and estimates as to how many women are multiorgasmic vary widely from 10% to 30% (Clifford, 1978; Masters & Johnson, 1966) to up to 67% of heterosexual women (Wolfe, 1982) and 50% of lesbians (Masters & Johnson, 1979). It is possible that most women have the capacity; but, social learning and who one's partner is affect individual preference and expressiveness.

Men are not considered to be multiorgasmic, although there are sporadic accounts of heterosexual men who *may* be multiorgasmic (Knox, 1984; Robbins & Jensen, 1977). Apparently they have several orgasms but ejaculate only once, after which they do not experience orgasm again. Masters and Johnson (1979) found no multiorgasms among 100 gay men they studied.

DURATION OF CYCLE People vary widely in the length of time they spend in foreplay—the excitement phase of the sexual response cycle. However, there is much less variance in intercourse. Several studies have looked at the length of time from the beginning of intromission (penile insertion) to ejaculation. Two early studies reported that about three-fourths of American men who attempted to delay orgasm could not do so effectively, with 40% ejaculating in less than 5 minutes, 34% between 5 and 10 minutes, 17% in 15 to 20 minutes, and 9% in 30 minutes or more (Dickinson & Beam, 1931; Kinsey et al., 1948). So, the whole sexual response cycle may vary in length (primarily in the excitement and plateau phases), but male orgasm occurs within 5 minutes of insertion about half of the time.

NEUROENDOCRINE REGULATION OF SEXUAL BEHAVIOR

Human and animal research suggests that the nervous and endocrine systems work together to control sexual behavior. A landmark study with cats has supported Masters and Johnson's data about the importance of the autonomic nervous system and the balance of parasympathetic-sympathetic impulses involved in erection, emission, and ejaculation (Seamans & Langworthy, 1938). Also, lesions in the brains of animals, primarily rats, can result in changes in sexual activity (Whalen, 1977). Lesions in the hypothalamus, depending on location, result in either the reduction of sex drive in male and female rats or increased ejaculation frequency and reduced refractory period in male rats.

Electrical stimulation of the hypothalamus causes an impressive increase of sexual activity in male rats. Normally, male rats can ejaculate no more than 8 times in 4 hrs; however, in 3 hrs and 40 mins one electrically stimulated rat achieved 174 mounts without insertion and 81 with insertion, 45 of these with ejaculation (Vaughn & Fisher, 1962).

Research with human subjects has found similar but not as dramatic results, suggesting that the hypothalamus, in response to other cortical inputs, mediates the sexual response cycle in human beings. Stimulation in a region of the temporal lobes near the hypothalamus causes subjects to report feelings of erotic pleasure and even orgasm-like experiences (Whalen, 1977). The hypothalamus controls homeostasis of the autonomic nervous system, which directs the sexual cycle through reflexes in the spinal cord. The excitement and early plateau phases are induced by parasympathetic impulses. Emission (the movement of semen in preparation for ejaculation) is dependent on an equilibrium of parasympathetic and sympathetic impulses, whereas ejaculation is the result of sympathetic impulses (Berkow & Fletcher, 1987). This autonomic process is easily disrupted by psychological influences on the hypothalamus.

Although nerve damage and vascular abnormalities may impair sexual function, they are rarely the cause of sexual dysfunction (Berkow & Fletcher, 1987; Masters & Johnson, 1970). Hormones, however, do regulate secondary sex characteristics, reproductive cycles, and sexual function. Communication between the cortex and hypothalamus is neuronal, whereas communication between the hypothalamus, pituitary, and gonads is hormonal (Marieb, 1989; Masters & Johnson, 1986; Whalen, 1977).

Hormones control the reproductive cycle and the production and maturation of oocytes and sperm. Hormones influence sex drive, but they do not control it (Masters & Johnson, 1986). Even though sex drive is influenced by the concentration of testosterone, estrogen, and progesterone, there are some cases where this is not evident and behavior belies the level of hormones (for example, a man with low testosterone or a woman with low estrogen levels can have normal sex drives and function). Hormones, then, provide only a background for sexual responsiveness and reproduction.

The sexual response cycle is under the direct control of the central nervous system; therefore, it is easily disrupted by psychological factors. Some of these factors include stress, worry, guilt, fear, religious and moral restrictions and inhibitions, or any stimulus that evokes the sympathetic nervous system ("fight or flight") during the excitement phase (Masters & Johnson, 1970). The brain, then, containing all of one's memories, experiences, likes and dislikes, is interposed on this otherwise reflexive process. The brain also responds to environmental and self-generated stimuli and can initiate the sexual excitement phase, without physical stimulation of the genitals, but presumably only if the autonomic nervous system is in a parasympathetic mode. The paradox is that sexual excitement occurs when one is sufficiently autonomically *relaxed.*

The state of the autonomic nervous system is the key to initiating sexual activity. If the appetitive conditions are conducive, and the ANS is in a *parasympathetic* mode, the excitement phase can occur reflexively when triggered either by a physical stimulus to the genitals *or* by mental stimuli such as memories or fantasy. However, in order to conclude sexual activity two additional conditions must be met: (a) there must be physical stimulation of the genital region, *and* (b) the CNS must trigger a shift of the ANS from the parasympathetic phase to the *sympathetic* phase.

It is the shift to a sympathetic phase that coincides with orgasm. Orgasm is not solely a reflex—it cannot occur just from physical stimulation of the genitals—because people whose spinal cords are severed (so the CNS is out of the circuit) do not have full orgasmic function. Also, orgasm is not solely under mental control and requires at least a minimal degree of physical stimulation of the genital region. Not a single one of Masters and Johnson's (1966) subjects was able to achieve an orgasm through fantasizing; all required some direct physical stimulation. Sexual function, therefore, reproductive function, depends on a combination of physical stimulation and mental readiness.

Masters and Johnson (1966, 1970) believed strongly that biopsychosocial factors combine to produce the human sexual response. They also concluded that, although the sexual response is instinctual, "molded and transmitted genetically . . . (it is) subject to both immediate and continued *learning* processes" (1966, p. 140; emphasis added). This recognizes the importance of conditioning in human sexual behavior. The role of conditioning is of primary importance in understanding sexual dysfunction, which Masters and Johnson spent the rest of their careers treating. Masters and Johnson's research also helped to dispel a number of myths about the human sexual response.

SEXUAL MYTHS

These myths were held by the general public, and even some physicians promoted them at one time. However, Masters and Johnson's data strongly contradict them.

CLITORAL VERSUS VAGINAL ORGASM

Since women who masturbate usually do so by touching the clitoris, Sigmund Freud reasoned that it must be an immature form of sexual stimulation compared to intercourse in which the penis stimulates the vagina (Gagnon, 1977). This pronouncement of Freud's was echoed by psychoanalysts for many years. Women who could not have an orgasm by stimulation of the vagina were told that they were sexually immature and that an orgasm by clitoral stimulation is a poor substitute.

Anatomy, however, contradicts Freud because the clitoris is richly supplied with sensory nerve endings, whereas the vagina is not (Ellis, 1961). What Freud did not know was that during intercourse, even when there is no attempt to stimulate the clitoris directly, it still receives indirect stimulation from thrusts of the penis. In fact, the clitoris is most receptive to direct stimulation *only* during the excitement phase. It becomes hypersensitive and, in order to reduce direct stimulation, it retracts in the plateau phase when orgasm nears. Continued direct stimulation of the clitoris is not preferred by most women at that time, and may be experienced as painful. Nevertheless, it is the continued *indirect* stimulation of the clitoris that initiates orgasm. The clitoris is women's primary organ of sexual *stimulation*, whereas the vagina is the primary organ of orgasmic *expression* (Masters & Johnson, 1966). This separation of the female's organs of stimulation and response differs from the male's anatomy, where the penis functions in both capacities.

ORGASM

Marriage manuals, women's magazines, and even some authorities used to assert that simultaneous orgasms were a mark of achievement, indicating superior sexual functioning and true compatibility. In fact, when partners attempt to synchronize their orgasms, they often become distracted and experience *less* sexual pleasure. Also, men and women have different orgasmic responses. Men can experience only one, whereas many women are capable of experiencing multiple orgasms. Masters and Johnson (1970) recommended that each person be responsible for the timing of his or her own orgasm, while mutually communicating what is wanted from the partner. Heterosexual couples should take into account that half of males reach orgasm within five minutes of intromission.

Knox (1984) has compiled data from a variety of sources about the percent of men and women experiencing orgasm in different conditions (see Table 13.1-1), and with the exception of masturbation, men and women differ greatly in these conditions. Men are far more likely to have experienced orgasm when dreaming, regularly during intercourse, and during their first intercourse experience. More women have never experienced an orgasm (which may be because these women never masturbated), while half of women who do experience orgasm have had multiple orgasms.

From these data we can conclude that men and women tend to experience orgasm differently under different conditions. This suggests that mutually satisfying sexual experiences may not be dependent on orgasm. One study of 42 couples found that they reported more sexual pleasure when orgasm did *not* occur (Waterman & Chiauzzi, 1982). In fact, given that so few women report orgasms during intercourse, sex therapists today consider that a woman is functioning normally if she can have an orgasm *in the presence of* a partner. This definition does not require intercourse or even the partner's help.

Therefore, although many people are preoccupied with orgasm, it is only one part of a sexual interaction, which may also include physical communications of affection, love, tenderness, and esteem. Nevertheless, these differences in men's and women's sexual experiences suggest the potential for misunderstanding that can contribute to sexual dysfunction in couples.

Table 13.1-1 **PERCENT OF WOMEN AND MEN EXPERIENCING ORGASM UNDER DIFFERENT CONDITIONS**

CONDITION	WOMEN (%)	MEN (%)
Masturbating	90	99
Dreaming	40	80
Regularly during intercourse	30	99
During first intercourse	10	99
Never experienced orgasm	5–10	1
Multiple orgasms	50	5

Pregnant women can enjoy sexual activity for the most part without harm to the fetus.

WOMEN'S SEXUALITY DURING MENSTRUATION AND PREGNANCY

Most women actually enjoy intercourse more during menstruation, especially during the second half of the period. Some men worry about continuing to have sex when a woman is pregnant. Yet, most women desire intercourse during pregnancy even up until they go into labor, although not always at the same frequency. They prefer about as frequent intercourse during the second trimester, however. There is little evidence that the woman or fetus are harmed by intercourse during the first six months of pregnancy. For women who have a history of spontaneous miscarriage, there is some danger during the early stages of pregnancy, and the opinion of an obstetrician-gynecologist should be sought in these cases.

PENIS SIZE

The belief that the size of a man's penis is related to either virility or the amount of enjoyment he can impart in sex is unfounded. There is only a weak correlation between the size of the penis when flaccid and when erect. Small, flaccid penises can double in size, whereas large penises may not enlarge as much. This leads to less variation among men in erect penis size. Nevertheless, size makes no difference in vaginal intercourse because the vagina is a potential space, which means it expands to fit the penis, so a large one receives and gives no more friction. However, psychologically, some men and women may perceive that a larger penis is more stimulating.

AGING AND SEX

Men and women who are in good general health typically continue to enjoy sex years beyond age 60. If regular levels of sexual activity are consistently maintained and there is no physical problem that intervenes, men have continued to remain sexually active into their 80s. The same may be said of women into their 70s, except that the scarcity of men tends to have the effect of decreasing women's sexual activity as they age. The sexual habits and interests of older adults tend to parallel those established when they were younger, but there is a general decrease in sexual activity and frequency (Masters & Johnson, 1981).

FIRST SEX WITH PARTNER

It is generally agreed by researchers that the overwhelming majority of American teenagers have had intercourse by the time they are 19 years of age. One study asked relatively equal numbers of young African American and European American men, aged 15 to 19, and women, aged 17 to 21, what was the context of the relationship within which they had their first sexual experience with a partner (Table 13.1-2; Zelnik & Shah, 1983). Very few young people in this

Table 13.1-2	RELATIONSHIP CONTEXT FOR YOUNG MEN'S AND WOMEN'S FIRST SEXUAL PARTNER	

RELATIONSHIP	% OF WOMEN (*N* = 936)	% OF MEN (*N* = 670)
Recently met	4	9
Friends	7	34
Dating	24	20
Going steady	55	36
Engaged	9	1

Source: Zelnick, M., & Shah, F. K., 1983, First intercourse among young Americans, Family Planning Perspectives, *15, 64–70.*

sample waited to be engaged or married for their first experience, and women had about as much likelihood of having had sex premaritally as men.

The frequency of partners in the "recently met" category may have important health implications because there would be little awareness of the partner's sexual history and trustworthiness. Although small, this category was almost 10% for men. Also, since "dating" was separated from "going steady," perhaps some of the men and women whose first partner was in the "dating" category also did not have a well-established relationship with their partner on which to base trust. This suggests that perhaps a fourth of first-time sex may take place under conditions of minimal knowledge and heightened risk of sexually transmitted diseases.

SEXUAL FANTASY

Given the role of the brain in the human sexual response, it is reasonable to assume that fantasy may affect sexual behavior. In fact, 70% of women and 80% of men fantasize about sex (Kinsey et al., 1948; Kinsey et al., 1953). Fantasies also occur quite frequently *during* sex (Masters & Johnson, 1966), a fact that many people find embarrassing or troublesome in a committed relationship, but which research suggests is quite normal. College students report using fantasy to increase general sexual arousal or the attractiveness of their

Table 13.1-3   FANTASIES OF COLLEGE STUDENTS DURING SEX

THEME	WOMEN (%)	MEN (%)
Oral-genital sex	61	51
Others finding you sexually irresistible	55	53
An imaginary lover	44	24
A former lover	43	41
Others giving in after resisting you at first	37	24
Forcing others to have sexual relations with you	24	16
Being forced or overpowered into a sexual relationship	21	36
Group sex	19	14
Observing others engaging in sex	18	13
Others observing you engaging in sexual intercourse	15	20
Being rejected or sexually abused	11	13
A member of the same sex	3	9
Animals	1	4

Source: Adapted from Sue, D., 1979, Erotic fantasies of college students during coitus, Journal of Sex Research, 4, 299–305.

partner (Sue, 1979). The frequencies of various fantasy themes reported by students are listed in Table 13.1-3.

Kinsey believed that sexual fantasy and behavior are separate, a view that is supported by research suggesting that there is little or no relationship between people's fantasies and their behavior (Friday, 1980; Sue, 1979). In other words, people may have fantasies that they never act on. Some have suggested that sexual fantasies are unhealthy (for example, Offit, 1977), but research has failed to support that viewpoint, indicating that a positive relationship exists between fantasizing and sexual satisfaction (Zimmer, Bouchardt, & Fischle, 1983).

■

MODULE SUMMARY

This concludes this module on the human sexual response. Before continuing with the next module on sexual dysfunction, review these major points:

1. The findings of early researchers of human sexuality such as Alfred Kinsey caused much consternation in the American public.
2. Masters and Johnson were the first to report on laboratory studies of human sexuality. They described four phases of the human sexual response: excitement, plateau, orgasm, and resolution. Helen Kaplan later added the appetitive phase, which comes before the other four.
3. The appetitive phase precedes sexual excitement, is purely psychological, and represents the minimal conditions that must be met before a person feels comfortable with sex.
4. The excitement phase is a physiological reflex mediated at the level of the spinal cord that can be initiated by direct physical contact of the genitals or by purely mental stimulation. It brings about sexual arousal but requires that the ANS be in a parasympathetic phase. There is erection in the male and vaginal lubrication in the female.
5. The plateau phase is also largely parasympathetic, and physiological changes are less dramatic than in the excitement phase. It can vary in length, during which time the penis may become somewhat more enlarged and the testes become markedly elevated, while the clitoris retracts.
6. The orgasm phase is the briefest. It is initiated by a rapid switch of the ANS from the parasympathetic to the sympathetic state. This occurs under control of the cortex, but orgasm cannot be accomplished by the brain alone; it also requires direct physical stimulation of the genitals. Orgasm is marked by contractions of the prostate and urethra in men and the vagina in women. Half of men ejaculate within five minutes of penetration, while most women require more time.

7. The resolution phase is a period of reduced tension characterized by a subjective sense of well-being. Women may be multiorgasmic and return immediately to the plateau phase to experience additional orgasms, whereas men enter the refractory period, during which they cannot have another orgasm.

8. Hormones control the sexual and reproductive cycles. However, the brain and hypothalamus, through the autonomic nervous system, control the sexual response cycle.

9. The clitoris is women's primary organ of sexual stimulation; whereas, it is the vagina that contracts during orgasm. Direct stimulation of the clitoris is conducive to a sexual response primarily during the excitement phase but can be counterproductive during the late plateau and orgasm phases.

10. Each partner should be responsible for the timing of his or her own orgasm while mutually communicating what is wanted to the partner. Simultaneous orgasms can be distracting and limit sexual pleasure. Men and women vary greatly in the experience and conditions of orgasm. Almost all men have orgasm during intercourse, whereas half of women do not. Because of this, a woman is considered sexually healthy if she can have an orgasm in the presence of a partner. This does not require the partner's participation.

11. Women are usually sexually receptive during pregnancy and there is little evidence of any harm from it.

12. Penis size is unrelated to either virility or satisfaction of a partner, except in a psychological sense. Differences in penis size are not as variable during erection as in the flaccid state.

13. Aging does reduce sexual activity and frequency somewhat, but sexual function can continue until late in life in those who are in good health and remain active.

14. The overwhelming majority of people fantasize about sex, many while they are with a partner. Fantasies vary widely, and Kinsey first proposed that fantasy is not the same as behavior.

SEXUAL DYSFUNCTION

The psychologist that Maria and Steve were referred to began by trying to understand their current sexual functioning and discovered that not only was Maria having painful intercourse, but also recently, when she was receptive to Steve's sexual overtures, he could not maintain an erection. This upset Steve a great deal, but Maria had to admit that she was relieved. The psychologist also learned that Steve and Maria were arguing a lot, something they had never done before and a sign that their sexual dysfunction was beginning to affect their relationship.

Sexual dysfunctions are among the most troubling interpersonal problems an otherwise healthy person can encounter. They can be a source of anxiety, guilt, and frustration. They can contribute to low self-esteem and concerns about one's ability to relate to and to please another person. They may also interfere with reproductive abilities as they did with Steve and Maria. Ultimately, they may isolate a person from intimate relationships, resulting in the loss of social support, which is important in overall physical and psychological health.

Sexual dysfunction is used to describe "inhibition in the appetitive or psychophysiologic changes that characterize the complete sexual response cycle" (APA, 1987, p. 290). Although there may be underlying physiological factors, the diagnosis is not made if the dysfunction is due entirely to a major medical illness such as prostate cancer, cervical cancer, or diabetes.

Just as they had been among the first to research the human sexual response, Masters and Johnson (1970) also conducted one of the first and most comprehensive studies of sexual dysfunction and treatment. There were 790 sexually dysfunctional subjects in the study. Two hundred eighty-seven were from married couples in which 1 partner had a problem and 446 were from married couples in which both partners had a problem for a total of 733 people with sexual dysfunctions. The remaining 57 subjects were 54 single men and 3 single women who were treated with partner surrogates. The subjects were middle-class, with above average income, and 73% had attended college. They had been referred to the Reproductive Biology Research Foundation's

Institute in St. Louis by physicians or other therapists. Because they had to travel to St. Louis for treatment, the subjects were highly self-motivated. Approximately ½ had received prior therapy for their problem.

Again, Masters and Johnson's research has some important limitations. These subjects were not representative of the population at large, but even more importantly, there was no comparison to a nontreatment or placebo group. Since the study of sexual *response* is descriptive research, there is no need for a comparison group, as long as we recognize that what is described may only hold for people who are similar to the sample. The same is true for the *descriptions* of the sexual dysfunctions here. However, when data are given for the *effectiveness* of treatment, it is necessary to realize that interpretation is severely hampered by the lack of an appropriate comparison group.

CAUSES OF DYSFUNCTION

Masters and Johnson (1970) categorized the causes of sexual dysfunction as *current* and *historical*, but there is not such a clear distinction in practice. They were trying to emphasize that current causes develop from past problems, but keep in mind that past problems could also be current problems.

CURRENT CAUSES

Masters and Johnson describe two current, interactive causes of sexual dysfunction: "fear of performance" and the "spectator role." **Fear of performance** is anxiety about one's ability to perform sexually. "Perform" is crucial, because it captures the sense of effort involved in the action and the feeling that one must give a performance just as an actor does. That is the way people with sexual dysfunctions describe their feelings about sexual behavior, and it distances them psychologically from what is otherwise a partly reflexive response.

Fear of performance is "the greatest known deterrent to effective sexual functioning, simply because it so completely distracts the fearful individual from his or her natural responsivity by blocking reception of sexual stimuli . . ." (Masters & Johnson, 1970, p. 12–13). From a biopsychosocial perspective, what happens is that sexual performance is cognitively appraised as a threat, which activates the sympathetic nervous system and disrupts the delicate parasympathetic-sympathetic balance required for the complete sexual response cycle.

Gradually, fear of performance causes the adoption of the **spectator role**. In this role, the person becomes acutely sensitive to how she or he is doing— preoccupied with self-evaluation and self-judgment. This further blocks the person from "egoless" participation in the kind of abandonment and "loss of self" that people often describe happening during fulfilling sex. Instead, the person in the spectator role becomes an observer and critic of his or her own responses, no longer able to freely accept the give and take of sexual activity. Becoming the focus of one's own attention further inhibits the natural response, contributing to increased fear of performance. Fear of performance and the spectator role are the current but not the primary cause of sexual dysfunction.

HISTORICAL CAUSES

The historical causes may be categorized as physiological or psychosocial.

PHYSIOLOGICAL   Masters and Johnson (1970) considered a number of physiological problems as historical causes of sexual dysfunction. Although this category initially included major medical illnesses, today it is used for minor physiological problems only (APA, 1987). Some examples are infections of the penis or vagina, incisions made in the vagina during childbirth, metabolic disturbances, trauma to genital nerves or blood vessels, or menopause when it reduces vaginal lubrication. Most of these are readily ruled out by a medical history and examination. When they are ruled out, then psychological antecedents are assumed to be the cause of the dysfunction.

PSYCHOSOCIAL   Masters and Johnson (1970) described a number of possible psychosocial causes of sexual dysfunction (see Box 13.2-1). Research suggests that these are far more common than physiological causes of sexual dysfunction.

Maria and Steve were both developing fear of performance, and the psychologist was able to determine that religious orthodoxy and sociocultural factors played a role as historical causes of the current problem. Maria had associated guilt with sex from early religious training, but this was not the primary problem. She also characterized her upbringing as one that discouraged women from experiencing their sexuality. In particular, she was raised in a Hispanic culture where her father was the dominant figure in the family. She was his favorite, and they were very close until adolescence, when she began to mature physically. Then her father grew more distant. Maria knew that her father felt he had lost his little girl when she married Steve. She also felt that when she had her own children, her father would never think of her as his little girl again.

Box 13.2-1 PSYCHOSOCIAL ANTECEDENTS OF SEXUAL DYSFUNCTION AS DESCRIBED BY MASTERS AND JOHNSON

Alcohol and Drugs   Masters and Johnson primarily focused on the role of excessive alcohol intake, which lowers sexual inhibitions while it interferes with erections. However, many other drugs, both licit and illicit, are known to interfere with the sexual response cycle in men and women. Any substance that affects the autonomic nervous system may upset the balance necessary for the cycle to occur. Necessary medications such as antidepressants or antihypertensives are well known for disrupting the sexual response cycle. So, too, is cocaine, which inflates one's belief in one's sexual prowess while reducing one's ability to function sexually.

Homosexual Inclinations/Fears   Masters and Johnson suggested that being homosexually inclined and trying to function heterosexually could cause sexual dysfunction (this would not include bisexuals, who by definition are sexually functional with either sex). People in this situation may have been more common at the time Masters and Johnson did their initial studies. Today, it is also reasonable to consider the role of homophobia (Weinberg, 1972) as a potential cause of sexual dysfunction, such that a person with a heterosexual inclination (or even a homosexual one) might fear the slightest thoughts or fantasies of homosexuality in him or herself and become dysfunctional.

Inaccurate Counseling   Before Masters and Johnson's research, very little accurate information was known about the human sexual response, which is evident in the myths described in Module 13.1, page 582. Therefore, physicians and other professionals gave poor advice. There is still bad advice given on the basis of poor research (for example, "The Hite Report" by Hite, 1976; "The G-spot" by Hock, 1983).

Psychosexual Trauma   This is an important, if sometimes overlooked, cause of sexual dysfunction. Such traumas may result from physical assault, such as rape, or a humiliating and embarrassing experience. For example, when a married woman is raped, both she *and* her husband are at risk for sexual dysfunction.

Religious Orthodoxy   This dysfunction occurs when one or both partners has negative attitudes, guilt, and anxiety about sex because they were brought up with strict religious beliefs. If people have the "fear of God" instilled in them from an early age, even though they may be in a sanctified union, it is sometimes difficult for them to overcome their fear and guilt about sex.

Sociocultural Background   Like religious orthodoxy, nonreligious beliefs about sex shared by the culture at large can also be a source of dysfunction. These are believed to affect women more than men, because our society has tended to tolerate or even encourage men's sexual expressiveness, while discouraging women's sexual expressiveness. Masters and Johnson believed that American culture discouraged women from their full genetically assigned role, which involves physiologically intense sexual arousal and multiple orgasms, thereby contributing a large part to women's sexual dysfunctions.

Although slightly guilty about it, Maria was fully sexually functional until the couple decided to try to have children. At that point, she felt that she would be signifying her mature womanhood and "putting a knife in" her father. She could not be his little girl if she had children of her own. This feeling combined with her religious guilt about sex to interfere with her enjoyment of intercourse and reproduction. As she became aware of this change in her feelings, she became anxious. Her anxiety developed into fear of performance and put her in the spectator role during sex.

In the meantime, Steve had thought that Maria was losing interest in him, that she no longer found him attractive. He started to worry about that and began to have trouble maintaining an erection. Until the interview with the psychologist, Steve knew nothing about his wife's concerns, but he was anxious that he had a sexual problem that would make him even less attractive to her. Steve was on the way to developing fear of performance, too. Maria and Steve's sexual dysfunction demonstrates the interdependence of sexual functioning in a couple and the effects of psychosocial factors on a largely physiological function.

THEORIES OF SEXUAL DYSFUNCTION

Before Masters and Johnson's formulation of historical and current causes of sexual dysfunction, psychodynamic theorists like Sigmund Freud traced them to repressed conflicts. The sexual dysfunction itself was viewed as merely a symbolic symptom of the conflict, and the dysfunctional behavior was seen to have a functional role. For example, a man who ejaculates too quickly would be explained as acting out repressed hostility toward his mother with other women. Freud considered that his entire theory was psychosexual, but ironically, psychoanalysis has reported few successful treatments of sexual dysfunction. Today, even psychoanalysts use behavioral techniques to assist in their work with sexually dysfunctional people (LoPiccolo, 1977).

Masters and Johnson's own theoretical position is primarily behavioral. They view the human sexual response cycle as a natural reflexive process that is, nevertheless, vulnerable to disruption by experience and conditioning. Anxiety, humiliation, and fear can disrupt the sexual response cycle. If, by avoiding sexual relationships, a person's anxiety, humiliation, and fear are decreased, then he or she may begin to avoid sexual behavior and even intimate relationships through escape or avoidance conditioning. Maria's avoidance of intercourse and relief when Steve had difficulty maintaining an erection is an example of escape/avoidance conditioning, but fortunately, the couple received help before it took hold. Also, Steve's own anxiety began to interfere with his ability to maintain an erection, so escape/avoidance conditioning could also have begun to affect him.

Although Masters and Johnson's conceptualization remains the most widely accepted, other theorists have contributed refinements. Some emphasize cognitive factors by focusing on the role of irrational thinking in sexual dysfunctions (Ellis, 1971). Consistent with this cognitive emphasis, research has revealed that people with sexual dysfunction often lack knowledge and skill (LoPiccolo & Hogan, 1979). Cognitive-behavioral treatments use sexual education, skill training, and cognitive restructuring to treat fear of performance.

The role of anxiety has also been a subject for conjecture. Kaplan (1974) believes that a person who wants to please his or her partner *too* much can become anxious and develop fear of performance. However, the entire role of anxiety in the sexual response cycle has also come under scrutiny. Early research first suggested that anxiety may actually *increase* rather than block genital arousal (Barlow, Sakheim, & Beck, 1983; Hoon, Wincze, & Hoon, 1977), contradicting Masters and Johnson's hypothesis. However, it appears that this holds only for well-functioning people, because later research indicates that anxiety decreases arousal in people with sexual dysfunctions (Beck, Barlow, Sackheim, & Abramson, 1984).

One difficulty researchers have is how to determine the specific phase in the response cycle as it relates to autonomic nervous system functioning. Earlier in the excitement phase anxiety should decrease arousal, but in the later phases it should facilitate orgasm by sympathetic activation. This demonstrates that the human sexual response is not as neatly divided into phases as it seems, but rather the phases blend together.

■■■

DESCRIPTION OF SEXUAL DYSFUNCTIONS

Four general categories of sexual dysfunction affect men and women: desire, arousal, orgasm, and pain (APA, 1987). Dysfunction may be evident during sex with a partner or during masturbation, and there is no reference to whether the partner is of the same sex or the opposite sex. The same categories have, in fact, been found to be relevant for diagnosing sexual dysfunction in gay men (Paff, 1985).

Many authorities believe that the symptoms of most of these dysfunctions are very common but transitory. Almost everyone will experience problems with sexual desire or arousal on some occasions. Therefore, in order for a diagnosis of sexual dysfunction to be made, it must be *recurrent* and *persistent* (APA, 1987).

DESIRE DISORDERS

Desire disorders affect the appetitive and the early sexual excitement phases, and they are the same in both sexes. They include two categories: (a) **hypoactive sexual desire disorder**, which occurs when a person has few or no sexual fantasies and/or urges, although he or she may still engage in sexual behavior; and (b) **sexual aversion disorder**, in which a person avoids sexual activity entirely. Chronic desire disorders are believed to be related to traumatic events occurring in childhood or adolescence, active suppression of sexual fantasies, or low levels of testosterone. Psychoactive and antihypertensive medication and hormonal deficiencies can also cause decreased desire, but it more often results from boredom in a relationship and depression (Berkow & Fletcher, 1987), and it develops in relationships that are characterized by anger, distrust, poor communication, and power struggles (Stuart, Hammond, & Pett, 1987). When boredom is the cause, there will be a loss of interest in one's sexual partner, but sexual desire remains normal with others. In contrast, depression usually affects general, not just sexual, desire. It is estimated that about 20% of the adult population has hypoactive sexual desire disorder (APA, 1987), which may just be one end of the normal distribution. How much desire should a person have? Unfortunately, there is little research. Interestingly, there is no corresponding category of *hyper*active sexual desire disorder (although there are categories for hyperactive sexual *behavior*).

AROUSAL DISORDERS

Arousal disorders affect the excitement phase and are different in men and women. **Female sexual arousal disorder**, which used to be called "frigidity," occurs when a woman has an inadequate vaginal lubrication-swelling response (resulting in discomfort during intercourse) or when there is a lack of the subjective sense of pleasure and excitement during sex.

Maria was beginning to develop female sexual arousal disorder. She was having difficulty maintaining a sense of pleasure and excitement, at first due to historical causes but then due to fear of performance. As the mood became conducive to sex, she became anxious and could not remain relaxed, in a parasympathetic state. This probably led to inadequate vaginal lubrication and discomfort when intercourse was attempted, which caused her to believe that there was something physically wrong with her. Because she had been sexually functional with Steve before, Maria's situation is acute rather than chronic.

Chronic female sexual arousal disorder may result from sexual ignorance (of the genital anatomy, particularly of the different roles of the clitoris and vagina), the association of sex with sin and guilt, or fear of intimacy (Berkow & Fletcher, 1987; Masters & Johnson, 1970). This makes it difficult for the woman to communicate her needs to a partner in order to increase her sexual satisfaction. Many physical conditions (for example, endometriosis, vaginitis, diabetes, multiple sclerosis, and medications such as oral contraceptives, anti-hypertensives, and tranquilizers) can cause this disorder; however, the over-whelming majority of cases are caused by marital discord, inadequate stimulation by the partner, depression, and stress.

Male erectile disorder, which used to be called "impotence," is the inability to attain or sustain an erection through to completion of the sexual activity or when there is a lack of the subjective sense of pleasure and excite-ment during sex. Kaplan (1974) described a variety of manifestations of erec-tile dysfunction (for example, normal erection lost on penetration, erection during oral-genital sex but not during intercourse).

Men, because of their genital anatomy, have a particularly difficult role in sex. The fact that their primary physiological response, erection, is obvious may make men more prone to develop the spectator role and fear of perfor-mance. Erectile dysfunction is almost always due to psychosocial factors (Berkow & Fletcher, 1987; Masters & Johnson, 1970; Rosen & Rosen, 1981). This is usually easy to determine, for if there is an erection under any other cir-cumstances (for example, while masturbating or sleeping), then the physio-logical mechanism for erection is intact, and the cause must be psychogenic.

It is normal for many men to have situational erectile dysfunction, in which they have a problem with a certain partner, in a particular place, or at a certain time. That is why erectile dysfunction is only diagnosed when it occurs *across* partners or situations. As Steve began to worry that Maria might be los-ing her attraction to him, he was starting to develop situational male erectile disorder.

In the adult male population, about 7% of men report difficulty obtaining any erection at all, and 9% report difficulty maintaining one (Mohr & Beutler, 1990). When the problem is chronic, it is usually due to sexual guilt or fear of intimacy. When it is acute, it is usually the result of anxiety or stress. In Steve's case, it was caused by anxiety that Maria was losing interest in him. Recent research suggests that in half of all cases, an underlying physical con-dition such as diabetes (the most common cause), syphilis, alcoholism, multi-ple sclerosis, antihypertensives, sedatives, or amphetamines may play a role, although they are usually not the primary cause (Mohr & Beutler, 1990).

ORGASM DISORDERS

Males are subject to two types of orgasm disorders. In **premature ejaculation**, ejaculation occurs with minimal stimulation *and* before the person wishes it.

Ejaculation may occur before, upon, or immediately after penetration. Recall that half of men ejaculate within five minutes of penetration, which is usually less time than it takes a woman to achieve orgasm. Therefore, in order to satisfy a woman, men must learn how to delay penetration and ejaculation.

Whether or not ejaculation is premature depends on a variety of factors: age, novelty of the sexual partner or situation, amount of stimulation, and frequency of sexual activity may all influence it. Also, one's own and one's partner's expectations about how long it "should" take to ejaculate influence the judgment of "premature." This is the most common sexual dysfunction for men and is estimated to affect 30% (APA, 1987). Perhaps that is because so many factors, some of them subjective, influence it.

Anxiety is almost always associated with premature ejaculation (Masters & Johnson, 1970). It is fairly common in adolescent males who are just learning how to function sexually and may be associated with guilt about sex, fear of discovery, fear of sexually transmitted diseases, or fear of performance (Berkow & Fletcher, 1987). These same factors may also cause premature ejaculation in adults.

Inhibited male orgasm is a rare phenomenon in which there is a delay or absence of orgasm following a normal and adequate excitement phase. When it occurs it is usually in connection with vaginal intercourse, and orgasm remains possible under other conditions such as masturbation. Aging may retard orgasm and must be taken into account. There are a few physical conditions that can inhibit male orgasm, such as diabetes, antihypertensive medication, and some tranquilizers; however, psychogenic causes are presumed to predominate.

Inhibited female orgasm is more common. Again, there must be delay or absence of orgasm following a normal and adequate excitement phase. Some women are only able to experience orgasm during direct clitoral stimulation and not (indirectly) during intercourse. This is considered a normal variation of the female sexual response and is not usually diagnosed as inhibited female orgasm. However, if there is reason to suspect that it is occurring as a result of psychogenic and not biologic factors, the diagnosis is made.

About 20% of adult women report that they rarely experience orgasm (Kinsey et al., 1953), and about 10% of women do not experience orgasm at all through any source of stimulation (Berkow & Fletcher, 1987). This latter group, who have never experienced orgasm, are referred to as "**anorgasmic.**" Some sex therapists do not consider anorgasmia a disorder at all, because such women are sexually responsive and have all of the other phases of the sexual response cycle—they lack only the physiological response of orgasm (Kaplan, 1974). Interestingly, women who have less masturbatory experience are more likely to be anorgasmic, suggesting that masturbation may help some women learn how to be orgasmic (Kinsey et al., 1953; Hoon & Hoon, 1978).

Inhibited female orgasm is an appropriate diagnosis only when a woman has been orgasmic. Most inhibited female orgasm is attributed to psychosocial factors such as guilt or fear of letting go or of losing control. Sometimes lack of knowledge on the part of the woman or her partner may also be involved. Finally, inhibited female orgasm may be the result of conditioning by the let-down of prior sexual experiences that were terminated before the woman's own orgasm. This also demonstrates the interpersonal context in which sexual dysfunction develops.

PAIN DISORDERS

Vaginismus is an involuntary spasm of the muscles of the outer third of the vagina, making penetration difficult and interfering with intercourse. It is assumed to be a conditioned response caused by past experience with painful intercourse or a psychosexual trauma like rape. Infections may make pain more likely and thus contribute to its development.

Finally, **dyspareunia** is any genital pain in men or women occurring before, during, or after intercourse. It may be the result of infection or exacerbated by it. It may also be caused by anatomical abnormalities.

INCIDENCE

The incidence of the various categories of sexual dysfunction is difficult to determine. One survey of 289 members of the American Association of Sex Educators, Counselors, and Therapists reported that desire disorders are the most common problems encountered in therapy, supporting Kaplan's (1974) inclusion of this category as a preliminary phase in the sexual response cycle (Kilmann et al., 1986). The least common problems encountered are vaginismus, inhibited male orgasm, and male erectile disorder (when erection could not be attained at all).

INTERPERSONAL CONTEXT

Although it does not appear so from the descriptions of the sexual dysfunctions, there is a major emphasis on the *interpersonal* context within which they occur. Often, when one partner is experiencing a sexual dysfunction, the other is, too, as we saw with Maria and Steve. Sometimes a dysfunction in one partner leads to the development of one in the other. For example, sometimes vaginismus develops in a wife when her husband has erectile dysfunction (Masters & Johnson, 1970), and nonorgasmic women are often found to be married to husbands who are not skilled at or understanding about sex (Kaplan, 1974; LoPiccolo, 1977). Even if only one partner has a dysfunction, there will often be distress in the relationship for both.

PREVENTION OF SEXUAL DYSFUNCTIONS

Since underlying physical factors are rarely the cause of sexual dysfunction, prevention should focus on the psychosocial factors. Many people are unaware of the delicate neuroendocrine and autonomic balance that is necessary for the human sexual response and, in particular, the role of the brain and one's psychological state. Also, many people with sexual dysfunctions are ignorant of sexual anatomy and function. Therefore, sex education would seem to be a necessary preventive focus.

Sex education has been defined as more than just "naming the parts" and a few moral pronouncements. Instead, it is necessary to discuss the biopsychosocial and interpersonal aspects of sex, the meaning of being a man or woman, and the need to take responsibility for one's sexuality (Schiller, 1980). In the absence of good sex education, people can still learn on their own by visiting a public library where several good resources on human sexuality and reproduction are usually found: Masters, Johnson, and Kolodny's (1986) *Masters and Johnson on Sex and Human Loving*, and for men, Zilbergeld's (1979) *Male Sexuality*.

TREATMENT OF SEXUAL DYSFUNCTION

MASTERS AND JOHNSON'S TREATMENT

Most sex therapy uses a comprehensive treatment approach that includes as its centerpiece Masters and Johnson's (1970) original behavioral techniques. They preferred to treat people in couples, and most of their early treatment was with married partners. However, they also provided treatment for gay and lesbian couples and researched the use of sexual surrogates for single people, reporting equally good results. Other research also supported the use of sexual surrogates (Sommers, 1980); however, Masters and Johnson abandoned their use because of the possibility of legal problems and the tendency for surrogates to fall in love with higher-status clients. Today, sexual surrogates are rarely used in sex therapy.

Masters and Johnson began by using a formal, two-week intensive treatment program requiring residence near their clinic (Kolodny, Masters, & Johnson, 1979). Although different techniques are employed for each of the disorders, there is a uniform general procedure.

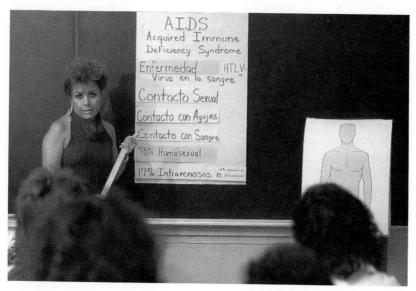

Sex education class

The first day consists of an interview, a detailed sexual history, and a physical examination to rule out underlying physiological problems. On the second day, there is an open discussion during which the therapists present the diagnosis, prognosis, and an outline of the treatment plan.

In most situations, treatment begins with sensate focus exercises, which are first described by the therapists and then carried out in private by the couple. **Sensate focus** was developed by Masters and Johnson to encourage mutual exploration and discovery of one's total physical (not just sexual) responsiveness in a relaxed situation. It uses touch, massage, and fondling. Specific rules are given: (a) both partners are nude; (b) there can be no intercourse, no touching of genitals, and a male may not touch a female's breasts; (c) partners take turns (approximately 20 minutes) touching and massaging each other; and (d) the partner being touched is to pay attention to pleasurable feelings and communicate whether something is pleasurable or not.

Sensate focus decreases anxiety about intimate physical contact. It is actually systematic desensitization (see Module 2.2, page 50), and it reduces fear of performance (since none is allowed) and removes one from the spectator role (since the partner receiving the sensate focus must attend to his or her own sensations, not responses).

Although sensate focus continues, after the third day treatment becomes individualized depending on the person and the problem, but the techniques used are largely behavioral. For example, treatment of premature ejaculation begins with the use of the "squeeze technique." It involves slightly aversive counterconditioning by squeezing the penis in a particular manner that causes the male to lose the urge to ejaculate and sometimes up to 30% of full erection.

Another example of Master and Johnson's behavioral approach is the treatment of vaginismus. It first involves anatomical education and a demonstration of the involuntary vaginal muscle reflex to both partners. Therapy consists of systematic desensitization, employing a series of dilators in graduated sizes used by the partner under the woman's guidance. The treatments for premature ejaculation and vaginismus involve more steps that are too involved to describe here, but their behavioral basis should be evident.

EFFECTIVENESS

In their initial study, described at the beginning of this module, Masters and Johnson reported overall success rates on completion of treatment of 83% for men and 81% for women (Masters & Johnson, 1970). They also followed 215 of the married couples for 6 years and reported that treatment was still successful for 72% of them at the end of this period. However, remember that Masters and Johnson had no comparison group, so it is impossible to know how many people would have improved on their own without treatment.

However, studies by other researchers have used adequate comparison groups and have tended to support Masters and Johnson's treatment results. These studies have demonstrated that combined cognitive-behavioral therapy is one of the most successful approaches in treating sexual dysfunctions (Heiman & LoPiccolo, 1983; Matthews, Bancroft et al., 1983; Nunes & Bandeira, 1980; Obler, 1973; Schumacher, 1977).

Nevertheless, sex therapy is not uniformly effective. On 5-year follow-up, Masters and Johnson (1970) reported that 93% of premature ejaculation cases and 82% of inhibited male orgasm cases were successfully treated, compared to only 69% of male erectile disorder after insertion and only 59% of male erectile disorder insufficient to establish insertion. For women on 5-year follow-up, 82% of those with anorgasmia and 75% of women who were situationally nonorgasmic were successfully treated. Therapists report that the highest success rates are obtained for premature ejaculation, which is consistent with Masters and Johnson's early findings, and for inhibited orgasm (excluding anorgasmia) and desire disorders (Kilmann et al., 1986).

More recent studies of the effectiveness of sex therapy have a slightly lower rate of success than these early reports. For example, a recent review of therapy for erectile disorder found that two-thirds were satisfied with their improvement up to six years after treatment (Mohr & Beutler, 1990). The lower success rates in recent studies could be due to the fact that Masters and Johnson's subjects were self-selected and highly motivated. Recent studies have also continued to show a differential rate of success, depending on the dysfunction, but generally are consistent with the different rates obtained by Masters and Johnson.

MODIFICATIONS OF TREATMENT

Many professionals who treat sexual dysfunctions today have modified some of the features of Masters and Johnson's original procedure. For example, they do not use the dual-sex teams that Masters and Johnson thought were necessary for the comfort of men and women patients (for example, Zilbergeld & Evans, 1980) and some have adapted the techniques for group therapy. Almost all have dropped Masters and Johnson's intensive residential 2-week format in favor of nonresidential, weekly sessions in a therapist's office. Treatment is still brief, however, lasting only about 10 to 12 sessions.

A review of research suggests that sex therapy is equally successful regardless of whether a single or dual-sex team is used, or the gender of the therapist, or the format of the treatment (intensive residential versus weekly; Libman, Fichten, Brender, 1985). There is, however, some variability in treatment effectiveness due to who the person is, what the problem is, and the specific treatment approach used (Springer, 1981). Some individuals who do not respond to the brief behavioral approach may have severe psychopathology (Kaplan, 1979). In other cases, a couple may have other fundamental relationship problems such as incompatibility of interests, lack of affection, and frequent arguments, which make treatment much less effective (Whitehead & Mathews, 1986). For the more troubled individuals and couples, a combination of psychodynamic and behavioral therapy has been suggested (Obler, 1982).

Maria and Steve's psychologist used a modification of Masters and Johnson's treatment. Two sessions were devoted to history taking and exploration of the couple's problems. The diagnoses and their historical and current causes were explained to the couple at the third session. Both Maria and Steve were knowledgeable about sexual anatomy and function, so the education aspect of treatment was brief.

The psychologist then explained the sensate focus exercises, and the couple was assigned to do them three times between the fourth and fifth sessions. At the fifth session, the couple discussed their experiences during the sensate focus exercises, which were then modified to allow genital pleasuring but not intercourse. The process was repeated, and by the seventh session, the couple were engaging in pleasurable intercourse. The couple continued for three more sessions, during which they explored and renewed their feelings about having children. Maria also discussed and clarified her feelings about her father and decided to try to open communication with him.

Although this example of treatment is brief, the result is not extraordinary. Therapy for sexual dysfunction is considered to be one of the most successful of psychological interventions. Couples with long-standing problems usually have a poorer prognosis, but Maria and Steve's problem was dealt with early, before it could become entrenched. As a monogamous couple, Maria and Steve are fortunate because today people who are sexually active face another serious health problem—sexually transmitted diseases.

SEXUALLY TRANSMITTED DISEASES

Sexually transmitted diseases (STDs), also called venereal diseases, are among the most persistent health problems in the United States. STDs are infectious diseases but are not spread by "casual contact," which means that they cannot be transmitted to another by nonintimate touch or breathing the same air. They are spread primarily by intimate sexual contact. STDs are among the most common communicable diseases in the world. In the United States, bacterial STDs such as gonorrhea, syphilis, and chlamydia were the most common until recently, but now viral STDs like genital herpes and AIDS (see Module 10.3) are beginning to cause more concern (see Box 13.2-2).

PREVENTION AND THE ROLE OF HEALTH PSYCHOLOGISTS

Despite medical advances that can readily detect and often cure STDs or render them noninfectious, their incidence has risen dramatically, especially from the 1950s to 1970s (Berkow & Fletcher, 1987). Medical control of STDs consists of early diagnosis and treatment and "partner tracing."

Partner tracing is an active public health approach to secondary intervention. It is mandated by many states and counties and is usually under the jurisdiction of public departments of health. When an STD is "reportable" under the law (typically, this includes only gonorrhea and syphilis), physicians must inform health officials whenever a patient is treated. Health officials contact patients and encourage them to reveal the names and addresses of all of their recent sexual partners. Health officials then contact the sexual partners, inform them that they have been exposed, and ask them to come in for free testing or to see their own doctor.

All of this is done confidentially, and the identity of treated patients who supply the names of sexual partners is not revealed. Nevertheless, partner tracing does compromise some of the most intimate aspects of personal privacy. It is deemed necessary because many people with STDs are asymptomatic or believe they are "cured" if symptoms go away on their own, yet they can still infect others.

Box 13.2-2   COMMON SEXUALLY TRANSMITTED DISEASES

Gonorrhea   Also known as "the clap."

Cause: Bacterium that invades the urethra, cervix, rectum, pharynx, or eyes, usually through sexual contact. About 3 million Americans are infected annually (Berkow & Fletcher, 1987).

Symptoms: Most common site of infection in males is the urethra. After an incubation period of 2 to 14 days, there is mild discomfort, with painful urination and a discharge of pus from the penis. If untreated, it may affect the entire male duct system and cause constriction of the urethra. Women commonly are infected vaginally, and symptoms begin after 7 to 21 days. They are usually mild, consisting of abdominal pain, vaginal discharge, and uterine bleeding, however in about 20% of cases the woman may be asymptomatic. Usually the cervix and deep reproductive sites are infected.

Health Consequences: If untreated, it can result in pelvic inflammatory disease and sterility. Occasionally, gonorrhea may spread throughout the body and cause infections of other organs such as the heart and brain.

Treatment: If caught early, gonorrhea is usually easily eliminated with penicillin or other antibiotics. Recently, due to the widespread incidence of the disease, the bacterium is becoming resistant to the standard treatment, and additional regimens are being used.

Syphilis

Cause: A bacterium that enters through mucous tissue or through cuts in the skin. It, too, is primarily spread by sexual contact, primarily genital-oral and genital-rectal, and sometimes kissing and close body contact, although it can also be transmitted from mother to child. There are about 400,000 new cases of syphilis in the United States annually (Berkow & Fletcher, 1987). This is about 20 cases per 100,000 population, which represents a dramatic increase, since the widespread use of penicillin had reduced the incidence to 4 cases per 100,000 between 1949 and 1980 (Cimons, 1991).

Symptoms: Within hours of infection, syphilis is found in the lymph system from which it spreads throughout the body. The incubation period is usually 3 to 4 weeks, but may last up to 13 weeks. The first sign of infection may be a red, painless ulcer called a *chancre* at the site of infection. In males, the chancre usually appears on the penis, but with women it usually occurs in the vagina or cervix, where it may go unnoticed. The chancre denotes the primary stage of syphilis.

Health Consequences: In contrast to gonorrhea, which usually affects specific sites, syphilis is a systemic disease, affecting many parts of the body. The *secondary stage* occurs within 6 to 12 weeks following the first stage. There is a pink generalized skin rash and many symptoms characteristic of mild influenza. There may be anemia, and the hair may fall out in clumps. People are most contagious during the primary and secondary stages. The symptoms usually go away on their own within 6 weeks. That is the start of the *latency period*, which begins about 1 year after infection, and there may be no further symptoms at all. More typically, the *tertiary stage* develops about 3 to 10 years after infection. During this stage large lesions can develop in any organ, most typically the brain, skin, and oral cavity, and death can occur.

Treatment: The treatment of choice is penicillin for all stages of syphilis, and prognosis is excellent. However, any damage to the body before treatment is permanent.

Urethritis and Chlamydia

Cause: Chlamydia was once lumped together with several other STDs that were referred to collectively as "nonspecific or nongonococcal urethritis or cervicitis." As the various antigens that cause urethritis or cervicitis (inflammation of the urethra or cervix) have been identified, the bacterium, chlamydia, was found to be responsible for most cases, although there are also other infectious agents sometimes involved. Although accurate rates are hard to come by, chlamydia is believed to be the most common STD, affecting perhaps 3 to 4 million Americans a year. About 1 in 5 men and 1 in 3 women who have gonorrhea also have chlamydia.

Symptoms: The incubation period is between 7 and 28 days. Chlamydia is sometimes called a "silent infection" because its symptoms are mild and often overlooked. Most women are asymptomatic, although occasionally there is a mild pain or burning sensation, vaginal discharge, and irregular menses. Men are more likely to notice the mild symptoms that include discomfort in the urethra, penile discharge, and dried secretions at the lips of the penis that are more evident in the morning.

Health Consequences: The most serious consequence of chlamydia in women is sterility, while the most serious consequences in men are pervasive urogenital infection and arthritis. Newborns can be infected in the birth canal, causing eye and respiratory tract infections. Occasionally, chlamydia can cause proctitis and pharyngitis through genital-oral and genital-rectal contact.

Treatment: Treatment, which is considered very effective, consists of penicillin injections or oral tetracycline. Unfortunately, because it can go completely unnoticed, chlamydia is easily spread and can result in serious consequences in those who are asymptomatic.

Genital Herpes

Cause: Herpes is the most common viral STD, although AIDS, which is much more serious, is increasing rapidly. Ninety-five percent of genital herpes is caused by the herpes simplex virus type 2, and 5% is caused by type 1 (the same virus that causes "cold sores" around the mouth). Herpes is spread by contact with another person, but only at the time the ulcers are present.

Symptoms: It causes painful, circular, reddened ulcers on the skin that usually heal in about 10 days. These "blisters" are more nuisance than health threat. The first sores usually develop 4 to 7 days after initial contact and are the most painful outbreak. They may occur anywhere on the penis, labia, clitoris, vagina, cervix, anus, or rectum. After healing, the virus continues to remain dormant in local sensory nerves from where it may cause periodic recurring ulcerations.

Health Consequences: Herpes is not usually a major health threat. However, there may be a relationship between herpes and cervical cancer. Very rarely, and usually only in immunosuppressed individuals, the herpes virus can affect the joints, liver, lungs, or brain.

Treatment: Unlike the bacterial STDs described above, there is no cure for genital herpes. However, an oral medication, *acyclovir,* can reduce the pain and duration of first-time lesions and reduce the frequency of recurrences. Research has suggested that there is a relationship between stress and the frequency of recurrent outbreaks of herpes, indicating that relaxation training and stress reduction techniques may be effective in reducing outbreaks after infection (Longo & Clum, 1989).

Unfortunately, the rising incidence of STDs indicates that partner tracing has not been successful, although it may have slowed the increase. There are many reasons for this. First, it is not implemented uniformly. Second, public health service budgets are limited. Third, in a society as mobile as ours, not all exposed sexual partners can be identified and contacted. Fourth, it is voluntary—people who are contacted cannot be forced to be tested or treated. Finally, many perceive it as an invasion of privacy, and it is embarrassing, which probably means that sexual contacts are underreported. So, despite effective medical treatment and partner tracing, STDs remain a major health problem.

Psychosocial factors also account for the fact that these treatable diseases remain a major health problem. Primary among them are changes in sexual behavior in the latter twentieth century. People are engaging in more frequent and varied sexual activity, which offers STDs a greater opportunity to spread. Also, medical improvements in contraception have eliminated one centuries-old restraint on sexual activity—unwanted pregnancy.

That is why advances in medical diagnosis and the effectiveness of treatment alone are not enough to eliminate STDs. There is hope for inducing immunity against infection, but this is not yet possible. Nor does it appear that partner tracing can eliminate STDs. Therefore, primary prevention has taken on more importance in the battle to control STDs. The advent of AIDS has contributed a deadly urgency to prevention efforts (see Module 10.3).

Prevention is a matter that health psychologists have been interested in for a long time. Just how people can be influenced to engage in healthier behaviors is currently a topic of major research interest by health psychologists (for example, Gochman, 1988). Changing health behavior involves large-scale public health efforts that have only been researched sporadically and with respect to a few health problems (see Module 3.2, page 90).

There is also little research on prevention of STDs. It is known that sex between healthy partners and within a monogamous relationship is considered safest. After that, condoms do help prevent the spread of most STDs by presenting a barrier to bacteria or viruses, but condoms are not a complete solution (Berkow & Fletcher, 1987). First, they are not always effective. On very rare occasions they break, and although latex condoms are considered the strongest, they degenerate when exposed to oil-based lubricants, causing them to become permeable to viruses. Second, many people perceive condoms as a "barrier" to close physical contact. They won't use them or aren't prepared in advance to use them, or even if prepared, they forget to use them in the heat of passion.

Does this raise your anxiety? With the current high prevalence of STDs in general and the lethal consequences of AIDS in particular, there is good reason to be anxious about sexual contact. Any sex that is not in the context of a relationship between monogamous healthy partners or where condoms are not used must be considered a serious health risk. Therefore, anxiety is adaptive if it increases the likelihood that risky sex will be avoided or a condom will be used. However, research on AIDS has shown that fear, although it may be a necessary factor, is not sufficient to change sexual practices (see Module 3.2, page 94). People must believe that they are at risk, there must be specific things they can do to protect themselves, and they must believe that what they do will be effective.

Masters and Johnson (1986) made several recommendations to help minimize one's chances of contracting or spreading an STD (see Box 13.2-3). Health authorities believe that these precautions are not necessary for people who are in a monogamous relationship in which both partners have been

---

Box 13.2-3 WAYS OF REDUCING SEXUALLY TRANSMITTED DISEASE RISK

Being informed about the symptoms helps protect against being exposed and alerts you to when treatment is needed.

Being observant of yourself and your partner. This means checking for sores, rashes, discharges (and you romantics take notice—you cannot check out your partner in the dark). Masters and Johnson describe the "short-arm inspection," referring to an examination for penile gonorrhea and urethritis used by physicians and prostitutes alike. The penis is milked from its base to the head to check for discharge. Masters and Johnson maintain that a visual and short-arm inspection may all be done as part of foreplay, without having to announce it to your partner. If you see anything suspicious, don't proceed!

Be selective; remember that you are not just having sex with your partner but with all of your partner's past partners. Anonymous sex or sex with someone you hardly know is more dangerous because you don't know your partner's past and you do not know if you can believe what he or she tells you about it. Even with a partner you know well, do not hesitate to discuss STDs and possible past exposure to them.

Be honest about your health status. If you think you have an STD, refrain from sex altogether, and tell your partner who can then watch for symptoms or see the doctor.

Be cautious and use protective measures. That means no exchange of bodily fluids without a barrier. Condoms are very effective, intravaginal chemical contraceptives reduce the woman's risk of contracting gonorrhea if exposed, and urinating immediately after sex can flush infectious agents from the urethra and slightly reduce the risk of infection. If you think you have been exposed, abstain from sex and contact your doctor.

Be tested and treated immediately if necessary. Treatment can be obtained from your own doctor, a campus medical service, or community clinic. Many states and counties provide public health clinics where treatment is confidential and free or inexpensive. Early diagnosis and treatment can alleviate the serious complications of STDs. Also, be sure your partner gets tested and treated or you may be reinfected.

medically screened for STDs (including a test for antibodies to HIV) and where both partners are completely faithful.

Therefore, health authorities recommend that, at the beginning of any new relationship, both partners should be screened for STDs, have the HIV test, and receive the results *together*. They also recommend that both partners continue to observe sexual precautions until they are retested for HIV infection six months later. *Only* after the second HIV test is negative may the suggested precautions be dispensed with as long as the partners continue to remain monogamous. Although these precautions may seem to take the romance out of sex, consider Shapespeare's words, "To fear the worst oft cures the worse."

■■■

MODULE SUMMARY

1. Masters and Johnson were among the first to study human sexual dysfunction. Although there were limitations on their research, it has been supported by subsequent research.
2. Physiological antecedents sometimes cause sexual dysfunction, but mostly it is caused by psychosocial antecedents. Masters and Johnson formulated both historical and current psychosocial causes of sexual dysfunction. Historical causes include alcohol and drugs, homosexual inclination and fears, inaccurate counseling, psychosexual trauma, religious orthodoxy, and sociocultural background. The current cause is fear of performance that brings about a spectator role in sex.
3. There are two theories of sexual dysfunction. One, the psychodynamic, has received little verification; the other, the behavioral, is primarily represented by Masters and Johnson's work.
4. Desire disorders affect the appetitive and early excitement phases of the human sexual response cycle. They include hypoactive sexual desire disorder and sexual aversion disorder.
5. Arousal disorders affect the later excitement phase and include female sexual arousal disorder and male erectile disorder (which used to be called impotence).
6. Orgasm disorders include premature ejaculation and inhibited male orgasm in men and inhibited female orgasm in women. About 10% of women are anorgasmic and do not experience orgasm. Today's definition of healthy female sexual functioning requires only that a woman achieve an orgasm in the presence of a partner.
7. Pain disorders include vaginismus in females and dyspareunia, which can affect men and women.

8. Today, sexual dysfunction is considered in the context of interpersonal relationships, and rarely does it affect only one partner.

9. Sex education is a useful method to prevent sexual dysfunction, but people can still educate themselves by visiting libraries, because there are many excellent references.

10. Most treatment of sexual dysfunction follows Masters and Johnson's original method with some modifications. Such treatment is largely behavioral and begins with a physical evaluation and thorough interview. Treatment usually begins with sensate focus exercises to help the couple relax and discover one another physically. Individualized behavioral techniques are used after sensate focus, depending on the diagnosis.

11. Treatment varies in effectiveness. It is most effective for premature ejaculation and inhibited female orgasm and less effective for male erectile disorder.

12. Sexually transmitted diseases are a major health problem. Although most are easily treatable, they continue unabated, and with the advent of AIDS, have taken a deadly turn. Sexually transmitted diseases cannot be spread by casual contact but require intimate sexual contact.

13. It is hard to prevent STDs because of the behavioral and privacy issues involved. Partner tracing may have reduced the increase in STDs but has not controlled them. There is, unfortunately, very little research into the psychosocial factors in preventing the spread of STDs. Abstinence is the best protection, and the use of condoms can reduce them.

14

IMPROVING HEALTH AND
WELL-BEING

When the four freshmen college students first met in their dorm suite, they were sure the computer had gone haywire in matching them up. Jake had been a linebacker for his high school football team and still went to the gym every day to pump iron. He came from a closeknit, supportive family, and his idea of a balanced meal was to eat all *the items on the McDonald's menu. Doug was brimming with self-confidence and planned on being the head of a major corporation by age 35. He had a bet with his father that he could quit smoking by the end of the semester, but he feared it was a bet he would lose. Greg was a strict vegetarian and had already run three marathons. He was glad to be away from home where several of his friends had gotten heavily involved with drugs and had urged him to join them. Bob liked beer, and to him heavy exercise was a walk to the elevator. Weight control had always been a problem, but making friends never had been.*

Although they differed greatly in their backgrounds, personalities, and behaviors, these four young men arrived at school in good health. But which of their personal characteristics encouraged continued good health, and which were leading them toward trouble? Could they change if they wanted to, and how could they bring wanted change about?

In this final chapter, we will attempt to bring together four main themes that address these matters. These themes have been woven throughout the book, but we will focus directly on them here since they relate to the full range of health psychology's concerns. These themes are (a) lifesyle, (b) personality, (c) personal control, and (d) social support. In addressing each, we will attempt to offer recommendations for healthy living, in this way summarizing and extending information presented throughout this book.

■■■■

LIFESTYLE

Illness can strike at any time and without apparent reason. The most careful person may come down with the flu, and the fittest individual may discover a tumor. Yet, one of the strongest lessons we have learned recently is that people can affect their odds. Who you are and what you do can place you at greater or lesser risk, affecting the likelihood that you will remain healthy or develop problems.

Risk factors refer to those aspects of individuals associated with the appearance of health problems. While they do not *cause* the problem, they affect the probability that it will occur. Some risk factors, such as genetics, are fixed and cannot be changed. All other things equal, people who are born into a family with a history of heart disease go through life at a greater risk of coronary problems than those who are not.

But most risk factors are modifiable, and many of these refer to a person's lifestyle. **Lifestyle**, all of those voluntary decisions that people make about how to act on an everyday basis, makes a tremendous difference. How you live your life plays a major role in determining whether or not you will feel and actually be healthy and whether you will encounter a wide range of illnesses and diseases. Doug's smoking and Bob's excess weight raise their odds of health problems, whereas Jake's and Greg's exercise routines tilt the odds in their favor.

In the classic Alameda County study discussed in Module 3.1 (pages 65–66), researchers discovered that health habits were not only associated with whether people lived or died but also with how healthy they were (Berkman & Breslow, 1983; Camacho & Wiley, 1983). Since then, numerous surveys in America and throughout the world have been done on the beliefs, values, and actual behavior of people in relationship to lifestyle (Aaro et al., 1986; Fries & Bowen, 1990; Harris & Guten, 1979; Wardle & Steptoe, 1991). Table 14.1 presents the results of one such national survey. Breaking these figures down by gender, we can see that the behavior of females is more positively healthy in just about each of the areas listed, with the exception of physical activity.

In addition to gender, wide differences in behavior exist according to social class, age, religious, and racial and ethnic groupings. For instance, a higher percentage of blacks smoke compared to their white counterparts, whereas heavy drinking is more prevalent among whites than blacks (USDHHS, 1992). In a large-scale study of active Mormons in California, Enstrom (1989) found that only 9% of the males in the sample smoked, and that 0% reported using alcohol. It is hardly surprising that the general health of this group is very good, and that rates of cancer and cardiovascular disease are low. Recognizing the importance of lifestyle in disease, the U.S. government has generated a set of ambitious goals for health-related lifestyle and disease control for the year 2000. To meet these goals, considerable efforts have been exerted to inform and educate the public as well as to make services more accessible (USDHHS, 1992).

Having reviewed the general issue of lifestyle, we will take a brief look at several of the most important behaviors, summarizing the findings of earlier chapters and offering guidelines for healthy behavior.

Substance Use

People choose to use cigarettes, alcohol, and illegal drugs for a variety of reasons, each having to do with the momentary pleasure they provide. Taking a drag on a cigarette or drinking a few beers can relieve tension, but these behaviors can also cause a great many short- and long-term problems. How can these habits be controlled, and in what ways can these problems be avoided?

CIGARETTES   The best advice anyone can get about cigarette smoking is simple: don't. Tobacco is implicated in 1 out of every 6 deaths in the United

Table 14.1	PERCENTAGE OF AMERICAN ADULTS ENGAGING IN VARIOUS HEALTH-RELATED BEHAVIORS (1985)		
	ALL ADULTS 18+	MALES	FEMALES
Heavy drinkers*	25	35	12
Drinking and driving [†]	17	22	9
Currently smoke	30	33	28
Heavy smokers[††]	27	32	21
Exercise regularly	40	43	38
Very physically active[§]	28	34	22
Overweight (by 20% or more)	24	26	22
Trying to lose weight	56	48	64
Wear seat belts most or all of the time	36	34	38

*Consumed 5 or more drinks in a day at least 5 times in past year.
[†]Drove a car at least once in past year after having had too much to drink.
[††]Smoke 25 or more cigarettes per day.
[§]Expend an average of 3 or more kilocalories per kilogram per day.

Source: *Health United States 1990, 1991,* U.S. Department of Health and Human Services, Pub. No. (PHS) 91-1232, Hyattesville, MD.

States, approximately 400,000 per year (Office on Smoking and Health, 1989). For men, the risk of lung cancer among smokers is 22 times higher than those who never take up the habit, and cigarette smoking is responsible for 40% of all coronary heart disease deaths among those under 65. Women who smoke during pregnancy not only put themselves at risk but also risk the lives of their unborn children (Kleinman & Madans, 1985).

Before the publication of the Surgeon Generals' first report on smoking, few people were aware of the health hazards of tobacco. In the years since, the prevalence of smoking has declined. Figure 14.1 demonstrates this trend for smoking (as well as marijuana and alcohol) for the segment of the population between age 18 and 25. Still, smoking rates remain high among segments of the population, especially blue collar workers and those with little education. Almost two-thirds of the tenth graders in America have tried smoking, and almost 20% report having smoked a pack or more in the past month. In spite of the health risks involved, one-fourth of all pregnant women smoke throughout the full term of their pregnancy (National Center for Health Statistics, 1989).

Based on the review of smoking behavior in Module 7.2, we can offer several recommendations that might be useful for Doug:

Figure 14.1   PERCENTAGE OF AMERICANS AGED 18–25 USING SPECIFIC SUBSTANCES, 1974–1990

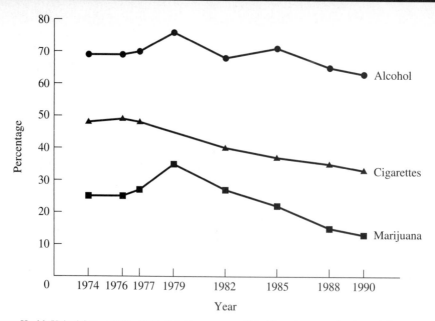

Source: Health United States 1991, *1992, U.S. Department of Health and Human Services, Pub. No. (PHS) 92-1232, Hyattesville, MD.*

1. Resist beginning to smoke, and help young people to do so. Smoking usually starts as the result of peer pressure or the desire to identify with someone. These sorts of pressures can be resisted.
2. Self-quitting is possible. Try to quit cold turkey during a nonstressful period rather than try to taper off. Think of positive reasons for quitting, and provide yourself with rewards for abstaining.
3. Drug therapies such as nicotine patches can be useful, but these should complement rather than substitute for changes in thoughts and behavior. Behavioral and cognitive therapy can also be very helpful.
4. Fight against relapse. Do not let an occasional slip or slight weight gain serve as a rationalization for smoking again. Enlist friends in supporting your efforts to quit.

ALCOHOL   By the time of their senior year in high school, 9 out of 10 Americans have tried alcohol at least once, and anywhere from 70 to 96% of American college students drink at least occasionally (Kivilan et al, 1989). Although drinking does not pose a serious problem for the majority of the public, about 18 million people do experience some form of problem associated with alcohol (National Institute on Alcohol Abuse and Alcoholism, 1987). The most serious is liver disease, although drinking has been implicated in approximately half of all homocides, suicides, and motor vehicle fatalities (Perrine, Peck & Fell, 1988).

For those who have alcohol-related problems, many different alternatives have been proposed, including medical treatments and a range of psychotherapeutic, behavioral, and cognitive therapies. Recently, skills training approaches have been proposed to help college students gain self-control over their drinking (Marlatt & George, 1988; Kivilan et al., 1990). Several of these techniques might be useful in helping Bob to drink responsibly:

1. Monitor your drinking. Determine the circumstances under which you drink, and how much you drink.
2. Identify and create limits for yourself. Recognize the extent to which you drink through direct or indirect peer pressure, and develop ways of resisting.
3. Find alternative ways of reducing stress and relaxing. Recognize that drinking is only one way of attempting to improve your emotional state.
4. Practice *placebo drinking*. At parties or other social occasions, drink nonalcoholic beverages or at least alternate alcoholic with nonalcoholic drinks to reduce the amount of alcohol consumed.
5. Engage in *lifestyle rebalancing*. When you become health oriented and make other healthy changes in diet, tobacco, or exercise, excessive drinking becomes inconsistent with a concern for your body and your health.

Drinking, a popular pastime on many college campuses, can be a serious personal problem for some students.

I L L E G A L   D R U G   U S E   The use of illicit drugs is one of society's greatest concerns, especially among the young and poor. Twenty-one million Americans admit to having used cocaine at least once, and 1 in 10 high school seniors has at least experimented with its use. Almost 44% of all high school seniors have tried marijuana at least once, and 21 million Americans report that they have used it in just the last year (USDHHS, 1992). The use of crack and other similar drugs has been called an epidemic in America's inner cities.

Obviously, the best way to avoid a drug problem is never to try drugs in the first place. However, the majority of those who try a drug one time do not progress into stronger drugs or greater usage. People with low self-esteem are more likely to give in to peer pressure to use drugs, and those who are alienated are less likely to heed society's message of "Just Say No." Once people develop a drug habit, especially if a physical dependence is involved, drug abuse is very hard to stop.

Although many different types of treatment programs have been proposed, the success rates of these programs, both short and long term, have been difficult to document. For any kind of program to be successful, four elements must be present:

1. You must be motivated to quit.
2. You must learn skills that allow you to achieve your goals without reliance upon drugs.

3. You must change your environment so the same factors that led to the initial use of drugs will not encourage and facilitate future use.
4. You must become involved in aftercare that involves continued support, monitoring, and lifestyle change.

NUTRITION AND DIET   Nutrition and weight control are two topics that many Americans are almost obsessive about. And well they might be. For those people who neither smoke nor drink, eating patterns can determine long-term health prospects more than any other lifestyle choice (USDHHS, 1992). At least one-fourth of the American public is overweight, and in combination with physical inactivity, diet has been associated with 5 of the 10 leading causes of death, especially coronary heart disease. Jake's steady diet of cheeseburgers may be harmful to his health more than his exercise is helpful to it, and Bob's excess weight is a potential cause for concern.

People who desire to lose weight often want a "quick fix." They turn to fad diets, fasting, appetite suppressants, and other methods that show little long-term success, even if they provide immediate results. The end result may be yo-yo dieting, an unhealthy pattern wherein a person's weight goes up and down repeatedly. Expanding on the concept of the "undiet" (Polivy and Herman, 1983), a number of suggestions can be offered for someone like Bob:

1. Eat to satisfy hunger. Try not to eat because you are stressed, upset, or see food in front of you.
2. Try to make peace with your setpoint. The body's regulatory mechanisms provide a fairly firm set of upper and lower limits that are likely to be maintained in the absence of extreme behavior.
3. Eat the right foods. Fats, oils and sweets should be consumed sparingly, reducing your intake of dietary fat to no more than 30% of calories. Eat a diet with plentiful portions of breads, cereals, rice, pasta, fruits, and vegetables.
4. The only road to weight maintenance involves a permanent modification of behaviors and thoughts. Changing eating patterns temporarily only guarantees that the weight will reappear eventually.
5. Exercise regularly. Exercise not only burns off calories but also can affect metabolism rate. Regular exercise may even be able to readjust your setpoint downward (Bennett & Gurin, 1982).

EXERCISE

Some people exercise regularly, making running, walking, or sports a central part of their schedules. Others believe in the value of exercise but never quite get around to doing it on a regular basis. Still others prefer the sedentary life, living according to the statement, "Whenever the impulse to exercise comes

Jogging can bring great benefits for the mind as well as the body.

over me, I lie down until it passes away" (McEvoy in Straus, 1968). Almost one-fourth of American adults report that they do not engage in any form of physical activity in their leisure time, and less than 10% of the population exercises at least 3 times a week at a level vigorous enough to improve their cardiorespiratory fitness (USDHHS, 1992).

Regular physical activity has many benefits. Not only can it help prevent disease, but it can also help people manage conditions that range from coronary heart disease and hypertension to diabetes and depression (Harris et al., 1989). Exercise has been associated with lowered rates of colon cancer and stroke (Powell et al., 1987; Salonen, Puska, & Tuomilehto, 1982), and as we have already noted above, it is an important element in most weight reduction programs. Some experts have suggested that it can actually increase your life expectancy (Paffenbarger et al., 1986).

Exercise has many positive effects on the body. It can produce a lower heart rate, and it creates positive changes in neurotransmitter and hormone levels, blood lipids, clotting factors, and glucose tolerance (Holmes & McGilley, 1987; Leon, 1989). Animal studies with a variety of species have shown that exercise not only reduces but also can even reverse artherosclerosis (Kramsch et al., 1981). The psychological effects of exercise are equally great. Studies have demonstrated that exercise can improve self-image and self-esteem as well as concentration. It is also associated with improvements in sleep, energy, and stress levels, as well as decreases in anxiety, hostility, and depression (King et al., 1989; Sime, 1984).

Experts disagree about the manner in which exercise produces positive effects. Some argue that physiological changes produced by activity produce direct physical benefits and an improved mental state. Others assert that exercise increases the person's sense of control and self-esteem, which influences disease resistance and health. Regardless of the manner by which it works, exercise has important positive effects on people both physiologically and psychologically and therefore represents a perfect example of the mind–body connection at work.

Although exercise can be very beneficial, it can also involve risks if not done cautiously. Let us offer some guidelines for a healthy exercise program:

1. Aerobic exercise—activities such as running, walking quickly, cycling, or swimming—require increased oxygen over a period of time. These sorts of activities are excellent to improve cardiorespiratory fitness.
2. Aerobic exercise three times a week for 30 minutes each should improve fitness and health. The exercise should elevate your heart rate to a prescribed level (suggested as 80% of your maximum for a young, healthy person) for a minimum of 20 minutes. To calculate this figure, subtract your age from 220, and take 80% of the result.
3. Start modestly. Beginners should work hard enough to cause heavy breathing (and accelerated heart pace). However, you should monitor the intensity of the workout carefully to avoid muscle strains, injury, or exhaustion.
4. Set goals for yourself. These goals should be specific, such as the number and length of exercise periods, the target heart rate you want to obtain, or the number of miles you want to cover in a specified period of time.
5. Select enjoyable activities that fit your lifestyle and schedule. Join a health club and work out with others if that fits your preferences and budget, ride a stationary bicycle if you would rather work out at home, or take runs or vigorous walks with a friend.

PERSONALITY AND INDIVIDUAL DIFFERENCES

Lifestyle is one health-related factor that differentiates us all. Yet people such as Jake, Doug, Greg, and Bob differ in many other ways. Personality is another critical factor that helps determine our exposure to, perception of, and reactions to threats to our physical well-being.

The search for a link between personality, emotion, and health can be traced back over 2,000 years to thinkers such as Hippocrates and Galen. In the twentieth century, Sigmund Freud and his followers focused attention on the relationship between personality and physical ailments, looking to the psychosomatic connection between unconscious conflict, mental disturbance, and organic disease. More recently, research on stressful life events has further highlighted and clarified this relationship between "psyche" and "soma" (Friedman, 1990; Friedman & Booth-Kewley, 1987).

This line of thinking leads to important questions such as, why do some people engage in activities that place them at risk, while others do not? And why do some people become ill when exposed to stress, while others seem to experience few if any negative effects? More generally, is there a "disease-prone personality" that is related to a range of physical illnesses; or, can we find specific personality traits and types that are associated with specific diseases?

In recent years, the study of relationships between personality and illness has accelerated greatly. Howard Friedman (1991) has asserted that personality may actually be an important *causal* factor in the development and progression of disease. Certainly the work in the Type A behavior pattern, as reviewed in Module 11.1, points to its role as a cause in the development of cardiac illness (Matthews, 1988; Rosenman, 1990).

Concerning the question of the generality between personality and disease, the evidence is mixed. Stanwyck and Anson (1986) looked at the combined results of 68 separate studies of illness and personality that utilized the MMPI, a widely respected instrument that measures psychological and emotional problems. Using complex statistical techniques, they found five different clusters of diseases, each related in a logical and clinically meaningful way to its own distinct MMPI profile. Friedman and Booth-Kewley (1987), using a technique known as meta-analysis, reviewed the results of 101 different studies covering a wide variety of diseases and personality measures. They found that a profile consisting of depression, anger, hostility, and anxiety played a strong causal role in coronary heart disease, and they believe that a case can be made for this profile as a general disease-prone personality.

MECHANISMS OF ACTION

Personality and disease might be related via several different pathways. Two of these routes, which represent complementary rather than competing explanations, seem particularly important. According to the first, known as the *personality induced hyperreactivity model*, people with certain personality traits show an exaggerated physiological reaction to stress (Suls & Rittenhouse, 1990).

As shown in Figure 14.2a, this model proposes that people with certain characteristics, Type A for example, appraise situations as more stressful than others and are more vigilant about potential sources of stress. These extreme or constant appraisals prompt elevated sympathetic and neuroendocrine responses, which strain bodily organs and organ systems. As a result of the frequency or the intensity of the body's reactions, the person runs a greater risk of developing health problems.

A second model, known as the *dangerous behaviors model*, proposes a pathway between personality and illness that is indirect rather than direct. According to this model (see Figure 14.2b), certain personality traits lead people to engage in activities that place them at greater risk. For example, people who are depressed are less likely to eat properly or take good care of themselves. Therefore, personality affects health and illness by encouraging positive or negative behaviors such as exercise, drug abuse, or smoking.

CHARACTERISTICS AND TRAITS

In trying to identify specific individual differences that link personality to health, researchers have investigated a great many personality traits and pat-

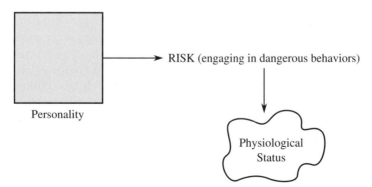

Figure 14.2   TWO MODELS OF THE LINKAGE BETWEEN PERSONALITY AND DISEASE

(a) The personality-induced hyperreactivity model.

(b) The dangerous behaviors model.

Source: Suls, J., & Rittenhouse, J. D., 1990, Models of linkages between personality and disease. In H. Friedman (Ed), Personality and disease, New York: Wiley.

terns. Two of the more interesting and promising directions they have pursued will be discussed here. These are Rotter's concept of locus of control and McClelland's study of achievement, affiliation, and power motives.

LOCUS OF CONTROL   People vary greatly in the extent to which they believe that the events around them are subject to their personal control. In developing the concept of **locus of control**, Julian Rotter proposed that some people, known as *internals*, hold a generalized belief that events are determined by their own actions and therefore feel in control of their lives. Others, known as *externals*, perceive that events are beyond their personal control and believe that outcomes are determined by fate, luck, or other people (Rotter, 1966; 1975).

Noting the potentially important implications that this might have for a range of health behaviors, several researchers have worked on developing a Health Locus of Control Scale (Wallston, Wallston, & DeVellis, 1978; Lau & Ware, 1981). They have found that internals wear seat belts more often (Williams, 1972) and are more likely to quit smoking or be nonsmokers in the first place (Wallston & Wallston, 1981). To account for several inconsistent findings, however, Lau (1988) has suggested that in order for internals to engage in health protective behaviors, they must also place a strong value on health.

MOTIVE PATTERNS   Closely related to the study of personality traits is the study of personal needs and motives. Although all of these terms are sometimes used interchangeably, needs or motive patterns drive behavior. They represent internal tendencies to respond in a given way to external circumstances–in a sense, "pulling" or predisposing a person toward specific forms of action (Murray, 1938).

David McClelland and his colleagues have conducted extensive research on needs such as the power motive (the need to control), the achievement motive (the need to excel), and the affiliative motive (the need to be liked or accepted; McClelland, 1985). He believes that standard personality tests have had only limited success in identifying relationships between health and specific traits because they rely on people's self-reports on questionnaires and interviews. Instead, McClelland has measured *implicit motives* by using people's "associative thought streams." To do so, he analyzes the stories that people write in response to pictures patterned after the projective Thematic Apperception Test (TAT). These implicit motives, he believes, are based on emotional learning, and are therefore "linked directly with automatically controlled physiological systems that govern healthy functioning of the body" (McClelland, 1989, p. 675).

Using McClelland's approach, research has shown a strong and consistent relationship between implicit motive patterns and health. Insulin-dependent diabetics tend to be moderate to high in the need for affiliation and low in the need for power, a pattern known as the "Easygoing Affiliative Syndrome" (McClelland et al., 1988). Affiliative trust, which represents a desire for positive rather than cynical or mistrustful relationships, has been related to higher ratios of helper to suppressor T-cells, which is an indicator of strengthened immune function (McKay, 1987). Those with a strong sense of *agency*, which is defined as being high in the needs for power and achievement (or at least one of these in combination with a low need for affiliation), feel a strong sense of control over their lives and tend to have good overall health (Jemmott, 1987; McClelland, 1989).

In addition to these findings, McClelland's research has demonstrated that programs of intervention may be able to affect motive patterns and thereby have a positive impact on health. In a recent program (Hellman et al., 1990; Hellman, 1987), patients in a community health plan practiced a series of exercises to learn relaxation, meditation, and guided imagery. They also learned to recognize that their thoughts, feelings, and bodily reactions were intimately tied together in order to make them "shapers of their own destiny rather than passive victims of what was happening in their lives" (McClelland, 1989, p. 279). The results of this project and McClelland's long-term program show significant changes in motive patterns such as agency, as well as improvements in health. These findings suggest that motive patterns are not just a reflection of these changes. Rather, they play a causal role, preceding improvements in health over a 10-year period.

PERSONALITY AND GOOD HEALTH

We have seen a good deal of recent interest in the search for the "disease-prone personality." Yet, health psychology's positive orientation really ought to be leading us away from "disease" concerns and toward questions about the "disease-resistant" or the "healthy" personality. Although it is still in the minority, some research of this sort does exist. For instance, McClelland has reported that while affiliative cynicism is associated with poor health, affiliative trust is related to good health. And Kobasa's concept of *hardiness* (Funk, 1992; Kobasa, 1979; Kobasa et al., 1985) and Schier and Carver's (1987) concept of *dispositional optimism* are two important health-relevant personality concepts that have been phrased in positive terms.

Since personality can be an important contributor to good and poor health, another critical question poses itself: Can people change their personalities and grow in beneficial ways, or is personality set by the time a person reaches adulthood? The answer here is a positive one. Although personality traits do not change easily or quickly, people can exert significant influence over their characteristics and traits, especially when they *seek* to change.

Just as we have seen that motive patterns can be altered, evidence also exists that the Type A behavior pattern is amenable to change. As discussed in

Module 11.1, Ethel Roskies and her colleagues at the University of Montreal have developed a 10-week treatment program for Type A individuals (Roskies, 1987; Roskies et al., 1986). The program is broken down into 8 modules (see Table 14.2) in which people learn to modify the way in which they think and the manner in which they respond to situations, both physically and cognitively. In essence, the attempt is to turn people from Type A responders more to Type B responders.

Although unable to find any changes in physiological reactivity from the beginning to the end of the program, the Montreal Type A Intervention Program has strongly demonstrated that it is possible to change the ways in which people react behaviorally. Whether these changes will be maintained or reflected in future health remains to be determined. Yet this example and

Table 14.2   MODULES AND SKILLS FROM THE MONTREAL TYPE A INTERVENTION PROJECT

MODULES	SKILLS TAUGHT
1. *Introduction to the program*	General overview
2. *Relax:* Learning to control physical stress responses	Self-monitoring of physical and emotional tension signs; progressive muscular relaxation
3. *Control yourself:* Learning to control behavioral stress responses	Self-monitoring of behavioral signs of tension; incompatible behaviors, delay, communication skills
4. *Think productively:* Learning to control cognitive stress responses	Self-monitoring of self-talk; cognitive restructuring
5. *Be prepared:* Learning to anticipate and plan for predictable stress situations	Identification of recurrent stress triggers; stress inoculation training
6. *Cool it:* Learning emergency braking in unpredictable stress situations	Identification of signs of heightened tension; application of physical, behavioral, and cognitive controls; anger control
7. *Building stress resistance:* Learning to plan for rest and recuperation	Identification of pleasurable activities; problem solving
8. *Protect your investment:* Stress management as a lifelong investment	Relapse prevention

Source: Adapted from Roskies, E. 1987, Stress management for the healthy Type A, *New York: Guilford Press.*

others like it offer hope that personality can be changed, that these changes are reflected in greater psychological well-being, and that they may lead to better physical health as well.

Control

The concept of control is one of the most pervasive issues in all of health psychology. To have a sense of control, to believe that positive outcomes follow from actions you are capable of carrying out is critical. Having a sense of control makes it easier to deal with life's everyday problems, and it encourages people to make efforts to help themselves. A loss of control makes stress even more difficult to handle and can lead people to give up, even when trying might be just the thing they need.

Research in a number of different traditions has demonstrated that the ability to control events, or even the *feeling* that you can make a difference (sometimes referred to as the "illusion of control"), can have a wide range of physiological, cognitive, and emotional effects. For example, research with rats has demonstrated that when stress is uncontrollable or inescapable, more corticosteroid is released, and immune function is compromised (Maier, Laudenslager & Ryan, 1985). In humans, catecholemine excretion is affected when workers have control over their jobs (Frankenhaeuser & Johansson, 1982).

A number of different formulations of control have been offered such as the individual difference variable, internal-external locus of control, discussed a few pages ago. Two other related formulations of the control concept are self-efficacy and learned helplessness.

Self-Efficacy

In Module 3.1, we discussed Bandura's concept of **self-efficacy** (Bandura, 1977; 1982). Compared to locus of control, self-efficacy grows out of a different tradition in psychology, social learning theory, but it points in a similar direction. To have a sense of self-efficacy is to make a judgment about oneself in relation to *specific tasks*, to believe that you can organize and carry out behavior even if the circumstances are novel, unpredictable, or stressful. In essence, it involves the belief that "I can do" (Schunk & Carbonari, 1984). When people have a feeling of self-efficacy, they believe that they have effective options. They do not need to avoid situations because of self-doubts, and they experience relatively few negative emotions in the face of difficult choices. Once they act, they are willing to expend a great deal of effort, and persist in the face of difficulties.

Self-efficacy forms the mediating link between intention and action. As we noted in the Theory of Reasoned Action (Module 3.1), people may intend to perform an action, but they will actually do so only if they believe they can succeed. Therefore, it is not surprising that self-efficacy has been associated with health-related behaviors as varied as quitting smoking (DiClemente, 1981), controlling weight, (Strecher et al., 1986) and using condoms to avoid AIDS (Coates, Morin, & McKusick, 1987).

LEARNED HELPLESSNESS

On the other end of the continuum of control, and growing out of a more clinical orientation in psychology, is the concept of **learned helplessness.** Martin Seligman and his colleagues (Seligman, 1975) initially developed this concept to describe a situation whereby individuals, through repeated failures to affect outcomes, come to believe that their behaviors do not make a difference. Imagine trying to improve a grade in a course, but no matter how hard you try or what you do, the result is still the same. Eventually, you would likely give up, especially if you experienced *personal helplessness*, a sense that there is nothing *you* could do to make a difference (Abramson, Seligman, & Teasdale, 1978). Unfortunately, people who experience learned helplessness not only give up on things in the present, but also they tend to give up trying altogether, even when a new and effective means of control presents itself. As a result, it is not surprising that learned helplessness is associated with lowered self-esteem and depression (Seligman, 1975).

Not all people develop learned helplessness in the face of failed efforts at control. To account for this, Peterson and Seligman (1987) revised the learned helplessness formulation, introducing the concept of *explanatory style*. Explanatory style is a habitual way by which people explain bad things that happen to them. People who adopt a *pessimistic* explanatory style explain bad events in a way that is internal ("It's *my* fault"), stable ("It's not going to get better"), and global ("It's going to ruin everything"). This style leads to a strong sense of helplessness, which is associated with depression, poor health and immune function, and high levels of morbidity (Peterson, Seligman & Vaillant, 1988; Peterson, 1988; Kamen, Rodin, & Seligman, 1987). Those who adopt an *optimistic* style (making external, unstable and specific attributions for problems) are less likely to experience learned helplessness and its negative consequences.

GAINING A SENSE OF CONTROL

As we have noted throughout the book, people have to believe in their ability to make a difference in order to try. Doug will not try to quit smoking if he does not believe he can, and Bob likely will not work hard to lose weight if he believes his efforts are doomed to failure. On the other hand, Greg must have believed in his ability to run 26 miles in order to train for the marathon, and when Jake suffered setbacks in his exercise program, he probably blamed them on temporary, changeable factors.

People can avoid learned helplessness and gain a greater sense of control by adopting a more optimistic attributional style. To demonstrate this, Wilson and Linville (1985) took a group of freshmen at Duke University who were experiencing academic difficulty and taught them to develop an optimistic attributional style to account for their problems. Assisted by juniors and seniors who had experienced early difficulties themselves, the freshmen learned to explain their difficulties in adapting to school by looking at sources that were external rather than internal ("College life places many demands on people that are hard to get used to"), unstable rather than stable ("Things will definitely improve"), and specific rather than global ("It's just one part of my life"). Only 5% of the troubled students who were taught the optimistic style dropped out of school, whereas 25% of those in a control group that received standard counseling dropped out.

The mechanisms for increasing self-efficacy and feeling in control are common to many of the self-regulation guidelines offered for specific lifestyle changes. We can summarize these here, offering some broad-based recommendations for gaining a sense of control:

1. Set goals for yourself. Make sure these are specific, attainable, and relatively short term. Once you reach these, continue to set other measurable, reachable goals.
2. Look at others who have been or are being successful. Be encouraged by their successes, learn from them, see the similarities between them and you.
3. Don't blame yourself for setbacks. Focus on areas of your life that are going well, and anticipate improvements.
4. Reward yourself. When you meet your goals, buy new clothes if you have lost weight. Get yourself a new CD for going a week without cigarettes. Feel good about your accomplishments.
5. At first you may want to avoid environments that tempt you too much in order to protect a fragile sense of self-efficacy. Although long-term avoidance is not appropriate, eventually you will find that you can face temptation and not give in. When you resist, see recommendation 4.

Social Support

People do not exist in a vacuum. They constantly seek and offer **social support**, and this is one of the most important themes in all of health psychology. To have support means to be involved in social relationships, to be connected with other people. Someone who has support can say, as Ringo Starr has, "I get by with a little help from my friends." In the presence of support you feel loved, valued, and cared for, and you know that you have resources available to you above and beyond your own. Friends, relatives, lovers, roommates, coworkers, and spouses all can serve as sources of social support.

Social support has a wide impact. It can affect the manner in which people cope with stress, and it can be a key determinant in the development of psychological and physical illness. It can also affect the progression of illness and recovery from it, as well as the initiation and maintenance of behavior change. A significant way of improving health is to increase one's social support, and insufficient social support can be considered a risk factor for morbidity and mortality (House, Landis, and Umberson, 1988).

THE STRUCTURE AND FUNCTIONS OF SUPPORT

While few people are without *any* sources of support, people differ in the structure of their social ties. The quantity and quality of social ties and the degree to which people are imbedded in social networks varies greatly. Men, for instance, are generally tied into more extensive social networks, but women's contacts are more personal and intense (Belle, 1987; Shumaker & Hill, 1991). Adult males often note that their wife is their only confidant, whereas women are likely to cite their friends about as often as their husbands as people with whom they share information and on whom they rely (Powers & Bultena, 1976).

Social support serves many different functions (House, 1981; Wills, 1985). One key function is emotional. Having someone to share problems with allows people to vent their emotions and allows others to offer reassurance and nurturance. We all feel better knowing that the people around us will cheer us up when ill or back us up when threatened. A second function is informational, involving the giving and receiving of advice and guidance. We can learn from others and have a wider repertoire of coping than if we faced life alone. A third major function is tangible. Friends can lend you money when you are short, help tutor you if you are having academic problems, or get you from one place to another if injured.

THE LINKS BETWEEN SUPPORT AND HEALTH

Two general viewpoints have been offered on the way in which support works. The first, known as the *buffering model*, suggests that social support serves as a source of protection (that is, a buffer) against the harmful effects of stress (Cohen & McKay, 1984). According to this model, social support allows people to appraise a stressor as less threatening and allows them to cope with it better. The second model, known as the *main effects model* (Cohen & Syme, 1985), deals with the value of social support independent of stress. It asserts that support is a positive and useful resource, and it suggests that its benefits are great even when people are not exposed to stress.

Self-help and support groups, which can be extremely useful, have been created for a wide variety of problems and health threats.

Support is linked to health in several ways. Social support gives people a better sense of control over events, and as we have seen, this can have beneficial health effects. Also, people who have social support may be less likely to engage in health-threatening behaviors. They may be less threatened by stress and therefore feel less need to smoke, or they may be encouraged by friends and family and helped to give up cigarettes. Recently, researchers have demonstrated that social support can reduce morbidity and mortality directly as a result of effects on the neuroendocrine, immunologic, and cardiovascular systems (Cohen, Kaplan & Manuck, 1991; Berkman, 1982).

Social support has been linked to a great many populations and health issues, but its role among the elderly (Bowling & Browne, 1991; Krause and Markides, 1990) and AIDS patients has been a topic of recent interest (McGough, 1990; Stall et al., 1990). In addition, a good deal of research has focused on the role of social support in the etiology and progression of the two leading causes of death, heart disease and cancer. In relation to heart disease, social support, as a stress buffer, may weaken physiological reactivity and inhibit the development of vascular lesions, lessening the likelihood of acute clinical events such as heart attacks and arrythmias (Kamark, Manuck, and Jennings, 1989; Shumaker & Czajkowski, 1991). Concerning cancer, social support has been closely associated with immune functioning, especially natural killer cell activity and secretory immunoglobulin (Jemmott & Migliore, 1988; Levy et al., 1990). The seeking of support is also a key coping pattern in cancer patients that seems to be effective in diminishing the distress that cancer patients experience (Dunkel-Schetter et al., 1992).

ENHANCING SUPPORT

Some people feel that it is a test of their integrity to weather a storm on their own, or they avoid others when in distress so as not to be a burden. Research and experience both show that this is not an adaptive way to handle problems. Some specific suggestions for enhancing support include the following:

1. Make use of your friends. Don't be afraid to ask for assistance and in doing so to disclose aspects of yourself. Females are more likely than males to share feelings and emotions, but the benefits are equal for both sexes.
2. Share interests with others. Whether it is a gym class or a club of Renaissance music fanciers, find others with similar interests. People with one thing in common often find that they share other interests and characteristics.
3. Offer support to others. Support that is given as well as received is beneficial, and those who offer support often find that the exchange of mutual support is the result.
4. Let others assist you in achieving your goals. Although programs such as Weight Watchers and Alcoholics Anonymous are not free of problems, they do bring people together to encourage, pressure, and praise one another into doing good things for themselves.
5. Find a support group. Whether formally or informally organized, support groups exist for almost every kind of problem and condition. Group members provide successful models for one another, share information, and provide a source of emotional release.

IN CONCLUSION

As we stated back in Chapter 1, health psychology deals with the factors that determine the ways people stay healthy, the reasons they become ill, and the manner by which they react to illness. In contrast to the narrowly defined biomedical model, we have taken the position that health and illness are determined by the interaction of biological, personal, environmental, and social variables. In this final chapter, we have focused on four overarching themes that seem to pervade all of the specific topics, conditions, and diseases we have addressed and that contribute equally to good health and health enhancement.

The message here is that people are not passive recipients of good or bad health. *You* shape your body and your environment. *You* can exert control, muster support, and live a healthy lifestyle. Who you are and what you do greatly affects your odds of staying well and of coping successfully with stress and illness. This does not mean that you should be neurotically obsessed with the health outcome of every action nor blame yourself when you become ill. But it does suggest that you can utilize the knowledge gained by health psychologists for your own good. In the coming years, this body of knowledge will expand exponentially, and it will be applied in medical practice and public policy. We invite you to join in its creation and in its use—to your good health.

SUMMARY

1. Lifestyle, all those voluntary decisions we make daily about how to act, affects our risk of health problems. Wide differences exist in lifestyle according to age, gender, race, class, and ethnicity.

2. Cigarette smoking constitutes a great health risk. Recommendations for quitting include using positive self-rewards, physiological mechanisms such as drug patches, and the use of social support to avoid relapse.

3. Alcohol, used widely among adults, represents a problem for about 18 million Americans. Students who fear they may have a problem ought to monitor their drinking, create limits for themselves, and rebalance their lifestyles so that excessive drinking no longer feels appropriate.

4. People who become addicted to illegal drugs must be highly motivated in order to quit. They should learn skills so they can achieve goals without a reliance on drugs, change their environment to resist relapse, and become involved in aftercare.

5. Diet is one of the most important lifestyle choices a person can make. People should avoid yo-yo dieting by permanently modifying their patterns of eating and thinking about food.

6. Exercise brings about many positive effects, both psychological and physiological. People should choose an exercise program that fits into their personal styles and preferences and set specific, reachable goals for themselves.

7. Personality can affect health and disease. The existence of a "disease-prone" personality is a topic of debate, although anger, depression, hostility, and anxiety seem associated with a great many health problems.

8. Personality can affect disease through different routes. Certain personality traits may (a) lead to an exaggerated physiological response to stress and (b) predispose people to engage in behaviors that place them at greater risk.

9. People known as internals believe that events are determined by their own actions. Externals believe that events are determined by others, fate, or luck. Internals are more likely to wear seat belts and to quit smoking.

10. By measuring implicit motives, such as the need for achievement, the need for affiliation, and the need for power, it is possible to identify important motive patterns. Research has uncovered several clear relationships between health and a variety of specific patterns.

11. People are capable of making changes in their personality, especially when they seek to change. Hardiness and dispositional optimism are two positively oriented personality variables associated with health.

12. Self-efficacy, a sense that "I can do," forms the mediating link between intention and action. People engage in behavior only when they feel they can accomplish their goals.

13. Learned helplessness involves a feeling that there is nothing a person can do to make a difference. People who experience learned helplessness often become depressed and may give up trying even when effort might help them to succeed.

14. People can avoid or overcome learned helplessness by adopting an optimistic explanatory style. By adopting this style, they come to believe that negative events are not their fault, that specific setbacks only represent one part of their life, and that events will change for the better.

15. Social support can come from a variety of sources such as family, friends, and roommates. Others can provide emotional support, informational support, or even tangible support, each serving to buffer the person against stress. Although some people avoid others when troubled, it is best to seek them out and share problems.

16. Knowledge in health psychology grows almost daily. Students are invited to utilize and apply it—even to join in its development—in order to lead healthier and happier lives in the years to come.

GLOSSARY

absorption The process by which the digested constituents of food pass out of the digestive system into the bloodstream.

activities of daily living (or ADLs) Involve the basic physical abilities needed for everyday functioning such as dressing, shopping, and using transportation.

addiction Devoting or surrendering oneself to a habit, appetite, or behavior.

A-delta fibers Carry the localized, sharp, pricking, but brief pain sensations.

adherence The extent to which a person's behavior is consistent with the advice given by a health care practitioner. (*See also* compliance.)

adrenal glands Located on top of each kidney, they release hormones called corticosteroids and catecholamines that prepare the body for activity and affect processes throughout the body.

aging Changes that accompany increasing chronological age: *primary aging* is the physical and largely *genetic* process of gradual deterioration and *secondary aging* is the result of *nongenetic* factors like disease, abuse, and disuse that occur throughout the lifespan.

AIDS dementia complex Global deterioration in mental functioning due to HIV infection of the brain occurring at the end stage of the disease.

AIDS-related complex (ARC) A midstage of HIV infection characterized by nonlethal opportunistic infections.

alcoholism Physical dependence, blackouts, and memory impairment caused by the consumption of alcohol: *primary alcoholism* is probably not genetic and easier to treat, while *secondary alcoholism* may have a genetic basis and occurs primarily in males.

alimentary canal A coiled, hollow, muscular tube approximately 10 meters (30 feet) in length, beginning at the mouth and ending at the rectum; the digestive tract.

allergens Any nonpathogenic foreign materials present in the environment. These usually trigger no immune response in the majority of people, but for unknown reasons the humoral branch of the immune systems of hypersensitive individuals reacts to them.

amenorrhea The absence of menstruation; a result of anorexia nervosa.

androgen Sex hormones such as testosterone.

anecdote A report of someone's experience or a brief narrative of an interesting or biographical event.

aneurysm A weak vessel wall that blows out like a balloon and can burst under pressure, leading to internal bleeding; major cause of hemorrhagic stroke.

anorexia nervosa "Nervous loss of appetite"; an eating disorder that involves extremes of dieting and exercise to the point of starvation; perhaps better conceived of as a fear of weight.

anorgasmic Women who do not experience orgasm through any source of stimulation.

antibody Chemicals manufactured by plasma B-cells to match the surface features of a particular antigen; these attach to the antigen, slowing it down and marking it for destruction by killer T-cells, macrophages, and NK cells.

antigens Potentially pathogenic foreign substances that trigger a response by the immune system.

aphasia Problems using or comprehending language: *expressive aphasia* is difficulty producing fluent, coherent speech, while the ability to make the basic sounds of speech and understand language remains intact and *receptive aphasia* is difficulty understanding language, while the ability to speak fluently remains intact.

applied psychologists Utilize psychological knowledge in consultation; their goal is to prevent the development of distress and maladaptive behavior.

arteriosclerosis When arteries become thick and lose their elasticity; sometimes called "hardening of the arteries."

assay A laboratory analysis of a substance such as a hormone taken in a sample of urine, blood, or tissue.

asthma Heightened sensitivity of the immunologic response in the respiratory system; related to chronic obstructive pulmonary disease.

asymptomatic The phase of an infection before symptoms are clinically significant.

atherosclerosis Narrowing of the arteries; occurs when fat is deposited along artery walls.

attachment An active, affectionate two-way relationship between parent and child necessary for normal emotional and physical development.

autoimmune disorder A breakdown in the immune system's ability to distinguish between self and nonself in which it attacks body tissue.

autonomic nervous system (ANS) Consists of a network of neural pathways running throughout the body: The *sympathetic division mobilizes* the body for action by concentrating energy resources for muscular activity, while the *parasympathetic division demobilizes* the body and promotes relaxation and energy conservation.

aversion therapy Aversive stimulus is paired with a stimulus that elicits an unwanted response.

avoidance conditioning Learning in order to avoid unpleasant consequences.

axons Long projections from the soma of neurons that transmit impulses to other neurons.

behavior modification Changing behavior through the principles of operant conditioning. It is used to condition voluntary behaviors that may be quite complex. Behaviors can be increased or decreased depending on the consequences that follow them. *Reinforcement* is the general term for the consequences: *Reward* will increase the likelihood of a behavior occurring again, while *punishment* will decrease it.

behavioral health An interdisciplinary field concerned primarily with the enhancement of health in healthy individuals. In addition to psychologists, it involves dieticians, epidemiologists, and health educators, among others.

behavioral medicine An interdisciplinary field concerned with the development and integration of behavioral psychology and biomedical science and techniques relevant to health and illness and the application of this knowledge and these techniques to prevention, diagnosis, treatment and rehabilitation. In addition to psychologists, it involves sociologists, biologists, and physicians, among others.

behavioral risk factors Behaviors that are cofactors in the expression of disease, like smoking and cancer. (*See* risk factor.)

behaviorism The study of how behavior is learned through conditioning.

bile A yellow-green, watery solution produced by the liver that breaks down the relatively large fat globules in food into fatty droplets that can be acted on by enzymes.

B-lymphocytes (B-cells) Involved in the humoral immune response, these become plasma cells and secrete antibody to a specific invader.

biofeedback Providing feedback about the status of physiological processes in order to help people learn to control them.

biomedical model The predominant medical model of illness; it is dualistic, mechanistic, reductionistic, and disease-oriented.

biopsychology A subfield of psychology that studies brain function and the relationship between physiology and mental states (also called physiological psychology).

biopsychosocial model A holistic model that incorporates interactions among biological, psychological, and social factors as causes of disease.

blood-brain barrier A biological barrier that protects the delicate neurons from toxins and infectious agents that may be present in the blood.

body-mass index A method of determining desirable weight; it is a ratio calculated by dividing the weight in kilograms (1 kg = 2.2 pounds) by the square of the height in meters (1 m = 39.4 inches).

bone marrow The soft, central part of large bones where red and white cells are manufactured.

bradykinin A potent pain-producing chemical that is manufactured when cells are injured and causes free nerve endings to send pain impulses to the brain.

brain The organ of the mind; stores and retrieves memories, formulates plans, and or-ganizes and carries out basic goal-directed and complex behavior; may be the executive homeostatic coordinator of the body.

brainstem A bulge in the spinal cord where it enters the skull; consists of the medulla and the pons.

bronchitis An oversecretion of mucus in the lower respiratory system, produces cough and structural changes in the bronchi that impair lung ventilation; related to chronic obstructive pulmonary disease.

bulimia nervosa "Continuous nervous hunger"; an eating disorder that involves cycles of binge eating followed by purging (self-induced vomiting or diarrhea).

carbohydrate Constituent of food that is metabolized by cells in the body to provide energy.

carcinogens Substances that are suspected to cause cancer by damaging DNA and interfering with normal regulation of cell growth.

cardiac arrest When the heart stops beating.

cardiac invalidism When patients become dependent and helpless and believe that they are less able than they actually are.

case study Research involving a single subject: a *clinical case study* is an in-depth report of an illness and its treatment while a *research case study* is used by behavioral psychologists when a single individual's behavior is studied as a variable and is manipulated.

catecholamines Substances produced by the adrenal glands and the brain that function as both neurotransmitters and hormones.

cellular response One of two branches of the immune system, it involves cells that are capable of moving through body tissue to attack invaders—T-cells, NK cells, and macrophages.

central control trigger Presumed feed-forward ability of the brain to transmit messages through large, rapidly conducting efferent fibers to the pain gateway in the spinal cord, opening or closing it.

central nervous system (CNS) Consists of the brain and spinal cord; it is where information *processing* takes place.

cerebellum Also known as the "little brain," it is a large and distinctive structure attached to the back surface of the brainstem; involved in the coordination of movement, equilibrium, and balance, it also mediates commands for voluntary muscle movements that originate from other brain centers.

cerebral infarction An area of dead brain tissue caused by oxygen deprivation resulting from obstruction in blood flow.

cervix A narrow canal that connects the uterus to the vagina.

C fibers Carry the diffuse, dull, burning, aching, and longer-lasting pain sensations.

cholesterol A fat-like substance needed by the body; found in all foods of animal origin (meat and dairy products) and some oils; a build-up in the arteries can cause heart attack or stroke. *High-density lipoprotein (HDL)* transports cholesterol from the arteries to the liver and *low-density lipoprotein (LDL)* transports cholesterol from the liver to the arteries. The *risk ratio* is the *ratio* of total cholesterol to HDL; it is now considered to be a better predictor of a future heart attack than total cholesterol.

chronic obstructive pulmonary disease (COPD) A relatively new diagnostic category that includes the related respiratory disorders of asthma, bronchitis, and emphysema. People with COPD have frequent pulmonary infections, dyspnea, and they may develop respiratory failure, which can cause death.

classical conditioning Used to condition involuntary behaviors such as basic physiological responses. Two stimuli that occur together become associated with the same response. The *unconditioned stimulus* is one that is naturally associated with the response. The *conditioned stimulus* is one that is not naturally associated with the response but eventually, by occurring together with the unconditioned stimulus many times, becomes able to elicit the response itself. A response is called *unconditioned* when it is associated only with the unconditioned stimulus, but it is called the *conditioned* after it becomes associated with the conditioned stimulus.

climacteric Changes involving the reproductive system in middle age; women experience menopause, the cessation of ovulation and menstruation.

clinical psychologists Utilize psychological knowledge in a therapeutic way with individuals or small groups.

clitoris A small rounded structure that extends slightly from the body external to and above the vagina. It is biologically homologous to the penis and enlarges slightly during stimulation through the same vascular mechanisms that cause the penis to become erect, but it responds more slowly than the penis and it does not lengthen appreciably. It also retracts just before orgasm. It is the only human organ whose sole function is in sex.

cognitive appraisal A transactional theory of stress in which perception of the environmental stressor and one's coping abilities determine whether or not a physiological stress response occurs. *Primary appraisal* is made of an event or situation which may be categorized as either: Irrelevant or good ("benign-positive"), thereby leading to no stress-response; or stressful (involving a harm, loss, or threat). *Secondary appraisal* is an ongoing evaluation of one's ability and resources to cope with events judged to be harmful, threatening, or challenging. *Reappraisal* is an acknowledgement that we are constantly re-evaluating and changing our appraisals in the face of new information.

cognitive-behavioral therapy Combines cognitive techniques with behavior therapy.

cognitive redefinition A method people seem to use naturally to change their perception of stress.

cognitive rehabilitation A diverse set of interventions designed to remedy the effects of brain damage on intellectual, behavioral, and personality functioning.

cognitive therapy A variety of approaches that have as their goal changing maladaptive thought patterns and beliefs that affect people behaviorally and emotionally. Also used to refer to therapy that is applied for purposes of cognitive rehabilitation.

coma A state in which the "vegetative" processes necessary for life proceed, but the normal sleep-wake cycle is disrupted and there is no conscious mental activity.

commonsense epidemiology The process wherein people generate hypotheses about actual and potential health problems and engage in a search for additional information to understand and confirm them.

compensation A conscious learning process in which a new sequence is learned to replace an old one disrupted by brain damage. (*See also* substitution of function.)

compliance The extent to which a person follows the advice of a health care practitioner. The term *adherence* is preferred by some because "compliance" and "noncompliance" have often been associated with patient blame.

consultation An indirect method of service usually involved with primary intervention and health promotion.

contiguity of reinforcement The principle that the timing of reinforcement influences the result of operant conditioning—reinforcement or punishment that follows the response most closely in time has the stronger effect.

contralateral Refers to the fact that motor and sensory functions of the body are mediated by the opposite hemisphere of the brain; (e.g., movement of the *right* hand is coordinated by the *left* hemisphere).

conversion hysteria Physical symptoms caused by unconscious mental conflicts. (*See also* somatoform.)

coping Any cognitive or behavioral effort that one uses to manage specific demands appraised as exceeding one's resources: *problem-focused coping* is any action that attempts to change the stressor and/or the environment, while *emotion-focused coping* is an attempt to change the cognitive aspects of stress.

coronary bypass Major surgery during which the patient's own veins from another part of the body are used to move blood around blocked and damaged coronary arteries and restore blood supply to the heart.

correlation coefficient Degree of association between two variables; expressed as a number from zero to ± 1.

cortex The convoluted outer folding of brain tissue visible when the skull is removed; consists of the two hemispheres of the brain.

corticosteroids Hormones produced by the adrenal glands that regulate metabolism and the production of energy.

cortisol A corticosteroid hormone produced by the adrenal glands that is anti-inflammatory and suppresses part of the immune system.

counterconditioning Replacing a conditioned response that is unwanted or unhealthy with a new incompatible response.

cross-sectional study A special case of retrospective designs which uses groups made up of subjects at different ages.

crowding The psychological perception of confinement in a high-density environment.

cynical hostility Resentful, suspicious, and angry distrust of others; appears to be the lethal part of Type A related to CHD.

deactivation of behavior Lethargic and emotionally lacking in responsiveness; impaired ability to engage in social relationships caused by damage to the frontal lobes. (*See also* deregulation of behavior.)

delirium tremens The result of alcoholism; it includes gross disorientation, cognitive disruption, impaired motor coordination and tremor, and fleeting hallucinations when withdrawal is attempted.

dementia A profound impairment of intellectual functioning involving thought, feeling, memory, and behavior.

dendrites Tree-like structures attached to the soma of neurons that receive impulses from other neurons.

density The physical condition of high population in limited space.

dependent variable A measurable outcome in an experiment; what the experimenter hopes to affect.

depersonalization The way in which hospitals may remove the individuality of patients, subjecting them to routines and treatment patterns in which individual preferences and needs are ignored.

depressants These reduce CNS arousal and promote relaxation.

deregulation of behavior Spontaneous and poorly coordinated responses and outbursts of emotion and behavior caused by damage to the frontal lobes (*See also* deactivation of behavior.)

detoxification Traditional hospital-based medical treatment directed toward treating the physical symptoms of withdrawal from alcohol or drugs.

developmental health psychology Concerned with the interrelationship of health, behavior, and aging.

diagnosis related group (DRG) system The classification of hospital patients into categories so that hospitals are reimbursed a fixed dollar amount for patients in a given grouping regardless of length of stay, encouraging fast and efficient treatment.

diffuse impairments In Neuropsychology, a general disruption of cognitive abilities due to generalized brain dysfunction.

digestion The process of breaking food down into its constituents.

disability Refers to the interaction between an individual with a specific impairment and a specific handicapping environment.

disease A characteristic grouping of physical signs and symptoms usually associated with a pathogen.

disease prototypes Idealized conceptions that people hold about the way in which symptoms go together for any given health problem.

disregulation theory A theory that explains how control and pain interact to affect immune system functioning.

diuretic Substance which, when ingested, causes the excretion of sodium, thereby increasing the loss of fluids from the body.

double-blind An experiment in which neither the subjects nor the experimenters know which group the subjects are in (the treatment or the placebo).

drive A physiological state of the brain that impels behavior: *Primary drives* are basic and inborn drives that include thirst, hunger, aggression, and sex, while *secondary drives* are learned through conditioning.

dualist (dualism) One who believes that the mind and body are separate entities.

duodenum Connects the stomach to the small intestine.

dyspareunia Any genital pain in men or women occurring before, during, or after intercourse.

dyspnea Breathing difficulty sometimes referred to as "air hunger."

embolus A loose piece of a thrombus, a clump of foreign matter, or a gas bubble that is carried by the blood until it lodges in a narrowed artery.

emetic A drug that produces nausea and vomiting; emetics are used in the treatment of alcohol addiction.

emotional lability The expression of dramatic emotionality such as laughing or crying, either without provocation or with minimal provocation.

emphysema Destructive changes in the alveolar walls causing loss of elasticity in the lungs and also the destruction of pulmonary capillaries. The loss of elasticity causes the airways to collapse during expiration, obstructing them. Related to chronic obstructive pulmonary disease.

endocrine system A set of glands that communicate with each other and with other organs by secreting hormones directly into the bloodstream.

endorphin Pain-killing neurotransmitters similar to the opiates.

enkephalin An endorphin.

enzymes Molecules that act as catalysts in biochemical reactions, and are responsible for the process of digestion itself.

epidemiology A branch of medicine that studies how a disease occurs or spreads in a population.

epinephrine One of the catecholamines produced exclusively by the adrenal glands; prepares the body for action and is involved in the response to stress (also called "adrenalin").

esophagus A mucus-lined, muscular, collapsed tube about 10 inches long that routes food from the pharynx to the stomach.

essential hypertension High blood pressure of unknown origin.

estrogen Present in both genders; manufactured in the testes and ovaries; promotes general physical development and the development of secondary sex characteristics (e.g., breast development, widening of the pelvis), and, with progesterone, initiates the maturation of the reproductive system and regulates the uterine cycle. It mediates vaginal lubrication, vaginal elasticity, and the condition and function of the breasts. It has no known function in males, except that too much reduces sex drive in males and causes erectile problems and enlargement of the breasts; absence of estrogen in women does not reduce sex drive.

eustress Refers to "good," nonharmful stressors.

euthanasia Mercy killing usually of terminal patients for whom there is little quality of life left.

experiment A type of scientific study involving random assignment and manipulation of independent variables; experiments can help establish cause-and-effect relationships among variables.

failure to thrive Delay in achieving expected height, weight, or motor development caused by emotional neglect and inattention and not by any known organic factor.

fallopian tubes Ducts approximately 10 cm (4 inches) long connecting the ovaries to the uterus.

fat A variety of compounds that cannot be dissolved in water; a rich source of energy and the primary means the body has to store energy in reserve. Fat must first be converted into simple carbohydrates before it can be metabolized by the cells to provide energy.

fear of performance Anxiety about one's ability to function sexually and the greatest single deterrent to effective sexual functioning, because it completely distracts the fearful individual from his or her natural responsivity by blocking reception of sexual stimuli. (*See also* spectator role.)

female sexual arousal disorder A disorder of arousal which used to be called "frigidity" and occurs during sexual activity when a woman has an inadequate vaginal lubrication-swelling response (resulting in discomfort during intercourse) or when there is a lack of the subjective sense of pleasure and excitement during sex.

fetal alcohol syndrome (FAS) Retarded growth and mental retardation caused by consumption of alcohol during pregnancy; characterized by slow prenatal and postnatal development, body malformations, brain dysfunctions, hyperactivity, attention deficits, learning disabilities, and motor impairments in childhood.

focal impairment In neuropsychology, a limited disruption of cognitive abilities, leaving many others intact.

frontal lobes Located in the front of the cerebrum, these are the largest areas in the human forebrain; involved in planning, organizing, initiating, and monitoring behavior. Personality and attention are greatly affected by damage to the frontal lobes, but the frontal lobes are not the sole focus for intelligence or memories.

general adaptation syndrome (GAS) The general physiological response to stress and strain described by Hans Selye that has three stages: *Alarm* is equivalent to the fight-or-flight response of the sympathetic nervous system; *resistance* follows alarm and is the use of energy to adapt to a stressor, but involves few outward signs of the initial heightened arousal of fight-or-flight strain; *exhaustion* is the final stage occurring after prolonged resistance, when the body's energy reserves are exhausted and breakdown occurs.

generalize Refers to applying the results of an experiment to other people.

genes Individual particles of deoxyribonucleic acid or *DNA,* which contain, in a chemical code, the description of the human being's entire physical structure. The genes are linked in threadlike structures called *chromosomes.*

germ theory Based on the biomedical model; the belief that a specific pathogen causes a disease.

gerontology The study of the aging process.

glia cells Provide a structural framework for neurons and are involved in important supportive metabolic functions for them; probably function as the blood-brain barrier.

glucagon Manufactured by the pancreas; causes the release of glucose into the bloodstream and stimulates the production of glucose by the liver.

glucose A simple carbohydrate that provides most of the body's energy needs.

gonads The only endocrine glands that differ anatomically and functionally in the two sexes: Ovaries and testes.

habilitation Acquiring an ability or capacity for the first time.

hallucinogens Drugs that produce distortions of perception.

handicap Refers to limitations of environments—such as architectural barriers—rather than people.

hassles Experiences and conditions of daily living that have been appraised as salient and harmful or threatening.

health Freedom from illness, homeostatic balance, and optimum physical, mental, and social functioning.

health behavior Any action taken by a person in the absence of signs or symptoms aimed at remaining well or improving one's state of health.

Health Belief Model A theory of health behavior which proposes that people act as a function of three main factors: a perceived threat to health, a perception of effective means to combat that threat, and a belief in their ability to carry out the required behaviors.

health education Any combination of learning experiences designed to teach people to make voluntary adaptations in their behavior that will facilitate good health.

health maintenance organization (HMO) A form of managed care in which enrolled members prepay premiums to receive comprehensive health care from practitioners affiliated with the organization.

health promotion The science and art of assisting people to change and re-orient their lifestyles toward a state of optimal health.

health psychology A subfield of psychology that involves researchers and practitioners who are interested in both illness and wellness. Incorporates the focus of behavioral health and behavioral medicine, but unlike them, it is not interdisciplinary.

helper T-cells Receive the identity of foreign invaders from macrophages, pass it along to and direct killer T-cells and B-cells to target an invader.

hemispheres One of two halves of the cortex; each hemisphere is divided into four lobes which have specialized functions. The *left hemisphere* processes information more sequentially and logically, and is responsible for language processes such as speaking and writing, whereas the *right hemisphere* processes spatial information, complex patterns, and emotions.

heritability A numerical value that indicates the relative importance of genetic influences.

holists (or holism) One who believes that the mind and body are one.

homeostasis Refers to normal, balanced functioning of the elements of a system; achieved by feedback of information: *Positive feedback* increases activity while *negative feedback* decreases it.

hormones Chemical messengers analogous to neurotransmitters, except that they are usually involved in the long-term regulation of ongoing functions of the body, like reproduction, growth, and metabolism.

hospice Provides an alternative to hospital care for people who are terminally ill; has the goal of easing the patient's passing in a warm and supportive environment with a minimum of pain.

humoral response One of two branches of the immune system, it involves the B-cells that move through the blood stream and secrete antibody.

hypercholesterolemia Abnormally high levels of cholesterol in the blood; generally >250 mg/ml.

hyperventilation Shallow, rapid breathing that increases oxygen intake but upsets the balance of carbon dioxide in the blood.

hypoactive sexual desire disorder A disorder of desire which occurs when a person has few or no sexual fantasies and/or urges, although he or she may still engage in sexual behavior.

hypothalamus A small structure under the thalamus; it organizes and propels the goal-seeking behavior found in such basic biological drives as drinking, eating, sexuality, and aggression; it is also the interface between the brain and three very important functions: maintenance of homeostasis, control of the autonomic nervous system, and regulation of the endocrine system.

hypothesis The best prediction or tentative answer to a research problem or question.

illness A broader term than disease; involves a person's beliefs about the state of their physical wellbeing.

illness behavior Any action taken by a person faced with uncertainty to clarify and understand one's health status and seek help.

impairment Refers to limitations of specific organs or functions.

incidence The frequency of new cases of a disease during a specific period of time.

incubation period The time between infection with a pathogen and the appearance of clinical symptoms.

independent variable Something that is manipulated to cause a change in a dependent variable; what the experimenter hopes will affect the dependent variable.

induction Procedures that are used to help people enter a hypnotic trance.

infarct Area of dead tissue due to oxygen deprivation resulting from a blockage of blood flow.

infertility When a couple who are not using contraception have not been able to conceive after one year of trying.

inflammation A local immune response that first involves constriction of blood vessels, preserving blood and permitting clotting, then dilation of blood vessels, which results in warmth, redness, and swelling.

inhibited female orgasm Delay or absence of orgasm following a normal and adequate excitement phase; more common than the male counterpart.

inhibited male orgasm A rare phenomenon in which there is a delay or absence of orgasm following a normal and adequate excitement phase.

insight therapy Those forms of psychological treatment that assume that disordered behaviors, emotions, and thoughts are due to conflicting needs and drives of which the person is unaware; utilizes a "talking cure."

insulin Manufactured by the pancreas; decreases blood sugar by causing cell membranes to open, permitting glucose to be absorbed.

interactionism Descartes' solution to the mind-body separateness posed by dualism; preserves their separateness but assumes that they interact at a certain location such as the pineal gland.

interferon A chemical produced by B-cells that travels to other cells, helping them to better resist viral infection.

interleukin A chemical that helps T-cells mature into killer T-cells; it also travels through the bloodstream to the brain, where it affects neurotransmitters and neuroendocrine functions.

intervention Directly applying knowledge about health and illness to change people's lives; *primary intervention* is concerned with the prevention of illness and the promotion of optimum physical, mental, and social well-being; *secondary intervention* is concerned with establishing whether or not certain symptoms mean that a disease process is present; and *tertiary intervention* is concerned with the treatment of people whose disease is already fully established, arresting it, and rehabilitating them.

ischemia Area of tissue receiving decreased oxygen due to an insufficient flow of blood.

jargon Specialized language or terminology used by the members of a profession; medical jargon can either facilitate or hinder good communication.

killer T-cells Attack specific invading viruses, fungi, parasites, and cancer cells at the direction of the helper T-cells.

labia Folds of skin, labia minor (inner) and labia major (outer), that enclose the clitoris and vaginal opening.

large intestine Part of the alimentary canal. A tube about 1.5 m (5 feet) long consisting of several regions, including the colon, rectum, and anus. It does not produce any enzymes or have any active role in chemical digestion, but there are bacteria present that carry on a small amount of digestion.

lay referral network All those family and friends who supply information, interpret symptoms, and make recommendations to people when they believe they have (or may have) a medical problem.

learned helplessness The tendency to take no action to avert unpleasant or unhealthful consequences; developed by repeated failure to affect outcomes in situations that are uncontrollable.

leukocytes General term for the white blood cells of the immune cells.

life event Any major occurrence that requires a person to adjust or adapt to it, such as marriage, divorce, or changing jobs.

lifestyle The sum total of all those voluntary decisions that people make about how to act on an everyday basis.

limbic system A group of interconnected structures surrounding the thalamus and hypothalamus that is also part of the cortex; involved with emotions.

locus of control Where a person places the responsibility for her or his successes and failures; refers to people's generalized beliefs as to whether outcomes are determined by their own actions (internal locus of control) or forces beyond their control, such as others or chance (external locus of control).

longitudinal study Special case of prospective designs that follows a single group of subjects over time as they age.

lymph Fluid in the lymph system containing a concentration of lymphocytes.

lymph nodes Thickenings of lymph vessels that contain concentrations of leukocytes, which filter foreign material from the lymph.

lymphocyte A type of leukocyte; includes the constituents of the immune system cellular response.

macrophages Nonspecific lymphocytes that specialize in destroying bacteria and cellular debris of any type; they pass the identity of foreign invaders on to helper T-cells.

male erectile disorder A disorder of arousal which used to be called "impotence" in which there is inability to attain or sustain an erection through to completion of the sexual activity, or when there is a lack of the subjective sense of pleasure and excitement during sex.

managed care Any form of health care delivery in which cost, access, and quality of health care services are coordinated and controlled.

matching Research technique which involves making groups equivalent on certain variables—like age—that could influence a dependent variable.

Medicaid Joint-federal-state program of public health insurance; this program helps to cover (non-hospital) health care costs for those in financial need.

medical psychologists Focus on the prevention and treatment of illness from a strong clinical perspective; the field is similar to behavioral medicine but not interdisciplinary.

medical students' disease Although no actual disease is involved, some students often come to believe that they are suffering from the medical problem being studied at the time; a phenomenon that often affects anxious and fatigued medical students.

Medicare A form of public health insurance, this is a federal program that covers people over 65 in order to help pay for hospital costs.

medulla Regulates nonconscious processes such as breathing and circulation of the blood.

metastasize When unregulated cancer cells spread to other parts of the body through the lymph or blood.

modeling Behavior change that occurs from watching another person perform a behavior. There is no reinforcement of the observer. Instead, the observation of the reinforcement of the model is the mechanism of learning.

myofascial pain The most common of all pain syndromes, it is mild to moderate transient pain without explanation.

natural killer cells (NK cells) Nonspecific lymphocytes that specialize in destroying tumors and viruses.

neglect syndrome A common visual disorder in right hemisphere lesions in which a patient may fail to recognize or process stimuli on the left side of the visual field.

neonatal period The first four weeks of life.

neoplastic Cells that grow in an unregulated manner; usually cancerous.

neurons Single cells that are specialized to receive, process, and transmit information.

neuropsychology The study of brain-behavior relationships.

neurotransmitters Molecules that travel across the synapse between the terminal buttons and the dendrites; they either **excite** the receiving neuron, *increasing* its potential to transmit a new impulse, or **inhibit** the receiving neuron, *decreasing* its potential to transmit a new impulse.

nitrites Food additives in processed meats such as hot dogs that may become carcinogenic after ingestion.

norepinephrine One of the catecholamines produced by the adrenal glands (and elsewhere in the body) that prepares the body for action and is involved in the response to stress; it is also a neurotransmitter (also called "noradrenalin").

occipital lobes Located at the back of each hemisphere, these process visual material.

oocytes Immature eggs. (*See also* ovum.)

operant conditioning Used to condition complex, voluntary behavior through altering its consequences of reinforcement.

opportunistic infections Infections occurring in people with immune deficiency; they are caused by common pathogens that are easily controlled by a healthy immune system.

optimistic bias A cognitive factor in maintaining unhealthful behavior; it is the belief that one can engage in an unhealthy behavior because one will be able to stop engaging in it before it can have unhealthy consequences.

osteoporosis A reduction in bone tissue mass that leaves older people more vulnerable to fractures from even slight pressure.

ovarian cycle Cycle which usually lasts 28 days and during which several oocytes will grow; culminates in the ovulation, or release, in 11 to 14 days, of usually a single oocyte.

ovaries Female endocrine glands located in the lower abdominal cavity; they produce the ova, or eggs, as well as two hormones: estrogen and progesterone.

ovum A single fertilized egg; *ova* (eggs) contain one-half of the genetic material necessary to create a new individual.

pain A partly physiological and partly psychological experience that seizes attention in the presence of threatening or actual tissue damage. *Acute pain* is a relatively brief sensation, defined for research purposes as lasting less than 6 months, and related to the potential for or extent of injury. *Chronic pain* is pain that lasts more than 6 months. There are several types of chronic pain. *Chronic progressive pain* originates from an organic condition that is malignant; it is continuous, but increases in intensity as the underlying organic condition worsens. *Prechronic pain* is a transition period between acute and nonprogressive chronic pain during which pain is either overcome or psychological factors, particularly hopelessness, may contribute to the development of chronic-recurrent or chronic intractable-benign pain. *Chronic recurrent pain* is alternating periods of intense pain and no pain that arises from a benign condition (one that is not worsening). *Chronic intractable-benign pain* is more or less persistent pain that arises from a benign condition.

pain gateway Interneurons located in the grey matter of the spinal cord that have the ability to modulate the transmission of pain impulses along the A-delta and C-fibers.

pancreas Located in the abdomen near the stomach, it has several endocrine and nonendocrine functions; it produces glucagon and insulin, two hormones necessary for metabolism and the regulation of sugar in the blood. Also the major enzyme-producing organ, it excretes pancreatic juice, an alkaline fluid that contains a variety of enzymes, into the duodenum to mix with food and digest it.

paraplegia Loss of function of the lower part of the body, usually involving the legs.

parietal lobes Located above the temporal lobes, these contain the sensory cortex and process tactile and kinesthetic information; they also play a role in integrating sensory information from the temporal and occipital lobes and monitoring the body's position in space.

pathogen A foreign agent that disrupts the normal operation of the body.

penis Composed of three cylindrical cavities of erectile tissue separated by bands of muscle tissue; in its flaccid state, it permits elimination of urine from the bladder, in its erect state it permits ejaculation of semen.

peripheral nervous system Consists of all of the neural pathways that lie outside the brain and spinal cord; it is most like a network of telephone lines carrying messages to and from distant locations.

peristalsis A wave-like motion that propels food throughout the alimentary canal.

phagocytosis A process by which lymphocytes engulf and destroy invaders.

phantom limb pain Pain that is perceived to be coming from an amputated limb or from an area of the body which has nonfunctional sensory nerve fibers.

pharynx A common passageway for food, fluids, and air.

physical dependence A state of physiological adaptation to a substance, characterized by *tolerance* and *withdrawal*. *Tolerance* occurs when the body accommodates to a certain level of a substance such that the dose must be increased in order to achieve the same effects. *Withdrawal* is the uncomfortable physiological changes and accompanying psychological symptoms that occur when a substance is discontinued.

physiological toughening Strengthening the mind-body's ability to resist stress through deliberate exposure to intermittent stressors.

pituitary Sometimes referred to as the "master gland," it produces a number of hormones that affect the other endocrine glands.

placebo Treatment added to an experiment to control for the effects that people's expectations and/or knowledge about experiments might exert on dependent variables.

plasma cells B-cells that secrete antibody to a specific antigen.

plasticity The ability of one area of the brain to substitute for another; assumed to be at a peak before the age of thirteen.

polygraphic monitoring Non-invasive electrical devices that are attached to the body to measure blood pressure, heart rate, respiration, and perspiration, all indicators of the sympathetic response.

pons Brainstem structure that regulates sleep and arousal.

PRECEDE model A model of health education that encourages careful planning and evaluation of programs and that focuses on predisposing, reinforcing, and enabling factors in problem definition and project implementation.

premature ejaculation Ejaculation that occurs with minimal stimulation *and* before the person wishes it.

preterm birth Delivery before the 37th week of gestation.

prevalence The *proportion* of a population that has a disease at a specific point in time.

primary immune deficiency Usually the result of a genetic defect, this usually becomes evident at a young age.

primary immune response One in which the immune system has had no prior experience with the antigen.

problem drinking Psychological dependence on alcohol and impaired social relationships and/or work performance due to the consumption of alcohol.

progesterone Present in both genders, it promotes lactation and, with estrogen, initiates the maturation of the reproductive system and regulates the uterine cycle; its function is not entirely understood, but it appears that it inhibits the sex drive.

prospective study Begins with subjects who do not have the condition or disease of interest and looks forward in time. Subjects are followed over a period of time to see who develops the disease. *Longitudinal* studies are prospective designs that follow a single group of subjects over time as they age.

prostate gland About the size of a walnut and located just below the bladder; sperm accumulate in the prostate, where they await ejaculation, at which time they are mixed with various fluids to form semen.

protein The basic building material for all body tissues: bones, muscles, and organs.

psychoactive substance Any chemical substance that is capable of influencing central nervous system activity.

psychological dependence A strong *desire* or *compulsion* to take a substance in order to produce feelings of pleasure or to avoid feelings of discomfort.

psychoneuroimmunology An interdisciplinary field on the forefront of research into the mind-body relationship as it affects the immune system.

psychosomatic medicine Refers to the treatment of real physical symptoms and disease through a holistic mind-body approach; the term *psychosomatic* is not to be confused with *somatoform*.

quadriplegia Extensive loss of function involving the arms and legs.

randomly assigned Refers to the method that subjects in an experiment are assigned to independent variable or their levels; all subjects must have an equal probability of being assigned to each of the groups.

reactance A feeling that one's freedom is being threatened, accompanied by actions aimed at restoring control over the situation.

reactivity The speed and responsiveness of the physiological changes involved in arousal when compared to a resting baseline level of relaxation.

rehabilitation To restore a former capacity.

reinforcement The general term for behavioral consequences in operant conditioning; *reward* will increase the likelihood of a behavior occurring again while *punishment* will decrease it.

refractory period Part of the resolution phase of the human sexual response cycle for men when no further sexual excitement or erection is possible.

relaxation training Consists of learning two behaviors that result in the reduction of tension in the body: deep breathing and muscle relaxation. *Progressive muscle relaxation* consists of having patients learn the difference between a state of tension and a state of relaxation in muscles by alternately and deliberately tensing, holding, and relaxing them. *Progressive muscle relaxation with controlled breathing* combines muscle relaxation with features borrowed from Eastern traditions such as yoga.

replicate To repeat an experiment in order to see if the same results are obtained.

reserve capacity The ability of the body's organ systems to put forth several times more effort than usual under demand.

reticular formation A major brainstem center for the sleep-wake cycle.

retrospective study A study that looks backward from a specific point in time. Subjects who already have a particular condition or disease are matched with a group of subjects who do not have the condition or disease and then the histories of both groups are searched for factors that differ between them. **Cross-sectional** studies are *retrospective* designs which use groups made up of subjects at different ages.

risk factors Characteristics or activities of the individual which affect the probability that a given health problem will occur. Some risk factors (e.g., genetics) are non-modifiable; whereas others (e.g., behavioral factors) are subject to modification.

salivary glands Located both inside and outside the oral cavity, they release saliva, a watery fluid that contains enzymes that digest carbohydrate.

scientific method A systematic method to obtain and observe data in an unbiased manner; does not accept superstition, rather makes use of logical reasoning and empiricism. *Theories* are sets of organized and related ideas about natural phenomena. Scientific studies are usually conducted to test theory-related *hypotheses,* which are the best predictions or tentative answers to a research problem or question. Studies must be *replicated,* that is, repeated, usually by other researchers in other circumstances, before the results are accepted by the scientific community at large.

secondary gains Situational rewards that sometimes occur with the sick role.

secondary immune deficiency Occurs in people who had previously normal immune function, and is more common than primary immune deficiency; an example is AIDS.

secondary immune response One in which the body is reinfected with an antigen that the immune system has had previous experience with; involves memory T-cells and B-cells.

self-efficacy A belief that one is competent and effective. People with a sense of self-efficacy are likely to attempt behavioral modifications based on their belief that they have the ability to accomplish their goals.

self-regulation The ability to effectively control one's behavior.

semen A milky alkaline substance produced by the prostate that activates mature sperm; contains simple carbohydrates and other substances that provide energy and a hospitable medium for the delicate sperm.

sensate focus Developed by Masters and Johnson to encourage mutual exploration and discovery of one's total physical (not just sexual) responsiveness and used in sex therapy; uses touch, massage, and fondling.

sexual aversion disorder A disorder of desire in which a person may avoid sexual behavior entirely.

sexual dysfunction Inhibition in the appetitive or psychophysiologic changes that characterize the complete sexual response cycle. More likely the result of psychosocial factors than physiological factors.

sexually transmitted diseases (STDs) Also called venereal diseases, these are infectious diseases, but are not spread by "casual contact," which means that they cannot be transmitted to another by nonintimate touch or breathing the same air; they are spread primarily by intimate sexual contact.

sick role behavior Any action taken by a person once labeled as ill to restore or rehabilitate one's health.

sign An objective indicator, such as body temperature or blood pressure, that health practitioners use to diagnose and treat disease.

single-blind An experiment in which the subjects are kept unaware of whether they belong to the treatment or the placebo group.

sleep apnea Intermittent periods of decreased breathing during sleep that are occasionally life-threatening.

small for date Newborns that weigh less than 90% of normal babies of the same age.

small intestine The longest section of the alimentary canal, approximately 6 m (20 feet) in length; the site of nearly all nutrient absorption.

social support Refers to information transmitted to people indicating that they are loved, valued, and cared for; also refers to the number of social relationships and their quality. The presence of support is an aid in coping with stress and illness.

social marketing The adaptation of methods and approaches from commercial marketing to the arena of ideas and positive (health-related) causes.

soma The body of a cell.

somatic nervous system Made up of neural pathways that carry information *from* the periphery of the body *to* the spinal cord (also called *afferent* pathways).

somatoform Psychological disorders characterized by physical symptoms that are generated by psychological processes; incorporates *conversion hysteria.*

spectator role Caused by fear of performance; when the person becomes acutely sensitive to how she or he is doing sexually; preoccupied with self-evaluation and self-judgment. Blocks the person from "egoless" participation in the kind of abandonment and "loss of self" that people often describe as occurring during fulfilling sex.

sperm Small single cells produced in the testes; each has a head containing 23 chromosomes (one-half of the normal complement of 46 necessary to produce a human being), a middle section that provides energy, and a tail that lashes to drive the sperm forward.

sphincter Circular band of muscles that acts as a valve in the body.

spinal cord The major pathway between the brain and the peripheral nervous system.

spleen Located in the left side of the abdominal cavity beneath the diaphragm, it serves as a reservoir for leukocytes while they mature; blood flowing through the spleen is constantly cleansed of debris and bacteria by macrophages.

stomach An expandable cavity about 25 cm (10 inches) long that can hold between 1.5 and 4.0 liters (1 to 2 quarts); it mechanically breaks down and mixes food, digests protein, and temporarily holds food.

stimulants Arouse the brain, leading to increased alertness and elevation of mood.

strain Describes the psychological and physiological reactions of an individual to ongoing stress.

stress buffer Any variable that prevents or reduces the harmful consequences of exposure to stress.

stressors The external component of stress, represented by the environmental events that precede the recognition of stress. *Acute stressors* are of the briefest duration, lasting a few seconds to a couple of days, and having no lasting impact on health. *Chronic stressors* are nonacute

stressors of the longest duration, lasting from weeks to years, that may have the most unhealthful consequences. *Intermittent stressors* are the most variable in duration, occurring periodically and alternating with periods of calm; they may increase stress-resistance.

substance abuse Any external behavior by which addiction is inferred.

substance P Neurotransmitter involved in the transmission of pain impulses by A-delta and C-fibers.

substitution of function Recovery of function after brain damage that has a basis in the structure of the brain itself. (*See also* "compensation.")

suppressor T-cells These keep track of the activity of antigens and helper T-cells and turn down the immune response when the antigen is neutralized.

symptom Any sensation that is recognized and labeled as a departure from normal feeling or functioning. Symptoms indicate disease or dysfunction to the individual.

synapse Microscopic fluid-filled gap between terminal buttons and dendrites.

systematic desensitization A classical conditioning therapy developed to treat anxiety disorders. Involves pairing relaxation training with an anxiety hierarchy. It works through counterconditioning, which occurs when an incompatible response— relaxation—is associated with a stimulus that once produced anxiety.

systems theory Recognizes that a system is comprised of interdependent elements in a state of homeostasis.

temporal lobes Located along the outer side of the cerebrum in front of the occipital lobes, process auditory information.

teratogens Risk factors that are related to birth defects.

terminal buttons Small knobs at the ends of axons.

testes The primary male sex organs; endocrine glands located in the scrotum that produce sperm as well as several sex hormones called androgens.

testosterone An androgen; one of the sex hormones present in both sexes, manufactured in the testes, ovaries, and adrenal glands; it initiates the maturation of the reproductive system and the development of secondary sex characteristics (e.g., changes in voice and distribution and growth of hair during puberty), and it is the principle biological determinant of sex drive.

thalamus The major relay center above the brainstem through which all incoming sensory information, with the exception of smell, passes on its way to the cortex.

theory A set of organized and related ideas about natural phenomena.

Theory of Reasoned Action An attitude-based theory that proposes that people will act to improve their health when they have a positive attitude toward the act, believe that others would have them act in this way, and believe that they can exert control over the desired outcome.

thrombus A clot of blood that forms on atherosclerotic tissue.

thymus An endocrine gland that lies deep behind the sternum in the center of the chest cavity and where T-cells mature; it has neural connections to the CNS and produces hormones that are essential for normal immune system development.

thyroid Endocrine gland located in the throat near the larynx; it produces hormones that regulate physical growth and metabolism.

T-lymphocytes (T-cells) Involved in the cellular immune response, they specialize in destroying specific tumors or viruses.

tonsils A ring of lymphatic tissue that surrounds the entrance to the pharynx; their function is largely a mystery, but it is known that macrophages migrate from there to the oral cavity.

transaction An interaction that takes into account the ongoing relationship between the individual and the environment.

transient ischemic attack (TIA) An episode of temporary obstruction of the arteries that supply the brain.

Type A Initially conceptualized as an aggressive, hard-driving, and competitive style of behavior, believed to be related to a higher incidence of CHD. Type A individuals were characterized as achievement-oriented, with easily aroused hostility and an exaggerated sense of time urgency.

Type B Initially conceptualized as a relaxed easy-going behavior style, believed to be related to a lower incidence of CHD. Type B individuals were characterized as lacking in competitiveness, hostility, and a sense of time urgency.

uplifts Experiences and conditions of daily living that have been appraised as salient and positive or favorable.

urethra A narrow tube that carries ejaculate from the prostate through the length of the penis to its head, where it is ejected.

uterus (womb) An expandable muscular cavity located centrally in the pelvic area behind the bladder.

vagina Muscular tube approximately 8 to 10 cm (3 to 4 inches) long connecting to the uterus; a "potential space" that expands and widens to give birth and to accept the penis during sexual arousal.

vaginismus An involuntary spasm of the muscles of the outer third of the vagina that interferes with intercourse.

vulnerability Refers to an individual's lack of actual resources—physical or social—to cope with a particular situation.

Wernicke-Korsakoff Syndrome Neuron damage resulting in memory impairment, confusion, drowsiness, and gait disturbance; probably affects about 10% of alcoholics and may be linked to poor nutrition.

yo-yo dieting Frequent weight fluctuations due to "on-again, off-again" diet cycles, may be the reason for the association of obesity and poor health.

REFERENCES

Aaro, L.E., Wold, B., Kannis, L., & Rimpela, M. (1986). Health behavior in school children. A WHO cross-national survey. *Health Promotion, 1*, 17–33.

Abbott, A.V., Peters, R.K., & Vogel, M.E. (1988). Temporal stability and overlap of behavioral and questionnaire assessments of Type A behavior in coronary patients. *Psychosomatic Medicine, 50*, 123–138.

Abbott, A.V., Peters, R.K., & Vogel, M.E. (1990). Type A behavior and exercise: A follow-up study of coronary patients. *Journal of Psychosomatic Research, 34*, 153–162.

Abraham, S., Collins, G., & Nordsieck, M. (1971). Relationship of childhood weight status to morbidity in adults. *Public Health Reports, 86*, 273–284.

Abrams, D.B., Niaura, R.S., Carey, K.B., Monti, P.M., & Binkoff, J.A. (1986). Understanding relapse and recovery in alcohol abuse. *Annals of Behavioral Medicine, 8*, 27–32.

Abramson, L.Y., Garber, J., & Seligman, M.E.P. (1980). Learned helplessness in humans: An attributional analysis. In J. Garber & M.E.P. Seligman (Eds.), *Human helplessness: Theory and applications*. New York: Academic Press.

Abramson, L.Y., Seligman, M.E.P., & Teasdale, J.D. (1978). Learned helplessness in humans: Critique and reformulation. *Journal of Abnormal Psychology, 87*, 49–74.

Achenbach, T.M. (1982). *Developmental psychopathology* (2nd ed.). New York: Wiley.

Acheson, R.M., & Williams, D.R.R. (1980). Epidemiology of cerebrovascular disease: Some unanswered questions. In F.C. Rose (Ed.), *Clinical neuroepidemiology*. Baltimore: University Park Press.

Achterberg, J., Kenner, C., & Casey, D. (1989). Behavioral strategies for the reduction of pain and anxiety associated with orthopedic trauma. *Biofeedback and Self-Regulation, 14*, 101–114.

Achterberg, J., Lawlis, G.F., Simonton, O.C., Matthews-Simonton, S. (1977). Psychological factors, blood factors and blood chemistries as disease outcome predictors for cancer patients. *Multivariate Experimental Clinical Research, 3*, 107–122.

Achterberg-Lawlis, J. (1988). Musculoskeletal disorders. In E.A. Blechman & K.D. Brownell (Eds.), *Handbook of behavioral medicine for women*. New York: Pergamon.

Adams, J.H., Corsellis, J.A.N., & Duchen, L.W. (1984). *Greenfield's Neuropathology* (4th ed.). New York: Wiley.

Ader, R. (1983). Developmental psychoneuroimmunology. *Developmental Psychobiology, 16*, 251–267.

Ader, R., & Cohen, N. (1985). Behavior and the immune system. In W.D. Gentry (Ed.), *Handbook of behavioral medicine* (pp. 117–173). New York: Guilford Press.

Ader, R., Felten, D.L., & Cohen, N. (Eds.). (1991). *Psychoneuroimmunology*. New York: Academic Press.

Adessor, V.J. (1985). Cognitive factors in alcohol and drug use. In M. Galizio & S.A. Maisto (Eds.), *Determinants of substance abuse: Biological, psychological, and environmental factors*. New York: Plenum.

Affleck, G., Tennen, H., Pfeiffer, C., & Fifield, J. (1987). Appraisals of control and predictability in adapting to a chronic disease. *Journal of Personality and Social Psychology, 53*, 273–279.

Agras, W.S. (1987). *Eating disorders: Management of obesity, bulimia, and anorexia nervosa*. New York: Pergamon.

Agras, W.W., Schneider, J.A., Arnow, B., Raeburn, S.D., & Telch, C.F. (1989). Cognitive-behavioral and response-prevention treatments for bulimia nervosa. *Journal of Consulting and Clinical Psychology, 57*, 215–221.

Ahmed, P.I., Kolker, A., & Coelho, G.V. (1979). Toward a new definition of health: An overview. In P.I. Ahmend & G.V. Coelho (Eds.), *Toward a new definition of health: Psychosocial dimensions* (pp. 7–22). New York: Plenum.

Aiello, J.R., Epstein, Y.M., & Karlin, R.A. (1975). Effects of crowding on electrodermal activity. *Sociological Symposium, 14*, 43–57.

Ainsfield, E., Casper, V., Nozyce, M., & Cunningham, N. (1990). Does infant crying promote attachment? An experimental study of the effects of increased physical contact on the development of attachment. *Child Development, 61,* 1617–1627.

Ainsworth, T.H. (1984). The health promotion concept. In M.P. O'Donnell & T.H. Ainsworth (Eds.), *Health promotion in the workplace,* New York: Wiley.

Aivazyan, T.A., Zaitsev, V.P., Salenko, B.B., Yurenev, A.P., & Patrusheva, I.F. (1988). Efficacy of relaxation techniques in hypertensive patients. *Health Psychology, 7* (Suppl.), 193–200.

Ajzen, I. (1985). From intentions to actions: A theory of planned action. In J. Kuhl & J. Beckman (Eds.), *Action control: From cognition to behavior.* New York: Springer.

Ajzen, I., & Fishbein, M. (1977). Attitude-behavior relations: A theoretical analysis and review of empirical research. *Psychological Bulletin, 84,* 888–918.

Ajzen, I., & Fishbein, M. (1980). *Understanding attitudes and predicting social behavior.* Englewood Cliffs, NJ: Prentice-Hall.

Alan Guttmacher Institute. (1976). *Eleven million teenagers.* New York: Author.

Alexander, F. (1950). *Psychosomatic medicine.* New York: Norton.

Alexander, M.A., & Bauer, R.E. (1988). Cerebral palsy. In V.B. VanHasselt, P.S. Strain, & M. Hersen (Eds.), *Handbook of developmental and physical disabilities.* New York: Pergamon Press.

Alexander, A.B., & Smith, D.D. (1979). Clinical applications of EMG biofeedback. In R.J. Gatchel & K.P. Price (Eds.), *Clinical applications of biofeedback: Appraisal and status.* New York: Pergamon Press.

Alexander, J.A. (1984). Blood pressure and obesity. In J.D. Matarazzo, S.M. Weiss, J.A. Herd, N.E. Miller, & S.M. Weiss (Eds.), *Behavioral health: A handbook of health enhancement and disease prevention.* New York: Wiley.

Allen, M.T., Lawler, K.A., Matthews, K.A., Rakaczky, C.J., & Jamison, W. (1987). Type A behavior pattern, parental history of hypertension, and cardiovascular reactivity in college males. *Health Psychology, 6,* 113–130.

Alloy, L.B., & Abramson, L.Y. (1980). The cognitive component of human helplessness and depression: A critical analysis. In J. Garber & M.E.P. Seligman (Eds.), *Human helplessness: Theory and applications.* New York: Academic Press.

Altman, I. (1978). Crowding: Historical and contemporary trends in crowding research. In A. Baum & Y.M. Epstein (Eds.), *Human response to crowding* (pp. 3–29). Hillsdale, NJ: Erlbaum.

American Academy of Pediatrics. (1986). *Positive approaches to day care dilemmas: How to make it work.* Elk Grove, IL: Author.

American Association of Retired Persons (AARP). (1986). *A profile of older Americans.* Washington, DC: Author.

American Diabetes Association. (1986). *Diabetes: Fats you need to know.* Alexandria, VA: Author.

American Heart Association. (1984). *Heart facts, 1984.* Dallas, TX: Author.

American Hospital Association. (1992). *Hospital Statistics 1992.* Chicago: American Hospital Associaton.

American Psychiatric Association. (1987). *Diagnostic and statistical manual of mental disorders* (3rd ed.) Washington, DC: Author.

American Psychological Association Task Force on Health Research (1976). Contributions of psychology to health research: Patterns, problems, and potentials. *American Psychologist, 31,* 263–274.

Anda, R.F., Williamson, D.F., Escobedo, L.G., Mast, E.E., Giovino, G.A., & Remington, P.L. (1990). Depression and the dynamics of smoking. *Journal of the American Medical Association, 264,* 1541–1545.

Andersen, B.L. (1989). Health psychology's contribution to addressing the cancer problem: Update on accomplishments. *Health Psychology, 8,* 683–703.

Andersen, B.L. (1992). Psychological interventions for cancer patients to enhance the quality of life. *Journal of Consulting and Clinical Psychology, 60,* 552–568.

Anderson, C.A., & Arnoult, L.H. (1989). An examination of perceived control, humor, irrational beliefs, and positive stress as moderators of the relation between negative stress and health. *Basic and Applied Social Psychology, 10,* 101–117.

Anderson, D.E. (1987). Experimental behavioral hypertension in laboratory animals. In S. Julius & D.R. Bassett (Eds.), *Handbook of hypertension: Vol. 9. Behavioral factors in hypertension.* North Holland: Elsevier.

Anderson, E.A. (1987). Preoperative preparation for cardiac surgery facilitates recovery, reduces psychological distress, and reduces the incidence of acute postoperative hypertension. *Journal of Consulting and Clinical Psychology, 55,* 513–520.

Anderson, K.O., Bradley, L.A., Young, L.D., McDaniel, L.K., & Wise, C.M. (1985). Rheumatoid arthritis: Review of psychological factors related to etiology, effects, and treatment. *Psychological Bulletin, 98,* 358–387.

Anderson, N.B., Lane, J.D., Taguchi, F., & Williams, R.B., Jr. (1989). Patterns of cardiovascular responses to stress as a function of race and parental hypertension in men. *Health Psychology*, *8*, 525–540.

Anderson, N.B., William, R.B., Jr., Lane, J.D., Haney, T., Simpson, S., & Houseworth, S.J. (1986). Type A behavior, family history of hypertension, and cardiovascular responsivity among black women. *Health Psychology*, *5*, 393–406.

Anderson, W.T. & Helm, D.T. (1979). The physician-patient encounter: A process of reality negotiation. In E.G. Jaco (Ed.) *Patients, physicians, and illness* (3rd ed.). New York: Free Press.

Andersson, B., & Larsson, B. (1961). Influences of local temperature changes in the preoptic area and rostral hypothalamus on the regulation of food and water intake. *Acta Physiologica Scandinavica*, *52*, 75–89.

Andrasik, F., Blake, D.D., & McCarran, M.S. (1986). A biobehavioral analysis of pediatric headache. In N.A. Krasnegor, J.D. Arasteh, & M.F. Cataldo (Eds.), *Child health behavior: A behavioral pediatrics perspective*. New York: Wiley.

Andrasik, F., Blanchard, E.B., & Edlund, S.R. (1985). Physiological responding during biofeedback. In S.R. Burchfield (Ed.), *Stress: Psychological and physiological interactions*. Washington, DC: Hemisphere.

Antoni, M.H., Baggett, L., Ironson, G., LaPerriere, A., August, S., Klimas, N., Schneiderman, N., & Fletcher, M.A. (1991). Cognitive-behavioral stress management, intervention buffers, distress responses, and immunologic changes following notification of HIV-1 seropositivity. *Journal of Consulting and Clinical Psychology*, *59*, 906–915.

Antoni, M.H., Schneiderman, N., Fletcher, M.A., Goldstein, D.A., Ironson, G., & LaPerriere A. (1990). Psychoneuroimmunology and HIV-1. *Journal of Consulting and Clinical Psychology*, *58*, 38–49.

Antonovsky, A. (1979). *Health, stress, and coping*. San Francisco: Jossey-Bass.

Ardlie, N.G., Glew, G., & Schwartz, C.J. (1966). Influence of catecholamines on nucleotide induced platelet aggregation. *Nature*, *212*, 415–417.

Arling, G. (1987). Strain, social support, and distress in old age. *Journal of Gerontology*, *42*, 107–113.

Armor, D.J., Polich, J.M., & Stambul, H.B. (1978). *Alcoholism and treatment*. New York: Wiley.

Armstead, C.A., Lawler, K.A., Gordon, G., Cross, J., Gibbons, J. (1989). Relationship of racial stressors to blood pressure responses and anger expression in black college students. *Health Psychology*, *8*, 541–557.

Aronow, W.S., Harris, C.N., Isbell, M.W., Rokaw, M.D., & Imparato, B. (1972). Effect of freeway travel on angina pectoris. *Annals of Internal Medicine*, *77*, 669–676.

Aronowitz, E., & Bromberg, E.M. (Eds.) (1984). *Mental health and long-term physical illness*. Canton, MA: Prodist.

Ary, D.V., & Biglan, A. (1988). Longitudinal changes in adolescent cigarette smoking behavior: Onset and cessation. *Journal of Behavioral Medicine*, *11*, 361–382.

Asch, A. (1984). The experience of disability: A challenge for psychology. *American Psychologist*, *39*, 529–536.

Ascione, F., James, M., Austin, S., & Shimp, L. (1980). Seniors and pharmacists: Improving the dialogue. *American Pharmacist*, *5*, 30–32.

Ashley, M.J., & Rankin, J.G. (1988). A public health approach to the prevention of alcohol-related health problems. In L. Breslow, J.E. Fielding, & L.B. Lave (Eds.), *Annual review of public health* (Vol. 9). Palo Alto, CA: Annual Reviews.

Aspinwall, L.G., Kemeny, M.E., Taylor, S.E., Schneider, S.G., & Dudley, J.P. (1991). Psychosocial predictors of Gay Men's AIDS risk-reduction behavior. *Health Psychology*, *10*, 432–444.

Auerbach, S.M. (1989). Stress management and coping research in the health care setting: An overview and methodological commentary. *Journal of Consulting and Clinical Psychology*, *57*, 388–395.

Avogaro, P., Cazzolato, G., Belussi, F., & Bittolo Bon, G. (1982). Altered apoprotein comsumption of HDL_2 and HDL_3 in chronic alcoholics. *Artery*, *10*, 317–368.

Baekeland, L., Lundwall, L., & Kissin, B. (1975). Methods for the treatment of chronic alcoholism: A critical appraisal. In R.J. Gibbons (Ed.), *Research Advances in Alcohol and Drug Problems* (vol. 2). New York: Wiley.

Baer, P.E., Garmezy, L.B., McLaughlin, R.J., Pokorny, A.D., Wernick, M.J. (1987). Stress, coping, family conflict, and adolescent alcohol use. *Journal of Behavioral Medicine*, *10*, 449–466.

Bageley, C. (1979). Control of the emotions, remote stress, and the emergence of breast cancer. *Indian Journal of Clinical Psychology*, *6*, 213–220.

Baille, A., Mattick, R.P., & Webster, P. (1990). *Review of published treatment outcome literature on smoking cessation: Preparatory readings for the Quality Assurance Project Smoking Cessation Expert Committee* (National Campaign Against Drug Abuse, National Drug and Alcohol Research Center, Working Paper No. 1). Sydney, Australia: University of New South Wales.

Bakal, D.A. (1979). *Psychology and medicine: Psychological dimensions of health and illness*. New York: Springer.

Baker, L.J., Dearborn, M., Hastings, J.E., & Hamberger, K. (1984). Type A behavior in women: A review. *Health Psychology*, *3*, 477–497.

Balint, M., Hung, J., Joyce, D., Marinker, M., and Woodcock, J. (1970). *Treatment or diagnosis: A study of repeat prescription in general practice.* Toronto: J.B. Lippincott.

Balkwell, C. (1981). Transition to widowhood: A review of the literature. *Family Relations, 30,* 117–127.

Balkwell, C. (1985). An attitudinal correlate of the timing of a major life event: The case of morale in widowhood. *Family Relations, 34,* 577–581.

Ballinger, C.B. (1981). The menopause and its syndromes. In J.G. Howells (Ed.), *Modern perspectives in the psychiatry of middle age* (pp. 279–303). New York: Brunner/Mazel.

Bandura, A. (1977). Self-efficacy: Toward a unifying theory of behavioral change. *Psychological Review, 84,* 191–215.

Bandura, A. (1982). Self-efficacy mechanism in human agency. *American Psychologist, 37,* 122–147.

Bandura, A. (1986). *Social foundations of thought and action: A social cognitive theory.* Englewood Cliffs, N.J.: Prentice-Hall.

Bandura, A., Reese, L., & Adams, N.E. (1982). Microanalysis of action and fear arousal as a function of differential levels of perceived self-efficacy. *Journal of Personality and Social Psychology, 43,* 5–21.

Barbarin, O.A., Hughes, D., & Chesler, M.A. (1985). Stress, coping, and marital functioning among parents of children with cancer. *Journal of Marriage and the Family, 47,* 473–480.

Barber, J. (1986). Hypnotic analgesia. In A.D. Holzman & D.C. Turk (Eds.), *Pain management: A handbook of psychological treatment approaches.* New York: Pergamon.

Barber, T.X. (1980). *Medicine, suggestive therapy, and healing: Historical and psychophysiological considerations.* Framingham, MA: Cushing Hospital.

Barber, T.X. (1982). Hypnosuggestive procedures in the treatment of clinical pain: Implications for theories of hypnosis and suggestive therapy. In T. Millon, C.J. Green, & R.B. Maegher, Jr. (Eds.), *Handbook of clinical health psychology.* New York: Plenum Press.

Bardana, E.J., Jr., & Montanaro, A. (1986). Tight building syndrome. *Immunology and Allergy Practice, 8,* 74–88.

Bardo, M.T., & Risner, M.E. (1986). Biochemical substrates of drug abuse. In M. Galizio & S.A. Maisto (Eds.), *Determinants of substance abuse: Biological, psychological, and environmental factors.* New York: Plenum.

Barlow, D.H., Sakheim, D.K., & Beck, J.G. (1983). Anxiety increases sexual arousal. *Journal of Abnormal Psychology, 92,* 49–54.

Barnlund, D.C. (1993). The mystification of meaning: Doctor-patient encounters. In B.C. Thronton & G.L. Kreps (Eds.), *Perspectives on health communication.* Prospect Heights, IL: Waveland Press.

Barrera, M.E., Rosenbaum, P.L., & Cunningham, C.E. (1986). Early home intervention with low-birth-weight infants and their parents. *Child Development, 57,* 20–33.

Barry, P., & O'Leary, J. (1989). Roles of the psychologist on a traumatic brain injury rehabilitation team. *Rehabilitation Psychology, 34,* 83–90.

Barsky, A.J. (1988). *Worried sick: Our troubled quest for wellness.* Boston: Little, Brown.

Bartlett, E.E., Higginbotham, J.C., Cohen-Cole, S., & Bird, J. (1990). How do primary care residents manage patient non-adherence? *Patient Education and Counseling, 16,* 53–60.

Barton, J., Chassin, L., Presson, C.C., & Sherman, S.J. (1982). Social image factors as motivators of smoking initiation in early and middle adolescence. *Child Development, 53,* 1499–1511.

Barton, M.L., & Zeanah, C.H. (1990). Stress in the preschool years. In L.E. Arnold (Ed.), *Childhood stress* (pp. 193–221). New York: John Wiley & Sons.

Bartrop, R.W., Luckhurst, E., Lazarus, L., & Kiloh, L.G. (1977). Depressed lymphocyte function after bereavement. *Lancet, 1,* 834–836.

Batchelor, W.F. (1988). AIDS 1988. *American Psychologist, 43,* 853–858.

Battista, R.N., & Fletcher, S.W. (1988). Making recommendations on preventive practices: Methodological issues. In R.N. Battista & R.S. Lawrence (Eds.), *Implementing preventive services* (pp. 53–67). New York: Oxford University Press.

Bauer, R.M., Greve, K.W., Besch, E.L., Schramke, C.J., Crouch, J., Hicks, A., Ware, M.R., & Lyles, W.B. (1992). The role of psychological factors in the report of building-related symptoms in sick building syndrome. *Journal of Consulting and Clinical Psychology, 60,* 213–219.

Baum, A., Grunberg, N.E., & Singer, J.E. (1982). The use of physiological and neuroendocrinological measurements in the study of stress. *Health Psychology, 1,* 217–236.

Baum, A., & Nesselhof, E.A. (1988). Psychological research and the prevention, etiology, and treatment of AIDS. *American Psychologist, 43,* 900–906.

Baum, A., & Paulus, P.B. (1987). Crowding. *Handbook of Environmental Psychology, I,* 533–536.

Baum, A., Singer, J.E., & Baum, C.S. (1981). Stress and the environment. *Journal of Social Issues, 37,* 4–35.

Baum-Baicker, C. (1985). The psychological benefits of moderate alcohol consumption: A review of the literature. *Drug and Alcohol Dependence, 15,* 305–322.

Bauman, L.J., & Leventhal, H. (1985). "I can tell when my blood pressure is up, can't I?" *Health Psychology, 4,* 203–218.

Bauman, L.J., Cameron, L.D., Zimmerman, R.S., & Leventhal, H. (1989). Illness representations and matching labels with symptons. *Health Psychology, 8,* 449–469.

Beard, R.J. (1975). The menopause. *British Journal of Hospital Medicine, 12,* 631–637.

Beautrais, A.L., Fergusson, D.M., & Shannon, F.T. (1982). Life events and childhood morbidity: a prospective study. *Pediatrics, 70,* 935–940.

Beck, A., & Katcher, A. (1983). *Between pets and people.* New York: Putnam.

Beck, A.T. (1987). Cognitive therapy. In J.K. Zeig (Ed.), *The evolution of psychotherapy.* New York: Brunner/Mazel.

Beck, J.G., Barlow, D.H., Sackheim, D.K., & Abrahamson, D.J. (1984). *Sexual responding during anxiety: Clinical versus nonclinical patterns.* Paper presented at the 18th annual convention of the Association for Advancement of Behavior Therapy, Philadelphia. As cited in Barlow, D.H. (1986). Causes of sexual dysfunction: The role of anxiety and cognitive interference. *Journal of Consulting and Clinical Psychology, 54,* 140–148.

Beck, K. (1981). Driving while under the influence of alcohol: Relationship of attitudes and beliefs in a college population. *American Journal of Drug and Alcohol Abuse, 8,* 377–388.

Becker, M.H. (Ed.) (1974). *The Health Belief Model and personal health behavior.* Thorofare, NJ: Charles B. Slack.

Becker, M.H. (1985). Patient adherence to prescribed therapies. *Medical Care, 23,* 539–555.

Becker, M.H. (1986). The tyranny of health promotion. *Public Health Review, 14,* 15–25.

Becker, M.H. (1991). In hot pursuit of health promotion: Some admonitions. In S.M. Wiess, J.E. Fielding, & A. Baum, (Eds.). *Health at work.* Hillsdale, NJ: Erlbaum.

Becker, M.H. & Joseph, J.G. (1988). AIDS and behavioral change to reduce risk: A review. *American Journal of Public Health, 78,* 394–410.

Becker, M.H., & Maiman, L.A. (1975). Sociobehavioral determinants of compliance with health and medical care recommendations. *Medical Care, 13,* 10–24.

Beecher, H.K. (1946). Pain of men wounded in battle. *Annals of Surgery, 123,* 96–105.

Beecher, H.K. (1956). Relationship of significance of wound to pain experience. *Journal of the American Medical Association, 161,* 1609–1613.

Behrman, R.E. (1985). Preventing low birth weight: A pediatric perspective. *Journal of Pediatrics, 107,* 842–854.

Behrman, R.E., & Vaughn, V.C. (1983). *Nelson textbook of pediatrics* (12th ed.). Philadelphia: Saunders.

Beisecker, A.E. and Beisecker, T.D. (1990). Patient information-seeking behaviors when communicating with doctors. *Medical Care, 28,* 19–28.

Belar, C.D., & Kibrick, S.A. (1986). Biofeedback in the treatment of chronic back pain. In A.D. Holzman & D.C. Turk (Eds.), *Pain management: A handbook of psychological treatment approaches.* New York: Pergamon.

Belar, C.D., Wilson, E., & Hughes, H. (1982). Health psychology training in doctoral programs. *Health psychology, 1,* 289–299.

Belbin, R.M. (1967). Middle age: What happens to ability? In R. Owen, *Middle age.* London: BBC.

Bell, I.R. (1987). Environmental illness and health: The controversy and challenge of clinical ecology for mind-body health. *Advances, 4,* 45–55.

Bell, P.A., Fisher, J.D., Baum, A., & Greene, T.E. (1990). *Environmental psychology.* Fort Worth, TX: Holt, Rinehart and Winston.

Belle, D. (1987). Gender differences in the social moderators of stress. In R.C. Barnett, L. Biener, and G.K. Baruch (Eds.), *Gender and stress.* New York: Free Press.

Bellet, S., Roman, L., & Katis, J. (1969). The effects of automobile driving on catecholamine and adrenocortical excretion. *The American Journal of Cardiology, 24,* 365–368.

Belloc, N. (1973). Relationship of health practices and mortality. *Preventive Medicine, 2,* 67–81.

Belloc, N.B. and Breslow, L. (1972). Relationship of physical health status and health practices. *Preventive Medicine, 13,* 409–421.

Bengston, V., Cuellar, J.A., & Ragan, P. (1975, October 29). *Group contrasts in attitudes toward death: Variation by race, age, occupational status, and sex.* Paper presented at the annual meeting of the Gerontological Society, Louisville, KY.

Ben-Sira, Z. (1985). Primary medical care and coping with stress and disease: The inclination of primary care practitioners to demonstrate affective behavior. *Social Science and Medicine, 21,* 485–498.

Bennett, F.C., Robinson, N.M., & Sells, C.J. (1983). Growth and development of infants weighing less than 800 grams at birth. *Pediatrics, 7,* 319–323.

Bennett, P., & Carroll, D. (1990). Stress management approaches to the prevention of coronary heart disease. *British Journal of Clinical Psychology, 29,* 1–12.

Bennett, W., & Gurin, J. (1982). *The dieter's dilemma: Eating less and weighing more.* New York: Basic Books.

Benson, H. (1975). *The relaxation response.* New York: Morrow.

Berenson, G.S., Arbeit, M.L., Hunter, S.M., Johnson, C.C., & Nicklas, T.A. (1991). Cardiovascular health promotion for elementary school children. The Heart Smart Program. *Annals of the New York Academy of Sciences, 623,* 299–313.

Berger, B.G., & Owen, D.R. (1983). Mood alteration with swimming—swimmers really do "feel better." *Psychosomatic Medicine, 45,* 425–433.

Berger, T.W. (1984). Long-term potentiation of hippocampal synaptic transmission affects rate of behavioral learning. *Science, 224*, 627–630.

Berkanovic, E., Telesky, C., & Reeder, S. (1981). Structural and social psychological factors in the decision to seek medical care for symptoms. *Medical Care, 19*, 693–709.

Berkman, L.F., Breslow, L. (1983). *Health and ways of living: The Alameda County Study.* New York: Oxford University Press.

Berkman, L.F., Breslow, L., & Wingard, D.L. (1983). Health practices and mortality risk. In L.F. Berkman & L. Breslow (Eds.), *Health and ways of living: The Alameda County study.* New York: Oxford University Press.

Berkman, L.F., & Syme, S.L., (1979). Social networks, host resistance, and mortality: A nine-year follow-up study of Alameda County residents. *American Journal of Epidemiology, 109*, 186–204.

Berkow, R., & Fletcher, A.J. (1987). *The Merck manual of diagnosis and therapy* (15th ed.). Rahway, New Jersey: Merck Sharp & Dohme Research Laboratories.

Berkowitz, R.I., Agras, W.S., Korner, A.F., Kraemer, H.C., & Zeanah, C.H. (1985). Physical activity and adiposity: A longitudinal study from birth to childhood. *Journal of Pediatrics, 106*, 734–738.

Berlyne, D. (1960). *Conflict, arousal, and curiosity.* New York: McGraw-Hill.

Bernard, L.C., & Belinsky, D. (1992). Hardiness, stress, and maladjustment: Effects on self-reported retrospective health problems and prospective health center visits. *Journal of Social Behavior and Personality, 7*, 1–14.

Bernstein, I.L. (1991). Aversion conditioning in response to cancer and cancer treatment. *Clinical Psychology Review, 11*, 185–191.

Bertakis, K.D. (1977). The communication of information from physician to patient: A method for increasing patient retention and satisfaction. *Journal of Family Practice, 5*, 217–222.

Besedovsky, H.O., Sorkin, E., Felix, D., & Haas, H. (1977). Hypothalamic changes during the immune response. *European Journal of Immunology, 7*, 323–325.

Best, J.A., Thomson, S.J., Santi, S.M., Smith, E.A., & Brown, K.S. (1988). Preventing cigarette smoking among school children. In L. Breslow, J.E. Fielding, & L.B. Lave (Eds.), *Annual review of psychology* (Vol. 9). Palo Alto, CA: Annual Reviews.

Bhagat, R.S. & Ford, D.L., Jr. (1990). Work and non-work issues in the management of occupational careers in the 1990's. In J.C. Quick, J.D. Quick, J. Hermalin, & R. Hess (Eds.), *Prevention in human services* (Vol. 8, No. 1). Binghamton, NY: Haworth Press.

Bibace, R., & Walsh, M.E. (1979). Developmental stages in children's conceptions of illness. In G.C. Stone, F. Cohen, & N.E. Adler (Eds.), *Health psychology—A handbook.* San Francisco: Jossey-Bass.

Bieliauskas, L.A., Shekelle, R.B., Garron, D.C., Maliza, C., Ostfield, A.M., & Raynor, W.J. (1979). Psychological depression and cancer mortality. *Psychosomatic Medicine, 41*, 77–78.

Biglan, A., Severson, H., Ary, D., Faller, C., Gallison, C., Thompson, R., Glasgow, R., & Lichtenstein, E. (1987). Do smoking prevention programs really work? Attrition and the internal and external validity of an evaluation of a refusal skills training program. *Journal of Behavioral Medicine, 10*, 159–171.

Bindra, D. (1985). Motivation, the brain, and psychological theory. In S. Koch & D.E. Leary (Eds.), *A century of psychology as science.* New York: McGraw-Hill.

Binstock, R.H. (1987). Health care: Organization use and financing. In G.L. Maddox (Ed.), *The encyclopedia of aging* (p. 308). New York: Springer.

Birren, J.E. (1974). Translations in gerontology—from lab to life: Psychophysiology and speed of response. *American Psychologist, 29*, 808–815.

Birren, J.E., Woods, A.M., & Williams, M.V. (1980). Behavioral slowing with age: Causes, organization, and consequences. In L.W. Poon (Ed.), *Aging in the 1980's.* Washington, DC: American Psychological Association.

Bishop, G.D. (1990, August). *Understanding the understanding of illness.* Paper presented at the annual meeting of the American Psychological Association, Boston.

Bishop, G.D. & Converse, S.A. (1986). Illness representations: A prototype approach. *Health Psychology, 5*, 95–114.

Blackwell, B., Griffin, B., Magill, M., and Bencze, R. (1978). Teaching medical students about treatment compliance. *Journal of Medical Education, 53*, 672–675.

Blair, A.J., Lewis, V.J., & Booth, D.A. (1989). Behaviour therapy for obesity: The role of clinicians in the reduction of overweight. Special Issue: Health Psychology: Perspectives on theory, research and practice. *Counselling Psychology Quarterly, 2*, 289–301.

Blake, J. (1990). *Risky times.* New York: Workman Publishing.

Blalock, J.E. (1988). Immunologically-mediated pituitary-adrenal activation. In G.P. Chrousos, D.L. Loriaux, & P.W. Gold (Eds.), *Mechanisms of physical and emotional stress* (pp. 217–222). NY: Plenum.

Blalock, J.E. (1989). A molecular basis for bidirectional communication between the immune and neuroendocrine systems. *Physiological Reviews, 69*, 1–30.

Blalock, J.E. & Smith, E.M. (1985). A complete regulatory loop between the immune and neuroendocrine systems. *Federal Proceedings, 44,* 1776–1779.

Blanchard, E.B. (1987). Long-term effects of behavioral treatment of chronic headache. *Behavior Therapy, 18,* 375–385.

Blanchard, E.B., & Andrasik, F. (1982). Psychological assessment and treatment of headache: Recent development and emerging issues. *Journal of Consulting and Clinical Psychology, 50,* 859–879.

Blanchard, E.B., & Andrasik, F. (1985). *Management of chronic headaches: a psychological approach.* New York: Pergamon Press.

Blanchard, E.B., Andrasik, F., Guarnieri, P., Neff, D.F., & Rodichok, L.D. (1987). Two-, three-, and four-year follow-up on the self-regulatory treatment of chronic headache. *Journal of Consulting and Clinical Psychology, 55,* 257–259.

Blanchard, E.B., & Andrasik, F., Neff, D.F., Arena, J.G., Ahles, T.A., Jurish, S.E., Pallmeyer, T.P., Saunders, N.L., & Teders, S.J. (1982). Biofeedback and relaxation training with three kinds of headache: Treatment effects and their prediction. *Journal of Consulting and Clinical Psychology, 50,* 562–575.

Blanchard, E.B., Jaccard, J., Andrasik, F., Guarnieri, P., & Jurish, S.E. (1985). Reduction in headache patients' medical expenses associated with biofeedback and relaxation treatments. *Biofeedback and Self-Regulation, 10,* 63–68.

Blanchard, E.B., Khramelashvili, V.V., McCoy, G.C., Aivazyan, T.A., McCaffrey, R.J., Salenko, B.B., Musso, A., Wittrock, D.A., Berger, M., Gerardi, M., & Pangburn, L. (1988). The USA-USSR collaborative cross-cultural comparison of autogenic training and thermal biofeedback in the treatment of mild hypertension. *Health Psychology, 7,* (Suppl.), 175–192.

Blanchard, E.B., McCoy, G.C., Wittrock, D., Musso, A., Gerardi, M., & Pangburn, L. (1988). A controlled comparison of thermal biofeedback and relaxation training in the treatment of essential hypertension. *Health Psychology, 7,* (Suppl.), 19–33.

Blaney, N.T. (1985). Smoking: Psychophysiological causes and treatments. In N. Schneiderman & J.T. Tapp (Eds.), *Behavioral medicine: The biopsychosocial approach.* NJ: Erlbaum.

Blankenhorn, D.H., Nessim, S.A., Johnson, R.L., Sanmarco, M.E., Azen, S.P., & Cashin-Hempill, L. (1987). Beneficial effects of combined colestipol-niacin therapy on coronary atherosclerosis and coronary venous bypass grafts. *Journal of the American Medical Association, 257,* 3233–3240.

Blankstein, K.R., Flett, G.L., & Koledin, S. (1991). The Brief College Student Hassles Scale: Development, validation, and relation with pessimism.

Journal of College Student Development, 32, 258–264.

Bleiberg, J. (1986). Psychological and neuropsychological factors in stroke management. In P.E. Kaplan & L.J. Cerullo (Eds.), *Stroke rehabilitation.* Boston: Butterworth.

Blinn, L.M. (1990). Adolescent mothers's perceptions of their work lives in the future: Are they stable? *Journal of Adolescent Research, 5,* 206–221.

Block, A.R., Kremer, E.F., & Gaylor, M. (1980a). Behavioral treatment of chronic pain: The spouse as a discriminative cue for pain behavior. *Pain, 9,* 243–252.

Block, A.R., Kremer, E.F., & Gaylor, M. (1980b). Behavioral treatment of chronic pain: Variables affecting treatment efficacy. *Pain, 8,* 367–375.

Block, M.A. (1976). Don't place alcohol on a pedestal. *Journal of the American Medical Association, 235,* 2103–2104.

Bloom, J.R. (1982). Social support, accommodation to stress, and adjustment to breast cancer. *Social Science and Medicine, 16,* 1329–1338.

Bloom, P. (1980). Evaluating social marketing programs: Problems and prospects. In R. Bagozzi, K. Bernhardt, P. Bosch, D. Cravens, J. Hair, Jr., & C. Scott (Eds.), *Marketing in the 80's: Changes and challenges.* Chicago: American Marketing Association.

Bloom, S.W. (1963). *The doctor and his patient: A sociological interpretation.* New York: Russell Sage.

Blumenthal, J.A., Emery, C.F., Walsh, M.A., Cox, D.R., Kuhn, C.M., Williams, R.B., & Williams, R.S. (1988). Exercise training in healthy Type A middle-aged men: Effects of behavioral and cardiovascular responses. *Psychosomatic Medicine, 50,* 418–433.

Bohlen, J.G., Held, J.P., & Sanderson, M.O. (1980). The male orgasm: Pelvic contractions measured by anal probe. *Archives of Sexual Behavior, 9,* 503–521.

Bohman, M., Sigvardsson, S., & Cloninger, C.R. (1981). Maternal inheritance of alcohol abuse. *Archives of General Psychiatry, 38,* 965–969.

Boll, T.J., & Barth, J.T. (1981). Neuropsychology of brain damage in children. In S.B. Filskov & T.J. Boll (Eds.), *Handbook of clinical neuropsychology.* New York: John Wiley & Sons.

Bonica, J.J. (1976). Organization and function of a multidisciplinary pain clinic. In M. Weisenberg & B. Tursky (Eds.), *Pain: New perspectives in therapy and research.* New York: Plenum.

Bonica, J.J. (1980a). Conclusion. In J.J. Bonica (Ed.), *Pain.* New York: Raven Press.

Bonica, J.J. (1980b). Pain research and therapy: Past and current status and future needs. In L. Ng & J.J. Bonica (Eds.), *Pain, discomfort, and humanitarian care.* New York: Elsevier.

Booth, D.A. (1977). Satiety and appetite are conditioned reactions. *Psychosomatic Medicine, 39,* 76–81.

Booth-Kewley, S., & Friedman, H.S. (1987). Psychological predictors of heart disease: A quantitative review. *Psychological Bulletin, 101,* 343–362.

Boranic, M. (1980). Central nervous system and immunity. *Lijec Vjesn, 102,* 602–608.

Bordieri, J.E., & Drehmer, D.E. (1988). Causal attribution and hiring recommendations for disabled job applicants. *Rehabilitation Psychology, 33,* 239–247.

Boring, E.G. (1950). *A history of experimental psychology* (2nd ed.). Englewood Cliffs, NJ: Prentice-Hall.

Borkan, G.A., Sparrow, D., Wisniewski, C., & Vokonas, P.S. (1986). Body weight and coronary disease risk: Patterns of risk factor change associated with long-term weight change. The Normative Aging Study. *American Journal of Epidemiology, 124,* 410–419.

Borkovec, T.D., Johnson, M.C., & Block, D.L. (1984). Evaluating experimental designs in relaxation training. In R.L. Woolfolk & P.M. Lehrer (Eds.), *Principles and practice of stress management.* New York: Guilford Press.

Borkovec, T.D., & Sides, J. (1979). Critical procedural variables related to the physiological effects of progressive relaxation: A review. *Behavior Research and Therapy, 17,* 119–125.

Bortner, R.W., & Rosenman, R.H. (1967). The measurement of pattern A behavior. *Journal of Chronic Diseases, 20,* 466–475.

Bosedovsky, H., del Rey, A., Sorkin, E., DaPrada, M., & Keller, H.H. (1979). Immunoregulation mediated by the sympathetic nervous system. *Cellular Immunology, 48,* 346–355.

Bosley, F., & Allen, T.W. (1989). Stress management training for hypertensives: Cognitive and physiological effects. *Journal of Behavioral Medicine, 12,* 77–90.

Botvin, G.J., & Wills, T.A. (1985). Personal and social skills training: Cognitive-behavioral approaches to substance abuse prevention. In C.S. Bell & R. Battjes (Eds.), *Prevention research: Deterring drug abuse among children and adolescents* (NIDA Research Monograph 63). Washington, DC: U.S. Government Printing Office.

Bouchard, C. (1991). Is weight fluctuation a risk factor? *New England Journal of Medicine, 324,* 1887–1889.

Bouchard, C., Bray, G.A., & Hubbard, V.S. (1990). Basic and clinical aspects of regional fat distribution. *American Journal of Clinical Nutrition, 52,* 946–950.

Bouchard, C., Tremblay, A., Despres, J.-P., Nadeau, A., Lupien, P.J., Theriault, G., Dussault, J., Moorjani, S., Pinault, S., & Gournier, G. (1990). The response to long-term overfeeding in identical twins. *The New England Journal of Medicine, 322,* 1477–1482.

Bound, J., Duncan, G.J., Laren, D.S., & Oleinick, L. (1991). Poverty dynamics in widowhood. *Journal of Gerontology, 46,* S115-S124.

Bourne, P.G., Alford, J.A., & Bowcock, J.Z. (1966). Treatment of skid row alcoholics with disulfiram. *Quarterly Journal of Studies on Alcohol, 27,* 42–48.

Bowlby, J. (1982). *Attachment and loss: Vol. 1. Attachment* (2nd ed.). London: Hogarth.

Bowling, A. & Browne, P.D. (1991). Social networks, health, and emotional well-being among the oldest old in London. *Journal of Gerontology, 46,* 520–532.

Boyce, W.T., & Chesterman, E. (1990). Life events, social support, and cardiovascular reactivity in adolescence. *Journal of Developmental and Behavioral Pediatrics, 11,* 105–111.

Boyce, W.T., Jensen, E.W., Cassel, J.C., Collier, A.M., Smith, A.H., & Ramey, C.T. (1977). Influence of life events and family routines on childhood respiratory tract illness. *Pediatrics, 60,* 609–615.

Boyd, J.R., Covington, T.R., Stanascek, W.F., and Coussans, R.T. (1974). Drug defaulting. Part II. Analysis of noncompliant patterns. *American Journal of Hospital Pharmacy, 31,* 485–491.

Bradford, L.P. (1986). Can you survive retirement? In R.H. Moos (Ed.), *Coping with life crises: An integrated approach.* New York: Plenum.

Bradley, B.W., & McCanne, T.R. (1981). Autonomic responses to stress: The effects of progressive relaxation, the relaxation response, and expectancy of relief. *Biofeedback and Self-Regulation, 6,* 235–251.

Bradley, C. (1979). Life events and the control of diabetes mellitus. *Journal of Psychosomatic Research, 23,* 159– 162.

Bradley, L.A., Prokop, C.K., Gentry, W.D., Van der Heide, L.H., & Prieto, E.J. (1981). Assessment of chronic pain. In C.K. Prokop & L.A. Bradley (Eds.), *Medical psychology: Contributions to behavioral medicine.* New York: Academic Press.

Bradley, L.A., Prokop, C.K., Margolis, R., & Gentry, W.D. (1978). Multivariate analysis of the MMPI profiles of low back pain patients. *Journal of Behavioral Medicine, 1,* 253–272.

Bradley, L.A., & Van der Heide, L.H. (1984). Pain-related correlates of MMPI profile subgroups among back pain patients. *Health Psychology, 3,* 157–174.

Bradley, R.H., & Casey, P.M. (1984). Home environments of low SES nonorganic failure-to-thrive infants. *Merrill-Palmer Quarterly, 30,* 393–402.

Brand, A.H., Johnson, J.H., & Johnson, S.B. (1986). Life stress and diabetic control in children and adolescents with insulin-dependent diabetes. *Journal of Pediatric Psychology, 11,* 481–495.

Brandsma, J.M., Maultsby, M.C., & Welsh, R.J. (1980). *The outpatient treatment of alcoholism: A review and comparative study.* Baltimore: University Park Press.

Bray, G.A. (1976). *The obese patient.* Philadelphia: Saunders.

Bray, G.A. (1984). The role of weight control in health promotion and disease prevention. In J.D. Matarazzo, S.M. Weiss, J.A. Herd, N.E. Miller, & S.M. Weiss (Eds.), *Behavioral health: A handbook of health enhancement and disease prevention.* New York: Wiley.

Brecher, E.M., & the Editors of *Consumer Reports.* (1972). *Licit and illicit drugs.* Mount Vernon, NY: Consumers Union.

Brehm, J. (1966). *A theory of psychological reactance.* New York: Academic Press.

Brehm, S.S. & Brehm, J. (1981). *Psychological reactance.* New York: Academic Press.

Brennan, A.F., Barrett, C.L., & Garretson, H.D. (1987). The utility of McGill Pain Questionnaire subscales for discriminating psychological disorder in chronic pain patients. *Psychology and Health, 1,* 257–272.

Breslow, L., Fielding, J., Hermann, A.A., & Wilbur, C.S. (1990). Worksite health promotion: Its evolution and the Johnson & Johnson experience. *Preventive Medicine, 19,* 13–21.

Brewster, A.B. (1982). Chronically ill hospitalized children's concepts of their illness. *Pediatrics, 69,* 355–362.

Bricker, D., & Bricker, W. (1971). Toddler research and intervention project report: Year I. *IMRID Behavioral Science Monograph 20.* Nashville, TN: Institute on Mental Retardation and Intellectual Development, George Peabody College.

Brobeck, J.R. (1948). Food intake as a mechanism of temperature regulation. *Yale Journal of Biology and Medicine, 20,* 545–552.

Brodsky, C.M. (1983). "Allergic to everything": A medical subculture. *Psychosomatics, 24,* 731–742.

Brody, B. (1945). *Bioenergetics and growth.* New York: Hafner.

Bromet, E. (1980). *Preliminary report on the mental health of Three Mile Island residents.* Pittsburgh, PA: Western Psychiatric Institute, University of Pittsburgh.

Brook, J.S., Whiteman, M., & Gordon, A.S. (1983). Stages in drug use in adolescence: Personality, peer, and family correlates. *Developmental Psychology, 19,* 269–277.

Brook, J.S., Whiteman, M., Gordon, A.S., & Cohen, P. (1986). Dynamics of childhood and adolescent personality traits and adolescent drug use. *Developmental Psychology, 22,* 403–414.

Brookmeyer, R. (1991). Reconstruction and future trends of the AIDS epidemic in the United States. *Science, 253,* 37–42.

Brooks, W.H., Cross, R.J., Roszman, T.L., & Markesbery, W.R. (1982). Neuroimmunomodulation: Neuroanatomical basis for impairment and facilitation. *Annals of Neurology, 12,* 56–61.

Brown, B. (1970). Recognition of aspects of consciousness through association with EEG alpha activity represented by a light signal. *Psychophysics, 6,* 442–446.

Brown, H., Adams, R.G., & Kellam, S.G. (1981). A longitudinal study of teenage motherhood and symptoms of distress: Woodlawn Community Epidemiological Project. In R. Simmons (Ed.), *Research in community and mental health,* Vol. 2. Greenwich, CT: JAI Press.

Brown, J.D., & Siegel, J.M. (1988). Exercise as a buffer of life stress: A prospective study of adolescent health. *Health Psychology, 7,* 341–353.

Brown, J.L. (1987). Hunger in the U.S. *Scientific American, 256,* 37–41.

Brown, L.K., DiClemente, R.J., & Reynolds, L.A. (1991). HIV prevention for adolescents: Utility of the Health Belief Model. *AIDS Education and Prevention, 3,* 50–59.

Brown, S.S. (1985). Can low birth-weight be prevented? *Family Planning Perspectives, 17,* 112–118.

Brownell, K.D. (1982a). The addictive disorders. In C.M. Franks, G.T. Wilson, P.C. Kendall, & K.D. Brownell (Eds.), *Annual review of behavior therapy: Theory and practice* (Vol. 8). New York: Guilford Press.

Brownell, K.D. (1982b). Obesity: Understanding and treating a serious prevalent and refractory disorder. *Journal of Consulting and Clinical Psychology, 52,* 820–840.

Brownell, K.D. (1984a). Behavioral medicine. In G.T. Wilson, C.M. Franks, K.D. Brownell, & P.C. Kendall, *Annual review of behavior therapy: Therapy and practice* (Vol. 9). New York: Guilford Press.

Brownell, K.D. (1984b). The addictive disorders. In G.T. Wilson, C.M. Franks, K.D. Brownell, & P.C. Kendall, *Annual review of behavior therapy: Therapy and practice* (Vol. 9). New York: Guilford Press.

Brownell, K.D. (1986a). Social and behavioral aspects of obesity in children. In N.A. Krasnegor, J.D. Arasteh, & M.F. Cataldo (Eds.), *Child health behavior: A behavioral pediatrics perspective.* New York: Wiley.

Brownell, K.D. (1986b). Public health approaches to obesity and its management. In L. Breslow, J.E. Fielding, & L.B. Lave (Eds.), *Annual review of public health* (Vol. 7). Palo Alto, CA: Annual Reviews.

Brownell, K.D. (1991a). Personal responsibility and control over our bodies: When expectation exceeds reality. *Health Psychology, 10*, 303–310.

Brownell, K.D. (1991b). Dieting and the search for the perfect body: Where physiology and culture collide. *Behavior Therapy, 22*, 1–12.

Brownell, K.D., & Jeffrey, R.W. (1987). Improving long-term weight loss: Pushing the limits of treatment. *Behavior Therapy, 18*, 353–374.

Brownell, K.D., Kelman, M.S., & Stunkard, A.J. (1983). Treatment of obese children with and without their mothers: Changes in weight and blood pressure. *Pediatrics, 71*, 515–523.

Brownell, K.D., & Kramer, F.M. (1989). Behavioral management of obesity. *Medical Clinica of North America, 73*, 185–201.

Brownell, K.D., Marlatt, G.A., Lichtenstein, E., & Wilson, G.T. (1986). Understanding and preventing relapse. *American Psychologist, 41*, 765–782.

Brownell, K.D., & Stunkard, A.J. (1981). Couples training, pharmacotherapy, and behavior therapy in the treatment of obesity. *Archives of General Psychiatry, 38*, 1224–1229.

Brownell, K.D., & Wadden, T.A. (1992). Etiology and treatment of obesity: Understanding a serious, prevalent, and refractory disorder. *Journal of Consulting and Clinical Psychology, 60*, 505–517.

Brownlee-Duffeck, M., Peterson, L., Simonds, J.F., Goldstein, D., Kilo, C., & Hoette, S. (1987). The role of health beliefs in the regimen adherence and metabolic control of adolescents and adults with diabetes mellitus. *Journal of Consulting and Clinical Psychology, 55*, 139–144.

Bruch, H. (1973). *Eating disorders. Obesity, anorexia nervosa and the person within.* New York: Basic Books.

Bruch, H. (1978). *The golden cage: The enigma of anorexia nervosa.* Cambridge, MA: Harvard University Press.

Bruch, H. (1982). Anorexia nervosa: Therapy and theory. *American Journal of Psychiatry, 139*, 1531–1538.

Buckalew, L.W. (1991). Patients' compliance: The problem and directions for psychological research. *Psychological Reports, 68*, 348–350.

Bukstein, O.G., Brent, D.A., Kaminer, Y. (1989). Comorbidity of substance abuse and other psychiatric disorders in adolescents. *American Journal of Psychiatry, 146*, 1131–1141.

Bullen, B.A., Reed, R.R., & Mayer, J. (1964). Physical activity of obese and nonobese adolescent girls appraised by motion picture sampling. *American Journal of Clinical Nutrition, 14*, 211–223.

Bulloch, K. (1985). Neuroanatomy of lymphoid tissue: A review. In R. Guillemin, M. Cohen, & T. Menechuk (Eds.), *Neural modulation of immunity* (pp. 111–141). New York: Raven Press.

Burbach, D.J., & Peterson, L. (1986). Children's concepts of physical illness: A review and critique of the cognitive-developmental literature. *Health Psychology, 5*, 307–325.

Burge, S., Hedge, S., Wilson, S., Bass, J.H., & Robertson, A. (1987). Sick building syndrome: A study of 4,373 office workers. *Annals of Occupational Hygiene, 31*, 493–504.

Burnam, M.A., Pennebaker, J.W., & Glass, D.C. (1975). Time consciousness, achievement-striving, and the Type A coronary-prone behavior pattern. *Journal of Abnormal Psychology, 84*, 76–79.

Burrell, C.D. & Levy, R.A. (1985). Therapeutic consequences of noncompliance. In *Improving medication compliance: Proceedings of a symposium.* Reston, VA: National Pharmaceutical Council.

Burton, I. (1990). Factors in urban stress. *Jounal of Sociology and Social Welfare, 17*, 79–92.

Bush, C., Ditto, B., & Feuerstein, M. (1985). A controlled evaluation of paraspinal EMG biofeedback in the treatment of chronic low back pain. *Health Psychology, 4*, 307–321.

Busse, E.W. (1987). Primary and secondary aging. In G.L. Maddox (Ed.), *The encyclopedia of aging* (p. 534). New York: Springer.

Butters, N., & Brandt, J. (1985). The continuity hypothesis: The relationship of long-term alcoholism to the Wernicke-Korsakoff syndrome. *Recent Developments in Alcoholism, 3*, 207–226.

Buxton, M.N., Arkey, Y., Lagos, J., Deposito, F., Lowenthal, F., & Simring, S. (1981). Stress and platelet aggregation in hemophiliac children and their family members. *Research Communications in Psychology, Psychiatry and Behavior, 6*, 21–48.

Byrne, D.G., & Rosenman, R.H. (1986). The Type A behaviour pattern as a precursor to stressful life-events: A confluence of coronary risks. *British Journal of Medical Psychology, 59*, 75–82.

Byrne, D., Steinburg, M., & Schwartz, M. (1968). Relationship between repression-sensitization and physical illness. *Journal of Abnormal Psychology, 73*, 154–155.

Byrne, P.S. & Long, B.E.L. (1976). *Doctors talking to patients.* London: Royal College of General Practitioners.

Cacioppo, J.T., Anderson, B.L., Turnquist, D.C., & Petty, R.E. (1986). Psychophysiological comparison processes: Interpreting cancer symptoms. In B.L. Anderson (Ed.), *Women with cancer: Psychological perspectives.* New York: Springer-Verlag.

Cacioppo, J.T., Petty, R.E., & Marshall-Goodell, B. (1985). Physical, social, and inferential elements of psychophysiological measurement. In P. Karoly (Ed.), *Measurement strategies in health psychology.* New York: Wiley.

Caggiula, A.W., Christakis, G., Farrand, M., Hulley, S.B., Johnson, R., Lasser, N.L., Stamler, J., & Widdowson, G. (1981). The Multiple Risk Factor Intervention Trial (MRFIT):/IV. Intervention on blood lipids. *Preventive Medicine, 10,* 443–475.

Calhoun, J.B. (1962). Population density and social pathology. *Science, 206,* 139–148.

Calnan, M., & Rutter, D.R. (1986). Preventive health practices and their relationship with socio-demographic characteristics. *Health Education Research, 1,* 247–253.

Camacho, T.C., & Wiley, J.A. (1983). Health practices, social networks, and change in physical health. In L.F. Berkman & L. Breslow (Eds.), *Health and ways of living: The Alameda County Study.* New York: Oxford University Press.

Cannon, W.B. (1929). *Bodily changes in pain, hunger, fear, and rage.* Boston: Branford. (Original work published 1915)

Cannon, W.B. (1932). *The wisdom of the body.* New York: Norton.

Caplan, G. (1964). *Principles of preventive psychiatry.* New York: Basic Books.

Carey, W.B., Hegvik, R.L., McDevitt, S.C. (1989). Temperamental factors associated with rapid weight gain and obesity in middle childhood. *Annual Progress in Child Psychiatry and Child Development,* pp. 316–327.

Carmelli, D., Chesney, M.A., Ward, M.W., & Rosenman, R.H. (1985). Twin similarity in cardiovascular stress response. *Health Psychology, 4,* 413–423.

Carmelli, D., Rosenman, R.H., & Chesney, M. (1987). Stability of the Type A structured interview and related questionnaires in a 10-year follow-up of an adult cohort of twins. *Journal of Behavioral Medicine, 10,* 513–525.

Carmelli, D., Rosenman, R.H., Chesney, M., Fabsitz, R., Lee, M., & Borhani, N. (1988). Genetic heritability and shared environmental influences of Type A measures in the NHLBI twin study. *American Journal of Epidemiology, 127,* 1041–1052.

Carmody, T.P., Fey, S.G., Pierce, D.K., Connor, W.E., & Matarazzo, J.D. (1982). Behavioral treatment of hyperlipidemia: Techniques, results, and future directions. *Journal of Behavioral Medicine, 5,* 91–116.

Carmody, T.P., Istvan, J., Matarazzo, J.D., Connor, S.L., & Connor, W.E. (1986). Application of social learning theory in the promotion of heart-healthy diets: The Family Heart Study dietary intervention model. *Health Education Research, 1,* 13–27.

Carmody, T.P., Matarazzo, J.D., & Istvan, J.A. (1987). Promoting adherence to heart-healthy diets: A review of the literature. *Journal of Compliance in Health Care, 2,* 105–124.

Carron, H. (1984). Management of low back pain. In C. Benedetti, C.R. Chapman, & G. Moricca (Eds.), *Advances in pain research and therapy: Vol. 7. Recent advances in the management of pain.* New York: Raven Press.

Caron, H.S., & Roth, H.P. (1971). Objective assessment of cooperation with an ulcer diet: Relation to antacid intake and to assigned physician. *American Journal of Medical Science, 261,* 61–66.

Carrington, P. (1978). *Clinically standardized meditation (CSM) instructor's kit.* Kendall Park, NJ: Pace Educational Systems.

Carruthers, M. (1981). "Field studies": Emotion and beta-blockade. In M.J. Christie & P.G. Mellett (Eds.), *Foundations of psychosomatics* (pp. 223–241). Chichester, England: Wiley.

Carver, C.S., DeGregorio, E., & Gillis, R. (1981). Challenge and Type A behavior among intercollegiate football players. *Journal of Sport Psychology, 3,* 140–148.

Carver, C.S., & Glass, D.C. (1978). Coronary-prone behavior pattern and interpersonal aggression. *Journal of Personality and Social Psychology, 36,* 361–366.

Carver, C.S., & Humphries, C. (1982). Social psychology of the Type A coronary-prone behavior pattern. In G.S. Saunders & J. Suls (Eds.), *Social psychology of health and illness* (pp. 33–64). Hillsdale, NJ: Erlbaum.

Case, R.B., Heller, S.S., Case, M.B., & Moss, A.J. (1985). Type A behavior and survival after acute myocardial infarction. *New England Journal of Medicine, 312,* 737–741.

Case, R.B., Moss, A.J., Case, N., McDermott, M., & Eberly, S. (1992). Living alone after myocardial infarction: Impact on prognosis. *Journal of the American Medical Association, 267,* 515–519.

Cassel, R.N. (1987). Use of select nutrients to foster wellness. *Psychology: A Quarterly Journal of Human Behavior, 24,* 24–29.

Cassileth, B.R., Lusk, E.J., Miller, D.S., Brown, L.L., & Miller, C. (1985). Psychosocial correlates of survival in advanced malignant diseases. *New England Journal of Medicine, 312,* 1551–1555.

Castelli, W.P., Garrison, R.J., Wilson, P.W., Abbott, R.D., Kalousdian, S., & Kannel, W.B. (1986). Incidence of coronary heart disease and lipoprotein cholesterol levels: The Framingham Study. *Journal of the American Medical Association, 256,* 2835–2838.

Castelnuovo-Tedesco, P. (1981). The psychological consequences of physical trauma and defects. *International Review of Psychoanalysis, 8,* 145–154.

Cataldo, M.F., Dershewitz, R.A., Wilson, M., Christophersen, E.R., Finney, J.W., Fawcett, S.B., & Seekins, T. (1986). Childhood injury control. In N.A. Krasnegor, J.D. Arasteh, & M.F. Cataldo (Eds.), *Child health behavior: A behavioral pediatrics perspective.* New York: Wiley.

Catania, J.A., Coates, T.J., Stall, R., Bye, L., Kegeles, S.M., Capell, F., Henne, J., McKusick, L., Morin, S., Turner, H., & Pollack, L. (1991). Changes in condom use among homosexual men in San Francisco. *Health Psychology, 10*, 190–199.

Cattanach, L., & Rodin, J. (1988). Psychosocial components of the stress process in bulimia. *International Journal of Eating Disorders, 7*, 75–88.

Caudill, B.D., & Marlatt, G.A. (1975). Modeling influences in social drinking: An experimental analogue. *Journal of Consulting and Clinical Psychology, 43*, 405–415.

Cauwells, J.M. (1983). *Bulimia: The binge-purge compulsion*. Garden City, NY: Doubleday.

Cautela, J.R. (1977). Toward a Pavlovian theory of cancer. *Behavior Therapy, 6*, 117–142.

Cay, E.L., Vetter, N.J., Philip, A.E., & Dugard, P. (1972). Psychological status during recovery from an acute heart attack. *Journal of Psychosomatic Research, 16*, 425–435.

Centers for Disease Control. (CDC) (1985). Recommendations for preventing transmission of infection with human t-lymphotropic virus type III/lymphadenopathy-associated virus in the workplace. *Morbidity and Mortality Weekly Reports, 34*, 681–686, 691–696.

Centers for Disease Control. (CDC) (1988). Update: Acquired immunodeficiency syndrome (AIDS)—worldwide. *Morbidity and Mortality Weekly Reports, 37*, 286–288.

Centers for Disease Control. (CDC) (1992, May). *HIV/AIDS surveillance*. Atlanta: Department of Health and Human Services.

Champion, V.L. (1990). Breast self-examination in women 35 and older: A prospective study. *Journal of Behavioral Medicine, 13*, 523–538.

Chaney, E.F., O'Leary, M.R., & Marlatt, G.A. (1978). Skill training with alcoholics. *Journal of Consulting and Clinical Psychology, 46*, 1092–1104.

Channon, S., deSilva, P., Hemsley, D., Perkins, R.E. (1989). A controlled trial of cognitive-behavioural and behavioural treatment of anorexia nervosa. *Behaviour Research and Therapy, 27*, 529–535.

Chapman, C.R. (1978). Pain: The perception of noxious events. In R.A. Sternbach (Ed.), *The psychology of pain*. New York: Raven Press.

Chapman, C.R. (1980). Pain and perception: Comparison of sensory decision theory and evoked potential methods. In J.J. Bonica (Ed.), *Pain*. New York: Raven Press.

Chapman, C.R. (1984). New directions in the understanding and management of pain. *Social Science and Medicine, 19*, 1261–1277.

Chapman, C.R., Casey, K.L., Dubner, R., Foley, K.M., Gracely, R.H., & Reading, A.E. (1985). Pain measurement: An overview. *Pain, 22*, 1–31.

Chapman, S.L., & Brena, S.F. (1985). Pain and society. *Annals of Behavioral Medicine, 7*, 21–24.

Chiriboga, D.A. (1982). Adaptation to marital separation in later and earlier life. *Journal of Gerontology, 37*, 109–114.

Christensen, L.B. (1991). *Experimental methodology*. Boston: Allyn and Bacon.

Christian, J.J. (1955). Effects of population size on the adrenal glands and reproductive organs of male mice in populations of fixed size. *The American Journal of Physiology, 182*, 292–300.

Christoffel, K.K., & Forsyth, B.W. (1989). Mirror image of environmental deprivation: Severe childhood obesity of psychosocial origin. *Child Abuse & Neglect, 13*, 249–256.

Ciaranello, R.D. (1983). Neurochemical aspects of stress. In N. Garmezy & M. Rutter (Eds.), *Stress, coping, and development in children*. New York: McGraw-Hill.

Cimons, M. (1991, January 25). Illicit drug use falls to 47.9% for young adults. *Los Angeles Times*, p. A4.

Cimons, M. (1992, February 12). AIDS epidemic worsening, agency finds. *Los Angeles Times*, p. A6.

Cimmons, M. (1991, May 17). Nation's syphilis rate worst since 1949, despite drug cure. *Los Angeles Times*, p. A4.

Cioffi, D. (1991). Beyond attentional strategies: A cognitive-perceptual model of somatic interpretation. *Psychological Bulletin, 109*, 25–41.

Citron, M.L., Johnston-Early, A., Boyer, M., Krasnow, S.H., Hood, M., & Cohen, M.H. (1986). Patient-controlled analgesia for severe cancer pain. *Archives of Internal Medicine, 146*, 734–736.

Clark, J.A., Potter, D.A., & McKinlay, J.B. (1991). Bringing social structure back into clinical decision-making. *Social Science and Medicine, 32*, 853–866.

Clark, W.B., & Cahalan, D. (1976). Changes in problem drinking over a four-year span. *Addictive Behaviors, 1*, 251–259.

Clarke-Stewart, A. (1977). *Child care in the family: A review of research and some propositions for policy*. New York: Academic Press.

Cleary, P.D., Edgman-Levitan, S., McMullen, W., & Delbanco, T.L. (1992). The relationship between reported problems and patient summary evaluations of hospital care. *Quality Review Bulletin, 18*, 53–59.

Clearly, P.D., Edgman-Levitan, S., Roberts, M., Maloney, T.W., McMullen, W., Walker, J.D., & Delbanco, T.L. (1991). Patients evaluate their hospital care: A national survey. *Health Affairs, 10*, 254–267.

Clifford, R.E. (1978). Subjective sexual experience in college women. *Archives of Sexual Behavior, 7*, 183–197.

Cloninger, C.R. (1991). D_2 Dopamine receptor gene is associated but not linked with alcoholism.

Journal of the American Medical Association, 266, 1833–1834.

Cluss, P. A., & Fireman, P. (1985). Recent trends in asthma research. *Annals of Behavioral Medicine, 7*, 11–16.

Coates, R.A., Soskoline, C.L., Calzavara, L., Read, S.E., Fanning, M.M., Shepherd, F.A., Klein, M.M., & Johnson, J.K. (1987). The reliability of sexual histories in AIDS-related research: Evaluation of an interview-administered questionnaire. *Canadian Journal of Public Health, 77*, 343–348.

Coates, T.J., Morin, S.F., & McKusick, L. (1987). Behavioral consequences of AIDS anti-body testing among gay men. *Journal of the American Medical Association, 258*, 1989.

Cobb, S. (1976). Social support as a moderator of life stress. *Psychosomatic Medicine, 38*, 300–314.

Cobrinick, P., Hood, R., & Chused, E. (1959). Effects of maternal narcotic addiction on the newborn infant. *Pediatrics, 24*, 288–290.

Cockerham, W.C. (1989). *Medical sociology* (4th ed.). Englewood Cliffs, NJ: Prentice-Hall.

Coe, R.M. (1978). *Sociology of medicine* (2nd ed.). New York: McGraw-Hill.

Cohen, F., & Lazarus, R.S. (1983). Coping and adaptation in health and illness. In D. Mechanic (Ed.), *Handbook of health, health care, and the health professions*. New York: Free Press.

Cohen, R.Y., Brownell, K.D., & Felix, M.R. (1990). Age and sex differences in health habits and beliefs of schoolchildren. *Health Psychology, 9*, 208–224.

Cohen, S. (1986a). The implications of crack. *Drug Abuse & Alcoholism Newsletter, 15*, No. 6.

Cohen, S. (1986b). Just say no. *Drug Abuse & Alcoholism Newsletter, 15*, No. 3.

Cohen, S. (1988). Social support and physical illness. *Health Psychology, 7*, 269–297.

Cohen, S., Kamarck, T., & Mermelstein, R. (1983). A global measure of perceived stress. *Journal of Health and Social Behavior, 24*, 385–396.

Cohen, S., Kaplan, J.R., Cunnick, J.E., Manuck, S.B., & Rabin, B.S. (1992). Chronic social stress, affiliation, and cellular immune response in nonhuman primates. *Psychological Science, 3*, 301–304.

Cohen, S., Kaplan, J.R., & Manuck, S.B. (1991). Social support and coronary heart disease: Underlying psychologic and biologic mechanism. In S.A. Schumaker & S.M. Czajkowski (Eds.), *Social support and cardiovascular disease*. New York: Plenum.

Cohen, S., & Lichtenstein, E. (1990). Partner behaviors that support quitting smoking. *Journal of Consulting and Clinical Psychology, 58*, 304–309.

Cohen, S., Lichtenstein, E., Prochaska, J.O., Rossi, J.S., Gritz, E.R., Carr, C.R., Orleans, C.T., Schoenbach, V.J., Biener, L., Abrams, D., Di-Clemente, C., Curry, S., Marlatt, G.A., Cummings, K.M., Emont, S.L., Giovino, G., Ossip-Klein, D. (1989). Debunking myths about self-quitting: Evidence from 10 prospective studies of persons who attempt to quit smoking by themselves. *American Psychologist, 44*, 1355–1365.

Cohen, S. & Matthews, K.A. (1987). Social support, Type A behavior, and coronary artery disease. *Psychosomatic Medicine, 49*, 325–330.

Cohen, S., & McKay, G. (1984). Social support, stress, and the buffering hypothesis: A theoretical analysis. In A. Baum, J.E. Singer, & S.E. Taylor (Eds.), *Handbook of psychology and health*, Vol. 4. Hillsdale, NJ: Erlbaum.

Cohen, S. & Syme, S.L. (1985). Issues in the study and application of social support. In S. Cohen, S. & S.L. Syme (Eds.), *Social support and health*. New York: Academic Press.

Cohen, S. Tyrrell, D.A.J., & Smith, A.P. (1991). Psychological stress and susceptability to the common cold. *The New England Journal of Medicine, 325*, 606–612.

Cohen, S., & Williamson, G.M. (1991). Stress and infectious disease in humans. *Psychological Bulletin, 109*, 5–24.

Cohen, S., & Wills, T.A. (1985). Stress, social support, and the buffering hypothesis. *Psychological Bulletin, 98*, 310–357.

Cohen, S.I., & Hajioff, J. (1972). Life events and the onset of acute closed-angle glaucoma. *Journal of Psychosomatic Research, 16*, 335–341.

Colletti, G., & Brownell, K.D. (1983). The physical and emotional benefits of social support: Application to obesity, smoking, and alcoholism. In M. Hersen, R.M. Eisler, & P.M. Miller (Eds.), *Progress in behavior modification*. New York: Academic Press.

Collins, A., & Frankenhaeuser, M. (1978). Stress responses in male and female engineering students. *Journal of Human Stress, 4*, 43–48.

Collins, D.L., Baum, A., & Singer, J. (1983). Coping with chronic stress at Three Mile Island: Psychological and biochemical evidence. *Health Psychology, 2*, 149–166.

Comstock, L., & Slome, C. (1973). A health survey of students. I: Prevalence of problems. *Journal of American College of Health Associations, 22*, 150–155.

Cone, J.D. (1988). Prevention. In V.B. VanHasselt, P.S. Strain, & M. Hersen (Eds.), *Handbook of developmental and physical disabilities*. New York: Pergamon Press.

Connell, C.M., D'Augelli, A.R. (1990). The contribution of personality characteristics to the relationship between social support and perceived physical health. *Health Psychology, 9*, 192–207.

Conrad, P. (1986). The myth of cut-throats among premedical students: On the role of stereotypes in justifying failure and success. *Journal of Health and Social Behavior, 27*, 153–160.

Consumer Reports. (1991, October). *A pyramid topples at the USDA*. Yonkers, NY: Author.

Contrada, R.J. (1989). Type A behavior, personality hardiness, and cardiovascular responses to stress. *Journal of Personality and Social Psychology, 57*, 895–903.

Contrada, R.J., & Krantz, D.S. (1988). Stress, reactivity, and Type A behavior: Current status and future directions. *Annals of Behavioral Medicine, 10*, 64–70.

Contrada, R.J., Wright, R.A., & Glass, D.C. (1985). Psychophysiological correlates of Type A behavior: Comments on Houston (1983) and Holmes (1983). *Journal of Research in Personality, 19*, 12–30.

Conway, T.L., Vickers, R.R., Ward, H.D., & Rahe, R.H. (1981). Occupational stress and variation in cigarette, coffee, and alcohol consumption. *Journal of Health and Social Behavior, 22*, 155–165.

Cooper, C.J., & Marshall, J. (1976). Occupational sources of stress: A review of the literature relating to coronary heart disease and mental ill health. *Journal of Occupational Psychology, 49*, 11–28.

Costello, R.M. (1975). Alcoholism treatment and evaluation: In search of methods. *International Journal of the Addictions, 10*, 251–275.

Costello, R.M., Baillargeon, J.G., Biever, P., & Bennett, R. (1980). Therapeutic community treatment for alcohol abusers: A one-year multivariate outcome evaluation. *International Journal of the Addictions, 15*, 215–232.

Cottington, E.M., Matthews, K.A., Talbott, E., & Kuller, L.H. (1986). Occupational stress, suppressed anger, and hypertension. *Psychosomatic Medicine, 48*, 249–260.

Cousins, N. (1979). *Anatomy of an Illness*. New York: Norton.

Coyne, J.C., & DeLongis, A. (1986). Going beyond social support: The role of social relationships in adaptation. *Journal of Consulting and Clinical Psychology, 54*, 454–460.

Cox, G.L., & Merkel, W.T. (1989). A qualitative review of psychosocial treatments for bulimia. *Journal of Nervous and Mental Diseases, 177*, 77–84.

Cox, T. (1978). *Stress*. Baltimore: University Park Press.

Cox, T., & Mackay, C. (1982). Psychosocial factors and psychophysiological mechanisms in the aetiology and development of cancer. *Social Science and Medicine, 16*, 381–396.

Cox, V.C., Paulus, P.B., McCain, G., & Karlovac, M. (1982). The relationship between crowding and health. In A. Baum & J.E. Singer (Eds.), *Advances in environmental psychology: Vol. 4. Environment and health*. Hillsdale, NJ: Erlbaum.

Cox, W.M., & Klinger, E. (1988). A motivational model of alcohol use. *Journal of Abnormal Psychology, 97*, 168–180.

Coyne, J.C., Holroyd, K. (1982). Stress, coping, and illness: A transactional perspective. In T. Millon, C. Green, & R. Meagher (Eds.), *Handbook of clinical health psychology*. New York: Plenum.

Crabbe, J.C., McSwigan, J.D., & Belknap, J.K. (1985). The role of genetics in substance abuse. In M. Galizio & S.A. Maisto (Eds.), *Determinants of substance abuse: Biological psychological, and environmental factors*. New York: Plenum.

Craun, A.M., & Deffenbacher, J.L. (1987). The effects of information, behavioral rehearsal, and prompting on breast self-exams. *Journal of Behavioral Medicine, 10*, 351–365.

Creer, T.L. (1979). *Asthma therapy: A behavioral health care system for respiratory disorders*. New York: Springer.

Creer, T.L. (1988). Asthma. In W. Linden (Ed.), *Biological barriers in behavioral medicine*, (pp. 221–255). New York: Plenum Press.

Creer, T.L. & Winder, J.A. (1986). The self-management of asthma. In K.A. Holroyd & T.L. Creer (Eds.), *Handbook of self-management in health psychology and behavioral medicine* (pp. 269–303). New York: Academic Press.

Crisp, A.H. (1967). The possible significance of some behavioral correlates of weight and carbohydrate intake. *Journal of Psychosomatic Research, 11*, 117–131.

Crisp, A.H., Palmer, R.L., & Kalucy, R.S. (1976). How common is anorexia nervosa? A prevalence study. *British Journal of Psychiatry, 128*, 549–554.

Crome, P., Curl, B., Boswell, M., Corless, D., & Lewis, R.R. (1982). Assessment of a new calendar pack—the "C-Pack". *Age and Aging, 11*, 275–279.

Croog, S.H. (1983). Recovery and rehabilitation of heart patients: Psychosocial aspects. In D.S. Krantz & J.S. Singer (Eds.), *Handbook of psychology and health* (Vol. III, pp. 295–334). Hillsdale, NJ: Erlbaum.

Croog, S.H., & Fitzgerald, E.R. (1978). Subjective stress and serious illness of a spouse: Wives of heart patients. *Journal of Health and Social Behavior, 9*, 166–178.

Croog, S.H., & Levine, S. (1977). *The heart patient recovers*. New York: Human Sciences Press.

Cross, R.J., Brooks, W.H., Roszman, T.L., & Markesbery, W.R. (1982). Hypothalamic-immune interactions: effect of hypophysectomy on neuroimmunomodulation. *Journal of Neurological Science, 53*, 557–566.

Curran, D.K. (1987). *Adolescent suicidal behavior*. Washington, DC: Hemisphere.

Curry, S., Marlatt, G.A., & Gordon, J.R. (1987). Abstinence violation effect: Validation of an attributional construct with smoking cessation. *Journal of Consulting and Clinical Psychology, 55*, 145–149.

Curry, S., Wagner, E.H., & Grothaus, L.C. (1990). Intrinsic and extrinsic motivation for smoking cessation. *Journal of Consulting and Clinical Psychology, 58*, 310–316.

Curtiss, F.R. (1991). Managed health care. In J.E. Fincham & A.I. Wertheimer (Eds.), *Pharmacy and the U.S. health care system.* Binghamton, NY: Haworth Press.

Cutrona, C.E. (1990). Stress and social support—In search of optimal matching. *Journal of Social and Clinical Psychology, 9*, 3–14.

Dahlberg, C.C. (1977, June). Stroke. *Psychology Today*, pp. 121–128.

Dahlgren, L., & Willander, A. (1989). Are special treatment facilities for female alcoholics needed? A controlled 2-year follow-up study from a specialized female unit (EWA) versus a mixed male/female treatment facility. *Alcoholism: Clinical and Experimental Research, 13*, 499–504.

Daniels, D., & Moos, R.H. (1990). Assessing life stressors and social resources among adolescents: Applications to depressed youth. *Journal of Adolescent Research, 5*, 268–289.

Dantzer, R. (1982). Donnees recentes sur la psychophysiologie de l'anxiete. [Recent trends in psychophysiology of anxiety]. *Encephale, 8*, 107–118. (From *Psychological Abstracts*, 1983, *69*, Abstract No. 05128)

Dantzer, R., & Kelley, K.W. (1989). Stress and immunity: An integrated view of relationships between the brain and the immune system. *Life Sciences, 44*, 1995–2008.

Dattore, P.J., Shontz, F.C., & Coyne, L. (1980). Premorbid personality differentiation of cancer and noncancer groups: A list of the hypotheses of cancer proneness. *Journal of Consulting and Clinical Psychology, 48*, 388–394.

Daut, R.L., & Cleeland, C.S. (1982). The prevalence and severity of pain in cancer. *Cancer, 50*, 1913–1918.

Davidson, L.M., Baum, A., & Collins, D.L. (1982). Stress and control-related problems at Three Mile Island. *Journal of Applied Social Psychology, 12*, 349–359.

Davidson, L.M., Fleming, R., & Baum, A. (1987). Chronic stress, catecholamines, and sleep disturbance at Three Mile Island. *Journal of Human Stress, 13*, 75–83.

Davies, D.L. (1962). Normal drinking in recovered alcohol addicts. *Quarterly Journal of Studies on Alcohol, 24*, 321–332.

Davis, G.P., & Park, E. (1981). *The heart: The living pump.* Washington, DC: U.S. News Books.

Davison, G.C., & Neale, J.M. (1990). *Abnormal Psychology* (5th ed.). New York: Wiley.

Dawber, T.R. (1980). *The Framingham study: The epidemiology of atherosclerotic disease.* Cambridge, MA: Harvard University Press.

Dawson, D.A., Cynamon, M., & Fitti, J.E. (1987). *National Center for Health Statistics Advance Data* (No. 146), *19*.

DeBusk, R.F., Haskell, W.L., Miller, N.H., Berra, K., & Taylor, C.B. (1985). Medically directed at-home rehabilitation soon after clinically uncomplicated acute myocardial infarction: A new model for patient care. *American Journal of Cardiology, 55*, 251–257.

DeJong, G., & Lifchez, K. (1983). Physical disability and public policy. *Scientific American, 248*, 40–49.

DeJong, W. (1989). Condom promotion: The need for a social marketing program in America's inner cities. *American Journal of Health Promotion, 3*, 5–16.

DeJong, W. & Winsten, J.A. (1990). The use of mass media in substance abuse prevention. *Health Affairs, 9*, 30–46.

Delbanco, T.L. (1992). Enriching the doctor-patient relationship by inviting the patient's perspective. *Annal of Internal Medicine, 116*, 414–418.

DeLeon, P.H., Forsythe, P., & VandenBos, G.R. (1986). Federal recognition of psychology in rehabilitation programs. *Rehabilitation Psychology, 31*, 47–56.

Delin, C.R., & Lee, T.H. (1992). Drinking and the brain: Current evidence. *Alcohol & Alcoholism, 27*, 117–126.

DeLongis, A., Coyne, J.C., Dakof, G., Folkman, S., & Lazarus, R.S. (1982). Relationship of daily hassles, uplifts, and major life events to health status. *Health Psychology, 1*, 119–136.

DeLucia, J.L., & Kalodner, C.R. (1990). An individualized cognitive intervention: Does it increase the efficacy of behavioral interventions for obesity? *Addictive Behaviors, 15*, 473–479.

Dembroski, T.M., & Costa, P.T. (1988). Assessment of coronary-prone behavior: A current overview. *Annals of Behavioral Medicine, 10*, 60–63.

Dembroski, T.M., MacDougall, J.M., Costa, P.T., Jr., & Grandits, G.A. (1989). Components of hostility as predictors of sudden death and myocardial infarction in the Multiple Risk Factor Intervention Trial. *Psychosomatic Medicine, 51*, 514–522.

Dembroski, T.M., MacDougall, J.M., Herd, J.A., & Shields, J.L. (1983). Perspectives on coronary-prone behavior. In D.S. Krantz, A. Baum, & J.E. Singer (Eds.), *Handbook of psychology and health: Vol. 3. Cardiovascular disorders and behavior.* Hillsdale, NJ: Erlbaum.

Dembroski, T.M., MacDougall, J.M., Shields, J.L., Petitto, J., & Lushene, R. (1987). Components of the Type A coronary-prone behavior pattern and cardiovascular responses to psychomotor performance challenge. *Journal of Behavioral Medicine, 1*, 159–176.

Dembroski, T.M., MacDougall, J.M., Williams, R.B., Haney, T.L., & Blumenthal, J.A. (1985).

Components of Type A, hostility, and anger-in: Relationship to angiographic findings. *Psychosomatic Medicine, 47,* 219–233.

Dennis, C., Houston-Miller, N., Schwartz, R.G., Ahn, D.K., Kraemer, H.C., Gossard, D., Juneau, M., Taylor, C.B., & DeBusk, R.F. (1988). Early return to work after uncomplicated myocardial infarction: Results of a randomized trial. *Journal of the American Medical Association, 260,* 214–220.

Denny, F.W., & Clyde, W.A. (1983). Acute respiratory tract infections: An overview. In W.A. Clyde & F.W. Denny (Eds.), *Workshop on acute respiratory diseases among children of the world. Pediatric Research, 17,* 1026–1029.

DePiano, F.A., & Salzberg, H.C. (1979). Clinical applications of hypnosis to three psychosomatic disorders. *Psychological Bulletin, 86,* 1122–1124.

Despres, J.P., Moorjani, S., Lupien, P.J., Tremblay, A., Nadeau, A., & Bouchard, C. (1990). Regional distribution of body fat, plasma lipoproteins, and cardiovascular disease. *Arteriosclerosis, 10,* 497–511.

DeQuattro, V., Loo, R., Yamada, D., & Foti, F. (1985). Blood pressure and sympathoadrenal tone in Type A behavior: A review of the stress responsiveness studies. In A. Zanchetti & P. Turner (Eds.), *Towards preventative treatment of coronary-prone behavior* (pp. 25–34). New York: Hans Huber.

Des Jarlais, D.C. & Bailey, W. (1990, June). *Almost banning bleach: An empirical study of AIDS policy development in the U.S.* Paper presented at the Sixth International Congress on AIDS, San Francisco.

Des Jarlais, D.C., Friedman, S.R., Casriel, C., & Kott, A. (1987). AIDS and preventing initiation into intravenous (IV) drug use. *Psychology and Health, 1,* 179–194.

DeVries, H., Wiswell, R., Bulbulin, R., & Moritani, T. (1981). Tranquilizer effects of exercise. *American Journal of Physical Medicine, 60,* 57–66.

Diamond, E.L. Massey, K.L., & Covey, D. (1989). Symptom awareness and blood glucose estimation in diabetic adults. *Health Psychology, 8,* 15–26.

Diamond, E. L., Schneiderman, N., Schwartz, D., Smith, J.C., Vorp, R., & Pasin, R.D. (1984). Harassment, hostility, and Type A as determinants of cardiovascular reactivity during competition. *Journal of Behavioral Medicine, 7,* 171–189.

Dickens, B.M., Doob, A.N., Warwick, O.H. & Winegard, W.C. (1982). *Report of the Committee of Inquiry into Allegations Concerning Drs. Linda and Mark Sobell.* Toronto: Addiction Research Centre.

Dickinson, R.L., & Beam, L. (1931). *A thousand marriages.* Baltimore: Williams & Wilkins.

DiClemente, C.C. (1981). Self-efficacy and smoking cessation maintenance: A preliminary report. *Cognitive Therapy and Research, 5,* 175–187.

DiClemente, C.C., & Prochaska, J.O. (1985). Processes and stages of self-change: coping and competence in smoking behavior change. In S. Shiffman & T.S. Wills (Eds.), *Coping and substance use.* Orlando, FL: Academic.

Diekstra, R.F. (1990). Psychology, health, and health care. Special Issue: The development of health psychology: An international perspective. *Psychology and Health, 4,* 51–63.

Diehl, A.K., Bauer, R.L., & Sugarek, N.J. (1987). Correlates of medication compliance in non-insulin-dependent diabetes mellitus. *Southern Medical Journal, 80,* 332–335.

Dienstbier, R.A. (1989). Arousal and physiological toughness: Implications for mental and physical health. *Psychological Review, 96,* 84–100.

Dienstbier, R.A., Crabbe, J., Johnson, G.O., Thorland, W., Jorgensen, J.A., Sadar, M.M., & Lavelle, D.C. (1981). Exercise and stress tolerance. In M.H. Sacks & M.L. Sacks (Eds.), *Psychology of running* (pp. 192–210). Champaign, IL: Human Kinetics.

Dienstbier, R.A., LaGuardia, R.L., Barnes, M., Tharp, G., Schmidt, R. (1987). Catecholamine training effects from exercise programs: A bridge to exercise-treatment relationships. *Motivation and Emotion, 11,* 297–318.

Dienstbier, R.A., LaGuardia, R.L., & Wilcox, N.S. (1987). The relationship of temperament to tolerance of cold and heat: Beyond "cold hands—warm heart." *Motivation and Emotion, 11,* 269–295.

Dienstfrey, H. (1991). Neal Miller, the dumb autonomic nervous system, and biofeedback. *Advances, 7,* 33–44.

Dienstfrey, H. (1992). What makes the heart healthy? A talk with Dean Ornish. *Advances, 8,* 25–45.

Dillard, K.D., & Pol, L.B. (1982). The individual economic costs of teenage childbearing. *Family Relations, 31,* 249–259.

Diller, L., & Gordon, W.A. (1981). Rehabilitation and clinical neuropsychology. In S.B. Filskov & T.J. Boll, *Handbook of clinical neuropsychology.* New York: John Wiley and Sons.

Dillman, D., & Tremblay, K., Jr. (1977). The quality of life in rural America. *Annals of the American Academy of Political and Social Sciences, 429,* 115–129.

Dillon, K.M., Minchoff, B., & Baker, K.H. (1985). Positive emotional states and enhancement of the immune system. *International Journal of Psychiatry in Medicine, 15,* 13–18.

DiMatteo, M.R. (1979). A social psychological analysis of physician-patient rapport: Toward a science of the art of medicine. *Journal of Social Issues, 35,* 12–33.

DiMatteo, M.R. and DiNicola, D.D. (1982). *Achieving patient compliance.* New York: Pergamon Press.

DiMatteo, M.R., Hays, R.D., & Prince, L.M. (1986). Relationship of physicians' nonverbal skill to patient satisfaction, appointment noncompliance, and physician workload. *Health Psychology, 5,* 581–594.

DiMatteo, M.R., Prince, L.M., & Taranta, A. (1979). Patients' perceptions of physicians' behavior: Determinants of patient commitment to the therapeutic relationship. *Journal of Community Health, 4,* 280–290.

DiMatteo, M.R., Taranta, A., Friedman, H.S., & Prince, L.M. (1980). Predicting patient satisfaction from physicians' nonverbal communication skills. *Medical Care, 18,* 376–387.

Dimsdale, J.E., Pierce, C., Schoenfeld, D., Brown, A., Zusman, R., & Graham, R. (1986). Suppressed anger and blood pressure: The effects of race, sex, social class, obesity, and age. *Psychosomatic Medicine, 48,* 430–436.

Dishman, R.K. (1982). Compliance/adherence in health-related exercise. *Health Psychology, 1,* 237–267.

Dishman, R.K., Sallis, J.F., & Orenstein, D.R. (1985). The determinants of physical activity and exercise. *Public Health Reports, 100,* 158–171.

Ditto, P.H., & Hamilton, J.L. (1990). Expectancy processes in the health care interaction sequence. *Journal of Social Issues, 46,* 97–124.

Ditto, P., Jemmott, J.B., III, & Darley, J.M. (1988). Appraising the threat of illness: A mental representational approach. *Health Psychology, 7,* 183– 201.

Dixon, N.F. (1980). Humor: A cognitive alternative to stress? In I.G. Sarason & C.D. Spielberger (Eds.), *Stress and anxiety* (Vol. 7). Washington, DC: Hemisphere.

Doehrman, S.R. (1977). Psychosocial aspects of recovery from coronary heart disease: A review. *Social Science and Medicine, 11,* 199–218.

Doherty, W.J., & Jacobson, N.S. (1982). Marriage and the family. In B. Wolman (Ed.), *Handbook of developmental psychology.* Englewood Cliffs, NJ: Prentice-Hall.

Dohrenwend, B.S., & Dohrenwend, B.P. (Eds.). (1981). *Stressful life events and their contexts.* New York: Prodist.

Dohrenwend, B.S., & Dohrenwend, B.P. (1984). Symptoms, hassles, social supports, and life events: The problem of confounded measures. *Journal of Abnormal Psychology, 93,* 222–230.

Dolecek, T.A., Milas, N.C., Van Horn, L.V. Farrand, M.E., Gorder, D.D., Duchene, A.G., Dyer, J.R., Stone, P.A., & Randall, B.L. (1986). A long-term nutrition experience: Lipid responses and dietary adherence patterns in the Multiple Risk Factor Intervention Trial. *Journal of the American Dietetic Association, 86,* 752–758.

Doll, R., & Hill, A.B. (1956). Lung cancer and other causes of death in relation to smoking: A second report on the mortality of British doctors. *British Medical Journal,* 1071–1081.

Doll, R., & Peto, R. (1981). *The causes of cancer.* New York: Oxford University Press.

Dollard, J., & Miller, N.E. (1950). *Personality and psychotherapy: An analysis in terms of learning, thinking, and culture.* New York: McGraw-Hill.

Dorian, B.J., Keystone, E., Garfinkel, P.E., & Brown, G.M. (1982). Aberrations in lymphocyte subpopulations and functions during psychosocial stress. *Clinical-Experimental Immunology, 50,* 132–138.

Dowling, J. (1983). Autonomic measures and behavioral indices of pain sensitivity. *Pain, 16,* 193–200.

Dracup, K. (1985). A controlled trial of couples' group counseling in cardiac rehabilitation. *Journal of Cardiopulmonary Rehabilitation, 5,* 436–442.

Dreher, H. (1992). Behavioral medicine's new marketplace of clinical applications: A report on a conference. *Advances, 8,* 46–69.

Dubbert, P.M. (1992). Exercise in behavioral medicine. *Journal of Consulting and Clinical Psychology, 60,* 613–618.

Dubuisson, D., & Melzack, R. (1976). Classification of clinical pain descriptions by multiple group discriminant analysis. *Experimental Neurology, 51,* 480–487.

Duffy, F.H., Als, H., & McAnulty, G.B. (1990). Behavioral and electrophysiological evidence for gestational age effects in healthy preterm and full-term infants; studies two weeks after expected due date. *Child Development, 61,* 1271–1286.

Dugan, S.O. (1984). Pain. In S.N. McIntire & A.L. Cioppa (Eds.), *Cancer nursing: A developmental approach.* New York: Wiley.

Duncan, D.F. (1990). Health education and health psychology: A comparison through content analysis of representative journals. *Psychological Reports, 66,* 1057–1058.

Dunkel-Schetter, C., Feinstein, L.G., Taylor, S.E., & Falke, R.L. (1992). Patterns of coping with cancer. *Health Psychology, 11,* 79–87.

Durel, L.A., Carver, C.S., Spitzer, S.B., Llabre, M.M., Weintraub, J.K., Saab, P.G., & Schneiderman, N. (1989). Associations of blood pressure with self-report measures of anger and hostility among black and white men and women. *Health Psychology, 8,* 557–576.

Durnin, J.V., Lonegran, M.E., Good, J., & Ewan, A. (1974). Cross-sectional nutritional and anthropometric study with an interval of 7 years on 611 young adolescent school children. *British Journal of Nutrition, 31,* 169–179.

Duszynski, K.R., Shaffer, J.W., & Thomas, C.B. (1981). Neoplasm and traumatic events in childhood: Are they related? *Archives of General Psychiatry, 38,* 327–331.

Dyer, E. (1963). Parenthood as crisis: A re-study. *Marriage and Family Living, 25,* 196–201.

Eckenrode, J. (1984). Impact of chronic and acute stressors on daily reports of mood. *Journal of Personality and Social Psychology, 46,* 907–918.

Eckert, E.D., Goldberg, S.C., Halmi, K.A., Casper, R.C., & Davis, J.M. (1979). Behavior therapy in anorexia nervosa. *British Journal of Psychiatry, 134,* 55–59.

Eckhardt, M.J., Harford, T.C., Kaelber, C.T., Parker, E.S., Rosenthal, L.S., Ryback, R.S., Salmoiraghi, G.C., Vanderveen, E., & Warren, K.R. (1981). Health hazards associated with alcohol consumption. *Journal of the American Medical Association, 246,* 648–666.

Edelmann, R.J., & Golombok, S. (1989). Stress and reproductive failure. Special Issue: Psychology and infertility. *Journal of Reproductive and Infant Psychology, 7,* 79–86.

Edleson, J., & Fitzpatrick, J.L. (1989). A comparison of cognitive-behavioral and hypnotic treatments of chronic pain. *Journal of Clinical Psychology, 45,* 316–323.

Edwards, G., Hensman, C., Hawker, A., & Williamson, V. (1967). Alcoholics Anonymous: The anatomy of a self-help group. *Social Psychiatry, 1,* 195–204.

Edwards, G., & Owens, R.G. (1984). The clinical ecology debate: Some issues arising. *Bulletin of the British Psychological Society, 37,* 325–328.

Edye, B.V., Mandryk, J.A., Frommer, M.S., Healey, S., & Ferguson, D.A. (1989). Evaluation of a worksite programme for the modification of cardiovascular risk factors. *Medical Journal of Australia, 151,* 542–543.

Egbert, L.D., Batit, G.E., Welch, C.E., & Bartlett, M.K. (1964). Reduction of postoperative pain by encouragement and instruction of patients: A study of doctor-patient rapport. *New England Journal of Medicine, 270,* 825–827.

Egeland, B., & Farber, E.A. (1984). Infant-mother attachment: Factors related to its development and changes over time. *Child Development, 55,* 753–771.

Eisenger, R.A. (1971). Psychosocial predictors of smoking recidivism. *Journal of Health and Social Behavior, 12,* 355–362.

Eisenger, R.A. (1972). Psychosocial predictors of smoking behavior change. *Journal of Health and Social Behavior, 13,* 137–144.

Eiser, C. (1985). *The psychology of childhood illness.* New York: Springer-Verlag.

Eliot, R.S., & Buell, J.C. (1983). The role of the central nervous system in sudden cardiac death. In T.M. Dembroski, T. Schmidt, & G. Blunchen

(Eds.), *Biobehavioral bases of coronary-prone behavior.* New York: Plenum.

Ellis, A. (1961). *The folklore of sex.* New York: Grove.

Ellis, A. (1971). Rational-emotive treatment of impotence, frigidity, and other sexual problems. *Professional Psychology, 2,* 346–349.

Ellis, A. (1987). The evolution of rational-emotive therapy (RET) and cognitive behavior therapy. In J.K. Zeig (Ed.), *The evolution of psychotherapy.* New York: Brunner/Mazel.

Emmons, R.A. (1986). Personal strivings: An approach to personality and subjective well-being. *Journal of Personality and Social Psychology, 51,* 1058–1068.

Emmons, R.A., & King, L.A. (1988). Conflict among personal strivings: Immediate and long-term implications for psychological and physical well-being. *Journal of Personality and Social Psychology, 54,* 1040–1048.

Emrick, C.D., & Hansen, J. (1983). Assertions regarding effectiveness of treatment for alcoholism: Fact or fantasy? *American Psychologist, 38,* 1078–1088.

Enander, A.E., & Hygge, S. (1990). Thermal stress and human performance. *Scandinavian Journal of Work, Environment and Health, 16,* (Suppl. 1), 44–50.

Eng, H.J. (1991). The U.S. health care system. In J.E. Fincham & A.I. Wertheimer (Eds.), *Pharmacy and the U.S. health care system.* Binghampton, NY: Haworth Press.

Engel, G.L. (1977). The need for a new medical model: A challenge for biomedicine. *Science, 196,* 129–136.

Engel, G.L. (1980). The clinical application of the biopsychosocial model. *American Journal of Psychiatry, 137,* 535–544.

English, E.H., & Baker, T.B. (1983). Relaxation training and cardiovascular response to experimental stressors. *Health Psychology, 2,* 239–259.

Engstrom, D. (1984). A psychological perspective of prevention in alcoholism. In J.D. Matarazzo, S.M. Weiss, J.A. Herd, N.E. Miller, & S.M. Weiss (Eds.), *Behavioral health: A handbook of health enhancement and disease prevention.* New York: Wiley.

Enos, W.F., Holmes, R.H., & Beyer, J. (1953). Coronary disease among U.S. soldiers killed in action in Korea. *Journal of the American Medical Association, 152,* 1090–1093.

Enright, M.F., Resnick, R., DeLeon, P.H., Sciara, A.D., & Ranney, F. (1990). The practice of psychology in hospital settings. *American Psychologist, 45,* 1059–1065.

Enright, M.R., Welch, B.L., Newman, R., & Perry, B.M. (1990). The hospital: Psychology's challenge in the 1990's. *American Psychologist, 45,* 1057–1058.

Enstrom, J.E. (1989). Health practices and cancer mortality among active California Mormons. *Journal of the National Cancer Institute, 81,* 1807– 1814.

Epp, L. (1986). *Achieving health for all: A framework for health promotion in Canada.* Toronto: Health and Welfare Canada.

Epstein, L.H., Grunberg, N.E., Lichtenstein, E., & Evans, R.I. (1989). Smoking research: Basic research, intervention, prevention, and new trends. *Health Psychology, 8,* 705–721.

Epstein, Y.M. (1982). Crowding stress and human behavior. In G.W. Evans (Ed.), *Environmental stress.* Cambridge, England: Cambridge University Press.

Eriksen, M.P., LeMaistre, C.A., & Newell, G.R. (1988). Health hazards of passive smoking. In L. Breslow, J.E. Fielding, & L.B. Lave (Eds.), *Annual review of public health* (Vol. 9). Palo Alto, CA: Annual Reviews.

Erikson, K.T. (1976). Loss of community at Buffalo Creek. *American Journal of Psychiatry, 133,* 302–305.

Essau, C.A., & Jamieson, J.L. (1987). Heart rate perception in the Type A personality. *Health Psychology, 6,* 43– 54.

Evans, F.J. (1985). Expectancy, therapeutic instructions, and the placebo response. In L. White, B. Tursky, & G.E. Schwartz (Eds.), *Placebo: Theory, research, and mechanisms* (pp. 215– 228). New York: Guilford Press.

Evans, G.W. (1979). Behavioral and physiological consequences of crowding in humans. *Journal of Applied Social Psychology, 9,* 27–46.

Evans, G.W., & Cohen, S. (1987). Environmental stress. In D. Stokols & I. Altman (Eds.), *Handbook of environmental psychology* (Vol. 1, pp. 571–610). New York: Wiley-Interscience.

Evans, P.D. (1990). Type A behaviour and coronary heart disease: When will the jury return? *British Journal of Psychology, 81,* 147–157.

Evans, P.D., Pitts, M.K., & Smith, K. (1988). Minor infection, minor life events, and the four day desirability dip. *Journal of Psychosomatic Research, 32,* 533–539.

Evans, R.I. (1976). Smoking in children: Developing a social psychological strategy of deterrence. *Preventive Medicine, 5,* 122–127.

Evans, R.I. (1984). A social inoculation strategy to deter smoking in adolescents. In J.D. Matarazzo, S.M. Weiss, J.A. Herd, N.E. Miller, & S.M. Weiss (Eds.), *Behavioral health: A handbook of health enhancement and disease prevention.* New York: Wiley.

Evans, R.I. (1988). Health promotion—science or ideology? *Health Psychology, 7,* 203–219.

Evans, R.I., Rozelle, R.M., Lasater, T.M., Dembroski, T.M., & Allen, B.P. (1970). Fear arousal, persuasion, and actual versus implied behavioral change: New perspective utilizing a real-life dental hygiene program. *Journal of Personality and Social Psychology, 16,* 220–227.

Evans, R.I., Rozelle, R.M., Maxwell, S.E., Raines, B.E., Dill, C.A., Guthrie, T.J., Henderson, A.H., & Hill, D.C. (1981). Social modeling films to deter smoking in adolescents: Results of a three-year field investigation. *Journal of Applied Psychology, 66,* 399–414.

Evans, R.I., Smith, C.K., & Raines, B.E. (1984). Deterring cigarette smoking in adolescents: A psychosocial-behavioral analysis of an intervention strategy. In A. Baum, S.E. Taylor, & J.E. Singer (Eds.), *Handbook of psychology and health: Vol. 4. Social psychological aspects of health.* Hillsdale, NJ: Erlbaum.

Eysenck, H.J. (1982). *Personality, genetics, and behavior: Selected papers.* New York: Praeger.

Eysenck, H.J. (1984). Lung cancer and the stress-personality inventory. In C.L. Cooper (Ed.), *Psychosocial stress and cancer.* Chichester, England: Wiley.

Eysenck, H.J. (1987). Anxiety, learned helplessness, and cancer: A causal theory. *Journal of Anxiety Disorders, 1,* 87–104.

Faden, R.R., Becker, C., Lewis, C., Freeman, J., & Faden, A.I. (1981). Disclosure of information to patients in medical care. *Medical Care, 19,* 718–733.

Fairburn, C.G. (1980). Self-induced vomiting. *Journal of Psychosomatic Research, 24,* 193– 197.

Fairburn, C.G. (1988). The current status of the psychological treatment for bulimia nervosa. 31st Annual conference of the Society for Psychosomatic Research. *Journal of Psychosomatic Research, 32,* 635–645.

Falkner, B., & Light, K.C. (1986). The interactive effects of stress and dietary sodium on cardiovascular reactivity. In K.A. Matthews, S.M. Weiss, T. Detre, T.M. Dembroski, B. Falkner, S.B. Manuck, & R.B. Williams (Eds.), *Handbook of stress, reactivity, and cardiovascular disease.* New York: Wiley.

Farkas, G., & Rosen, R.C. (1976). The effects of alcohol on elicited male sexual response. *Studies in Alcohol, 37,* 265–272.

Farquhar, J.W., Maccoby, N., Wood, P.D., Alexander, J.K., Breitrose, H., Brown, W.B., Jr., Haskell, W.L., McAlister, A.L., Meyer, A.J., Nash, J.D., & Stern, M.P. (1977). Community education for cardiovascular health. *Lancet, i,* 1192–1195.

Faust, I. (1984). The role of the fat cell in energy balance physiology. In A.J. Stunkard & E. Stellar (Eds.), *Eating and its disorders.* New York: Plenum.

Fawzy, F.I., Cousins, N., Fawzy, N.W., Kemeny, M.E., Elashoff, R., & Morton, D. (1990a). A structured psychiatric intervention for cancer patients, I. Changes over time in methods of coping and affective disturbance. *Archives of General Psychiatry, 47,* 720–725.

Fawzy, F.I., Kemeny, M.E., Fawzy, N.W., Elashoff, R., Morton, D., Cousins, N., & Fahey, J.L. (1990b). A structured psychiatric intervention for cancer patients, II. Changes over time in immunological measures. *Archives of General Psychiatry, 47,* 729–735.

Feindler, E.L., & Fremouw, W.J. (1983). Stress inoculation training for adolescent anger problems. In D. Meichenbaum & M.E. Jaremko (Eds.), *Stress reduction and prevention.* New York: Plenum Press.

Feinglos, M.N., & Surwit, R.S. (1988). *Behavior and diabetes mellitus.* Kalamazoo, MI: The Upjohn Company.

Fekken, G.C., & Jakubowski, I. (1990). Effects of stress on the health of Type A students. *Journal of Social Behavior and Personality, 5,* 473–480.

Felten, S.Y., & Felten, D.L. (1991). Innervation of lymphoid tissue. In R. Ader, D.L. Felton, & N. Cohen (Eds.), *Psychoneuroimmunology* (2nd ed. pp. 27–69). New York: Academic Press.

Ferguson, A. (1991). Food sensitivity or self-deception? *The New England Journal of Medicine, 323,* 476–478.

Fernandez, E. (1986). A classification system of cognitive coping strategies for pain. *Pain, 26,* 141–151.

Feuerstein, M., Labbe, E.E., & Kuczmierczyk, A.R. (1986). *Health psychology: A psychobiological perspective.* New York: Plenum Press.

Fichten, C.S., Robillard, K., Judd, D., & Amsel, R. (1989). College students with physical disabilities: Myths and realities. *Rehabilitation Psychology, 34,* 243–257.

Fielding, J.E. (1985). Smoking: Health effects and control. *New England Journal of Medicine, 313,* 491–498, 555–561.

Fielding, J.E. (1991a). Smoking control at the workplace. *Annual Review of Public Health, 12,* 209–234.

Fielding, J.E. (1991b). The challenges of work-place health promotion. In S.M. Weiss, J.E. Fielding, & A. Baum (Eds.), *Health at work.* Hillsdale, NJ: Erlbaum.

Fillmore, K.M., & Caetano, R. (1980 May). *Epidemiology of occupational alcoholism.* Paper presented at the National Institute on Alcohol Abuse and Alcoholism's Workshop on Alcohol Abuse in the Workplace, Reston, VA.

Filskov, S.B., Grimm, B.H., & Lewis, J.A. (1981). Brain-behavior relationships. In S.B. Filskov & T.J. Boll (Eds.), *Handbook of clinical neuropsychology.* New York: John Wiley & Sons.

Fineberg, H.V. (1988). Education to prevent AIDS: Prospects and obstacles. *Science, 239,* 592–596.

Fingarette, H. (1988). *Heavy drinking: The myth of alcoholism as a disease.* Berkeley, CA: University of California Press.

Finlayson, A., & McEwen, J. (1977). *Coronary heart disease and patterns of living.* New York: Watson.

Fischer, C.S. (1976). *The urban experience.* New York: Harcourt Brace Jovanovich.

Fischer, J.D. (1988). Possible effects of reference group-based social influence on AIDS-risk behavior and AIDS prevention. *American Psychologist, 43,* 914–920.

Fishbein, M., Ajzen, I., & McArdle, J. (1980). Changing the behavior of alcoholics: Effects of persuasive communication. In I. Ajzen and M. Fishbein (Eds.), *Understanding attitudes and predicting behavior.* Englewood Cliffs, NJ: Prentice-Hall.

Fishbein, M., Jaccard, J.J., Davidson, A.B., Ajzen, I., & Loken, B. (1980). Predicting and understanding family planning behavior. In I. Ajzen & M. Fishbein (Eds.), *Understanding attitudes and predicting behavior.* Englewood Cliffs, NJ: Prentice-Hall.

Fisher, E.B., Lichtenstein, E., & Haire-Joshu, D. (in press). Multiple determinants of tobacco use and cessation. In C.T. Orleans & J. Slade (Eds.), *Nicotine addiction: Principles & Management.* New York: Oxford.

Fisher, E.B., & Rost, K. (1986). Smoking cessation: A practical guide for the physician. *Clinics in Chest Medicine, 7,* 551–565.

Flanders, W.D., & Rothman, K.J. (1982). Interaction of alcohol and tobacco in laryngeal cancer. *American Journal of Epidemiology, 115,* 371–379.

Flay, B.R. (1985). Psychosocial approaches to smoking prevention: A review of findings. *Health Psychology, 4,* 449–488.

Flay, B.R., Ryan, K.B., Best, J.A., Brown, K.S., Kersell, M.W., D'Avernas, J.R., & Zanna, M.P. (1985). Are social-psychological smoking prevention programs effective? The Waterloo Study. *Journal of Behavioral Medicine, 8,* 37–59.

Fleming, I., Baum, A., Davidson, L.M., Rectanus, E., & McArdle, S. (1987). Chronic stress as a factor in physiological reactivity to challenge. *Health Psychology, 6,* 221–237.

Flor, H., Kerns, R.D., & Turk, D.C. (1987). The role of spouse reinforcement, perceived pain, and activity levels of chronic pain patients. *Journal of Psychosomatic Research, 31,* 251–259.

Flora, J.A., Maibach, E.W., & Maccoby, N. (1989). The role of media across four levels of health promotion intervention. *Annual Review of Public Health, 10,* 181–202.

Foley, K.M. (1985). The medical treatment of cancer pain. *New England Journal of Medicine, 313,* 84–95.

Folkman, S., & Lazarus, R.S. (1985). If it changes it must be a process: Study of emotion and coping during three stages of a college examination.

Journal of Personality and Social Psychology, 48, 150–170.

Folks, D.G., Freeman, A.M., Sokol, R.S., & Thurstin, A.H. (1988). Denial: Predictor of outcome following coronary bypass surgery. *International Journal of Psychiatry in Medicine, 18*, 57–66.

Follette, W.T., & Cummings, N.A. (1967). Psychiatric services and medical utilization in a prepaid health plan setting. *Medical Care, 5*, 25–35.

Follick, M.J., Ahern, D.K., & Auberger, E.W. (1985). Development of an audiovisual taxonomy of pain behavior: Reliability and discriminant validity. *Health Psychology, 4*, 555–568.

Follick, M.J., Ahern, D.K., Attanasio, V., & Riley, J.F. (1985). Chronic pain programs: Current aims, strategies, and needs. *Annals of Behavioral Medicine, 7*, 17–20.

Fontana, A.F., Kerns, R.D., Rosenberg, R.L., & Colonese, K.L. (1989). Support, stress, and recovery from coronary heart disease: A longitudinal causal model. *Health Psychology, 8*, 175–193.

Ford, A.B. (1976). *Urban health in America.* New York: Oxford University Press.

Ford, D.H., & Urban, H.B. (1963). *Systems of psychotherapy: A comparative study.* New York: Wiley.

Fordyce, W.E. (1974). Pain viewed as learned behavior. In J.J. Bonica (Ed.), *Advances in neurology* (Vol. 4). New York: Raven Press.

Fordyce, W.E. (1976). *Behavioral methods for chronic pain and illness.* St. Louis: Mosby.

Fordyce, W.E. (1978). Learning processes in pain. In R.A. Sternbach (Ed.), *The psychology of pain.* New York: Raven Press.

Fordyce, W.E., Brockway, J.A., Bergman, J.A., & Spengler, D. (1986). Acute back pain: A control-group comparison of behavioral vs. traditional management methods. *Journal of Behavioral Medicine, 9*, 127–140.

Fordyce, W.E., Fowler, R., Lehmann, J., DeLateur, B., Sand, P., & Treischmann, R. (1973). Operant conditioning in the treatment of chronic pain. *Archives of Physical Medicine and Rehabilitation, 54*, 399–408.

Fordyce, W.E., & Steger, J.C. (1979). Behavioral management of chronic pain. In O.F. Pomerleau & J.P. Brady (Eds.), *Behavioral medicine: Theory and practice.* Baltimore: Williams & Wilkins.

Foreyt, J.P. (1987). Issues in the assessment and treatment of obesity. *Journal of Consulting and Clinical Psychology, 55*, 677–684.

Forman, M.R., Trowbridge, F.L., Gentry, E.M., Marks, J.S., & Hogelin, G.C. (1986). Overweight adults in the United States: The behavioral risk factor surveys. *American Journal of Clinical Nutrition, 44*, 410–416.

Forster, J.L., Jeffrey, R.W., Schmid, T.L., & Kramer, L.M. (1988). Preventing weight gain in adults: A pound of prevention. *Health Psychology, 7*, 515–525.

Fox, B.H. (1978). Premorbid psychological factors as related to cancer incidence. *Journal of Behavioral Medicine, 1*, 45–133.

Fox, B.H. (1981). Psychosocial factors in the immune system in human cancer. In R. Ader (Ed.), *Psychoneuroimmunology.* New York: Academic Press.

Fox, B.H. (1983). Current theory of psychogenic effects on cancer incidence and prognosis. *Journal of Psychosocial Oncology, 1*, 17–31.

Frame, P.S. (1986). A critical review of adult health maintenance. Part 3: Prevention of cancer. *Journal of Family Practice, 22*, 511–520.

Frank, R.G., Gluck, J.P., & Buckelew, S.P. (1990). Rehabilitation: Psychology's greatest opportunity? *American Psychologist, 45*, 757–761.

Frankenhaeuser, M. (1986). A psychobiological framework for research on human stress and coping. In M.H. Appley & R. Trumbull (Eds.), *Dynamics of stress: Physiological, psychological, and social perspectives.* New York: Plenum.

Frankenhaeuser, M., & Johansson, G. (1982). Stress at work: Psychobiological and psychosocial aspects. Paper presented at the 20th International Congress of Applied Psychology, Edinburgh.

Frankl, V. (1963). *Man's search for meaning.* New York: Washington Square.

Fredrickson, M., & Matthews, K.A. (1990). Cardiovascular responses to behavioral stress and hypertension: A meta-analytic review. *Annals of Behavioral Medicine, 12*, 30–39.

Freedman, J.L., Klevansky, S., & Ehrlich, P.I. (1971). The effect of crowding on human task performance. *Journal of Applied Social Psychology, 1*, 7–26.

Freidson, E. (1970). *Profession of medicine. A study in the sociology of applied knowledge.* New York: Dodd, Mead.

Freidson, E. (1961). *Patients' views of medical practice.* New York: Russell Sage.

French, T.M., & Alexander, F. (1941). Psychogenic factors in bronchial asthma. *Psychosomatic Medicine Monographs*, No. 4.

Frick, M.H., Elo, O., Haapa, K., Heinonen, O.P., Heinsalmi, P., Helo, P., Huttunen, J.K., Kaitaniemi, P., Koskinen, P., Manninen, V., Mäenpää, H., Mälkönen, M., Hänttäri, M., Norola, S., Pasternack, A., Pikkarainen, J., Romo, M., Sjöblom, T., & Nikkilä, E.A. (1987). Helsinki Heart Study: Primary prevention trial with gemfibrozil in middle-aged men with dyslipidemia: Safety of treatment, changes in risk factors, and incidence of coronary heart disease. *New England Journal of Medicine, 317*, 1237–1245.

Fricton, J.R. (1982). Medical evaluation of patients with chronic pain. In J. Barber & C. Adrian (Eds.), *Psychological approaches to the management of pain.* New York: Brunner/Mazel.

Friday, N. (1980). *Men in love: Men's sexual fantasies: The triumph of love over rage.* New York: Delacorte.

Fried, P.A., Watkinson, B., & Willan, A. (1984). Marijuana use during pregnancy and decreased length of gestation. *Obstetrics and Gynecology, 150,* 23–27.

Friedman, H.S. (1990). *Personality and disease.* New York: Wiley.

Friedman, H.S. (1991). *The self-healing personality.* New York: Henry Holt.

Friedman, H.S. (1982). Nonverbal communication in medical interaction. In H.S. Friedman & M.R. DiMatteo (Eds.), *Interpersonal issues in health care.* New York: Academic Press.

Friedman, H.S. & Booth-Kewley, S. (1987). The disease-prone personality: A meta-analytic view of the construct. *American Psychologist, 42,* 539–555.

Friedman, H.S., & Booth-Kewley, S. (1988). Validity of the Type A construct: A reprise. *Psychological Bulletin, 104,* 381–384.

Friedman, H.S. & DiMatteo, M.R. (1979). Health care as an interpersonal process. *Journal of Social Issues, 35,* 1–11.

Friedman, L.A., & Kimball, A.W. (1986). Coronary heart disease mortality and alcohol consumption in Framingham. *American Journal of Epidemiology, 124,* 481–489.

Friedman, M., & Rosenman, R.H. (1974). *Type A behavior and your heart.* New York: Knopf.

Friedman, M., Thoresen, C.E., Gill, J.J., Powell, L.H., Ulmer, D., Thompson, L., Price, V.A., Rabin, D.D., Breall, W.S., Dixon, T., Levy, R., & Bourg, E. (1986). Alteration of Type A behavior and its effect on cardiac recurrences in post myocardial infarction patients: Summary results of the recurrent coronary prevention project. *American Heart Journal, 112,* 653–665.

Friedman, M., & Ulmer, D. (1984). *Treating Type A behavior and your heart.* New York: Knopf.

Fries, E., & Bowen, D.J. (June, 1990). Social desirability of health-related behaviors. Paper presented at the American Psychological Society meeting, Dallas.

Fries, H., Nillius, J., & Peterson, F. (1974). Epidemiology of secondary amenorrhea. *American Journal of Obstetrics and Gynecology, 118,* 473–479.

Fries, J.F., & Crapo, L.M. (1981). *Vitality and aging.* San Francisco: Freeman.

Frishman, W., Razin, A., Swencionis, E., & Sonnenblick, E.H. (1981). Beta-adrenoceptor blockade in anxiety states: A new approach to therapy. *Cardiovascular Reviews and Reports, 2,* 447–459.

Froese, A., Hackett, T.P., Cassem, N.H., & Silverberg, E.L. (1974). Trajectories of anxiety and depression in denying and nondenying acute myocardial infarction patients during hospitalization. *Journal of Psychosomatic Research, 18,* 413–420.

Fuchs, V.R., & Hahn, J.S. (1990). How does Canada do it? A comparison of expenditures for physicians' services in the United States and Canada. *New England Journal of Medicine, 323,* 884–890.

Fullam, F.A. (1991). Implementing patient-centered care in an emergency room. *Picker/Commonwealth Report, 1,* 2.

Funk, S. C. (1992). Hardiness: A review of theory and research. *Health Psychology, 11,* 335–345.

Funk, S.C., & Houston, K. (1987). A critical analysis of the Hardiness Scale's validity and reliability. *Journal of Personality and Social Psychology, 53,* 572–578.

Gagnon, J.H. (1977). *Human sexualities.* Chicago: Scott, Foresman.

Gaind, R.N., & Jacoby, R. (1978). Benzodiazepines causing aggression. In R.N. Gaind & B.L. Hudson (Eds.), *Current themes in psychiatry.* London: Macmillan.

Galizio, M., & Maisto, S.A. (1985). Toward a biopsychosocial theory of substance abuse. In M. Galizio & S.A. Maisto (Eds.), *Determinants of substance abuse: Biological, psychological, and environmental factors.* New York: Plenum.

Gallup Opinion Index. (1973). Princeton, NJ: American Institute of Public Opinion, No. 102.

Gannon, L.R., Haynes, S.N., Cuevas, J., & Chavez, R. (1987). Psychophysiological correlates of induced headaches. *Journal of Behavioral Medicine, 10,* 411–423.

Garfinkel, P.E., & Garner, D.M. (1982). *Anorexia nervosa: A multidimensional perspective.* New York: Brunner/ Mazel.

Garfinkel, P.E., & Garner, D.M. (1983). The multidetermined nature of anorexia nervosa. In P.L. Darby, P.E. Garfinkel, D.M. Garner, & D.V. Coscina (Eds.), *Anorexia nervosa: Recent developments in research.* New York: Liss.

Garfinkel, P.E., & Garner, D.M. (1984). Bulimia in anorexia nervosa. In R.C. Hawkins, W.J. Fremouw, & P.F. Clement (Eds.), *The binge-purge syndrome: Diagnosis, treatment and research.* New York: Springer.

Garner, D.M., Garfinkel, P.E., & Bemis, K.M. (1982). A multidimensional psychotherapy for anorexia nervosa. *International Journal of Eating Disorders, 1,* 3–46.

Garner, D.M., Garfinkel, P.E., Schwartz, D., & Thompson, M. (1980). Cultural expectations of thinness in women. *Psychological Reports, 47,* 483–491.

Garner, D.M., & Wooley, S.C. (1991). Confronting the failure of behavioral and dietary treatments for obesity. *Clinical Psychology Review, 11,* 729– 780.

Garrity, T.F., & Marx, M.B. (1979). Critical life events and coronary disease. In W.D. Gentry &

R.B. Williams (Eds.), *Psychological aspects of myocardial infarction and coronary care* (2nd ed.). St. Louis: Mosby.

Garvey, A.J., Heinhold, J.W., & Rasner, B. (1989). Self-help approaches to smoking cessation: A report from the normative aging study. *Addictive Behaviors, 14,* 23–33.

Gazzaniga, M.S. (1970). *The bisected brain.* New York: Appleton-Century-Crofts.

Gebhardt, D.L., & Crump, C.E. (1990). Employee fitness and wellness programs in the workplace. Special Issue: Organizational psychology. *American Psychologist, 45,* 262–272.

Geiser, D.S. (1989). Psychosocial influences on human immunity. *Clinical Psychology Review, 9,* 689–715.

Gelhorn, E., & Kiely, W.F. (1972). Mystical states of consciousness: Neurophysiological and clinical aspects. *Journal of Nervous and Mental Disease, 154,* 399–40.

Gentry, W.D. (1984). Behavioral medicine: A new research paradigm. In W.D. Gentry (Ed.), *Handbook of behavioral medicine.* New York: Guilford.

Gentry, W.D., & Kobasa, S.C. (1984). Social and psychological resources mediating stress-illness relationships in humans. In W.D. Gentry (Ed.), *Handbook of behavorial medicine* (pp. 87–116). New York: Guilford.

Gentry, W.D., & Matarazzo, J.D. (1981). Medical psychology: Three decades of growth and development. In L.A. Bradley & C.K. Prokop (Eds.), *Medical psychology: Contributions to behavioral medicine.* New York: Academic Press.

Georgas, J., Giokoumaki, E., Georgoulias, N., Koumandakis, E., & Kaskarelis, D. (1984). Psychosocial stress and its relation to obstetrical complications. *Psychotherapy and Psychosomatics, 41,* 200–206.

George, L., & Gwyther, L. (1984). The dynamics of caregiving burden: Changes in caregiver well-being over time. *Gerontologist, 23,* 249.

Gerbert, B., Maguire, B.T., Bleecker, T., Coates, T.J., McPhee, S.J. (1991). Primary care physicians and AIDS. *Journal of the American Medical Association, 266,* 2837–2842.

Gerbert, B., Stone, G., Stulbarg, M., Gullin, D.S., & Greenfield, S. (1988). Agreement among physicians' assessment methods: Searching for the truth among fallible methods. *Medical Care, 26,* 519–532.

Gergen, P.J., Mullally, D.I., & Evans, R. (1988). National survey of prevalence of asthma among children in the United States, 1976 to 1980. *Pediatrics, 81,* 1–7.

German, P.S. & Burton, L.C. (1989). Medication and the elderly: Issues of prescription and use. *Journal of Aging and Health, 1,* 4–34.

Geschwind, N. (1979). Specializations of the human brain. In *Scientific American* editors of, *The brain: Readings from Scientific American.* San Francisco: W.H. Freeman.

Gil, K.M., Keefe, F.J., Sampson, H.A., McCaskill, C.C., Rodin, J., & Crisson, J.E. (1988). Direct observation of scratching behavior in children with atopic dermatitis. *Behavior Therapy, 19,* 213–227.

Gilbert, D.G. (1979). Paradoxical tranquilizing and emotion-reducing effects of nicotine. *Psychological Bulletin, 86,* 643–661.

Gilford, R. (1984). Contrasts in marital satisifaction throughout old age: An exchange theory analysis. *Journal of Gerontology, 39,* 325–333.

Gilford, R. (1986). Marriages in later life. *Generations, 10,* 16–20.

Gill, J.S., Price, V.A., Friedman, M., Thoresen, E.E., Powell, L.H., Ulmer, D., Brown, B., & Drews, F.R. (1985). Reduction in Type A behavior in healthy middle-aged American military officers. *American Heart Journal, 110,* 503–514.

Gill, J.S., Zezulka, A.V., Shipley, M.J., Gill, S.K., & Beevers, D.G. (1986). Stroke and alcohol consumption. *New England Journal of Medicine, 315,* 1041–1046.

Gintner, G.G. (1988). Relapse prevention in health promotion: Strategies and long-term outcome. Special Issue: Behavioral medicine and the mental health counselor. *Journal of Mental Health Counseling, 10,* 123–135.

Glantz, M.D. (1992). A developmental psychopathology model of drug abuse vulnerability. In M.D. Glantz & R. Pickens (Eds.), *Vulnerability to drug abuse.* Washington, DC: American Psychological Association.

Glaser, R., Kiecolt-Glaser, J.K., Bonneau, R., Malarkey, W., & Hughes, J. (1992). Stress-induced modulation of the immune response to recombinant hepatitis B vaccine. *Psychosomatic Medicine, 54,* 22–29.

Glaser, R., Rice, J., Speicher, C.E., Stout, J.C., & Kiecolt-Glaser, J. (1986). Stress depresses interferon production concomitant with a decrease in natural killer cell activity. *Behavioral Neuroscience, 100,* 675–678.

Glasgow, R.E., Klesges, R.C., Mizes, J.S., & Pechacek, T.F. (1985). Quitting smoking: Strategies used and variables associated with success in a stop-smoking contest. *Journal of Consulting and Clinical Psychology, 53,* 905–912.

Glasgow, R.E., McCaul, K.D., & Schafer, L.C. (1987). Self-care behaviors and glycemic control in Type I diabetes. *Journal of Chronic Diseases, 40,* 399–412.

Glasgow, M.S., & Engel, B.T. (1987). Clinical issues in biofeedback and relaxation therapy for hypertension. In J.P. Hatch, J.G. Fisher, & J.D. Rugh (Eds.), *Biofeedback,* (pp. 81–121). New York: Plenum.

Glasner, P.D., & Kaslow, R.A. (1990). The epidemiology of human immunodeficiency virus infection. *Journal of Consulting and Clinical Psychology, 58,* 13–21.

Glass, D.C. (1977). *Behavior patterns, stress, and coronary disease.* Hillsdale, NJ: Erlbaum.

Glass, D.C., Snyder, M.L., & Hollis, J. (1974). Time urgency and the Type A coronary-prone behavior pattern. *Journal of Applied Social Psychology, 4,* 125–140.

Glass, D.C., Ross, D.T., Isecke, W., & Rosenman, R.H. (1982). Relative importance of speech characteristics and content of answers in the assessment of behavior pattern A by the Structured Interview. *Basic and Applied Social Psychology, 3,* 161–168.

Glasser, W. (1976). *Positive addiction.* New York: Harper & Row.

Glassman, A.H., Helzer, J.E., Covey, L.S., Cottler, L.B., Stetner, F., Tipp, J.E., & Johnson, J. (1990). Smoking, smoking cessation, and major depression. *Journal of the American Medical Association, 264,* 1546–1549.

Glenn, S.W., Parsons, O.A., & Stevens, L. (1989). Effects of alcohol abuse and familial alcoholism on physical health in men and women. *Health Psychology, 8,* 325–341.

Glick, R., & Cerullo, L.J. (1986). Subarachnoid and parenchymal hemorrhage. In P.E. Kaplan & L.J. Cerullo (Eds.), *Stroke rehabilitation.* Boston: Butterworth.

Gliedman, J., & Roth, W. (1980). *The unexpected minority: Handicapped children in America.* New York: Harcourt Brace Jovanovich.

Glynn, C.J., Lloyd, J.W., & Folkard, S. (1981). Ventilatory responses to chronic pain. *Pain, 11,* 201–212.

Gochman, D.S. (1988). *Health behavior: Emerging research perspectives.* New York: Plenum.

Goffman, E. (1961). *Asylums.* Garden City, NY: Doubleday.

Goggins, F.C., Odgers, R.P., Luscombe, S.M., & Foust, R. (1989). Chemical dependency and anxiety disorders. *Psychiatric Hospital, 20,* 79–83.

Goldberg, E.L., & Comstock, G.W. (1980). Epidemiology of life events: Frequency in general populations. *American Journal of Epidemiology, 111,* 736–752.

Golombok, S. (1989). Causes, effects and treatment of long-term benzodiazepine use: A review of psychological perspectives. *Human Psychopharmacology, 4,* 15–22.

Gonder-Frederick, L.A., Cox, D.J., Bobbitt, S.S., & Pennebaker, J.W. (1989). Mood changes associated with blood glucose fluctuations in insulin-dependent diabetes mellitus. *Health Psychology, 8,* 45–59.

Goodall, T.A., & Halford, W.K. (1991). Self-management of diabetes mellitus: A critical review. *Health Psychology, 10,* 1–8.

Goodwin, D.W. (1986). Heredity and alcoholism. *Annals of Behavioral Medicine, 8,* 3–6.

Goodwin, D.W., Schulsinger, F., Knop, J., Mednick, S., & Guze, S. (1977). Psychopathology in adopted and nonadopted daughters of alcoholics. *Archives of General Psychiatry, 34,* 1005–1009.

Gorder, D.D., Dolecek, T.A., Coleman, G.G., Tillotson, J.L., Brown, H.B., Lenz-Litzow, K., Bartsch, G.E., & Grandits, G. (1986). Dietary intake in the Multiple Risk Factor Intervention Trial (MRFIT): Nutrient and food group changes over 6 years. *Journal of the American Dietetic Association, 86,* 744–751.

Gordis, L. (1984). General concepts for use of markers in clinical trials. *Controlled Clinical Trials, 5,* 481–487.

Gordon, E.D., Minnes, P.M., & Holden, R.R. (1990). The structure of attitudes toward persons with a disability, when specific disability and context are considered. *Rehabilitation Psychology, 35,* 79–90.

Gordon, T., Castelli, W.P., Hjortland, M.C., Kannel, W.B., & Dawber, T.R. (1977). High density lipoprotein as a protective factor against coronary heart disease. The Framingham Study. *American Journal of Medicine, 62,* 707–714.

Gordon, T., & Doyle, J.T. (1987). Drinking and mortality: The Albany study. *American Journal of Epidemiology, 125,* 263–270.

Gordon, T., & Kannel, W.B. (1984). Drinking and mortality: The Framingham Study. *American Journal of Epidemiology, 120,* 97–107.

Gordon, W.A., & Diller, L. (1983). Stroke: Coping with a cognitive deficit. In T.G. Burish & L.A. Bradley (Eds.), *Coping with chronic disease: Research and applications.* New York: Academic.

Gorman, D.R. (1988). Assessment of a screening method for heart disease. *Family Practice, 5,* 297–301.

Gortmaker, S., Eckenrode, J., & Gore, S. (1982). Stress and the utilization of health services: A time series and cross-sectional analysis. *Journal of Health and Social Behavior, 23,* 25–38.

Gotestam, K.G., & Agras, W.S. (1989). Bulimia nervosa: Pharmacologic and psychologic approaches to treatment. *Nordisk Psykiatrisk Tidsskrift, 43,* 543–551.

Gottlieb, M.S., Schanker, H.M., Fan, P.T., Saxon, A., Weisman, J.D. (1981). Pneumocystis pneumonia—Los Angeles. *Morbidity and Mortality Weekly Report, 30,* 250–252.

Gottman, J.M., & Katz, L.F. (1989). Effects of marital discord on young children's peer interaction and health. *Developmental Psychology, 25,* 373–381.

Grand, S.A., Bernier, J.E., & Strohmer, D.C. (1982). Attitudes toward disabled persons as a function of social context and specific disability. *Rehabilitation Psychology, 27,* 165–174.

Graham, S., Snell, L.M., Graham, J.B., & Ford, L. (1971). Social trauma in the epidemiology of cancer of the cervix. *Journal of Chronic Diseases, 24*, 711–725.

Grant, I., & Heaton, R.K. (1990). Human immunodeficiency Virus-Type 1 (HIV-1) and the brain. *Journal of Consulting and Clinical Psychology, 58*, 22–30.

Green, K.L. (1989). Healthy workers: Whose responsiblity? *Advances, 6*, 12–14.

Green, L.W., Kreuter, M.W., Deeds, S.G., & Partridge, K.B. (1980). *Health education planning: A diagnostic approach*. Palo Alto, CA: Mayfield.

Green, L.W., Mullen, P.D., & Stainbrook, G.L. (1985). Programs, to reduce drug errors in the elderly: Direct and indirect evidence from patient education. In *Improving medication compliance: Proceedings of a symposium*. Reston, VA: National Pharmaceutical Council.

Greenberg, M.T., & Crinic, K.A. (1988). Longitudinal predictors of developmental status and social interactions in premature and full-term infants at age two. *Child Development, 59*, 554–570.

Greene, W.A., & Swisher, S.N. (1969). Psychological and somatic variables associated with the development and course of monozygotic twins discordant for leukemia. *Annals of the New York Academy of Sciences, 164*, 394–408.

Greenfield, S., Kaplan, S.H., & Ware, J.E., Jr. (1985). Expanding patient involvement in care: Effects on patient outcomes. *Annals of Internal Medicine, 102*, 520–528.

Greenfield, S., Kaplan, S.H., Ware, J.E., Jr., Yano, E.M., & Frank, H.J. (1988). Patient participation in medical care: Effects on blood sugar control and quality of life in diabetes. *Journal of General Internal Medicine, 3*, 448–457.

Greer, S., & Morris, T. (1978). The study of psychological factors in breast cancer: Problems of method. *Social Science and Medicine, 12*, 129–134.

Greer, S., Morris, T., & Pettingale, K.W. (1979). Psychological response to breast cancer: effect on outcome. *Lancet, 2*, 785–787.

Gregory, W.L., & Burroughs, W.J. (1989). *Introduction to applied psychology*. Glenview, IL: Scott, Foresman and Company.

Grob, G.N. (1983). Disease and environment in American history. In D. Mechanic (Ed.), *Handbook of health, health care, and the health professions*. New York: Free Press.

Gross, J., & Rosen, J.C. (1988). Bulimia in adolescents: Prevalence and psychosoical correlates. *International Journal of Eating Disorders, 7*, 51–61.

Grossman, H.J. (Ed., 1983). *Classification in mental retardation*. Washington, D.C.: American Association on Mental Deficiency.

Grossman, S.P. (1979). The biology of motivation. In M. Rosenzweig & L.W. Porter (Eds.), *Annual review of psychology: 1979* (Vol. 30). Palo Alto, CA: Annual Reviews.

Group Health Association of America (1988). *HMO Industry Profile*. (Vol. 2). *Utilization patterns*. Washington, DC: Research and Analysis Department GHAA.

Grunberg, N.E., & Bowen, D.J. (1985). Coping with the sequelae of smoking cessation. *Journal of Cardiopulmonary Rehabilitation, 5*, 285–289.

Guastello, S.J. (1992). Accidents and stress-related health disorders among bus operators: Forecasting with catastrophe theory. In J.C. Quick, L.R. Murphy, & J.J. Hurrell, Jr. (Eds.), *Stress and well-being at work*. Washington, D.C.: American Psychological Association.

Guck, T.P., Skultety, F.M., Meilman, P.W., & Dowd, E.T. (1985). Multidisciplinary pain center follow-up study: Evaluation with a no-treatment control group. *Pain, 21*, 295–306.

Guidubaldi, J., & Cleminshaw, H.K. (1985). Divorce, family health, and child adjustment. Special Issue: The family and health care. *Family Relations Journal of Applied Family and Child Studies, 34*, 35–41.

Gurr, M.I., Jung, R.T., Robinson, M.P., & James, W.P.T. (1982). Adipose tissue cellularity in man: The relationship between fat cell size and number, the mass and distribution of body fat, and the history of weight gain and loss. *International Journal of Obesity, 6*, 419–436.

Gustafsson, P.A., Kjellman, N.I.M., & Cederblad, M. (1986). Family therapy in the treatment of severe childhood asthma. *Journal of Psychosomatic Research, 30*, 369–374.

Hadlow, J., & Pitts, M. (1991). The understanding of common health terms by doctors, nurses, and patients. *Social Science and Medicine, 32*, 193–196.

Hall, J.A., & Dornan, M.C. (1988a). Meta-analysis of satisfaction with medical care: Description of research done in and analysis of overall satisfaction levels. *Social Science and Medicine, 26*, 637–644.

Hall, J.A., & Dornan, M.C. (1988b). What patients like about their medical care and how often they are asked: A meta-analysis of the satisfaction literature. *Social Science and Medicine, 27*, 935–939.

Hall, J.A., & Dornan, M.C. (1990). Patient sociodemographic characteristics as predictors of satisfaction with medical care: A meta-analysis. *Social Science and Medicine, 30*, 811–818.

Hall, J.A., Roter, D.L., & Katz, N.R. (1988). Meta-analysis of correlates of provider behavior in medical encounters. *Medical Care, 26*, 657–675.

Hall, R.S. (1988). The virology of AIDS. *American Psychologist, 43*, 907–913.

Hall, S.M., & Hall, R.G. (1982). Clinical series in the behavioral treatment of obesity. *Health Psychology, 1*, 359–372.

Halmi, K.A. (1982). Cyroheptadine for anorexia nervosa. *Lancet, i*, 1357–1358.

Hamberger, K., & Lohr, J. (1984). *Stress and stress management: Research and applications.* New York: Springer.

Hamburg, D.R., Elliot, G.R., & Parron, D.L. (1982). *Health behavior: Frontiers of research in the biobehavioral sciences.* Washington, DC: National Academy.

Hamilton, M.K., Gelwick, B.P., & Meade, C.J. (1984). The definition and prevalence of bulimia. In R.C. Hawkins, W.J. Fremouw, & P.F. Clement (Eds.), *The binge-purge syndrome: diagnosis, treatment and research.* New York: Springer.

Hamlett, K.W., & Curry, J.F. (1990). Anorexia nervosa in adolescent males: A review and case study. *Child Psychiatry and Human Development, 21,* 79–94.

Hammond, E.C., & Horn, D. (1954). The relationship between human smoking habits and death rates. *Journal of the American Medical Association, 155,* 1316–1328.

Hansen, W.B., Graham, J.W., Sobel, J.L., Shelton, D.R., Flay, B.R., & Johnson, C.A. (1987). The consistency of peer and parent influences on tobacco, alcohol, and marijuana use among young adolescents. *Journal of Behavioral Medicine, 10,* 559–579.

Hanson, C.L., Henggeler, S.W., & Burghen, G.A. (1987). Models of associations between psychosocial variables and health-outcome measures of adolescents with IDDM. *Diabetes Care, 10,* 752–758.

Hanson, C.L., & Pichert, J.W. (1986). Perceived stress and diabetes control in adolescents. *Health Psychology, 5,* 439–452.

Harburg, E., Erfurt, J.C., Havenstein, L.S., Chape, C., Schull, W.J., & Schork, M.A. (1973). Socioecological stress, suppressed hostility, skin color, and black-white male blood pressure: Detroit. *Psychosomatic Medicine, 35,* 276–296.

Harrell, J.P. (1980). Psychological factors and hypertension: A status report. *Psychological Bulletin, 87,* 482–501.

Harris, D.M., & Guten, S. (1979). Health-protective behaviors: An exploratory study. *Journal of Health and Social Behavior, 20,* 17–29.

Harris, P.R. (1980). *Promoting health, preventing disease: Objectives for the nation.* Washington, DC: U.S. Government Printing Office.

Harris, S.S., Casperson, C.J., DeFriese, G.H., & Estes, E.H. (1989). Physical activity counseling for healthy adults as a primary preventive intervention in the clinical setting. *Journal of the American Medical Association, 261,* 3590–3598.

Hart, K.E. (1990, April). *Attitudes toward AIDS versus cancer patients.* Paper presented at the meeting of the Western Psychological Association, Los Angeles, CA.

Hartig, T., Mang, M., & Evans, G.W. (1991). Restorative effects of natural environment experiences. *Environment and Behavior, 23,* 3–26.

Hartmann, H. (1958). *Ego psychology and the problem of adaptation.* New York: International Universities.

Hartz, A.J., Rupley, D.C., & Rimm, A.A. (1984). The association of girth measurements with disease in 32,856 women. *American Journal of Epidemiology, 119,* 71–80.

Harwood, A. (1971). The hot-cold theory of disease. *Journal of the American Medical Association, 216,* 1153–1158.

Haskell, W.L. (1984). Overview: Health benefits of exercise. In J.D. Matarazzo, S.M. Weiss, J.A. Herd, N.E. Miller, & S.M. Weiss, (Eds.), *Behavioral health: A handbook of health enhancement and disease prevention.* New York: Wiley.

Haskell, W.L. (1985). Exercise programs for health promotion. In J.C. Rosen & L.J. Solomon (Eds.), *Prevention in health psychology.* Hanover, NH: University Press of New England.

Haskell, W.L., Camargo, C., Jr., Williams, P.T., Vranizan, K.M., Krauss, R.M., Lindgren, F.T., & Wood, P.D. (1984). The effect of cessation and resumption of moderate alcohol intake on serum high-density lipoportein subfractions. *New England Journal of Medicine, 310,* 805–810.

Hatfield, M.O. (1990). Stress and the American worker. *American Psychologist, 45,* 1162–1164.

Hathaway, S.R., & McKinley, J.C. (1967). *The Minnesota Multiphasic Personality Inventory Manual.* New York: Psychological Corporation.

Hauenstein, M.S., Schiller, M.R., & Hurley, R.S. (1987). Motivational techniques of dieticians counseling individuals with Type II diabetes. *Journal of the American Diabetic Association, 87,* 37–42.

Haug, M.R., & Lavin, B. (1983). *Consumerism in medicine: Challenging physician authority.* Beverly Hills, CA: Sage.

Havik, O.E., & Maeland, J.G. (1988). Verbal denial and outcome in myocardial infarction patients. *Journal of Psychosomatic Research, 32,* 145–157.

Havik, O.E., & Maeland, J.G. (1990). Pattern of emotional reactions after a myocardial infarction. *Journal of Psychosomatic Research, 34,* 271–285.

Hawton, K., Cole, D., O'Grady, J., & Osborn, M. (1982). Motivational aspects of deliberate self-poisoning in adolescents. *British Journal of Psychiatry, 141,* 286–290.

Hayes, D., & Ross, C.E. (1987). Concern with appearance, health beliefs, and eating habits. *Journal of Health and Social Behavior, 28,* 120–130.

Haynes, R.B. (1976). Strategies for improving compliance: A methodologic analysis and review. In D.L. Sackett & R.B. Haynes (Eds.), *Compliance with therapeutic regimens*. Baltimore: John Hopkins University.

Haynes, R.B. (1979). Introduction. In R.B. Haynes, D.W. Taylor, & D.L. Sackett (Eds.), *Compliance in health care*. Baltimore: Johns Hopkins.

Haynes, R.B., Taylor, D.W., Sackett, D.L., Gibson, E.S., Berkholz, C.D., & Mukherjee, J. (1980). Can simple clinical measurement detect patient noncompliance? *Hypertension, 2*, 757–764.

Haynes, R.B., Wang, E., & Gomes, M.D. (1987). A critical review of interventions to improve compliance with prescribed medications. *Patient Education and Counseling, 10*, 155–166.

Haynes, S.G., Feinleib, M., & Eaker, E.D. (1983). Type A behavior and the ten-year incidence of coronary heart disease in the Framingham heart study. In R.H. Rosenman (Ed.), *Psychosomatic risk factors and coronary heart disease*. Berne: Huber.

Haynes, S.G., Feinleib, M., & Kannel, W.B. (1980). The relationship of psychosocial factors to coronary heart disease in the Framingham Study: I. Methods and risk factors. *American Journal of Epidemiology, 107*, 362–383.

Health Care Financing Administration. (1981). *Long-term care: Background and future directions*. Washington, DC: U.S. Department of Health and Human Services.

Health Care Financing Administration. (1987). National health expenditure, 1986–2000. *Health Care Financing Review, 8*, 1–36.

Hebb, D.D. (1955). Drives and the C.N.S. (conceptual nervous system). *Psychological Review, 62*, 243–254.

Hechtman, L., Weiss, G., & Perlman, T. (1984). Hyperactives as young adults: Past and current substance abuse and antisocial behavior. *American Journal of Orthopsychiatry, 54*, 415–425.

Hediger, H. (1965). Environmental factors influencing the reproduction of zoo animals. In F. Beach (Ed.), *Sex and behavior*. New York: Wiley.

Heiby, E.M., Gafarian, C.T., & McCann, S.C. (1989). Situational and behavioral correlates of compliance to a diabetic regimen. *Journal of Compliance in Health Care, 4*, 101–116.

Heiman, J.R. & LoPiccolo, J. (1983). Effectiveness of daily versus weekly therapy in the treatment of sexual dysfunction. Unpublished manuscript, State University of New York at Stony Brook.

Heimstra, N.W. (1973). The effects of smoking on mood change. In W.L. Dunn, Jr. (Ed.), *Smoking behavior: Motives and incentives*. Washington, DC: Winston.

Heimstra, N.W., & McFarling, L.H. (1978). *Environmental psychology* (2nd ed.). Monterey, CA: Brooks/Cole.

Heinrich, R.L., Cohen, M.J., Naliboff, B.D., Collins, G.A., & Bonnebakker, A.D. (1985). Comparing physical and behavior therapy for chronic low back pain on physical abilities, psy-

chological distress, and patients' perceptions. *Journal of Behavioral Medicine, 8*, 61–78.

Heisel, J.S., Locke, S.E., Kraus, L.J., & Williams, M. (1986). Natural killer cell activity and MMPI scores of a cohort of college students. *American Journal of Psychiatry, 143*, 1382–1386.

Hellman, C.J.C. (1987). *The physiological, psychological, and economic effects of group behavioral medicine interventions for primary care patients*. Unpublished doctoral dissertation, Harvard University, Cambridge, MA.

Hellman, C.J.C., Budd, M., Borysenko, J., McClelland, D.C., & Benson, H. (1990). A study of the effectiveness of two group behavioral medicine interventions for patients with psychosomatic complaints. *Behavioral Medicine, 16*, 165–173.

Helmstadter, G.C. (1970). *Research concepts in human behavior*. New York: Appleton-Century-Crofts.

Helzer, J.E., Robins, L.N., Taylor, J.R., Carey, K., Miller, R.H., Combs-Orne, T., & Farmer, A. (1985). The extent of long-term moderate drinking among alcoholics discharged from medical and psychiatric treatment facilities. *New England Journal of Medicine, 312*, 1678–1682.

Henbest, R.J. & Steward, M. (1990). Patient-centeredness in the consultation. 2: Does it really make a difference? *Family Practice, 7*, 28–33.

Hendler, N.H. (1984). Chronic pain. In H.B. Roback (Ed.), *Helping patients and their families cope with medical problems*. San Francisco: Jossey-Bass.

Hendren, R.L. (1990). Stress in adolescence. In L.E. Arnold (Ed.), *Childhood stress* (pp. 247–264). New York: John Wiley & Sons.

Hennig, P., & Knowles, A. (1990). Factors influencing women over 40 years to take precautions against cervical cancer. *Journal of Applied Social Psychology, 20*, 1612–1621.

Henrich, M. (1989). Making stress management relevant to worksite wellness. Special Issue: Mind-body health at work. *Advances, 6*, 55–60.

Henry, J.P. (1990). The arousal of emotions: Hormones, behavior, and health. *Advances, 6*, 59–62.

Henry, J.P., & Cassel, J.C. (1969). Psychosocial factors in essential hypertension: Recent epidemiologic and animal experimental evidence. *American Journal of Epidemiology, 90*, 171–200.

Herd, J.A. (1978). Physiological correlates of coronary-prone behavior. In T. Dembroski, S. Weiss, J. Shields, S. Haynes, & M. Feinleib (Eds.), *Coronary-prone behavior*. New York: Springer.

Herd, J.A., & Weiss, S.M. (1984). Overview of hypertension: Its treatment and prevention. In J.D. Matarazzo, S.M. Wiess, J.A. Herd, N.E. Miller, & S.M. Weiss (Eds.), *Behavioral health: A handbook of health enhancement and disease prevention*. New York: Wiley.

Herity, B., Moriarty, M., Daly, L., Dunn, J., & Bourke, G.J. (1982). The role of tobacco and alcohol in the aetiology of lung and larynx cancer. *British Journal of Cancer, 46*, 961–964.

Herman, C.P. (1987). Social and psychological factors in obesity: What we don't know. In H. Weiner & A. Baum (Eds.), *Perspectives in behavioral medicine: Eating regulation and discontrol* (pp. 175–187). Hillsdale, NJ: Erlbaum.

Herning, R.I., Jones, R.T., Bachman, J., & Mines, A.H. (1981). Puff volume increases when low-nicotine cigarettes are smoked. *British Medical Journal, 283*, 187–189.

Heuch, I., Kvale, G., Jacobsen, B.K., & Bjelke, E. (1983). Use of alcohol, tobacco and coffee, and risk of pancreatic cancer. *British Journal of Cancer, 48*, 637–643.

Hibbard, J.H. (1988). Age, social ties, and health behaviors: An exploratory study. *Health Education Research, 3*, 131–139.

Hilgard, E.R. (1975). The alleviation of pain by hypnosis. *Pain, 1*, 213–231.

Hilgard, E.R. (1978). Hypnosis and pain. In R.A. Sternbach (Ed.), *The psychology of pain.* New York: Raven Press.

Hilgard, E.R. (1979). The Stanford hypnotic susceptibility scales as related to other measures of hypnotic responsiveness. *American Journal of Clinical Hypnosis, 21*, 68–83.

Hilgard, E.R., & Hilgard, J.R. (1983). *Hypnosis in the relief of pain* (rev. ed.). Los Altos, CA: Kaufman.

Hinds, M.W., Kolonel, L.N., Hankin, J.H., & Lee, J. (1984). Dietary vitamin A, carotene, vitamin C, and risk of lung cancer in Hawaii. *American Journal of Epidemiology, 119*, 227–237.

Hindi-Alexander, M., & Cropp, G.J.A. (1984). Evaluation of a family asthma program. *Journal of Allergy and Clinical Immunology, 74*, 505–510.

Hingson, R., Alpert, J.J., Day, N., Dooling, E., Kayne, H., Morelock, S., Oppenheimer, E., & Zuckerman, B. (1982). Effects of maternal drinking and marijuana use on fetal growth and development. *Pediatrics, 70*, 539–546.

Hingson, R., Zuckerman, B., Amaro, H., Frank, D.A., Kayne, H., Sorenson, J.R., Mitchell, J., Parker, S., Morelock, S., & Timperi, R. (1986). Maternal marijuana use and neonatal outcome: Uncertainly posed by self-reports. *American Journal of Public Health, 76*, 667–669.

Hinkle, L.E. (1974). The effect of exposure to cultural change, social change, and changes in interpersonal relationships on health. In B.S. Dohrenwend & B.P. Dohrenwend (Eds.), *Stressful life events: Their nature and effects* (pp. 9–44). New York: Wiley.

Hiroto, D.S., & Seligman, M.E.P. (1975). Generality of learned helplessness in man. *Journal of Personality and Social Psychology, 31*, 311–327.

Hite, S. (1976). *The Hite report.* New York: Macmillan Co.

Hjermann, I., Velve B.K., Holme, I., & Leren, P. (1981). Effect of diet and smoking intervention on the incidence of coronary heart disease. *Lancet, 2*, 1303–1310.

Hobbs, D., & Cole, S. (1976). Transition to parenthood: A decade replication. *Journal of Marriage and the Family, 38*, 723–731.

Hobbs, D., & Wimbish, J. (1977). Transition to parenthood by black couples. *Journal of Marriage and the Family, 39*, 677–689.

Hochbaum, G. (1958). *Participation in medical screening programs: A sociopsychological study.* (Public Health Service Publication No. 572). Washington, DC: U.S. Government Printing Office.

Hock, Z. (1983). The G spot. *Journal of Sex and Marital Therapy, 9*, 166–167.

Hoelscher, T.J., Lichstein, K.L., & Rosenthal, T.L. (1986). Home relaxation practice in hypertension treatment: Objective assessment and compliance induction. *Journal of Consulting and Clinical Psychology, 54*, 217–221.

Hoffman, J.W., Benson, H., Arns, P.A., Stainbrook, G.L., Landsberg, G.L., Young, J.B., & Gill, A. (1982). Reduced sympathetic nervous system responsivity associated with the relaxation response. *Science, 215*, 190–192.

Hofman, A., Walter, H.J., Connelly, P.A., & Vaughn, R.D. (1987). Blood pressure and physical fitness in children. *Hypertension, 9*, 188–191.

Hofstetter, A., Schutz, Y., Jequier, E., & Wahren, J. (1986). Increased 24-hour energy expenditure in cigarette smokers. *New England Journal of Medicine, 314*, 79–82.

Holahan, C. (1986). Environmental psychology. *Annual Review of Psychology, 37*, 381–407.

Holahan, C.K., Holahan, C.J., & Belk, S. (1984). Adjustment in aging: The roles of life stress, hassles, and self-efficacy. *Health Psychology, 3*, 315–328.

Holden, C. (1987). Is alcoholism treatment successful? *Science, 236*, 20–22.

Holland, J.C., & Tross, S. (1985). The psychosocial and neuropsychiatric sequelae of the acquired immunodeficiency snydrome and related disorders. *Annals of Internal Medicine, 103*, 760–764.

Hollon, S.D., & Beck, A.T. (1986). Cognitive and cognitive-behavioral therapies. In S.L. Garfield & A.E. Bergin (Eds.), *Handbook of psychotherapy and behavior change* (3rd ed., pp. 443–482). New York: Wiley.

Holloway, R.L., Matson, C.C., & Zismer, D.K. (1989). Patient satisfaction and selected physician behaviors: Does the type of practice make a difference? *Journal of the American Board of Family Practice, 2*, 87–92

Holmes, D.M. (1986). The person and diabetes in psychosocial context. *Diabetes Care, 9*, 194–206.

Holmes, D. S. (1984). Meditation and somatic arousal reduction: A review of the experimental evidence. *American Psychologist, 39,* 1–10.

Holmes, D. S. & McGilley, B. M. (1987). Influence of a brief aerobic training program on heart rate and subjective response to a psychologic stressor. *Psychosomatic Medicine, 49,* 366–374.

Holmes, J.A. (1990). Differential effects of avoidant and attentional coping strategies on adaptation to chronic and recent-onset pain. *Health Psychology, 9,* 577–584.

Holmes, T.H. (1979). Development and application of a quantitative measure of life change magnitude. In J.E. Barrett, R.M. Rose, & G.L. Klerman (Eds.), *Stress and Mental Disorder.* New York: Raven.

Holmes, T.H., & Masuda, M. (1974). Life change and illness susceptibility. In B.S. Dohrenwend & B.P. Dohrenwend (Eds.), *Stressful life events: Their nature and effects.* New York: Wiley.

Holmes, T.H., & Rahe, R.H. (1967). The Social Readjustment Rating Scale. *Journal of Psychosomatic Research, 11,* 213–218.

Holroyd, K.A., Andrasik, F. (1982). Do the effects of cognitive therapy endure? A two-year follow-up of tension headache sufferers treated with cognitive therapy or biofeedback. *Cognitive Therapy and Research, 6,* 325–334.

Holroyd, K.A., Andrasik, F., & Westerbrook, T. (1977). Cognitive control of tension headache. *Cognitive Therapy and Research, 1,* 121–133.

Holroyd, K.A., & Gorkin, L. (1983). Young adults at risk for hypertension: Effects of family history and anger management in determining responses to interpersonal conflict. *Journal of Psychosomatic Research, 27,* 131–138.

Holroyd, K.A., Nash, J.M., & Pingel, J.D. (1991). A comparison of pharmacological (Amitriptyline HCL) and nonpharmacological (cognitive-behavioral) therapies for chronic tension headaches. *Journal of Consulting and Clinical Psychology, 59,* 387–393.

Holroyd, K.A., & Penzien, D.B. (1985). Client variables and the behavioral treatment of recurrent tension headache: A meta-analytic review. *Journal of Behavioral Medicine, 9,* 515–536.

Holzman, A.C., Rudy, T.E., Gerber, K.E., Turk, D.C., Sanders, S.H., Zimmerman, J., & Kearns, R.D. (1985). Chronic pain: A multiple-setting comparison of patient characteristics. *Journal of Behavioral Medicine, 8,* 411–422.

Homer, C.J., James, S.A., & Siegal, E. (1990). Work-related psychosocial stress and risk of preterm, low birthweight delivery. *Advances, 7,* 13–16.

Hoon, E.F., & Hoon, P.W. (1978). Styles of sexual expression in women: Clinical implications of multivariate analyses. *Archives of Sexual Behavior, 7,* 105–116.

Hoon, P., Wincze, J., & Hoon, E. (1977). A test of reciprocal inhibition: Are anxiety and sexual arousal in women mutually inhibitory? *Journal of Abnormal Psychology, 86,* 65–74.

Horan, M.J. (1988). Introduction: Hypertension research perspective in the United States. *Health Psychology, 7* (Suppl.), 9–14.

Horn, J.C., & Meer, J. (1987). The vintage years. *Psychology Today, 21,* 76–90.

Hornbrook, M.C., & Berki, S.E. (1985). Practice mode and payment method. Effects on use costs, quality, and access. *Medical Care, 23,* 484–511.

Horne, R.L., & Picard, R.S. (1979). Psychosocial risk factors for lung cancer. *Psychosomatic Medicine, 41,* 503–514.

Horowitz, M., & Kaltreider, N. (1977). Brief therapy of the stress response syndrome. *Psychiatric Clinics of North America, 2,* 365–377.

Horton, A.M., & Wedding, D. (1984). *Clinical and behavioral neuropsychology.* New York: Praeger.

Hough, R.L., Fairbank, D.T., & Garcia, A.M. (1976). Problems in the ratio measurement of life stress. *Journal of Health and Social Behavior, 17,* 70–82.

House, J.S. (1981). *Work stress and social support.* Reading, MA: Addison-Wesley.

House, J.S., Landis, K.R., & Umberson, D. (1988). Social relationships and health. *Science, 241,* 540–545.

House, J.S., Kessler, R.C., Herzog, A.R., Mero, R.P., Kinney, A.M., & Breslow, M.J. (1990). Age, socioeconomic status, and health. *Milbank Quarterly, 68,* 383–411.

House, J.S., Robbins, C., & Metzner, H.L. (1982). The association of social relationships and activities with mortality: Prospective evidence from the Tecumseh Community Health Study. *American Journal of Epidemiology, 116,* 123–140.

House, J.S., & Smith, D.A. (1985). Evaluating the health effects of demanding work on and off the job. In T.F. Drury (Ed.), *Assessing physical fitness and physical activity in population-base surveys* (pp. 481–508). Hyattsville, MD: National Center for Health Statistics.

Householder, J., Hatcher, R., Burns, W., & Chasnoff, I. (1982). Infants born to narcotic-addicted mothers. *Psychological Bulletin, 92,* 453–468.

Houston, B.K. (1986). Psychological variables and cardiovascular and neuroendocrine reactivity. In K.A. Matthews, S.M. Weiss, T. Detre, T.M. Dembroski, B. Falkner, S.B. Manuck, & R.B. Williams (Eds.), *Handbook of stress, reactivity, and cardiovascular disease.* New York: Wiley.

Houston, B.K. (1988). Division 38 survey: Synopsis of results. *The Health Psychologist, 10,* 2–3.

Houts, P.W., Miller, R.W., Tokuhata, G.K., & Ham, K.S. (1980, April 8). *Health-related behavioral impact of the Three Mile Island nuclear incident.* Report submitted to the TMI Advisory Panel on Health Research Studies of the Pennsylvania Department of Health, Part I.

Hovland, C.I., Janis, I.L., & Kelley, J.J. (1953). *Communication and persuasion.* New Haven, CT: Yale University.

Howarth, E. (1965). Headache, personality, and stress. *British Journal of Psychiatry, 111,* 1193–1197.

Hubert, H.B. (1986). The importance of obesity in the development of coronary risk factors and disease: The epidemiologic evidence. In L. Breslow, J.E. Fielding, & L.B. Lave (Eds.), *Annual review of public health* (Vol. 7). Palo Alto, CA: Annual Reviews.

Huffman, L.C., & del Carmen, R. (1990). Prenatal stress. In L.E. Arnold (Ed.), *Childhood stress,* pp. 141–171. New York: John Wiley & Sons.

Hughes, G.H., Hymowitz, N., Ockene, J.K., Simon, V., & Vogt, T.M. (1981). The Multiple Risk Factor Intervention Trial (MRFIT). V. Intervention on smoking. *Preventive Medicine, 10,* 476–500.

Hughes, P.L., Wells, L.A., Cunningham, C.J. & Ilstrup, D.M. (1986). Treating bulimia with desipramine. *Archives of General Psychiatry, 43,* 182–186.

Hulka, B.S., (1979). Patient-clinician interactions and compliance. In R.B. Haynes, D.W. Taylor, & D.L. Sackett (Eds.), *Compliance in health care.* Baltimore: Johns Hopkins University.

Hull, C.L. (1943). *Principles of behavior.* New York: Appleton.

Hull, C.L. (1951). *Essentials of behavior.* New Haven: Yale University.

Hull, E.M., Young, S.H., & Ziegler, M G. (1984). Aerobic fitness affects cardiovascular and catecholamine response to stressors. *Psychophysiology, 21,* 353–360.

Hull, J.G., & Bond, C.F. (1986). Social and behavioral consequences of alcohol consumption and expectancy: A meta-analysis. *Psychological Bulletin, 99,* 347–360.

Hull, J.G., Young, R.D., & Jouriles, E. (1986). Applications of the self-awareness model of alcohol consumption: Predicting patterns of use and abuse. *Journal of Personality and Social Psychology, 51,* 790–796.

Hull, J.G., Van Treuren, R.R., & Virnelli, S. (1987). Hardiness and health: A critique and an alternative approach. *Journal of Personality and Social Psychology, 53,* 518–530.

Hunt, B., & Hunt, M. (1974). *Prime time.* New York: Stein & Day.

Hunt, W.A., Barnett, L.W., & Branch, L.G. (1971). Relapse rates in addiction programs. *Journal of Clinical Psychology, 27,* 455–456.

Hunter, C., Jr. (1982). Freestanding alcohol treatment centers—A new approach to an old problem. *Psychiatric Annals, 12,* 396–408.

Hunter, M., & Philips, H.C. (1981). The experience of headache: An assessment of the qualities of tension headache pain. *Pain, 10,* 209–219.

Hunter, R.C.A., Lohrenz, J.G., & Schwartzman, A.E. (1964). Nosophobia and hypochondriasis in medical students. *Journal of Nervous and Mental Diseases, 139,* 147–152.

Hurd, P.D., & Blevin, J. (1984). Aging and color of pills. *New England Journal of Medicine, 310,* 202.

Hussar, D.A. (1985). Improving patient compliance: The role of the pharmacist. In *Improving Medication Compliance: Proceedings of a symposium.* Reston, VA: National Pharmaceutical Council.

Hyman, B.T., Van Hoesen, G.W., Damasio, A.R., & Barnes, C.L. (1984). Alzheimer's disease: Cell-specific pathology isolates the hippocampal formation. *Science, 225,* 1168–1170.

Ikard, F.F., Green, D.E., & Horn, D. (1969). A scale to differentiate between types of smoking as related to the management of affect. *International Journal of Addictions, 4,* 649– 659.

Ikard, F.F., & Tomkins, S. (1973). The experience of affect as a determinant of smoking behavior: A series of validity studies. *Journal of Abnormal Psychology, 81,* 172–181.

Imber, S., Schultz, E., Funderburk, F., Allen, R., & Flanner, R. (1976). The fate of the untreated alcoholic: Toward a natural history of the disorder. *Journal of Nervous and Mental Disorders, 162,* 238–247.

Ingersoll, G.M., Orr, D.P., Herrold, A.J., & Golden, M.P. (1986). Cognitive maturity and self-management among adolescents with insulin-dependent diabetes mellitus. *Journal of Pediatrics, 108,* 620–623.

Inui, T.S., Carter, W.B., Percoraro, R.E., Pearlman, M.D., & Dohan, J.J. (1980). Variations in patient compliance with common long-term drugs. *Medical Care, 18,* 986–993.

Inui, T.S., Yourtee, E.L., & Williamson, J.W. (1976). Improved outcomes in hypertension after physician tutorials: A controlled trial. *Annals of Internal Medicine, 84,* 646–651.

Iosub, S., Bamji, M., Stone, R.K., Gromisch, D.S., & Wasserman, E. (1987). More on human immune deficiency virus embryopathy. *Pediatrics, 80,* 512–516.

Irwin, M., Daniels, M., Bloom, E.T., Smith, T.L., & Weiner, H. (1987). Life events, depressive symptoms, and immune function. *American Journal of Psychiatry, 144,* 437–441.

Irwin, M., Daniels, M., Risch, S.C., Bloom, E.T., & Weiner, H. (1988). Plasma cortisol and natural killer cell activity during bereavement. *Biological Psychiatry, 24,* 173–178.

Israel, A.C., Silverman, W.K., & Solotar, L.C. (1988). The relationship between adherence and weight loss in a behavioral treatment program for overweight children. *Behavior Therapy, 19,* 25–33.

Isselbacher, K.J., Adams, R.D., Braunwald, E., Petersdorf, R.G., & Wilson, J.D. (1980). *Harrison's principles of internal medicine* (9th ed.). New York: McGraw-Hill.

Jaccard, J.J., & Davidson, A.R. (1972). Toward an understanding of family planning behaviors: An initial investigation. *Journal of Applied Social Psychology, 2*, 228–235.

Jacob, R.G., Forman, S.P., Kraemer, H.C., Farquhar, J.W., & Agras, W.S. (1985). Combining behavioral treatments to reduce blood pressure: A controlled outcome study. *Behavioral Modification, 9*, 32–54.

Jacobsen, P.B., Perry, S.W., & Hirsch, D.A. (1990). Behavioral and psychological responses to HIV antibody testing. *Journal of Consulting and Clinical Psychology, 58*, 31–37.

Jacobson, A.M., Hauser, S.T., Wolfsdorf, J.I., Houlihan, J., Milley, J.E., Herskowitz, R.D., Wertlieb, D., & Watt, E. (1987). Psychologic predictors of compliance in children with recent onset of diabetes mellitus. *Journal of Pediatrics, 110*, 805–811.

Jacobson, E. (1938). *Progressive relaxation: A physiological and clinical investigation of muscle states and their significance in psychology and medical practice* (2nd ed.). Chicago: University of Chicago.

Jaffe, J.H. (1985). Drug addiction and drug abuse. In *Goodman and Gilman's The pharmacological basis of therapeutic behavior.* New York: Macmillan.

Jalali, B., Jalali, M., Crocetti, G., & Turner, F. (1980). Adolescence and drug use: Toward a more comprehensive approach. *American Journal of Orthopsychiatry, 51*, 120–130.

James, S.A. (1987). Psychosocial precursors of hypertension: A review of the epidemiologic evidence. Circulation, 76, (Suppl. I), I-60–I-66.

James, S.A., Hartnett, S.A., & Kalsbeek, W.D. (1983). John Henryism and blood pressure differences among black men. *Journal of Behavioral Medicine, 6*, 259–278.

James, S.A., Strogatz, D.W., Wing, S.B., & Ramsey, D.L. (1987). Socioeconomic status, John Henryism, and hypertension in blacks and whites. *American Journal of Epidemiology, 126*, 664–673.

Janis, I.L., (1958). *Psychological stress.* New York: Wiley.

Janis, I.L. (1983). Inoculation as an inherent coping mechanism. In D. Meichenbaum & M.E. Jaremko (Eds.), *Stress reduction and prevention.* New York: Plenum.

Janis, I.L., & Feshbach, S. (1953). Effects of fear-arousing communications. *Journal of Abnormal and Social Psychology, 48*, 78–92.

Jansen, M.A., Methorst, G.J., Kerkhof, A.J. (1990). Health psychology in international perspective: A summary and some thoughts for the future. Special Issue: The development of health psychology: An international perspective. *Psychology and Health, 4*, 83–89.

Janz, N.K., & Becker, M.H. (1984). The health belief model: A decade later. *Health Education Quarterly, 11*, 1–47.

Janz, N.K., Becker, M.H., & Hartman, P.E. (1984). Contingency contracting to enhance patient compliance. A review. *Patient Education and Counseling, 5*, 165–178.

Jaremko, M.E. (1983). Stress inoculation training for social anxiety, with emphasis on dating anxiety. In D. Meichenbaum & M.E. Jaremko (Eds.), *Stress reduction and prevention.* New York: Plenum.

Jason, L.A., Jayaraj, S., Blitz, C.C., Michaels, M.H., & Klett, L.E. (1990). Incentives and competition in a worksite smoking cessation intervention. *American Journal of Public Health, 80*, 205–206.

Jeffrey, D.B., & Lemnitzer, N. (1981). Diet, exercise, obesity, and related health problems: A macroenvironmental analysis. In J.M. Ferguson & C.B. Taylor (Eds.), *The comprehensive handbook of behavioral medicine: Vol. 2—Syndromes & special areas* (pp. 47–66). New York: SP Medical & Scientific Books.

Jeffrey, R.W., Hellerstedt, W.L., & Schmid, T.L. (1990). Correspondence programs for smoking cessation and weight control: A comparison of two strategies in the Minnesota Heart Health Program. *Health Psychology, 9*, 585–598.

Jeffrey, R.H., Pheley, A.M., Forster, J.L., Kramer, F.M., & Snell, M.K. (1988). Payroll contracting for smoking cessation: A worksite pilot study. *American Journal of Preventive Medicine, 4*, 83–86.

Jemerin, J.M., Boyce, W.T. (1990). Psychobiological differences in childhood stress response: II. Cardiovascular markers of vulnerability. *Journal of Developmental and Behavioral Pediatrics, 11*, 140–150.

Jemmott, J.B., III. (1987). Social motives and susceptibility to disease: Stalking individual differences in health risks. *Journal of Personality, 55*, 267–298.

Jemmott, J.B., III & Locke, S.E. (1984). Psychosocial factors, immunologic mediation, and human susceptibility to infectious disease. *Psychological Bulletin, 95*, 52–77.

Jemmott, J.B., III, & Migliore, K. (1988). Academic stress, social support, and secretory immunoglobulin A. *Journal of Personality and Social Psychology, 55*, 803–810.

Jenkins, C.D. (1988). Epidemiology of cardiovascular disease. *Journal of Consulting and Clinical Psychology, 56*, 324–332.

Jenkins, C.D., Rosenman, R.H., & Zyzanski, S.J. (1974). Prediction of clinical coronary heart disease by a test for the coronary prone behavior pattern. *New England Journal of Medicine, 290*, 1271–1275.

Jenkins, C.D., Zyzanski, S.J., & Rosenman, R.H. (1979). *Jenkins Activity Survey.* New York: Psychological Corporation.

Jennings, G., Nelson, L., Nestel, P., Esler, M., Korner, P., Burton, D., & Bazelmans, J. (1986). The effects of changes in physical activity on major cardiovascular risk factors, hemodynamics, sympathetic function, and glucose utilization in man: A controlled study of four levels of activity. *Circulation*, *73*, 30–40.

Jensen, M.P., & Karoly, P. (1991). Control beliefs, coping efforts, and adjustment of chronic pain. *Journal of Consulting and Clinical Psychology*, *59*, 431–438.

Jepson, C., & Chaiken, S. (1986, August). *The effect of anxiety on the systematic processing of persuasive communications.* Paper presented at the annual meeting of the American Psycholocial Association, Washington, DC.

Jessor, R. (1984). Adolescent development and behavioral health. In J.D. Matarazzo, S.M. Weiss, J.A. Herd, N.E. Miller, & S.M. Weiss (Eds.), *Behavioral health: A handbook of health enhancement and disease prevention.* New York: Wiley.

Jewett, D.L., Fein, G., & Greenberg, M.H. (1991). A double-blind study of symptom provocation to determine food sensitivity. *The New England Journal of Medicine*, *323*, 429–433.

Job, R.F.S. (1985). Reported attitudes, practices, and knowledge in relation to drunk driving: The effects of the introduction of random breath testing in New South Wales. In S. Kaye & G.W. Meier, (Eds.), *Alcohol, drugs and traffic safety: Proceedings of the Ninth International Conference on Alcohol, Drugs, and Traffic Safety.* Washington, DC: National Highway Traffic Safety Commission.

Job, R.F.S. (1988). Effective and ineffective use of fear in health promotion programs. *American Journal of Public Health*, *78*, 163–167.

Johnson, C.A., Pentz, M.A., Webert, M.D., Dwyer, J.H., Baer, N., MacKinnon, D.P., Hansen, W.B., & Flay, B.R. (1990). Relative effectiveness of comprehensive community programming for drug abuse prevention with high-risk and low-risk adolescents. *Journal of Consulting and Clinical Psychology*, *58*, 447–456.

Johnson, D. (1980). Doctor talk. In L. Michaels & C. Ricks (Eds.), *The state of the language.* Berkeley, CA: University of California.

Johnson, J.H. (1986). *Life events as stressors in childhood and adolescence.* Newbury Park, CA: Sage.

Johnson, J.V., & Hall, E.M. (1988). Job strain, work place social support, and cardiovascular disease: A cross-sectional study of a random sample of the Swedish working population. *American Journal of Public Health*, *78*, 1336–1342.

Johnson, S.B. (1980). Psychosocial factors in juvenile onset diabetes: A review. *Journal of Behavioral Medicine*, *3*, 95–116.

Johnson, S.B. (1985). The family and the child with chronic illness. In D.C. Turk & R.D. Kearns (Eds.), *Health, illness, and families: A life-span perspective.* New York: Wiley.

Johnston, D.W. (1989). Prevention of cardiovascular disease by psychological methods. *British Journal of Psychiatry*, *154*, 183–194.

Johnston, L.D., Bachman, J.G., & O'Malley, P.M. (1987). *National trends in drug use and related factors among American high school students and young adults, 1975–1986.* Rockville, MD: National Institute on Drug Abuse, U.S. Department of Health and Human Services (Publication No. ADM 87–1535).

Jones, B.M. (1973). Memory impairment on the ascending and descending limbs of the blood alcohol curve. *Journal of Abnormal Psychology*, *82*, 24–32.

Jones, B.M., & Parsons, O.A. (1971). Imparied abstracting ability in chronic alcoholics. *Archives of General Psychiatry*, *24*, 71–75.

Jones, M.C. (1968). Personality correlates and antecedents of drinking patterns in males. *Journal of Consulting and Clinical Psychology*, *32*, 2–12.

Jones, M.C. (1971). Personality antecedents and correlates of drinking patterns in women. *Journal of Consulting and Clinical Psychology*, *36*, 61– 69.

Jones, R.A. (1990). Expectations and delay in seeking medical care. *Journal of Social Issues*, *46*, 81–95.

Jones, R.A., & Wiese, H.J. (1982, August). *Provider and consumer differences in perceived relationships among symptoms.* Paper presented at the annual meeting of the American Psychological Association, Washington, DC.

Jones, R.A., Wiese, H.J., Moore, R.W., & Halay, J.V. (1981). On the perceived meaning of symptoms. *Medical Care*, *19*, 710–717.

Jones, W.H.S. (1923). On decorum and the physician. In E. Capps, T.E. Page, & W.H.D. Rouse (Eds.), *Hippocrates* (Loeb Classic Library, Vol. 2). London: William Hermann; New York: G.P. Putnam.

Jorgensen, R.S., & Houston, B.K. (1981). Family history of hypertension, gender, and cardiovascular reactivity and sterotypy during stress. *Journal of Behavioral Medicine*, *4*, 175–190.

Joseph, J.G., Montgomery, S.B., Emmons, C., & Kessler, R.C. (1987). Magnitude and determinants of behavioral risk reduction: Longitudinal analysis of a cohort at risk for AIDS. *Psychology & Health*, *1*, 73–95.

Joseph, J.G., Montgomery, S.B., Kirscht, J., Kessler, R.C., Ostrow, D.G., Emmons, C.A., & Phair, J.P. (1987, June). *Behavioral risk reduction in a cohort of homosexual men: Two year follow-up.* Paper presented at the Third International Conference on AIDS, Washington, DC.

Joyce, C. (1984, November). A time for grieving. *Psychology Today*, *18*, 42–46.

Justin, R.G. (1988). Adult and adolescent attitudes toward death. *Adolescence*, *23*, 429–435.

Kahn, K.L., Keeler, E.B., Sherwood, M.J., Rogers, W.H., Draper, D., Bentow, S.S., Reinisch, E.J., Rubenstein, L.V., Kosecoff, J., & Brook, R.H. 1990). Comparing outcomes of care before and after implementation of the DRG-based prospective payment system. *Journal of the American Medical Association, 264*, 1984–1988.

Kalechstein, A., Triplett, J., Rolfe, E., Rotstein, K., & Cochran, S.D. (1988, April). *Little white lies: Sexual dishonesty among college students.* Paper presented at the meeting of the Western Psychological Association, Burlingame, CA.

Kamarck, T.W. (1990). Social support reduces cardiovascular reactivity to psychological challenge: A laboratory model. *Psychosomatic Medicine, 52*, 42–58.

Kamarck, T.W., & Lichtenstein, E. (1985). Current trends in clinic-based smoking control. *Annals of Behavioral Medicine, 7*, 19–23.

Kamarck, T.W., Manuck, S.B., & Jennings, J.R. (1989, April). *Social support reduces cardiovascular reactivity to behavioral challenge: A laboratory model.* Paper presented at the meeting of The Society of Behavioral Medicine, San Francisco.

Kamen, L.P., Rodin, J., & Seligman, M.E.P. (1987). *Explanatory style and immune functioning.* Unpublished manuscript, University of Pennsylvania, Philadelphia.

Kaminer, Y., & Bukstein, O. (1989). Adolescent chemical use and dependence: Current issues in epidemiology, treatment and prevention. *Acta Psychiatrica Scandinavica, 79*, 415–424.

Kandel, D. (1974). Inter- and intragenerational influences of adolescent drug use. *Journal of Social Issues, 30*, 107–135.

Kandel, D., & Faust, R. (1975). Sequence and stages in patterns of adolescent drug use. *Archives of General Psychiatry, 32*, 923–932.

Kandel, D.B. (1982). Epidemiological and psychosocial perspectives on adolescent drug use. *Journal of the American Academy of Child Psychiatry, 20*, 328–347.

Kandil, O., & Borysenko, M. (1987). Decline of natural killer cell target binding and lytic activity in mice exposed to rotation stress. *Health Psychology, 6*, 89–99.

Kane, R.I., Wales, J., Bernstein, L., Leibowitz, A., & Kaplan, S. (1984, April 21). A randomized controlled trial of hospice care. *Lancet*, 890–894.

Kanfer, F.H. (1971). The maintenance of behaviors by self-generated stimuli and reinforcement. In A. Jacobs & L.B. Sachs (Eds.), *The psychology of private events: Perspectives on covert response systems* (pp. 39–59). New York: Academic.

Kannel, W.B., & Abbott, R.D. (1984). Incidence and prognosis of unrecognized myocardial infarction. *New England Journal of Medicine, 311*, 1144–1147.

Kanner, A.D., Coyne, J.C., Schaefer, C., & Lazarus, R.S. (1981). Comparisons of two modes of stress measurement: Daily hassles and uplifts versus major life events. *Journal of Behavioral Medicine, 4*, 1–39.

Kanner, R. (1986). Pain management. *Journal of the American Medical Association, 256*, 2110–2114.

Kanouse, D.E., Berry, S.H., Gorman, E.M., Yano, E.M., & Carson, S. (1991a). Response to the AIDS epidemic: A survey of homosexual and bisexual men in Los Angeles County. (Report No. R-4031-LACH). Santa Monica, CA: Rand.

Kanouse, D.E., Berry, S.H., Gorman, E.M., Yano, E.M., Carson, S., & Abrahamse, A. (1991b). AIDS-related knowledge, attitudes, beliefs, and behaviors in Los Angeles County. (Report No. R-4054-LACH). Santa Monica, CA: Rand.

Kaplan, H. (1974). *The new sex therapy.* New York: Brunner/Mazel.

Kaplan, H. (1979). *Disorders of desire.* New York: Brunner/Mazel.

Kaplan, H.I. (1985). Psychological factors affecting physical conditions (psychosomatic disorders). In H.I. Kaplan & B.J. Saddock (Eds.), *Comprehensive textbook of psychiatry IV* (pp. 1106–1113). Baltimore, MD: Williams & Wilkins.

Kaplan, N.M. (1986). Dietary aspects of the treatment of hypertension. In L. Breslow, J.E. Fielding, & L.B. Lave (Eds.), *Annual review of public health* (Vol. 7). Palo Alto, CA: Annual Reviews.

Kaplan, R.M. (1991). Health-related quality of life in patient decision-making. *Journal of Social Issues, 47*, 69–90.

Kaplan, R.M., & Hartwell, S.L. (1987). Differential effects of social support and social network on physiological and social outcomes in men and women with Type II diabetes mellitus. *Health Psychology, 6*, 387–398.

Kaplan, S.H., & Ware, J.E., Jr. (1989). The patient's role in health care and quality assessment. In N. Goldfield & D.B. Nash (Eds.), *Providing quality care.* Philadelphia: American College of Physicians.

Kaplan, S.L., Busner, J., Weinhold, C., Lenon, P. (1987). Depressive symptoms in children and adolescents with cancer: A longitudinal study. *Journal of the American Academy of Child & Adolescent Psychiatry, 26*, 782–787.

Karlin, R.A., Epstein, Y.M., & Aiello, J.R. (1978). A setting-specific analysis of crowding. In A. Baum & Y.M. Epstein (Eds.), *Human response to crowding.* Hillsdale, NJ: Erlbaum.

Karlin, R.A., Rosen, L., & Epstein, Y.M. (1979). Three into two doesn't go: A follow-up of the effects of overcrowded dormitory rooms. *Personality and Social Psychology Bulletin, 5*, 391–395.

Karoly, P. (1985). The assessment of pain: Concepts and procedures. In P. Karoly (Ed.), *Measurement strategies in health psychology.* New York: Wiley.

Kasl, S.V., & Berkman, L.F. (1981). Some psychosocial influences on the health status of the elderly: The perspective of social epidemiology. In J.L. McGaugh & S.B. Kiesler (Eds.), *Aging: Biology and behavior.* New York: Academic.

Kasl, S.V. & Cobb, S. (1966). Health behavior, illness behavior, and sick role behavior. *Archives of Environmental Health, 12,* 246–266.

Kasl, S.V., Evans, A.S., & Niederman, J.C. (1979). Psychosocial risk factors in the development of infectious mononucleosis. *Psychosomatic Medicine, 41,* 445–466.

Kastenbaum, R. (1985). Dying and death: A life-span approach. In J.E. Birren & K.W. Schaie (Eds.), *Handbook of the psychology of aging* (2nd ed), pp. 619–643. New York: Van Nostrand.

Katz, S., Branch, L.G., Branson, M.H., Papsidero, J.A., Beck, J.C., & Greer, D.S. (1983). Active life expectancy. *New England Journal of Medicine, 309,* 1218–1224.

Keefe, F.J. (1982). Behavioral assessment and treatment of chronic pain: Current status and future directions. *Journal of Consulting and Clinical Psychology, 50,* 896–911.

Keefe, F.J., & Block, A.R. (1982). Development of an observation method for assessing pain behavior in chronic low back pain patients. *Behavior Therapy, 13,* 363–375.

Keefe, F.J., Dunsmore, J., & Burnett, R. (1992). Behavioral and cognitive-behavioral approaches to chronic pain: Recent advances and future directions. *Journal of Consulting and Clinical Psychology, 60,* 528–536.

Keesey, R.E. (1980). A set-point analysis of the regulation of body weight. In A.J. Stunkard (Ed.), *Obesity.* Philadelphia: Saunders.

Keesey, R.E. (1986). A set-point theory of obesity. In K.D. Brownell & J.P. Foreyt (Eds.), *Handbook of eating disorders: Physiology, psychology, and treatment of obesity, anorexia, and bulimia* (pp. 63–87). New York: Basic Books.

Keesey, R.E., & Powley, T.L. (1975). Hypothalamic regulation of body weight. *American Scientist, 63,* 558–565.

Keesey, R.E., & Powley, T.L. (1986). The regulation of body weight. In M.R. Rosenzweig & L.W. Porter (Eds.), *Annual Review of psychology: 1986* (Vol. 37). Palo Alto, CA: Annual Reviews.

Keil, J.E., Tyroler, H.A., Sandifer, S.H., & Boyle, E.J. (1977). Hypertension: Effects of social class and racial admixture. The results of a cohort study in the Black population of Charleston, South Carolina. *American Journal of Public Health, 67,* 634–639.

Keita, G.P., & Jones, J.M. (1990). Reducing adverse reaction to stress in the workplace. *American Psychologist, 45,* 1137–1141.

Kellner, R. (1986). *Somatization and hypochondriasis.* New York: Praeger.

Kelly, J.A., & Murphy, D.A. (1992). Psychological interventions with AIDS and HIV: Prevention and treatment. *Journal of Consulting and Clinical Psychology, 60,* 576–585.

Kelly, J.A., St. Lawrence, J.S., Diaz, Y.E., Stevenson, L.Y., Haruth, A.C., Brasfield, T.L., Kalichman, S.C., Smith, J.E., & Andrew, M.E. (1991). HIV risk behavior reduction following intervention with key opinion leaders of population: An experimental analysis. *American Journal of Public Health, 81,* 168–171.

Kelly, J.A., St. Lawrence, J.S., Betts, R., Brasfield, T.L., & Hood, H.V. (1990). A skills-training group intervention model to assist persons in reducing risk behaviors for HIV infection. *AIDS Education and Prevention, 2,* 24–35.

Kelsey, J.L., & Hochberg, M.C. (1988). Epidemiology of chronic musculoskeletal disorders. In L. Breslow, J.E. Fielding, & L.B. Lave (Eds.), *Annual review of public health* (Vol. 9). Palo Alto, CA: Annual Reviews.

Kempe, C.H. (1971). Pediatric implications of the battered baby syndrome. *Archives of Disease in Childhood, 46,* 28.

Kemper, H.C., Snel, J., Verschuur, R., Storm-van Essen, L. (1990). Tracking of health and risk indicators of cardiovascular diseases from teenager to adult: Amsterdam Growth and Health Study. *Preventive Medicine, 19,* 642–655.

Kendall, R.E. (1965). Normal drinking by former alcohol addicts. *Quarterly Journal of Studies on Alcohol, 26,* 247–257.

Kenkel, P.J. (1988). Managed care will dominate within a decade—experts. *Modern Health Care, 18,* 31.

Keown, C., Slovic, P., & Lichtenstein, S. (1984). Attitudes of physicians, pharmacists, and laypersons toward seriousness and need for disclosure of perscription drug side effects. *Health Psychology, 3,* 1–12.

Kerr, J.K., Skok, R.L., & McLaughlin, T.F. (1991). Characteristics common to females who exhibit anorexic or bulimic behavior: A review of current literature. *Journal of Clinical Psychology, 47,* 846–853.

Kerr, N., & Meyerson, L. (1987). Independence as a goal and a value of people with physical disabilities: Some caveats. *Rehabilitation Psychology, 32,* 173–180.

Kertez, A. (1983). *Localization in neuropsychology.* New York: Academic.

Kessler, L.G., Burns, B.J., Shapiro, S., Tischler, G.L., George, L.K., Hough, R.L., Bodison, D., & Miller, R.H. (1987). Psychiatric diagnoses of medical service users: Evidence from the epidemiologic catchment area program. *American Journal of Public Health, 77*, 18–24.

Ketterlinus, R.D., Henderson, S.H., & Lamb, M.E. (1990). Maternal age, sociodemographics, prenatal health, and behavior: Influences on neonatal risk status. *Journal of Adolescent Health Care, 11*, 423–431.

Keys, A. (1979). Is overweight a risk factor for coronary heart disease? *Cardiovascular Medicine, 4*, 1233–1243.

Keys, A., Brozek, J., Henschel, A., Mickelsen, O., & Taylor, H.L. (1950). *The biology of human starvation.* 2 vols. Minneapolis: University of Minnesota.

Kiecolt-Glaser, J.K., Dura, J.R., Speicher, C.E., Trask, O.J., & Glaser, R. (1991). Spousal caregivers of dementia victims: Longitudinal changes in immunity and health. *Psychosomatic Medicine, 53*, 345–362.

Kiecolt-Glaser, J.K., Dyer, C.S., & Shuttleworth, E.C. (1988). Upsetting social interactions and distress among Alzheimer's disease family caregivers: A replication and extension. *American Journal of Community Psychology, 116*, 825–837.

Kiecolt-Glaser, J.K., & Glaser, R. (1987). Psychosocial moderators of immune function. *Annals of Behavioral Medicine, 9*, 16–20.

Kiecolt-Glaser, J.K., & Glaser, R. (1988). Psychological influences in immunity: Implications for AIDS. *American Psychologist, 43*, 892–898.

Kiecolt-Glaser, J.K., & Glaser, R. (1992). Psychoneuroimmunology: Can psychological interventions modulate immunity? *Journal of Consulting and Clinical Psychology, 60*, 569–575.

Kiecolt-Glaser, J.K., Glaser, R., Strain, E.C., Stout, J.C., Tarr, K.K., Holiday, J.E., & Speicher, C.E. (1986). Modulation of cellular immunity in medical students. *Journal of Behavioral Medicine, 9*, 311–320.

Kiecolt-Glaser, J.K., Glaser, R., Williger, D., Stout, J., Messick, G., Sheppard, S., Ricker, D., Romisher, S.C., Briner, W., Bonnell, G., & Donnerberg, R. (1985). Psychosocial enhancement of immunocompetence in a geriatric population. *Health Psychology, 4*, 25–41.

Kilmann, P.R., Boland, J.P., Norton, S.P., Davidson, E., & Caid, C. (1986). Perspectives of sex therapy outcome: A survey of AASECT providers. *Journal of Sex and Marital Therapy, 12*, 116–138.

Kilo, C., & Williamson, J.R. (1987). *Diabetes: The facts that let you regain control of your life.* New York: Wiley.

Kim, K.K., & Grier, M.R. (1981). Pacing effects of medication instruction for the elderly. *Journal of Gerontological Nursing, 7*, 464–468.

Kimmel, D.C. (1980). *Adulthood and aging* (2nd ed.). New York: Wiley.

Kindelan, K., & Kent, G. (1987). Concordance between patients' information preferences and general practitioners' perceptions. *Psychology and Health, 1*, 399–409.

King, A.C., Taylor, C.B., Haskell, W.L., & DeBusk, R.F. (1989). Influence of regular aerobic exercise on psychological health: A randomized controlled trial of healthy middle-aged adults. *Health Psychology, 8*, 305–324.

Kinsey, A.C., Pomeroy, W.B., & Martin, C.E. (1948). *Sexual behavior in the human male.* Philadelphia: Saunders.

Kinsey, A.C., Pomeroy, W.B., Martin, C.E., & Gebhard, P.H. (1953). *Sexual behavior in the human female.* Philadelphia: Saunders.

Kirkley, B.G., Schneider, J.A., Agras, W.J., & Bachman, J.A. (1985). Comparison of two group treatments for bulimia. *Journal of Consulting and Clinical Psychology, 53*, 43–48.

Kirscht, J.P., Becker, M., Haefner, D., & Maiman, L. (1978). Effects of threatening communications and mothers' health beliefs on weight change in obese children. *Journal of Behavioral Medicine, 1*, 147–157.

Kittle, F., Kornitzer, M., DeBacker, G., & Dramaix, M. (1982). Metrological study of psychological questionnaires with reference to social variables: The Belgian Heart Disease Prevention Project (BHDPP). *Journal of Behavioral Medicine, 5*, 9–36.

Kivilan, D.R., Coppel, D.B., Fromme, K., Williams, E., & Marlatt, G.A. (1989). Secondary prevention of alcohol-related problems in young adults at risk. In K.D. Craig & S.M. Weiss (Eds.), *Prevention and early intervention: Biobehavioral perspectives.* New York: Springer.

Kivilan, D.R., Marlatt, G.A., Fromme, K., Coppel, D.B., & Williams, E. (1990). Secondary prevention with college drinkers: Evaluation of an alcohol skills training program. *Journal of Consulting and Clinical Psychology, 58*, 805–810.

Klatsky, A.L., Friedman, G.D., & Siegelaub, A.B. (1981). Alcohol and mortality: A ten-year Kaiser-Permanente experience. *Annals of Internal Medicine, 95*, 139–145.

Klass, P.A. (1987). *Not an entirely benign procedure.* New York: Signet.

Klein, L.E., German, P.S., Levine, D.M., Feroli, E.R., and Ardery, J. (1984). Medication problems among outpatients: A study with emphasis on the elderly. *Archives of Internal Medicine, 144*, 1185–1188.

Klein, N., Hack, M., Gallagher, J., & Fanaroff, A.A. (1985). Preschool performance of children with normal intelligence who were very low-birth-weight infants. *Pediatrics, 75*, 531–537.

Kleinke, C.L., & Spangler, A.S. (1988). Psychometric analysis of the audiovisual taxonomy for assessing pain behavior in chronic back-pain patients. *Journal of Behavioral Medicine, 11*, 83–94.

Kleinman, A. (1988). *The illness narratives: Suffering, healing, and the human condition.* New York: Basic Books.

Kleinman, J.C., & Madans, J.H. (1985). The effects of maternal smoking, maternal stature, and educational attainment on the incidence of low birthweight. *American Journal of Epidemiology, 121,* 843–855.

Klesges, R.C., & Cigrang, J.A. (1989). Worksite smoking cessation programs: Clinical and methodological issues. In M. Hersen, R.M. Eisler, and P.M. Miller (Eds.), *Progress in behavior modification.* New York: Russell Sage.

Klesges, R.C., Klesges, L.M., & Meyers, A.W. (1991). Relationship of smoking status, energy balance, and body weight: Analysis of the second National Health and Nutrition Examination Survey. *Journal of Consulting and Clinical Psychology, 59,* 899–905.

Klitzman, S., & Stellman, J.M. (1989). The impact of the physical environment on the psychological well-being of office workers. Special Issue: Festschrift for Jack Elinson. *Social Science and Medicine, 29,* 733–742.

Knapp, R.J. (1987, July). When a child dies. *Psychology Today, 21,* 60–67.

Kneier, A.W., & Temoshok, L. (1984). Repressive coping reactions in patients with malignant melanoma as compared to cardiovascular disease patients. *Journal of Psychosomatic Research, 28,* 145–155.

Knittle, J.L. (1975). Early influences on development of adipose tissue. In G.A. Bray (Ed.), *Obesity in perspective.* Washington, DC: U.S. Government Printing Office.

Knowles, J.H. (1977). The responsibility of the individual. In J.H. Knowles (Ed.), *Doing better and feeling worse: Health in the United States* (pp. 57–80). New York: Norton.

Knox, D. (1984). *Human sexuality: The search for understanding.* St. Paul, MN: West.

Knox, R.A. (October 6, 1991). Critiquing hospital care. *Boston Globe Good Health Magazine, 4,* 16–17.

Kobasa, S.C. (1979). Stressful life events and health: An inquiry into hardiness. *Journal of Personality and Social Psychology, 37,* 1–11.

Kobasa, S.C. (1982a). Commitment and coping in stress resistance among lawyers. *Journal of Personality and Social Psychology, 42,* 707–717.

Kobasa, S.C. (1982b). The hardy personality: Toward a social psychology of stress and health. In G.S. Sanders & J. Suls (Eds.), *Social psychology of health and illness* (pp. 3–32). Hillsdale, NJ: Erlbaum.

Kobasa, S.C., Maddi, S.R., & Courington, S. (1981). Personality and constitution as mediators in the stress-illness relationship. *Journal of Health and Social Behavior, 22,* 368–378.

Kobasa, S.C., Maddi, S.R., & Kahn, S. (1982). Hardiness and health: A prospective study. *Journal of Personality and Social Psychology, 42,* 168–177.

Kobasa, S.C., Maddi, S.R., & Puccetti, M.C. (1982). Personality and exercise as buffers in the stress-illness relationship. *Journal of Behavioral Medicine, 5,* 391–404.

Kobasa, S.C., Maddi, S.R., Puccetti, M.C., & Zola, M.A. (1985). Effectiveness of hardiness, exercise, and social support as resources against illness. *Journal of Psychosomatic Research, 29,* 525–533.

Kochanska, G. (1991). Patterns of inhibition to the unfamiliar in children of normal and affectively ill mothers. *Child Development, 62,* 250–263.

Kog, E., & Vandereycken, W. (1985). Family characteristics of anorexia nervosa and bulimia: A review of the research literature. *Clinical Psychology Reviews, 5,* 159–180.

Kohler, T., & Haimerl, C. (1990). Daily stress as a trigger of migraine attacks: Results of thirteen single-subject studies. *Journal of Consulting and Clinical Psychology, 58,* 870–872.

Kolata, G. (1985). Why do people get fat? *Science, 227,* 1327–1328.

Kolodny, R.C., Masters, W.H., & Johnson, V.E. (1979). *Textbook of sexual medicine.* Boston: Little, Brown.

Koltun, A., & Stone, G.C. (1986). Past and current trends in patient noncompliance research: Focus on diseases, regimens-programs, provider-disciplines. *The Journal of Compliance in Health Care, 1,* 21–32.

Koop, C.E. (1985). Keynote address. In *Improving medication compliance: Proceedings of a symposium.* Reston, VA: National Pharmaceutical Council.

Koop, C.E. (1986). *The Surgeon General's report on acquired immune deficiency syndrome.* Washington, DC: U.S. Government Printing Office.

Korsch, B.M., Gozzi, E.K., & Francis, V. (1968). Gaps in doctor-patient communication. 1. Doctor-patient interaction and patient satisfaction. *Pediatrics, 42,* 855–871.

Kosa, J., & Robertson, L. (1975). The social aspects of health and illness. In J. Kosa & I. Zola (Eds.), *Poverty and health: A sociological analysis.* Cambridge, MA: Harvard University.

Kosten, T.A., Kosten, T.R., & Rounsaville, B.J. (1989). Personality disorders in opiate addicts show prognostic specificity. *Journal of Substance Abuse Treatment, 6,* 163–168.

Kosten, T.R., Jacobs, S.C., & Kasl, S.V. (1985). Terminal illness, bereavement, and the family. In D.C. Turk & R.D. Kearns (Eds.), *Health, illness, and families: A life-span perspective.* New York: Wiley.

Kotler, P. (1982). *Marketing for nonprofit organizations* (2nd ed.). Englewood Cliffs, NJ: Prentice-Hall.

Kozlowski, L. T. (1984). Pharmacological approaches to smoking modification. In J. D. Matarazzo, S. M. Weiss, J. Herd, N. E. Miller, & S. M. Weiss (Eds.), *Behavioral health: A handbook of health enhancement and disease prevention.* New York: Wiley.

Kozlowski, L. T., Wilkinson, D. A., Skinner, W., Kent, C., Franklin, T., & Pope, M. (1989). Comparing tobacco cigarette dependence with other drug dependencies. *Journal of the American Medical Association, 261,* 898–901.

Kramsch, D. M., Aspen, A. J., Abramowitz, B. M., Kreimendahl, T., & Hood, W. B., Jr. (1981). Reduction of coronary atherosclerosis by moderate conditioning exercise in monkeys on an atherogenic diet. *New England Journal of Medicine, 305,* 1483–1489.

Krantz, D. S., Arabian, J. M., Davis, J. E., & Parker, J. S. (1982). Type A behavior and coronary artery bypass surgery: Intraoperative blood pressure and perioperative complication. *Psychosomatic Medicine, 44,* 273–284.

Krantz, D. S., Baum, A., & Weideman, M. V. (1980). Assessment of preferences for self-treatment and information in health care. *Journal of Personality and Social Psychology, 39,* 977–990.

Krantz, D. S., & Deckel, A. W. (1983). Coping with coronary heart disease and stroke. In T. G. Burish & L. A. Bradley (Eds.), *Coping with chronic disease: Research and applications.* New York: Academic.

Krantz, D. S., Contrada, R. J., Hill, D. R., & Friedler, E. (1988). Environmental stress and biobehavioral antecedents of coronary heart disease. *Journal of Consulting and Clinical Psychology, 56,* 333–341.

Krantz, D. S., & Durel, L. A. (1983). Psychobiological substrates of the Type A behavior pattern. *Health Psychology, 2,* 393–412.

Krantz, D. S., & Glass, D. C. (1984). Personality, behavior patterns, and physical illness: Conceptual and methodological issues. In W. D. Gentry (Ed.), *Handbook of behavioral medicine* (pp. 38–86). New York: Guilford.

Krantz, D. S., & Manuck, S. B. (1984). Acute psychophysiologic reactivity and risk of cardiovascular disease: A review and methodological critique. *Psychological Bulletin, 96,* 435–464.

Krause, J. S., & Crewe, N. M. (1987). Prediction of long-term survival of persons with spinal cord injury: An 11-year prospective study. *Rehabilitation Psychology, 32,* 205–213.

Krause, N. & Markides, K. (1990). Measuring social support among older adults. *International Journal of Aging and Human Development, 30,* 37–53.

Krause, N., & Stryker, S. (1984). Stress and well-being: The buffering role of locus of control beliefs. *Social Science and Medicine, 18,* 783–790.

Kremer, E. F., Atkinson, J. H., Jr., & Ignelzi, R. J. (1981). Measurement of pain: Patient preference does not confound pain measurement. *Pain, 10,* 241–248.

Kreutzer, J. S., Gordon, W. A., & Wehman, P. (1989). Cognitive remediation following traumatic brain injury. *Rehabilitation Psychology, 34,* 117–130.

Krop, J. (1986). Clinical ecology: Future prospect of preventive medicine. *Journal of Orthomolecular Medicine, 1,* 5–12.

Krueger, D. W. (1981–1982). Emotional rehabilitation of the physical rehabilitation patient. *International Journal of Psychiatry in Medicine, 11,* 183–191.

Krueger, D. W. (1984). Psychological rehabilitation of physical trauma and disability. In D. W. Krueger (Ed.), *Rehabilitation psychology.* Rockville, MD: Aspen.

Krupat, E. (1983). The doctor-patient relationship: A social psychological analysis. In R. F. Kidd & M. J. Saks (Eds.), *Advances in Applied Social Psychology* (Vol. 2). Hillsdale, NJ: Erlbaum.

Krupat, E. (1985). *People in cities: The urban environment and its effects.* New York: Cambridge University.

Ku, L., & Fisher, D. (1990). The attitudes of physicians toward health care cost-containment policies. *Health Services Research, 25,* 25–42.

Kuntzleman, C. T. (1978). *Rating the exercises.* New York: Morrow.

Kusnecov, A., King, M. G., & Husband, A. J. (1989). Immunomodulation by behavioural conditioning. *Biological Psychology, 28,* 25–39.

Lacey, J. H., & Birtchnell, S. A. (1986). Abnormal eating behavior. In M. J. Christie & P. G. Mellett (Eds.), *The psychosomatic approach: Contemporary practice of wholeperson care.* New York: Wiley.

Lader, M. (1984). Pharmacological methods. In R. L. Wollfolk & P. M. Lehrer (Eds.), *Principles and practice of stress management.* New York: Guilford.

Lagercrantz, H., & Slotkin, T. A. (1986). The "stress" of being born. *Scientific American, 254,* 100–107.

Lago, D., Delaney, M., Miller, M., & Grill, C. (1989). Companion animals, attitudes toward pets, and health outcomes among the elderly: A long-term follow-up. *Anthrozoos, 3,* 25–34.

Lando, H. A. (1977). Successful treatment of smokers with a broad-spectrum behavioral approach. *Journal of Consulting and Clinical Psychology, 45,* 361–366.

Lang, A. R., & Marlatt, G. A. (1982). Problem drinking: A social learning perspective. In R. J.

Gatchel, A. Baum, & J.E. Singer (Eds.), *Handbook of psychology and health* (Vol. 1). Hillsdale, NJ: Erlbaum.

Langer, E.J., & Rodin, J. (1976). The effects of choice and enhanced personal responsibility for the aged: A field experiment in an institutional setting. *Journal of Personality and Social Psychology, 34,* 191–198.

Langford, H. G., Blaufox, D., Oberman, A., Hawkins, M., Curb, J.D., Cutter, G.R., Wassertheil-Smoller, S., Pressel, S., Babcock, C., Abernethy, J.D., Hotchkiss, J., & Tyler, M. (1985). Dietary therapy slows the return of hypertension after stopping prolonged medication. *Journal of the American Medical Association, 253,* 657–664.

Langosch, W. (1984). Behavioral interventions in cardiac rehabilitation. In S. Steptoe & A. Matthews (Eds.), *Health care and human behaviour.* London: Academic.

Lang, A.R., Goeckner, D.J., Adessor, V.J., & Marlatt, G.A. (1975). Effects of alcohol on aggression in male social drinkers. *Journal of Abnormal Psychology, 84,* 508–518.

Larson, E.B., Olsen, E., Cole, W., & Shortell, S. (1979). The relationship of health beliefs and a postcard reminder to influenza vaccination. *Journal of Family Practice, 8,* 1207–1211.

Larson, L.N. (1991). Financing health care in the United States. In J.E. Fincham & A.I. Wertheimer (Eds.), *Pharmacy and the U.S. health care system.* Binghampton, NY: Haworth.

LaRue, A., & Jarvik, L.F. (1982). Old age and biobehavioral changes. In B.B. Wolman (Ed.), *Handbook of developmental psychology.* Englewood Cliffs, NJ: Prentice-Hall.

Lasagna, L. (1977). The role of benzodiazepines in nonpsychiatric medical practice. *American Journal of Psychiatry, 134,* 656–658.

Latiolais, C.J., & Berry, C.C. (1969). Misuse of prescription medications by outpatients. *Drug Intelligence and Clinical Pharmacy, 3,* 270–277.

Lau, R.R. (1988). Beliefs about control and health behavior. In D.S. Gochman, *Health behavior: Emerging research perspectives* (pp. 43–63.). New York: Plenum.

Lau, R.R., Bernard, T.M., & Hartman, K.A. (1989). Further explorations of common-sense representations of common illnesses. *Health Psychology, 8,* 195–219.

Lau, R.R., & Hartman, K.A. (1983). Common-sense representations of common illnesses. *Health Psychology, 2,* 167–185.

Lau, R.R., & Klepper, S. (1988). The development of illness orientations in children aged 6 through 12. *Journal of Health and Social Behavior, 29,* 149–168.

Lau, R.R., & Ware, J.E., Jr. (1981). Refinements in the measurement of health-specific locus-of-control beliefs. *Medical Care, 19,* 1147–1158.

Laudenslager, M. L, Ryan, S.M., Drugan, R.C., Hyson, R.L., & Maier, S.F. (1983). Coping and immunosuppression: Inescapable but not escapable shock suppresses lymphocyte proliferation. *Science, 221,* 568–570.

Laurie, P. (1967). *Drugs.* Middlesex, England: Penguin.

Lavey, R.S., & Taylor, C.B. (1985). The nature of relaxation therapy. In S.R. Burchfield (Ed.), *Stress: Psychological and Physiological interactions.* Washington, DC: American Psychological Association.

Lazarus, A.A. (1971). *Behavior therapy and beyond.* New York: McGraw-Hill.

Lazarus, A.A., & Wilson, G.T. (1976). Behavior modification: Clinical and experimental perspectives. In B.B. Wolman (Ed.), *The therapist's handbook: Treatment methods of mental disorders.* New York: Van Nostrand Reinhold.

Lazarus, R.S. (1984). Puzzles in the study of daily hassles. *Journal of Behavioral Medicine, 7,* 375–389.

Lazarus, R.S., & Folkman, S. (1984a). Coping and adaptation. In W.D. Gentry (Ed.), *Handbook of behavioral medicine.* New York: Guilford.

Lazarus, R.S., & Folkman, S. (1984b). *Stress, appraisal, and coping.* New York: Guilford.

Lazarus, R.S., & Folkman, S. (1989). *Manual for the Hassles and Uplifts Scales.* Palo Alto, CA: Consulting Psychologists.

Lazarus, R.S., & Launier, R. (1978). Stress-related transactions between person and environment. In L.A. Pervin & M. Lewis (Eds.), *Perspectives in interactional psychology.* New York: Plenum.

LeBow, M.D. (1977). Can lighter become thinner? *Addictive Behaviors, 2,* 87–93.

Lebra, T.S. (1972). Religious conversion and elimination of the sick role. In W. Lebra (Ed.), *Transcultural research in mental health.* Hawaii: University of Hawaii.

Lecos, C.W. (1989). *Planning a diet for a healthy heart.* Department of Health and Human Services (HHS Publication No. FDA 89–2220). Rockville, MD: Department of Health and Human Services.

Lee, C., & Owen, N. (1986). Exercise persistence: Contributions of psychology to the promotion of regular physical activity. *Australian Psychologist, 21,* 427–466.

Lee, D. D-P., DeQuattro, V., Allen, J., Kimura, S., Aleman, E., Konugres, G., & Davison, G. (1988). Behavioral versus beta-blocker therapy in patients with primary hypertension: Effects on blood pressure, left ventricular function and mass, and the pressor surge of social stress anger. *American Heart Journal, 116,* 637–644.

Lefcourt, H.M., & Martin, R.A. (1986). *Humor and life stress: Antidote to adversity.* New York: Verlag.

Lehrer, P.M., Sargunaraj, D., & Hochron, S. (1992). *Journal of Consulting and Clinical Psychology, 60*, 639–643.

Lehrer, S. (1980). Life change and gastric cancer. *Psychosomatic Medicine, 42*, 499–502.

Leibel, R.L., Berry, E.M., & Hirsch, J. (1983). Biochemistry and development of adipose tissue in man. In H.L. Conn, E.A. DeFelice, & P. Kuo (Eds.), *Health and obesity* (pp. 21–48). New York: Raven.

LeMasters, E.E. (1957). Parenthood as crisis. *Marriage and Family Living, 19*, 352–355.

Leon, A.S. (1989). Effects of physical activity and fitness on health. In National Center for Health Statistics, *Assessing Physical Fitness and Physical Activity in Population-Based Surveys*, (DHHS Pub. No. [PHS] 89–1253). Hyattesville, MD: U.S. Dept. of Health and Human Services.

Lerner, D.J., & Kannel, W.B. (1986). Patterns of coronary heart disease mortality in the sexes: A 26-year follow-up of the Framingham population. *American Heart Journal, 111*, 383–390.

Lester, B.M. (1979). A synergistic process approach to the study of prenatal malnutrition. *International Journal of Behavioral Development, 2*, 377– 394.

Lester, R., & Van Theil, D.H. (1977). Gonadal function in chronic alcoholic men. *Advances in Experimental Medicine and Biology, 85A*, 339–414.

Lett, B.T. (1975). Long-delay learning in the T-maze. *Learning and Motivation, 6*, 80–90.

Levenkron, J.C., & Moore, G.L. (1988). Type A behavior pattern: Issues for intervention research. *Annals of Behavioral Medicine, 10*, 78–83.

Levenstein, J.H., Brown, J.B., Weston, W.W., Stewart, M., McCracken, E.C., & McWhinney, I. (1989). Patient-centered clinical interviewing. In M. Stewart & D. Roter (Eds.), *Communicating with medical patients*. Beverly Hills, CA: Sage.

Leventhal, H., & Avis, N. (1976). Pleasure, addiction, and habit: Factors in smoking behavior? *Journal of Abnormal Psychology, 85*, 478–488.

Leventhal, H., & Cleary, P.D. (1980). The smoking problem: A review of the research and theory in behavioral risk modification. *Psychological Bulletin, 88*, 370–405.

Leventhal, H., Easterling, D.B., Coons, H.L., Luchterhand, C.M., & Love, R. (1986). Adaptation to chemotherapy treatments. In B.L. Anderson (Ed.), *Women with Cancer: Psychological Perspectives*. New York: Springer-Verlag.

Leventhal, H., Leventhal, E.A., & Van Nguyen, T. (1985). Reactions of families to illness: Theoretical models and perspectives. In D.C. Turk & R.D. Kearns (Eds.), *Health illness, and families: A life-span perspective*. New York: Wiley.

Leventhal, H., Meyer, D., & Nerenz, D. (1980). The common sense representation of illness danger. In S. Rachman (Ed.), *Medical Psychology* (Vol. 2). Elmsford, NY: Pergamon.

Leventhal, H., Nerenz, D.R., & Steele, D. J. (1984). Illness representations and coping with health threats. In A. Baum, S.E. Taylor, and J.E. Singer (Eds.), *Handbook of psychology and health* (Vol. 4) *Social psychological aspects of health*. Hillsdale, NJ: Erlbaum.

Leventhal, H., Prohaska, T.R., & Hirschman, R.S. (1985). Preventive health behavior across the life span. In J.C. Rosen & L.J. Solomon (Eds.), *Prevention in health psychology*. Hanover, NH: University Press of New England.

Leventhal, H., Safer, M.A., Cleary, P.D., & Gutmann, M. (1980). Cardiovascular risk modification by community-based programs for life-style change: Comments on the Stanford study. *Journal of Consulting and Clinical Psychology, 48*, 150–158.

Leventhal, H., Zimmerman, R., & Gutmann, M. (1984). Compliance: A self-regulation perspective. In W.D. Gentry (Ed.), *Handbook of behavioral medicine* (pp. 369–436). New York: Guilford.

Levi, L. (1990). Occupational stress. *American Psychologist, 45*, 1142– 1145.

Levine, C., & Dubler, N.N. (1990). HIV and childbearing: I. Uncertain risks and bitter realities: The reproductive choices of HIV-infected women. *Milbank Quarterly, 68*, 321–351.

Levine, D.M. (1984, June). *Improving patient compliance*. Paper presented to 33rd Pharmaceutical Conference, Rutgers University, New Brunswick, NJ.

Levine, J.D., Gordon, N.C., & Fields, H.L. (1978). The mechanism of palcebo analgesia. *Lancet, ii*, 654–657.

Levine, R.V., Lynch, K., Miyake, K., & Lucia, M. (1989). The Type A city: Coronary heart disease and the pace of life. *Journal of Behavioral Medicine, 12*, 509–524.

Levitz, L., & Stunkard, A.J. (1974). A therapeutic coalition for obesity: Behavior modification and patient self-help. *American Journal of Psychiatry, 131*, 423–427.

Levor, R.M., Cohen, M.J., Naliboff, B.D., McArthur, D., & Heuser, G. (1986). Psychosocial precursors and correlates of migraine headache. *Journal of Consulting and Clinical Psychology, 54*, 347–353.

Levy, S. (Ed.) (1982). *Biological mediator of stress and disease: Neoplasms*. New York: Elsevier-North Holland.

Levy, S.M. (1985). *Behavior and cancer: Life-style and psychosocial factors in the initiation and progression of cancer*. San Francisco: Jossey-Bass.

Levy, S.M., Herberman, R.B., Whiteside, T., Sanzo, K., Lee, J., & Kirkwood, J. (1990). Perceived social support and tumor estrogen/progesterone receptor status as predictors of natural killer cell activity in breast cancer patients. *Psychosomatic Medicine, 52,* 73–85.

Lewin, K. (1935). *A dynamic theory of personality.* New York: McGraw-Hill.

Lewis, M., Thomas, D.A., & Worobey, J. (1990). Developmental organization, stress, and illness. *Psychological Science, 1,* 316–318.

Lewinsohn, P.M., Mermelstein, R.M., Alexander, C., & MacPhillamy, D.J. (1985). The Unpleasant Events Schedule: A scale for the measurement of aversive events. *Journal of Clinical Psychology, 41,* 483–498.

Lex, B.W. (1991). Some gender differences in alcohol and polysubstance abusers. *Health Psychology, 19,* 121–132.

Ley, P. (1982a). Giving information to patients. In J.R. Eiser (Ed.), *Social psychology and behavioral medicine.* New York: Wiley.

Ley, P. (1982b). Understanding, memory, satisfaction, and compliance. *British Journal of Clinical Psychology, 21,* 241–254.

Lezak, M.D. (1983). *Neuropsychological assessment* (2nd ed.). New York: Oxford University.

Lia-Hoaberg, B., Rode, P., Skovholt, C.J., Oberg, C.N., Berg, C., Mullett, S., & Choi, T. (1990). Barriers and motivators to prenatal care among low-income women. *Social Science and Medicine, 30,* 487–495.

Libman, E., Fichten, C.S., & Brender, W. (1985). The role of therapeutic format in the treatment of sexual dysfunction: A review. *Clinical Psychology Review, 5,* 103–117.

Lichtenstein, E., & Glasgow, R.E. (1992). Smoking cessation: What have we learned over the past decade? *Journal of Consulting and Clinical Psychology, 60,* 518–527.

Lichtenstein, E., & Mermelstein, R.J. (1984). Review of approaches to smoking treatment: Behavior modification strategies. In J. D. Matarazzo, S.M. Weiss, J.A. Herd, N.E. Miller, & S.M. Weiss (Eds.), *Behavioral health: A handbook of health enhancement and disease prevention.* New York: Wiley.

Lied, E.R., & Marlatt, G.A. (1979). Modeling as a determinant of alcohol consumption: Effect of subject sex and prior drinking history. *Addictive Behavior, 4,* 47–54.

Linden, W. (1988). *Biological barriers in behavioral medicine.* New York: Plenum.

Linn, M.W., Linn, B.S., & Stein, S.R. (1982). Satisfaction with ambulatory care and compliance in older patients. *Medical Care, 20,* 606–614.

Lipid Research Clinics Program. (1984). The Lipid Research Clinics coronary primary prevention trial results II. The relationship of reduction in the incidence of coronary heart disease to cholesterol lowering. *Journal of the American Medical Association, 253,* 365–374.

Lipowski, Z.J. (1977). Psychosomatic medicine in the seventies: An overview. *American Journal of Psychiatry, 134,* 233–244.

Lipowski, Z.J., (1986). What does the word "psychosomatic" really mean? A historical and semantic inquiry. In M.J. Christie & P.G. Mellett (Eds.), *The psychosomatic approach: Contemporary practice and whole-person care.* New York: Wiley.

Lipton, H.L. (1982). The graying of America: Implications for the pharmacist. *American Journal of Hospital Pharmacy, 39,* 131–135.

Liskow, B. (1982). Substance induced and substance use disorders: Barbiturates and similarly acting sedative hypnotics. In J.H. Greist, J.W. Jefferson, & R.L. Spitzer (Eds.), *Treatment of mental disorders.* New York: Oxford University.

Lissner, L., Odell, P.M., D'Agostino, R.B., Stokes, J., Kreger, B.E., Belanger, A.J., & Brownell, K.D. (1991). Variability of body weight and health outcomes in the Framingham population. *New England Journal of Medicine, 324,* 1839–1844.

Livingston, I.L. (1988). Co-factors, host susceptibility, and AIDS: An argument for stress. *Journal of the National Medical Association, 80,* 49–59.

Lobo, M.L. (1990). Stress in Infancy. In L.E. Arnold (Ed.), *Childhood stress* (pp. 173–192). New York: John Wiley & Sons.

Locke, S.E., Hurst, M.W., Williams, R.M., & Heisel, I.S. (1978). *The influences of psychosocial factors on human cell-mediated immune function.* Paper presented at the meeting of the American Psychosomatic Society, Washington, D.C.

Loda, F.A. (1980). Day care. *Pediatrics in Review, 1,* 277–281.

Loeser, J.D. (1980). Low back pain. In J.J. Bonica (Ed.), *Pain.* New York: Raven.

Logue, A.W. (1986). *The psychology of eating and drinking.* New York: W.H. Freeman.

London, P. (1986). *The modes and morals of psychotherapy* (2nd ed.). New York: Hemisphere.

Long, B.C. (1984). Aerobic conditioning and Stress Inoculation: A comparison of stress-management interventions. *Cognitive Therapy and Research, 8,* 517–542.

Long, B.C. (1985). Stress-management interventions: A 15-month follow-up of aerobic conditioning and stress inoculation training. *Cognitive Therapy and Research, 9,* 471–478.

Long, C.J. (1981). The relationship between surgical outcome and MMPI profiles in chronic back patients. *Journal of Clinical Psychology, 37,* 744–749.

Long, R.T., Lamont, J.H., Whipple, B., Bandler, L., Blom, G.E., Burgin, L., & Jessner, L. (1958). A psychosomatic study of allergic and emotional factors in children with asthma. *American Journal of Psychiatry, 114,* 890–899.

Longo, D.J., & Clum, G.A. (1989). Psychosocial factors affecting genital herpes recurrences: Linear vs mediating models. *Journal of Psychosomatic Research, 33,* 161–166.

Lonsdale, D. (1986). Three circles of health: Application of Boolean algebra in health assessment. *International Journal of Biosocial Research, 8,* 80–83.

LoPiccolo, J. (1977). Direct treatment of sexual dysfunction in the couple. In J. Money & H. Musaph (Eds.), *Handbook of sexology.* New York: Elsevier/North Holland.

LoPiccolo, J., & Hogan, D.R. (1979). Multidimensional treatment of sexual dysfunction. In O.R. Pomerleau & J.P. Brady (Eds.), *Behavioral medicine: Theory and practice.* Baltimore: Williams & Wilkins.

Lorber, J. (1975). Good patients and problem patients: Conformity and deviance in a general hospital. *Journal of Health and Social Behavior, 16,* 213–225.

Lowenstein, A., & Rosen, A. (1989). The relation of widows' needs and resources to perceived health and depression. *Social Science and Medicine, 29,* 659– 667.

Lowinson, J.H., Ruiz, P., Millman, R.B., & Langrod, J.G. (Eds.) (1992). *Substance abuse: A comprehensive textbook* (2nd ed.). Baltimore: Williams and Wilkins.

Lubin, B., Nathan, R.G., & Matarazzo, J.D. (1978). Psychologists in medical education: 1976. *American Psychologist, 33,* 339–343.

Lubin, J.H., Richter, B.S., & Blot, W.J. (1984). Lung cancer risk with cigar and pipe use. *Journal of the National Cancer Institute, 73,* 377–381.

Luepker, R.V., & Perry, C.L. (1991). The Minnesota Heart Health Program. Education for youth and parents. *Annals of the New York Academy of Sciences, 623,* 314–321.

Luft, H.S. (1981). *Health maintenance organizations: Dimensions of performance.* New York: Wiley.

Lundin, D.V. (1978). Medication taking behavior and the elderly: A pilot study. *Drug Intelligence and Clinical Pharmacy, 12,* 518–522.

Lunn, S., Skydsbjerg, M., Schulsinger, H., Parnas, J., Pedersen, C., & Mathiesen, L. (1991). A preliminary report on the neuropsychologic sequelae of Human Immunodeficiency Virus. *Archives of General Psychiatry, 48,* 139–142.

Luria, A.R. (1973). *The working brain: An introduction to neuropsychology.* New York: Basic Books.

Lussier, A. (1980). The physical handicap and the body ego. *International Journal of Psychoanalysis, 61,* 179–185.

Lynch, K. (1960). *The image of the city.* Cambridge, MA: MIT Pr.

Maccoby, N., & Alexander, J. (1979). Reducing heart disease risk using the mass media: Comparing the effects on three communities. In R.F. Munoz, L.R. Snowden, & J.G. Kelly (Eds.), *Social and psychological research in community settings* (pp. 69–100). San Francisco: Jossey-Bass.

MacDougall, J.M., Dembroski, T.M., Dimsdale, J.E., & Hackett, T.P. (1985). Components of Type A hostility and anger-in: Further relationships to angiographic findings. *Health Psychology, 4,* 137–152.

MacDougall, J.M., Dembroski, T.M., & Krantz, D.S. (1981). Effects of types of challenge on pressor and heart rate responses in Type A and B women. *Psychophysiology, 18,* 1–9.

MacDougall, J.M., Dembroski, T.M., & Musante, L. (1979). The Structured Interview and questionnaire methods of assessing coronary-prone behavior in male and female college students. *Journal of Behaviroal Medicine, 2,* 71–83.

Mackay, C.J., & Cooper, C.L. (1985). Occupational stress and health: Some current issues. In C.L. Cooper & I.T. Robertson (Eds.), *International review of industrial and organizational psychology* (pp. 167–199). Chichester, England: Wiley.

MacKinnon, D.P., Johnson, C.A., Pentz, M.A., Dwyer, J.H., Hansen, W.B., Flay, B.R., & Wang, E.Y-I. (1991). Mediating mechanisms in a school-based drug prevention program: First-year effects of the Midwestern Prevention Project. *Health Psychology, 10,* 164–172.

MacRae, J.R. & Siegel, S. (1987). Extinction of tolerance to the analgesic effect of morphine. *Behavioral Neuroscience, 101,* 790–796.

Maddux, J.E., Roberts, M.C., Sledden, E.A., & Wright, L. (1986). Developmental issues in child health psychology. *American Psychologist, 41,* 25– 34.

Maddux, J.E., & Rogers, R.W. (1983). Protection motivation and self-efficacy: A revised theory of fear appeals and attitude change. *Journal of Experimental Social Psychology, 19,* 469– 479.

Maguire, G.P., Lee, E.G., Barington, D.J., Kuchemann, C.S., Crabtree, R.J., & Cornell, C.E. (1978). Psychiatric morbidity in the first year after mastectomy. *British Medical Journal, 1,* 963– 965.

Mahoney, M.J., Thoresen, C.E., & Danaher, B.G. (1972). Covert behavior modification: An experimental analysis. *Journal of Behavior Therapy and Experimental Psychiatry, 3,* 7–14.

Maier, S.F., Laudenslager, M.L., & Ryan, S.M. (1985). Stressor controllability, immune function, and endogenous opiates. In F.R. Brush & J.B. Overmier (Eds.), *Affect, conditioning and cognition: Essays on the determinants of behavior.* Hillsdale, N.J.: Erlbaum.

Malmo, R.B. (1975). *On emotions, needs, and our archaic brain.* New York: Holt, Rinehart & Winston.

Manfredi, M., Bini, G., Cruccu, G., Accornero, N., Beradelli, A., & Medolago, L. (1981). Congenital absence of pain. *Archives of Neurology, 38,* 507–511.

Manson, J.E., Colditz, G.A., Stampfer, M.J., Willett, W.C., Rosner, B., Monson, R.R., Speizer, F.E., & Hennekens, C.H. (1990). A prospective study of obesity and risk of coronary heart disease in women. *New England Journal of Medicine, 322,* 882–889.

Manuck, S.B., Cohen, S., Rabin, B.S., Muldoon, M.F., & Bachen, E.A. (1991). Individual differences in cellular immune response to stress. *Psychological Science, 2,* 111–115.

Manuck, S.B., Craft, S., Gold, K.J. (1978). Coronary-prone behavior pattern and cardiovascular response.

Marcus, D. (1989). Anorexia nervosa reconceptualized from a psychosocial transactional perspective. *American Journal of Orthopsychiatry, 59,* 346–354.

Marcus, M.D., Wing, R.R., & Hopkins, J. (1988). Obese binge eaters: Affect, cognitions, and response to behavioral weight control. *Journal of Consulting and Clinical Psychology, 56,* 433–439.

Marieb, E.N. (1989). *Human anatomy and physiology.* Redwood City, CA: Benjamin/Cummings.

Marion, R.W., Wiznia, A.A., Hutcheon, G., & Rubinstein, A. (1986). Human T-cell lymphotropic virus type III (HTLV-III) embryopathy. *American Journal of Diseases of Children, 140,* 638–640.

Markowitz, J.S., & Gutterman, E.M. (1986). Predictors of psychological distress in the community following two toxic chemical incidents. In A.H. Lebovits, A. Baum, & J.E. Singer (Eds.), *Advances in environmental psychology* (Vol. 6, pp. 89–107). Hillsdale, NJ: Erlbaum.

Marks, J. & Parry, A. (1987). Syringe exchange program for drug addicts. *Lancet, i,* 691–692.

Marks, G., Richardson, J.L., & Maldonado, N. (1991). Self-disclosure of HIV infection to sexual partners. *American Journal of Public Health, 81,* 1321–1322.

Marlatt, G.A. (1983). The controlled-drinking controversy: A commentary. *American Psychologist, 38,* 1097–1110.

Marlatt, G.A., Demming, B., & Reid, J. (1973). Loss of control drinking in alcoholics: An experimental analog. *Journal of Abnormal Psychology, 81,* 233–241.

Marlatt, G.A., & George, W.H. (1988). Relapse prevention and the maintenance of optimal health. In S. Shumaker, E. Schron, & J.K. Ockene (Eds.), *The adoption and maintenance of behaviors for optimal health.* New York: Springer.

Marlatt, G.A., & Gordon, J.R. (1980). Determinants of relapse: Implications for the maintenance of behavior change. In P.O. Davidson & S.M. Davidson (Eds.), *Behavioral medicine: Changing health lifestyles.* New York: Brunner/Mazel.

Marlatt, G.A., & Rohsenow, D.J. (1980). Cognitive processes in alcohol use: Expectancy and the balanced placebo design. In N. Mello (Ed.), *Advances in substance abuse: Behavioral and biological research.* Greenwich, CT: Jai.

Maron, D.J., & Fortmann, S.P. (1987). Nicotine yield and measures of cigarette smoke exposure in a large population: Are lower-yield cigarettes safer? *American Journal of Public Health, 77,* 546–549.

Marshall, J.R. (1978, September). Changes in aged white male suicides: 1948–1972. *Journal of Gerontology, 33,* 763–768.

Marston, H.M. (1975). Crowding and animal behavior. In E. Krupat (Ed.), *Psychology is social.* Glenview, IL: Scott, Foresman.

Marteau, T.M., Johnston, M., Baum, J.D., & Block, S. (1987). Goals of treatment in diabetes: A comparison of doctors and parents of children with diabetes. *Journal of Behavioral Medicine, 10,* 33–48.

Martin J.R., & Wollitzer, A.O. (1988). The prevalence, secrecy, and psychology of purging in a family practice setting. *International Journal of Eating Disorders, 7,* 515–519.

Maslach, C., & Jackson, S.E. (1982). Burnout in health professions: A social psychological analysis. In G.S. Sanders & J. Suls (Eds.), *Social psychology of health and illness.* Hillsdale, NJ: Erlbaum.

Mason, J., Preisinger, J., Sperling, R., Walther, V., Berrier, J., & Evans, V. (1991). Incorporating HIV education and counseling into routine prenatal care: A program model. *AIDS Education and Prevention, 3,* 118–123.

Mason, J.W. (1975). A historical view of the stress field. *Journal of Human Stress, 1,* 22–36.

Masters, W.H., & Johnson, V.E. (1966). *Human sexual response.* Boston: Little, Brown.

Masters, W.H., & Johnson, V.E. (1970). *Human sexual inadequacy.* Boston: Little, Brown.

Masters, W.H., & Johnson, V.E. (1979). *Homosexuality in perspective.* Boston: Little, Brown.

Masters, W.H., & Johnson, V.E. (1981). Sex and the aging process. *Journal of the American Geriatrics Society, 29,* 385–390.

Masters, W.H., Johnson, V.E., & Kolodny, R.C. (1986). *Masters and Johnson on sex and human loving.* Boston: Little, Brown.

Masur, F.T. (1981). Adherence to health care regimens. In C.K. Prokop & L.A. Bradley (Eds.), *Medical psychology: Contributions to behavioral medicine.* New York: Academic.

Matarazzo, J.D. (1980). Behavioral health and behavioral medicine: Frontiers for a new health psychology. *American Psychologist, 35*, 807–817.

Matarazzo, J.D. (1982). Behavioral health's challenge to academic, scientific, and professional psychology. *American Psychologist, 37*, 1–14.

Matarazzo, J.D. (1984). Behavioral health: A 1990 challenge for the health sciences professions. In J.D. Matarazzo, S.M. Weiss, J.A. Herd, N.E. Miller, & S.M. Weiss (Eds.), *Behavioral health: A handbook of health enhancement and disease prevention.* New York: Wiley.

Matarazzo, J.D. (1987). Relationships of health psychology to other segments of psychology. In G.C. Stone, S.M. Weiss, J.D. Matarazzo, N.E. Miller, J. Rodin, C.D. Belar, M.J. Follick, & J.E. Singer (Eds.), *Health psychology: A discipline and a profession* (pp. 41– 59). Chicago: University of Chicago.

Matas, L., Arend, R., & Sroufe, L.A. (1978). Continuity of adaptation in the second year: The relationship between quality of attachment and later competence. *Child Development, 49*, 547–556.

Matheny, K.B., & Cupp, P. (1983). Control, desirability, and anticipation as moderating variables between life changes and illness. *Journal of Human Stress, 9*, 14–23.

Mathews, A., & Ridgeway, V. (1984). Psychological preparation for surgery. In A. Steptoe & A. Mathews (Eds.), *Health care and human behaviour.* London: Academic.

Mathews, R.M., & Seekins, T. (1987). An interactional model of independence. *Rehabilitation Psychology, 32*, 165–172.

Maton, K.I. (1989). The stress-buffering role of spiritual support: Cross-sectional and prospective investigations. *Journal for the Scientific Study of Religion, 28*, 310–323.

Mattar, M.E., Markello, J., & Yaffee, S.J. (1975). Inadequacies of ambulatory children. *Journal of Pediatrics, 87*, 137–141.

Matthews, A.M., Bancroft, J., Whitehead, A., Hackmann, A., Julier, D., Bancroft, J., Gath, D., & Shaw, P. (1983). The behavioural treatment of sexual inadequacy: A comparative study. *Behaviour Research and Therapy, 14*, 427–436.

Matthews, K.A. (1982). Psychological perspectives on the Type A behavior pattern. *Psychological Bulletin, 91*, 293–323.

Matthews, K.A. (1988). Coronary heart disease and Type A behaviors: Update on and alternative to the Booth-Kewley and Friedman (1987) quantitative review. *Psychological Bulletin, 104*, 373–380.

Matthews, K.A., Glass, D.C., Rosenman, R.H., & Bortner, R.W. (1977). Competitive drive, pattern A, and coronary heart disease: A further analysis of some of the data from the Western Collaborative Group Study. *Journal of Chronic Diseases, 30*, 489–498.

Matthews, K.A., Siegel, J.M., Kuller, L.H., Thompson, M., & Varat, M. (1983). Determinants of decisions to seek medical treatment by patients with acute myocardial infarction syndromes. *Journal of Personality and Social Psychology, 44*, 1144–1156.

Mattson, M.E., Pollack, E.S., & Cullen, J.W. (1987). What are the odds that smoking will kill you? *American Journal of Public Health, 77*, 425–431.

Mattsson, A. (1977). Long-term physical illness in childhood: A challenge to psychosoical adaptation. In R.H. Moos (Ed.), *Coping with physical illness* (pp. 183–199). New York: Plenum.

Mausner, B. (1973). An ecological view of cigarette smoking behavior. *Journal of Abnormal Psychology, 81*, 115–126.

Mayer, J. (1955). Regulation of energy intake and the body weight: The glucostatic theory and the lipostatic hypothesis. *Annals of the New York Academy of Science, 63*, 15–43.

Mayer, J. (1968). *Overweight: Causes and control.* Englewood Cliffs, N.J.: Prentice-Hall.

Mayer, J. (1975). *A diet for living.* New York: Plenum.

Mayer, J. (1980). The best diet is exercise. In P.J. Collipp (Ed.), *Childhood obesity* (2nd ed.). Littleton, MA: PSG.

Mayer, W. (1983). Alcohol abuse and alcoholism: The psychologist's role in prevention, research, and treatment. *American Psychologist, 38*, 1116– 1121.

Mayes, B.T., Sime, W.E., & Ganster, D.C. (1984). Convergent validity of Type A behavior pattern scales and their ability to predict physiological responsiveness in a sample of female public employees. *Journal of Behavioral Medicine, 7*, 83–108.

Mays, V.M., & Cochran, S.D. (1988). Issues in the perception of AIDS risk and risk reduction activities by black and Hispanic/Latina women. *American Psychologist, 43*, 949–957.

McCaleb, M.L., & Meyers, R.D. (1981). Cholecystokinin acts on the hypothalamic "noradrenergic system" involved in feeding. *Peptides, 1*, 47–49.

McCarthy, C.M., & Thorpe, K.E. (1986). Financing for health care. In S. Jonas (Ed.), *Health care delivery in the United States.* New York: Springer.

McCaul, K.D., & Glasgow, R.E. (1985). Preventing adolescent smoking: What have we learned about treatment construct validity? *Health Psychology, 4*, 361–387.

McCaul, K.D., & Malott, J.M. (1984). Distraction and coping with pain. *Psychological Bulletin, 95*, 516–533.

McCaul, K.D., Monson, N., & Maki, R.H. (1992). Does distraction reduce pain-produced distress among college students? *Health Psychology, 11*, 210– 217.

McClelland, D.C. (1985). *Human motivation.* Glenview, IL: Scott, Foresman.

McClelland, D.C. (1989). Motivational factors in health and disease. *American Psychologist, 44,* 675–683.

McClelland, D.C., Brown, D., Patel, V., & Kelner, S.P., Jr. (1988). *Affiliation motivation and eating behavior in insulin-dependent diabetics.* Unpublished manuscript, Boston University, Boston, MA.

McClelland, D.C., & Kirshnit, C. (1988). The effect of motivational arousal through films on salivary immunoglobulin. *Psychology and Health, 2,* 31–52.

McClelland, D.C., Ross, G., Patel, V. (1985). The effect of an academic examination on salivary norepinephrine and immunoglobulin levels. *Journal of Human Stress, 11,* 52–59.

McCord, W., McCord, J., & Gudeman, J. (1959). Some current theories of alcoholism. *Quarterly Journal of Studies on Alcoholism, 20,* 727–749.

McCord, W., McCord, J., & Gudeman, J. (1960). *Origins of alcoholism.* Stanford, CA: Stanford University.

McCormack, T. (1981). The new criticism and the sick role. *Canadian Review of Sociology, 18,* 30–47.

McCrady, B.S. (1988). Alcoholism. In E.A. Blechman & K.D. Brownell (Eds.), *Handbook of behavioral medicine for women.* New York: Pergamon.

McCranie, E.W., & Brandsma, J.M. (1988). Personality antecedents of burnout among middle-aged physicians. *Behavioral Medicine, 14,* 30–36.

McCranie, E.W., Watkins, L.O., Brandsma, J.M., & Sisson, B.D. (1986). Hostility, coronary heart disease (CHD) incidence, and total mortality: Lack of association in a 25-year follow-up study of 478 physicians. *Journal of Behavioral Medicine, 9,* 119–126.

McCubbin, H.I., McCubbin, M.A., Patterson, J.M., Cauble, A.E., Wilson, L.R., & Warwick, W. (1983). CHIP—coping health inventory for parents: An assessment of parental coping patterns in the care of the chronically ill child. *Journal of Marriage and the Family, 45,* 359–370.

McCubbin, J.A., Surwit, R.S., & Williams, R.B., Jr. (1985). Endogenous opiate peptides, stress reactivity, and risk for hypertension. *Hypertension, 7,* 808–811.

McCubbin, J.A., Surwit, R.S., & Williams, R.B., Jr. (1988). Opiod dysfunction and risk for hypertension: Naloxone and blood pressure responses during different types of stress. *Psychosomatic Medicine, 50,* 8–14.

McCutchan, J.A. (1990). Virology, immunology, and clinical course of HIV infection. *Journal of Consulting and Clinical Psychology, 58,* 5–12.

McFadden, E.R., Jr. (1984). Pathogenesis of asthma. *Journal of Allergy and Clinical Immunology, 73,* 413–424.

McFadden, E.R., & Austen, K.F. (1980). Lung diseases caused by immunologic and environmental injury. In T.R. Harrison (Ed.), *Principles of internal medicine* (9th ed., pp. 1203–1210). New York: McGraw-Hill.

McGill, J.C., Lawlis, G.F., Selby, D., Mooney, V., & McCoy, C.E. (1983). The relationship of Minnesota Multiphasic Personality Inventory (MMPI) profile clusters to pain behaviors. *Journal of Behavioral Medicine, 6,* 77–92.

McGinnis, J.M., Shopland, D., & Brown, C. (1987). Tobacco and health: Trends in smoking and smokeless tobacco consumption in the United States. In L. Breslow, J.E. Fielding, & L.B. Lave (Eds.), *Annual review of public health,* (Vol. 8). Palo Alto, CA: Annual Reviews.

McGlashan, T.H., Evans, E.J., Orne, M.T. (1969). The nature of hypnosis analgesia and the placebo response to experimental pain. *Psychosomatic Medicine, 31,* 227–246.

McGough, N. (1990). Assessing social support of people with AIDS. *Oncology Nursing Forum, 17,* 31–35.

McGuire, F.L. (1982). Treatment of the drinking driver. *Health Psychology, 1,* 137–152.

McKay, J. (1987). Trust vs. cynicism: The relationship of affiliative orientation to immunocompetence and illness frequency. Unpublished doctoral dissertation, Harvard University, Cambridge, MA.

McKenney, J.W., & Harrison, W.L. (1976). Drug-related hospital admissions. *American Journal of Hospital Pharmacy, 33,* 792–795.

McKinney, R.S., Hofshire, P.J., Buell, J.C., & Eliot, R.S. (1984). Hemodynamic and biochemical responses to stress: The necessary link between Type A behavior and cardiovascular disease. *Behavioral Medicine Update, 6,* 16–21.

McKinnon, W., Weisse, C.S., Reynolds, C.P., Bowles, C.A., & Baum, A. (1989). Chronic stress, leukocyte subpopulations, and humoral response to latent variables. *Health Psychology, 8,* 389–402.

McKusick, L. (1988). The impact of AIDS on practitioner and client. *American Psychologist, 43,* 935–940.

McLarnon, L.D., & Kaloupek, D.G. (1988). Psychological investigation of genital herpes recurrence: Prospective assessment and cognitive-behavioral intervention for a chronic physical disorder. *Health Psychology, 7,* 231–249.

McMinn, M.R. (1984). Mechanisms of energy balance in obesity. *Behavioral Neuroscience, 98,* 375–393.

McNamara, S.S., Molot, M.A., Stremple, J.F., & Cutting, R.T. (1971). Coronary artery disease in combat casualties in Vietnam. *Journal of the American Medical Association, 216,* 1185.

McNeilly, M., & Zeichner, A. (1989). Neuropeptide and cardiovascular responses in intravenous catherization in normotensive and hypertensive blacks and whites. *Health Psychology, 8*, 483–488.

McReynolds, W.T., Green, L., & Fisher, E.B., Jr. (1983). Self-control as choice management with reference to the behavioral treatment of obesity. *Health Psychology, 2*, 261–276.

Mechanic, D. (1968). *Medical sociology: A selective view.* New York: Free Press.

Mechanic, D. (1972). Social psychologic factors affecting the presentation of bodily compliants. *New England Journal of Medicine, 286*, 1132–1139.

Mechanic, D. (1976a). *The growth of bureaucratic medicine.* New York: Wiley.

Mechanic, D. (1976b). Stress, illness, and illness behavior. *Journal of Human Stress, 2*, 2–6.

Mechanic, D. (1979). Development of psychological distress among young adults. *Archives of General Psychiatry, 36*, 1233–1239.

Mehnert, T., Kraus, H.H., Nadler, R., & Boyd, M. (1990). Correlates of life satisfaction in those with disabling conditions. *Rehabilitation Psychology, 35*, 3–17.

Meichenbaum, D. (1977). *Cognitive behavior modification: An integrative approach.* New York: Plenum.

Meichenbaum, D. (1985). *Stress inoculation training.* New York: Pergamon.

Meichenbaum, D., & Cameron, R. (1983). Stress inoculation training: Toward a general paradigm for training coping skills. In D. Meichenbaum & M.E. Jaremko (Eds.), *Stress reduction and prevention.* New York: Plenum.

Meichenbaum, D., & Jaremko, M.E. (Eds.). (1982). *Stress prevention and management: A cognitive-behavioral approach.* New York: Plenum.

Meichenbaum, D., & Turk, D.C. (1976). The cognitive-behavioral management of anxiety, anger and pain. In P.O. Davidson (Ed.), *The behavioral management of anxiety, depression, and pain.* New York: Brunner/Mazel.

Melzack, R. (1975). The McGill Pain Questionnaire: Major properties and scoring methods. *Pain, 1*, 277–299.

Melzack, R., & Torgerson, W.S. (1971). On the language of pain. *Anesthesiology, 134*, 50–59.

Melzack, R., & Wall, P.D. (1965). Pain mechanisms: A new theory. *Science, 150*, 971–979.

Melzack, R., & Wall, P.D. (1982). *The challenge of pain.* New York: Basic Books.

Methorst, G.J., Jansen, M.A., & Kerkhof, A.J. (1990). Training in health psychology: An international look. Special Issue: The development of health psychology: An international perspective. *Psychology and Health, 4*, 19–30.

Metropolitan Life Insurance Company. (1983). *Statistical bulletin.* New York: Author.

Meyer, A.J., Nash, J.D., McAlister, A.L., Maccoby, N., & Farquhar, J.W. (1980). Skills training in a cardiovascular health education campaign. *Journal of Consulting and Clinical Psychology, 48*, 129–142.

Meyer, D., Leventhal, H., & Gutmann, M. (1985). Common-sense models of illness: The example of hypertension. *Health Psychology, 4*, 115–135.

Meyer, R.J., & Haggerty, R.J. (1962). Streptococcal infections in families. *Pediatrics, 29*, 539–549.

Michel, C., & Battig, K. (1989). Separate and combined psychophysiological effects of cigarette smoking and alcohol consumption. *Psychopharmacology, 97*, 65–73.

Michela, J.L. (1987). Interpersonal and individual impacts of a husband's heart attack. In A. Baum & J.E. Singer (Eds.), *Handbook of psychology and health* (Vol. 5, pp. 255–301.). Hillsdale, NJ: Erlbaum.

Millar, W.J., & Stephens, T. (1987). The prevalance of overweight and obesity in Britain, Canada, and the the United States. *American Journal of Public Health, 77*, 38–41.

Miller, E., Craddock-Watson, J.E., & Pollack, T.M. (1982, October 9). Consequences of confirmed maternal rubella at successive stages of pregnancy. *Lancet*, 781–784.

Miller, J.D., & Cisin, I.H. (1983). *Highlights from the National Survey on Drug Abuse: 1982.* (DHHS Publication No. 83–1277). Washington, DC: U.S. Government Printing Office.

Miller, L.C., Murphy, R., & Buss, A.H. (1981). Consciousness of body: Private and public. *Journal of Personality and Social Psychology, 41*, 397–406.

Miller, M. (1978, October). Geriatric suicide: The Arizona study. *Gerontologist, 18*, 488–495.

Miller, N.E. (1944). Experimental studies of conflict. In J.M. Hunt (Ed.), *Personality and the behavior disorders* (Vol. 1). New York: Ronald.

Miller, N.E. (1959). Liberalization of basic S-R concepts: Extension to conflict behavior, motivation, and social learning. In S. Koch (Ed.), *Psychology: A study of a science* (Vol. 2). New York: McGraw-Hill.

Miller, N.E. (1969). Learning of visceral and glandular responses. *Science, 163*, 434–445.

Miller, N.E. (1980). A perspective on the effects of stress and coping on disease and health. In S. Levine & H. Ursin (Eds.), *Coping and health* (pp. 323– 354). New York: Plenum.

Miller, N.E. (1983). Behavioral medicine: Symbiosis between laboratory and clinic. *Annual Review of Psychology, 34*, 1–31.

Miller, S.M., Brody, D.S., & Summerton, J. (1988). Styles of coping with threat: Implications for health. *Journal of Personality and Social Psychology, 54*, 142–148.

Miller, S.M. & Mangan, L.E. (1983). Interacting effects of information and coping style in adapting to gynecological stress: Should the doctor tell all? *Journal of Personality and Social Psychology, 45*, 223–236.

Miller, W.R., & Hester, R.K. (1980). Treating the problem drinker: Modern approaches. In W.R. Miller (Ed.), *The addictive behaviors: Treatment of alcoholism, drug abuse, smoking, and obesity.* New York: Pergamon.

Miller, W.R., & Hester, R.K. (1986). Inpatient alcoholism treatment: Who benefits? *American Psychologist, 41,* 794–805.

Minkler, M. (1989). Health education, health promotion, and the open society: An historical perspective. *Health Education Quarterly, 16,* 17–30.

Minuchin, S., Rosman, B.L., & Baker, L. (1978). *Psychosomatic families: Anorexia nervosa in context.* Cambridge, MA: Harvard University.

Mishler, E.G. (1984). *The discourse of medicine: Dialectics of medical interviews.* Norwood, NJ: Ablex.

Mitchell, J.C. (Ed.) (1969). *Social networks in urban situations.* Manchester, England: Manchester University.

Mitchell, J.E., Hatsukami, D., Eckert, E.D., & Pyle, R.I. (1985). Characteristics of 275 patients with bulimia. *American Journal of Psychiatry, 142,* 482–485.

Mittlemark, M.B., Murray, D.M., Luefker, R.V., Pechacek, T.F., Pikie, P.L., & Pallonen, U.E. (1987). Predicting experimentation with cigarettes: The Childhood Antecedents of Smoking Study (CASS). *American Journal of Public Health, 77,* 206–208.

Mofenson, H.C., & Greensher, J. (1978). Childhood accidents. In R.A. Hoekelman, S. Blatman, P.A. Brunell, S.B. Friedman, & H.H. Seidel (Eds.), *Principles of pediatrics.* New York: McGraw-Hill.

Mohr, D.C., & Beutler, L.E. (1990). Erectile dysfunction: A review of diagnostic and treatment procedures. *Clinical Psychology Review, 10,* 123–150.

Montgomery, R.J.V., Gonyea, J.G., & Hooyman, N.R. (1985). Caregiving and the experience of subjective and objective burden. *Family Relations, 34,* 19–26.

Montgomery, S.B., Joseph, J.G., Becker, M.H., Ostrow, D.G., Kersher, R.C., & Kirscht, J.P. (1989). The Health Belief Model in understanding compliance with preventive recommendations for AIDS: How useful? *AIDS Education and Prevention, 1,* 303–323.

Moolgavkar, S.H. (1983). A model for human carcinogenesis: Hereditary cancers and premalignant lesions. In R.G. Crispen (Ed.), *Cancer: Etiology and prevention.* New York: Elsevier Biomedical.

Moore, J.E., Armentrout, D.P., Parker, J.C., & Kivilan, D.R. (1986). Empirically derived pain-patient MMPI subgroups: Prediction of treatment outcome. *Journal of Behavioral Medicine, 9,* 51–63.

Moore, R.D., Hidalgo, J., Sugland, B.W., & Chaisson, R.E. (1991). Zidovudine and the natural history of the Acquired Immunodeficiency Syndrome. *The New England Journal of Medicine, 324,* 1412–1416.

Moos, R.H., Cronkite, R.C., & Finney, J.W. (1982). A conceptual framework for alcoholism treatment evaluation. In E.M. Pattison & E. Kaufman (Eds.), *Encyclopedic handbook of alcoholism.* New York: Gardner.

Moos, R.H., & Finney, J.W. (1983). The expanding scope of alcoholism treatment evaluation. *American Psychologist, 38,* 1036–1044.

Moos, R.H., & Schaefer, J.A. (1986). Life transitions and crises: A conceptual overview. In R.H. Moos (Ed.), *Coping with life crises: An integrated approach.* New York: Plenum.

Morbidity and Mortality Weekly Report. (1987, January 16). *Infant mortality among blacks.* Washington, DC: U.S. Department of Health and Human Services, Public Health Service.

Morbidity and Mortality Weekly Report. (1991, January 25). *Mortality attributable to HIV infection in the United States, 1981–1990.* Washington, DC: U.S. Department of Health and Human Services, Public Health Service.

Moriskey, D.E. (1986). Nonadherence to medical recommendations for hypertensive patients: Problems and potential solutions. *Journal of Compliance in Health Care, 1,* 5–20.

Moriskey, D.W., Green, L.W. & Levine, D.M. (1986). Concurrent and predictive validity of a self-reported measure of medication adherence. *Medical Care, 24,* 67–78.

Mosbach, P., & Leventhal, H. (1988). Peer group identification and smoking: Implications for intervention. *Journal of Abnormal Psychology, 97,* 238–245.

Mostofsky, D. (1981). The recurrent paraxymal of the CNS. In S.M. Turner (Ed.). *Handbook of clinical behavior therapy.* New York: Wiley.

Mowrer, O.H. (1947). On the dual nature of learning—A reinterpretation of "conditioning" and "problem-solving." *Harvard Educational Review, 17,* 102–148.

Mullen, P.D., Hersey, J.C., & Iverson, D.C. (1987). Health behavior models compared. *Social Science and Medicine, 24,* 973–981.

Muller, J.E., Ludmer, P.L., Willich, S.N., Tofler, G.H., Aylmer, G., Klangos, I., & Stone, P.H. (1987). Circadian variations in the frequency of sudden cardiac death. *Circulation, 75,* 131–138.

Muranaka, M., Lane, J.D., Suarez, E.C., Anderson, N.B., Suzuki, J., & Williams, R.B., Jr. (1988a). Stimulus-specific patterns of cardiovascular reactivity in Type A and B subjects: Evidence for enhanced vagal reactivity in Type B. *Psychophysiology, 25,* 330–338.

Muranaka, M., Monou, H., Suzuki, J., Lane, J.D., Anderson, N.B., Kuhn, C.M., Schanberg, S.M., McCown, N., & Williams, R.B., Jr. (1988b). Physiological responses to catecholamine infusions in Type A and Type B men. *Health Psychology, 7,* (Suppl.), 145–163.

Murray, H.A. (1938). *Explorations in personality.* New York: Oxford University.

Murray, M., Swan, A.V., Johnson, M.R.D. & Bewley, B.R. (1983) Some factors associated with increased risk of smoking by children. *Journal of Child Psychology and Psychiatry, 24,* 223– 232.

Murrell, S.A., Himmelfarb, S., & Phifer, J.F. (1988). Effects of bereavement loss and pre-event status on subsequent physical health in older adults. *International Journal of Aging and Human Development, 27,* 89–107.

Myers, H.F. (1982). Stress, ethnicity, and social class: A model for research with Black populations. In E.E. Jones & S. Korchin (Eds.), *Minority mental health* (pp. 118–148). New York: Praeger.

Myers, K., Hale, C.S., Mykytowycs, R., & Hughes, R.L. (1971). Density, space, sociality, and health. In A.H. Esser (Eds.), *Behavior and environment.* New York: Plenum.

Myrsten, A., Andersson, K., Frankenhaeuser, M., & Elgerot, A. (1975). Immediate effects of cigarette smoking as related to different smoking habits. *Perceptual and Motor Skills, 40,* 515–523.

Myska, M.J., & Pasewark, R.A. (1978, December). Death attitudes of residential and non-residential rural aged persons. *Psychological Reports, 43,* 1235–1238.

Naeye, R.L., & Peters, E.C. (1984). Mental development of children whose mothers smoked during pregnancy. *Obstetrics and Gynecology, 64,* 601.

Nagy, E., & Berczi, I. (1979). Immunodeficiency in hypophysectomized rats. *Fed. Proceedings, Federation of American Societies for Experimental Biology,* 38, 1355.

Nathan, P.E. (1985). Prevention of alcoholism: A history of failure. In J.C. Rosen & L.J. Solomon (Eds.), *Prevention in health psychology.* Hanover, NH: University Press of New England.

Nathan, P.E., (1986). Outcomes of treatment for alcoholism: Current data. *Annals of Behavioral Medicine, 8,* 40–46.

Nathanson, C.A., & Lorenz, G. (1982). Women and health: The social dimensions of biomedical data. In J.Z. Giele (Ed.), *Women in the middle years.* New York: Wiley.

National Cancer Institute. (1980). *Breast cancer: A measure of progress in public understanding* (U.S. Department of Health and Human Services/National Institutes of Health Publication No. 81–2291). Washington, DC: U.S. Government Printing Office.

National Center for Health Statistics. (1970). *Selected symptoms of psychological distress.* (Public Health Services Series 11, No. 357). Washington, DC: U.S. Government Printing Office.

National Center for Health Statistics. (1989). *Current Estimate from the National Health Interview Survey, United States, 1988. Vital and Health Statistics. Series 10, No. 173* (DHHS Pub. No. PHS 89–1501). Hyattesville, MD: U.S. Dept. of Health and Human Services.

NIAAA (National Institute on Alcohol Abuse and Alcoholism, 1974). *Alcohol and health* (Publication No. 017–024–003999–9). Washington, DC: U.S. Government Printing Office.

NIAAA (National Institute on Alcohol Abuse and Alcoholism, 1981). *First statistical compendium on alcohol and health.* (Publication No. 81–1115). Washington, DC: U.S. Government Printing Office.

NIAAA (National Institute on Alcohol Abuse and Alcoholism, 1983). *Fifth special report to the U.S. Congress on alcohol and health.* (Publication No. 84–1291). Washington, DC: U.S. Government Printing Office.

NIAAA (National Institute on Alcohol Abuse and Alcoholism, 1986). *Media alert: FAS awareness campaign: My baby, strong and healthy.* Rockville, MD: National Clearinghouse for Alcohol Information.

NIAAA (National Institute on Alcohol Abuse and Alcoholism, 1987). *Sixth Special Report to the U.S. Congress on Alcohol and Health.* Washington, DC: U.S. Dept. of Health and Human Services.

NIAID (National Institute of Allergy and Infectious Diseases, 1981). *Self-management educational programs for childhood asthma: Vol. 2. Manuscripts.* Bethesda, MD: Author.

NIDA (National Institute on Drug Abuse, 1983). *Population projections, based on the National Survey on Drug Abuse, 1982.* Rockville, MD: National Institute on Drug Abuse.

NIDA (National Institute on Drug Abuse, 1986). *Capsules: Overview of the 1985 household survey on drug abuse.* Rockville, MD: Author.

National Institutes of Health. (1985). *National cancer program: 1983–1984 director's report and annual plan, FY 1986–1990.* (NIH Publication No. 85–2765). Washington, DC: U.S. Government Printing Office.

National Institute for Occupational Safety and Health. (1988). *A proposed national strategy for the prevention of work-related psychological disorders.* Cincinnati, OH: Author.

National Opinion Research Center. (1987, July). *General Social Survey, 1972–1987.* Chicago: Author.

NRC (National Research Council, 1989). *Diet and health: Implications for reducing chronic disease risk.* Washington, DC: U.S. Government Printing Office.

Navia, B.A., Jordan, B.D., & Price, R.W. (1986). The AIDS dementia complex: I. clinical features. *Annals of Neurology, 19,* 517–524.

Neale, A.V., Tilley, B.C., & Vernon, S.W. (1986). Marital status, delay in seeking treatment, and survival from breast cancer. *Social Science and Medicine, 23,* 305–312.

Neff, J.A., & Husaini, B.A. (1982). Life events, drinking patterns, and depressive symptomatology: the stress-buffering effects of alcohol consumption. *Journal of Studies on Alcohol, 43,* 301–318.

Nelson, F.L., & Faberow, N.L. (1980, November). Indirect self-destructive behavior in the elderly nursing home patient. *Journal of Gerontology, 34,* 949–957.

Nelson, G.D. & Moffit, P.B. (1988). Safety belt promotion: Theory and practice. *Accident Analysis and Prevention, 20,* 27–38.

Nelson, G.E. (1984). *Biological principles with human perspectives* (2nd ed.). New York: Wiley.

Neugarten, B., Wood, V., Kraines, R., & Loomis, B. (1963). Women's attitudes towards the menopause. *Vita Humana, 6,* 140–151.

Newberger, C.M., Newberger, E.H., & Harper, G.P. (1976). The social ecology of malnutrition in childhood. In J.D. Lloyd-Still (Ed.), *Malnutrition and intellectual development.* Littleton, MA: Publishing Sciences Group.

Newberne, P.M., & Supharkarn, V. (1983). Nutrition and cancer: A review, with emphasis on the role of vitamins C and E and selenium. *Nutrition and cancer, 5,* 107–119.

Newcomb, M.D., & Bentler, P.M. (1986). Cocaine use among adolescents: Longitudinal associations with social context, psychopathology, and use of other substances. *Addictive Behaviors, 11,* 263–273.

Newcomb, M.D., Maddahian, E., & Bentler, P.M. (1986). Risk factors for drug use among adolescents: Concurrent and longitudinal analyses. *American Journal of Public Health, 76,* 525–531.

Newman, R.I., & Seres, J. (1986). The interdisciplinary pain center: An approach to the management of chronic pain. In A.D. Holzman & D.C. Turk (Eds.), *Pain management: A handbook of psychological treatment approaches.* New York: Pergamon.

Newman, S. (1984a). Anxiety, hospitalization, and surgery. In R. Fitzpatrick, J. Hinton, S. Newman, G. Scambler, & J. Thompson (Eds.), *The experience of illness.* London: Tavistock.

Newman, S. (1984b). The psychological consequences of cerebrovascular accident and head injury. In R. Fitzpatrick, J. Hinton, S. Newman, G. Scambler, & J. Thompson (Eds.), *The experience of illness.* London: Tavistock.

New York Times/CBS News Poll. (1984, September 23). Prolonging life by machine. *The New York Times,* p. 56.

Nicassio, P.M., Wallston, K.A., Callahan, L.F., Herbert, M., & Pincus, T. (1985). The measurement of helplessness in rheumatoid arthritis: The development of the Arthritis Helplessness Index. *Journal of Rheumatology, 12,* 462–467.

Nieburg, P., Marks, J.S., McLaren, N.M., & Remington, P.L. (1985). The fetal tobacco syndrome. *Journal of the American Medical Association, 253,* 2998–2999.

Niederland, W. (1965). Narcissistic ego impairment in patients with early physical malformations. *Psychoanalytic Study of the Child, 20,* 518–534.

Nigl, A.J. (1984). *Biofeedback and behavioral strategies in pain treatment.* New York: Medical and Scientific Books.

Nisbett, R. (1972). Hunger, obesity, and the ventromedial hypothalamus. *Psychological Review, 79,* 433–453.

Nooman, Z.M., Schmidt, H.G., & Ezzat, E.S. (1990). *Innovation in medical education: An evaluation of its present status.* New York: Springer-Verlag.

Norback, D., Michel, I., Widstrom, J. (1990). Indoor air quality and personal factors related to the sick building syndrome. *Scandinavian Journal of Work, Environment, and Health, 16,* 121–128.

Norell, S.E. (1981). Accuracy of patient interviews and estimates by clinical staff determining medication compliance. *Social Science and Medicine, 15,* 57–61.

Norman, S.A., Marconi, K.M., Schezel, G.W., Schechter, C.F., & Stolley, P.D. (1985). Beliefs, social normative influences, and compliance with antihypertensive medication. *American Journal of Preventive Medicine, 1,* 10–17.

Novaco, R.W., Stokols, D., Campbell, J., & Stokols, J. (1979). Transportation stress and community psychology. *American Journal of Community Psychology, 4,* 361–380.

Novin, D., Robinson, B.A., Culbreth, L.A., & Tordoff, M.G. (1983). Is there a role for the liver in the control of food intake? *American Journal of Clinical Nutrition, 9,* 233–246.

Nunes, J.S., & Bandeira, C.S. (1980). A sex therapy clinic in Portugal: Some results and a few questions. In R. Forleo & W. Pasini (Eds.), *Medical sexology* (pp. 605–608). Littleton, MA: PSG Publishing.

Nuttbrock, L. (1986). The management of illness among physically impaired older people: An interactionist interpretation. *Social Psychology Quarterly, 49,* 180–191.

Nyquist, R.H., & Bors, E. (1967). Mortality and survival in traumatic spinal cord injury over a period of nine years. *Paraplegia, 5,* 22–48.

Oates, R.K., Peacock, A., & Forrest, D. (1985). Long-term effects of nonorganic failure to thrive. *Pediatrics, 75,* 36–40.

Obler, M. (1973). Systematic desensitization in sexual disorders. *Journal of Behavior Therapy and Experimental Psychiatry, 4,* 93–101.

Obler, M. (1982). A comparison of a hypnoanalytic/behavior modification technique and a cotherapist-type treatment with primary orgasmic dysfunctional females: Some preliminary results. *Journal of Sex Research, 18,* 331–345.

Office on Smoking and Health (1989). *Reducing the health consequences of smoking: 25 years of progress. A report of the Surgeon General* (DHHS Publication No. CDC 89–8411). Washington, DC: U.S. Dept. of Health and Human Services.

Office of Technology Assessment (1985). *Smoking-related deaths and financial costs.* Washington, DC: Office of Technology Assessment.

Offit, A. (1977). *The sexual self.* New York: Ballantine.

Offutt, C., & La Croix, J.M. (1988). Type A behavior pattern and symptom reports: A prospective investigation. *Journal of Behavioral Medicine, 11,* 227–237.

Olafsson, O. & Svensson, P. (1986). Unemployment related lifestyle changes and health disturbances in adolescents and children in Western countries. *Social Science and Medicine, 22,* 1105–1113.

Oldenberg, B., Perkins, R.J., & Andrews, G. (1985). Controlled trial of psychological intervention in myocardial infarction. *Journal of Consulting and Clinical Psychology, 53,* 852–859.

Oldridge, N.B., & Streiner, D.L. (1990). The Health Belief Model: Predicting compliance and dropout in cardiac rehabilitation. *Medicine and Science in Sports and Exercise, 22,* 678–683.

Olds, J., & Milner, P. (1954). Positive reinforcement produced by electrical stimulation of the septal area. *Journal of Comparative and Physiological Psychology, 47,* 419–427.

Olds, M.E., & Fobes, J.L. (1981). The central basis of motivation: Intracranial self-stimulation studies. In M.R. Rosenzweig & L.W. Porter (Eds.), *Annual review of psychology: 1981.* Palo Alto, CA: Annual Reviews.

O'Leary, A. (1985). Self-efficacy and health. *Behavior Research & Therapy, 23,* 437–451.

O'Leary, K.D., & Wilson, G.T. (1987). *Behavior therapy: Application and outcome.* Englewood Cliffs, NJ: Prentice-Hall.

Olson, J.M., & Zanna, M.P. (1987). Understanding and promoting exercise: A social psychological perspective. *Canadian Journal of Public Health, 78,* S1–S7.

Olton, D.S., & Noonberg, A.R. (1980). *Biofeedback: Clinical applications in behavioral medicine.* Englewood-Cliffs, NJ: Prentice-Hall.

Orleans, C.T., & Barnett, L.R. (1984). Bulimarexia: Guidelines for behavioral assessment and treatment. In R.C. Hawkins, W.J. Fremouw, & P.F. Clement (Eds.), *The binge-purge syndrome.* New York: Springer.

Orme-Johnson, D.W., & Farrow, J.T. (Eds.). (1977). *Scientific research on the transcendental meditation program, Vol. I.* New York: Maharishi European Research University.

Orne, M.T. (1977). Mechanisms of hypnotic pain control. In J.J. Bonica & D. Albe-Fessard (Eds.), *Advances in pain research and therapy* (Vol. 1, pp. 717–726). New York: Raven.

Orne, M.T. (1980). Hypnotic control of pain: Toward a clarification of the different psychological processes involved. In J.J. Bonica (Ed.), *Pain.* New York: Raven.

Ornish, D., Brown, S.E., Scherwitz, L.A., Billings, J.H., Armstrong, W.T., Ports, T.A., McLanahan, S.M., Kirkeeide, R.L., Brand, R.J., & Gould, K.L. (1990). Can lifestyle changes reverse coronary artery disease? *Lancet, 336,* 129–133.

Ornstein, R., & Sobel, D. (1989). Coming to our senses. *Advances, 6,* 49–56.

Orth, J.E., Stiles, W.B., Scherwitz, L., Hennrikus, D., & Vallbona, C. (1987). Patient exposition and provider explanation in routine interviews and hypertensive patients' blood pressure control. *Health Psychology, 6,* 29–42.

Ostrea, E.M., & Chavez, C.J. (1979). Perinatal problems (excluding neonatal withdrawal) in maternal drug addiction: A study of 830 cases. *Journal of Pediatrics, 94,* 292–295.

Oxtoby, M.J. (1990). Perinatally acquired human immunodeficiency virus infection. *Pediatric Infectious Disease Journal, 9,* 609–619.

Oyebode, F., Boodhoo, J.A., & Schapira, K. (1988). Anorexia nervosa in males: Clinical features and outcome. *International Journal of Eating Disorders, 7,* 121–124.

Paff, B.A. (1985). Sexual dysfunction in gay men requesting treatment. *Journal of Sex and Marital Therapy, 11,* 3–18.

Paffenbarger, R.S., Jr., Hyde, R.T., Wing, A.L., & Hsieh, C-C. (1986). Physical activity, all-cause mortality, and longevity of college alumni. *New England Journal of Medicine, 314,* 605–613.

Pagel, M.D., Smilkstein, G., Regen, H., Montano, D. (1990). Psychosocial influences on new born outcomes: A controlled prospective study. *Social Science and Medicine, 30,* 597–604.

Pallonen, U.E., Murray, D.M., Schmid, L., Pirie, P., & Luepker, V. (1990). Patterns of self-initiated smoking cessation among young adults. *Health Psychology, 9,* 418–426.

Palmblad, J. (1981). Stress and immunologic competence: Studies in man. In R. Ader (Ed.), *Psychoneuroimmunology.* New York: Academic.

Panico, S., Celentano, E., Krogh, V., Jossa, F., Farinaro, E., Trevisan, M., & Mancini, M. (1987). Physical activity and its relationship to blood pressure in school children. *Journal of Chronic Diseases, 40,* 925–930.

Pardine, P., & Napoli, A. (1983). Physiological reactivity and recent life-stress experience. *Journal of Consulting and Clinical Psychology, 51,* 467–469.

Parikh, R., M., Lipsey, J.R., Robinson, R.G., & Price, T.R. (1988). A two year longitudinal study of poststroke mood disorders: Prognostic factors related to one and two year outcome. *International Journal of Psychiatry in Medicine, 18,* 45–56.

Parker, H.J., & Chan, F. (1990). Psychologists in rehabilitation: Preparation and experience. *Rehabilitation Psychology, 35,* 239–248.

Parker, G. (1977). Cyclone Tracy and Darwin evacuees. On the restoration of the species. *British Journal of Psychiatry, 130,* 548–555.

Parkes, C.M., Benjamin, B., & Fitzgerald, R. (1969). Broken heart: A statistical study of increased mortality among widows. *British Medical Journal, 4,* 740–743.

Parmelee, A.H. (1986). Children's illnesses: Their beneficial effects on behavioral development. *Child Development, 57,* 1–10.

Parsons, O.A. (1975). Brain damage in alcoholics: Altered states of consciousness. In M.M. Gross (Ed.), *Alcohol intoxication and withdrawal.* New York: Plenum.

Parsons, O.A. (1977). Neuropsychological deficits in chronic alcoholics: Facts and fancies. *Alcoholism: Clinical and Experimental Research, 1,* 51–56.

Parsons, O.A. (1986). Alcoholics' neuropsychological impairment: Current findings and conclusions. *Annals of Behavioral Medicine, 8,* 13–19.

Parsons, O.A., & Farr, S.P. (1981). The neuropsychology of alcohol and drug abuse. In S.B. Filskov & T.J. Boll (Eds.), *Handbook of clinical neuropsychology.* New York: Wiley-Interscience.

Parsons, T. (1951). *The social system.* New York: Free Press.

Parsons, T. (1975). The sick role and the role of the physician reconsidered. *Milbank Memorial Fund Quarterly, 53,* 257–278.

Parsons, T. (1978). *Action theory and the human condition.* New York: Free Press.

Pascoe, G.C. (1983). Patient satisfaction in primary health care: A literature review and analysis. *Evaluation and Program Planning, 6,* 185–210.

Pauling, L. (1980). Vitamin C therapy of advanced cancer. *New England Journal of Medicine, 302,* 694–698.

Paulus, P. (1988). *Prison crowding: A psychological perspective.* New York: Springer-Verlag.

Pavlov, I.P. (1927). *Conditioned reflexes.* New York: Dover.

Peck, C.A., & Cooke, T.P. (1983). Benefits of early childhood mainstreaming. *Analysis and Intervention in Developmental Disabilities, 3,* 1–22.

Peck, C.J., Fordyce, W.E., & Black, R.G. (1978). The effect of the pendency of claims for compensation upon behavior indicative of pain. *Washington Law Review, 53,* 251–278.

Peele, S. (1981). Reductionism in the psychology of the eighties: Can biochemistry eliminate addiction, mental illness, and pain? *American Psycholo- gist, 36,* 807–818.

Peele, S. (1984). The cultural context of psychological approaches to alcoholism: Can we control the effects of alcohol? *American Psychologist, 39,* 1337–1351.

Peele, S. (1989). *Diseasing of America: Addiction treatment out of control.* Boston: Houghton Mifflin.

Peele, S. (1991, December). What we know about treating alcoholism and other addictions. *The Harvard Mental Health Letter, 8,* 5–7.

Pell, S., & Fayerweather, W.E. (1985). Trends in the incidence of myocardial infarction and in associated mortality and morbidity in a large employed population, 1957–1983. *New England Journal of Medicine, 312,* 1005–1011.

Pelletier, K.R., & Herzing, D.L. (1988). Psychoneuroimmunology: Toward a mindbody model. *Advances, 5,* 27–56.

Pendery, M.L., Maltzman, I.M., & West, L.J. (1982). Controlled drinking by alcoholics? New findings and a re-evaluation of a major affirmative study. *Science, 217,* 169–175.

Pendleton, D., & Bochner, S. (1980). The communication of medical information as a function of patients' social class. *Social Science and Medicine, 14A,* 669–673.

Pennebaker, J.W. (1980). Perceptual and environmental determinants of coughing. *Basic and Applied Social Psychology, 1,* 83–91.

Pennebaker, J.W. (1982). *The psychology of physical symptoms.* New York: Springer-Verlag.

Pennebaker, J.W., & Brittingham, J.L. (1982). Environmental and sensory cues affecting the perception of physical symptoms. In A. Baum and J. Singer (Eds.), *Advances in environmental psychology,* (Vol. 4). Hillsdale, NJ: Erlbaum.

Pennebaker, J.W., Kiecolt-Glaser, J.K., & Glaser, R. (1988). Disclosure of traumas and immune function: Health implications for psychotherapy. *Journal of Consulting and Clinical Psychology, 56,* 239–245.

Pennebaker, J.W., & Skelton, J.A. (1981). Selective monitoring of bodily sensations. *Journal of Personality and Social Psychology, 41,* 213–223.

Perri, M.G., McAllister, D.A., Gange, J.J., Jordan, R.C., McAdoo, W.G., & Nezu, A.M. (1988). Effects of four maintenance programs on the long-term management of obesity. *Journal of Consulting and Clinical Psychology, 56,* 529–534.

Perri, M.G., Nezu, A.M., Patti, E.T., & McCann, K.L. (1989). Effect of length of treatment on weight loss. *Journal of Consulting and Clinical Psychology, 57,* 450–452.

Perrin, E.C., & Gerrity, P.S. (1981). There is a demon in your belly: Children's understanding of illness. *Pediatrics, 67,* 841–849.

Perrin, E.C., & Shapiro, E. (1985). Health locus of control beliefs of healthy children, children with a chronic physical illness, and their mothers. *Journal of Pediatrics, 107,* 627–633.

Perrine, M., Peck, R., & Fell, J. (1988). Epidemiological perspectives on drunk driving. In *Surgeon General's workshop on drunk driving: Background papers.* Washington, DC: U.S. Department of Health and Human Services.

Pert, C.B. (1987). The wisdom of the receptors: Neuropeptides, the emotions, and bodymind. *Advances, 3,* 8–16.

Peters, H.P., Albrecht, G., Hennen, L., & Stegelmann, H.U. (1990). "Chernobyl" and the nuclear power issue in West German public opinion. Special Issue: Psychological fallout from the Chernobyl nuclear accident. *Journal of Environmental Psychology, 10,* 121–134.

Petersen, A.C. (1987). Those gangly years. *Psychology Today, 21,* 28–34.

Peterson, C. (1982). Learned helplessness and health psychology. *Health Psychology, 1,* 153–168.

Peterson, C. (1988). Explanatory style is a risk factor for illness. *Cognitive Therapy and Research, 12,* 117–130.

Peterson, C., & Seligman, M.E.P. (1987). Explanatory style and illness. *Journal of Personality, 55,* 237–265.

Peterson, C., Seligman, M.E.P., & Vaillant, G.E. (1988). Pessimistic explanatory style is a risk factor for physical illness: A thirty-five-year longitudinal study. *Journal of Personality and Social Psychology, 55,* 23–27.

Peterson, J.L., & Marin, G. (1988). Issues in the prevention of AIDS among black and hispanic men. *American Psychologist, 43,* 871–877.

Peto, R., Doll, R., Buckley, J.D., & Spron, M.B. (1981). Can dietary beta-carotene materially reduce human cancer rates? *Nature, 290,* 201–208.

Pettingale, K.W., Morris, T., Greer, S., & Haybittle, J.L. (1985). Mental attitudes to cancer: An additional prognostic factor: *Lancet, 1,* 750.

Petzel, S.R., & Cline, D.W. (1978). Adolescent suicide: Epidemiological and biological aspects. *Adolescent Psychiatry, 6,* 239–266.

Piaget, J. (1983). Piaget's theory. In P.H. Mussen (Ed.), *Handbook of child psychology,* Vol. 1. New York: Wiley.

Pill, R. & Stott, N.C.H. (1982). Concepts of illness causation and responsibility: Some preliminary data from a sample of working class mothers. *Social Science and Medicine, 16,* 43–52.

Pincus, T., Callahan, L.F., & Burkhauser, R.V. (1987). Most chronic diseases are reported more frequently by individuals with fewer than 12 years of formal education in the age 18–64

United States population. *Journal of Chronic Diseases, 40,* 865–874.

Pinkerton, S.S., Hughes, H., & Wenrich, W.W. (1982). *Behavioral medicine: Clinical applications.* New York: Wiley & Sons.

Piot, P., Plummer, F.A., Mhalu, F.S., Lamboray, J.L., Chin, J., & Mann, J.M. (1988). AIDS: An international perspective. *Science, 239,* 573–579.

Piran, N., Kennedy, S., Garfinkel, P.E., & Owens, M. (1985). Affective disturbance and eating disorders. *The Journal of Nervous and Mental Disease, 173,* 395–400.

Pitts, J.S., Schwankovsky, L., Thompson, S.C., Cruzen, D.E., Everett, J., & Freedman, D. (1991, August). *Do people want to make medical decisions?* Paper presented at the annual meeting of the American Psychological Association, San Francisco.

Pohorecky, L. (1991). Stress and alcohol interaction: An update of human reseach. *Alcoholism: Clinical and Experimental Research, 15,* 438–459.

Pokorny, A.D. (1968). Myths about suicide. In H.L.P. Resnik (Ed.), *Suicidal behaviors.* Boston: Little, Brown.

Polich, J.M., Armor, D.J., & Braiker, H.B. (1980). *The course of alcoholism: Four years after treatment.* New York: Wiley.

Polivy, J., & Herman, C.P. (1983). *Breaking the diet habit: The natural weight alternative.* New York: Basic Books.

Polivy, J., & Herman, C.P. (1987). Diagnosis and treatment of normal eating. *Journal of Consulting and Clinical Psychology, 55,* 635–644.

Polivy, J., & Thomsen, L. (1988). Dieting and other eating disorders. In E.A. Blechman & K.D. Brownell (Eds.), *Handbook of behavioral medicine for women.* New York: Pergamon.

Pomerleau, O.F. (1982). A discourse on behavioral medicine: Current status and future trends. *Journal of Consulting and Clinical Psychology, 50,* 1030–1039.

Pope, C.R. (1978). Consumer satisfaction in a health maintenance organization. *Journal of Health and Social Behavior, 19,* 291–303.

Pope, H.G., & Hudson, J.I. (1984). *New hope for binge eaters: Advances in the understanding and treatment of bulimia.* New York: Harper & Row.

Pope, H.G., & Hudson, J.I. (1989). Pharmacologic treatment of bulimia nervosa: Research findings and practical suggestions. Special Issue: Eating disorders. *Psychiatric Annals, 19,* 483–487.

Pope, H.G., Hudson, J.I., Jonas, J.M., & Yurgelun-Todd, D. (1983). Bulimia treated with imipramine: A placebo-controlled double-blind study. *American Journal of Psychiatry, 140,* 554–558.

Pope, H.G., Hudson, J.I., & Yurgelun-Todd, D. (1984). Anorexia nervosa and bulimia among 300 suburban women shoppers. *American Journal of Psychiatry, 141,* 292–293.

Pope, H.G., Ionescu-Pioggia, M., & Aizley, H.G. (1990). Drug use among college undergraduates in 1989: a comparison with 1969 and 1978. *American Journal of Psychiatry, 147*, 998–1001.

Porikos, K.P., Hesser, M.F., & Van Itallie, T.B. (1982). Caloric regulation in normal-weight men maintained on a palatable diet of conventional foods. *Physiology & Behavior, 29*, 293–300.

Porterfield, A.L. (1987). Does sense of humor moderate the impact of life stress on psychological and physical well-being? *Journal of Research in Personality, 21*, 306–317.

Powell, K.E., Caspersen, C.J., Koplan, J.P., & Ford, E.S. (1989). Physical activity and chronic disease. *American Journal of Clinical Nutrition, 49*, 999–1006.

Powell, K.E., Thompson, P.D., Caspersen, C.J., & Kendrick, J.S. (1987). Physical activity and the incidence of coronary heart disease. In L. Breslow, J.E. Fielding, & L.B. Lave (Eds.), *Annual review of public health, 8*, Palo Alto, CA: Annual Reviews.

Powell, L.H., Friedman, M., Thoresen, C.E., Gill, J.J., & Ulmer, D.K. (1984). Can the Type A behavior pattern be altered after myocardial infarction? A second year report from the Recurrent Coronary Prevention Project. *Psychosomatic Medicine, 46*, 293–313.

Powell, L.H., & Thoresen, C.E. (1988). Effect of Type A behavioral conseling and severity of prior acute myocardial infarction on survival. *American Journal of Cardiology, 62*, 1159–1163.

Powers, E. & Bultena, G. (1976). Sex differences in intimate friendships in old age. *Journal of Marriage and the Family, 38*, 739–747.

Prevention Research Center. (1986). *Prevention index '86: A report card on the nation's health* [Summary Report]. Emmaus, PA: Rodale.

Pribram, K.H. (1981). Emotions. In S.B. Filskov & T.J. Boll (Eds.), *Handbook of clinical neuropsychology*. New York: Wiley.

Prochaska, J.O., & DiClemente, C.C. (1983). Stages and processes of self-change of smoking: Towards an integrative model of change. *Journal of Consulting and Clinical Psychology, 51*, 390–395.

Prochaska, J.O., DiClemente, C.C., & Norcross, J.C. (1992). In search of how people change: Applications to addictive behaviors. *American Psychologist, 47*, 1102–1114.

Prohaska, T.R., Keller, M.L., Leventhal, E.A., & Leventhal, H. (1987). Impact of symptoms and aging attribution on emotions and coping. *Health Psychology, 6*, 495–514.

Putallaz, M., & Gottman, J. (1981). Social skills and group acceptance. In S. Asher & J. Gottman (Eds.), *The development of children's friendships*. Cambridge: Cambridge University.

Pyle, R.L., Mitchell, J.E., & Eckert, E.D. (1981). Bulimia: A report of 34 cases. *Journal of Clinical Psychiatry, 42*, 60–64.

Pyle, R.L., Mitchell, J.E., Eckert, E.D., Halvorsen, P.A., Neuman, P.A., & Goff, G.M. (1983). the incidence of bulimia in freshman college students. *International Journal of Eating Disorders, 2*, 75–85.

Pyle, R.L., Mitchell, J.E., Eckert, E.D., Hatsukami, D., Pomeroy, C., & Zimmerman, R. (1990). Maintenance treatment and 6-month outcome for bulimic patients who respond to initial treatment. *American Journal of Psychiatry, 147*, 871–875.

Quarantelli, E.L., & Dyness, R.R. (1972). When disaster strikes. *Psychology Today, 5*, 66–70.

Quick, J.C., & Quick, J.D. (1984). *Organizational stress and preventive management*. New York: McGraw-Hill.

Rachman, S.J., & Wilson, G.T. (1980). *The effects of psychological therapy*. New York: Pergamon.

Radloff, L.S. (1977). The CES-D Scale: A self-report depression scale for research in the general population. *Journal of Applied Psychological Measurement, 1*, 385–401.

Rahe, R.H. (1974). The pathway between subjects' recent life changes and their near-future illness reports: Representative results and methodological issues. In B.S. Dohrenwend & B.P. Dohrenwend (Eds.), *Stressful life events: Their nature and effects*. New York: Wiley.

Rahe, R.H. (1984). Developments in life change measurement: Subjective life change unit scaling. In B.S. Dohrenwend & B.P. Dohrenwend (Eds.), *Stressful life events & their contexts*. New Brunswick, NJ: Rutgers University.

Rahe, R.H., & Holmes, T.H. (1965). Social, psychologic, and psychophysiologic aspects of inguinal hernia. *Journal of Psychosomatic Research, 8*, 487–491.

Raichle, M.E., De Vivo, D.C., & Hanaway, J. Disorders of cerebral circulation. (1978). In S.G. Eliasson, A.L. Prensky, & W.B. Hardin, Jr. (Eds.), *Neurological pathophysiology* (2nd ed.). New York: Oxford University.

Rainwater, N., & Alexander, A.B. (1982). Respiratory disorders: Asthma. In D.M. Doleys, R.L. Meredith, & A.R. Ciminero (Eds.), *Behavioral medicine: Assessment and treatment strategies* (pp. 435–446). New York: Plenum.

Rakoff, V. (1983). Multiple determinants of family dynamics in anorexia nervosa. In P.L. Darby, P.E. Garfinkel, D.M. Garner, & D.V. Coscina (Eds.), *Anorexia nervosa: Recent developments in research* (pp. 29–40). New York: Liss.

Rand, C.S.W., & Stunkard, A.J. (1983). Obesity and psychoanalysis: Treatment and four-year follow-up. *American Journal of Psychiatry, 140*, 1140–1144.

Rappaport, J., & Chinsky, J.M. (1974). Models for delivery of service from a historical and conceptual perspective. *Professional Psychology, 5*, 42–50.

Ravussin, E., Lillioja, S., Knowler, W.C., Christin, L., Freymond, D., Abbott, W.G.H., Boyce, V., Howard, B.V., & Bogardus, C. (1988). Reduced rate of energy expenditure as a risk factor for body-weight gain. *New England Journal of Medicine, 318*, 462–472.

Ray, E.B., & Donohew, L. (Eds.). (1990). *Communication and health: Systems and applications.* Hillsdale, NJ: Lawrence Erlbaum.

Razin, A.M. (1984). Coronary artery disease. In H.B. Roback (Ed.), *Helping paitents and their families cope with medical problems.* San Francisco: Jossey-Bass.

Redd, W.H., & Andrykowski, M.A. (1982). Behavioral intervention in cancer treatment: Controlling aversion reactions to chemotherapy. *Journal of Consulting and Clinical Psychology, 50*, 1018–1029.

Reed, S.D., Katkin, E.S., & Goldband, S. (1986). Biofeedback and behavioral medicine. In F.H. Kanfer & A.P. Goldstein (Eds.), *Helping people change: A textbook of methods* (3rd ed.). Elmsford, NY: Pergamon.

Rees, J. (1984). ABC's of asthma: Precipitating factors. *British Medical Journal, 288*, 1512–1513.

Reichard, S., Livson, F., & Peterson, P. (1962). *Aging and personality: A study of 87 older men.* New York: Wiley.

Reis, H.T., Wheeler, L., Kernis, M.H., Spiegel, N., & Nezlek, J. (1985). On specificity in the impact of social participation on physical and psychological health. *Journal of Personality and Social Psychology, 48*, 456–471.

Reitan, R.M., & Davison, L.A. (1974). *Clinical neuropsychology: Current status and applications.* Washington, DC: V.H. Winston & Sons.

Reitan, R.M., & Wolfson, D. (1985). *Neuroanatomy and neuropathology: A clinical guide for neuropsychologists.* Tuczon, AZ: Neuropsychology Press.

Revicki, D.A., & May, H.J. (1985). Occupational stress, social support, and depression. *Health Psychology, 4*, 61–77.

Review Panel on Coronary-Prone Behavior and Coronary Heart Disease. (1981). A critical review. *Circulation, 63*, 1199–1215.

Reynolds, D.V. (1969). Surgery in the rat during electrical anesthesia induced by focal brain stimulation. *Science, 164*, 444–445.

Reynolds, P.P. (1991). Professionalism and residency reform. *Bulletin of the New York Academy of Medicine, 67*, 369–377.

Rezek, M. (1976). The role of insulin in the glucostatic control of food intake. *Canadian Journal of Physiology and Pharmacology, 54*, 650–665.

Rhodewalt, F., & Marcroft, M. (1988). Type A behavior and diabetic control: Implications of psychological reactance for health outcomes. *Journal of Applied Social Psychology, 18*, 139–159.

Rhodewalt, F., & Zone, J. B, (1989). Appraisal of life change, depression, and illness in hardy and nonhardy women. *Journal of Personality and Social Psychology, 56*, 81-88.

Rice, F.P. (1990). *The adolescent: Development, relationships, and culture* (6th ed.). Boston, MA: Allyn & Bacon.

Rich, C.L., Warstradt, G.M., Nemiroff, R.A., Fowler, R., & Young, D., (1991). Suicide, stressors, and the life cycle. *American Journal of Psychiatry, 148*, 524–527.

Richards, J., Derham, D., Aeillo, J., Burnes, T., Liener, L., & Wastell, L. (1989). Changes in medication use following participation in a stress management course. *Behaviour Change, 6*, 19–28.

Richards, J.S., Nepomuceno, C., Riles, M., & Suer, Z. (1982). Assessing pain behavior: The UAB Pain Behavior Scale. *Pain, 14*, 395.

Richardson, J.L. (1986). Perspectives on compliance with drug regimens among the elderly. *Journal of Compliance in Health Care, 1*, 33–45.

Richter-Heinrich, E., Homuth, B., Henrich, B., Knust, U., Schmidt, K.H., Weidemann, E., & Gohlke, H.R. (1988). Behavioral therapies in essential hypertensives: A controlled study. In T. Elbert, W. Langosch, A. Steptoe, & D. Vaitl (Eds.), *Behavioral medicine in cardiovascular disorders*, (pp. 113–127). London: Wiley.

Ried, L.D., & Christensen, D.B. (1988). A psychosocial perspective in the explanation of patients' drug-taking behavior. *Social Science and Medicine, 27*, 277–285.

Riley, V. (1979). Introduction: stress-cancer contradictions—a continuing puzzlement. *Cancer Detection Preview, 2*, 159–162.

Riley, V. (1981). Psychoneuroendocrine influences on immunocompetence and neoplasia. *Science, 212*, 1100–1109.

Rimm, D.C., & Cunningham, H.M. (1985). Behavior therapies. In S.J. Lynn & J.P. Garske (Eds.), *Contemporary psychotherapies: Models and methods.* Columbus, OH: Charles E. Merrill.

Rimm, D.C., & Masters, J.C. (1979). *Behavior therapy: Techniques and empirical findings* (2nd ed.). New York: Academic.

Rintala, D.H., Young, M.E., Hart, K.A., Clearman, R.R., & Fuhrer, M.J. (1992). Social support and the well-being of persons with spinal cord injury living in the community. *Rehabilitation Psychology, 37*, 155–163.

Roan, S. (1990, May 8). Risky business. *Los Angeles Times*, E1.

Roan, S. (1991, November 13). Bold new approaches explored in hunt for clues to prevention. *Los Angeles Times*, A14.

Robbins, M.B., & Jensen, G.D. (1977). Multiple orgasm in males. In R. Gemme & C. Wheeler (Eds.), *Progress in sexology* (pp. 323–328). New York: Plenum.

Roberts, A.H. (1986). The operant approach to the management of pain and excess disability. In A.D. Holzman & D.C. Turk (Eds.), *Pain management: A handbook of psychological treatment approaches.* New York: Pergamon.

Robertson, I.H., & Heather, N. (1982). A survey of controlled drinking treatment in Britain. *British Journal of Alcohol and Alcoholism, 17,* 102–105.

Robinson, D. (1979). *Talking out of alcoholism: The self-help process of Alcoholics Anonymous.* London: Croom, Helm.

Robinson, R.G., & Benson, D.F. (1981). Depression in aphasia patients: Frequency, severity, and clinical-pathological correlations. *Brain and Language, 14,* 282–291.

Roche, D. (1989). Psychology, society, and the management of addiction. *The Irish Journal of Psychology, 10,* 82–99.

Rodin, J. (1976). Crowding, perceived choice, and response to controllable and uncontrollable outcomes. *Journal of Experimental Social Psychology, 12,* 564–578.

Rodin, J.A. (1987). Weight change following smoking cessation: The role of food intake and exercise. *Addictive Behaviors, 12,* 303–317.

Rodin, J., & Baum, A. (1978). Crowding and helplessness: Potential consequences of density and loss of control. In A. Baum & Y.M. Epstein (Eds.), *Human response to crowding* (pp. 389–401). Hillsdale, NJ: Erlbaum.

Rodin, J., & Plante, T. (1989). The psychological effects of exercise. In R.S. Williams & A. Wellece (Eds.), *Biological effects of physical activity* (pp. 127–137). Champaign, IL: Human Kinetics.

Rodwin, V.G. (1990). Comparative health systems. In A.R. Kovner (Ed.), *Health care delivery in the United States.* New York: Springer.

Roemer, M.I. (1980). Private health insurance in a national health program: The U.S. experience. *Journal of Public Health Policy, 1,* 166–176.

Rogers, C.R. (1961). *On becoming a person: A therapist's view of psychotherapy.* Boston: Houghton Mifflin.

Rogers, W.H., Draper, D. Kahn, K.L., Keeler, E.B., Rubenstein, L.V., Kosecoff, J., & Brook, R.H. (1990). Quality of care before and after implementation of the DRG-based prospective payment system. A summary of effects. *Journal of the American Medical Association, 264,* 1989–1994.

Rogot, E. (1974). Smoking and mortality among U.S. veterans. *Journal of Chronic Diseases, 27,* 189–203.

Rohsenow, D.J. (1982). Social anxiety, daily moods, and alcohol use over time among heavy social drinking men. *Addictive Behaviors, 7,* 311–315.

Romieu, I., Willett, W.C., Stampfer, M.J., Colditz, G.A., Sampson, L., Rosner, B., Hennekens, C.H., & Speizer, F.E. (1988). Energy intake and other determinants of relative weight. *American Journal of Clinicial Nutrition, 47,* 406–412.

Rona, R.J., Angelico, F., Antonini, R., Arca, M., Brenci, G., Del Ben, M., Gedda, L., Hayward, D., Heller, R.F., Lewis, B., Montali, A., Pandozi, C., Ricci, G., & Urbinati, G.C. (1985). Plasma cholesterol response to a change in dietary fat intake: A collaborative twin study. *Journal of Chronic Disease, 38,* 927–934.

Ronis, D.L., & Kaiser, M.K. (1989). Correlates of breast self-examination in a sample of college women: Analyses of linear structural relations. *Journal of Applied Social Psychology, 19,* 1068–1084.

Room, R., & Day, N. (1974). Alcohol and mortality. In M. Keller (Ed.), *Second special report to the U.S. Congress: Alcohol and health.* Washington, DC: U.S. Government Printing Office.

Rorabaugh, E. (1979). *The alcoholic republic: An American tradition.* New York: Oxford University.

Rose, G., Tunstall-Pedoe, H.D., & Heller, R.F. (1983). U.K. heart disease prevention project: Incidence and mortality results. *Lancet, 2,* 1062–1065.

Rose, J.E., Ananda, S., & Jarvik, M.E. (1983). Cigarette smoking during anxiety-provoking and monotonous tasks. *Addictive Behaviors, 8,* 353–359.

Rosen, J.C., & Gross, J. (1987). Prevalence of weight reducing and weight gaining in adolescent boys and girls. *Health Psychology, 6,* 131–147.

Rosen, J.C., & Leitenberg, H. (1982). Bulimia nervosa: Treatment with exposure and response prevention. *Behavior Therapy, 13,* 117–124.

Rosen, R.C., & Rosen, L. (1981). *Human sexuality.* New York: Knopf.

Rosenblatt, R.A. (1990, December 21). U.S. medical spending soars 11% during 1989. *Los Angeles Times,* A4.

Rosengren, W. (1980). *Sociology of medicine: Diversity, conflict, and change.* New York: Harper and Row.

Rosenman, R.H. (1978). The interview method of assessment of the coronary-prone behavior pattern. In T. Dembroski, S. Weiss, J. Shields, S. Haynes, & M. Feinleib (Eds.), *Coronary-prone behavior.* New York: Springer.

Rosenman, R.H. (1990). Type A behavior pattern: A personal overview. *Journal of Social Behavior and Personality, 5,* 1–24.

Rosenman, R.H., Brand, R.J., Jenkins, C.D., Friedman, M., Straus, R., & Wurm, M. (1975). Coronary heart disease in the Western Collaborative Group Study: Final followup experience of 8 $\frac{1}{2}$ years. *Journal of the American Medical Association, 233,* 872–877.

Rosensteil, A., & Keefe, F. (1983). The use of coping strategies in chronic low back pain patients: Relationships to patient characteristics and current adjustment. *Pain, 17,* 33–44.

Rosenstock, I. M. (1966). Why people use health services. *Milbank Memorial Fund Quarterly, 44,* 94–124.

Rosenstock, I. M. (1990). The Health Belief Model: Explaining health behavior through expectancies. In K. Glanz, F. M. Lewis, & B. K. Rimer (Eds.), *Health behavior and health education.* San Francisco: Jossey-Bass.

Rosenstock, I. M. & Kirscht, J. (1979). Why people use health services. In G. Stone, F. Cohen, & N. E. Adler (Eds.), *Health Psychology.* San Francisco: Jossey-Bass.

Rosenstock, I.M., Strecher, V.J., & Becker, M.H. (1988). Social learning theory and the Health Belief Model. *Health Education Quarterly, 15,* 173–183.

Rosetti-Ferreira, M.C. (1978). Malnutrition and mother-infant asynchrony: Slow mental development. *International Journal of Behavioral Development, 1,* 207–219.

Roskies, E. (1987). *Stress management for the healthy Type A.* New York: Guilford.

Roskies, E., Seraganian, P., Oseasohn, R., Hanley, J.A., Collu, R., Martin, N., & Smilga, C. (1986). The Montreal Type A Intervention Project: Major findings. *Health Psychology, 5,* 45–69.

Roskies, E., Spevack, M., Surkis, A., Cohen, C., & Gilman, S. (1978). Changing the coronary-prone (Type A) behavior pattern in a nonclinical population. *Journal of Behavioral Medicine, 1,* 201–216.

Rosman, B.L., Minuchin, S., & Liebman, R. (1975). Family lunch session: An introduction to family therapy in anorexia nervosa. *American Journal of Orthopsychiatry, 45,* 846–852.

Rosman, B.L., Minuchin, S., & Liebman, R. (1976). Input and outcome of family therapy of anorexia nervosa. In J.L. Claghorn (Ed.), *Successful psychotherapy.* New York: Brunner/Mazel.

Ross, E.D. (1981). The aprosodias. *Archives of Neurology, 38,* 561–569.

Ross, E.D. (1982). The divided self. *The Sciences, 22,* 8–12.

Ross, J.L. (1977). Anorexia nervosa: An overview. *Bulletin of the Menninger Clinic, 41,* 418–436.

Ross, L.E., Wheaton, B., & Duff, R.S. (1981). Client satisfaction and the organization of medical practice: Why time counts. *Journal of Health and Social Behavior, 22,* 243–255.

Ross, M.W., & Rosser, B.S. (1989). Education and AIDS risk: A review. *Health Education Research, 4,* 273–284.

Rossiter, L.F., Langwell, K., Wan, T.T., & Rivnyak, M. (1989). Patient satisfaction among elderly enrollees and disenrollees in Medicare health maintenance organizations. Results from the National Medicare Competition Evaluation. *Journal of the American Medical Association, 262,* 57–63.

Roter, D.L. (1984). Patient question asking in physician-patient interaction. *Health Psychology, 3,* 395–410.

Roter, D.L., & Hall, J.A. (1992). *Doctors talking with patients—patients talking with doctors.* Westport, CT: Auburn House.

Roth, D.L., & Holmes, D.S. (1985). Influence of physical fitness in determining the impact of stressful life events on physical and psychological health. *Psychosomatic Medicine, 47,* 164–173.

Roth, D.L., Wiebe, D.J., Fillingim, R.B., & Shay, K.A. (1990). Life events, fitness, hardiness, and health: A simultaneous analysis of proposed stress-resistance effects. *Journal of Personality and Social Psychology, 57,* 136–142.

Roth, H.P., & Caron, H.S. (1978). Accuracy of doctors' estimates and patients' statements on adherence to a drug regimen. *Clinical Pharmacological Theory, 19,* 361–370.

Roth, S., & Cohen, L.J. (1986). Approach, avoidance, and coping with stress. *American Psychologist, 41,* 813–819.

Rothwell, N., & Stock, M. (1979). A role for brown adipose tissue in diet-induced thermogenesis. *Nature, 281,* 31–35.

Rotter, J.B. (1966). Generalized expectancies for internal versus external control of reinforcement. *Psychological Monographs, 80,* (Whole No. 609).

Rotter, J.B. (1975). Some problems and misconceptions related to the construct of internal vs. external control of reinforcement. *Journal of Consulting and Clinical Psychology, 43,* 56–67.

Rotton, J. (1992). Trait humor and longevity: Do comics have the last laugh? *Health Psychology, 11,* 262–266.

Rovario, S., Holmes, D.S., & Holmstein, R.D. (1984). Influence of a cardiac rehabilitation program on the cardiovascular, psychological, and social functioning of cardiac patients. *Journal of Behavioral Medicine, 7,* 61–81.

Rowlison, T., & Felner, R.D. (1988). Major life events, hassles, and adaptation in adolescence: Confounding in the conceptualization and measurement of life stress and adjustment revisited. *Journal of Personality and Social Psychology, 55,* 432–444.

Ruback, R., & Pandey, J. (1991). Crowding, perceived control, and relative power: An analysis of households in India. *Journal of Applied Social Psychology, 21,* 315–344.

Rubin, D.H., Krasilnikoff, P. A., Leventhal, J. M., Weile, B., & Berget, A. (1986, August 23). Effect of passive smoking on birth-weight. *Lancet,* 415–417.

Ruble, D.N. (1972). Permenstrual symptoms: A reinterpretation. *Science, 197,* 291–292.

Rush, T.V. (1979). Predicting treatment outcomes from juvenile and young adult clients in the Pennsylvania substance-abuse system. In G.M. Beschner & A.S. Friedman (Eds.), *Youth drug abuse.* Lexington, MA: Lexington Books.

Rutter, D.R., & Quine, L. (1990). Inequalities in pregnancy outcome: A review of psychosocial and behavioural mediators. *Social Science and Medicine, 30,* 553–568.

Rutter, M. (1983). Stress, coping, and development: Some issues and some questions. In N. Garmezy & M. Rutter (Eds.), *Stress, coping, and development in children.* New York: McGraw-Hill.

Ryan, C.M., & Morrow, L.A. (1992). Dysfunctional buildings or dysfunctional people: An examination of the Sick Building Syndrome and allied disorders. *Journal of Consulting and Clinical Psychology, 60,* 220–224.

Ryan, W. (1971). *Blaming the victim.* New York: Random House.

Rzewnicki, R., & Forgays, D.G. (1987). Recidivism and self-cure of smoking and obesity: An attempt to replicate. *American Psychologist, 42,* 97–100.

Sackett, D.L. (1976). A compliance practicum for the busy practitioner. In R.B. Haynes, D.W. Taylor, & D.S. Sackett (Eds.), *Compliance in health care.* Baltimore: Johns Hopkins University.

Sackett, D.L. & Snow, J.C. (1979). The magnitude of compliance and noncompliance. In R.B. Haynes, D.W. Taylor, & D.L. Sackett (Eds.) *Compliance in health care.* Baltimore: Johns Hopkins University.

Saegert, S., & Winkel, G.H. (1990). Environmental psychology. *Annual Review of Psychology, 41,* 441–477.

Safer, M.A., Tharps, Q.J., Jackson, T.C., & Leventhal, H. (1979). Determinants of three stages of delay in seeking care at a medical care clinic. *Medical Care, 17,* 11–29.

Safranek, R., & Schill, T. (1982). Coping with stress: Does humor help? *Psychological Reports, 51,* 222.

Salans, L.B., Knittle, J.L., & Hirsch, J. (1968). The role of adipose cell size and adipose tissue insulin sensitivity in the carbohydrate intolerance of human obesity. *Journal of Clinical Investigation, 47,* 153–165.

Sallis, J.F., Dimsdale, J.E., & Caine, C. (1988). Blood pressure reactivity in children. *Journal of Psychosomatic Research, 32,* 1–12.

Sallis, J.F., & Nader, P.R. (1988). Family determinants of health behaviors. In D.S. Gochman (Ed.), *Health behavior: emerging research perspectives.* New York: Plenum.

Salonen, J.T., Heinonen, O.P., Kottke, T.E., & Puska, P. (1981). Change in health behaviour in relation to estimated coronary heart disease risk during a community-based cardiovascular diseases prevention programme. *International Journal of Epidemiology, 10,* 343–354.

Salonen, J.T., Puska, P., & Tuomilehto, J. (1982). Physical activity and risk of myocardial infarction, cerebral stroke, and death: A longitudinal study in Eastern Finland. *American Journal of Epidemiology, 115,* 526–537.

Salovey, P., & Birnbaum, D. (1989). Influence of mood on health-relevant cognitions. *Journal of Personality and Social Psychology, 57,* 539–551.

Sanders, M.R., Rebgetz, M., Morrison, M., Bor, W., Gordon, A., Dadds, M., Shepherd, R. (1989). Cognitive-behavioral treatment of recurrent nonspecific abdominal pain in children: An analysis of generalization, maintenance, and side effects. *Journal of Consulting and Clinical Psychology, 57,* 294–300.

Sanders, S.H. (1985). Chronic pain: Conceptualization and epidemiology. *Annals of Behavioral Medicine, 7,* 3–5.

Sandler, J. (1975). Aversion methods. In F.H. Kanfer & A.P. Goldstein (Eds.), *Helping people change: A textbook of methods.* New York: Pergamon.

Santiago, J.V. (1984). Effect of treatment on the long term complications of IDDM. *Behavioral Medicine Update, 6,* 26–31.

Santisteban, G.A., Riley, V., Spackman, D.H. (1977). Stress-related factors in the neoplastic process. *Proceedings of the American Association for Cancer Research, 18,* 172.

Sarason, M.B., & Sarason, B.R. (1984). Life changes, moderators of stress, and health. In A. Baum, S.E. Tayor, & J.E. Singer (Eds.), *Handbook of psychology and health: Social psychological aspects of health* (Vol. 4, pp. 279–299). Hillsdale, NJ: Erlbaum.

Sattler, J.M. (1988). *Assessment of children.* San Diego, CA: Author.

Sayette, M.A., & Mayne, T.J. (1990). Survey of current clinical and research trends in clinical psychology. *American Psychologist, 45,* 1263–1266.

Schachter, S. (1971). Some extraordinary facts about obese humans and rats. *American Psychologist, 26,* 129–144.

Schachter, S. (1980). Unitary pH and the psychology of nicotine addiction. In P.O. Davidson & S.M. Davidson (Eds.) *Behavioral medicine: Changing health lifestyles.* New York: Brunner/Mazel.

Schachter, S. (1982). Recidivism and self-cure of smoking and obesity. *American Psychologist, 37,* 436–444.

Schachter, S., Goldman, R., & Gordon, A. (1968). Effects of fear, food deprivation, and obesity on eating. *Journal of Personality and Social Psychology, 10,* 107–116.

Schachter, S., & Gross, L. (1968). Manipulated time and eating behavior. *Journal of Personality and Social Psychology, 10,* 98–106.

Schachter, S., Silverstein, B., Kozlowski, L.T., Perlick, D., Herman, C.P., & Liebling, B. (1977). Studies of the interaction of psychological and pharmacological determinants of smoking. *Journal of Experimental Psychology: General, 106,* 3–40.

Schachter, S., & Singer, J.E. (1962). Cognitive, social, and physiological determinants of emotional state. *Psychological Review, 69,* 379–399.

Schaefer, C., Coyne, J.C., & Lazarus, R.S. (1981). The health-related functions of social support. *Journal of Behavioral Medicine, 4,* 381–406.

Schaeffer, M.A., McKinnon, W., Baum, A., Reynolds, C.P., Rikli, P., Davidson, L.M., & Fleming, I. (1985). Immune status as a function of chronic stress at Three Mile Island. *Psychosomatic Medicine, 47,* 85 (abstract).

Schafer, L.C., Glasgow, R.E., & McCaul, K.D. (1982). Increasing the adherence of diabetic adolescents. *Journal of Behavioral Medicine, 5,* 353–362.

Schaps, E., Moskowitz, J., Malvin, J., & Schaeffer, G. (1984). *The Napa drug abuse prevention project: Research findings.* (DHHS Publication No. [ADM] 84–1339). Washington, DC: U.S. Government Printing Office.

Scherer, K.R. (1986). Voice, stress, and emotion. In M.H. Appley & R. Trumbull (Eds.), *Dynamics of stress: Physiological, psychological, and social perspectives.* New York: Plenum.

Schier, M.F., & Carver, C.S. (1987). Dispositional optimism and physical well-being: The influence of generalized outcome expectancies on health. *Journal of Personality, 55,* 169–210.

Schiller, P. (1980). New advances in sex education. In R. Forleo & W. Pasini (Eds.), *Medical sexology* (pp. 466–476). Littleton, MA: PSG Publishing.

Schlesier-Stropp, B. (1984). Bulimia: A review of the literature. *Psychological Bulletin, 95,* 247–257.

Schlesinger, H.J., Mumford, E., & Glass, G.V. (1980). Mental health services and medical utilization. In G. Vandenbos (Ed.), *Psychotherapy: From practice to research to policy* (pp. 71–102). Beverly Hills, CA: Sage.

Schmall, V.L., & Pratt, C. (1986). Special friends: Elders and pets. *Generations, 10,* 44–45.

Schnall, P.L., Pieper, C., Schwartz, J.E., Karasek, R.A., Schlussel, Y., Devereux, R.B., Ganau, A., Alderman, M., Warren, K., & Pickering, T.G. (1990). The relationship between "job strain," workplace diastolic blood pressure, and left ventricular mass index. *Journal of the American Medical Association, 263,* 1929–1935.

Schneider, J.A., O'Leary, A., & Agras, W.S. (1987). The role of perceived self-efficacy in recovery from bulimia: A preliminary examination. *Behavioral Research and Therapy, 25,* 429–432.

Schneiderman, N., Antoni, M.H., Ironson, G., LaPerriere, A., & Fletcher, M.A. (1992). Applied psychological science and HIV-1 spectrum disease. *Applied & Preventive Psychology, 1,* 67–82.

Schneiderman, N., Chesney, M.A., & Krantz, D.S. (1988). Biobehavioral aspects of cardiovascular disease: Progress and prospects. *Health Psychology, 8,* 649–676.

Schottenfeld, D. (1979). Alcohol as a co-factor in the etiology of cancer. *Cancer, 43,* 1962–1966.

Schroeder, D.H., & Costa, P.T., Jr. (1984). Influence of life events stress on physical illness: Substantive effects or methodological flaws? *Journal of Personality and Social Psychology, 46,* 853–863.

Schuckit, M.A. (1985). Genetics and the risk for alcoholism. *Journal of the American Medical Association, 254,* 2614–2617.

Schulz, R., Scheckler, W.E., Girard, C., & Barker, K. (1990). Physician adaptation to health maintenance organizations and implications for management. *Health Services Research, 25,* 43–64.

Schulz, R., Tompkins, C., Wood, D., & Decker, S. (1987). The social psychology of caregiving: The physical and psychological costs of providing support to the disabled. *Journal of Applied Social Psychology, 17,* 401–428.

Schuman, M. (1982). Biofeedback in the management of chronic pain. In J. Barber & C. Adrian (Eds.), *Psychological approaches to the management of pain.* New York: Brunner/Mazel.

Schumm, W.R., & Bugaighis, M.A. (1986). Marital quality over the marital career: Alternative explanations. *Journal of Marriage and the Family, 48,* 165–168.

Schunk, D.H., & Carbonari, J.P. (1984). Self-efficacy models. In J.D. Matarazzo, S.M. Weiss, J.A. Herd, N.E. Miller, & S.M. Weiss, *Behavioral health.* New York: Wiley.

Schwartz, D.M., Thompson, M.G., & Johnson, C.L. (1982). Anorexia nervosa and bulimia: The sociocultural context. *International Journal of Eating Disorders, 1,* 20–36.

Schwartz, G.E. (1982). Testing the biopsychosocial model: The ultimate challenge facing behavioral medicine? *Journal of Consulting and Clinical Psychology, 50,* 1040–1053.

Schwartz, G.E. (1983). Social psychophysiology and behavioral medicine: A systems perspective. In J.T. Cacioppo, R.E. Petty & D. Shapiro (Eds.), *Social psychophysiology: A sourcebook* (pp. 592–608). New York: Guilford.

Schwartz, G.E. (1984). Psychobiology of health: A new synthesis. In B.L. Hammonds & C.J. Scheirer (Eds.), *Psychology and health: The master lecture series* (Vol. 3, pp. 149–193). Washington, DC: American Psychological Association.

Schwartz, G.E., & Weiss, S.M. (1978). Behavioral medicine revisited: An amended definition. *Journal of Behavioral Medicine, 1,* 249–251.

Schwartz, L.B., & Brunzell, J.D. (1981). Increase of adipose tissue lipoprotein lipase activity with weight loss. *Journal of Clinical Investigation*, *67*, 1425–1430.

Schwartz, R.H., Hayden, G.F., Getson, P.R., & DiPaola, A. (1986). Drinking patterns and social consequences: A study of middle-class adolescents in two private pediatric practices. *Pediatrics*, *77*, 139–143.

Scitovsky, A., Benham, L., & McCall, N. (1979). Use of physician services under two prepaid plans. *Medical Care*, *17*, 441–460.

Scofield, M.E., & Frank, J. (1989). Corporate barriers to mind-body strategies. Special Issue: Mind-body health at work. *Advances*, *6*, 41–46.

Seamans, J.H., & Langworthy, O.R. (1938). Observations on the neurophysiology of sexual function in the male cat. *Journal of Urology*, *40*, 836.

Searles, J.S. (1988). The role of genetics in the pathogenesis of alcoholism. *Journal of Abnormal Psychology*, *97*, 153–167.

Sears, S.J., & Milburn, J. (1990). School-age stress. In L.E. Arnold (Ed.), *Childhood stress* (pp. 223–246). New York: John Wiley & Sons.

Seeman, J. (1989). Toward a model of positive health. *American Psychologist*, *44*, 1099–1109.

Seifter, E., Rettura, G., Padawer, J., & Fryburg, D. (1983). Nutritional and other agents modify the stress component of tumor growth. *Advances*, *1*, 12–17.

Seliger, S. (1986). Stress can be good for you. In M.G. Walraven & H.E. Fitzgerald (Eds.), *Annual editions: Psychology 86/87*. Guildford, CT: Dushkin.

Seligman, M.E.P. (1975). *Helplessness: On depression, development, and death*. San Francisco: Freeman.

Selye, H. (1956). *The stress of life*. New York: McGraw-Hill.

Selye, H. (1974). *Stress without distress*. Philadelphia: Lippincott.

Selye, H. (1976). *Stress in health and disease*. Reading, MA: Butterworth.

Selye, H. (1979). *The stress of my life: A scientist's memoirs*. New York: Van Nostrand Reinhold.

Selye, H. (1985). History and present status of the stress concept. In A. Monat & R.S. Lazarus (Eds.), *Stress and coping* (2nd ed.). New York: Columbia University.

Selwyn, P.A. (1986). AIDS—What is now known. Psychological aspects, treatment prospects. *Hospital Practice*, *21*, 125.

Severson, H.H., & Lichtenstein, E. (1986). Smoking prevention programs for adolescents: Rationale and review. In N.A. Krasnegor, J.D. Arasteh, & M.F. Cataldo (Eds.), *Child health behavior: A behavioral pediatrics perspective*. New York: Wiley.

Shanfield, S.B. (1990). Return to work after an acute myocardial infarction: A review. *Heart and Lung*, *19*, 109–117.

Shangold, M.M. (1979). The health care of physicians: Do as I say and not as I do. *Journal of Medical Education*, *54*, 668.

Shapiro, D.H. (1985). Meditation and behavioral medicine: Application of a self-regulation strategy to the clinical management of stress. In S.R. Burchfield (Ed.), *Stress: Psychological and physiological interactions*. Washington, DC: Hemisphere.

Shapiro, D., & Goldstein, I.B. (1982). Biobehavioral perspectives on hypertension. *Journal of Consulting and Clinical Psychology*, *50*, 841–858.

Shaw, L., & Ehrlich, A. (1987). Relaxation training as a treatment for chronic pain caused by ulcerative colitis. *Pain*, *29*, 287–293.

Shedler, J., & Block, J. (1990). Adolescent drug use and psychological health. *American Psychologist*, *45*, 612–630.

Shiels, J.F., Young, G.J., & Rubin, R.J. (1992). O Canada: Do we expect too much from its health system? *Health Affairs*, *11*, 7–20.

Shekelle, R.B., Gale, M., & Norusis, M. (1985). Type A score (Jenkins Activity Survey) and risk of recurrent coronary heart disease in the Aspirin Myocardial Infarction Study. *American Journal of Cardiology*, *56*, 221–225.

Shekelle, R.B., Hulley, S.B., Neaton, J.D., Billings, J.H., Borhani, N.O., Gerace, T.A., Jacobs, D.R., Lasser, N.L., Mittelmark, M.B., & Stamler, J. (1985). The MRFIT Behavior Pattern Study: II. Type A behavior and incidence of heart disease. *American Journal of Epidemiology*, *122*, 559–570.

Shekelle, R.B., Raynor, W.J., Ostfield, A.M., Garron, D.C., Bieliauskas, L.A., Liu, S.C., Maliza, C., & Paul, O. (1981). Psychological depression and 17-year risk of death from cancer. *Psychosomatic Medicine*, *43*, 117–125.

Shelton, J.L., & Levy, R.L. (1981). *Behavioral assignments and treatment compliance: A handbook of clinical strategies*. Champaign, IL: Research Press.

Shepard, D.S., Forster, S.B., Stason, W.B., Solomon, H.S., McArdle, P.J., & Gallagher, S.S. (1979, April). *Cost-effectiveness of intervention to improve compliance with anti-hypertensive therapy*. Paper presented at the National Conference on High Blood Pressure Control, Washington, DC.

Sher, K.J., & Levinson, R.W. (1982). Risk for alcoholism and individual differences in the stress-response-dampening effect of alcohol. *Journal of Abnormal Psychology*, *91*, 350–367.

Sherr, L., Palmer, C., Goldmeier, D., & Green, J. (1986). AIDS information. *Lancet*, *ii*, 1040.

Sheridan, E.P., Matarazzo, J.D., Boll, T.J., Perry, N.W., Jr., Weiss, S.M., & Belar, C.D. (1988). Postdoctoral education and training for clinical service providers in health psychology. *Health Psychology, 7,* 1–17.

Sherr, L. (1990). Fear arousal and AIDS: Do shock tactics work? *AIDS, 4,* 361–364.

Schneidman, E.S. (1987). A psychological approach to suicide. In G.R. VandenBos & B.K. Bryant (Eds.), *Cataclysms, crises, and catastrophes: Psychology in action.* Washington, DC: American Psychological Association.

Shopland, D.R., & Brown, C. (1985). Changes in cigarette smoking prevalence in the U.S.: 1955 to 1983. *Annals of Behavioral Medicine, 7,* 5–8.

Shumacher, S. (1977). Effectiveness of sex therapy. In R. Gemme & C.C. Wheeler (Eds.), *Progress in sexology* (pp. 141–151). New York: Plenum.

Shumaker, S.A., & Czajkowski, S.M. (Eds.). (1991). *Social support and cardiovascular disease.* New York: Plenum.

Shumaker, S.A., & Hill, D.R. (1991). Gender differences in social support and physical health. *Health Psychology, 10,* 102–111.

Shuval, J., Antonovsky, A., & Davies, A.M. (1973). Illness: A mechanism for coping with failure. *Social Science and Medicine, 7,* 259–265.

Siegal, M. (1988). Children's knowledge of contagion and contamination as causes of illness. *Child Development, 59,* 1353–1359.

Siegel, J.M. (1984). Anger and cardiovascular risk in adolescents. *Health Psychology, 3,* 293–313.

Siegel, J.M. (1992). Anger and cardiovascular health. In H.S. Friedman, *Hostility, coping, and health* (pp. 49–64). Washington, DC: American Psychological Association.

Siegel, J.M., Johnson, J.H., & Sarason, I.G. (1979). Life changes and menstrual discomfort. *Journal of Human Stress, 5,* 41–46.

Siegel, K., Mesagno, F.P., Chen, J.Y., & Christ, G. (1987, June). *Factors distinguishing homosexual males practicing safe and risky sex.* Paper presented at the Third International Conference on AIDS, Washington, DC.

Siegel, S., & Ellsworth, D.W. (1986). Pavlovian conditioning and death from apparent overdose of medically prescribed morphine: A case report. *Bulletin of the Psychonomic Society, 24,* 278–280.

Siegler, I. (1989). Developmental health psychology. In G.R. VandenBos & M. Storandt (Eds.), *The adult years: Continuity and change* (pp. 119–142). Washington, DC: American Psychological Association.

Siegler, I.C., & Costa, P.T. (1985). Health behavior relationships. In J.E. Birren & K.W. Schaie (Eds.), *Handbook of the psychology of aging* (2nd ed), pp. 144–166. New York: Van Nostrand.

Siegman, A.W., Dembroski, T.M., & Ringel, N. (1987). Components of hostility and the severity of coronary artery disease. *Psychosomatic Medicine, 49,* 127–135.

Silber, S.J. (1980). *How to get pregnant.* NY: Charles Scribner's Sons.

Siller, J.A., Chipman, A., Ferguson, L., & Vann, D.H. (1967). *Studies in reaction of disability: Vol. II. Attitudes of the nondisabled toward the physically disabled.* New York: New York University, School of Education.

Siller, J.A., Ferguson, L.T., Vann, D.G., & Holland, B. (1967). *Studies in reactions to disability XII: Structure of attitudes toward the physically disabled.* New York: New York University, School of Education.

Silver, B.V., & Blanchard, E.G. (1978). Biofeedback and relaxation training in the treatment of psychophysiological disorders: Or are the machines really necessary? *Journal of Behavioral Medicine, 1,* 217–239.

Silver, R.L., & Wortman, C.B. (1980). Coping with undesirable life events. In J. Garber & M.E.P. Seligman (Eds.), *Human helplessness: Theory and applications.* New York: Academic.

Sime, W.E. (1984). Psychological benefits of exercise. In J.D. Matarazzo, S.M. Weiss, J.A. Herd, N.E. Miller, & S.M. Weiss (Eds.), *Behavioral health.* New York: Wiley.

Simon, E.P. (1991). Interim home care meets both patient and hospital needs. *Picker/Commonwealth Report, 1,* 7.

Simone, C.B. (1983). *Cancer and nutrition.* New York: McGraw-Hill.

Simons-Morton, B.G., Brink, S., & Bates, D. (1987). Effectiveness and cost-effectiveness of persuasive communications and incentives in increasing safety belt use. *Health Education Quarterly, 14,* 167–179.

Sims, E.A.H. (1974). Studies in human hyperphagia. In G. Bray & J. Bethune (Eds.), *Treatment and management of obesity.* New York: Harper & Row.

Sims, E.A.H. (1976). Experimental obesity, dietary-induced thermogenesis, and their clinical implications. *Clinics in Endocrinology and Metabolism, 5,* 377–395.

Sims, E.A.H., & Horton, E.S. (1968). Endocrine and metabolic adaptation to obesity and starvation. *American Journal of Clinical Nutrition, 21,* 1455–1470.

Singer, J.E., Lundberg, U., & Frakenhaeuser, M. (1978). Stress on the train: A study of urban commuting. In A. Baum, J.E. Singer, & S. Valins (Eds.), *Advances in environmental psychology* (Vol. 1, pp. 41–56). Hillsdale, NJ: Erlbaum.

Sisson, R.W., & Azrin, N.H. (1986). Family-member involvement to initiate and promote treatment of problem drinkers. *Journal of Behavior Therapy and Experimental Psychiatry, 17*, 15–21.

Skelton, J.A. (1980, August). *Symptomatic experience and judgments of the health-relevance of verbal stimuli.* Paper presented at the annual meeting of the American Psychological Association, Montreal.

Skelton, J.A., & Pennebaker, J.W. (1978, August). *Dispositional determinants of symptom reporting: Correlational evidence.* Paper presented at the annual meeting of the American Psychological Association, Toronto.

Skelton, J.A., & Pennebaker, J.W. (1982). The psychology of physical symptoms and sensations. In J. Sanders and J. Suls (Eds.), *The social psychology of health and illness.* Hillsdale, NJ: Erlbaum.

Skelton, M., & Dominian, J. (1973). Psychological stress in wives of patients with myocardial infarction. *British Medical Journal, 2*, 101.

Skinner, B.F. (1953). *Science and human behavior.* New York: Macmillan.

Skinner, H.A., Jackson, D.N., & Hoffman, H. (1984). Alcoholic personality types: Identification and correlates. *Journal of Abnormal Psychology, 83*, 658–666.

Sklar, L.S., & Anisman, H. (1981). Stress and cancer. *Psychological Bulletin, 89*, 369–406.

Skoraszewski, M.J., Ball, J.D., & Mikulka, P. (1991). Neuropsychological functioning of HIV-infected males. *Journal of Clinical and Experimental Neuropsychology, 13*, 278–290.

Skov, P., Valbjorn, O., Pederson, Bo-V., Gravesen, S., et al. (1990). Influence of indoor climate on the sick building syndrome in an office environment. *Scandinavian Journal of Work, Environment, and Health, 16*, 363–371. (From *Psychological Abstracts, 1991, 78*, Abstract No. 10437)

Sloand, E.M., Pitt, E., Chiarello, R.J., & Nemo, G.J. (1991). HIV testing: State of the art. *Journal of the American Medical Association, 266*, 2861–2866.

Slochower, J.A. (1983). *Excessive eating: The role of emotions and environment.* New York: Human Sciences.

Slochower, J., Kaplan, S.P., & Mann, L. (1981). The effects of life stress and weight on mood and eating. *Appetite, 2*, 115–125.

Smart, R.G. (1976). Spontaneous recovery in alcoholics: A review and analysis of the available research. *Drug and Alcohol Dependence, 1*, 277–285.

Smith, A. (1981). Principles underlying human brain functions in neuropsychological sequelae of different neuropathological processes. In S.B. Filskov & T.J. Boll (Eds.), *Handbook of clinical neuropsychology* (pp. 175–226). New York: John Wiley & Sons.

Smith, A.A., Knight, J., & Eveline, B. (1990). The abilities of very low-birth-weight children and

their classroom controls. *Developmental Medicine and Child Neurology, 32*, 590–601.

Smith, C.T. (1985). Health care delivery system changes: A special challenge for teaching hospitals. *Journal of Medical Education, 60*, 1–8.

Smith, G.P. (1984). Gut hormone hypothesis of postprandial satiety. In A.J. Stunkard & E. Stellar (Eds.), *Eating and its disorders.* New York: Plenum.

Smith, G.S., & Kraus, J.F. (1988). Alcohol and residential, recreational, and occupational injuries: A review of the epidemiologic evidence. In L. Breslow, J.E. Fielding, & L.B. Lave (Eds.), *Annual review of public health* (Vol. 9). Palo Alto, CA: Annual Reviews.

Smith, M., Colligan, M., Horning, R.W., & Hurrel, J. (1978). *Occupational comparison of stress-related disease incidence.* Cincinnati: National Institute for Occupational Safety and Health.

Smith, M.C. (1985). The cost of noncompliance and the capacity of improved compliance to reduce health care expenditures. In *Improving medication compliance: Proceedings of a symposium.* Reston, VA: National Pharmaceutical Council.

Smith, R.E., & Nye, S.L. (1989). Comparison of induced affect and covert rehearsal in the acquisition of stress management coping skills. *Journal of Counseling Psychology, 36*, 17–23.

Smith, R.G. (1970). Personality and smoking: A review of the empirical literature. In W.A. Hunt (Ed.), *Learning mechanisms in smoking.* Chicago: Aldine.

Smith, R.P., Woodward, N.J., Wallston, B.S., Wallston, K.A., Rye, P., & Zylstra, M. (1988). Health care implications of desire and expectancy for control in elderly adults. *Journals of Gerontology, 43*, P1-P7.

Smith, T.W. (1989). Interactions, transactions, and the Type A pattern: Additional avenues in the search for coronary-prone behavior. In A.W. Siegman & T.M. Dembroski (Eds.), *In search of coronary-prone behavior: Beyond Type A* (pp. 91–116). Hillsdale, NJ: Erlbaum.

Smith, T.W., & Frohm, K.D. (1985). What's so unhealthy about hostility? Construct validity and psychosocial correlates of the Cook and Medley HO scale. *Health Psychology, 4*, 503–520.

Smith, T.W., Turner, C.W., Ford, M.H., Hunt, S.C., Barlow, G.K., Stults, B.M., & Williams, R.R. (1987). Blood pressure reactivity in adult male twins. *Health Psychology, 6*, 209–220.

Smyer, M.A., McHale, S.M., Birkel, R., & Madle, R.A. (1988). Impairments, handicapping environments, and disability: A life-span perspective. In V.B. Van Hasselt, P.S. Strain, & M. Hersen, *Handbook of developmental and physical disabilities.* New York: Pergamon.

Sobal, J., & Stunkard, A.J. (1989). Socioeconomic status and obesity: A review of the literature. *Psychological Bulletin, 105*, 260–275.

Sobel, D.S. (1990). The placebo effect: Using the body's own healing mechanisms. In R. Ornstein & C. Swencionis (Eds.), *The healing brain: A scientific reader* (pp. 63–74). New York: Guilford.

Sobell, M.B., & Sobell, L.C. (1973). Individualized behavior therapy for alcoholics. *Behavior Therapy, 4,* 49–72.

Sobell, M.B., & Sobell, L.C. (1978). *Behavioral treatment of alcohol problems: Individualized therapy for controlled drinking.* New York: Plenum.

Solomon, G.F. (1985). The emerging field of psychoneuroimmunology with a special note on AIDS. *Advances, 2,* 6–19.

Solomon, G.F., & Temoshok, L. (1987). A psychoneuroimmunologic perspective on AIDS research: Questions, preliminary findings, and suggestions. Special Issue: Acquired Immune Deficiency Syndrome (AIDS). *Journal of Applied Social Psychology, 17,* 286–308.

Sommers, F.G. (1980). Treatment of male sexual dysfunction in a psychiatric practice integrating the sexual therapy practitioner (surrogate). In R. Forleo & W. Pasini (Eds.), *Medical sexology* (pp. 593–598). Littleton, MA: PSG Publishing.

Sommers-Flanagan, J., & Greenberg, R.P. (1989). Psychosocial variables and hypertension: A new look at an old controversy. *Journal of Nervous and Mental Disease, 177,* 15–24.

Sorbi, M., Tellegen, B., & du Long, A. (1989). Long-term effects of training in relaxation and stress-coping in patients with migraine: A 3-year follow-up. *Headache, 29,* 111–121.

Sorensen, G., Pechacek, T., & Pallonen, U. (1986). Occupational and worksite norms and attitudes about smoking cessation. *American Journal of Public Health, 76,* 544–549.

Sorensen, G., Jacobs, D.R., Pirie, P., Folsom, A., Luepker, R., & Gillum, R. (1987). Relationships among Type A behavior, employment experiences, and gender: The Minnesota Heart Survey. *Journal of Behavioral Medicine, 10,* 323–336.

Sorenson, J.L., & Guydish, J.R. (1991). Adopting effective interventions. In J.L. Sorenson, L.A. Wermuth, D.R. Gibson, K.H. Choi, J.R. Guydish, & S.L. Batki (Eds.), *Preventing AIDS in drug users and their sexual partners.* New York: Guilford.

Sorlie, P., Gordon, T., & Kannel, W.B. (1980). Body build and mortality—the Framingham study. *Journal of the American Medical Association, 243,* 1828–1831.

Sours, J.A. (1980). *Starving to death in a sea of objects: The anorexia nervosa syndrome.* New York: Aronson.

Spear, J.E. (1987). Comparing the triple allergenic theory with a core belief/maladaptive solution approach to emotional problems. *Medical Hypnoanalysis Journal, 2,* 75–81.

Speisman, J.C., Lazarus, R.S., Mordkoff, A., Davison, L. (1964). Experimental demonstration of stress based on ego-defense theory. *Journal of Abnormal and Social Psychology, 68,* 367–380.

Spence, S.H. (1989). Cognitive-behavioral therapy in the management of chronic occupational pain of the upper limits. *Behaviour Research & Therapy, 27,* 435–446.

Sperry, L. (1984). Nutritional perspectives in wellness medicine: A primer for health and mental health professionals. *Individual Psychology: A Journal of Adlerian Theory, Research, and Practice, 40,* 384–400.

Spiegel, D. (1991). A psychosocial intervention and survival time of patients with metastatic breast cancer. *Advances, 7,* 10–19.

Spiegel, D., Bloom, J., Kraemer, H.C., & Gottheil, E. (1989). Effect of psychosocial treatment on survival of patients with metastatic breast cancer. *Lancet, 2,* 888–891.

Sprafka, J.M., Folsom, A.R., Burke, G.L., Hahn L.P., & Pirie, P. (1990). Type A behavior and its association with cardiovascular disease prevalence in Blacks and Whites: The Minnesota Heart Survey. *Journal of Behavioral Medicine, 13,* 1–13.

Springer, K.J. (1981). Effectiveness of treatment of sexual dysfunction: Review and evaluation. *Journal of Sex Education and Therapy, 7,* 18–22.

Srole, L. (1972). Urbanization and mental health: Some reformulations. *American Scientist, 60,* 576–583.

Sroufe, L.A. (1979). Socioemotional development. In J. Osofsky (Ed.), *Handbook of infant development.* New York: Wiley.

Stall, R.D., Coates, T.J., & Hoff, C. (1988). Behavioral risk reduction for HIV infection among gay and bisexual men. *American Psychologist, 43,* 878–885.

Stall, R.D., Ekstrand, M., Pollack, L., McKusick, L., & Coates, T.J. (1990). Relapse from safer sex: The next challenge for AIDS prevention efforts. *Journal of Acquired Immune Deficiency Syndrome, 3,* 1181–1187.

Stall, R.D., Wiley, J.A., McKusick, L., Coates, T.J., & Ostrow, D. (1986). Alcohol and drug use during sexual activity and compliance with safe sex guidelines for AIDS: The AIDS Behavioral Research Project. *Health Education Quarterly, 13,* 359–371.

Stamler, J. (1985a). Coronary heart disease: Doing the "right thing." *New England Journal of Medicine, 312,* 1053–1055.

Stamler, J. (1985b). The marked decline in coronary heart disease mortality rates in the United States, 1968–1981: Summary of findings and possible explanations. *Cardiology, 72,* 11–22.

Stamler, J., Farinaro, E., Mojonnier, L.M., Hall, Y., Moss, D., & Stamler, R. (1980). Prevention and control of hypertension by nutritional-hygiene means. *Journal of the American Medical Association, 243*, 1819–1823.

Stanwyck, D.J., & Anson, C.A. (1986). Is personality related to illness? Cluster Profiles of aggregated data. *Advances, 3*, 4–15.

Starfield, B. (1991). Primary care and health. A cross-national comparison. *Journal of the American Medical Association, 266*, 2268–2271.

Starfield, B., Katz, H., Gabriel, A., Livingston, G., Benson, P., Hankin, J., Horn, S., & Steinwachs, D. (1984). Morbidity in childhood—a longitudinal view. *The New England Journal of Medicine, 310*, 824–829.

Stark, M.J. (1992). Dropping out of substance abuse treatment: A clinically oriented review. *Clinical Psychology Review, 12*, 93–116.

Starr, P. (1982). *The social transformation of American medicine.* New York: Basic Books.

Stason, W., Neff, R., Miettinen, O., & Jick, H. (1976). Alcohol consumption and nonfatal myocardial infarction. *American Journal of Epidemiology, 104*, 603–608.

Steig, R.L., & Williams, R.C. (1983). Cost effectiveness study of multidisciplinary pain treatment of industrial-injured workers. *Seminars in Neurology, 3*, 370–376.

Steiger, H. (1976). Understanding the psychologic factors in rehabilitation. *Geriatrics, 31*, 68–73.

Stein, J.A., Newcomb, M.D., & Bentler, P.M. (1987). An 8-year study of multiple influences on drug use and drug use consequences. *Journal of Personality and Social Psychology, 53*, 1094–1105.

Stein, M. (1982a). Stress, brain, and immune function. *The Gerontologist, 22*, 203.

Stein, M. (1982b). Biophychosocial factors in asthma. In L.J. West & M. Stein (Eds.), *Critical issues in behavioral medicine* (pp. 159–182). Philadelphia: J.B. Lippencott.

Stein, M., Schiavi, R., & Camerino, M. (1976). Influence of brain and behavior on the immune system. *Science, 191*, 435–440.

Steinbrook, R., (1988, December 6). AIDS slowdown in 3 key cities seen. *Los Angeles Times*, p. 1.

Stern, J.S. (1984). Is obesity a disease of inactivity? In A.J. Stunkard & E. Stellar (Eds.), *Eating and its disorders.* New York: Raven.

Sternberg, D.E. (1989). Dual diagnosis: Addiction and affective disorders. *Psychiatric Hospital, 20*, 71–77.

Sterns, H.L., Barrett, G.V., & Alexander, R.A. (1985). Accidents and the aging individual. In J.E. Birren & K.W. Schaie (Eds.), *Handbook of the psychology of aging.* New York: Van Nostrand Reinhold.

Stevens, J.H., Turner, C.W., Rhodewalt, F., & Talbot, S. (1984). The Type-A behavior pattern and carotid artery atherosclerosis. *Psychosomatic Medicine, 46*, 105–113.

Stevenson, D.D. (1991). Allergy and headache. *Headache Quarterly, 2*, 9–16.

Stewart, M., & Roter D. (1989). Introduction. In M. Stewart & D. Roter (Eds.), *Communicating with medical patients.* Beverly Hills, CA: Sage.

Stiles, W.B., Putnam, S.M., James, S.A., & Wolf, M.H. (1979a). Dimensions of patient and physician roles in medical screening interviews. *Social Science and Medicine, 13A*, 335–341.

Stiles, W.B., Putnam, S.M., Wolf, M.H., & James, S.A. (1979b). Interaction exchange structure and patient satisfaction with medical interviews. *Medical Care, 17*, 667–681.

Stokols, D., & Novaco, R. (1981). Transportation and well-being: An ecological perspective. In I. Altman, J. Wohlwill, & P. Everett (Eds.), *Human behavior and environment: Advances in theory and research.* New York: Plenum.

Stone, A.A. (1987). Evidence that secretory IgA antibody is associated with daily mood. *Journal of Personality and Social Psychology, 52*, 988–993.

Stone, G.C. (1979a). Health and the health system: A historical overview and conceptual framework. In G.C. Stone, F. Cohen, & N.E. Adler, (Eds.), *Health psychology—A handbook* (pp. 1–17). San Francisco: Jossey-Bass.

Stone, G.C. (1979b). Patient compliance and the role of the expert. *Journal of Social Issues, 35*, 34–59.

Stone, G.C. (1982). *Health Psychology:* A new journal for a new field. *Health Psychology, 1*, 1–6.

Stone, G.C. (Ed.). (1983). National Working Conference on Education and Training in Health Psychology [Special Issue]. *Health Psychology, 2* (Suppl.).

Straus, M.B. (Ed.), (1968). *Familiar medical quotations.* Boston: Little, Brown.

Strecher, V.J., DeVellis, B.M., Becker, M.H., & Rosenstock, I.M. (1986). The role of self-efficacy in achieving health behavior change. *Health Education Quarterly, 13*, 73–92.

Strickland, B.R. (1978). Internal-external expectatancies and health-related behaviors. *Journal of Consulting and Clinical Psychology, 46*, 1192–1211.

Striegel-Moore, R., & Rodin, J. (1985). Prevention of obesity. In J.C. Rosen & L.J. Solomon (Eds.), *Prevention in health psychology.* Hanover, NH: University Press of New England.

Striegel-Moore, R., Silberstein, L.R., & Rodin, L.R. (1986). Toward an understanding of risk factors for bulimia. *American Psychologist, 41*, 246–263.

Stroebel, C.F., & Glueck, B.C. (1976). Psychophysiological rationale for the application of biofeedback in the alleviation of pain. In M. Weisenberg & B. Tursky (Eds.), *Pain: New perspectives in therapy and research.* New York: Plenum.

Strong, C.A. (1895). The psychology of pain. *Psychological Review, 2*, 329–347.

Strong, J., Cramond, T., Maas, F. (1989). The effectiveness of relaxation techniques with patients who have chronic low back pain. *Occupational Therapy Journal of Research, 9,* 184–192.

Stroufe, L.A., Fox, N.E., & Pancake, V.R. (1983). Attachment and dependency in a developmental perspective. *Child Development, 54,* 1615–1627.

Strubbe, J.H., Steffens, A.B., & deRuiter, L. (1975). Plasma insulin and the time pattern of feeding in the rat. *Physiology and Behavior, 18,* 81–86.

Stuart, F.M., Hammond, D.C., & Pett, M.A. (1987). Inhibited sexual desire in women. *Archives of Sexual Behavior, 16,* 91–106.

Stuart, R.B. (1967). Behavioral control of overeating. *Behavior Research and Therapy, 5,* 357–365.

Stunkard, A.J. (1979). Behavioral medicine and beyond: The example of obesity. In O.F. Pomerleau & J.P. Brady (Eds.), *Behavorial medicine: Theory and practice* (pp. 279–298). Baltimore, MD: Williams & Wilkins.

Stunkard, A.J. (1986). Childhood obesity. *Science, 232,* 20–21.

Stunkard, A.J. (1987). Conservative treatments for obesity. *American Journal of Clinical Nutrition, 45,* 1142–1154.

Stunkard, A.J. (1988). Some perspectives on human obesity: Its causes. *Bulletin of the New York Academy of Medicine, 64,* 902–923.

Stunkard, A.J., Cohen, R.Y., & Felix, M.R. (1989). Weight loss competitions at the worksite: How they work and how well. *Preventive Medicine, 18,* 460–474.

Stunkard, A.J., Harris, J.R., Pedersen, N.L., & McClearn, G.E. (1990). The body-mass index of twins who have been reared apart. *New England Journal of Medicine, 322,* 1483–1487.

Stunkard, A.J., & Mahoney, M.J. (1976). Behavioral treatment of the eating disorders. In H. Lutenberg (Ed.), *Handbood of behavior modification and behavioral therapy.* Englewood Cliffs, NJ: Prentice-Hall.

Sue, D. (1979). Erotic fantasies of college students during coitus. *Journal of Sex Research, 15,* 229–305.

Sullivan, D.F. (1974). Conceptual problems in developing an index of health. *Vital and Health Statistics,* Series 2, No. 17. (DHEW Publication No. HRA 74–1017). Washington, DC: U.S. Government Printing Office.

Suls, J., & Mullen, B. (1981). Life changes and psychological distress: The role of perceived control and desirability. *Journal of Applied Social Psychology, 11,* 379–389.

Suls, J., & Rittenhouse, J.D. (1987). Personality and health: An introduction. *Journal of Personality, 55,* 155–167.

Suls, J. & Rittenhouse, J.D. (1990). Models of linkages between personality and disease. In H. Friedman (Ed.), *Personality and disease.* New York: Wiley.

Suls, J., & Sanders, G.S. (1989). Why do some behavioral styles place people at coronary risk? In A. Siegman & T. Dembroski (Eds.), *In search of coronary-prone behavior: Beyond Type A* (pp. 1–20). Hillsdale, NJ: Erlbaum.

Suls, J., Sanders, G.S., & Lebrecque, M.S. (1986). Attempting to control blood pressure without systematic instruction: When advice is counterproductive. *Journal of Behavorial Medicine, 9,* 567–578.

Suls, J., & Wan, C.K. (1989). Effects of sensory and procedural information on coping with stressful medical procedures and pain: A meta-analysis. *Journal of Consulting and Clinical Psychology, 57,* 372–379.

Sundet, K., Finset, A., & Reinvang, I. (1988). Neuropsychological predictors in stroke rehabilitation. *Journal of Clinical and Experimental Neuropsychology, 10,* 363–379.

Sundstrom, E. (1978). Crowding as a sequential process: Review of research on the effects of population density on humans. In A. Baum & Y.M. Epstein (Eds.), *Human response to crowding.* Hillsdale, NJ: Erlbaum.

Sundstrom, E. (1986). *Work places: The psychology of the physical environment in offices and factories.* New York: Cambridge.

Surgeon General's Report on Nutrition and Health (1988). (Public Health Service Pub. No. 88–50210). Washington, DC: U.S. Dept. of Health and Human Services.

Surwit, R.S., & Feinglos, M.N. (1988). Stress and autonomic nervous system in Type II diabetes: A hypothesis. *Diabetes Care, 11,* 83–85.

Surwit, R.S., Feinglos, M.N., & Scovern, A.W. (1983). Diabetes and behavior: A paradigm for health psychology. *American Psychologist, 38,* 255–262.

Svanum, S., & Schladenhauffen, J. (1986). Lifetime and recent alcohol consumption among male alcoholics. *Journal of Nervous and Mental Diseases, 17,* 214–220.

Svarstad, B., (1976). Physician-patient communication and patient conformity with medical advice. In D. Mechanic (Ed.), *The growth of bureaucratic medicine.* New York: Wiley.

Swain, M.A., & Steckel, S.B. (1981). Influencing adherence among hypertensives. *Research in Nursing and Health, 4,* 213–218.

Swan, G.E., Carmelli, D., & Rosenman, R.H. (1986). Spouse-pair similarity on the California Psychological Inventory with reference to husband's coronary heart disease. *Psychosomatic Medicine, 48,* 172–186.

Swanson, B., Bieliauskas, L.A., Kessler, H.A., Zeller, J.M., & Cronin-Stubbs, D. (1991). Infrequent neuropsychological impairment in asymptomatic persons infected with the human immunodeficiency virus. *The Clinical Neuropsychologist, 5,* 183–189.

Syrjala, K.L., & Chapman, C.R. (1984). Measurement of clinical pain: A review and integration of research findings. In C. Benedetti, C.R. Chapman, & G. Moricca (Eds.), *Advances in pain research and therapy: Vol. 7. Recent advances in the management of pain.* New York: Raven.

Szasz, T.S., & Hollender, M.H. (1956). The basic models of the doctor-patient relationship. *Archives of Internal Medicine, 35,* 156–184.

Taggart, P., Gibbons, D., & Sommerville, W. (1969). Some effects of motor-car driving on the normal and abnormal heart. *British Medical Journal, 4,* 130–134.

Tagliacozzo, D.L., & Mauksch, H.O. (1970). The patient's view of the patient's role. In E.G. Jaco (Ed.), *Patients, physicians, and illness* (2nd ed.). New York: Free Press.

Task Force On Psychology and the Handicapped. (1984). Final report of the Task Force on Psychology and the Handicapped. *American Psychology, 39,* 545–550.

Taubman, A.H. (1975). Noncompliance in initial prescription filling. *Apothecary, 9,* 14.

Taylor, C.B., Bandura, A., Ewart, C.K., Miller, N.H., DeBusk, R.F. (1985). Exercise testing to enhance wives' confidence in their husbands' cardiac capability soon after clinically uncomplicated acute myocardial infarction. *American Journal of Cardiology, 55,* 635–638.

Taylor, S.E. (1979). Hospital patient behavior: Reactance, helplessness, or control? *Journal of Social Issues, 35,* 156–184.

Taylor, S.E. (1983). Adjustment to threatening events: A theory of cognitive adaptation. *American Psychologist, 38,* 1161–1173.

Telch, C.F., Agras, W.S., & Rossiter, E.M. (1988). Binge eating increases with increasing adiposity. *International Journal of Eating Disorders, 7,* 115–119.

Telch, C.F., & Telch, M.J. (1985). Psychological approaches for enhancing coping amount cancer patients: A review. *Clinical Psychology Review, 5,* 325–344.

Temoshok, L., Zich, J., Solomon, M.D., & Stites, D.P. (1987, November). An intensive psychoimmunologic study of men with AIDS. Paper presented at the First Research Workshop on the Psychoneuroimmunology of AIDS, Tiburon, CA.

Tennant, C. (1988). Psychosocial causes of duodenal ulcer. *Australian and New Zealand Journal of Psychiatry, 22,* 195–201.

Teshima, H., Nagata, S., Kinara, H., & Sogawa, H. (1986). Psychobiological studies on the onset of allergic diseases: A Japanese approach. *Advances, 3,* 143–149.

Theorell, T., Ahlberg-Hulten, G., Sigala, F., Perski, A., Soderholm, M., Kallner, A., & Eneroth, P. (1990). A psychosocial and biomedical comparison between men in sex contrasting service occupations. *Work and Stress, 4,* 51–63.

Theorell, T., & Rahe, R.H. (1975). Life change events, ballistocardiography, and coronary death. *Journal of Human Stress, 1,* 18–24.

Thompson, D.R., & Meddis, R. (1990). Wives' responses to counseling early after myocardial infarction. *Journal of Psychosomatic Research, 34,* 249–258.

Thompson, E.L. (1978). Smoking education programs 1960–1976. *American Journal of Public Health, 68,* 250–257.

Thompson, J.K., Jarvie, G.J., Lahey, B.B., & Cureton, K.J. (1982). Exercise and obesity: Etiology, physiology, and intervention. *Psychological Bulletin, 91,* 55–78.

Thompson, S.C. (1981). Will it hurt less if I can control it? A complex answer to a simple question. *Psychological Bulletin, 90,* 89–101.

Thompson, S.C., Nanni, C., & Schwankovsky, L. (1990). Patient-oriented interventions to improve communication in a medical visit. *Health Psychology, 9,* 390–404.

Thompson, S.C., Sobolew, S. A., Graham, M.A., & Janigian, A.S. (1989). Psychosocial adjustment following a stroke. *Social Science and Medicine, 28,* 239–247.

Thompson, W.R., & Thompson, D.L. (1987). Effects of exercise compliance on blood lipids in post-myocardial infarction patients. *Journal of Cardiopulmonary Rehabilitation, 7,* 332–341.

Thoresen, C.E., & Kirmil-Gray, K. (1983). Self-management psychology and the treatment of childhood asthma (Pt. 2). *Journal of Allergy and Clinical Immunology, 72,* 596–606.

Thoresen, C.E., & Mahoney, M.J. (1974). *Behavioral self-control.* New York: Holt, Rinehart Winston.

Thoresen, C.E., & Powell, L.H. (1992). Type A behavior pattern: New perspectives on theory, assessment, and intervention. *Journal of Consulting and Clinical Psychology, 60,* 595–604.

Thorndike, E.L. (1898). Animal intelligence. *Psychological Monographs, 1,* (whole No. 8).

Timpe, K.P. (1990). Modern information technologies and the role of psychology in work design. Special Issue: Organisational psychology and the new technologies. *Irish Journal of Psychology, 11,* 157–169.

Tindall, W.N., Beardsley, R.S., & Kimberlin, C.L. (1989). *Communication skills in pharmacy practice.* Philadelphia: Lea and Febiger.

Tischenkel, N.J., Saab, P.G., Schneiderman, N., Nelesen, R.A., Pasin, R. DeC., Goldstein, D.A., Spitzer, S.B., Woo-Ming, R., & Weidler, D.J. (1989). Cardiovascular and neurohumoral responses to behavioral challenge as a function of race and sex. *Health Psychology, 8,* 503–524.

Tobler, N.S. (1986). Meta-analysis of 143 adolescent drug prevention programs: Quantitative outcome results of program participants compared to a control or comparison group. *Journal of Drug Issues, 16,* 537–568.

Tomkins, S.S. (1966). Psychological model for smoking behavior. *American Journal of Public Health, 56* (Suppl. 12), 17–20.

Tomkins, S.S. (1968). A modified model of smoking behavior. In E.F. Borgatta & R.R. Evans (Eds.), *Smoking, health, and behavior.* Chicago: Aldine.

Tompkins, S.S. (1988). Post-stroke depression in primary support persons: Predicting those at risk. *Journal of Consulting and Clinical Psychology, 56,* 502–508.

Tosteson, D.C. (1990). New pathways in general medical education. *New England Journal of Medicine, 322,* 234–238.

Totman, R. (1982). Psychosomatic theories. In J.R. Eiser (Ed.), *Social psychology and behavioral medicine.* New York: Wiley.

Totman, R., Kiff, J., Reed., S.E., & Craig, J.W. (1980). Predicting experimental colds in volunteers from different measures of recent life stress. *Journal of Psychosomatic Research, 24,* 155–163.

Tracey, T.J., Sherry, P., & Keitel, M. (1986). Distress and help-seeking as a function of person-environment fit and self-efficacy: A causal model. *American Journal of Community Psychology, 14,* 657–676.

Travell, J. (1976). Myofascial trigger points: A clinical view. In J.J. Bonica & D. Albe-Fessard (Eds.), *Advances in pain research and therapy* (Vol. 1). New York: Raven.

Trotta, P. (1980). Breast self-examination: Factors influencing compliance. *Oncology Nursing Forum, 7,* 13–17.

Trumbull, R., & Appley, M.H. (1986). A conceptual model for examination of stress dynamics. In M.H. Appley & R. Trumbull (Eds.), *Dynamics of stress: Physiological, psychological, and social perspectives.* New York: Plenum.

Tuckett, H.D., Boulton, M., Olson, C., & Williams, A. (1985). *Meetings between experts: An approach to sharing ideas in medical consultations.* London: Tavistock.

Turk, D.C. (1978). Cognitive behavioral techniques in the management of pain. In J.P. Foreyt & D.P. Rathjen (Eds.), *cognitive behavior therapy.* New York: Plenum.

Turk, D.C., Litt, M.D., Salovey, P., & Walker, J. (1985). Seeking urgent pediatric treatment: Factors contributing to frequency, delay, and appropriateness. *Health Psychology, 4,* 43–59.

Turk, D.C., Meichenbaum, D., & Berman, W.H. (1979). Application of biofeedback for the regulation of pain: A critical review. *Psychological Bulletin, 86,* 1322–1338.

Turk, D.C., Meichenbaum, D., & Genest, M. (1983). *Pain and behavioral medicine: A cognitive-behavioral perspective.* New York: Guilford.

Turk, D.C., Rudy, T.E., & Salovey, P. (1984). Health protection: Attitudes and behaviors in LPNs, teachers, and college students. *Health Psychology, 3,* 189–210.

Turk, D.C., Rudy, T.E., & Salovey, P. (1986). Implicit models of illness. *Journal of Behavorial Medicine, 9,* 453–474.

Turk, D.C., & Speers, M.A. (1983). Diabetes mellitus: A cognitive-functional analysis of stress. In T.G. Burish & L.A. Bradley (Eds.), *Coping with chronic disease: Research and applications.* New York: Academic.

Turk, D.C., Wack, J.T., & Kearns, R.D. (1985). An empirical examination of the "pain-behavior" construct. *Journal of Behavioral Medicine, 8,* 119–130.

Turner, J.A. (1982). Comparison of group progressive-relaxation training and cognition-behavioral group therapy for chronic low back pain. *Journal of Consulting and Clinical Psychology, 50,* 757–765.

Turner, J.A., & Chapman, C.R. (1982a). Psychological interventions for chronic pain: A critical review: I. Relaxation training and biofeedback. *Pain, 12,* 1–21.

Turner, J.A., & Chapman, C.R. (1982b). Psychological interventions for chronic pain: A critical review: II. Operant conditioning, hypnosis, and cognitive-behavior therapy. *Pain, 12,* 23–46.

Turner, J.A., & Clancy, S. (1988). Comparison of operant-behavioral and cognitive-behavorial group treatment for chronic low back pain. *Journal of Consulting and Clinical Psychology, 56,* 261–266.

Turner, J.A., Clancy, S., McQuade, K.J., & Cardenas, D.D. (1990). Effectiveness of behavioral therapy for chronic low back pain: A component analysis. *Journal of Consulting and Clinical Psychology, 58,* 573–579.

Turner, J.A., Herron, L.D., & Pheasant, H.C. (1981). MMPI prediction of outcome following back surgery. *Pain Supplement, 1,* S244 (Abstract).

Turner, J.A., & Romano, J.M. (1984). Evaluating psychologic interventions for chronic pain: Issues and recent developments. In C. Benedetti, C.R. Chapman, & G. Moricca (Eds.), *Advances in pain research and therapy: Vol. 7, Recent advances in the management of pain.* New York: Raven.

Turner, R.J., & McLean, P.D. (1989). Physical disability and psychological distress. *Rehabilitation Psychology, 34,* 225–242.

Tweed, D.L., Shern, D.L., & Ciarlo, J.A. (1988). Disability dependence, and demoralization. *Rehabilitation Psychology, 33,* 143–154.

Tyson, M.E., & Favell, J.E. (1988). Mental retardation in children. In V.B. VanHasselt, P.S. Strain, & M. Hersen (Eds.), *Handbook of developmental and physical disabilities.* New York: Pergamon.

Udvarhelyi, I.S., Jennison, K., Phillips, R.S. & Epstein, A.M. (1991). Comparison of the quality of ambulatory care for fee-for-service and prepaid patients. *Annals of Internal Medicine, 115,* 394–400.

Uhlenberg, P., & Meyers, M.A.P. (1981). Divorce and the elderly. *Gerontologist, 21,* 276–282.

U.S. Bureau of the Census (1975). *Historical statistics of the United States, colonial times to 1970, Part 1.* Washington, DC: U.S. Government Printing Office.

U.S. Bureau of the Census (1983). *America in transition: An aging society* (Current Population Reports, Series P-23, No. 128). Washington, DC: U.S. Government Printing Office.

U.S. Bureau of the Census (1985). *Statistical abstracts of the United States, 1986* (106th ed.). Washington, DC: U.S. Government Printing Office.

U.S. Bureau of the Census (1986). *Statistics.* Washington, DC: U.S. Government Printing Office.

U.S. Bureau of the Census (1989). *Statistical abstract of the United States, 1989.* Washington, DC: U.S. Government Printing Office.

U.S. Bureau of the Census (1990). *Statistical abstract of the United States, 1990.* Washington, DC: U.S. Government Printing Office.

USDHEW (U.S. Dept. of Health, Education, and Welfare, 1979a). *Healthy people: Surgeon General's report on health promotion and disease prevention* (Publication No. PHS 79–55071). Washington, D.C.: U.S. Government Printing Office.

USDHEW (U.S. Dept. of Health, Education, and Welfare, 1979b). *Smoking and health: A report of the Surgeon General* (Publication No. PHS 79–50066). Washington, D.C.: U.S. Government Printing Office.

U.S. Department of Health, Education, and Welfare and U.S. Public Health Service, Center for Disease Control (1964). *Smoking and health: Report of the advisory committee to the Surgeon General of the Public Health Service* (Pub. No. 1103). Washington, DC: U.S. Government Printing Office.

USDHHS (U.S. Dept. of Health and Human Services, 1981). *Alcohol and health.* Rockville, MD: National Institute on Alcohol Abuse and Alcoholism.

USDHHS (U.S. Dept. of Health and Human Services, 1982). *Prevention `82.* (Publication No. 82–50157). Washington, DC: U.S. Government Printing Office.

USDHHS (U.S. Dept. of Health and Human Services, 1984). *The 1984 Report of the Joint National Committee on Detection, Evaluation, and Treatment of High Blood Pressure.* (Publication No. NIH 84–108.) Washington, DC: U.S. Government Printing Office.

USDHHS (U.S. Dept. of Health and Human Services, 1985). *Charting the nation's health: Trends since 1960* (Publication No. PHS 85–1251). Washington, DC: U.S. Government Printing Office.

USDHHS (U.S. Dept. of Health and Human Services, 1986a). *Prevalence of selected chronic conditions: United States, 1979–81* (Publication No. PHS 86–1583). Washington, DC: U.S. Government Printing Office.

USDHHS (U.S. Dept. of Health and Human Services, 1986b). *Coping with AIDS: Psychological and social considerations in helping people with HTLV-III infection* (Publication No. 85–1432). Washington, DC: U.S. Government Printing Office.

USDHHS (U.S. Dept. of Health and Human Services, 1986c). *The health consequences of involuntary smoking: A report of the Surgeon General* (Publication No. 87–8398). Washington, DC: U.S. Government Printing Office.

USDHHS (U.S. Dept. of Health and Human Services, 1986d). *Health status of the disadvantaged: Chartbook: 1986* (Publication No. HRS-P-DV86–2). Washington, DC: U.S. Government Printing Office.

USDHHS (U.S. Dept. of Health and Human Services, 1986e). *Health, United States, 1986 and Prevention Profile* (Publication No. PHS 87–1232). Washington, DC: U.S. Government Printing Office.

USDHHS (U.S. Dept. of Health and Human Services, 1987). *Smoking and health: A national status report* (Publication No. HHS/PHS/CDC 87–8396). Washington, DC: U.S. Government Printing Office.

USDHHS (U.S. Dept. of Health and Human Services, 1988). *The health consequences of smoking. Nicotine addiction: A report of the surgeon general* (Publication No. 88–8406). Washington, DC: U.S. Government Printing Office.

USDHHS (U.S. Dept. of Health and Human Services, 1989). *Reducing the health consequences of smoking. 25 years of progress: A report of the Surgeon General* (Publication No. 89–8411). Rockville, MD: Department of Health and Human Services.

USDHHS (U.S. Dept. of Health and Human Services, 1990). *Smoking and health: A national status report* (2nd ed., revised) (Publication No. CDC 87–8396). Washington, DC: U.S. Government Printing Office.

USDHHS (U.S. Dept. of Health and Human Services, 1992). *Healthy People 2000: National Health Promotion and Disease Prevention Objectives* (Publication No. PHS 91–50213). Washington, DC: U.S. Government Printing Office.

USPHS (U.S. Public Health Service, 1964). *Smoking and Health: Public Health Service Report of the Advisory Committee to the Surgeon General* of the *Public Health Service* (Publication No. 1103). Washington, DC: U.S. Government Printing Office.

Ungar, S.J. (1989, January 15). AIDS cases in Africa: an everyone epidemic. *Los Angeles Times.*

Urban, B.J., France, R.D., Steinberger, E.K., Scott, D.L., & Maltbie, A.A. (1986). Long-term use of narcotic/antidepressant medication in the management of phantom limb pain. *Pain, 24,* 191–196.

Valdiserri, R.O., Lyter, D.W., Kingsley, L.A., Leviton, L.C., Schofield, J.W., Huggins, J., Ho, M., & Rinaldo, C.R. (1987). The effect of group education on improving attitudes about AIDS risk reduction. *New York State Journal of Medicine, 87,* 272–278.

Valenstein, E.S. (1973). *Brain control.* New York: Wiley.

Valentine, D.P. (1982). The experience of pregnancy: A developmental process. *Family Relations, 31,* 243–248.

Valenzuela, M. (1990). Attachment in chronically underweight young children. *Child Development, 61,* 1984–1996.

Vaillant, G.E. (1977). *Adaptation to life.* Boston: Little, Brown.

Vaillant, G.E. (1979). The natural history of male psychologic health: Effects of mental health on physical health. *New England Journal of Medicine, 301,* 1249–1254.

Vandereycken, W. (1989). The place of behaviour therapy in the in-patient treatment of anorexia nervosa. *British Review of Bulimia and Anorexia Nervosa, 3,* 55–60.

VanderPlate, C., & Aral, S.O. (1987). Psychosocial aspects of genital herpes virus infection. *Health Psychology, 6,* 57–72.

VanderPlate, C., Aral, S.O., & Magder, L. (1988). The relationship among genital herpes simplex virus, stress, and social support. *Health Psychology, 7,* 159–168.

Van Egeren, L.F., Sniderman, L.D., & Roggelin, M.S. (1982). Competitive two-person interactions of Type-A and Type-B individuals. *Journal of Behavioral Medicine, 5,* 55–66.

van Gorp, W.G., Satz, P., Hinkin, C., Selnes, O., Miller, E.N., McArthur, J., Cohen, B., & Paz, D. (1991). Metacognition in HIV-1 seropositive asymptomatic individuals: Self-ratings versus objective neuropsychological performance. *Journal of Clinical and Experimental Neuropsychology, 13,* 812–819.

Van Houten, R. (1983). Punishment: From the animal laboratory to the applied setting. In S. Axelrod & J. Apsche (Eds.), *The effects of punishment on human behavior.* New York: Academic.

VanItallie, T.B. (1979). Adverse effects on health and longevity. *American Journal of Clinical Nutrition, 32,* 2723–2733.

Varni, J.W., Jay, S.M., Masek, B.J., & Thompson, K.L. (1986). Cognitive-behavioral assessment and management of pediatric pain. In A.D. Holzman & D.C. Turk (Eds.), *Pain management: A handbook of psychological treatment approaches.* New York: Pergamon.

Varni, J.W., & Thompson, K.L. (1986). Biobehavioral assessment and management of pediatric pain. In N.A. Krasnegor, J.D. Arasteh, & M.F. Cataldo (Eds.), *Child health behavior: A behavioral pediatrics perspective.* New York: Wiley.

Vaughn, E., & Fisher, A.E. (1962). Male sexual behavior induced by intracranial electrical stimulation. *Science, 137,* 758.

Verbrugge, L. (1979). Marital status and health. *Journal of Marriage and the Family, 41,* 467–485.

Vernon, D.T.A. (1974). Modeling and birth order in response to painful stimuli. *Journal of Personality and Social Psychology, 29,* 50–59.

Viegener, B.J., Perri, M.G., Nezu, A.M., Renjilian, D.A., McKelvey, W.F., & Schein, R.L. (1990). Effects of an intermittent, low-fat, low-calorie diet in the behavioral treatment of obesity. *Behavior Therapy, 21,* 499–509.

Vining, E., Accardo, P.J., Rubenstein, J.E., Farrell, S.E., & Roizen, N.J. (1976). Cerebral palsy: A pediatric developmentalist's point of view. *American Journal of Diseases of Children, 130,* 643–649.

Visintainer, M.A., Volpicelli, J.R., & Selisman, M.E. (1982). Tumor rejection in rats after inescapable or escapable shock. *Science, 216,* 437–439.

Volhardt, L.T. (1991). Psychoneuroimmunology: A literature review. *American Journal of Orthopsychiatry, 61,* 35–47.

Vuchinich, R.E., & Tucker, J.A. (1988). Contributions from behavioral theories of choice to analysis of alcohol abuse. *Journal of Abnormal Psychology, 97,* 181–195.

Wadden, T.A., & Brownell, K.D. (1984). The development and modification of dietary practices in individuals, groups, and large populations. In J.D. Matarazzo, S.M. Weiss, J.A. Herd, N.E. Miller, & S.M., Weiss (Eds.), *Behavioral health: A handbook of health enhancement and disease prevention.* New York: Wiley.

Wadden, T.A., Luborsky, L., Greer, S., & Crits-Christoph, P. (1984). The behavioral treatment of essential hypertension: An update and comparison with pharmacological treatment. *Clinical Psychology Review, 4,* 403–429.

Wadden, T.A., Stunkard, A.J., Brownell, K.D., & Day, S.C. (1984). Treatment of obesity by behavior therapy and very low calorie diet: A pilot investigation. *Journal of Consulting and Clinical Psychology, 52,* 692–694.

Wadden, T.A., Stunkard, A.J., & Liebschutz, J. (1988). Three-year follow-up of the treatment of obesity by very low calorie diet, behavior therapy, and their combination. *Journal of Consulting and Clinical Psychology, 56,* 925–928.

Wagner, B.M., Compas, B.E., & Howell, D.C. (1988). Daily and major life events: A test of an integrative model of psychosocial stress. *American Journal of Community Psychology, 16,* 189–205.

Waitzkin, H. (1984). Doctor-patient communication. *Journal of American Medical Association, 252,* 2441–2446.

Waitzkin, H. (1985). Information giving in medical care. *Journal of Health and Social Behavior, 26,* 81–101.

Waitzkin, H., & Stoeckle, J.D. (1976). Information control and the micropolitics of health care: Summary of an ongoing research project. *Social Science and Medicine, 10,* 263–276.

Wald, E.R., Dashevsky, B., Byers, C., Guerra, N., & Taylor, F. (1988). Frequency and severity of infections in day care. *Journal of Pediatrics, 112,* 540–546.

Wallace, L.M. (1986). Communcation variables in the design of pre-surgical preparatory information. *British Journal of Clinical Psychology, 25,* 111–118.

Waller, J.A. (1987). Injury: Conceptual shifts and preventive implications. In L. Breslow, J.E. Fielding, & L.B. Lave (Eds.), *Annual review of public health* (Vol. 8). Palo Alto, CA: Annual Reviews.

Wallston, B.S., Alagna, S.W., DeVellis, B.M., & DeVellis, R.F. (1983). Social support and physical health. *Health Psychology, 2,* 367–391.

Wallston, B.S., & Wallston, K.A. (1981). Health locus of control scales. In H.M. Lefcourt (Ed.), *Research with the locus of control construct,* (Vol. 1, pp. 189–243). New York: Academic.

Wallston, B.S., Wallston, K.A., & DeVellis, R. (1978). Development of the multidimensional health locus of control (MHLC) scales. *Health Education Monographs, 6,* 160–170.

Wallston, K.A. & Wallston, B.S. (1981). Health locus of control scales. In H.M. Lefcourt (Ed.), *Research with locus of control concept.* New York: Academic.

Ward, M.M., Chesney, M.A., Swan, G.E., Black, G.W., Parker, S.D., & Rosenman, R.H. (1986). Cardiovascular responses in Type A and Type B men to a series of stressors. *Journal of Behavioral Medicine, 9,* 43–49.

Wardle, J. & Steptoe, A. (1991). The European health and behavior survey: Rationale, methods, and initial results from the United Kingdom. *Social Science and Medicine, 33,* 925–936.

Ware, J.E., Jr., & Berwick, D.M. (1990). Patient judgments of hospital quality. Conclusions and recommendations. *Medical Care, 28,* 539–544.

Ware, J.E., Jr., Davies-Avery, A., & Stewart, A.L. (1978). The measurement and meaning of patient satisfaction. *Health and Medical Care Services Review, 1,* 2–15.

Ware, J.E., Jr., & Hays, R.D. (1988). Methods for measuring patient satisfaction with specific medical encounters. *Medical Care, 26,* 393–402.

Ware, J.E., Manning, W.G., Duan, N., Wells, K.B., & Newhouse, J.P. (1984). Health status and the use of outpatient mental health services. *American Psychologist, 39,* 1090–1100.

Waterman, C.K., & Chiauzzi, E.J. (1982). The role of orgasm in male and female sexual enjoyment. *Journal of Sex Research, 18,* 146–159.

Watson, D.B. (1983). The relationship of genital herpes and life stress as moderated by locus of control and social support. *Dissertation Abstracts International, 43,* 3857–3858.

Watson, M., Greer, S., Pruyn, J., & van den Borne, B. (1990). Locus of control and adjustment to cancer. *Psychological Reports, 66,* 39–48.

Watson, P.B. (1989). The hypothalamic/pituitary/-adrenal axis revisited. *Stress Medicine, 5,* 141–143.

Weg, R. (1987). Menopause: Biomedical aspects. In G.L. Maddox (Ed.), *The encyclopedia of aging* (pp. 433–437). New York: Springer.

Wegman, M.E. (1986). Annual summary of vital statistics—1985. *Pediatrics, 78,* 983–994.

Weinberg, G. (1972). *Society and the healthy homosexual.* New York: St. Martin's.

Weinberger, M., Hiner, S.L., & Tierney, W.M. (1987). In support of hassles as a measure of stress in predicting health outcomes. *Journal of Behavioral Medicine, 10,* 19–31.

Weiner, H. (1977). *Psychobiology and human disease.* New York: Elsevier.

Weiner, H. (1978). Emotional factors. In S.C. Werner & S.H. Ingbar (Eds.), *The Thyroid.* New York: Harper & Row.

Weiner, H. (1985). Respiratory disorders. In H.I. Kaplan & B.J. Shadock (Eds.), *Comprehensive textbook of psychiatry* (4th ed.). Baltimore, MD: Williams & Wilkins.

Weinstein, K.A., Davison, G.C., DeQuattro, V., & Allen, J.W. (1987). Type A behavior and cognitions: Is hostility the bad actor? *Health Psychology, 6,* 55–56 (abstract).

Weinstein, N.D. (1984). Why it won't happen to me: Perceptions of risk factors and susceptibility. *Health Psychology, 3,* 431–457.

Weinstein, N.D. (1987). Unrealistic optimism about susceptiblity to health problems: Conclusions from a community-wide sample. *Journal of Behavioral Medicine, 10,* 481–500.

Weinstein, N.D., & Lechandro, E. (1982). Egocentrism as a source of unrealistic optimism. *Personality and Social Psychology Bulletin, 8,* 195–200.

Weinstock, C. (1984). Further evidence on psychobiological aspects of cancer. *International Journal of Psychosomatics, 31*, 20–22.

Weisenberg, M. (1977). Pain and pain control. *Psychological Bulletin, 84*, 1008–1044.

Weiss, B.D., & Senf, J.H. (1990). Patient satisfaction survey instrument for use in health maintenance organizations. *Medical Care, 28*, 434–445.

Weiss, S.M. (1988). Stress management in the treatment of hypertension. *American Heart Journal, 116*, 645–649.

Weiss, S.M., Fielding, J.E., & Baum, A. (1991). *Health at work*. Hillsdale, NJ: Erlbaum.

Wellisch, D.K. (1981). Intervention with the cancer patient. In C.K. Prokop & L.A. Bradley (Eds.), *Medical psychology: Contributions to behavioral medicine*. New York: Academic.

Wenger, N.S., Linn, L.S., Epstein, M., & Shapiro, M.F. (1991). Reduction of high-risk sexual behavior among heterosexuals undergoing HIV antibody testing: A randomized clinical trial. *American Journal of Public Health, 81*, 1580–1585.

Wermuth, L.A., Sorenson, J.L., and Franks, P. (1991). Preventing AIDS: Policy implications. In J.L. Sorenson, L.A. Wermuth, D.R. Gibson, K.H. Choi, J.R. Guydish, & S.L. Batki (Eds.), *Preventing AIDS in drug users and their sexual partners*. New York: Guilford.

Werner, R., & Keys, C. (1988). The effects of changes in jail population densities on crowding, sick call, and spatial behavior. *Journal of Applied Social Psychology, 18*, 852–866.

West Berlin Human Genetics Institute. (1987). *Study on effects of nuclear radiation at Chernobyl on fetal development*.

Weston, W.W., Brown, J.B., & Stewart, M. (1989). Patient-centered interviewing. Part I: Understanding patients' experiences. *Canadian Family Physician, 35*, 147–151.

Whalen, R.E. (1977). Brain mechanisms controlling sexual behavior. In F.A. Beach (Ed.), *Human sexuality in four perspectives*. Baltimore: Johns Hopkins University.

White, D.R., & White, N.M. (1988). Causes and effects of obesity: Implications for behavioral treatment. In W. Linden (Ed.), *Biological barriers in behavioral medicine*, (pp. 35–62). New York: Plenum.

Whitehead, A., & Mathews, A. (1986). Factors related to successful outcome in the treatment of sexually unresponsive women. *Psychological Medicine, 16*, 373–378.

Whitlock, F.A., & Siskind, M. (1979). Depression and cancer: A follow-up study. *Psychological Medicine, 9*, 747–752.

Wiebe, D.J., & McCallum, D.M. (1986). Health practices and hardiness as mediators in the stress-illness relationship. *Health Psychology, 5*, 425–438.

Wiedenfeld, S.A., O'Leary, A., Bandura, A., Brown, S., Levine, S., & Raska, K. (1990). Impact of perceived self-efficacy in coping with stressor on components of the immune system. *Journal of Personality and Social Psychology, 59*, 1082–1094.

Wiens, A.N., & Menustik, C.E. (1983). Treatment outcome and patient characteristics in an aversion therapy program for alcoholism. *American Psychologist, 38*, 1089–1096.

Wikler, A. (1980). *Opiod dependence: Mechanisms and treatment*. New York: Plenum.

Wilcox, N.E., & Stauffer, E.S. (1972). Follow-up of 423 consecutive patients admitted to the Spinal Cord Centre, Rancho Los Amigos Hospital, 1 January to 31 December, 1967. *International Journal of Paraplegia, 10*, 115–122.

Wiley, J.A., & Camacho, T.C. (1980). Life-style and future health: Evidence from the Alameda County Study. *Preventive Medicine, 9*, 1–21.

Willenbring, M.L., Levine, A.S., & Morley, J.E. (1986). Stress induced eating and food preferences in humans: A pilot study. *International Journal of Eating Disorders, 5*, 855–864.

Willer, J.C., & Albe-Fessard, D. (1980). Electrophysiological evidence for a release of endogenous opiates in stress-induced analgesia in man. *Brain Research, 198*, 419–426.

Williams, A.F. (1972). Factors associated with seatbelt use in families. *Journal of Safety Research, 4*, 133–138.

Williams, D.A., Lewis-Faning, E., Rees, L., Jacobs, J., & Thomas, A. (1958). Assessment of the relative importance of the allergic, infective and psychological factors in asthma. *Acta Allergologista, 12*, 376–385.

Williams, D.A., & Thorn, B.E. (1989). An empirical assessment of pain beliefs. *Pain, 36*, 351–358.

Williams, J.M., Peterson, R.G., Shea, P.A., Schmedtje, J.F., Bauer, D.C., & Felten, D.L. (1981). Sympathetic innervation of murine thymus and spleen: Evidence for a functional link between the nervous and immune systems. *British Research Bulletin, 6*, 83–94.

Williams, R.B., & Barefoot, J.C. (1988). Coronary-prone behavior: The emerging role of the hostility complex. In B.K. Houston & C.R. Snyer (Eds.), *Type A behavior pattern: Current trends and future directions* (pp. 189–211). New York: Wiley.

Williams, R.B., Haney, T.L., Lee, K.L., Kong, Y., Blumenthal, J.A., & Whalen, R.E. (1980). Type A behavior hostility and coronary atherosclerosis. *Psychosomatic Medicine, 42*, 539–549.

Williamson, D.F., Madans, J., Anda, R.F., Kleinman, J.C., Giovino, G.A., & Byers, T. (1991). Smoking cessation and severity of weight gain in a national cohort. *New England Journal of Medicine, 324,* 739–745.

Wills, T.A. (1984). Supportive functions of interpersonal relationships. In S. Cohen & L. Syme (Eds.), *Social support and health.* New York: Academic.

Wills, T., & Shiffman, S. (1985). Coping and substance use: A conceptual framework. In S. Shiffman & T. Wills (Eds.), *Coping, stress, and drugs.* New York: Academic.

Wilson, A., Passik, S.D., Faude, J., Abrams, J., & Gordon, E. (1989). A hierarchical model of opiate addiction: Failures of self-regulation as a central aspect of substance abuse. *The Journal of Nervous and Mental Disease, 177,* 390–399.

Wilson, C.P. (1983). *Fear of being fat: The treatment of anorexia nervosa and bulimia.* New York: Aronson.

Wilson, G.T. (1980). Behavior modification and the treatment of obesity. in A.J. Stunkard (Ed.), *Obesity.* Philadelphia: Saunders.

Wilson, G.T. (1984). Toward the understanding and treatment of binge eating. In R.C. Hawkins, W.J. Frenouw, & P.F. Clement (Eds.), *The binge-purge syndrome.* New York: Springer.

Wilson, G.T., & Lawson, D.M. (1976). The effects of alcohol on sexual arousal in women. *Journal of Abnormal Psychology, 85,* 489–497.

Wilson, G., McCreary, R., Kean, J., & Baxter, J. (1979). The development of preschool children of heroin-addicted mothers: A controlled study. *Pediatrics, 63,* 135–141.

Wilson, G.T., Rossiter, E., Kleifield, E.I., & Lindholm, L. (1986). Cognitive-behavioral treatment of bulimia nervosa: A controlled evaluation. *Behaviour Research and Therapy, 24,* 277–288.

Wilson, T.D., & Linville, P.W. (1985). Improving the performance of college freshmen with attributional techniques. *Journal of Personality and Social Psychology, 49,* 287–293.

Wine, J.D. (1982). Evaluation anxiety: A cognitive-attentional construct. In H.W. Krohne & L. Laux (Eds.), *Achievement, stress, and anxiety.* New York: Hemisphere.

Winegarten, H.P. (1983). Conditioned cues elicit feeding in sated rats: A role for learning in meal initiation. *Science, 220,* 431–432.

Winett, R.A., King, A.C., & Altman, D.G. (1989). *Social psychology and public health.* New York: Pergamon.

Wing, R.R., Epstein, L.H., Nowalk, M.P., & Lamparski, D. (1986a). Behavioral self-regulation in the treatment of patients with diabetes mellitus. *Psychological Bulletin, 99,* 78–89.

Wing, R.R., Epstein, L.H., Nowalk, M.P., Scott, N., Koeske, R., & Hagg, S. (1986b). Does self-monitoring of blood glucose levels improve dietary competence for obese patients with Type II diabetes? *American Journal of Medicine, 81,* 830–836.

Wing, R.R., Nowalk, M.P., & Guare, J.C. (1988). Diabetes mellitus. In E.A. Blechman & K.D. Brownell (Eds.), *Handbook of behavioral medicine for women.* New York: Pergamon.

Winick, M., Morgan, B.L.G., Rozovski, J., & Marks-Kaufman, R. (1988). *The Columbia encyclopedia of nutrition.* New York: G.P. Putman's Sons.

Winkelstein, W., & Marmot, M. (1981). Primary prevention of ischemic heart disease: Evaluation of community interventions. *Annual Review of Public Health, 2,* 253–276.

Winters, R. (1985). Behavioral approaches to pain. In N. Schneiderman & J.T. Tapp (Eds.), *Behavioral medicine: The biopsychosocial approach.* Hillsdale, NJ: Erlbaum.

Wirsching, M., Stierlin, H., Hoffmann, F., Weber, G., Wirsching, B. (1982). Psychological identification of breast cancer patients before biopsy. *Journal of Psychosomatic Research, 26,* 1–10.

Wise, R.A. (1988). The neurobiology of craving: Implications for the understanding and treatment of addiction. *Journal of Abnormal Psychology, 97,* 118–132.

Wistuba, F. (1986). Significance of allergy in asthma from a behavioral medicine viewpoint. *Psychotherapy & Psychosomatics, 45,* 186–194.

Witte, K. (1991). The role of culture in health and disease. In L.A. Samovar & R.E. Porter (Eds.), *Intercultural communication: A reader.* Oxford: Pergamon.

Wolf, S. (1950). Effects of suggestion and conditioning on the action of chemical agents in human subjects—The pharmacology of placebos. *Journal of Clinical Investigation, 29,* 100–109.

Wolf, S.L., Nacht, M., & Kelly, J.L. (1982). EMG feedback training during dynamic movement for low back pain patients. *Behavior Therapy, 13,* 395–406.

Wolfe, L. (1980, September). The sexual profile of that Cosmopolitan girl. *Cosmopolitan,* pp. 254–265.

Wolinsky, F.D. (1980). The performance of health maintenance organizations: An analytic review. *Milbank Memorial Fund Quarterly, 58,* 537–587.

Wolinsky, F.D. (1988). Sick-role legitimation. In D.S. Gochman (Ed.), *Health behavior: Emerging research perspectives.* New York: Plenum.

Wolinsky, F.D. (1988). *The sociology of health.* Belmont, CA: Wadsworth.

Wolman, B.B. (1988). *Psychosomatic disorders.* New York: Plenum.

Wolpe, J. (1958). *Psychotherapy by reciprocal inhibition.* Stanford, CA: Stanford University.

Wolpe, J. (1987). The promotion of scientific therapy: A long voyage. In J.K. Zeig (Ed.), *The evolution of psychotherapy.* New York: Brunner/ Mazel.

Woodall, K.L., & Matthews, K.A. (1989). Familial environment associated with Type A behaviors and psychophysiological responses to stress in children. *Health Psychology, 8,* 403–426.

Woods, S.M., Natterson, J., & Silverman, J. (1966). Medical students' disease: Hypochondriasis in medical education. *Journal of Medical Education, 41*, 785–790.

Woodward, N.J., & Wallston, B.S. (1987). Age and health care beliefs: Self-efficacy as a mediator of low desire for control. *Psychology & Aging, 2*, 3–8.

Wooley, O.W., Wooley, S.C., & Dunham, R.B. (1972). Can calories be perceived and do they affect hunger in obese and nonobese humans? *Journal of Comparative and Physiological Psychology, 80*, 250–258.

Wooley, S.C. (1972). Physiologic versus cognitive factors in short-term food regulation in the obese and nonobese. *Psychosomatic Medicine, 34*, 62–68.

Woolhandler, S., & Himmelstein, D.U. (1990). The deteriorating administrative efficiency of the U.S. health care system. *New England Journal of Medicine, 324*, 1253–1258.

Wortman, C.B., & Dunkel-Schetter, C. (1987). Conceptual and methodological issues in the study of social support. In A. Baum & J.E. Singer (Eds.), *Handbook of psychology and health* (Vol. 5). Hillsdale, NJ: Erlbaum.

Wright, B. (1960). *Physical disability: A psychological approach.* New York: Harper & Row.

Wright, B.A. (1984). Developing constructive views of life with a disability. In D.W. Krueger (Ed.), *Rehabilitation psychology.* Rockville, MD: Aspen Publications.

Wright, L., Schaeffer, A.B., & Solomons, G. (1979). *Encyclopedia of pediatric psychology.* Baltimore, MD: University Park.

Wynder, E.L., & Graham, E.A. (1950). Tobacco smoking as a possible etiologic factor in bronchiogenic carinoma. *Journal of the American Medical Association, 143*, 329–336.

Wynne, E.A. (1978). Behind the discipline problem: Youth suicide as a measure of alienation. *Phi Delta Kappan, 59*, 307–315.

Wyper, M.A. (1990). Breast self-examination and the Health Belief Model: Variations on a theme. *Research in Nursing and Health, 13*, 421–428.

Yager, J. (1989). Psychological treatments for eating disorders. Special Issue: Eating Disorders. *Psychiatric Annals, 19*, 477–482.

Yankelovich, D. (1981). *New rules: Searching for self-fulfillment in a world turned upside down.* New York: Random House.

Yarnold, P.R., Mueser, K.T., Grau, B.W., & Brimm, L.G. (1986). The reliability of the student version of the Jenkins Activity Survey. *Journal of Behavioral Medicine, 9*, 401–414.

Yates, J., Chalmer, B., St. James, P., Follansbee, M., & McKegney, F. (1981). Religion in patients with advanced cancer. *Medical and Pediatric Oncology, 9*, 121–128.

Young, L.M., & Powell, B. (1985). The effects of obesity on the clinical judgments of mental health professionals. *Journal of Health and Social Behavior, 26*, 133–246.

Yuker, H.E., Block, J.R., & Young, J.H. (1966). *The measurement of attitudes toward disabled persons.* Albertson, NY: Human Resources Center.

Zagon, I.S., & McLaughlin, P.J. (1983). Naltrexone modulates tumor response in mice with neuroblastoma. *Science, 221*, 671–672.

Zakowski, S., Hall, M.H., & Baum, A. (1992). Stress, stress management, and the immune system. *Applied & Preventive Psychology, 1*, 1–13.

Zakowski, S.G., McAllister, C.G., Deal, M., & Baum, A. (1992). Stress, reactivity, and immune function in healthy men. *Health Psychology, 11*, 223–232.

Zarski, J.J. (1984). Hassles and health: A replication. *Health Psychology, 3*, 243–251.

Zarski, J.J., West, J.D., DePompei, R., & Hall, D.E. (1988). Chronic illness: Stressors, the adjustment process, and family-focused interventions. *Journal of Mental Health Counseling, 10*, 145–158.

Zedeck, S., & Mosier, K.L. (1990). Work in the family and employing organization. *American Psychologist, 45*, 240–251.

Zelnick, M., & Shah, F.K. (1983). First intercourse among young Americans. *Family Planning Perspectives, 15*, 64–70.

Zilbergeld, B. (1979). *Male sexuality.* New York: Bantam.

Zilbergeld, B., & Evans, M. (1980). The inadequacy of Masters and Johnson. *Psychology Today, 14*, 28–43.

Zimberg, S. (1985a). Psychiatric office treatment of alcoholism. In S. Zimberg, J. Wallace, & S.B. Blume (Eds.), *Practical approaches to alcoholism psychotherapy* (2nd ed.). New York: Plenum.

Zimberg, S. (1985b). Principles of alcoholism psychotherapy. In S. Zimberg, J. Wallace, & S.B. Blume (Eds.), *Practical approaches to alcoholism psychotherapy* (2nd ed.). New York: Plenum.

Zimmer, D., Bouchardt, E., & Fischle, C. (1983). Sexual fantasies of sexually distressed and nondistressed men and women: An empirical comparison. *Journal of Sex and Marital Therapy, 9*, 38–50.

Zimney, G.H. (1961). *Method in experimental psychology.* New York: Ronald.

Zimpfer, D.G. (1990). Group work for bulimia: A review of outcomes. *Journal for Specialists in Group Work, 15*, 239–251.

Zola, I.K. (1966). Culture and symptoms—an analysis of patients' presenting complaints. *American Sociological Review, 31*, 615–630.

Zola, I.K. (1973). Pathways to the doctor: From person to patient. *Social Science and Medicine, 7*, 677–689.

Zlutnick, S., & Taylor, C.B. (1982). Chronic pain. In D.M. Doleys, R.L. Meredith, & A.R. Ciminero (Eds.), *Behavioral medicine: Assessment and treatment strategies.* New York: Plenum.

Zucker, R.A., & Gomberg, E.S.L. (1986). Etiology of alcoholism reconsidered: The case for a bio-phychosocial process. *American Psychologist, 41,* 783–793.

Zuckerman, D.M., Kasl, S.V., & Ostfeld, A.M. (1984). Psychological predictors of mortality among the elderly poor: The role of religion, well-being, and social contacts. *American Journal of Epidemiology, 119,* 710–723.

ILLUSTRATION CREDITS

Page 352: © Carl Purcell/Photo
   Researchers
Page 356: © Martin/Custom Medical
   Stock
Page 364: © Hank Morgan/Rainbow

Chapter 9
Page 381: © Michael Sargent/The White
   House
Page 399: © Dan McCoy/Rainbow

Chapter 10
Page 411: © Lennart Nilsson, Boehringer
   Ingelheim International Gmbh
Page 435: ©1988 SIU
Page 445: © 1991 Kevin Beebe
Page 450: © Lennart Nilsson, Boehringer
   Ingelheim International Gmbh
Page 455: © Alon Reininger
Page 458: © Richard B. Levine

Chapter 11
Page 471: © Dan McCoy/Rainbow
Page 474: © Los Angeles Times Photo

Page 504: © Blair Seitz
Page 510: © George White

Chapter 12
Page 533: © George White
Page 544: © Steve Niedorf/Image Bank
Page 553: © Alistair Cowin/Image Bank

Chapter 13
Page 577: © Enzio Petersen/UPI
   Bettmann
Page 585: © Tony Freeman/Photo Edit
Page 600: © M. Richards/Photo Edit

Chapter 14
Page 616: © Bob Firth
Page 618: © Janeart Ltd./The Image
   Bank
Page 629: © Blair Seitz

AUTHOR INDEX

SUBJECT INDEX

Page numbers in boldface indicate where key terms are introduced.